THE COLLECTED STORIES OF GLYN JONES

Glyn Jones (1905–1995)

THE COLLECTED STORIES

OF

GLYN JONES

Edited, with an Introduction
by
TONY BROWN

UNIVERSITY OF WALES PRESS
CARDIFF
1999

© the short stories, the estate of Glyn Jones, 1999
© introduction and notes, the University of Wales, 1999

All enquiries regarding copyright on the works of Glyn Jones should be addressed
to Meic Stephens, the writer's lieterary executor and agent of his estate.

British Library Cataloguing-in-Publication Data.
A catalogue record for this book is available from the British Library.

ISBN 0–7083–1420–1

Published with the financial support of the Arts Council of Wales

THE ASSOCIATION FOR
WELSH WRITING IN ENGLISH
CYMDEITHAS LÊN SAESNEG CYMRU

Typeset at University of Wales Press
Printed in Great Britain by Bookcraft, Midsomer Norton, Avon

Contents

ø

Foreword

❧

This edition is part of a series of publications, sponsored by the Universities of Wales Association for the Study of Welsh Writing in English, bringing together collected editions of Welsh authors writing in English. The field has received relatively little attention in the past and it is hoped that, with the re-publication of major literary works from earlier this century and before, critical interest will be stimulated in writers who will handsomely repay such attention. The editions are conceived of on scholarly lines and are intended to give a rounded impression of the author's work, with introductions, bibliographical information and notes.

JOHN PIKOULIS
General Editor

In grateful memory

Kenneth Frederick Brown (1919–1995)

Acknowledgements

ॐ

My first debt of gratitude is, of course, to Glyn Jones himself, not only for his stories, but for his continuous support at the beginning of this project, for many conversations about his work, for his endless courtesy in answering questions about his stories, and for his friendship. I am also grateful to Doreen Jones for her unfailing kindness and her hospitality. My one regret is that this project could not have been completed in time for Glyn to see it.

I am deeply grateful to Glyn Jones's Literary Executor, Meic Stephens, for many conversations about Glyn Jones and his work and for the generous access he gave me after Glyn's death to manuscripts and papers, which yielded much valuable material relating to the stories and their publication. I am also grateful to Dr. Ceridwen Lloyd Morgan at the Manuscripts Department, National Library of Wales, for granting me access to uncatalogued material as Glyn Jones's papers were transferred to the Library and for her patience and expertise. Dr. John Pikoulis, the General Editor and a close friend of Glyn Jones, gave scrupulous and detailed textual advice and saved me from numerous errors; those which remain are, of course, my responsibility.

Friends and colleagues across Wales, and beyond, have been endlessly helpful in answering my questions not just about literary matters but about everything from horse medicine to railway alarm systems. In Bangor, I am grateful to Mrs. Glenda Carr for assistance with matters of translation, to Dr. Densil Morgan, Dr. Bruce Griffiths, Dr. Branwen Jarvis, Dr. Gwawr Jones, Dr. Dafydd Glyn Jones, Professor R. Merfyn Jones, Dr. Margaret Locherbie-Cameron, Mr. Brinley Rees and Mr. Tony Eccles. Some of these colleagues answered numerous queries about Welsh idioms and I am particularly grateful for the help which Mr. Jason Walford Davies (and his grandmother, Mrs. Olive Powell of Bancffosfelen, Carmarthenshire) gave me regarding Welsh idiomatic usages in Carmarthenshire. Mrs. Linda Jones, Research Administrator in the English Department at Bangor, gave me indispensable assistance at an early stage with the scanning and electronic manipulation of text. Professor M. Wynn Thomas (University of Wales, Swansea) assisted me, as ever, with the answers to many queries; I am particularly grateful to him for guiding me through the riches of Caniedydd yr Annibynnwyr. Valuable assistance in a variety of forms was also given to me by other friends and colleagues: Mrs. Joan Rees Franzinetti (University of Turin), Dr. Katie Gramich and Elinor Le Bourdon (Trinity College, Carmarthen), Dr. John Harris (University of Wales, Aberystwyth), Professor Dafydd Johnston (University of Wales, Swansea) and Professor Dai Smith (BBC, Cardiff). As will be apparent from the notes, the late Tudor Bevan's knowledge of Llansteffan and of the social and geographical background of Glyn Jones's work, shared with me in conversation and by his giving me a copy of his MA dissertation, was indispensable; he is sadly missed.

Perhaps my most important debt is to Nancy, Sara and Alys, who have put up with my being endlessly huddled in front of a word-processor when they could quite reasonably have expected me to be doing more sociable things.

Note on editorial procedure

❧

The text used for each story is that used in the first volume in which the story was collected (*The Blue Bed*, *The Water Music*, *Selected Stories* or *Welsh Heirs*), an editorial procedure which had Glyn Jones's approval. Where the story had previously appeared in a magazine, the texts have been compared and any significant variation is given in the Notes which follow the texts. Where a manuscript or typescript has survived, these have also been consulted and points of interest noted.

Typographical errors have been silently corrected. Glyn Jones's punctuation has been followed throughout, even when idiosyncratic, although some obvious slips have been silently corrected and a few points of punctuation slightly revised to avoid ambiguity.

Introduction

✎

The Making of a Writer

The Merthyr Tydfil into which Glyn Jones was born on 28 April 1905 was still one of the most dynamic industrial communities in Britain. While the census of 1801 had shown Merthyr, with a population of 7,700, to be the largest town in Wales, labour poured into the area through the nineteenth century as the iron, steel and coal industries boomed; by 1901 the population was 80,000. Given the energy of the core industries, Merthyr was a place where money could be made: it has been estimated that between 1905 and 1914 more than a quarter of a million pounds was spent by tradesmen on the construction or reconstruction of their shops in the area.[1] It was a volatile, and vulnerable, economy, sensitive to the fluxes of world trade; there were depressions in 1903–4 and 1908–9 and the iron industry had declined at the end of the nineteeth century, with the bulk of production of the Dowlais works being moved to Cardiff in 1891, to be closer to its supplies of imported ore. But the coal industry had continued to boom; by 1906, 43 per cent of the electorate of Merthyr Boroughs were classified as 'miners'. 1913 was a record year for the south Wales coalfield and three million tons of coal were produced from the pits of the newly incorporated Borough of Merthyr. Unemployment was down to 1.4 per cent; the locust years were yet to come.[2]

But the miners and iron-workers whom Glyn Jones passed in the streets of Merthyr as a boy lived a harsh and unrelenting life. Housing conditions in parts of the Borough were still poor, the Medical Officer of health reporting in 1901 that the death-rate from measles, scarlet fever, diphtheria and other infectious diseases was half as high again in Merthyr as for the rest of England and Wales. Working hours were long; in 1911, the local MP, Keir Hardie, claimed that some workers in Treharris worked 84 hours a week, with some weekend shifts of 36 hours.[3] Unsurprisingly, particularly in an area whose radical traditions went back through Chartism to the Rising of 1831, the miners of Merthyr were amongst the most militant in the coalfield. There were violent strikes in the Aberdare area in 1908 and 1909; 1910 saw the year-long Cambrian lock-out, with the riots in Tonypandy being echoed by violence in Merthyr and Aberdare. Following the

foundation of the Central Labour College in London, young activists
from the coalfield became familiar with Marxist analysis of the social
and economic forces which were pressing upon their communities.

While the first wave of workers into Merthyr had been from Welsh-
speaking west and mid Wales, later in the century workers poured into
the area from much further afield, from England and Ireland, even
from Spain and Italy. This raw, mixed, volatile, occasionally violent
community was the one in which the young Glyn Jones grew up:

> An early memory I have is of coming, unexpectedly, in a hollow up the
> mountain, on a thick ring of squatting miners in the centre of which stood two
> bare-fisted collier boys, facing each other, stripped to the waist, bleeding,
> sweating, and panting loudly. It was a sight which, however fascinating and
> powerfully moving, I knew I should not be watching. This sort of savagery had
> no support at all from the enlightened and chapel-going citizens of Merthyr.[4]

The episode is revealing not merely of contemporary Merthyr, but of
Glyn Jones's own response to that essentially masculine world of
physicality and violence; he is fascinated but aware of the transgressive
nature of that fascination – 'I knew I should not be watching'. Jones's
family were very decidedly among those 'chapel-going citizens': Clare
Street, where he lived with his parents and his brother, David Tydfilyn
(five years older than Glyn and known as 'Tyd'), was 'quite a tidy
street', that very south Walian adjective, referring of course not just to
the street's visual neatness but to its respectability.[5] The Jones's
neighbours were for the most part craftsmen or members of the
commercial lower middle classes: 'Davies the Plasterer, Irving the Hay
and Corn Merchant, Griffiths the Printer, Jenkins the Credit-draper,
Jones the Shopwalker' (*MPi* 70). Another neighbour was Arthur
Horner, at this stage a lay-preacher, not the Marxist and fiery miners'
leader he was later to become. It was a neighbourhood, though, which
provided enough colour for a future writer of fiction:

> There was Mr. Phillips the Overman, a quiet, ponderous genial man who would
> sometimes come home of a Saturday evening a bit the worse for wear. In this
> condition he would sit lachrymosely in the back-garden and play his little
> accordion, singing mournful Welsh hymns about death and crossing the Jordan
> while Mrs. Phillips threatened him viciously and called him a stupid fool and all
> manner of knave and wastrel. (*MPi* 72)

Nonconformity was still a dynamic force within the community;
indeed Glyn Jones had been born during the months of the great
religious revival which began in the autumn of 1904, usually named
after its most charismatic preacher, Evan Roberts, who preached to

large, enthusiastic crowds in Merthyr. (The *Western Mail* reported on 15 December 1904 that, after the meetings, people 'gather together in hundreds and sing and pray in the streets at Midnight'; many of these meetings were so large that they were held on the mountain, amidst the slag heaps above the town.)[6] As Kenneth Morgan has indicated, some of the energies released by the revival found expression in 'social Christianity, . . . a movement that worked within the religious bodies themselves, in contrast to the Marxist messianism of Ablett and the syndicalists'.[7] Indeed the social gospel of Christianity infused the Labour movement. As in other parts of Britain in the early years of the Socialist movement, the vision of a transformed social and economic order was frequently articulated in religious registers; the workers would build a New Jerusalem. The minutes of the Aberdare Socialist Society show discussions on topics such as 'The Sermon on the Mount' and 'Socialism and the Ten Commandments'.[8] The Jones family were members at Soar, the Welsh Independent chapel in Merthyr. Of Glyn Jones's parents, it is Mrs. Jones who appears to have been the more active member; as well as regularly attending services and weekly prayer meetings with the rest of the family, at one period she acted as unofficial secretary for the minister and also ran, with three or four other Sunday School teachers, a kind of youth club for the boys and girls of the chapel during the week.[9]

Unlike the majority of Merthyr's population, Margaret Jones's family had been in the Merthyr area for generations; her great-grandparents had farmed just down the valley from the town. Her mother died in childbirth and her father, a local government clerk in the town, departed for America, leaving his baby daughter to be brought up by his in-laws. She ultimately qualified as a teacher in 1900 – her father wrote from America to congratulate her and sent her $5 'to aid you to have the necessary books, hoping you will make good use of them, so in time you will not be a burden on your Grandma and Grandpa's back'.[10] It is clear that, almost inevitably, the nature of her upbringing left its mark on Mrs. Jones. She clearly laid great store by personal independence and social responsibility. Jones writes feelingly of his mother's thrift: at Christmas he and his brother did not receive the 'colourful, worthless presents' their friends did, no Snakes and Ladders or chocolate novelties: 'No, my mother's idea of a present to acknowledge the lighter side of Christmas was a good book, or a pair of shoes, or woollen gloves, or a new overcoat for Sundays' (*MPi* 74). There is no doubt that Glyn Jones's relationship with his mother was the most important influence on the growing imagination of the future writer. It is clear that, as a boy, Glyn Jones worshipped his mother;

even in old age he would refer to her with obvious emotion, to her religious faith and to her beauty. But the relationship was not a simple one. Mrs. Jones was clearly the forceful one in the family and her concern for order and respectability meant that her son was very aware of her as a moral presence as he grew: one recalls his reaction to seeing the boys fighting on the hillside. Unsurprisingly she also discouraged him from playing with some of the less reputable boys in the neighbourhood, like the Irish family who not only kept a small gymnasium where the boys boxed, but who would 'curse, and swear, play football on a Sunday, and wipe their noses on their sleeves' (*MPi* 73). Underlying his mother's concern for his behaviour, Jones thought when he looked back, was her concern that he should not grow to be irresponsible and feckless like her own father.[11] But unsurprisingly her son did not always welcome her close attention; as late as April 1933 he reflects in his Journal:

> I sometimes think 'What a wonderful thing is mother-love'. It prowls around the off-spring ready to fling out its claws at anyone or anything that menaces them, quite regardless of itself, how ridiculous it may look.
>
> But how horrible a thing it is when it wants to go on protecting and what is worse, when it assumes dictatorship over the offspring, although that offspring is better able to manage its own affairs than ever the mother would be. Mothers – your mate is the man you chose – not your sons or your daughters.

The resulting tensions – the son's guilty resentment at the constraints imposed by a deeply-loved mother – ultimately find their outlet at times in the fiction.

Glyn Jones's father's family had their origins in Llanybri, Carmarthenshire; Jones's great-grandfather had left the family farm and, like so many others, he and his family joined the long march east, into the industrial valleys, where he ultimately worked underground and became a member at Soar. His grandson, Glyn Jones's father, intended, like his future wife, to become a schoolteacher, but an attack of meningitis and the financial pressures on his parents – his father was a clerk with an insurance company in Merthyr – disrupted these plans and he became a messenger boy with the General Post Office (*DTT* 19); apart from service in France during the First World War, he worked in clerical positions for the GPO for the rest of his life. But he remained a cultured man, a man of books and ideas: 'a dreamer, fond of arguing with his like-minded friends in Sunday School or in the University's extra-mural classes . . . His real life was his inner, private one; he found greatest satisfaction in the world of theories, and dreams, and questions and doubts' (*MPi* 69).

The home in which Glyn Jones and his brother grew up was, therefore, one in which books and ideas were valued: in a talk given in the
1970s, Jones remembered that his mother's

> poetry books, studied for her teaching certificate, were about the house,
> underlined and annotated in pencil by her . . . My father's father had been a
> Welsh poet, and his books also, English and Welsh were in our bookcase in what
> we called in Merthyr 'the middle room'. To talk freely about poetry, and poets,
> was nothing strange in our home.[12]

The grandfather referred to, the impoverished insurance clerk, was the
Welsh poet Llwch-Haiarn (David William Jones), who had died five
years before Jones's birth, and who had been well known in the locality.
One remembers that the poet who was to become Glyn Jones's friend
in the 1930s, Dylan Thomas, also had a relative who had been a
distinguished Welsh-language poet, his great-uncle, Gwilym Marles; in
other words, it was precisely that class whose literary expression had
until this point been in Welsh which in this new generation, born in the
early years of the century into an inceasingly Anglicized Wales, would
for the first time write in English.

We get fleeting glimpses of the life of the teenage Glyn Jones from a
pocket diary given to him for Christmas in 1919 and which he kept
during 1920.[13] As we might expect, the diary shows his regular attendance at chapel activities: on a Sunday in January 'A young student
preached, very nervous'; the following Wednesday Jones attends one of
the regular young people's meetings, which included a debate on 'Who
has contributed most for the uplift of mankind, man or woman?' A later
debate is on 'The Church and its attitude towards gambling'. One Friday
he attends a 'Tea fight in Soar – complete washout. Lantern lecture there.
Slides upside down'. But his social life is not entirely centred on the
chapel; he has a healthy fifteen-year-old's interest in sport: he plays
football and he goes regularly to see Merthyr Town, in those days playing
in the Football League against such teams as Watford, Brighton and
Crystal Palace; he duly records the scores and the fact that there is a 'big
rumpus' at one game after which the 'Crowd waited for ref'. He also
carefully records the result of that year's Derby, as well as family news: his
brother Tyd is accepted at teacher training college in Cheltenham and, in
June, 'Dad heard joyful news of his success', his appointment to a post at
the GPO in Cardiff, although the family did not move to Cardiff until
Glyn Jones had followed his brother to college. In July, shortly after
breaking up from school, he is walking by the canal and the sharp ear of
the future writer is momentarily evident: 'Met funny sort of johnny. "Are
you acquainted with the rudiments of etiquette of society?" '

In August he is in Carmarthenshire, staying with his father's relatives, an annual visit to rural, Welsh-speaking Wales which continued throughout his life and provided him with another world about which to write, far away from the scruffy urban world of Merthyr. That countryside is seen in the fiction as sun-filled, often mysterious, sometimes funny and it is clear that the young boy enjoyed himself on the farm, Y Lan, where he stayed with his 'Uncle John' (actually his father's cousin) and his two unmarried sisters. The boy joined in the hay-making and accompanied his uncle to Llansteffan and to the races in Llanybri. On other occasions he went with his uncle, who bred horses, to the horse fairs at Carmarthen. But the strength of the ties the fifteen-year-old boy felt with his home is also evident: he carefully records the arrival of letters from Merthyr, three in four days one week, and the dates of his replies. He found life on the Carmarthenshire farm very different from that at his home in Clare Street in ways which again tell us much about the growing boy:

> I never saw a book, nor heard any song, nor any discussion of any literary, political, or religious subject, in my uncle's home . . . Although my uncle and his sisters were kind enough to me in their own dull way, life on the remote farm was sometimes rather lonely . . . there was nothing to read there . . . except the Bible, the Ready Reckoner, and the pretty almanac that advertised cattle-feed.
>
> (*MPi* 76–7; cf. *DTT* 77)

Even at fifteen, the boy would have missed the political debate with which he was evidently familiar in Merthyr, his interest encouraged perhaps by his father, who was for years a paid-up member of the Labour Party and took an active, though mainly theoretical, interest in contemporary politics (*DTT* 21). The fifteen-year-old Jones carefully records, in February, the result of a by-election in Paisley, won by Asquith, as well as the 'great demonstration' in Merthyr on 'Labour Day' (1 May). In later life Glyn Jones remembered that not only did he hear political debate at home – 'I had a brother . . . who was a great talker, and arguer, and debater all his life' – but that

> You couldn't *be* a schoolboy in Merthyr in those days and avoid politics. Politics were like the air we breathed – everywhere. One of my close friends in my grammar schooldays was called John Arnold Roberts . . . [his] father was . . . the headmaster of a school in Merthyr and he was also a red-hot Socialist. Arnold and I used to attend political meetings together when we were in form four and form five [i.e. when 14 and 15 years of age]; after Chapel on Sunday morning . . . we used to go up to Thomastown Park to listen with the crowd to firebrands like Tom Mann, the pioneer Socialist, and Mrs. Despard the Socialist and suffragette. All the famous Socialists used to come to Merthyr, including Bernard Shaw. During the week nights, we'd go to the Drill Hall, or the Rink

(no-one skated), whenever there was a political meeting, and enjoy the actual
speeches, and the marvellous heckling that used to go on – witty, devastating,
unanswerable.

(*Remembering Aloud* 4)

The stream of visiting Socialist celebrities were of course attracted to
the constituency which had been held by Keir Hardie until his death in
1915, and in Glyn Jones's boyhood Labour was making rapid and
significant progress in local elections in the area. These early years in
Merthyr inevitably orientated him politically, and the poverty he was
later to see in the slums of Cardiff and the streets of the Valleys as the
economy collapsed only confirmed him in his view of what was being
done to the working people of south Wales; although always sceptical of
professional politicians and political leaders, Glyn Jones was consistently to identify himself in the 1930s, and beyond, as a Socialist.

The day-to-day life of this Merthyr boyhood was to be vividly
recreated in short stories like 'Bowen, Morgan and Williams' and 'The
Water Music' and in his novel *The Island of Apples* (1965). But perhaps
it is celebrated most joyously of all in *A Day in July*, a radio play written
in the 1950s but published only recently.[14] Here the boys ramble along
the sun-filled streets and long to swim in the canal: 'On a hot July day
we often envied the boys who swam there, and ran naked up and down
the canal bank to dry themselves', but the canal is also 'used as the
drowning place for mangy dogs and unwanted cats . . . our mothers did
not approve of it'. And so the boys wander on, past the colliers coming
off shift – 'A thrilling whiff of pit-clothes drifts back in their wake' – to
the colliery yard: 'We pass blinkered ponies and grimy surface-men, we
walk the coal-glittering earth while the confluent and dissolving engine-
room steams drift about us . . . We stand in the sultry doorway of the
blacksmith's shop, with its delicious smell of burning hoof'. The boys
walk on, up out of the valley, to picnic on the mountain, lighting a fire
to cook the unlikely scraps of food they have brought with them:

> [A]rriving at our high shelf we dropped the school satchels in which we carried
> our food and performed in the wind a shouting and boisterous dance: we
> crowed like dawn cocks; we wallowed like tingling dolphins in the showers of
> wind; we bit like exultant pit-ponies put out to grass; we covered the mountain's
> sunlit back with the patterns of our exultation . . . And then we sat down and lit
> our grass fire in the shelter of the wall. We had forgotten to bring water so we
> had to boil our potatoes in lemonade.

On other days they hang around the colliery stables and ride the pit-
ponies up to the mountain to graze; one pony is handsome and

unpredictable – 'We feared and half worshipped him' – and the boy associates the thrill of riding this horse with a tunnel near the mine

> into which one could peep through an iron grating, a gloomy place of dark horror. Along it ran a coal-black river which disappeared at the end in a roaring waterfall, the oily water tumbled out of sight into the terror of infinite space, into cold black nothingness and annihilation. 'Lark' the wild horse and the black river, even in sunlight haunt me, in them I experience the fascination of all that is fearful.

Here are the roots of Glyn Jones's fictional world: the sensual world of the colliery town – the sunshine, the tang of coal dust – the joyous freedom of the natural world, with beneath it an awareness that there is a dark side to the world, an unfocused threat, that is both appalling and thrilling.

The image one gets, then, is of a livelier, more exuberant boy, than the rather introverted, detached, slightly unworldly, figure Glyn Jones recreates in some of his autobiographical writings. He was, for instance, a skilled mimic; it was an ability guaranteeing popularity in the classroom.[15] But the love of books was unquestionable: 'I was a boy with a romantic spirit and, like my father, a great reader. I would consume so many books that Mam would sometimes turn to me and say, "For goodness sake, take your nose out of that old book for change".'[16] At the age of 14, he would run home from school at lunchtime, leaving his friends, and quickly swallow some lunch in order to read a chapter or two of a book; he read his way through the children's adventure stories of Captain Marryat – *The Little Savage, Children of the New Forest, Mr. Midshipman Easy* – and then on to other stories of romantic adventure: Dumas' *The Three Musketeers, Twenty Years After* and *The Count of Monte Cristo*, Sir Walter Scott's *Ivanhoe, Quentin Durward* and *Kenilworth*, the novels of Robert Louis Stevenson and G. A. Henty, *Tom Brown's Schooldays* – all telling of worlds far away from Merthyr and all, of course, in English, books that were no doubt being read by boys of his age in Kent or Surrey: 'There were no books in Welsh at that time, in the school library nor in the town's public library, that were able to feed my imagination and the essential romantic element in my nature' (*Tyfi'n Gymro* 10).

How many Welsh-language books there were in the library at Cyfarthfa Castle Grammar School, to which Jones went in 1916, is uncertain, for while various Education Acts from 1870 onwards had made state secondary education available to all, the Act of 1889 establishing state secondary education in Wales had laid down that that education would be entirely in English:

I did not hear a word of Welsh nor any mention of Wales in the primary school in Merthyr, and in the grammar school . . . nobody taught us Welsh. No Welsh lessons at all. One of the staff was a poet, a chaired poet at the National Eisteddfod, but Sarnicol tried to teach us chemistry, not Welsh. And the same in the history lessons; we had the history of England, and Europe, not the history of Wales, not to mention the rich history of Merthyr itself. I left school without hearing about the business of Dic Penderyn, although every day on my way to the grammar school I walked past the place where the rising began in 1831; the history master lived only a hundred yards from the spot . . . But education in Merthyr in my time, as regards language, and content, and direction, was the same as education in Norfolk, say, or London, or Somerset, or anywhere else in England. (*Tyfi'n Gymro* 8–9)[17]

The school in which these young citizens of the British Empire were were being educated was a new one. The castle had been bought by Merthyr Corporation in 1908 from the Crawshay family, who had built it in 1825 on the profits from the Cyfarthfa ironworks, which they owned, and the school finally opened in 1913, with some 500 pupils. By the time Glyn Jones entered the school three years later, the Great War had broken out and, given the newness of the school and the shortage of teachers, away at the Front, there was 'a certain inevitable wartime laxity of discipline and effort'; he found it thus 'a heavenly place'. 'Staffed by the finest collection of characters and genial eccentrics in the whole education business',[18] the school was set in surroundings of great natural beauty; the castle was in a park with a lake and woods, while beyond the school to the north lay the Brecon Beacons, close enough to be reached on a bicycle for a brief hour of freedom even at lunch-time: 'an area of enchantment, of sunshine and blue lakes and woods, and the vast bareness of the mountains rising from the roadside, green and yellow with the thin cloud shadows lying transparent upon them in the heat' (*DTT* 28).

In school he had to cope with being apparently less able than Tyd, who had gone through school some five years ahead of him. Jones always recollects himself as having been both self-absorbed and rather lazy, although one notices that in that little pocket diary which he kept at the age of fifteen he carefully records that he is eighth in the class in the summer examinations. He also had to cope with several of the masters being friends of his parents – 'a devastating humiliation' – and members at Soar, who frequently visited the Jones home in Clare Street. (Mr. Evans, the physics master, would visit the Joneses on family holidays at Llansteffan, appearing, spade over shoulder, to dig for lugworms with Mr. Jones: 'In school he would heap insult after insult on my head for its inability to master the truths of natural

philosophy. And here he was calling my father "Bill"!')[19] Given this
relationship between teachers and parents, it seems likely that this boy
who was not outstanding academically, but read avidly and was
fascinated by art, history and, above all, literature, was nurtured and
encouraged, especially in a relatively small community, despite the
disruption caused by the war.

In his diary on 18 March 1920, Jones records, 'Received Golden
Treasury'. The volume, Palgrave's *Golden Treasury, with Additional
Poems* was a revelation to the young boy whose romantic tastes we have
already noted: the volume opened his imagination for the first time to
the rich world of English Romantic poetry, to the landscapes – both
outer and inner – of Wordsworth and Coleridge, the painful beauty of
Keats and, perhaps above all, the ornate, medieval England of Morris,
Rossetti and Tennyson. The teenage Jones became 'obsessed by poetry'
(*DTT* 27), by its sounds and imagery, by the very texture of its
language. It is from this time that Jones's lifelong fascination with
words dates, with the shapes and sounds of words at least as much as
their meanings, the sensual patterns you could make with them. He
notes how he became fascinated with the literary terms he found listed
at the back of one of his grammar books – 'such words as prolepsis,
litotes, and hendiadys' (*MPi* 79) and, again, while he learns their
meanings (although they were not part of the syllabus), he was mainly
struck by their strange sound and shape.

As he was to write years later:

> It is often said that a writer's mother tongue, the language he heard first from
> his mother . . . is the one he will inevitably use for his creative work . . . This I
> question. It seems to me that the language which captures his heart and
> imagination during the emotional and intellectual upheavals of adolescence, the
> language of his awakening, the language in which ideas – political, religious,
> aesthetic – and an understanding of personal and social relationships first dawn
> upon his mind, is likely to be the one of his creative work. (*DTT* 25)

Certainly it was thus for Glyn Jones. When he was born, the majority of
the people of Merthyr – just over 50 per cent in the census of 1901 –
could speak Welsh, but the actual use of the language was rapidly
eroding.[20] Apart from the impact of immigrant labour, children for
whom the language of the hearth was Welsh were taught only in
English from the time they entered school, and one imagines that
English very rapidly became the language of playground as well as the
classroom. Even at Soar things were changing, as they were in the
other Welsh chapels in Merthyr: the young people of the chapel no
longer had a secure grasp of a language they were using less and less,

and so, by the time that Glyn Jones became involved in the chapel, the week-night activities for the young people – the Band of Hope, Christian Endeavour, the Young People's Fellowship, the Gym Club, and so on – were all conducted in English – 'they saw that keeping the church going was more important than teaching a language' (*Tyfi'n Gymro* 9) – although the Sunday services were still held in Welsh. Thus by the time that Jones was an adolescent, he, and thousands like him, had virtually ceased to use their first language. English, the language of school and street, and of chapel activities, finally and inevitably, became the language of his home, as his parents, too, gradually began to speak English to him and his brother. The only Welsh he heard was from his Auntie Ann, his father's half-sister, who lived next door and who continued to speak to her brother in Welsh, from elderly relatives who lived over the mountain from Merthyr and, of course, from his relatives on the farm at Llansteffan, who had very little English. But it was a fragile connection: 'In such circumstances, what hope had anyone of being a Welsh-speaking Welshman – unless he was a fanatic or a hero – and I don't see myself in those categories' (*Tyfi'n Gymro* 9).

As he approached the end of his school career, Jones seems to have had little idea of what to do next. His interest in art had continued – he used to take his painting equipment with him to Llansteffan – and, rather surprisingly and presumably in her anxiety that her son make something of himself, his mother suggested he go to art college. Instead, he ultimately chose to follow Tyd to St. Paul's College, Cheltenham, to train as a teacher.[21] Glyn Jones never spoke in any detail of his years at St. Paul's, except to say that his time in that 'deadly, uninspiring place was one of the dullest periods of my life' (*MPii* 73): although his main subject was English literature, his love of poetry, he wrote later, 'was not enriched or extended to the slightest degree'.[22] It is hard to imagine an environment more alien to a chapel boy from Merthyr: St. Paul's was an Anglican foundation run like an English public school. And beyond the College, of course, was a well-heeled spa town to which many of its inhabitants had retired after years of service in the Indian army or civil service. The only pleasurable memory he had of these years was, characteristically, of leaving the town on his bike and cycling through the fields where flowers were being cultivated commercially, and drinking in their smells as he rode along.

On qualifying as a teacher, Glyn Jones considered teaching posts in Norwich and the north of England but ultimately he moved to Cardiff, to where his parents had removed during his years at Cheltenham, and after a brief period of unemployment he was appointed, in 1925, to a post in Wood Street School in what was then known as Temperance Town, an area near what was then called Cardiff General railway station. Despite being so near the town centre, this area of workers' houses, developed in the mid-nineteenth century on land reclaimed when the course of the Taff was altered, had become one of the worst slums in Cardiff. It was here in the rows of run-down terraced streets that Jones's pupils lived, 'among the poorest and most wretched in the city, ill fed, ill cared for, dressed in dirty, handed-on clothes often not much better than rags. Several came to school barefooted even in winter' (*DTT* 29). Many families struggled hard to do their best for their children, despite desperate poverty; other parents whom Jones came across were negligent, alcoholic and, not infrequently, criminal: 'one father was a convicted coiner, another operated an illicit still . . . another was involved in a brutal race-gang knifing near the school' (*DTT* 29). Prostitution was rife in the area – police tended to turn a blind eye to the brothels as long as there was no violence or breach of the peace – and several of the children's parents were brothel-keepers or prostitutes. Jones later recalled that many of the prostitutes were among the better mothers and their children, given the mother's income, were amongst the best-dressed. In such an environment, inevitably, many of the children, as Jones knew, were subject to violence and to sexual abuse, including prostitution. As he makes clear in what is one of the most deeply-felt passages in *The Dragon Has Two Tongues*, Glyn Jones had seen poverty in Merthyr, but never to this extent, and never with the associated criminality and vice. What he saw and experienced in the shabby streets around him in these years not only shocked him profoundly but gave him a vision of human nature, of what human lives were capable of suffering and enduring as well as the pain that humans could inflict one on another, unimaginably different from the values of Clare Street and Soar. It was an awareness he never forgot and which indelibly marked the developing imagination of the young man whose deepest emotional responses up to this point had been to the beauty of the natural world and the visions which the poets of *The Golden Treasury* had held up to him.

Given his temperament and background, Jones did his best to reach out to the children he taught, even visiting them at home when they were ill. Such visits, of course, made him all the more aware of the conditions in which some of his pupils lived: 'I visited one boy I was especially fond of – not a phrase you could use today of course – and found him in bed covered only with sacking.'[23] Such visits by an outsider cannot have always been welcomed, of course; the awkwardness and tensions that could result are evident in the episode near the beginning of 'I Was Born in the Ystrad Valley', written in response to the conditions he had seen.[24] There were inevitably less grim episodes, like the time when one lad, in court the previous week for shoplifting in Woolworth's, wrote about *Oliver Twist* – one wonders whose idea it was to study that text – 'The character I like least is the Artful Dodger because he pinches things.'[25] But for a young, inexperienced teacher, trying to teach such children cannot have been easy; to show the sympathy he obviously felt could all too easily be taken advantage of by children well-used to having to exploit any situation they could. A glimpse of the pressures Jones was under is given by an untitled fragment, written some time after 1929:[26]

> He was slow to accept that he had to dominate all these boys – dominate them or go down, be annihilated. He was unwilling to do it. He felt it wrong at the core of him to dominate anybody, subjecting them arbitrarily to his will and his different ideas. He wanted to be friendly with them, leading them on with their co-operation, never forcing discipline on them, but he found they weren't having any. They were rough boys from poor, even desperate, homes, vicious, dirty-minded many of them, spending their time after school on the streets in the worst parts of the town, with plenty of smart answers, cute, insolent, knowing too much, having a lot of mob courage. And when he tried being decent and helpful, treating them with respect and ordinary civilized decency, hardly any of them responded; most of them just ignored him and began wasting their time and a few of the worst thought he was soft, a bit of a pansy, and they tried scoring off him and being awkward.

This, one feels, has the ring of authentic experience, albeit carefully transposed into the third person. What follows this opening passage, though, sounds, in the image drawn of the teacher and in its rather strident imagery, rather more like wishful thinking:

> But [the boys] were mistaken. His nature was hot and passionate, and it made him mad seeing all this indifference and coarseness and resistance, and several times parents came up with threats and warnings, complaining he had been hurting the boys; but once he realised he had to be the boss he didn't give a damn who came. They could do what they threatened and more, he wouldn't stop until he was obeyed without question by every boy in the school. And when his head called him to his room to see a mother, he was composed, a bit contemptuous, sure of himself, with plenty of natural dignity, showing up pretty well in contrast to the silly threats of the woman . . . He was so self-assured and logical the mothers usually went away feeling they hadn't done much good, poor women, and wouldn't do it any more. They got no satisfaction out of him. He had poise, and he was completely self-contained, impossible to frighten . . . And bit by bit, forgetting tenderness, he got his classes where he wanted them. He found a way to discipline his anger, and even to simulate it, and yet let it blaze out steadily like a blown flame, directing it fiercely in a hot stream against a boy, burning out passionately his own shame and humiliation . . . After that he

would speak tenderly and often tears would come, the token of surrender. In time he was able to work upon them as on an organ, knowing the effect of a word or an inflection.

The fiery anger and the self-possessed poise seem equally unlikely; the fact that he wrote the piece at all is, one suspects, a measure of Jones's struggles in his Wood Street classroom in these early years.

Socially these years provided little relief from the stresses of teaching; indeed Glyn Jones writes of this period as being one of 'great loneliness and unhappiness'.[27] He knew virtually nobody in Cardiff and was back living with his parents, initially in Donald Street, Roath, and then in Pentyrch Street, Cathays. In the autumn of 1926, partly no doubt to make contact with other people, but also to undertake a more systematic study of English literature than that which had been available at Cheltenham, he joined an extra-mural class at the University College, run by a senior lecturer in English, Miss Catherine Maclean, a Wordsworth specialist; Miss Maclean, 'the first person I had ever spoken to about what excited me most at the time, namely contemporary literature' (*DTT* 30), became an invaluable friend and guide to the young Jones, who visited her home and discussed and borrowed books. His journals indicate the width of reading undertaken as part of his literature courses with her: the plays of Jonson, Webster and Marlowe, Shakespeare's comedies, the prose of Jeremy Taylor, lectures on the prose of Lamb, Hogg and Scott and the poetry of Keats, Clare, Byron and Emily Brontë, with later study of *Paradise Lost*, Swift, Fielding, Wordsworth and Browning. In in the academic sessions 1931–2 and 1932–3 Jones attended WEA classes in Charles Street, including a course in 'Philosophy and the Sciences', which involved the study of Descartes, Hegel and, later, Freud and Jung.

His 'Notes on Books' kept during these years show an intensity of reading and thinking that is a measure of Glyn Jones's intellectual curiosity and ambition in the period, especially given the energy he was also expending in the classroom and on marking and preparation. His reading in these years shows a continued political interest; as well as several books on William Morris, in September 1932 he is reading Maxton on Lenin, and notes: 'Here is obviously a great man, and yet seldom have great men been so obsessed by one idea to the exclusion of everything else even to their own personality.' This follows, and implicitly comments on, an entry which sounds, surely, a distinctly personal note; Jones has been reading John Clare:

Poor Clare. I am almost of the opinion that the sad lives of so many artists is due to the mal-adjustment of capitalism; artists feel themselves outcasts from society. Their work is unappreciated equally by the people, too often far too busy earning a living to bother about art, and by the capitalists who are intent on their business. In this way art becomes an arcane study of a few, losing touch with the vast multitude of people. The artist, having no audience and feeling himself quite out of touch with the system in which he lives, too often ends like Clare.

This loss of touch with ordinary people is a theme to which he will return even more urgently. A concern with the relation between artist and workers was, of course, a very current one in the 1930s, and Jones was avidly reading the politically-informed literature being produced elsewhere in Britain; he comments in his 'Notes on Books', 'Communism invaded English poetry about 1931 with McDearmid [*sic*]. First Hymn to Lenin.' He read Auden and his friends in *New Signatures* (1932) and *New Country* (1933) as well as one of their heroes, Wilfred Owen, copying 'Futility' and Owen's Preface into his notebook; Owen's elegiac, almost caressive compassion for the suffering men around him clearly appealed to Jones. He did not read uncritically, however; in June 1932 he is exasperated by Auden's *The Orators*: 'What is it all about? . . . Why do critics take such nonsense seriously?' Reading Ezra Pound's *Active Anthology* in 1933, he finds parts of Pound's Cantos 'excellent', while two of Bunting's poems are 'quite "Georgian"' and Zukovsky 'is often merely silly'.

His major discoveries in these years, however, were the poetry of D. H. Lawrence and Gerard Manley Hopkins. To some extent, perhaps, Jones identified with that other young man brought up in the chapel culture of a mining community, passionate about the beauty of the natural world, who trained as a teacher and who, out of all this, became an outstanding writer. Jones seems never to have been concerned with Lawrence's ideas about society; above all what he was thrilled by in the two volumes of Lawrence's poetry, which he bought in 1931, was, again, the almost tactile intensity of the language: 'L's extraordinary awareness of the life around him and his ability to crystallise his impressions in vivid and concrete, although often homely figures, e.g. "my shadow strains like a dog", etc.'[28] The description would equally fit the intense, linguistically vivid poetry and fiction which Jones was to write in the 1930s, upon some of which Lawrence was to be a profound influence. It was equally the rich verbal texture and sensual immediacy of Hopkins's language and imagery that drew Jones, with the additional element of Hopkins's fascination with the sound of poetry, a concern with aural structure and patterning which would coalesce with Jones's own awakening awareness of the aural effects of Welsh-language poetry.

This contact with Welsh-language culture came almost by accident in the late 1920s. His parents had become members of the Welsh Congregationalist chapel in Minny Street, Cathays; within walking distance of their home, it was an island of Welshness in the English-speaking terraced streets of Cathays. While Mr. Jones attended Sunday services and the Sunday School, given his hours of work, it was his wife who was the more active members of the chapel, again involving herself in all of its meetings. And again it is symptomatic of her continued hold on her son that she ensured that he accompanied her: 'I have to confess that the only reason I came to chapel at that time was to please Mam. Because I had little interest in the language of the chapel, Welsh, I had little interest in that which was going on . . . I came to chapel under protest' (*Tyfi'n Gymro* 11). However, in the chapel he gradually got to know a number of young people of his own age, working in Cardiff or studying at the University nearby, who were still living their everyday lives in Welsh:

> What was new and marvellous to me at that time was this: for the first time in my life I heard Welsh spoken naturally, as a first language, by people more or less the same age as me, from the same generation and background . . . talking about rugby and cricket in Welsh, and the cinema, and ordinary things like their digs in the city, and the strange landladies . . . and telling stories and jokes, all in Welsh. (*Tyfi'n Gymro* 12).

The link with the Welsh community at Minny Street chapel was crucial to Jones's future life – he was ultimately to be a member there for more than sixty years – reuniting him with the religious faith of his youth, with the Welsh language and, for the first time, bringing to his awareness the riches of the literature written in that language. Several of his new friends were studying Welsh but the key figure was Griffith John Jones, from Bedlinog, who was teaching Welsh in Cardiff and became a close friend. Jones's first awareness of the possibilities of Welsh poetry came from the great hymns of the *Caniedydd*, echoes of which are heard in several of his stories, but Griffith Jones introduced him to the *hen benillion*, the traditional verses originally to be sung to the harp. (Later, during the Second World War, while fire-watching in Cathays, the two men would pass the time by talking about Welsh poetry and reciting it to each other (*Remembering Aloud* 5).)[29] In the early 1930s Hughes and Son of Wrexham began to publish paperback editions of classical Welsh literature in a series called 'Y Ford Gron' (The Round Table): here Jones could read the Mabinogion, Emrys ap Iwan, Eben Fardd and above all the poetry of Dafydd ap Gwilym and the medieval *cywyddwyr*. The vivid imagery and intricate aural texture of the work of the *cywyddwyr* was a revelation to him: '[A]fter twenty years of indifference my Welsh was uncertain and limited; but I could take in enough to be swept off my feet by the unfamiliar music . . . by the brilliance of their imagery and their sharp response to the visual beauty of the world'(*DTT* 37). He immediately set out to study, with students from the chapel, the complexities of the *cynghanedd* used by these poets; by May of 1932 he was a member of an evening class taught by Saunders Lewis, studying W. J. Gruffydd's recent *Y Flodeugerdd Gymraeg* (1931); Jones's notebook from the course shows him making careful notes on the types of *cynghanedd*. By the mid-1930s, as he began to find his own voice as a poet, he was already translating from Welsh poetry.[30]

To meet Saunders Lewis at this time was, of course, to come into the orbit of a very potent force; Plaid Cymru had been founded just a few years earlier and several of Jones's friends, including Griff Jones, were enthusiastic members. But Jones never fell under Lewis's spell: 'I saw him quoted somewhere as saying that if he had been an Englishman he would have been a Tory. I doubt that he went on many of the Hunger Marches.'[31] (Jones continued to admire him as a critic, though; after hearing a lecture by Lewis in this period, he wrote to Keidrych Rhys, 'Saunders is in some ways the Pound of Wales – trying single-handed it seems to me to break the narrow parochial tradition of Welsh literature and criticism and prejudice; pointing all the time to France and the Middle Ages and to England even.')[32] Jones was always sympathetic to the nationalism of his friends, but as he looked around at south Wales in the 1930s, 'I just couldn't understand how on earth self-government for Wales, and still less Welsh culture, was going to improve the wretched condition of Western civilization and, closer to home, the poverty and unemployment that I came face to face with every day at school' (*MPii* 76):

> How do you persuade people who have lived on the dole, and suffered the Means Test, for perhaps ten or more years – how do you make them realise that the language and Welsh culture are important? What they want is a job and a good standard of living, for themselves and their children . . . They had never spoken the language, many of them, and so didn't feel the need for it . . . [A]t the time of its founding Plaid was overtaken by an enormous economic typhoon, which would probably have engulphed and obliterated altogether a party with less courage and dedication. (*Remembering Aloud* 6)

To this position Jones remained consistent throughout the 1930s and beyond; when Keidrych Rhys is to visit him in March 1937, Jones writes 'I shall be delighted to see you. We can talk about Welsh poetry, and ditto Nationalism. Myself, I'm a Socialist.'[33]

Given his immersion in literature, in English and in Welsh, in these early years in Cardiff, and the fascination with language which began in his schooldays, it is possibly surprising that it was not until about 1929–30 that he himself attempted to write poetry. His earliest works are imitations of the poetry he had been reading: Lawrence, Eliot, Pound and above all the poets by whom he had been dazzled in the *Golden Treasury*, especially Browning and William Morris. Several of the early poems are Morris transposed into a Welsh setting, a medieval Wales with the violent immediacy of Morris poems like 'The Haystack in the Flood', decorated with the dazzling, ornate detail that Jones had found in the Mabinogion and Tennyson's version of Arthurian romance. This elaborately decorative world, however, showed no trace of the grim reality of Wales in the 1930s. It is as if he had to keep the two sides of his life apart; faced day after day with the grim world of Wood Street, he perhaps needed the emotional release into this more beautiful world of his imagination. Or perhaps there was no way to reconcile the scruffy world his pupils inhabited with his private world of poetry. 'Gull' was inspired by a bird Jones saw from the window of his classroom in that grim building – it was built like a castle, with towers and fake arrow slits. The bird, up in the sunshine, free and apart, says the poet, 'bears my beating heart'. Indeed, in so many of these early poems, the speaker stands apart from the community and its stresses, alone on a hill, describing the sky and the landscape, often at dawn or sunset. It is a poetry not just of apartness but of an aching loneliness, a loneliness that provides a plangent undertone to much of Jones's poetry and indeed his short stories.[34]

Socially, however he was gradually becoming less alone; there were the friends he had met through the chapel and in 1929, while walking on the Wenallt to the north of Cardiff, he met Doreen Jones, the daughter of a local businessman. The meeting led to marriage, five years later, with the couple settling initially in the garden suburb of Rhiwbina before they moved to Manor Way (the road from Merthyr), where they lived for the rest of their sixty years together. But creatively Jones still felt isolated. There was no literary scene in Cardiff, no literary magazines – his early poems were published in *The Dublin Magazine*, in *Poetry* (Chicago) and then in London journals like Middleton Murray's *The Adelphi* – and he knew no other writers; as late as 1939 he wrote in his journal 'being an artist in Cardiff is like playing an away match – there's no-one to raise a shout for you'.

Thus, when, on one of his lunch-time visits to Cardiff Central Library, a short walk from the school, Jones came across a remarkable poem in *The Adelphi* by a young poet with the evidently Welsh name

'Dylan Thomas', Jones got the poet's address from the editor, Sir Richard Rees, and, in March 1934, wrote to this still-unknown young poet. Thomas wrote back promptly and was, characteristically, soon lecturing his new acquaintance on poetry – 'the emotional appeal in Auden wouldn't raise a corresponding emotion in a tick' – and politics – 'You are, I suppose, a good Socialist';[35] when Jones wrote about his own attempts to 'achieve a body of workers' poetry', Thomas replied, 'the trouble is that in attempting to write for the Workers one generally writes *down*. The thing to do is to bring the Workers *up* to what one is writing' (*Letters* 117). Jones soon visited Dylan in Cwmdonkin Drive and in May 1934 they visited Llansteffan (the home of Thomas's mother's family, as well as Jones's father's relatives) and Laugharne; then in the autumn they paid a memorable visit to Caradoc Evans in Aberystwyth (*DTT* 64–5). Dylan was already paying regular visits to London, to see other writers and editors and to push his work, moving there to live in November. Jones had also made sallies to the cultural capital, reviewing the Tate Gallery's Burne-Jones exhibition in *The Welsh Outlook* in 1933 and was now invited, when in London, to stay at the large ramshackle house in South Kensington that Thomas shared with two fellow artists from Swansea, the painters Mervyn Levy and Alfred Janes: 'Everything is in rather a mess . . . [T]he demon alcohol . . . has become a little too close and heavy a friend for some time now. Pile in with us, will you?' (*Letters* 179). Thomas had already been drawing his friend's work to the attention of editors in London ('By the way, Geoffrey Grigson is very interested in you and your poetry,' Thomas wrote in the autumn of 1934) and visits to Thomas brought Jones into contact with editors like Grigson, editor of *New Verse*, Middleton Murry and Sir Richard Rees, editors of *The Adelphi*, and Robert Herring, editor of *Life and Letters To-day*, as well as poets like Norman Cameron and Rayner Hepenstall, the latter of whom introduced him to R. A. Caton, whose Fortune Press was to publish Jones's first volume of poetry, *Poems* (1939).

But Jones was already concerned at what he saw of Thomas's London life-style and he feared for the 'prodigal manner' in which Thomas offered that friendship to those casual acquaintances with whom he came in contact in London. And he began to realize that the drinking, too, stemmed not just from an initial sense of liberation from the constraints of home and Swansea but from something more fundamental, from impulses that Jones never fully understood. His ambivalence – the affection underlying his impatience at Thomas's public behaviour and fears for the artistic effects of his life-style – is evident in an unpublished letter to Keidrych Rhys in March 1937:

I gather you don't like Dylan. He makes me pretty mad myself at times, being such an ass, a silly poseur, and yet I have a great affection for him. I've told him how absurd all this drinking and so on is, suicidal for a man like him, but it makes no difference, of course. It's a tremendous pity he kids himself so much. His work suffers I think – his 'Life and Letters' story is piffling. He hasn't the energy or the determination to acquire any background, so he is reduced to spinning fantasies out of his own navel. And soon his navel won't have any fantasy left.[36]

Jones was always sceptical of the cult of the artist as bohemian – Thomas's circle was to be sharply satirized in Jones's story 'The Tower of Loss' – and one suspects that this was in part precisely because of what he had seen happen to Thomas, though in part it was also a matter of temperament, for clearly the two young men whose backgrounds were in some ways so similar were temperamentally very different. During his visit to Laugharne with Jones in May 1934, Thomas had described him in a letter to Pamela Handsford Johnson as 'a nice, handsome young man with no vices. He neither smokes, drinks, nor whores' (*Letters* 135); Jones had presumably seen this letter when he wrote in his diary many years later, and without further comment, 'A prig to Dylan was one who didn't smoke at all, drank little and seldom committed adultery.'[37] The chapel-going, teetotal schoolmaster, still living in south Wales with his parents when he made his initial visits to Swansea and London, in every respect inhabited a different world from that of his friend; indeed, as Jones noted shrewdly in his journal in 1964, 'My friendship with Dylan was bound to lapse because I represented all that he was trying to get away from.'

But creatively the contact with Thomas, as well as with the London literary scene, was invaluable in these early years of Jones's career. He noted himself in his 'Sketch of the Author', published in *Poems*, that it was reading Thomas's work that ended his attempts to write 'a workers' poetry'; Dylan 'appeared completely unconcerned with the social or communal aspects of poetry' and this encouraged Jones to turn inwards and to explore 'the familiar images that . . . confronted me from the mirror maze'. The impact of Thomas's verse, as well as Jones's own interest in Surrealism, is evident in the dense, dazzling, often physiological imagery in poems like 'Sande' ('The winds pluck off his ripened flesh like leaves'), 'Easter', 'Rant' and 'Man', as well as the remarkable 'Biography' (1939), which catches the tensions of the period in vivid, energetic images of dream and nightmare.[38] It has sometimes been suggested that it was Thomas who urged Jones to write short stories.[39] However, although he certainly received encouragement from Thomas to write short stories – 'What about your story of the workman shitting over the cliff?' Thomas asks in March 1935 (*Letters* 186) – it seems likely that Jones had already begun to do so; he did not meet Thomas until April of 1934, while Jones's diaries show that by the autumn of 1934 he had not only competed four stories – 'Eden Tree', 'Cadi Hughes', 'Eben Isaac' and 'Knowledge' – but was awaiting decisions about them from editors. These stories, and 'I Was Born in the Ystrad Valley', probably written in 1935, show Jones writing in a number of styles, 'Knowledge' in fact being heavily indebted to D. H. Lawrence. But the two men certainly talked about short stories on that first visit to Cwmdonkin Drive and after one of his early visits Jones brought home with him typescript copies of three of the surrealist stories that were to appear in *The Map of Love* (1939): 'The Mouse and the Woman', 'The Visitor' and 'The Enemies'. Several of the stories that Jones collected in his first volume *The Blue Bed* (1937) and some of those in the first half of *The Water Music* (1944) are certainly shaded with tones and techniques that respond to the haunting world of Thomas's 'Jarvis Valley' stories, though Jones's own vision is rarely over-powered by that of his friend. While the way in which the natural world and the human body are mysteriously interfused in Thomas's stories – 'there was creation sweating out of the pores of the trees' ('The Enemies') – is echoed in some of Jones's landscapes – 'the body of the mountain . . . sloped into the night holding up a breast with both hands against the rubbing sky'('The Kiss') – we do not sense in Jones's stories Thomas's almost obsessive sense of the mercilessness of time and natural process; Jones's sense of mortality is less dynamic, more associated, often grotesquely so, with pain and physical suffering. We hear echoes of Thomas's tone and syntax at times in Jones's more mysterious, unlocated, fabular stories, with their unnamed characters –

The child knew the house from roof to cellar; he knew the irregular lawns and the gardener's shed where the flowers burst out of their jars . . . The gardener had no present to give the child, so he took out a key from his pocket and said: 'This is the key to the tower. On Christmas Eve I will unlock the door for you'.
(Dylan Thomas, 'The Tree')

The little girl sat in the cottage kitchen drawing a fire like a rose bunch, and a wine cup and a shooting star . . . 'Remember the bread, cariad, and the key, and the jump, and the clock face', said the old man, and he turned slowly away out of the garden. The little girl said, 'Good-bye, Rhys y Mynydd'.
(Glyn Jones, 'The Four-Loaded Man')

The child lay in bed . . . The night was windy and cold, he was warm under the sheets; the night was as big as a hill, he was a boy in bed.
(Dylan Thomas 'The Tree')

> When the child woke up his bedroom was full of light and the moon shining in
> had made a window upon his floor. hearing outside the noisy tide of trees
> roaring he left his warm bed and looked out into the blue cube of his world.
>
> (Glyn Jones, 'The Little Grave')

– but in such stories as 'The Little Grave', 'The Four-Loaded Man'
and 'The Wanderer', Jones's concern with compassion and with human
love and forgiveness is doctrinally more orthodox than Thomas's
disturbing, illogical world. At the same time none of the characters in
Thomas's early stories is described with the same fascinated,
occasionally bizarre, attention to detail which Jones lavishes on his
characters; nor do the rather isolated figures of Thomas's Jarvis Valley
stories inhabit the lively, sardonic, humorous village communities lived
in by Cadi Hughes or Eben Isaac or Revd. Roderick Price-Parry.
Reviewing *The Map of Love* in Gwyn Jones's *Welsh Review* in 1939,
Jones found the later fantasies like 'The Map of Love', 'less shapely
and satisfying' than the Jarvis Valley stories, which he saw as
'describing a landscape which lies perhaps between the territory of
Caradoc Evans and T. F. Powys'; their 'strange power' he saw as
deriving from 'the collocation of previously unrelated words and ideas
. . . into new combinations which constantly surprise us . . . Dylan
Thomas understands the Alchemy of the Word. He knows that an
adjective and a noun thrown together are as likely to be explosive as
two chemicals pounded in a mortar'.[40] Perhaps more than anything
this was what Glyn Jones found exciting and liberating in Thomas's
work: that one need not be bound by decorums of register and of
English literary practice. In the work of this other young Welsh writer
Jones found an echo of his own fascination with the novelty of English
words and confirmation of the startling effects that could be achieved
when incongruous words flashed together in unexpected and unconventional ways.

In 1937, the year in which Jones finally moved from Wood Street
School to a post at Allensbank Secondary Modern School in Cathays,
Cardiff, he saw the publication of his first volume of short stories, *The
Blue Bed and Other Stories*. Hamish Miles had written from Cape in June
of 1935 saying how much that he had enjoyed 'Eden Tree', which Cape
had published in *New Stories*; he had now seen 'Cadi Hughes' in *The
Adelphi* and wanted to know if Jones had sufficient material to form a
book.[41] Jones must have responded, for in April 1936 Jonathan Cape
himself wrote offering terms for the collection (originally to be called
Welsh Stories); Edward Garnett in one of his last reader's reports for
Cape had written that 'Glyn Jones is a genius . . . his stories have a

strange imaginative quality about them unlike anything else'. Rupert Hart Davis, then working with Cape, returned the proofs on 25 November 1936, commenting that 'I think it is one of the most remarkable first books I have ever read'. The book was published in January 1937, and in February E. P. Dutton accepted it for publication in the USA. The reviews of the book in the London press confirmed Garnett's enthusiasm. In the *Morning Post* (29 January 1937), H. E. Bates hailed 'an uncommon talent, prodigal but sure, sensuous but conscious . . . revelling in the luxury of words and yet having something fresh and powerful to declare'; in the *Observer* (7 February 1937), under the headline 'A Remarkable New Author', Richard Hughes praised a writer in whom 'words are alive, and immensely powerful . . . Such writers are rare: only one or two in a generation'; Edwin Muir in the *Listener* (10 March 1937) quoted at length from 'Wil Thomas' and 'Eben Isaac' to demonstrate their author's 'extraordinary command of language'. Perhaps most enthusiastic of all was Humbert Wolfe in the *Sunday Referee* (February 1937), who under the striking if imaginative headline 'A New D. H. Lawrence Emerges from the Pits', wrote that 'in Mr. Glyn Jones we may have a new D. H. Lawrence' and, in a long review which is in many respects the most responsive of all to the nature and tone of Jones's created world, draws attention to the quality of beauty in the writing that is, 'like Lawrence's . . . primarily tactual' and which gives a 'picture of the hearts and wild emotions hidden behind rags and filth'. These were reviews to gladden the heart and quicken the ambition of any young writer. The Welsh settings inevitably distracted some reviewers – the reviewer in the *Sunday Times* (7 February 1937) found the stories to be partly limited by the fact that they 'are all Welsh of the Welsh, inbred Welsh' – and confused others, especially in America, where the *Washington Post* review (22 May 1938) reported that the stories 'deal largely with Welsh coal miners' and 'are very tiring and on the whole incomprehensible'. Back in Merthyr, the Revd. M. Watcyn-Williams in the *Merthyr Express* was of course more in tune with Jones's concerns: in 'I Was Born in the Ystrad Valley', the 'sudden flooding of the heart of the hero with new love for his fellows takes one's breath away'; the reviewer goes on to hope that, reading the story, 'alert English people . . . will begin to understand the cry of the Special Areas, and to realise why three cultured, brilliant Welsh nationalists are in jail and, understanding, they will want to do something about it' or else 'the things Mr. Glyn Jones offers us as fiction might very well be despairing, desperate fact'. Other Welsh responses were less political. The newly founded *Wales* printed an extraordinary 'review' of the book by Margiad Evans: 'It touched me again and again with the ague of ecstasy. I wanted to clap and cry praise and run and bring the sun . . . The stories themselves grope and worry their way into the reader . . . With a spare hand he can lift one to the mouth of a paean' (*Wales*, 2, August 1937); Dylan Thomas wrote with delighted scorn to Keidrych Rhys that it sounded 'as though Miss Evans were, in the process of reviewing, being fucked with literary skill and Celtic ardour on the Blue Bed itself'.[42] By the end of June, Cape had sold 679 copies, while royalty statements show that by 1944 a further 600 copies had been sold, earning Jones £17. 4s. 6d, to add to his £30 advance; in addition Faber paid four guineas to publish 'Wil Thomas' in their 1937 anthology, *Welsh Short Stories*.

Glyn Jones's literary activities in the early 1930s were not, however, limited to his own writing. One Sunday morning in 1931 he was introduced after chapel to a young undergraduate who was studying English at University College, Cardiff. Seven years younger than Jones, Elwyn Davies had edited the undergraduate magazine at the University and in the summer of 1934 with another former editor, Harold Edwards, the young men decided to do something about the fact that there was no journal at all in Wales in which creative writers could publish their work; even *The Welsh Outlook*, which published articles on Welsh political and cultural matters, had closed in 1933. The new literary journal which they planned was to be 'Welsh, Celtic, and Left, the resurgence into literature of a race economically dispossessed'.[43] Having settled on the title *The Broad Arrow* – having connotations both of the prison and of the druidic Three Beams of Light – the next task was to raise capital. However, despite their enthusiasm and despite letters to Lady Rhondda ('to live in Wales is to live in a country culturally dead, or at least dying', wrote Jones), to Richard Hughes, and even to William Randolph Hearst at his castle at St. Donats, no money was forthcoming and the project foundered.

In Elwyn Davies, Jones found a friend, in Cardiff, with whom he could discuss his reading and his own writing. Davies shared Jones's enthusiasm for Lawrence – Jones loaned him Lawrence's poems – and for Roy Campbell. The two men also shared an interest in painting – Davies was already painting as an undergraduate and did so for the rest of his life – and in the summer of 1932 the the two chapel-going young men set off for Paris:

> Glyn called for me in his holiday best, carrying his suitcase. 'There's nice you look, Glyn', said Mam . . . Mam tolerated my trips abroad because she recognised that they were a part of my education, but they never won her whole-hearted approval . . . Yet, if they had to be, I couldn't do better than go with Glyn. Chapel matrons approved of Glyn – he was 'very faithful', teetotal, and a

'nice boy', in spite of his poetry . . . [I]n his company a wild throwing over of traces was unlikely.[44]

As they wandered the galleries and print-shops of Montparnasse, the streets of Montmartre, respectable Cardiff must have seemed a long way away. When they paid to take drawing lessons, they entered a studio to find a naked model on the dais: 'Glyn's expression did not change, and I tried to make mine look as if this was not a milestone in my Welsh Nonconformist career'; before long the two men were casually chatting to the models in the intervals between sketching, feeling rather worldly – 'I could not help feeling that all the propaganda we had heard back in Wales about the sins of the flesh tended to take nudity too seriously.'

It seems to have been during this trip that Glyn Jones first became alerted to the creative possibilities of Surrealism; he read Breton's 'Manifeste Surrealiste' (1924), of which an English translation had just been published in Paris, and subsequently read several theoretical works on the subject, including David Gascoyne's *A Short Survey of Surrealism* (1935); there is no record as to whether he visited the International Surrealist Exhibition at the New Burlington Galleries in the summer of 1936, as Dylan Thomas did (*Letters* 230–1), but by August of 1937 he had written a short article on Surrealism for Alun Llewelyn-Williams's Welsh-language journal *Tir Newydd* ('New Territory').[45] 'There is no need for you to feel diffident of your Welsh', wrote Llewelyn-Williams, presumably in response to qualms Jones had expressed. 'It . . . does not need much correcting, and is more correct, as it stands, than a great deal of stuff that appears in the Welsh press.' Llewelyn-Williams subsequently asked him to review Kate Roberts's volume of short stories, *Ffair Gaeaf*, and to contribute to a special issue devoted to the work of W. J. Gruffydd.[46]

When he loaned a copy of *Tir Newydd* to Keidrych Rhys, Rhys seems not to have been very impressed; 'No, it's not so marvellous,' Jones admitted. '[I]t suffers from the customary time-lag, but as a Welsh periodical it's very smart and contemporary' (August 1937). By now, however, Rhys was involved in producing something altogether smart, contemporary and Welsh. Jones had, of course, responded enthusiastic-ally to a letter from Rhys, proposing the establishment of a new magazine, offering Rhys both advice and practical assistance as well as material for publication; he agreed with Rhys that what was needed were new voices, not 'the rearguard', by which Jones took Rhys to mean 'Rhys Davies, Caradoc Evans, Richard Hughes. Would be good to do a good show without them first, I think. Might admit them later perhaps – if they'd come'(1 March 1937). But he did not agree with Rhys at all points, and said so; when he was sent a draft of a 'manifesto' for the first issue, Jones wrote back that he didn't think it was very good:

> If you have one at all, why not a fairly long and infinitely vigorous one that will give the readers a jerk so that when they have finished reading it they will wonder where the 'ell they are and what is going to happen next . . . I wouldn't say anything about small fry like Grigson and Roughton – why not burn up the paper with Eliot and Rapallo Pound, Windbag Lewis, the Fascists, with a cut at the pretentious nonsense of 'transition' . . . Then turn round and say we in Wales are on the side of Socialism, the people.
>
> (?March 1937)

When the first issue of *Wales* finally appeared in June 1937, Jones thought it looked 'very well indeed', although he reported to Rhys in August that

> Jack Jones and Gwyn Jones both denounce 'Wales' to me in extremely scornful and uncompromising language! But I am not surprised a bit. Both of them, I've realised for a long time, distrust if not dislike anything experimental, or revolutionary or fanciful. We remain friends however. They're both awfully food fellers. Rhys Davies likes it very much.
>
> (August 1937)

The first issue had included Jones's poem 'Scene' along with poems by Vernon Watkins, Idris Davies, and Rhys himself; it had opened with Dylan Thomas's 'Prologue to an Adventure', about which, to Jones's delight, the *Western Mail* received letters of protest, while a member of the BBC staff, a former London magistrate, told one bookseller that the piece warranted prosecution (letter to Rhys, August/September 1937).

Meanwhile, Jones and Rhys worked closely together; Rhys coming to stay with the Joneses in 1937 and in 1938. In the summer of 1937, Jones was correcting proofs of the second issue and offering Doreen's services as a typist. Rhys sent Jones material submitted for publication in the third issue, Jones responding with crisply discriminating recommendations for what should be included, most of which Rhys accepted.

In a covering letter (September 1937) Jones writes that he is reading Auden and Isherwood's *Letters from Iceland*, which had just been published: 'Amusing book with some crazy pictures. Couldn't we get Cape to send us somewhere like that, you and I?' and then, as a PS, he writes 'School Tuesday does seem awful'. A couple of weeks later he is writing to Rhys in more desperate terms:

> Teaching is getting intolerable. I get a devil of a struggle to go in day after day. I

would like to chuck the whole thing, it's all so senseless. Perhaps I will some day. My attraction is always towards the lowest and most helpless, the dispossessed. I am getting to hate more and more this comfortable middle-class world which seems to be getting me. I don't know which requires the more courage, to quit or to stand up to it. Probably the latter. But it's damned hard.

Do you know what I'm talking about or am I raving?

(September/October 1937)

It is perhaps one of the most revealing passages Glyn Jones ever wrote. Clearly the stresses of teaching were real and acute: 'Many writers have described the cruelty of teachers to children but few the cruelty of children to teachers', he had written in his journal in late 1936, and in the autumn of 1937 there is the curt but eloquent entry, 'Bugger school'. But the letter to Rhys speaks of a much more fundamental discontent, a profound sense that the middle-class life he was living, the respectability that had its roots in Clare Street, instilled by his mother, was somehow incomplete, unfulfilling. In the summer of 1937 he had copied, without comment, some words of Virginia Woolf into his diary, 'All this, my marriage and my job seem to be happening not to "me", but to some assumed and temporary flesh', and the frustration and alienation in the letter to Rhys is painfully echoed in Jones's journal the following month; the entry is written in Welsh, the language in which Jones writes his most intimate thoughts:

Tonight I felt full of anger and hatred, in coming back to this house . . . I walked in the middle of the road in order not to feel the 'smugness' which was coming out of the houses on every side. I felt like throwing the shoe I was carrying through one of the windows. The desire to escape was strong in me . . . I constantly feel like some kind of Ishmael – excluded from everything. This feeling has become part of my nature, worst luck.[47]

As in the letter to Rhys, a more authentic life was to be found elsewhere:

I'd like to give up all these things – house, my bourgeois life, and go down to Bute Street to live simply, without bothering with neighbours . . . possessions or anything else.[48]

This sense of longing for a life in closer contact with the 'non-respectable' working classes, a life conceived as simpler, more sensual, less emotionally constrained, seems at times to be mingled with guilt; indeed the longing seems likely to have had its origins in Jones's guilty awareness of the distance which respectability had constructed between himself and the working people around him in the streets of

Merthyr. These feelings can only have been made stronger by what he saw in the lives of his pupils in Temperance Town. And again one remembers his comments on John Clare, five years earlier. It is such feelings, clearly, that colour his growing impatience with D. H. Lawrence in this period: 'His world is too bourgeois. The problems afflicting his characters don't seem to have anything to do with our problems . . . He is a deserter of the working classes' (Journal, 28 August 1935). Given his earlier imaginative identification with Lawrence, one senses more personal emotion here too, especially when Jones writes, again in Welsh, the following year:

> Every artist born of the working class turns his back on his class by becoming an artist. Because the working class, most of them, care nothing for art.
>
> (Journal, May 1936)[49]

These tensions and these longings, clearly, contribute to Glyn Jones's construction of working people, particularly the working men, in the short stories which he was writing in these years.

It is these emotional impulses towards the working class, clearly, which also underlie Jones's Socialism. In 1932 he had written in his journal:

> These are some of the things I would like to see passing – exploitation, rank and privilege, poverty. This is the thing I should like to see remaining – the kindliness of the poor. These are the things I would like to see coming – the revolutionary mind to the workers, responsible state ownership, the classless society.
>
> (Journal, 24 October 1932)

But he had no illusions as to whether the 'revolutionary mind' was in fact coming to the workers of south Wales; having stood amongst some unemployed men outside the City Hall listening to the results of the general election of October 1935 which returned Tories to all three Cardiff constituencies, an episode that he used in his most political story 'I Was Born in the Ystrad Valley', Jones wrote:

> Some women near me were nearly in tears, saying, 'It's the damned upper classes have done it'.
> I should have said, 'No, it's us. If all working people voted Labour, Labour would govern'.
>
> (Journal, 15 October 1935)[50]

That 'us' is symptomatic of his emotional identification, and during the Spanish Civil War he joined in campaigning in Cardiff, albeit he found even such modest practical activity created anxiety which puzzled him:

> I am deeply wounded somewhere. This going from door to door hurts me terribly, heaven knows why. Giving out the Food for the Spanish People leaflets pains me, although all I have to do is push a leaflet through the letterbox.
>
> (Journal, late 1936)

Presumably, again, such public activity ran counter to deeply-rooted notions of respectability and privacy.

When Barcelona fell in 1939 he expresses his despair in his Journal: Europe seems like a ship slowly and inevitably going down: 'I feel as if my fate is pressing in on me'. This was not a mere rhetorical posture, for Glyn Jones clearly realized that the imminence of war was going to provide a challenge to his own deepest beliefs. On the same page he copied a line from Milton's *Areopagitica*: 'When I kill a man I kill a reasonable human being, the image of God' and then, in a separate entry, 'The real C.O. [conscientious objector] is one who wants to be allowed to serve his country in his own way'. For all his responsiveness to the world's beauty, an acute sense that pain and physical suffering were an inescapable presence in human life formed an equally powerful impulse in Glyn Jones's perception of the world he inhabited, suffering that came from illness, accident or the casual cruelty of others. The origins of this awareness, often vividly present in the writing, is difficult to trace with any certainty, though being brought up in a mining community would certainly have made him aware of the potential for sudden death or crippling injury and, clearly, what he saw in the homes of his pupils in Temperance Town gave him a glimpse of human behaviour which shocked him profoundly. Whatever the origins of this sense of human suffering, his deep, at times even guilty, compassion for his suffering fellow human beings was an essential part of Glyn Jones's temperament:

> At bottom there is worry and suffering and pain. And I add to the pain by the things I do. It is awful . . . Suffering and death. I see them all around me. The bitterness is not so much my own, but I see it in every man – Blood at the bottom of every man's cup.
>
> (Journal, 5 November 1934)[51]

Even if war came, he had no intention of adding to the world's suffering. The pacifist tradition had been strong in Merthyr and Jones became a member of the Peace Pledge Union, helping at a stall run by them with other pacifist groups on a Saturday morning in Cardiff

Market (*DTT* 33). As well as hearing the pacifist case being argued with vigour from the pulpit at Minny Street by the minister, Revd. R. J. Jones, he attended Quaker meetings: 'From a Christian point of view, and I considered myself to be a Christian by now, there was only one answer to these arguments, which was to refuse to support war of any kind' (*MPii* 80).

On 28 November 1940 Jones applied for provisional registration as a conscientious objector, stating in his application:

> I base my objection to war on humanitarian and Christian grounds. I believe the sufferings a modern war inflicts on its participants and the cruelties to which it subjects those, largely women and children, who play no part in it make it contrary to the spirit of Christianity and incompatible with the ideas of human brotherhood.[52]

His age and occupation made it extremely unlikely that he would be called up, but in the spring of 1942 he received notification that, since his occupation had become 'dereserved' from 1 January, he would have to appear before a local tribunal which would hear his case to be formally registered as a conscientious objector. Whilst being perfectly willing to appear, Jones pointed out in an undated letter the absurdity of this procedure: the tribunal could refuse his application and direct him into the forces or other work, despite the shortage of teachers, or it could grant his application in which case he would anyway lose his job, since Cardiff City Council's policy was not to employ teachers who were registered conscientious objectors. Nevertheless Jones was called to appear before the local tribunal at the Law Courts in Cardiff on 18 May 1942. As the date approached, he prepared himself thoroughly, carefully listing relevant biblical passages and scrupulously writing out pages of responses to questions which he might be asked:

> Men are prepared to do dangerous things and lay down their lives for you, while you claim a nice job. Is that right? It is true that at all times men do unpleasant and dangerous jobs and lay down their lives for us – I am not likely to forget those people, and I dedicated my first book to such people. But in warfare I am prepared not to let them defend me, as Ghandi is in India . . .[53]

> Do you think it would be a good thing if the British Empire was conquered?. . . I want to see the end of all Empires. In so far as the British Empire is one of power and exploitation and not one of brotherhood and help, I am prepared to see it go . . .

> Why won't you join the R.A.M.C.? When the war started I felt strongly attracted to the idea of joining the R.A.M.C. because I wanted to share the dangers and hardships of the men who were joining up. But when I looked more objectively at the matter I saw that the real function of the R.A.M.C. was to

keep the army fighting fit, to keep disease, fever, etc. away from it so it could go on with its fighting . . .

Keidrych Rhys, already in the army, and Gwyn Jones provided testimonials for the tribunal ('. . . parts of it Doreen thought too nice for words . . . I am glad that you put in the sentence about my views not being yours – that gives it a lot more value really'),[54] as did the Revd. R. J. Jones, from Minny Street, who also spoke on Jones's behalf at the tribunal. In the event, the questioning was brief, the application granted and an unconditional registration as a conscientious objector was issued to Jones on 22 May 1942.

However the previous day Jones had already received a letter from the City of Cardiff Education Committee notifying him, in the light of his registration, of his immediate suspension from his duties at Allensbank School and giving him one month's notice of the termination of his contract. Among letters of support from friends and sympathizers, was a letter and a cheque from colleagues at Allensbank. Jones wrote a letter to the Secretary of State for Education, R. A. Butler, pointing out the absurdity of the procedures: 'teachers in my age group have not been called up and if your instructions carry any weight they will not be called up'; if he had *applied* to join up, his age would have caused him to be turned down. But now began the task of finding a new job. Jones wrote dozens of letters of application or enquiry to schools and education committees all over Britain; one after another, back came the negative replies: 'My school will not sanction the appointment of a conscientious objector'; 'In view of the circumstances mentioned [in your letter], the Committee will not be able to consider an application from you'; 'You may take it that my Committee would not, under any circumstances, agree to the appointment of a conscientious objector.'

At the end of June, however, he obtained a post at Oldcastle Boys' School in Bridgend. The reaction was immediate and hostile. The staff at the school held a protest meeting and agreed unanimously to bring the matter to the attention of parents and the NUT; a deputation met representatives of the local council and one member of staff, signing himself 'Ex-Serviceman', brought the matter to the attention of the readers of the *Western Mail*: 'It seems . . . that 'conchie' teachers are not desirable in Cardiff schools and are welcome in Glamorgan county'.[55] The protests surrounding Jones's appointment continued into the summer, reported fully in the press, the *Western Mail* carrying regular reports and letters of protest.[56] Bridgend Urban District Council unanimously passed a resolution demanding that Glamorgan Education Authority dismiss Jones, one councillor urging that parents of boys at the school who had relatives in the Services should organize a strike if the appointment were maintained.[57] A vigorous debate took place at the education committee, when it was pointed out that three or four masters at the school who had served in the Great War, one of whom had been badly wounded, felt particularly angry at the appointment of a conscientious objector; in the event, however, the authority decided to take no action. Protests were still being made by Bridgend Council at the end the end of August, when the NUT wrote in support of Jones.[58] Inevitably when Glyn Jones had joined the staff in late June, he had received a cold reception. His distress is evident in a letter to the director of education seeking a transfer to another school: 'I have found it impossible to give of my best to the children in my care because of the atmosphere of hostility in which I am continually working . . . Half the members of the staff have spoken not a word to me yet and the remainder appear anxious to confine their remarks to replies when I speak to them first'. He received at least one abusive letter, addressed simply to 'The Conchie Teacher'. But no transfer was forthcoming and Jones remained at the school until he was appointed to a post at the Twyn School in Caerphilly in 1944.

His pacifism did not, of course, mean that Jones took no part in the war. He acted as a firewatcher in the city and as an A.R.P. ambulanceman. He and Doreen also looked after a succession of evacuated children. And nobody was out of danger: in 1941 six people were killed when bombs fell on Whitchurch, just down the road from them: 'Doreen and I heard the bombs whistling down and fell flat like a couple of legless reptiles.'[59] Inevitably his experiences only heightened Jones's sense of horror at the world around him, evident in entries on one page of his Journal:

> After Blitz: men approached tree – birds flew out – on way back – birds flew out again – examine tree – human meat blown there.
>
> Mr. L. – following lorry on bike – tarpaulin blows up – sees human meat inside – has to dismount – lorry full.
>
> Man shovelling out rubble – hand of child amongst it – woman sitting on doorstep, demented, saying – 'It's all right, I haven't got any children, I haven't got any children.'
>
> 'I am a faithful servant of my country but I am also a servant of God' (Thomas More).
>
> (Journal, early 1940s)

Despite the pressures that he was under, or possibly because of them, Glyn Jones continued to write through these years, both poems and short stories. In July 1943 he wrote to Jonathan Cape concerning the possibility of a second volume of short stories; Cape wrote back inviting him to send the stories, although it seemed unlikely that Cape could get them into print because of war-time paper restrictions.[60] In the event Jones sent his eleven stories to Routledge, from whom T. Murray Wragg wrote in February 1944 to say that readers had liked them immensely: '*Wat Pantathro* is . . . certainly the best short story that I have read in the last 15–20 years'.[61] Terms were quickly agreed, Jones receiving an advance against royalties of £25; when he returned his signed agreement Jones enclosed his latest story 'Price-Parry', to be added to the collection. *The Water Music and Other Stories* was published in December 1944 in time for Christmas and, in the strong market for short stories which existed in the war years, it sold rapidly: the first printing of just over 2,000 copies was sold out by the end of January, earning Jones some £77 in addition to his advance; a further printing of another 2,000 copies also sold out and royalty statements show that altogether the author earned over £193 from the sales of *The Water Music*, a not insubstantial amount at the time.

But the book was not only a financial success. If the reviews were not as extravagant as for Jones's first volume, they were certainly very positive. The volume showed a shift in subject matter and to some extent in technique. As well as unlocated, fable-like stories ('The Wanderer', 'The Saviour') similar to some of the stories in *The Blue Bed*, Jones had begun to write stories set in the south Wales valleys, usually seen through the eyes of boys not unlike his boyhood self, wandering the streets of a town not unlike Merthyr, though using experiences too from his years in the classroom. Rhys Davies in *The Welsh Review* (March 1945) noted the two types of story, the stories of boyhood – 'straightforward . . . can be enjoyed by all' – and the more fabular, poetic stories – 'his hot-house flowers, his orchids' – adding shrewdly, 'Their core is some veiled episode of mental anguish exploding into heavily-laden sentences, often of extreme beauty'. While Davies found the latter to be at times overwritten, he felt 'The Water Music' itself to be a triumph: 'Here, miraculously, the fusion [has] been achieved . . . In it the mere short story writer [has] become true poet. Or mere poet a superb story writer'.

Further afield, praise was equally forthcoming. In the *Listener* (20 January 1945) Edwin Muir found that in this collection Jones had gone 'far beyond' *The Blue Bed* and noted the 'Terror, dread, horror' which formed part of the 'unified vision of life' in the stories. The reviewer in *Reynolds News* (21 January 1945) noted that 'this is a golden age of the short story' and that Glyn Jones was 'outstanding among his contemporaries . . . His native gift of observing the apparently insignificant in people and things . . . is now matched by such mastery of language, such discipline and freedom, that all the time one wants to read passages aloud'. In the *Observer* (31 December 1944), Alan Pryce-Jones found the volume 'outstanding'. The only negative note came from the *TLS* (6 January 1945), in which the anonymous reviewer admired 'An Afternoon at Ewa Shad's' and 'Wat Pantathro', but felt that in the more poetic stories 'the reader is made more conscious of the author's flow of words than the claims of story-telling should surely permit' and that the 'relish for the physically up-setting is a further weakness'. One of the most astute reviews appeared in Welsh; in *Y Faner* (17 January 1945) Kate Roberts emphasized the similes, 'fresh and odd and yet always accurate', and compared the imagery with which Jones described the natural world with that of Dafydd ap Gwilym. She too noted the presence of two worlds, that of fable and that of the real world but pointed out that the author never seems to have his feet wholly on the ground: 'There is some sense of another world in all the stories'.

The post-war years saw Glyn Jones continue to divide his life between his creative world and his day-to-day routine as a teacher. (He moved to Glantaf Secondary School, Llandaf, Cardiff, in September 1956, where he taught English until his retirement in 1965.) And that creative world was extending in new directions. In May 1949 he wrote to Gwyn Jones: 'my novel has been with Nicholson and Watson for well over two months now. What are they doing with it?'[62] (As early as January 1937, Glyn Jones refers to 'a projected novel' in a letter to Keidrych Rhys, but no other evidence of it appears to have survived.) The novel finally appeared from Dent in 1956 as *The Valley, The City, The Village*. A *Bildungsroman* tracing the life of an artistic young Valleys boy to university and to a village not unlike Llansteffan, the novel has been criticized for a lack of unity, for being all too evidently the work of a short-story writer. In fact it is a genuinely experimental work, using a variety of narrative techniques, including such Welsh devices as *dyfalu* (the piling up of figurative effects).

During the 1950s Jone's creative life and his life as a teacher were brought together in two projects. In 1953 he was commissioned by Aneirin Talfan Davies at the BBC to write a verse-play for radio. *The Dream of Jake Hopkins* portrays a schoolmaster caught between the stultifying demands of educational bureaucracy ('And a list of all addresses – and the ages in a list – /And a list of all boys absent – and a list of every list / That you've listed in your thirty years of list begetting list', *CP* 25) and his compassion for the boys in his charge:

> Murphy's home is a ruin, with one double-bedder
> For swarms of young Murphys, the younger the madder . . .
>
> And Wayne's granny Williams is just as adoring;
> She keeps a sly brothel and lives on the whoring.
>
> (CP 25–6)

Jake is a man possessed of 'blessed memory', of childhood love and of natural beauty, but also haunted by the painful voice of 'undesired memory',

> remembering,
> Like a bitter regurgitation, shaven skulls,
> Striped pariah clothing, squalor, madness and defeat
> Encircled in barbed wire, glittering
> And brand new.
>
> (CP 34)

Near the end of the poem mystified parents ask: 'Why isn't Jake a Head?', though Jake, 'a middle-aged teacher, / Behind my moustache like a straw-haired Nietzsche' (*CP* 39), has no illusions and no such ambitions. In fact, in January 1951 Glyn Jones did apply for the post of headmaster of a junior school. He was never an ambitious man – 'As a headmaster / I'd have been a disaster' he quipped in his Journal in 1982 – but what he saw of the way promotions were obtained in south Wales, the corrupt network of personal connections and influence, the canvassing of councillors, infuriated him:

> I am hardly out of the room before the clerk comes out and recalls 'Mr Davies'. He is either head and shoulders above us or he has canvassed well.
>
> Q. What has T.H. got that I haven't got? A. A brother that's a councillor.
>
> (Journal, 3 Feb. 1951)

Jones began to draft a three-act play to reveal the corruption of appointments and promotions to teaching posts, but in the event he did so in a second novel, *The Learning Lark*, published by Dent in 1960. Despite the fact that the book dealt with the whole issue in an essentially comic manner, it aroused more controversy than any of Jones's other works, moving off the book pages to the news pages, not just of the *Western Mail* and the *South Wales Echo* but the *Empire News* (which serialized the novel) and the *Daily Mail* (which headlined the story: 'I am Shocked by this Tammany Hall'); more soberly, in *The Bookman* the young Alan Sillitoe compared it favourably with *Lucky*

Jim: one didn't as in that 'dead-end farce' recall 'only the funny bits, here one is aware of the other side of the coin as well, flashing darkly among the remembered laughs'.[63]

This was perhaps Jones's finest period of writing since the 1930s and it produced, in his third novel, *The Island of Apples* (Dent, 1965), his fictional masterpiece. The novel, again using the child's point-of-view to tell of young Dewi Davies's attraction to the romantic but mysterious stranger, Karl, alludes to the myth of Ynys Afallon, the land of eternal youth; ultimately it is a story of the potency of adolescent romanticism, its exciting illusions, and the pain of its loss. 'I suppose what I am trying to say in "I. of A",' Jones commented, 'is – "How beautiful is the ideal world, how completely enchanting, and how brittle"' (Journal, 1964).

Jones appears to have planned a third volume of short stories sometime in the late 1960s, to be called *The Golden Pony*, a full typescript of which survives. Presumably this was submitted unsuccessfully to publishers. In the event, when Dent published *Selected Short Stories* in 1971, Jones inserted three stories from the *Golden Pony* collection: 'The Boy in the Bucket', 'It's not by his Beak you can Judge a Woodcock', and the remarkable, previously unpublished 'Jordan'. The remainder of the stories did not see the light of day until the publication of Glyn Jones's last volume of short stories, *Welsh Heirs*, published in Wales, by Gomer, in 1977. Collecting as it does stories written over a period of a quarter of a century, from 'Lias Lewis' in the 1940s to 'The Tower of Loss' and the stories of the Jeffreys family, written in the 1960s, the volume shows the remarkable consistency, power and range of Glyn Jones's imagination: the comedy of 'Rhysie' and 'The Tower of Loss', the mystery of 'Rhamant Drist', the deeply compassionate 'Robert Jeffreys'.

The roots of that imagination one can only, of course, hint and gesture at. The mysterious alchemy by which the creative imagination of that 'nice, handsome young man with no vices', or the quiet, even-tempered, outwardly serene man that he became in his later years, could bring forth the surrealist anguish of 'The Wanderer' or 'The Apple-Tree', the heated frustration of 'The Saviour', or the gothic horror of 'Jordan', was something which even Glyn Jones was at a loss to explain. Asked on one occasion about the origins of 'Jordan', he immediately told of the cheapjacks that came to the markets of Carmarthenshire, but when pressed as to the origin and significance of the grotesque Jordan himself, with his hairless, scar-covered body, the author could only shrug, rest his finger on his temple and say 'I suppose it all came from up here somewhere . . . One writes what one has to write'.[64]

The Stories: Acts of Atonement

As we have seen, Kate Roberts, in her review of *The Water Music*, writes of the stories as being situated in 'another world'.[65] It is certainly a distinctive world. In the early fabular stories – 'Porth-y-Rhyd', 'The Apple-Tree', 'The Saviour', 'The Wanderer' – as well as stories like 'Eben Isaac', and the last part of 'I Was Born in the Ystrad Valley', the heat of the sun pours from the sky in a very un-Welsh fashion, creating an atmosphere of oppressive oddness and a landscape of harsh shadows, discomforting, alienating:

> In front of him was nothing except a laddered sea-sun on the sand, and the stones shagged black and green with weed, and stretching over him a thin white sky-skin with a crazy sun in it; when he turned to the shore, that too was empty in the distance and completely desolate. (this collection, p.87)

Indeed, the world of the stories is one that is often haunted by a sense of loneliness, of unfocused longing and a sense of· incompleteness, feelings similar to those we have seen expressed on occasion in Glyn Jones's journal.

To 'explain' the stories simply in terms of biographical factors is to be crudely reductive, to devalue indeed the power and rich variety of Jones's creative imagination. But there would seem to be a link, for instance, between the impatience and frustration with bourgeois respectability expressed so vehemently at times in the journal and the fascinated relish with which households so different from the respectability of Clare Street are described in the fiction: the extraordinary, chaotic, scruffy but vital household of the narrator's friend, Arthur Vaughan Morgan, in 'Bowen, Morgan and Williams', that other dilapidated, motherless house in 'Wat Pantathro' with its bare boards and broken plaster, and, above all, the scruffy, chaotic alternative household, with the cousin who 'smells of stale tobacco', that the little boy in 'The Boy in the Bucket' imagines, joyous, free and unrespectable:

> Lead me on. Lead me on to my dirty auntie – somewhere I have her – and her cousins of chaos, unreproved; to the household of children spotted like wallpaper . . . to the house of indifference and joy. (p.219)

We should, however, note that at the end of the story, the boy is clasped in the sanctuary of the arms of the mother whose disapproval he has feared so much: 'How beautiful she looked to his startled eyes . . . Never before had he smelt so sweetly the faint perfume of her, the breathed-in freshness of her presence' (p.223).

A variation on this impulse towards freedom from scrupulous domestic cleanliness and respectability is to be found in one of Glyn Jones's oddest stories, 'Eden Tree'.[66] The unnamed protagonist – he is 'a workman' – sees growing up as a process of becoming socialized and respectable, which inevitably involves the rejection of the 'otherness' of the dirty and the sordid. When you are young, he reflects,

> You shovelled your hands into the chilly dirt of the garden and then bit your nails; and bathed in the canal where they drowned dogs; and blew up a pig's bladder with your mouth to play football with. But bit by bit they got you clean – leave that alone, come away from there, don't dirty yourself . . . But gradually he saw that it was all bunk. Utterly pure water isn't even wet, and utterly pure salt is no good for potatoes. (p.77)

One remembers the boy's envy of the lads whose mothers did not forbid them to swim in the canal in 'A Day in July'. The workman ultimately rejects such notions of cleanliness and respectability as unnatural, inhibiting, limiting of natural impulse; he goes on to associate such a life with the non-organic, the isolated and the mechanical – '[W]hat was worse than touch me not was machinery' – and one night he has a bizarre and horrific vision of what this life has done to him: his own heart has become a machine:

> [T]here was nothing living about it, no flesh, no juices or pulsation . . . Flat-fingered cogs spun dryly into one another like dead catherine wheels; long polished steel rods slid accurately on and back through oily collars . . . and in the middle of it four brass-elbowed pistons tupped determinedly down into the steamy square of darkness. (pp.78–9)

He weeps tears of rage and shame: 'He felt much better after that. But he knew he wasn't whole yet' (p.79). How does one achieve wholeness? The story becomes even more allegorical and, as we shall see, the underlying themes and associations are wholly characteristic of Jones's fictional world. The workman digs in the countryside and finds 'tears'; he digs in the colliery and finds 'a cross'. Wholeness it seems, is a rejection of cleanliness and respectability and an acceptance, an embracing, not only of the unclean, even the squalid, but of pain and suffering:

> Take any common saying such as 'God was the Word' – well you can write brilliant books and answers about that, but only when something happens like childbirth, or a lot of suffering, and it wades into the middle of you and squats there giving orders that you begin to put your clothes on the beggars or run away into the woods. (p.80)

The iconography of the story is, not unusually, that of the New Testament. But, underlying this iconography, the impulses are essentially sensory and emotional. We find similar impulses and longings in Glyn Jones's long story of armed rebellion in the south Wales valleys, 'I Was Born in the Ystrad Valley'. The story begins with a section which is not political. The narrator, Wyn, remembers an episode (it is described in vivid detail) when he was a boy; the horse which pulled the coalman's delivery cart trapped him against the railings in the narrow lane outside the boy's house:

> I was in terror of his hot massiveness, of the great emanations of his strength in that narrow space between the cart shaft and the railings . . . feeling his flesh-warmth sweeping over the resistance of my naked face . . . At last with my ears bursting and the jerk of my heart hurting me I put out my hand palm flat and touched the soft muscle slab swelling above his leg. It was warm and soft, flat, beautiful to touch with the palm of my hand. (p.2)

It is, clearly, a powerfully erotic episode – in bed that night Wyn cannot sleep because he can smell the horse on his fingers and can see 'the forked vein rooted along the curve of his dry belly'; it is, again, a sensual contact with the physical world, with the organic 'other' and serves as a prelude to Wyn's impulses of sympathy for the 'unrespect-able other' of the workers and his involvement with the communist-led workers' uprising.

A related connection between eroticism and the profoundly com-passionate, between comradeship/brotherhood and an embracing of the organic, this time in the form of the shockingly sordid, comes in 'The Kiss'. Here another unnamed workman, a collier, mysteriously comes to life after apparently being killed in a pit accident. As he slowly comes to consciousness and makes his way down the hillside to his home, he begins to feel longings for sensual experience, a longing present even in the description of the landscape:

> Along one side of the road leading down to the village was a line of naked poplars all shoved sideways, swaying to one side like the long hair of earth blown up erect . . . The workman longed to speak again, longed to see the bodies of women and men moving once again with passionate or even commonplace movements as the restless urgency used them, hungered and thirsted to taste with his mouth, longed to smell living bread, to feel fire. If he could exist to touch flesh with his healed hands, never increasing suffering . . . (p.45)

The flesh that the collier does touch is indeed suffering: reunited with his brother, the collier slowly and gently unwinds the stained and stinking bandages with which the brother's hand is wrapped. The hand is finally revealed:

It was a great heavy mass of black flesh, soft and thick, swollen up with black
spongy decay and larger than twice its normal size, showing no trace anywhere
of veins or knuckles or the pink shine of fingernails or even of the shapes and
divisions of fingers. Beginning from the wholesome pale wrist-flesh and
spreading to the farthest tip, it was a shapeless black mass of stinking flesh like
some bad inward part cut from an animal, warm and soft throughout, not
divided up into fingers at all and with only a small bud of foul black flesh
sticking out at the side where the thumb should have been growing. The
workman, used to sights of the body diseased and lacerated, had never seen
anything to terrible or so pitiful . . . Very tenderly, with tears running down his
face, he bent forward and kissed the putrid flesh of his brother's hand. (p.48)

In the background, as the bandages are peeled away, the men's mother
breaks out in anguished weeping, urging the collier not to undo the
bandages; when he looks up after he has done so, she has fainted. The
precise nature of her objections is never made quite clear; however, the
strong impression one gets is of maternal objection to the confrontation
with the sordid, and also a tension between maternal restraint, her
concern with avoiding the disgusting hand, and male comradeship,
liberating, willing to embrace 'otherness'. Once again, too, tender concern for suffering is articulated in registers which are both highly
physical, even erotic, and also overtly religious: 'His love-acts were skilful,
and soothing to his brother, tender and reverential, and his calm absorption in this eucharistic task seemed child-like and complete' (p.47).

This extraordinary scene in many respects epitomizes the nexus of
emotions one senses so often in Glyn Jones's stories: an impulse to
transcend distaste for the physically disgusting, to break out of the
isolating fastidiousness of respectability, and make physical connection
with the non-respectable, to express loving, physical compassion for
that which is suffering. This impulse to identify with, to be at-one-with,
guiltily to *atone* for – we remember the religious registers – that which
the respectable self is moved to reject, aesthetically or morally, seems
to be at the heart of Glyn Jones's fictional world. In this way the
alienated self can gain a sense of completeness, wholeness, *at-one-ness*
with the communal, indeed with the proletarian, in the face of those
factors – educational, social, familial – which isolate it.

These impulses are articulated in political terms in 'I Was Born in
the Ystrad Valley'. The sensitive, emotionally intense Wyn, whom we
met above, goes to university in England and is gradually isolated from
his roots in the working-class south Wales valleys community:

Oh, it was delightful listening to the charming disinterested professors telling one
about beauty and talking about form and content and literary revolutions

... before the end of the year they had me just where they wanted me – I was one of their very nicest little doctored toms, a collier's son with the outlook of a French aesthete . . . [M]y great love of grandeur and sensuousness and style in all things [was] bringing about in me a subtle, spiritual betrayal of my people. (p.4)

We should not, of course, confuse Wyn simply with Glyn Jones, but Wyn's situation is clearly coloured by feelings and anxieties with which his creator was familiar; when Wyn ultimately begins to realize the falsity of his life, we hear echoes of sentiments we have seen in Glyn Jones's journal:

I was convinced that art is no concern of the working-class man, that directly he begins to write or paint or compose, by that very act he separates himself from his class and accepts the ideology of the middle classes. (p.6)

The squalid living conditions of the poor in south Wales are brought home to Wyn when he visits the home of a young boy from a youth club for unemployed boys where Wyn has been helping; there in the sordid one-room home in the slums of Cardiff, when the boy's father, silent and hostile, 'drawn and wild-looking', looks at him, Wyn experiences a moment of deep emotional awareness:

This wild look of terror and helplessness and desperation went like a stab through my loins, my heart beat in my belly, I was weak, ashamed, I could have wept at the pity of it . . . I saw a creature whom I loved with tenderness, for whose sake I would have died if that could have saved him further suffering . . . I understood for the first time in this upper chamber, love, and the cross and the washing of feet. (p.11)

Once again deep pity is registered in a complex of registers: sensual, almost Lawrentian, and religious. And it is this nexus of deep feelings, coupled with the realization that the ballot box is incapable of bringing about the necessary radical social and economic changes, which causes Wyn to join his friend, Alun, in organising the left-wing insurrection. When, the insurrection defeated, they finally part, Alun wishes Wyn good luck and he kisses him:

I said 'Good-bye, Alun,' and we separated. It was quite simple, but knowing that Alun had loved me was very sweet and as I walked back along that country road though the night I felt for the moment happy and almost triumphant, although I belonged to a defeated people. (p.39)

Again, as in 'The Kiss', brotherhood, loving comradeship, comes to epitomize Wyn's reintegration into working-class community, although the end of the story is complex, even evasive.[67] While Wyn merges mysteriously with the natural landscape, he is still ultimately apart from his people, and they are indeed defeated; what seems to matter more than their victory is Wyn's own self-realization, his coming to life emotionally and his contact with the suffering people and the organic world.

The envy of the lonely self for the companionship and sensual vitality perceived to be possible within the working class is in fact present in Glyn Jones's early poetry. The speaker in 'Hills', for example, standing, as do so many of the narrators in his poetry, alone on the hillside, thinks of the miners he has seen coming off shift:

> . . . the sound of their boots
> Like chattering of tipped hail over roofs;
> I can remember like applause the sound
> Of their speech and laughter, the smell of their pit-clothes.
>
> (*CP* 41)

But once again the narrator can only watch, cannot become part of the community which the men represent; and again, too, the solitary watcher is filled with compassion for the men and their hard lives. Or at least ostensibly so: in the third stanza the poem moves somewhat elusively into the third person and the unfocused feelings seem to be as much for the situation of lonely figure, perceived romantically on the hillside, as for the men:

> On the hillside, ambushed by rising stars,
> Beneath a pine-tree giving up its scent
> Into the night like some monstrous blossom,
> A man stands suffering, with tears salt
> And cold upon his mouth for very pity.
>
> (*CP* 41)

At one time it seems that Glyn Jones thought that his poetry itself might provide a means of establishing contact with the working classes, an intention, as we have seen, to which he refers in his correspondence with Dylan Thomas.

That attempt was abandoned – 'The workers work eight hours, have three R's education, and care nothing for poetry . . . I had no means of reaching them' (*CP* 136)[68] – but clearly Glyn Jones's imaginative, and emotional, response to the working classes continued. Duttons, the American publishers of *The Blue Bed*, included in a press release about the book a passage, provided by Jones and not otherwise published, in which he refers to having been brought up in 'one of the most distressed towns in the 'special areas' of Great Britain', a background which has made it difficult for him now 'to sympathize with the artificial sorrows of the intellectuals' and their literary quarrels:

> I've a tendency to think with Rousseau, speaking of the 'common people', that 'hardly anything else is worth considering', a tendency to feel that the real sorrows of the poor are the yardstick of all sorrows.

Later in the same piece he refers to his admiration for Whitman, another writer, clearly, whose deeply compassionate, emotional attraction to the physical life of the workers and the 'unrespectable' is an inextricable part of his vision of Democracy.[69]

In fact it is striking just how many of the protagonists of Glyn Jones's short stories *are* working men (often only identified as 'the workman'), even when there would appear to be no necessity in plot or narrative terms for them to be so. As well as the working men we have already seen in 'Eden Tree' and 'The Kiss', Tudur, for example, in the dream-like 'Porth-y-Rhyd', is also described as a 'workman' (he is in fact a fisherman). Tudur is alone on the sunlit but desolate shore in the first part of the story, 'Machludiad'; in the second half of the story, 'Codiad' he awakes to find a young woman sitting quietly in his room. He asks who she is:

> He thought she said 'Yourself', but he wasn't sure.
> 'How can you be myself?' he asked gently. 'You are a woman with breasts. I am Tudur Porth-y-Rhyd, a working man'. (p.89)

She tells him of a lost child, and of human suffering; he has apparently lost the woman he loved, 'and at her burial I saw blood in the bottom of every man's cup'. It is this loss and awareness of human mortality which has pushed him into the isolation of the first part of the story; the establishment of sympathy reunites him with others: at the end of the story he runs down to the shore to greet his father and his brother whose boat has landed as the woman is speaking.

A number of points link this enigmatic story to other stories about working men. Typical of Jones's construction of these figures, Tudur is portrayed not as physically robust but as 'delicately made' and is associated, as we have seen, with the feminine; in 'Knowledge', Jones's most Lawrentian story, the collier, Penn, is big and powerful but his flesh is 'white as a girl's' and his main hobby is growing roses ('his big hands went delicately into the thick of the rose bush'). Moreover, Tudur in the first part of 'Porth-y-Rhyd' cuts both his hands and his feet on the sharp stones of the shore ('He stood in a warm pool and wept with his hands bloody over his face and the bleeding wounds of his feet sending out red growths into the water'); in 'The Kiss', the unnamed collier as he comes back to life looks at his hands and sees that he has holes in the palms of his hands. Again, then, the working-man, portrayed in terms of delicacy even femininity, is perceived as suffering, but the iconography of sacrifice, of the ultimate act of atonement, is also clearly present.

The image of the workman as gentle but vital saviour is most explicit in the remarkable story entitled 'The Saviour'. A woman sits, her stick across her knees, outside her cottage while a young workman toils in her fields 'in the vertical pour of the sunlight'. She guards her daughter, who is locked inside. The young girl, a hunchback dressed in shapeless clothes, becomes increasingly hysterical, but the mother – 'Her savage face . . . dinted with shallow pockmarks, although peevish and masterful, . . . beginning to slobber and lose its formal solidity' (pp.99–100) – seems intent on keeping the girl from any contact with the workman. He does, however, manage to come to the girl's window at one point and she, terrified at defying the mother, passes a cup of water to him as he stands smiling outside: 'In the fierce sunlight his dense short hair shone clear yellow, almost lemon-coloured, and his eyebrows appeared in a pale and fluffy line with the intense blue eyes contracted beneath them' (p.104). When at the end of the story a violent thunderstorm breaks on the valley, the mother still refuses to let him into the house and he finally kicks in the door. At the end of the story, he and the girl are making their way down the hill, in the rain: 'the pity of the workman's hand glowed like a hot glass on the girl's wet arm'; the workman has struck and killed the mother, separating the girl 'from the hug and comfort of that tyrannical body'. Here more graphically than ever, the isolation of maternal constraint (although we notice the ambivalence of 'hug and comfort . . . tyrannical') has been broken by the action of the gentle working man; alienation has been transformed, it seems, into the freedom of more dynamic life.

The mother is one of the few villains in Glyn Jones's stories, and typically she is a character who cuts off her daughter from social contact. For the characters portrayed negatively in the stories are consistently those who deliberately isolate others, or more usually themselves, from the community, usually for motives of material gain or pride: in 'Robert Jeffreys', Dafydd Morris's grasping wife, Hannah, isolates both herself and her husband from the valley community when a local character, something of a simpleton, kills himself after Hannah threatens him with prosecution for stealing half an ounce of tobacco from the Morrises' shop (Dafydd afterwards feels himself as an 'Ishmael' in his loneliness); Revd. Price-Parry ('Price-Parry') holds himself coldly aloof from his parishioners out of pride in his descent from the Welsh princes until the ghostly appearance of one of his unrespectable parishioners melts his pride and reconciles him with his flock; Lias Lewis ('Lias Lewis') out of spiritual pride tries literally to look down on his sinful neighbours, only to crash to earth and to be reconciled with them in forgiveness before he dies.

The impulse towards non-exclusivity, towards loving, compassionate at-one-ness with others in the community, however disreputable, however unattractive, is, then, a key theme in Glyn Jones's stories. And 'non-exclusivity' could also be said to be a characteristic of Jones's writing technique. We have seen how in 'The Kiss' his narration does not avoid direct and unflinching attention to images and issues which might be excluded on grounds of aesthetic taste. Jones's employment, especially in the stories written in the 1940s, of a child-narrator or of a child's point-of-view has a similar effect: the child's perception – observant, unjudging, unconstrained by decorum – is a perfect means by which to engage the world's beauty, its squalor, its oddness; to engage its wholeness. The child can make the unconventional connections which the the adult mind would either not see or would reject on grounds of taste or inappropriateness. Thus the boy in 'Explosion' describes his teacher as having 'a bald spot at the back of his head surrounded by his black fuzzy hair like the pink spot under a dog's tail'; the narrator of 'The Boy in the Bucket', sitting in chapel, hears one of the congregation clear his throat with 'a loud cackle like trucks shunting'; the young narrator of 'An Afternoon at Ewa Shad's' sees bedclothes billow from a window 'like a large white cauliflower'. This inclusiveness of perception is not, of course, restricted to the stories narrated from the child's point-of-view; it is present throughout Jones's fiction. In 'Lias Lewis', for instance, Maddox the Minister has 'stiff black hair sticking out round his scalp like a bird's nest, and the large white egg of his bald-spot laid in the middle of it'. Such bizarre images, pulling together objects or images from fields of reference which are quite unconnected, remind us of Glyn Jones's interest in Surrealism and in writing which shows some 'suspension of the cerebral',[70] a technique which, Jones indicated, he utilized in the nightmarish description of human suffering in 'The Apple-Tree' and 'The Wanderer':

> In a passage between two windowless houses a daft negress danced with her back to him, howling over the sea-muds and the yellow fields brilliant under buttercups, keeping the stumbling pigeons in the air with her ape-like hands . . .

He hurried past her down the narrow grass-grown street and met the imbecile barefooted dwarf with the gigantic brass head and the fouled work-suit. (p.111)

Clearly, Glyn Jones kept the tactless, unblinking, unjudging stare of the child; he saw the world with an intensity that did not set up polite distances of taste between perceiver and perceived and, like the child, he does not avert his eyes:

Ewa Shad . . . was a funny-looking man, pale, with a big oval face and round popping eyes, whitish grey and very shiny and wet-looking. On his head he had a brown covering of my father's armpit hair, and now that he had taken off his red flannel muffler I could see the swelling wen hung in his neck like a little udder, half of it grimy and half of it clean and white. (p.134)

The stories contain a weird gallery of characters with wall eyes, wens, boils, birthmarks, or graveyard teeth. 'People *do* look odd, very often, if you look carefully', Glyn Jones once said to me. In a way such looking might be considered gratuitous, not in the sense of bad manners or bad taste, but because the elaborate descriptions of odd-looking characters can on occasion hold up the narrative momentum of the story. At the same time, such descriptions again manifest his fascination with the physicality of the world, with the tactile. While there is compassion for the bearer of such deformities, there is usually also something pleasurable in the detailed looking and describing. Something of the same nexus of feelings is present in that extraordinary description of Wil Thomas's eye, lost in an accident years before, as it now lies, apparently, in the minister's hand:

. . . fresh and glistening in the lamplight, with threads of thin steam rising from it and the nerve-roots hanging out between the preacher's fingers. It lay solid and big as a fine peeled egg, . . . polished like china in the lamplight with the pupil and the khaki iris gazing up at Wil in a fixed way he didn't like at all. (p.61)

There is the shudder of revulsion at the sheer tactile presence of the eye, but there is also the pleasure that is evidently being taken in the act of description, and then there is the flash of humour at the end. It is a complex of emotions wholly characteristic of Jones's fiction. One might argue, in fact, that the finest of Glyn Jones's stories – for example, 'An Afternoon at Ewa Shad's', 'Wat Pantathro', 'The Water Music' – derive their strength from the complexity of emotions which they contain, while one characteristic of some of the less successful – 'The Four-Loaded Man', 'The Little Grave', 'Rhamant Drist' – is that they, too overtly, invite a unified, simple emotional response and, in their careful simplicity, do not always avoid sentimentality. (Why '*Little Grave*'?)

Jones's use of that word 'odd' ('People *do* look odd'), though, is a revealing one. As I have argued elsewhere, both in his poetry and in his fiction, the physical world around him is frequently defamiliarized, is perceived as odd.[71] Everyday things are registered, especially in moments of emotion, as strange, as other. In his poem 'Esyllt', for example, as her lover leaves, the girl feels the moment to be 'unreal' and her eye is caught by 'this intense and silver snail calligraphy / Scrawled here in the sun across these stones' (*CP* 4), while the narrator of 'The Death of Prince Gronw', after stabbing his brother, looks up: 'I saw across the bank outside / Grass, like thin hairs along an arm' (*CP* 172). That last image might have appeared in one of the stories, where the strange, almost surreal, images as well as the descriptions of physical oddness, similarly create a sense of the otherness of the world; in other words, even as the narrators gaze in fascination at the world, stylistically the stories register a degree of estrangement from that world, an alienation from environment and community which we have seen as one of the stories' thematic concerns.

Something of the same defamiliarizing effect is, of course, created at times by Glyn Jones's use of the English language itself. He handles words in a way which is, again, almost tactile; they are objects, shaped into sentences and patterns, one feels at times, almost as a painter smoothes paint onto a canvas with a pallet knife. In this, as we have already suggested, he was not alone. He was of a generation for whom English was new and full of potential, a medium of which the writers were all the more aware *because* of their sense of that other language, the language of the hearth or of parents and relatives but not of the writers themselves. It is this novelty, the result of the cultural shifts which had taken place, which (along with communal recollection of older, Welsh rhetorical patternings) gave the people of south Wales their fascination with the effects which could be achieved with English words, in the pulpit and on the political platform, in the street and on the page. Thus Glyn Jones is very much of his generation when he writes in his poem 'Merthyr' *(CP* 41–4) that he 'fanc[ies] words'; one of the undergraduates, a native Welsh-speaker, in Jones's novel *The Valley, The City, The Village*, 'kept a little black book in which he collected big English words',[72] and Jones did something similar, noting down not just individual words which caught his attention, but idioms which he heard around him in Merthyr, Cardiff and Carmarthenshire. Jones's prose is manifestly not, in George Orwell's phrase prose 'like a windowpane';[73] it is designed to be seen and noticed. We are aware of the *craft* of Jones's language in his fiction as much as we are in his poetry, behind which of course is the conscious linguistic crafting and patterning he had found in Welsh-language poetry. Frequently in reading his fiction we are very aware not just of what is being described but of *how* it is being described, of signifier at least as much as signified.

One way in which the language draws attention to itself is a version of that 'alchemy' which he detected in Dylan Thomas, the way in which words from unrelated contexts, from quite distinct registers, can be pressed together to create striking effects. (The parallel with what has been said about the defamiliarizing effects of Jones's imagery is clear.) Thus, while in his poem 'Merthyr' words drawn from, for example, Greek myth ('cyclopean'), from alchemy ('alkahest') and astronomy ('aerolith') are very consciously juxtaposed with more domestic words ('toothpaste'), Americanisms ('bums'), slang ('posh') and local usages ('mitching'),[74] in the stories formal, technical and arcane vocabulary ('stringcourse', 'corbel', 'perihelion') are used alongside distinctively south Walian registers ('bosh', 'gambo', 'twti', 'cwtch'); the protagonist of 'The Water Music', himself, of course, a word-fancier, knows and uses words like 'vidame', 'hirundine' and 'scalene' as well as 'spit', 'gob', 'swig' and 'hairy'. Clearly, what we have here is a fascinating example of what the Russian critic Mikhail Bakhtin calls 'heteroglossia' ('other tonguedness' or linguistic division). Bakhtin argues that all discourse is in fact a blend of discourses (formal, demotic, jargon, technical, etc.) and he points to the methods by which writers like Fielding, Sterne and Dickens exploit the 'heteroglossia' and hybridity potential in English.[75] More recently, the Scottish critic Robert Crawford has pointed to the way in which such techniques are utilized in Modernist texts (*Ulysses*, *The Waste Land*) and Postmodernist writing, and especially to the ways in which in the contemporary world the self, and the literary text, has to be constructed in a decentred society composed of shifting, unstable values and registers in which none has ultimate authority.[76] He goes on to indicate the particular relevance of Bakhtin's ideas to literatures written away from the metropolitan, cultural imperialist centres; in considering the heteroglossia, the linguistic eclecticism, of Scottish writers like Hugh MacDiarmid, Sorley Maclean and Edwin Muir – whose poems are constructed from a rich variety of linguistic sources, both from Scotland and elsewhere – Crawford points to the existence and value of the dynamic interaction between cultures:

> We place too much emphasis on the apparently unchanging elements of a
> culture, tending towards an essentialist position which assumes some sort of

unaltering Scotland or Wales or Canada. In practice, though, such a commuity or tradition would be dead. It is only by remaining dynamic, by evolving, that a culture or a literary tradition continues to live.[77]

It is rewarding to consider the writing of Glyn Jones – and indeed of other 'Anglo-Welsh' writers – in this context; while his fascination with words is clearly to an extent a personal one, the heteroglossia, the jostle of registers we find in his work, is culturally symptomatic, especially given the generation in which he was writing, exemplifying the tensions and conflicts that exist along the borders between cultures, albeit those borders are, of course, far from stable and the cultures on either side far from unified ('For regional and national identities are never fixed, but are fluid, part of an on-going dialogic process'[78]).

A comparison with that most notorious of Welsh short-story writers, Caradoc Evans, visited in 1934 by Glyn Jones as he began to write his own stories, gives us a useful final perspective, linguistic and ideo-logical, on those stories. Glyn Jones was always generous in what he wrote about Evans, noting for example that, 'in spite of everything commonly urged against them', he read Evans's 'strange stories almost always with curiosity and respect, often with considerable admiration' (*DTT* 64). On the issue of Evans's language, Jones is careful and discriminating. While noting that Evans did translate Welsh idioms into English with a striking and estranging literalness – 'large money' (*arian mawr*), 'red penny' (*ceiniog goch*), 'kill your hay' (*lladd eich gwair*) etc. – Jones points out that nothing in Welsh relates to many of Evans's strange coinages; they are used, Jones argues, because Evans 'saw in the necessity to translate his characters' Welsh speech into English a splendid artistic opportunity' (*DTT* 73–4). It was presumably this example which alerted Glyn Jones to the same opportunity. In several of his stories set in rural Carmarthenshire, it is evident that we are to suppose the characters to be speaking in Welsh – for instance, 'Lias Lewis', 'Price-Parry' and 'It's not by his Beak you can Judge a Woodcock'[79] – and it is primarily (though not exclusively) in these stories that we find Jones also translating literally from Welsh idioms which will certainly be unfamiliar to his non-Welsh-speaking reader and will also strike the Welsh-speaker with a curious mixture of recognition and defamilarization: 'from the bottom of the nest' (*cyw gwaelod y nyth*, the youngest child); 'carrying water over the river' (*cyrchu dŵr dros yr afon*, carrying coals to Newcastle); 'my fiddle is in the thatch' (*rhoi'r ffidil yn y to*, to give up doing something).[80] But the overall effect is very different from the sardonic mockery of Evans; Jones plays with the language, and with idiomatic south Walian

English, with affection and pleasure; such idioms are, after all, not the formal registers of literature, but phrases which people use in their ordinary lives, usages which they share with one another; such idioms are markers of community.

This is, of course, symptomatic of the difference between Caradoc Evans's attitude to the community about which he writes and Glyn Jones's own concern for community. Here is none of Jones's tolerant inclusiveness:

> [E]very writer's version of a community is a partial one and Caradoc's range is narrower than that of most. He sees hypocrisy, cheating, lust with admirable clarity, but to gentleness, to sacrifice, to nobility, to tenderness between individuals he is largely indifferent.[81]

Even stylistically Evans is a 'leaver out' (*DTT* 75–6), Jones noting that not only does Evans almost totally ignore the natural beauty of west Wales but he also rarely gives detailed descriptions of his characters' appearance (though Jones cannot resist quoting, as if to prove the rule, a few elaborate descriptions which would not have been out of place in his own work). Perhaps most interesting of all is Glyn Jones's attempt to account for the bleak intensity of Caradoc Evans's work:

> Sometimes I am tempted to think that Caradoc's truly appalling vision of life is not to be explained by the facile reasons often given for it. In his stories he is not paying back the insults and humiliations of his first thirty years . . . [H]is best stories are less those things than a *cri-de-coeur*, an agonised cry of protest and indignation at the horror of life itself. Or they are his attempt to objectify, to make something out of, the emotions of bitterness with which the spectacle of existence on this planet have filled him.[82]

This is an insight which perhaps tells us as much about Glyn Jones as it does about Caradoc Evans, for, as we have seen, he was all too familiar with such agonized feelings about the world he saw around him. But for Jones bitterness was too limited a response; while human life could certainly be horrific, painful, ugly, it could also be beautiful, loving and compassionate. It is a vision most fully expressed in the final paean of praise at the end of 'The Water Music'.

In many respects Glyn Jones's response to the world is closer to that of a very different writer from Caradoc Evans. When Jones came to review the short stories of Kate Roberts, he immediately notes that 'one gets in her work on the whole very little description of the outward appearance of her characters', her main interest being, he says, 'not so much in the skins of her men as in their thoughts and feelings'.[83] However, Jones had huge admiration for Kate Roberts's work, and what he wrote in 1938 about the deep, inclusive humanity of her work, her awareness of both human suffering and of human dignity, might stand as a summation of his own short stories:

> What really differentiates her from the majority of the working-class writers, with their roots in the Great Slump of 1931, is the fact that she knows the different sources of the misery and the glory of human nature. Man does not live by bread alone, but also on identity, and love, and pride, and desire, and compassion for himself and for his fellow-men.

TONY BROWN

Notes

1. Kenneth O. Morgan, 'The Merthyr of Keir Hardie', *Merthyr Politics: The Making of a Working-Class Tradition* (Cardiff: University of Wales Press, 1966), 61.

2. J. W. England, 'The Merthyr of the twentieth century: a postscript', *Merthyr Politics*, 83.

3. Ibid., 84.

4. Unpublished holograph manuscript, headed 'Time of Winstone's fight, September 1965', apparently a short piece for radio on the occasion of one of Merthyr boxer Howard Winstone's world-title fights.

5. GJ's phrase is *digon parchus* ('quite respectable'). See Meic Stephens, 'The making of a poet – Part One', *Planet*, 112 (Aug./Sept. 1995), 68–79 (p.70). This piece is Meic Stephens's translation of the first half of GJ's autobiographical essay in *Y Llwybrau Gynt*, ed. Alun Oldfield-Davies (Llandysul: Gomer, 1971), 61–93. The second half of the essay was published as 'The making of a poet – Part Two', *Planet*, 113 (Oct./Nov. 1995), 73–84. Further references to these pieces, identified as *MPi* and *MPii* respectively, will be included in the text.

6. *The County Borough of Merthyr*, Archives Photographs Series (Chalford, Gloucs.: Chalford Press, 1994), 115.

7. *Merthyr Politics*, 76.

8. Ibid.

9. Glyn Jones, *The Dragon Has Two Tongues: Essays on Anglo-Welsh Writers and Writing* (London: Dent, 1968), 23. Further references to this book, identified as *DTT*, will be included in the text.

10. Undated letter to 'Maggie', Glyn Jones Papers, National Library of Wales. (At the time of writing much of this material is still to be catalogued. Where there are catalogue numbers these will be given. References to other unpublished material, including GJ's Journal, are to material in the NLW except where indicated.)

11. Conversation with the editor, 18 October 1992.

12. Unpublished holograph manuscript, entitled 'Remembering Aloud'. This is the text of a talk probably given in the early 1970s. Further references will be included in the text.

13. Diary in the Glyn Jones collection at Trinity College, Carmarthen.

14. The text was published in *New Welsh Review*, 32 (Spring 1996), 91–9. The play was broadcast on the BBC Welsh Home Service on 7 July 1955, with Stanley Baker as the Narrator.

15. Conversation with the editor, 22 February 1992.

16. Unpublished typescript, entitled *Tyfi'n Gymro* ('Growing to be a Welshman'), 10. This is the text, in Welsh, of an autobiographical talk given at Minny Street Chapel, sometime after 1985. The translations from this TS are my own. Further references will be included in the text.

17. Cf. *DTT* 26. Sarnicol was Thomas Jacob Thomas (1873–1945), who won the Chair at the 1913 National Eisteddfod and in the period 1898–1944 published ten volumes of poetry and prose.

18. From a short essay which GJ contributed to a booklet published by Cyfarthfa Castle School in 1963 to celebrate its fiftieth anniversary. Other facts about the school are from this booklet.

19. Ibid.

20. Gareth Hopkins, 'Population', *Merthyr Tyfil: A Valley Community* (Merthyr: Merthyr Teachers Centre Group, 1981) 389.

21. GJ indicated to the editor, 18 October 1992, that, primarily due to the efforts of his mother, Tyd had been kept out of the First World War by entering the pit as a trainee surveyor. It was after the war, in 1920, that he went to Cheltenham. He subsequently became a teacher in the Midlands and later an HMI.

22. Glyn Jones, 'Illuminations', *Poetry Wales*, 24/3 (1989), 43.

23. Conversation with the editor, 25 November 1994.

24. Conversation with the editor, 18 October 1992.

25. Unpublished Notebook, 1930s.

26. The piece is written on notepaper of the 'Western Produce Co. Ltd.', a company of which the father of Doreen Jones, whom GJ met in 1929, was a director.

27. 'Illuminations', 43.

28. Ibid.

29. The *hen benillion*, traditional verses for the harp, which were passed from generation to generation of the common folk, interested GJ for the rest of his life. A collection of his translations, with an Introduction by GJ, was published after his death: *A People's Poetry: Hen Benillion* (Bridgend: Seren, 1997).

30. See, for example, 'The Wind's Complaint' (from the Welsh of John Morris-Jones), *Collected Poems*, ed. Meic Stephens (Cardiff: University of Wales Press, 1996), 188. Further references, abbreviated as *CP*, are included in the text.

31. Letter to the editor, 18 February 1993.

32. GJ, letter to Keidrych Rhys, [c.1937], NLW MS 22745D.

33. GJ, letter to Keidrych Rhys, 18 March 1937, NLW MS 22745D.

34. On this aspect of GJ's poetry, see my essay-review of *Collected Poems*, 'Tones of loneliness', *New Welsh Review*, 39 (Winter 1997–8), 43–7.

35. Letter to GJ, *c.* 14 March 1934, Dylan Thomas, *The Collected Letters*, ed. Paul Ferris (London: Dent, 1985), 97. Further references, identified as *Letters*, are included in the text.

36. GJ, letter to Keidrych Rhys, 18 March 1937, NLW MS 22745D. All letters from GJ to Keidrych Rhys are in this collection at NLW. Further references are indicated by date in the text.

37. Diary entry, 1982.

38. When 'Easter' appeared in *New Verse*, Thomas wrote to GJ, 'I came to the vain and very boastful conclusion that it was strongly influenced by myself' (*Letters* 144).

39. GJ appears to imply as much in *DTT* 191 and in *Starting Out: A Memoir of the Literary Life in Wales* (Cardiff: University College, 1982), 12.

40. *Welsh Review*, 2/3 (1939), 179–80. Presumably GJ is alluding to, or half-remembering, Rimbaud's 'Alchimie du Verbe'; Rimbaud is cited by GJ in his 'Notes on Surrealism' (1937).

41. Hamish Miles, letter to GJ, 14 June 1935.

42. Letter to Keidrych Rhys, early July 1937, NLW MS 22745D.

43. GJ, letter to Keidrych Rhys, January 1937, NLW 22745D. On the attempt to found *The Broad Arrow*, see Elwyn Davies, 'The magazine that never was', *Anglo-Welsh Review*, 81 (1985), 97–106.

44. Elwyn Davies, 'Glyn Jones and I go to Paris', *New Welsh Review*, 4 (Spring 1989), 34–5. Other quotations in this paragraph are from the same essay (33–7).

45. 'Nodiadau ar Surrealistiaeth', *Tir Newydd* (November 1937), 11–14. Translated as 'Notes on Surrealism', *New Welsh Review*, 28 (Spring 1995), 20–2.

46. Alun Llywelyn-Williams, letters to GJ, 30 August 1937 and 20 December 1937.

47. Journal, October 1937. The translations of Welsh entries in the journal are my own.

48. Journal, July 1937. This entry is also in Welsh. Bute Street is a working-class street in Cardiff's dockland.

49. GJ uses the word *gwerin*: 'Mae pob artist yn enedigol o'r gwerin [*sic*] yn troi ei gefn ar ei ddosbarth trwy fod yn artist. Oherwydd nid yw'r werin, yn y mwyafrif, yn hidio dim am gelfyddid' [*sic*].

50. The full entry is given in the notes to 'I Was Born in the Ystrad Valley'.

51. One of the characters in GJ's novel, *The Valley, The City, The Village* (1956) sees the world as 'a mixture of madhouse and torture chamber'; when asked in an interview in July 1994 if this represented his own view, Glyn Jones said that it did, adding: 'The world can be a very cruel place' (videotaped interview, 'Writers in View' series, Arts Council of Wales, 1995).

52. All of the documents cited relating to GJ's conscientious objection were amongst his papers and are now in NLW.

53. *The Blue Bed* had been dedicated to 'The unknown heroes equal to the greatest heroes known'.

54. GJ, letter to Gwyn Jones, 6 May 1942, NLW Prof. Gwyn Jones Papers II, 9/2.

55. *Western Mail*, 29 June 1942.

56. See for example, 'Collier Tom Looks at a 'Conchie'', *Western Mail*, 16 July 1942, and ensuing correspondence.

57. *Western Mail*, 3 July 1942.

58. 'Bridgend Council and C.O. teacher', *Glamorgan Gazette*, 28 August 1942.

59. GJ, letter to Gwyn Jones, 2 March 1941, NLW Prof. Gwyn Jones Papers II, 9/2.

60. Jonathan Cape, letter to GJ, 20 July 1943.

61. T. Murray Wragg, letter to GJ, 15 February 1944.

62. Letter to Gwyn Jones, 8 May 1949, NLW Prof. Gwyn Jones Papers II, 9/2.

63. *Bookman* (January/February 1960).

64. Conversation with the editor, 22 February 1992, and 'Writers In View' interview, 1995.

65. *Y Faner*, 17 Ionawr 1945, 7.

66. A fuller discussion of some points made in the following discussion will be found in my "Praise . . . in my pain and in my enjoying': self and community in the short stories of Glyn Jones', *Fire Green as Grass: Studies in the Creative Impulse in Anglo-Welsh Poetry and Short Stories of the Twentieth Century*, ed. Belinda Humfrey (Llandysul: Gomer, 1995), 65–81.

67. On the debate about the ending of this story, see James A. Davies, 'Bed, farm and map: three responses to the troubled 1930s', *Seeing Wales Whole: Essays on the Literature of Wales*, ed. Sam Adams (Cardiff: University of Wales Press, 1998), 77–101, and the notes to the story.

68. For a fuller account of this concern with the workers in GJ's poetry, see 'Tones of loneliness', *New Welsh Review*, 39 (Winter 1997–8), 43–7.

69. In 'Remembering Aloud', GJ notes, 'A great poet – a Whitman, a Hopkins, some of the *cywyddwyr* – can speak with enormous power right to our hearts, their words can set us aglow'. In his Journal in 1973, GJ wrote, 'Ah, Walt, why were you never a Welshman? What a Welshman you would have been!'

70. Conversation with the editor, February 1982.

71. See 'Tones of loneliness'.

72. Glyn Jones, *The Valley, The City, The Village* (London: Dent, 1956), 105.

73. George Orwell, 'Why I Write', *Collected Essays, Journalism and Letters of George Orwell, vol. I*, ed. Sonia Orwell and Ian Angus (London: Secker & Warburg, 1968), p.7.

74. On the linguistic registers used in 'Merthyr', see John Pikoulis, 'Llansteffan, Merthyr, Samarkand: the question of beauty in the poetry of Glyn Jones', *Welsh Writing in English: A Yearbook of Critical Essays*, 5 (1999), 1–26.

75. Mikhail Bakhtin, 'Heteroglossia in the Novel', *Bakhtinian Thought: An Introductory Reader*, ed. Simon Dentith (London: Routledge, 1995), 195–224. The section is abstracted from Bakhtin's 'Discourse in the Novel', written in the mid-1930s.

76. Robert Crawford, *Identifying Poets: Self and Territory in Twentieth-Century Poetry* (Edinburgh: Edinburgh University Press, 1993).

77. Ibid., 13

78. Ibid. Crawford cites Bakhtin: 'One must not, however, imagine the realm of culture as some sort of spatial whole, having boundaries but also having internal territory. The realm of culture has no internal territory: it is entirely distributed along the boundaries, boundaries pass everywhere, through its every aspect' (*Problems of Dostoevsky's Poetics*, 1929).

79. See the notes to these stories.

80. On the effects of this use of translated Welsh idioms, see Katie Gramich's review of GJ's *Goodbye, What Were You?: Selected Writings*, in *New Welsh Review*, 26 (Autumn 1994), 73–4.

81. Manuscript draft of 'Three Anglo-Welsh Prose Writers', *Rann*, 19 (1953), 1–5.

82. Ibid.

83. Review of *Ffair Gaeaf a Storiau Eraill*, in *Tir Newydd*, 11 (Chwefror 1938), 18–19. My translation.

I Was Born in the Ystrad Valley

҂

I was born in the Ystrad Valley where my father was a collier. His people, frugal and independent peasant farmers from the west, had migrated to the coalfields two generations before I was born, but my mother was the unacknowledged love-child of a local squire and quack-herbalist, a fantastic playboy descended from the native princes of our county. I was born in a row of cottages belonging to the colliery company, within a quarter of a mile of a pit, and I was fascinated as a child by the exciting industrialism around me, and I absorbed and retained impressions of it with great readiness. I can easily remember even now the feel in my hands of the cold fern-like patterns made by the big-headed nails in the sole and the instep of my father's working boots, and the sharp smell of his pit-clothes as he stripped for his bath every evening before the kitchen fire.

I seem to be able to remember such early impressions not only with my mind but with the soft of my fingers, and my knees, and the delicate skin of my mouth, and even with the patient inward parts of the body which have an awareness and a sensitivity of their own although they are never touched and can see nothing. They seem to treasure vibrations to which the mind has remained rigid. I can remember in my throat the tock-tock of the big heavy coal-cart wheels going down the lane at the back of our cottages, the loose axle-block of the big wooden hubs giving out a broken tock-tock as the spokes turned over and the broad iron rim of the knocking wheel cut into the ground under the weight of the coal and the creaking wooden cart. Sometimes there was already a load of coals tipped in the narrow lane which had garden railings on one side and the river fence on the other, and any second cart had then to drive up over it to get past. I have still the hot resisted pressure against my eyeballs and the whole front of my body, and the weight and remembrance upon my shoulders of the energy issuing in a hot flood against them from the sweating body before me, from the big chestnut coal horse drawn up at our garden railings. His driver had backed him there hard before I could get out of the way, all the brass and the jerking chains of his heavy harness crashing through my ears, his slipping shoes shining the hard black earth, and his stuck back head furfolding the thick of his neck like a fern-spread. I stood in terror with my face close to the shaft chains and the wet skin of his flank, trapped, suffocating with fear, watching him breathing heavily above me as he rested, blown for the moment, the black sweat smoking under the harness leathers of his back and his gaping collar, and running in thin curves down under the powerful swell of his belly, where he was still dry-haired. I was small and I was frightened of him, afraid of the great shaggy hoof-cones sloped close to my feet, and the massive weight of his hot body, afraid of the barrage of his energy seeming to envelop me, to be collapsing about my head with terrible strength and power. I was in terror of his hot massiveness, of the great emanations of his strength in that narrow space between the cart shaft and the railings, fearing he would crush me, feeling his flesh-warmth sweeping over the resistance of my naked face, but I couldn't get away, I had to stand with my cornered heart pounding, fixed within the hot envelopment of his flesh and his warm animal smell, watching with fascination his soaking back, and the soft heavy muscles of his shoulder and his bright chestnut flank-skin close against my face, dry-haired, hard, stretched full with the great wind-gusts of his heavy breathing. At last with my ears bursting and the jerk of my heart hurting me I put out my hand palm-flat and touched the soft muscle slab swelling above his leg. It was warm and soft, flat, beautiful to touch with the palm of my hand and I held it there a long time sunk against the cushion of his shoulder, draining heat out of the great blooded body of the horse.

But that night I couldn't sleep with the strong animal smell on my fingers and the excitement of remembering a thick forked vein rooted along the curve of his dry belly, feeling it in the darkness to be flowing with a hot throb into my own grateful flesh.

And as I got older I developed a great craving for physical impressions and sensations of all sorts, and I fed this craving before I understood at all what it was leading me into. I used to press flowers against my eyelids, the hard buttons of the ox-eyes and the tender grape-froth of the white and purple lilac bunches, or place the cold blade of a knife flat along my thigh, or find pleasure in rubbing the fine hairs of my hand against the bark of the beech tree branches. And once, when I picked a dead swallow out of the wire netting, I spread the lovely blue lines of his wings across my naked loins. And all this time I lived in the steaming earth-crack of the Ystrad Valley, my father a collier and my two elder brothers working with him underground.

Ystrad was one of the five or six valleys that ran up from the seaboard into the mountains, radiating from a common junction like opened fansticks or the sinews spreading out into the fingers at the back of the wrist. Stepping at sunny midday from hill to hill across the imagined decks of the valley, one sees northward mountain ranges, tawny, muscular, leaking the whitewash of streams that weave in the distance and pour across a cliff-lip like a rope running fast out of a hawse-hole. Here the river pools are clear beneath the lime cliffs and the down drench of the birches, and the valley boys bathe bare with swimming flesh chinaed in empty water. The water is uneasy glass in the peak of the valley where the few farms are and the masty firs in triangular smoke and green, and the feet of mountain sheep peck at the pass-road that leads up out of the valley and curves for England.

Here no thick vein drains down under the side of the mountains, and no pulse beats in the earth of a deep hill, but this is an image of the valley before the holy bogies of the first locomotive carried coal out of her.

The first town dirties the water. Between the blown silks of smoke one sees the township huddled narrow against the river, houses terraced like bent rod-iron along the mountain sides, saving flat silt for pits and railways, long rows of grey streets spiney with vertebral chimneys curving over the shell-folds of the hills parallel to the river bed, or struggling up into the mountains. The grey bleak hills lean up from the streets on both sides, bare but for shorn turf as a steep roof-slope, in places cropping out into scabs of black rock or sliced into cliffs, but everywhere without a daffodil or the huge suck of a tree. And the black slag tips buttress them where there is room, rising with their grasses from the river. Sink to the little streets – three windows and a door, three windows and a door, three windows and a door.

Farther down, where the river runs like a length of opened vein, deep through the divided flesh of the hills, the stalks of two black stacks unravel into horizontal smoke, and the pit is bannered with it. Look at the things happening with the sun upon them, the muzzle of a two-inch sooty pipe sticking out of the big engine-room brickwork, eight feet up, coughing steam towards a clean flat board of sunbeam criss-crossed with metal winding gear, sloped through the coal-dust. The long shadow of the iron piping points like a swung pendulum back across the wall of brick armoured with disks of iron. Men move over the sequined earth lifting the steel tip of a boot across the little tram rails, talking, hanging the coconut fibre bag or the feed bucket over the brown pony's neck, knocking the cage up at the pit-mouth. The big wheel spokes spin opposite for chance above the pit-head and the tall straddle of gearing, and at the mouth of the shaft the long-drawn rope probes into the darkness, pouring steadily down like a line of firm liquid or stiff-spouting upward in a taut jet through the sunshine; the cables slacken, thicken into clamps and hooked couplings shackled to the iron cage rising above ground, that takes up with a clank on its lintel the pit-mouth wicket gate of iron. The fine dry drizzle of coal-dust has settled on sparkling skin and steel. Dug and shovelled lump coal is shoved out packed in the chalked trams, and by the locomotive sheds the pit sidings swerve towards the railroads shining like tight wire into the sun. Here the eight-spoked iron wheels of trucks squeal, shunted, stuffed with coal, three-humped with the black sugar of shovelled small coal, packed with upright loads of sweet-scented pine logs, the clean, equal pit props stripped white or matted with carrot-red sweet-smelling coverings of bark. The boiler house siren hoots the day shift up and the pit-road chatters like a drumskin with the heavy boots hail-showering over it.

I saw this, and more, when I was young, accepting it, fascinated by it. But since I see the track precede the wheel; where there are fifty pits someone will find the bones of the little wren, and under the concrete of the engine-room there is a crocus that will burn holes in it.

When I lived in the valleys as a child I never believed that any world really existed apart from the vivid, palpable one immediately around me day by day, the absorbing vital world of pits and colliers and machinery constantly impressing itself upon my senses as terrifying or beautiful, but when I went to a university in England I began to develop, to get cultured, and as long as I was there I swallowed what they told me, hook, line and sinker. I was a real and complete sucker, taking it all in as though it was so much incontrovertible gospel because most of the stuff sounded lovely, so refined and impartial, and of such tremendous importance, just what I had always wanted to hear. Oh, it was delightful listening to the charming disinterested professors telling one about beauty and talking about form and content and literary revolutions without any vulgar dogmatism, and without relating what they had to say at all to ordinary life; before the end of the first year they had me just where they wanted me – I was one of their very nicest little doctored toms, a collier's son with the outlook of a French aesthete. They had an easy and satisfying job with me because my naturally sensuous and impressionable nature, when it was directed by these charming middle-class professors to the high spots of English poetry and poetic prose (these two formed my most readily assimilated diet for three years), began to flourish, my eager sensibility began to expand like Jonah's gourd, or so it seemed to me, and I was growing into spiritual manhood, entering into a rich heritage, becoming the heir of a great culture and tradition. All this

now seems to me poppycock, so much pipe-smoke. I know, rather with
thankfulness than with disappointment and bitterness, that I am an
outsider, that this literature was not written for me or for anyone like
me. Daily it becomes clearer that my unlucky sensibility and my great
love of grandeur and sensuousness and style in all things were bringing
about in me a subtle, spiritual betrayal of my people. I did not even
notice in these years of satisfied sensuous craving that indifference to
the sufferings and aspirations of the class from which I had sprung is
the almost universal condition of English poetry, this poetry which the
teachers were clapping me on the back for absorbing with such ease
and willingness, and I couldn't see through so much skilfully-pulled
wool that the universality of Shakespeare's genius saw in my people
merely figures of fun and the material for comic relief, and never for a
moment creatures like his aristocrats, of suffering and passion. And yet
I should have known that the sufferings of the working classes are more
real than any I had read about in Shakespeare, because, in addition to
being spiritual, they are also economic, and therefore, so far as their
victims are concerned, completely inescapable. When I read books,
after I had joined the movement, about the inevitability of the fate
overtaking the Shakespearean hero, they used to make me tired,
because such a concept is so false, so unreal, meaning nothing to the
man in the actual grip of economic forces; these books showed clearly
their secluded and dilettante origins, because only the man in the
power of forces engendered by a society which he has not willed
struggles and suffers in the truly heroic manner. It amounts to this,
Macbeth was never for a moment bound by any law of man or nature
to murder Duncan, but if you are unemployed you are bound to suffer
however noble and blameless your life may be. But the college worked
the dope so painlessly under the skin of their willing victim that not
once in three years did any such idea disturb me although my father
was unemployed part of the time, and I never at all questioned the
validity of allowing the middle classes to write the country's literature
and at the same time criticize for me the product of their own class.
Later on, when I got back to the valleys, I became a bit saner and I
began to take immense pleasure in arranging lists of dates like the
following. 1830–1835: 'Paracelsus', 'Lady of Shalott', 'Lotus Eaters';
Reform Bill, Factory Legislation, Unrest in Ireland. 1842–1860: 'Bells
and Pomegranates', 'The Blessed Damozel'; Coal-mine and Factory
Legislation, Chartists at Kennington Common. Revolutions in France,
Austria, Germany and Italy.

It amused me to see what a sucker I had been. And from that time,
as far as I myself was concerned, I was convinced that art is no concern

of the working-class man, that directly he begins to write or paint or compose, by that very act he separates himself from his class and accepts the ideology of the middle classes, who at all times have produced the bulk of the country's poetry, music and pictures. I believe that the nature of the working class is to remain inarticulate and that the working-class man should express himself only through action and the class struggle. But it was a long time before I got to that stage of enlightenment.

When I left college the university gave me a job after a bit lecturing on art in the evenings in Cardiff. I was delighted and so were my parents and my two brothers. Sometimes, in addition, I used to give lectures in the valleys, and I had the nerve to talk to the unemployed about the Post-Impressionists, and eighteenth-century English Portraiture, and the Poetry and Painting of William Blake. And all the time I thought I was doing fine, being so helpful, and cultured and up to date in everything. And I nearly finished myself because a woman fell in love with me. After one of my lectures to the intelligentsia of Cardiff – it was on Toulouse-Lautrec – a very handsome girl in navy blue came up to me, carrying her hat in her hand, to ask me about something she had not understood properly. I often had people coming up like that and a fine lot they were when I lectured in bourgeois Cardiff, arty, conceited, gutsless, merely anxious to be impressive and to show off their knowledge. But this girl, I saw in a few minutes, wasn't kidding herself like so many of them, and I knew at once she was not drawing me towards an argument in which she hoped to justify her little ego by defeating the lecturer. She was far too sure of herself for that. She was puzzled and I was obviously the person to enlighten her, that's all there was to it. I had to respect her, her independence and her confidence, and her splendid sense of style when she spoke or moved about; she was delightful, her breasts under her thin blue dress were small and elegant, no bigger than a couple of hard tennis balls, and I admired very much her straight yellow hair tugged back flat over her head and her white skin and the full, rather high curve of her cheek-bones. And although her hair was yellow and her skin so pale she had dark brown eyes, rather long and narrow with bluish lids. All her features except her forehead were small, the mouth a sharp scarlet line, and the jaw delicate and well-marked, tapering into a small upcurving chin, but I suppose her features were elegant and firm, distinguished, without any trace of looseness rather than strictly beautiful. One thing I saw at once, she had plenty of style, mostly innate and unconscious. As we sat in a café that night I found out that her father was a well-known shipowner, a knight who had been very wealthy during the war and who was still a rich and influential man. I started to see her after that, even writing poems about her, saying how her face was like marble and her brow like a pebble a wave had handled smooth, and praising her for her gentleness, which I said was like her virginity, she was born with it. But I always admired her, acknowledging her intelligence and her sensitiveness and her distinction, and the wonderful poise she maintained between her gentleness and her splendid sense of style. But she never felt herself implicated any more than I did in the suffering around her, she never suspected her own responsibility. She was completely without affectation and she could see clearly enough her immediate obligations, being always sympathetic and generous, but when I saw the complete inadequacy of everything that was being done for my countrymen and tried to explain to her that some other sort of action was necessary she was bewildered, antagonistic, quite unable to understand what I was feeling. Her affection died when I mentioned revolution and she married a naval officer. R.I.P.

While I was doing this lecturing I became interested in a club for un-employed boys in Cardiff. I had gone to their rooms first to give them a talk on something or other, and after that I used often to call in and play cards or bagatelle with them in their army hut, and I enjoyed it because I had naturally always preferred the people of my own class as friends and companions to any other, even when I was at my artiest in college. Some of these boys were tough, already pretty disillusioned and inclined to be cynical about things, but I got on well with them because many of the people I had been brought up among were like that and I was used to it. I got to like one of them particularly, and I thought he liked me too, although he was the difficult, jeering sort, not likely to show it much. He was a pretty, rather small and delicately-made boy with a Welsh name. His eyes were blue and although he must have been about sixteen he had a mop of yellow curls. But he used the foulest language I have ever heard next to a pit haulier living near us in Ystrad. He was vital though, clever at most things, independent, not much of a mixer with the other boys, inclined, I thought, to sneer a bit at the enthusiasm they worked themselves into over football and boxing, a bit insolent and superior. But I could tell by his clothes and his broken boots that he was very poor.

The day of a general election in Cardiff, I went to visit him because he was ill and hadn't been to the club for a long time. I found he lived in rooms with his parents over a foul-looking empty shop in a very rough quarter, down where the seamen's lodging houses are. I went along a dark passage and up bare wooden stairs with the nail heads from the last carpet sticking up out of the wood, and the green plaster peeling damp off the chart-like walls. I passed a lot of shut doors on my way up but there was no sign of life anywhere, although I made a tremendous amount of noise because of the dim light, kicking the wooden risers so that they resounded up and down the hollow stairway. On one side of the stairs was a banister with a lot of the uprights missing that swayed when I touched it, and when I got to the top flight, about three stories up, I saw a lot of washing hanging on string against the wall of the passage that led to the door I was looking for. Everything was so depressing and dirty, there was so much squalor and neglect and hopelessness in the look of this building I began to be sorry I had come. I hated the furtive doorways I had passed on the stairs, and the stale human smell and the smell of damp the dim evil place was giving up. I began to be sorry I had not gone swimming with Alun.

When I knocked, a woman came to the door wiping her suddy hands on a canvas apron, while a curl of steam began to drift out over her head from the room behind her. I said 'Good morning. Does Gwilym Morgan live here, please?'

She said 'He does' without opening the door any farther. Then she stood silent, not trying to give me an opening to say anything, but only looking at me in her sullen challenging way. She was a tall, auburn-haired woman, straight and well-made, wearing a dirty white blouse cut off at the elbows that had worked out all round from the waist of her skirt and her apron. Her thick hair was untidy with work, beginning to come down, looping over her ears on both sides of her hard, bitter face. But she must one time have been beautiful, and I was bound to admire her even now, appreciating in the poor light the full upright heaviness of her figure and the weight in the thick coppery loops of her hair. But her resentful, unyielding look as she held the door half open began to irritate me, I felt how silly it was.

'I'm from the boys' club,' I said. 'I called round to see him. He's been ill, hasn't he?'

She said 'Yes' again, resisting me, not yielding me an inch of footing. I knew nothing of love for people then, I had no experience of their suffering and I was naturally irritable, quick-tempered, but I tried not to show my annoyance and I asked her quite gently if I could see him.

She hesitated a moment and then she said 'Come in, will you?' Her tone was still without concealment, reluctant and full of antagonism, but she led me through a tiny dark room where a zinc bath with washing in it steamed on two backless chairs, into a slightly larger and lighter room beyond. Right ahead of me, opposite the door by which I entered, was a fireplace with a few red cinders in the grate and a kettle on them. On the left stood an oilcloth-covered table before the window, the black-and-white check of the oilcloth worn into holes at the corners, and against the wall on the right was a black double bed of brass and iron where the boy was lying covered with a patchwork quilt. A man, who I supposed was his father, sat at the fireside with his back to the window and his feet on the steel fender. He glanced at me and nodded grudgingly as I entered and then looked away back into the fireplace. Although it was lighter here than in the room where the woman was doing her washing, the place was still quite dim to me at first because one of the window panes had been repaired with a sheet of plywood, and apart from that not much light could enter because the roof-slates of the next building came right up against glass. But I could see all the same the signs everywhere of poverty and defeat and hopelessness, the dirty sacking on the floor, and the few broken sticks of furniture and in the corners the patternless wallpaper bulging out lose in great thick bladders covered with dark shadows of dust.

The boy was sitting up in the bed, his curly hair untidy, his face white except for bright red patches on his cheek-bones that looked inflamed as though some pressure, some heavy object had rested upon them. But his blue eyes were shiny as glaze, and when he saw me he smiled queerly.

'Hullo, Gwilym,' I said, going up to him and taking his hand. 'How are you feeling these days?'

I sat down on the edge of the bed with my back against the cage of upright bars at the foot.

'I'm all right, thank you,' he answered in a curiously flat weary voice, and then I asked him all about his illness. But when he had told me how long he had been ill and how long in bed, and what he had had to eat, I found he couldn't or wouldn't say much more. And after a time I had a difficult job saying anything myself, because I began to feel how unwelcome I was, how little I was wanted by any of these people, especially by the silent man sitting at the fireside. I began to feel his active hostility towards me. I looked at him from time to time and noticed how thin and small and ill-fed he looked. He wore a cap but he had no collar and tie on, and the folds of skin from his jawline curved down into the prominent sinews of his neck. His ragged moustache looked notched and was fair in colour with a brown triangle of tobacco stain on the right hand side of his lip. He hadn't shaved, and the pale, sour skin of his cheeks and his neck looked stale and lifeless in the grey light coming flat across them, and his eyes seemed to be completely without colour. But his expression, like the woman's, was bitter and challenging, and I could see at once by the hostile, protesting glance he gave me as I entered that he was irritated, that he resented my visit as plainly as he could; although he said nothing he was telling me to cut the farce and the pretence and to get out. I was sorry he felt like that, but I hadn't come to see him anyway, so I tried my best to interest the boy, talking to him about the club as he sat up in the black iron bed covered with the blankets and the dark patchwork quilt.

'When you come back there'll be a chance of your going to camp,' I told him. 'They're talking of going down to Merthyr Mawr in the summer. Do you think you'll be able to come with us?' He shrugged his shoulders and looked up at his mother. 'I don't know,' he answered with his peculiar half-sneering smile.

As long as I sat at the bedside his mother stood a few paces behind my back as though she was waiting for me to get up and go, and whenever the boy spoke to me he looked past me and smiled up over my head at her. I became acutely conscious of this silent, intimate communication between the two, this sympathy which excluded me, which was hostile and menacing, and I seemed to be able to feel the ill-will and antagonism which the woman and her son felt towards me. Because the smile of this attractive boy was not one of pleasure or politeness but an expression, I felt sure, of the strangely-shown dislike he bore me, perhaps even of his contempt and hatred. I felt humiliated at this; I was astonished and distressed at the force of the malice, the active evil and bitterness which I felt these three people were directing towards me. I was deeply hurt at it, and then I began to feel my anger rising against them because of their injustice to me, my resentment growing even against this sick boy I imagined I had always loved so much. Why should I suffer the opposition of this child when all I wanted to do was to comfort him; why should the woman stand behind me and overwhelm me with her passionate hatred? I coloured and raged inwardly against them, but I tried not to show how deeply I resented their silence and their ill-will and their opposition, and I sat on the edge of the bed talking to the boy about the club and what they had been doing while he was ill. I even tried to bring his mother and father into the conversation, but they both resisted me, and I was defeated by their terrible hostile silences and their unwilling speech. I said to the man, 'Have you voted today, Mr. Morgan?'

He answered nothing and for a moment he continued to look into the sinking fire as though he hadn't heard. I was about to ask him again when he turned his face towards me. It was pitiful to look at, drawn and wild-looking, haggard, and I thought for the moment he would have broken out into sobs or into a cry of rage and hatred against me. I did not know at all what his expression meant, it was at once so full of anger and despair and extreme agony I was shocked by it, the hopelessness and the anguish of it were terrible to see; my own resentment disappeared before it, I felt as though a door had shut on some tumult in my brain. This wild look of terror and helplessness and desperation went like a stab low through my loins, my heart beat in my belly, I was weak, ashamed, I could have wept at the pity of it. In place of the man whom I was willing to hurt because he had hurt me I saw a creature whom I loved with tenderness, for whose sake I would have died if that could have saved him further suffering or one thought of bitterness more. I was hot with shame, I felt indignation growing within me that a look of such anguish and desperation could come into the face of any man, I saw like a flash all the suffering which had led to it and made it possible. What this man felt towards me was of no importance now, it was overborne and nullified by the gush of love I felt for him, my pity for his suffering and his despair. I understood for the first time in this upper chamber, love, and the cross, and the washing of feet. But I could no longer stay in that room with this fierce illumination breaking out within me, and I got away as quickly as I could. I had to be alone to see into many corners of my soul while this excess of light was upon me, I had to feel this strange fire warm in every member of my spirit.

The next day I went down to the civic park to hear the lord mayor reading out the election results from the city hall balcony. I had not slept much that night because I had felt so disturbed, and I went largely to steady myself by doing something among a crowd of people. I did not understand at all why the fact of suffering and misery should have become suddenly of such significance nor why Morgan, an unlikely stranger, had been the agent for such a vivid revelation. I saw poverty among the unemployed colliers every time I visited the valleys, but I had always accepted it, it had never dug itself into me as the loveliness of things had done. But today I was numb with reaction, feeling nothing clearly.

It was a lovely sunny day and a good crowd of people, between three and four thousand, was gathered in the park under the stone balcony waiting for the lord mayor to come out and read the figures. The crowd was loose-knit and I worked my way in towards Emrys Hughes, an unemployed communist leader I knew, whose black, hatless head I could see rising in the sunlight like a tree stump above the uneasy earth of the gathering. He had a few unemployed with him, all of them in overcoats although it was not a bit cold, and they were attracting a lot of attention by arguing and wisecracking and shouting out at anyone who appeared on the balcony. They were cheerful and talkative, confident the socialists would win two if not three seats in the city, and they could see the chance of a job again, or at any rate the end of the means test, with that sun on them and the air warming after winter. Emrys himself was tall and big-boned, a dark-skinned crop-haired chap with big hands and long arms that were always working from the elbows in front of his body, moving up and down with the fingers spread out when he was talking, almost with the action of a man lifting a big tankard to and from his mouth. But in spite of his black, pockmarked chin and his aggressive manner he was really only a windbag, and his revolutionary talk was mostly flim-flam. But the unemployed friends he had with him were interesting enough, full of half-baked ideas and with odds and ends from the *Communist Manifesto* at their fingertips. One of them was a powerful, biggish chap wearing a great grey bag of an overcoat and a broken cap with the eyelets missing, pouching back on his neck. He had a large rigid nose, sharp and curved, and his black teeth were thin, worn with decay until they looked like black needles or the narrow points of a comb. They called him Ern, and they listened when he said anything. The most talkative and exhibitionist was a fair, hatless little chap about twenty-two, with his hands deep in his trousers pockets, holding back his long overcoat and showing his light blue sweater with the roll collar beneath it. 'The board gave us a fine chicken last Christmas,' he said, just as I got up to the group, 'didn' they Emrys? Pity it was in a shell.' He was enjoying having an audience and he was making the most of it, saying anything. Many of the people near were laughing at him, especially the women, and as he made his remarks he jerked himself about as spry and cheeky as a little blue-breasted bird. Another of the men was short and stout, sullen, thick-waisted, with a red glossy face and very powerful glasses; his overcoat of heavy material would scarcely come round his swollen-looking figure, and at the shoulders it was ripped and the canvas and the white wadding were coming out. He had a blue and metal pencil stuck under his cap and along the tops of his ears a noticeable down of soft fur was showing in the sun. Half a dozen other men seemed to be with them including an Arab seaman wearing a trilby and a pink shirt and collar; he chewed a tooth cleaner all the time but said nothing.

'Any results yet?' I asked Emrys.

'Not yet, comrade,' he answered, 'but they can't be long now, it's struck quarter past.' With that a photographer belonging to Alun's newspaper came out on to the white stone balcony, and stood there a moment looking a bit lost, his thumb under his nostril. 'Ay, Archie, leave your nose alone,' shouted Blue-Breast, and although the photographer didn't know what was said he grinned and waved his hand-camera in our direction all the same. I looked up at the huge ornate façade of the city hall, dazzling white in the sunlight and backed by a silk-stretch of delicate blue sky; its whiteness and its bulk made it impressive, but it was not very beautiful because it dripped with unnecessary ornament that looked like a stucco of cream cheese; but it had a lovely clock tower, a carved finger, firm and ice-white in the sun, rising out of the middle of it. In a few minutes I saw a woman in a sable coat appear at one of the windows shaking her handkerchief to the crowd. I recognized her as the wife of one of the Conservative candidates, a woman who always attended art exhibitions and lectures on painting. 'That's done it,' said Ern, who saw her too. 'We're snookered in south, anyway. Look who's up there waving her handkerchief.' Some of the people began to cheer when they saw her, but Emrys's friends and a large section of the crowd started booing, and Blue-Breast began giving her loud raspberries. 'Co sammy, look at her overcoat,' he said. 'It would keep me in dole for a year and I'm a married man.' Just then the woman disappeared suddenly and the noise soon died down again, the people waiting for the lord mayor to come out with the results.

One of the women standing near Blue-Breast seemed to know him. 'I didn't know you was married,' she said, 'I thought you was courting that girl in the market.'

'I wish I was,' he answered. 'It's not so hot married on twenty-seven bob a week I can tell you.'

I looked round at the crowd; it was composed largely of poor people, most of them good-tempered and hopeful-looking, women, some of them with babies, as well as men. On the outskirts a lot of clerks and workmen in dungarees were standing with their bikes waiting to hear the results on their way home to dinner, and all around the edges of the park were the iron beech trunks, tall and naked in the sunshine, grey as girder steel, and overhead one or two long tufts of cloud caught like hawthorn wool in the clear sky.

In a few minutes the little lord mayor fussed out on to the sunny balcony to read the figures, accompanied by the two candidates and their wives. He was a stout little man in black with a white face and red eyes, wearing his gold plate and chain, and holding down with his palm the lid of white hair he brushed over his head to cover his baldness. The crowd became very excited when he read out the names of the candidates and for a long time he couldn't get order, largely because the woman in the sable coat behind him was waving her handkerchief excitedly, and kissing her hands to the crowd all the time.

'Speak up, Fog-eye,' shouted Blue-Breast, 'we can't hear you.' Through the uproar we heard the Conservative was in with a big majority. But the crowd wouldn't listen to him; he looked startled and uneasy at the hostility his appearance had aroused and he seemed glad to get back into the shelter of the building, not even stopping to have his photograph taken. The socialist, a nice-looking, fresh-complexioned boy not long out of Oxford, spoke quite cheerfully. He seemed thankful he had done so well.

'I knew it,' said Emrys. 'I knew it all along.' Although he was a communist he had been working for the socialists, but he hadn't thought much of the candidates from the start. 'I knew it,' he went on, his arms beginning to work. 'How can they expect to win? Look at their bourgeois candidates, one a barrister, another an ex-officer and this one with a private income. Where are all the working-class men who have given all their lives to the movement, sweating their eyeballs out before there was a cheque-book or a title in the party? They are the people who knows what the workers and the unemployed wants.'

'They're all the same, Em,' said Ern. 'Once they get to London they don't give a damn what we want. They can all be bribed, take it from me. Jesus Christ was the only one they couldn't square and they crucified him.' I knew about this man; he was a tough sailor, a bitter and cynical man who would never get a boat again because he had once persuaded a crew to refuse to sail in a tramp he held was unseaworthy and short-handed. He was disillusioned, embittered with everything, and it was strange to find this bit of sweetness about Jesus still intact in his nature.

In a few minutes, almost before the excitement, the cat-calls, following the first announcement had died down, the lord mayor hurried out again. He stood on the balcony appealing to the crowd for silence, frowning and flapping his hand excitedly with the paper in it in all directions as though he were trying to beat down the dog-noise, his soundless mouth saying 'Sh, sh,' shaped like a bugle end. Emrys took out his notebook and pencil in readiness. 'Who's your lady friend?' Blue-Breast yelled out as he caught sight of the Conservative candidate, a monocled ex-consul with a reputation for gallantry, but Ern told him to shut his gab.

The noise died down. The socialists had lost two divisions.

'Is this a distressed area?' shouted the man with the thick glasses, who hadn't said anything until then. His cry went like a missile over the crowd. For the moment, as he shouted out, he seemed oblivious of everything, his eyes moist with his disappointment and his voice full of anger and bitter protest. Then he became sullen and absorbed again. 'Well, I don't know, well, I don't know,' Emrys kept on repeating, nodding his head and looking disgusted and puzzled. He couldn't think of any Marxist phrase to explain this defeat and he was completely unable to account for it by any other means.

'It's all this propaganda,' said Blue-Breast with confidence, 'it's all this blasted capitalist propaganda in the papers and everywhere. The cunning devils have been here before, they can stampede the electorate whichever way they wants to, up to London for a wedding or a jubilee or into the polling booth to vote Tory. It's all according to what they wants them to do at the time.'

'Well, I don't know,' said Emrys, his thumb hissing over his chin. 'I'm up a gum-tree after that. I thought we had the north right in the blanket too.' He took a long end out of his waistcoat pocket and put his hand on my shoulder so that he could strike a match on the sole of his boot. 'I don't know,' he went on, pulling hard and frowning in the sun. 'Fancy anyone at all voting for a useless petticoat-chaser like that.'

'That's right,' said Blue-Breast, 'those damn capitalists are brought up like that, see. They don't believe in keeping a cow when they can buy milk, don't you worry. No sir.'

'Well there's still the central,' said Emrys. 'I wonder what those brainy buggers will do.'

In a few minutes the last result was delivered. Socialism had lost its three seats.

I began then to understand the look Gwilym Morgan's father had given me. Why should he vote, what had his years of struggling and defeat, his years of living in two attic rooms to do with a false thing like an election campaign, and what could he hope for from any result? He was disillusioned, he had been poor and neglected so long he knew that finally no one cared about him. But Emrys and his friends were enraged at the last announcement, bitterly disappointed, and they began to use filthy language in their moment of desperate frustration. They were betrayed, cruelly thwarted, they felt now no one cared a damn for their cause or their hardships, that the people who should have helped them with their votes had abandoned them, had played cynically for their own meagre safety. They felt very keenly, I could tell, this acute sense of having been sold and deserted through the selfishness of people who should have understood them, the mass traitors of their own class who were only slightly and temporarily more secure themselves, and they were unforgiving towards them. They felt they didn't matter as long as someone could keep them sweet and harmless in clubs and community houses and for the moment they were impatient, contemptuous of what had been done for them, seeing calculation and design in everything. They felt enraged at their own helplessness and they used filthy language in a sort of desperation.

Just as we were moving off, a fat youngish woman in black ran up with a big lump of toffee in her mouth and her breasts jumping about inside her black blouse like a pair of live things fighting. She had come too late for the results. 'Is it right there's three Conservatives in?' she asked eagerly, stopping her chewing, a worried look on her dark hairy face. 'Yes, that's right, three of the bastards,' said Blue Breast. 'Three!' she echoed incredulously, her brows contracting. 'It's them upper classes that's done it,' she went on. 'It's them sodding upper classes again.' 'Of course it's not, of course it's not,' said Ern with terrible bitterness. 'Can't you see it's us, you bloody fool? If the working classes voted socialist, the socialists would all be in.'

I went home disturbed and bewildered.

After those two days, the visit to Morgan's and the election results, I began to lose interest in my work; it seemed to be pointless, an activity like breaking records, a species of coconut carving, and my attitude towards art began to be, not that it was sinful, as my ancestors would have said, but that it was negligible, unsatisfying. I became obsessed more and more with the suffering and the monotony and the hopelessness I felt after my visit to Gwilym Morgan's to exist all round me, and at times this obsession became almost unbearable; I was a sort of agonized saint, conscious at all hours of a presence, not of God, but of universal suffering and death, and I began to despise all those concerned in any activity other than the service of the workers and the workless. But what tormented me was the acknowledgment that I myself was among the people I despised, because I could see no way in which I was able to lessen the sufferings of my class. I had no offering within myself to give. I was bitterly ashamed that I had ever gone to the Morgans's because my visit, I could see myself, was a fraud and an intrusion; I could give them nothing but meaningless talk, and their resentment was natural and justified. I had my private ecstasies, my appreciations, my acute sensibility, but I couldn't offer a sunset any longer to a workless man. That was something he couldn't put in his pocket.

A short time before this I had become intimate with a young journalist named Alun Vaughan, a man of my own age whose home was in the agricultural west, and whose widowed mother still lived in Llanilltyd, the village from which my own father's people had migrated when the coalfields began developing. I had known him slightly when he worked in Ystrad, and now he had got a job on a Cardiff paper, and as it happened he came to stay in the same lodgings so that we became pretty friendly. He was a big pleasant chap with black hair cut short and sticking up all over his head and a brownish face, a bit like a Japanese. He wore glasses with toric lenses and when he smiled his eyes became two of many curved lines in his face, and his mouth seemed to go oblong showing his gums and the small yellow squares of his teeth with the wide spaces between them. He had no interest at all in any of the arts nor any wish to understand them or to know anything about them, and our talk was chiefly concerned with people and conditions in the valleys. But he had accumulated somehow a vast corpus of erotic and bawdy stories so that he was a pleasant chap enough to know.

'What do you think of the election results, Alun?' I asked him one night.

'Rotten,' he said.

'But the valleys returned socialists.'

'Yes, but what's the use of that when Cardiff and so many other places like it prevent them from getting a majority?'

'That's true,' I answered. 'How do you account for the difference in the political outlook between two places so close together as Cardiff and the valleys, then?'

'The causes are economic I think, and partly psychological and snobbish. Cardiff is the clearing house, the shopping centre employing necessarily large armies of black coats who think, and their women keep them up to it, that they belong to the superior middle classes. They don't realize their interests are completely identified with those of the workers of the valleys whom they despise because of their Welsh accents and because they make water in the lanes the nights of the international Rugby matches. They can't see that their success depends entirely upon the prosperity of the valleys. And of course mushrooms have no roots.'

'Well, what can be done about it do you think?' I asked him. 'Have we to wait until everyone is converted to socialism before we can do anything?'

He smiled at me and said, 'I have my ideas about that.' Then he knocked his pipe out and went out to work.

But I wasn't in the mood at that time to let him get away with such an evasion as that, so the next chance I had I got at him. There was a report in his paper of the closing of another pit in the valleys. 'Look here,' I said, 'have you seen this?' He glanced where I was pointing and nodded, 'Yes,' he said, 'I wrote it.'

We were sitting upstairs in his bed-sitting-room and he was smoking a curved pipe with a clear amber stem. He looked big sitting on the low narrow bedroom chair, and he had swung his legs up on to the bed for comfort.

I asked him if he didn't think it was rotten and he agreed that it was.

'Well, if you do think so,' I said becoming needlessly excited, 'what do you think can be done about it?' And because he looked so indolent and indifferent, I said, 'You do care about it, don't you?'

'Of course I do,' he answered, grinning as though it were a joke, his eyes invisible behind the shine of the convex lenses, 'but you didn't expect me to put in a paragraph at the bottom of the report saying what I think about it all, did you?'

I was so troubled about this, it meant so much to me, I began to lose patience. I could easily have quarrelled with him then. But he said in the tender way he often used towards me, 'Don't get sore, Wyn. It hurts us all.'

I wasn't completely pacified and reassured by that, but he went on just the same, getting at last to what I had told him about Morgan and the election results. 'What was the reaction of that man in Bute Road to your question about voting? He knew obviously the hopelessness of waiting for a socialist majority because his experience had taught him that even if it came it wouldn't do him much good. His hope in politics is gone and he may be looking elsewhere. Then you saw the unemployed getting all balled up at the defeat of the party they hoped would be able to help them. Before long they will begin to get desperate, the more realistic of them, contemptuous of the salve of clubs and social services, impatient of waiting until a majority is prepared to vote socialist, and then they will begin to look elsewhere too. Where do you think they'll look?'

I knew what he was thinking. 'Not in this country,' I said.

He grinned again. 'In what country, Wyn?' he asked.

'Why, England,' I answered.

'What about Wales?' he went on, although I shook my head and said, 'Not a hope.' 'Perhaps there is not very much chance of a successful revolution here if we attempt it alone, but once we have begun perhaps we will not find ourselves alone for long. And no country is better suited in many ways for a revolution. Think of our history – where is the topography finer for guerrilla warfare against which mechanized armies are largely helpless?'

I began to think he was teasing me because he was grinning all the time.

'Where indeed,' I said and changed the subject.

But I couldn't forget this conversation, and a day or two later I said to him, 'Alun, were you serious about the possibility of a revolution in Wales?' I was smiling in self-defence. But he didn't grin as I had expected. He said, 'If there were a revolutionary movement in Wales, would you join it? Even if it meant violence?'

'I should want to know first its objects and who was sponsoring it,' I answered.

He went into his room and returned with an unnamed pamphlet in cyclostyled typescript. He laid it on the table and we read it together while he added comments and explanations. It was written side by side in English and Welsh. It began by describing the economic condition of the country, particularly the industrial south, the almost universal unemployment existing side by side with potential and actual wealth and displays of extravagance, material with which I was quite familiar already. 'Skip it,' said Alun, 'we know all this.' Then it went on to describe the disillusionment of the people as they lost faith in one political party after another. 'See this. Who could believe in empty clichéists and windbags like the local communists,' said Alun, 'or the Welsh Nationalists with their summer schools for spooners? Do you know their local leader? Typical, a pale intellectual with wadding in his ear.' The pamphlet then demanded a revolution of the workers and the workless, a 'resurgence from below,' organized and completely carried out without the help of middle-class money, organization or philosophy. It finished by sketching out roughly a plan of campaign and by appealing for the support of men of courage and goodwill. It was a queer document, quite cool and realistic, and with the issue stated clearly without any equivocal philosophic and political jargon, almost biblical in its simplicity and its directness. After studying it for several days I told Alun I would join the movement.

The movement was entirely secret. During the whole time I belonged to it, until I went up into the valley, I knew personally only four other members, Alun, a short-time stevedore and two unemployed colliers who had settled in Cardiff in the hope of finding work. There was of course no oratory or any inducement of position, no chance was given to anyone for personal display. When I joined I promised secrecy and obedience, that was all. Sometimes I was given papers and charts to study, but almost everything was conveyed to me by word of mouth from Alun. As my fidelity came to be assumed he disclosed to me bit by bit, sometimes with the aid of charts and maps, the extent of the organization. I was surprised and impressed, filled with admiration. By the time I had joined there was not a town or large village in Wales and the border that had not its arms caches and its interrelated groups of fives.

But the movement had methods of discipline. Once Alun took me down to the river to watch the police dragging out the body of a workman entangled under the iron stanchions of one of the bridges in town. His dead body was caught there among the sticks and the remains of an old mattress brought down by the water-flood, and when the tide had gone out of the river at the ebb people had seen it black and soaking lying mixed up with rubbish on the soft mud bank of the river bed.

'He was fond of children,' said Alun, 'but he couldn't keep his trap shut.' He grinned over the report of the inquest he was writing for his newspaper.

A week before the shooting began they sent me up to the far end of the Ystrad valley, and I was ordered to take instructions from a cell leader there who would meet me in the station of my native town. I went up by train with a revolver in the pocket of my overcoat. Knowing what I was expected to do I thought most likely I should be killed. But I was calm about it, this journey was my jump into Etna, pity directed outwards and become tolerable through action, action annihilating the self. I felt no hatred towards anyone although I was prepared for violence, but rather in moments of reflection and solitude, great love and tenderness, especially towards the sufferers of my own class, and I felt too a strange sense of exhilaration and capacity. I was capable, more powerful and assured than I had ever felt before, satisfied and elated with this sense of potency and assurance one clear determination had given me.

The train went puff and stop for about twenty miles, and it was evening when we drew into the terminus at the other end of the valley, a bleak empty barn of a station, huge and deserted, roofed like a conservatory where one or two dwarf black engines were spouting steam up into the resounding tunnel of the roof. When we got in they were lighting the hanging gas lamps, and under the end one on the empty platform I recognized the cell leader from Alun's description.

He took me into the inner room of an Italian refreshment bar where we were quite alone, and when we had ordered coffee he began questioning me and suggesting ways in which I could be useful to him, speaking all the time in Welsh.

He was a strange person, small and dark with yellowish skin, the colour of cheap paper but very soft and smooth, and his black hair going back in waves from his forehead with the symmetry of a wavy postmark. As he sat opposite in the clear electric light, reserved and watchful, a bit touchy, I noticed his brilliant pupil-black eyes, and the smallness of the bones of his thin yellow face showing like whale-bone in his nose and his jaw, and the hard nails of his tiny delicate hands tapping the scarlet glass top of the table like the elegant hands of a girl. His dark overcoat and his black scarf looked good, and he wore no hat. He was unwillingly speaking to me, his account of what he had carried out was grudging and meagre; he was reticent, suspicious of me, and I could feel his distrust and hostility challenging me. But I was unwilling that we should thwart each other like this, it was ridiculous between people who were to work together, so I managed to mention my father and mother, who still lived in one of the villages outside the town, and when he knew who I was he became less hostile and suspicious, telling me at last about himself and his people. And as he went on, sensing my sympathy, he began to speak with bitterness and indignation of what had happened to him, his black eyes moist and his soft wailing voice rising and falling in a whine of bewilderment and desperation. He had been unemployed for six years. When he left school he resisted the temptation to go underground with most of the boys of his age, thinking to better himself, and soon he got a job as an office boy with a firm of wholesale grocers. He went to night-school for several years and after getting some certificates he was taken on as a pay clerk in the colliery office, and while he was still young he became one of their cashiers. But when the colliery closed down he got the sack like everybody else, and he had been out ever since. His own history left him bewildered and outraged; the attack upon his innocent sense of security had made him a desperate and embittered man. Gradually he had withdrawn from all the organizations to which he had belonged, his chapel, his unemployed club and one political party after another, exasperated at their indifference or their inability to help him at all, and in desperation had joined our movement to which he had given the tireless energy of his now embittered and fanatical nature, and which in turn had given him identity and a function. He was easy for me to love; he spoke with the violence of a bewildered child enraged at an injustice at the hands of someone it has tried to satisfy. 'Look at me,' he sang in his passionate wailing voice, 'look at me, I worked hard, I did my job properly and I always tried to be decent and respectable. I never did anyone any wrong. And what's happened to me? I'm no better than anybody else, than if I'd never cared a damn about anything.' His eyes were full of tears and he passed his hand over his thick black hair.

That night in the Italian shop, although I loved this man, I saw no touch of greatness in him, or nobility, very little consideration beyond the bitterness of his own disappointment and misfortune. Later, I knew he had been shot selflessly covering the retreat of his men from Kiltanglwys, his small fragile body left thimbled with bullet holes on the mountain side. But that night I compared him with my father, a meek dignified man with too much pride it seemed to me for complaint or resistance, accepting the cruelty of an experience he did not understand although the growing sense of his uselessness and his endless failure to give my mother any hope of work were slowly killing him, reserving his suffering to himself, touching greatness in his refusal to find relief in hatred or violence or in any utterance of grief or bitterness.

The next day I left my hotel and went up the mountain for revolver practice. Soon after I joined the movement I started making myself a good revolver shot. (I think Alun must have reported this activity of mine to our superiors who surely took it as a sign of my seriousness and determination. Otherwise I was never sure why they selected me, whose job had lifted me on to the fringes of the middle classes, as their liaison officer in upper Ystrad.) First I bought a powerful air pistol which I used to practise with in our lodgings, fixing up a dartboard target and shooting at it across the room from the corner diagonally opposite. But a lot of the lead pellets used to come unstuck from the wood and drop on to the carpet and the landlady started to complain because she had to sweep them up. So then I got her to buy me a biscuit tin and when I had covered the dartboard with fresh coloured paper I fixed it into the bottom of the tin. I hung this up where the target had been before, and the tin held all the pellets that failed to stick in the wood. Later on I wanted a bigger range so I used to drawing-pin cigarette cards on the garden door and shoot at them from the kitchen steps. But when I bought a real revolver, a .455 Webley, my big difficulty was to find such a safe place to practise with it. In the end I used to go down to lonely parts of the coast with pieces of wood in my pocket and fire at them as they floated about on the water. But in summer it wasn't so easy to find a part of the coast where there were no bathers, and my last dodge was to cover the blocks of wood with luminous paint and fire at them after dark as they floated some distance out, tied with long pieces of string to the beach pebbles like little toy boats. By the end I could hit a chaffinch at a distance of sixty feet.

The night after my arrival the leader took me round the arms caches scattered over the slopes of the bleak mountains on both sides of the valley. There he showed me with his electric torch hundreds of rifles and revolvers and cases of ammunition packed into beautifully-cut holes in the ground that had been dug out there at night by squads of unemployed colliers belonging to our movement. Each of these dumps was wonderfully concealed although they had all been sunk near the lonely roads leading into the next valleys so that the buses and lorries we were to hire and commandeer could be driven up to them, loaded with arms and men and then sent back into the town and the villages for service. All these hidden guns and the ammunition cases had been brought to the valleys from lonely and inaccessible smuggling coves in Lleyn and Pembrokeshire a few at a time, carried under the samples of commercial travellers and piled up in vans pretending to belong to furniture removers and egg and butter merchants from the west.

The next day was Sunday and I decided to see my father and mother, as I thought for the last time. I had purposely not visited them because I wished them not to be implicated at all in what I was doing, and from this point of view I was sorry I had been sent into Ystrad at all. I went to the chapel where they were both members, when the evening service was on, and looked down through the glass window half-way up the stair leading into the gallery. I could see them standing with the congregation in the body of the chapel. I felt a gush of love for them seeing them standing there, side by side, singing the last blessing hymn, so quiet together. I felt the need for renunciation and sacrifice towards them. My mother in her narrow coat was slim as a young girl but ageing, an old woman at the stoop of her shoulders, her hair gone grey and lifeless. She held up her face to the shine of the light and sang her prayer with her eyes shut, calm and brave, and I knew she was so full of worry, so near the thought and fear of death. My eyes filled with tears watching her. My father's face was bowed low as he sang, his head bent as though he were beaten, defeated, and my bowels went weak with love and anguish at the sight of him. I was filled with passionate rebellion to see him thus, my father, an old man, so decent, so full of acceptance, going down suffering bitterly but with his lips dumb and without complaint or resistance. I hurried out of the building before anyone had seen me.

Very little happened in the week before the revolution started; everything seemed to be going on as usual in the valley – there was very little work and the unemployed colliers were to be seen daily standing about in groups at the street corners, often not knowing what to do with themselves. I got a letter in a Welsh code from Alun, saying, amongst other things, that he had heard that his mother was desperately ill, but that he couldn't go to see her because he had been ordered to stay in Cardiff in readiness. I felt sorry about this because I guessed how much they meant to each other, and I wrote him a long reply, reminding him of what we had arranged if the revolt failed and trying to tell him all that was happening. Actually very little was happening visibly. Everything in the town was going on quietly, without suspicion, although the last day or two many of the members of the groups of five were brought into closer contact with one another, so that they could receive their final instructions..

Then the last evening arrived. The rising had been planned for midsummer and even up at the arms cache on the bleak mountain where we were to meet the air was warm and almost still. From there we could see the town below with a fleece of smoke on its back, and above the mountain on the other side of the valley was a broad luminous board of sky where the sun had just gone down. There were about two hundred men gathered there receiving arms, and at the roadside about a dozen vans and lorries were drawn up in line ready to carry them into the town. I was to take charge of two of them with a chap called Llew Beynon, and we were to occupy the head police station in the town. Llew was a short, thick-set chap, an unemployed collier who had played scrum-half for the country several times when he was younger. He was dark and broad-shouldered, with a thin pale face and his lower jaw projecting beyond his upper teeth, and all over his cropped head were white cuts where the hair had never grown after scalp wounds he had received underground. He was wearing a blue jacket and a pair of green trousers with gold braid stripes down the sides that he had got from his brother-in-law, a cinema attendant a good bit taller than himself. They made him laugh a lot, and he showed me the tops coming up under his armpits and his braces shortened until they were no longer than the shoulderstraps on ladies' underwear. The others present, with the help of men from the other caches on the mountains, were to capture the railway station, and the post office and the bus centres, all of them at the same moment as far as was possible.

I came down the mountain road second, in a covered furniture van, the boys sitting on benches inside with the rifles on the floor boards. I was sitting beside the driver in front, and I could hear them through the three-ply behind my head talking and laughing inside, the younger men treating the thing externally as a joke, although I knew they were in dead earnest.

One of the men was describing how the means test man had questioned him, asking him about the amount of money he had in the bank. 'Two thousand pounds,' he answered. 'Now then,' said the means test man whom he imitated beautifully, 'we don't want any joking here.' 'Well, you started,' he answered. And I could hear Dai Tudor, well-known locally as a back-punching pub-fighter, making the boys laugh telling them how he had spat beer in Freedman the bookie's face and then hit him smack on the bar floor before he knew where he was. As we came round the corner of some tips, one brilliant talkative star swam out yellow into the middle sky. The driver of our van was a wag, a cheerful chap with plenty to say, who couldn't walk much because of his bad leg, but who managed to drive pretty well all the same. He was a thin-faced, bow-nosed chap in a cap and muffler, dark with a prominent Adam's apple and a birth mark along the side of his face like a piece of brown bread, and most of the way he was singing Welsh hymns about victory in Canaan in a pleasant light tenor voice. I knew him before; he was Charlie Evans, an unemployed bread-van driver, and he had shown his leg to all the women in the valley almost, when he was on his rounds, describing how the shrapnel had got into his thigh during the war. But he was a pleasant chap to have next to me at this moment because he didn't seem to realize at all the danger we were going into. He stopped half way through one of his hymns and asked me if I had ever tasted swan. I said, 'No I hadn't. Why?' Then he started telling me how just before Christmas four of his pals had gone up to the pond the unemployed had dug in the park and caught the two swans that lived there, with a garden rake and a rabbit net. The swans were named after a couple of local aldermen, I knew that much. Most of the ride he told me how the catching was done and why they didn't eat the giblets. At the crossroads where we were turning into the town the policeman waved us on and Charlie saluted him, and as we passed I heard the sound of loud disrespectful noises from inside the van. We drove slowly down the High Street and I was glad to see there were not many people about, although there were queues outside one of the three cinemas we passed. Everything was going on normally and the shops were closing because it was beginning to get dusk. We turned into the sidestreet where the police station was, and pulled the two vans as we had arranged across the road, one each side of the doorway, sticking out at right angles from the pavement so that nothing could pass. We poured over the tail-board with our guns and rushed up the steps into the station, some of Llew's men remaining on the vans and on top of the steps and the rest running round to the back to prevent anyone getting out that way. It was a bit dim inside the police station and the corridor smelt strongly of carbolic. The inspector in charge, a stern white-headed old man, with the bags under his eyes gauzed with lines and his moustaches waxed out like a couple of quills, happened to be coming along the corridor with the top buttons of his tunic open and a paper in his hand just as we rushed in. He had known me since I was a boy, because when he was a constable he had lived near us. I lowered my revolver. I thought I would let him speak first.

'Hullo, hullo, what's this?' he shouted in his harsh, bossy voice, coming towards us. 'What do you want, what do you want?' He didn't know at all what was happening, poor chap, seeing all these armed civilians rushing along his corridor, but his habit of authority flashed out at once, making his voice echo down the stone walls of the passage. And he wasn't scared at all of us either.

'We are taking charge of the building for a while, Mr. Richards.' I told him. 'Take it easy, sir, no harm will be done to you. Will you please call out your men, we would like to see them if you will be good enough.'

At first he didn't seem to be able to speak for anger.

'No harm will be done me,' he shouted in a sort of frenzy. 'No harm will be done me. Get out, get outside quick, or you'll suffer for it. You fools, don't you know what you're doing? You're in England, you fools.'

His white face had gone scarlet, he seemed almost hysterical, so I tried to calm him a little, feeling sorry for him, although we had no time to lose.

'Try not to get excited, sir,' I said. 'Let these two boys look after you a bit.' But just then, before I had finished speaking, and as I was signalling two of the boys forward, a door along the corridor opened and a sergeant and half a dozen constables came out ready to go on duty. When they saw us standing in the corridor with our rifles and the chief our prisoner, they looked so surprised and bewildered the boys began laughing and jeering. 'Come on, you sods,' shouted Rhys Charles. 'We'll give you a bit of your own damn ointment now.' Rhys had been blistered pretty often for lifting coal from the trucks in the sidings, and he was sore against the police because of it.

'All right, Rhys,' I said. 'See to them. But never mind the rough stuff yet.'

So Rhys and Dai Tudor and half a dozen others stepped forward towards the constables who were still standing in confusion in the dim corridor, crowding outside the door of their mess room, not knowing what to do. They moved back a pace or two but the sergeant, a big hefty stupid-looking chap with plenty of guts, as I knew, started shouting just as the chief had done, his voice resounding down the low stone corridor, asking us what the devil we were after, and offering to give us a chance to get out before it was too late. That made the boys grin and start back-chat, but the sergeant wasn't the chap to be ordered about easily by a lot of fellers half his size, even if they were armed, and I could tell his blood was rising dangerously, that he was ready to show fight. 'Take it easy, sergeant,' I said. 'We don't want to hurt anybody. All you have to do is to go with these boys for a bit until things are settled properly. There's a revolution on and you are unlucky as the representatives of the party in power. When we change places with them we shall be glad of your services.'

'You bolshies,' he shouted. 'You bloody bolshies, so that's your game is it?' His ham of a fist swung round in fury and hit little Teddy Joshua smack in the face, so that his head jerked back and crashed snap into the door panel behind him. I thought from the sound his neck was broken. He fell to the floor at once on top of his rifle and lay there in a heap without a whimper, the blood streaming from his mouth and both his nostrils. I thought what a terrible thing it is to see a man like that wounded on the floor. But the sergeant was down himself the next moment. Someone went down at his legs without warning, and the rest of the boys piled on to his shoulders and clung round him, striking at him and pulling at his belt and his helmet, until he overbalanced and fell forward to the floor at my feet. I believe, too, that someone fouled him badly, most likely Dai Tudor, because he screamed out in rage and pain; but after a few minutes of swearing and scuffling in the confined space, half a dozen of them had him prostrate and impotent on the floor of the corridor, while Harry Jones held the butt of his rifle six inches above his mouth. The fierce stupid face was raw along the left side and badly cut across the cheekbone, because the sergeant had not been able to throw out his arms when he was falling, and he had come down heavily on his face. All this time the other policemen had stood the far side of the struggle covered by myself and the others with me, and at the end by Llew's men, who had come in from the back of the station; they fidgeted to join in but they were afraid to do it, although the old chief kept on shouting, 'Help him, you cowards; help him you cowards' all the time. He couldn't do anything himself because his two guards were straining him back against the wall and I could hear one of them, Sammy Thomas, saying, 'Go easy mun, go easy little chief,' in a gentle soothing voice, as though he were speaking to a wilful child. In a few minutes we had the handcuffs on the sergeant, and then we got them all down into the cells.

But news travels quickly and mysteriously in the valleys, and when we got back to the station door there was a big crowd running together outside between the two vans. Right in front of us at the bottom of the steps was Phil Peg, a simple-minded chap with a wooden leg who led or followed every band and procession in the valley. When the people saw so many of us coming out with our guns they moved back a bit and some of them started to boo and the women to shout out, although I couldn't tell what. Llew was no good at impromptu public speaking, so I did my best to tell them that they were safe, that they had absolutely nothing to fear. I told them what we had done and what we intended to do, that we were fighting in their cause and were even ready to die for it. But it all sounded even to myself pretty glib, so much like a political election speech that I soon shut up, assuring the people once more that not one of them would be hurt or any part of their property damaged. After a bit they broke up into groups arguing about in the street but not attempting to do anything. In a few minutes it was dark. That night at the same pre-arranged time we captured the police station, the post office, the bus centres, the railway station and the signal boxes, the newspaper offices of the local weekly and the drill hall and barracks belonging to the territorial army. This was done the same summer evening the whole length of the valley, so that the entire means of transport and communication fell into our hands overnight, and there was not a gun or a bullet in six valleys that did not belong to us by the morning. The revolt in the valleys was as nearly perfect as a human organization can be, everything was foreseen and provided for. In other parts of Wales it was not so perfectly planned, and in Cardiff, as I had suspected, big business and the absence of any corporate feeling were too much for us.

Before the end of a fortnight we were starving.

During that fortnight we were pretty busy, but our activity, after we had locked up the police and a few people we could not trust, was entirely peaceful; because the people were with us, we had little real opposition to deal with. For me the time was more like the fortnight of a parliamentary election campaign than of a revolution, and I spent my days and often a good part of my nights in interviewing and persuading, and denying rumours and rushing about with Llew who was supposed to be in charge of propaganda. I was so completely absorbed in action I had no time for reflection or analysis of any kind, and I was completely happy. Every day aeroplanes flew low overhead but they dropped nothing more dangerous than leaflets describing how the rebellion had failed over the whole country, so they did not worry us much. The first day the dole was to be paid, we organized a monster march which ended up with speeches and hymn singing on the side of the mountain. We gave them a proportion of their dole too. Our people once, almost with their pennies, had founded a university.

At the end of five days Cardiff capitulated, and the warships steamed into the docks. But we were near the mountains right up at the far end of the valley, and we could hold out longer. We had sealed ourselves in by blasting the only road that led out of the valley at the far end, a road that went through the mountain pass and curved towards a barracks town the other side of the mountain ranges near the English border. In places that lonely road was only a shelf curving perilously round the steep shoulder of the hillside with a limestone cliff above it on one side and a steep escarpment dropping swiftly down into the river on the other. We never expected that they would march infantry against us over this road because the whole distance the troops would have been exposed to the rifle fire of our men inaccessibly hidden on the cliffs and among the mountain boulders, and we blasted the road because we were afraid they might attack us with tanks and armoured cars from this direction.

By the end of a week I could see what was going to happen, no trains were arriving because Cardiff had been captured, and we couldn't get any food by lorry because all the roads from east and west were bound to pass through Cardiff owing to the configuration of the country, before turning northwards into the valleys. There were a good many farms on the far edge of the coalfield, but the population of our town alone was fifty thousand, and what they could supply was quite inadequate. But the end came more quickly than I had expected.

We had established a camp or meeting place concealed from aeroplanes on Kiltanglwys, a hill behind the town. One afternoon the leader I had met the night I came into the valley asked me if I would go down with Llew Beynon to see if anything had arrived at the railway station. I remember that on that day Llew was wearing his green trousers and in the middle of his cheek he had a six-pointed plaster star covering a boil. He was telling me he had been told to call back for a job in the spring so often he was beginning to feel like a bloody cuckoo. It was a terribly gusty day, but mild and very sunny in the town, the wind hauling the smoke smartly up the chimneys and holding paper bags about in the air, head high, like shooting-range balls on the water jets, before ballooning them over the buildings. The sunny side of the main street looked shabby with grime and dilapidation, shop windows covered with thin sheets of dust, torn and sagging sunblinds, the various monotony of uninteresting shop-fronts and broken and rising flagstones everywhere. But the side in shadow was even worse, looking as though it could have eaten up many pounds of putty and drums of bright paint and varnish by the wagon load. And the town that sunny day seemed strangely deserted and quiet, almost as though it were a Sunday afternoon. There was a short approach leading off from the High Street to the station and just as we turned the corner into the building itself we came almost face to face with half a dozen soldiers in khaki forming up inside the entrance. I was startled, I hadn't expected their arrival as soon as this, and inside the hollow station I could see hundreds more getting out of the train and falling into their positions on the platform. They had arrived with so much secrecy that nobody knew anything about it, and there was no crowd about waiting to see them coming in. When the officer in charge of the nearest soldiers spotted us, Llew with his rifle slung over his shoulder and me with my Sam Browne, he shouted out something and at that his men turned quickly in our direction and started running towards us. They were only a few paces away, just inside the big sliding doors, and we had no time to lose. 'Quick, Llew,' I shouted, hitting his sleeve, and we dodged back from sight and ran for it along the short approach leading into the main street. Twenty steps at a good pace and we were in High Street once again where they couldn't shoot at us very well because there were just a few people about. As we turned the corner of the approach the wind got under the peak of my cap and jerked it back off my head, and the funny thing was I half turned round to run back after it. I could tell Llew was relying on me somehow, just waiting for me to tell him what to do, so I said 'Down High Street and sharp left at Broad Pavement,' giving him some objective, something to think about. All this time I could hear the officer shouting from time to time, and the quick beat of the soldiers running, the sound coming in the tempo of a dog scratching an itch out of his ear with his back paw; and the few people in High Street on both sides of the road began to stop as we passed, looking after us running like mad as near the pavement as we could, wondering what was happening, a woman far gone in carrying a child and a little girl with whitish-yellow hair, the wind under her cut hair holding it out for a moment in the sun as we passed like the inverted claw of a honeysuckle flower. We were running fast and we were both heavily-loaded, but I was conscious of no discomfort or difficulty in any part of my body; I seemed to be existing only in a small area near my eyes, I had a narrow clear ring of consciousness round my head at the level of my eyes, and apart from this my limbs and my breathing seemed to be working automatically without my knowledge or volition, but all the same with the sweetness of a used machine. And during the whole of this run I was less aware of fatigue or the fear of getting a bullet in my back than of the bright visual impressions shoaling in under the arches of my brows, the whole of the desolate neglected street seemed to be roaring into my brain, pouring back along the nerve throats as long as our flight continued. I didn't know at all how Llew felt but since we were running downhill and the wind was with us I supposed he was all right. The first time I was really conscious of him was when I saw he had collided with a dirty-looking bearded little man coming up the street carrying a big golden ball bigger than a man's head under his arm. It looked unreal this bright gilded ball in the drab town and I wondered who the hairy little foetus of a man in a blue serge suit could be, carrying a big gilt ball about in High Street and wearing a beard the yellow-brown of a tobacco-stained hand. When Llew went into him he dropped the ball with a heavy thud and it rolled without bouncing down alongside us in the gutter for a few yards. But although the little man sat down suddenly on the pavement with the impact and then spat on Llew's green trousers, it delayed us hardly at all, and I believed we were gaining on the soldiers. If we could get to the Broad Pavement we stood a chance of losing ourselves in the winding streets to the east of the town. We passed Simon's the pawn-broker, who, I noticed, because the sun was on his shop, had only two brass balls and an empty spike hanging over his doorway, and just there the High Street curved a little, giving us a chance to dodge down the Broad Pavement without being seen. So far we had done pretty well, we had not been shot at at all, and no one had attempted to stop us, although most of the people we passed slowed down or stopped to look at us as we ran by, and one or two shouted out although I don't know what. The Broad Pavement was a street of houses, completely deserted this quiet afternoon, and half-way along a woman wearing glasses put her head out of a downstairs window as we were running past and began to clean the glass. She put her head right into a sunbeam and the wind scattered her short hair as soon as she put it out. It was white, like a white chrysanthemum, and made up of little lambs-wool curls disordered in the gust of wind. She stared at us, with a yellow chamois leather in her hand, out of the narrow window-opening, and then she disappeared. For the moment we couldn't hear the soldiers chasing us, I thought most likely they were not sure which of the turnings at the bend in High Street we had taken, and before they came in sight again we turned left into a lane running back in the direction of the station. I was more conscious of the existence of the rest of my body now than I had been

in the first few minutes of action and excitement, but I still had this
unusual clarity in my recognition of physical objects and in my intuitive
knowledge of what I ought to do next. I meant to double back into
Kiltanglwys if possible to warn the men still there that the soldiers had
come, and I thought we had a good chance of doing it because I knew
the back streets of this place probably much better than the soldiers
who I thought, with the usual cunning of the enemy, were almost
certain to be English. In this long narrow lane which had garden walls
and back doors on both sides we passed a huge, fat, young woman
intent on her game, playing whip and top by herself with absorption,
half-way along; she was tremendous, with her vast arsage turned
towards us as we ran up the lane, and just when we got behind her the
wind lifted up her skirt as she stooped to whip her top and chucked it
up over her back. She had bright baggy drawers of butcher blue on, and
both of us laughed as we ran by. 'Emma Daley,' said Llew. I
remembered her, a bit of a simpleton the children used to tease. We
seemed by now almost certainly to have shaken off the soldiers but I
didn't want to go too far in one direction in case we should be seen
from a distance, so at the next junction in the lane we turned sharp
right disturbing a cat at an ash bin that streaked across the lane and
poured up a garden wall like an upward bucketful. Llew heaved his rifle
over after her, and it fell in a cucumber frame. We were taking a risk
going along this way because the lane led out on to a fairly important
street into which the soldiers might possibly have entered directly from
the station, but if we could get smartly across without meeting any of
them we could consider ourselves safe for the time because we would
be within easy reach of the mountain. We had almost certainly given the
soldiers a miss because I was pretty certain they wouldn't get much
change out of Emma Daley, even if she had seen us at all, and we had
passed very few other people really. At the end of the lane we stopped
and stood listening behind a telegraph post that had three upright
marks of manspiss on it like bails and wickets. We could hear the
ordinary street noises and bits of talk drifting towards us from two
women gossiping round the corner, one of them using a loud masterful
voice, and we had to smile hearing these fragments of what they were
saying to each other as we listened for the soldiers: 'Yes it was awful,
Mrs. What's-it,' the loud one was saying in her brassy tones, 'the body
burst inside the coffin . . . the new curate from the tin church . . . and he
was sick in the lavatory as well . . . spoilt the carpets of course . . . yes,
much better, but when I coughs I pees . . .'

But there was no noise that sounded at all like the soldiers marching,
so I put my revolver in my pocket and dumped my Sam Browne

behind the telegraph pole, and went into the street walking smartly. We saw the two women at the corner still talking away, one of them small and insignificant and the other taller, red-faced, stoutly-made; they were poor, both of them wore fringed shawls and they were hatless in the sun. It was then we had a fine piece of luck – nine or ten yards along a saloon car was drawn up at the kerb on our side with its back to us. I led Llew by the sleeve past the women, opened the rear door, signed him in, and then got in myself. There was hardly anyone about apart from the two women who took no notice of us, and the driver was so surprised when he turned round that he didn't know what to say.

'Look here, Freedman Brothers,' I said to him. 'Take us along the Brychan road, will you? We'll go round past the Brynna, please. Start up.' I showed him my gun and he coloured but got the car going without a word. I knew him, he was one of two brothers, Jewish bookies who had been making a pile in the valley. He was a big fat lazy-looking chap, clean-shaven with a pink girl-like complexion, and the back of his fat neck pimply and looking as though it were stuffed with wadding. We drove off without anyone noticing anything strange happening, and it was comfortable in the soft enclosed car. I didn't expect any funny stuff from our chauffeur, he was a kind-hearted chap and as well he was too scared of the gun held against his fat ham. He drove beautifully; I just reminded him at the different turnings which way to go and all he said the whole way was, 'Yes I know,' or, 'Right-o, kid,' in his queer guttural Jewish-Welsh speech. As we got up the mountain, it became more and more windy, the sand getting up off the road and spinning round in a body like a dancer, and the wind sometimes holding the car back and snorting hard into the bonnet. But he got us to the mountain path safely, he knew the roads and streets of the valley as he knew his own face. And we didn't see a soldier the whole way. We thanked him. 'That's all right, kid,' he said grinning, and running his finger round inside his collar. With that he reversed and drove off looking red and uncomfortable.

I found the leader and told him what we had seen. We decided to scatter, and when we had shaken hands all round I turned off westward across the valley fields making for Llanilltyd and the west where a boat might get me across to Ireland.

The leader, the man I had met on the night of my arrival in the valley, was the last to leave, and before he was off the mountain the soldiers had arrived, and he was shot and killed.

I kept to the mountains, making rapidly for the coast, meaning to pass through Llanilltyd, where Alun, I hoped, would be waiting for me. I had heard my father describe how my grandfather had once walked from Ystrad after work on a Saturday afternoon back to this village, the place his people had migrated from, arriving there about twelve noon the next day. I knew I couldn't do the distance in that time because I meant to travel only during the short nights, but it enabled me to make some sort of rough calculation, and I thought that, unless we were stopped, by the end of five days we should be at the coast ready to slip across to Ireland. It was lonely travelling by myself, and I spoke to no one except an old shepherd on the first morning who bought some food for me and let me sleep in his turf hut throughout the day. He was a lovely, bearded old man, a bit like one of the apostles, spending his time carving thumbsticks which he sold to some firm in London. When I left him, just as it was getting dark on the mountains, he prayed over me and gave me his blessing while the lights came out in the valleys far below and the clean-wicked stars emerged from the growing darkness of the sky. It was monotonous walking by night after a bit, there was only the occasional droning of planes overhead for excitement, and there was nothing to see except the car-beams swinging up the sky from time to time, moving round over the surface of the sky like a clock arm being set or a pointing dial finger, and, partly because I encountered very little danger, I didn't feel at all like a fugitive. I seemed to be keeping all my experiences, my disappointment at what had happened, and my fear of being captured and shot, right out on the edges of my being, although I was not doing this consciously. I was not permitting them to invade my consciousness as it were until I could more readily dominate them, and the only feeling I had at all acutely was boredom at the long lonely walks I had to take night after night over the mountains. But I knew that this fear and disappointment were slowly coiling into a tighter and tighter tension within me, gathering explosive force every moment their release was denied them.

The third night at about four in the morning I reached the village of Llanilltyd. I found Alun's house easily; it stood alone by the roadside, the last house before the church at the end of the village. He had described it accurately in his letter, and as I approached and drew near along the dark deserted road, I could see his sign outside one of the out-houses, an inconspicuous V tarred on the wall near the grass. There was a wide iron gate made of flat horizontal strips of iron in the wall surrounding the cottage and the close, where the outhouses were and the garden and the orchard, but the cottage had another little wooden gate before the front door. I looked round but could see no one about, it was so dark, and the low whitewashed wall before me was like a heap of dirty snow; I went silently into the dark garden and approached the first building, which looked like a stable, and directly I got on to the cement path leading to the door I heard someone stirring inside, and a voice saying, 'Who's there?' 'Alun,' I answered softly, 'it's me. It's Wyn.' In a few moments I was inside lying with Alun on some sacking on the empty stable floor, talking about what had happened to us. He lit a match to show me in, and his appearance made me smile, he looked so rough; he had a black eye and a scarf was wound round his mouth, and when he pulled it down to speak to me I saw his huge growth of bushy black beard. He had lost his glasses and when I made fun of his beard he said, 'Well, it's something to be proud of. You look as though your chin had been dipped in brown sugar.' We lay there for hours asking each other questions and describing the collapse of the revolt. 'It was terrible after the first day or two,' he said. 'We settled down on the place pretty well, we had the whole place bottled for forty-eight hours, but after that they began to recover from the shock a bit and to be awkward. Did you shoot anyone, Wyn?' I felt sure he was grinning at me as he often used to, to annoy me.

'There was hardly any shooting in Ystrad at all,' I answered. 'We had no one to shoot at. I thought once I should have to fire when the soldiers chased us but we got away all right without. The chief of the police died though, but that was with shame and bad temper.'

'I shot two damn dock rats from our movement,' he said, 'and that was all. When they knew it was all up, they tried to square themselves by getting the skids on me. They came into the office, where I was editing the news-sheet, with guns in their pockets, four of the toughest nuts I've ever seen, but the typist phoned up to me and I got a minute's start of them up the fire escape. I didn't kill them though, I'm afraid, and the other two beat it.' He went on for a long time telling me all that had happened; he had had a much more exciting time than I had, because opposition was more powerful and more determined in Cardiff than in Ystrad. He got his black eye and cut lip jumping off a lorry where the road forked left to Llanilltyd.

Only at the end did he tell me that his mother was lying dead in the house across the garden.

We slept in turns that night and the next afternoon we watched the funeral from the disused harness loft above the stable. The only person in Llanilltyd who knew Alun was in the village was his brother, a workman in the mart, who brought us food and told us everything that was going on. He shook hands with us both that morning because he knew we were going away directly after the funeral. The harness loft seemed pitch black when we got up through the trapdoor, with only one thin stick of solid light leaning rigid from a round coin on the floor out through a hole in the roof slates. And the heat there was stifling because there was almost no breeze at all. We pulled out some of the dusty sacking stuffed under the eaves, and then we were able to look out into the road, although from such a narrow vizor-slit we were not able to see much, only laterally – no sky and only the bottoms of the fruit trees white-limed as it were to the armpits. But a good stretch of grey road was in sight and some of the hedge-bank opposite where we could see the little blood-bowls of hundreds of brilliant corn-poppies set out for the sun, and the caked-up duck-pond with its chocolate mud netted with crack-lines at the roadside opposite. And we could see, too, the restless heat rising endlessly in tongues of colourless flame off the big iron gate, the unconsumed bonfire of the ironwork blazing invisibly in the heat-glare of the afternoon enveloping the bars in sheets of silent fire.

Close up there under the burning slates we found it hard to breathe, and the heat filled the air like uncomfortable powder.

Presently the men who were to walk in the funeral started to arrive, their boots grunting over the gritty road, standing about in groups outside the cottage or near the big garden gate. They were all dressed in grey or black, most of them had bowler hats on and heavy suits of stiff dark material, and we were near enough to see a cobweb of thin dust laid over the toecaps of their thick-soled polished boots. They moved about very little because of the heat, but stood in stiff groups in the smouldering roadway talking in low voices, one or two of them with grass in their mouths, hardly moving at all except to wipe the sweat off their faces with a handkerchief or to step back and acknowledge a friend or a newcomer. Alun knew most of them and he whispered to me about them as they came into our view. But he was suffering, I knew that, although he was pretending so hard to be philosophic and even indifferent because I was with him.

At last five or six men brought out the coffin with difficulty through the front door of the cottage, a long white box with nickel handles flashing in the sun, and laid it on the bier which stood on the green verge at the roadside. Then the mourners fell in in couples led by the vicar, and walked slowly on ahead, their hats tilted forward because the sun was on their faces, while four men carried the heavy bier, going slowly, their boots purring over the gritty road, finding it hard work in the heat of the afternoon. Behind the coffin walked a dozen relatives, men and women, all of them with bowed faces, and in the deepest mourning.

When they had gone out of sight along the road, the bright plate of the coffin-lid flashing from the edges with the movements of the bearers, Alun sat down on a box, gazing before him with an expression of bitterness and revolt on his face. I wasn't sure whether to speak or not, he looked so full of emotion, but before I could make up my mind he got up and said, 'Wyn, I'm going to the church-yard.'

'I wouldn't,' I said, although in a way I felt glad. 'You don't want to risk yourself. You couldn't do any good going.'

'I don't care,' he answered in a reckless tone, 'I want to see the burial and I'm going. You can wait here till I come back if you like.'

'If you're going I'm coming with you,' I answered, 'but let's go carefully. Can we get there without going by the road? Perhaps we can watch the ceremony without being seen ourselves at all.'

'All right,' he said, 'we'll go across the fields. It will mean getting through a few hedges but we can manage that, I expect. I must see the last of her.'

We climbed down from the loft, hurried through the far side of the orchard and set off up across the fields. There was no one about in the green silence, the hills around were targeted with sun-struck fields and the whole earth and the sky were deserted; from the top of the first green bend we could see no one except some tiny harvesters the sun picked out for us in a pear-shaped field miles off up the other side of the valley. As we approached the churchyard hedge we could hear the vicar reading the service, and we could make out the figures of the mourners through the thick hawthorn, standing among the gravestones. We went cautiously forward and lay flat in the long grass covering the bank where the hedge grew and we were able to see everything that was going on between the grey stems of the bushes. The mourners were quite near us because the grave had been broken close to the hedge: it was an oblong hole, sharp-edged, with the sides lined with fresh green branches of yew and laurel, and with a heap of clay and cream pebbles piled on the turf on both sides of it. From where we lay on the soft grass with our faces in the shadow of the hedge and the tiny machinery of the crickets active about us, we could see as a background to the group of mourners and the black polished tombstones the putty-white walls of the church simplified flat in the sun, with a row of torch lilies brilliant against it like the red ink zigzag line of a graph; and the worn file of stalagmite pinnacles above the coping-stone, and the castellated tower bound with the bright green arteries of the ivy creeper.

I began to feel myself weakening.

By the time we got there the coffin had already been let down and the vicar, a small round-headed man with cropped grey hair and half-lensed spectacles was reading the service in Welsh. When he said, 'Dust unto dust' he paused while the sexton, a rough-looking man who seemed to have been cutting the graveyard hay before the burial, snatched up some earth and threw it down indifferently on to the coffin. He unhooked his thumbs from the pockets of his breeches and carelessly tossed down the hard lumps of clay on to the coffin lid that resounded with a hollow thud out of the depths of the grave. The vicar shook out the dazzle of his sleeve and went on; Alun looked as though he would tear his way through the hawthorn hedge with his hands. She had meant so much to him; she was a fighter, small in body and often ill, and in pain, but it was she who had schemed and struggled to get him to college, taking on the job of cleaning the church when his father died and not listening to any advice or discouragement. Once he showed me her picture; it was of a small humorous woman with both her hands tucked up under the fringes of her shawl. He explained that her hands were incurably deformed with arthritis.

We lay there watching until the end of the service and no one saw us, although one of the mourners, a square, heavy, full-shouldered old man in a long green-black jacket, had his back so close to us that I could hear him breathing. I could see the double seams of his vented jacket and the strange texture of his hair which grew low over his neck, thick and short, soft as a grey moss or catkin fur. And on the greenish curve of his shoulder two brown shiny insects like fishing flies alighted, coupling in the sunlight. But we did not wait to see them shovelling in the barbarous earth, and by the end of the service I had made up my mind. 'Let's go now,' Alun whispered. 'I'm satisfied.' So we hurried back over the field, and when we were once more in the stable he said, 'And what now?' He seemed much better now it was all over.

I said, 'I'm going back, Alun.'

'Back? Back where?' he asked, in surprise.

'I'm going back to the valleys,' I said. 'What should I do in Ireland or America or any other place? I belong to the valleys and I'm going there. If I get shot, I get shot. I'm homesick at the quick of me already.'

'Don't go back, Wyn,' he said. 'They'll kill you in the valleys. It's a place of death. No man will escape alive from there.'

'No man like me will escape from there at all,' I answered. 'My destruction is more certain and terrible if I do escape than if I return and suffer the death of my body. I am so deeply implicated I have no meaning or existence apart from them. Only one thing troubles me, you have waited here in danger for five days when you might have been making your way out of the country.'

'Don't think of that, Wyn,' he answered. 'I should not have left until after my mother's funeral anyhow. If you think it is your life you must go.'

As I lay awake on the sacking that evening, listening to the un-expected rain falling heavily into the garden, I saw again the hopelessness and folly of my trying to escape, and I remembered Alun at the funeral with the people of the village before him, the scene that had made me homesick. About nine o'clock, just after it had become dark, we got up and gathered our things and went out. It had stopped raining, and when we were on the road outside the cottage he said, 'Good-bye, Wyn, good luck,' and he kissed me. I said 'Good-bye, Alun,' and we separated. It was quite simple, but knowing Alun had loved me was very sweet and as I walked back along that country road through the night I felt for the moment happy and almost triumphant, although I belonged to a defeated people. It was fine again then, but the full moon was heavy and green with rain. After I had left the village, I went down a narrow road where the cart-tracks were full of water, and I passed some woman I didn't know. She was small and poorly-dressed, and as she went by close against my shoulder I heard her crying bitterly to herself. She looked small and decent, simple, being dressed in quiet, dark clothes, a woman not yet old, only beginning to age, sobbing with her handkerchief held against her face as she went hurriedly down the road towards the village. I looked after her and saw her in the poor moonlight, the small, decent woman, hurrying on with her body stooping forward and her head bowed over both her hands with weeping, a small pitiful figure, passionate, her movements heedless and intense, concerned only with her own grief and absorbed under the night in the bitterness of her suffering. I sorrowed with her proudly, I bore for a moment in anguish one corner of her cross.

A few yards farther on I came to a stile at the end of a path leading down to the river through the long wet grass and the rushes. I stood on the round pale pebbles that looked in the moonlight like the shells of various-sized eggs under the willow bushes, and took out my revolver and flung it into the black flowing water, half-way across. It plunged in with a muted gulping sound, and I just saw a thin icicle of water erect itself for the moment where it had sunk. Then I threw a scattering handful of bullets in after it and went on towards the valleys.

And now I have come at last to the brim of the valley I was born in, and as I stand on the mountain above it the lights far below come out, frequent and beautiful, burning calmly under the water of darkness. I had expected success and death, but after everything I am still alive, a man, living flesh, but all the suffering I had beaten off in months of action descends upon me, and my body is down; this huge carrion strewn across the mountain tops is my dying flesh. The big birds circle over it between the sheer cliffs of my soles and my molten hair, each seeking a place to set down his dripping foot. Stone-crop breaks out like green fire along the folds of my flesh and the cock-owl that issued at sundown out of the thunders of my ears burst with his wings the hung webs of fishing spiders. From the marches of my loins the starlings rip themselves in a flock, they are sprayed across the clouds, they float swaying darkly like a carpet over my body and pour back over my face like the dark drops of a shower. Small creatures, the curlew and the gorcock find my brow and my hands. They drink at the twitching lips of my wounds; but the purple bubble-flame, the amber bloom above my cratered mouth, forbids the bats a roosting place inside my flesh, beneath the cave-roofs of my nostrils. Naked-headed heavy birds snarl from their cruel slate-hooks, they beat with their raw wing-bones against my bitten face. The burnt-wood raven also perches on the posts of my nipples and in the swirl and flesh-folds of my navel the big sea-hawks build. And now at last the vultures lift their beaks out of my eaten eyes.

The Kiss

୨ଡ଼

I

A dead lier deep in the coalfield and the cracking darkness filling the
pitted earth, stirred out of his first death wanting faintly with two
broken hands to push the pitch night back into the stones, feeling close
over his face the pressure of the imminent bleak rock, and the water,
and the light fingering of the tall earth roofing his grave. His body
ached in the ground, groaning with the chill of burial, suffering bitterly
from cold and the corruption opening his flesh. As he lay on his back,
weary, bearing the cold, watching with the indifference of death but
still painfully his stirring bewildered pulses, and the confusion of his
nostrils, he could feel from time to time the flicker of his beating heart,
tired, uneasy, vibrating like a moth caught under a cupped palm,
turning him sick, but at every movement pushing its warm wash of
blood farther over the levels of his body.

The darkness is kneeling on my chest, I can't draw breath.

And down into his feet, painfully filling his veins with the blood-
froth, and the pods of his rotten cold flesh. Then with a sickness filling
his belly and his mouth like bitter water he bent his knees, trying
languidly to rise off the rock-slab, but the blood shot up hot through
his thighs, molten, mounting like a tilted spirit-bubble through his
flesh, sinking his legs out straight again with agony. He groaned and
fell back, knowing there was no voice to call him Lazarus out of the
rock, to bring his feet rotting with death out on to the grass again.
There was only his own heart with its jet of blood spouting full up
through his throat into the chill of his skull and now suddenly breaking
like a rocket over his brain. And there were whispers perhaps. But
slowly, as his perception cleared of the blood-drench, his stroking heart
deepened and soft-hooted with more assurance, and soon he could feel
the regular beat of his pulses tapping softly like piano-hammers among
the bones of his wrists, soothing the flesh, and his hair all over his body
beginning to feed again upon his skin. His strength was slowly
returning to him, poured into his limbs, his blood was giving it up to
him like a grape-wall breathing warm on the hands in the darkness. He
was alive again. But even now he could feel a worm deep in his foot,
and his hands putrid, enduring cold and death. And when he foresaw

the burden of loving and the beginning of speech without judgment, like the difficult cutting of the tongue-string, it seemed one simple act was preferable to many, the dribbling of cut pulses easier than the acceptance of men. But even as he thought it he found himself rising giddily to his feet, unsteadied, with his heart hammering up under the roof of his skull and the blood heavy in his legs. He swayed and had to cling for support to the timbers, blinded and dizzy. But he had to get out. He groped his way in the pitch draught like wading through a current of snow-water to the hips, leaving the coal-fall behind him, making for the old workings that opened out on to the side of the mountain. In his pocket he pushed a piece of the rock that had killed him. When he at last reached the open air and the hard morning sun buffeting his eyes, the blood spouted up from his belly like a vomit, pouring out of his mouth, and he fell on his knees on the grass with his arm over his face. A few moments later, trying to rise, he fainted back on to the grass and lay there at full length in the sun with his stiff beard pointing up in a steep sharp cone out of his chin and the blood running among the coal-dust over his face.

II

The garden looked cold and black, and there was nothing alive in it. There were no weeds on the bready earth, and from the kitchen window the black meagre beds looked sour and poisonous. But right in the middle was a tree like a planted arm. The wind went into the five black branches from the east and the bleak leaves smoked out on the far side, tapping against the wall in a flock and then dropping deflected from the stone-work to the black earth. Darkness was going up the sky like a shutter.

A waking woman sat at the kitchen window. She was dressed in a black gown and a grey woollen shawl, and as was the custom among the women of the valleys she wore a man's cap covering her hair. She seemed to be seeing the garden for the first time, saying to herself:

Are my eyes open or my lids glass?

She watched the leaves jumping up off the garden, pecking at the wall and then falling back to the earth again. She was calculating, a bunch of lines gathered between her brows.

When will I be delivered of this son heavily loading my womb?

Then she laughed because she remembered she was old, the mother of men and women. Her face was thin, and white as an eggshell, but lined almost everywhere as though a broken hair-net were spread over it; and most noticeable were the small sharp lines radiating from the reeving-string of her mouth. Her thin blue lids slid out again from the hollows under her edgy brows, curving forward to cover over her eyes, and along the curved ridge of her nose, and over her cheek-bones, the skin was thin and tight, shining, faintly luminous. And as she sat at the window with her mouth open the naked veins tunnelled blue and prominent along the backs of her hands lying crossed over her lap for weariness.

She wondered how long she must wait for the knocking at her door.

Soon she was able to see nothing out of the window except a narrow tape of cold sky, the blue of clock-hands, showing over the garden wall, with one branch wagging before it still tagged with a few leaves. Her little clock struck hurriedly. The fire got up in the darkness and then sank down again, easing itself like an animal twisting for comfort, and then the night set in.

But even in the pitch darkness the old woman could hear the wind outside gnawing at the tree.

III

Inched against his opening eyelids was a stem growing from the green tangle of grasses. It was a daisy, lifting up the yellow flat catchment of its flower to the sun, gathering the tilted warmth like a funnel, pouring a light-thread down through its thin stem to meet sap that rose up from roots leeching hungrily at the arterial earth. It was a perfect blossom, an ochre disk with the petals crowding white and stiff round it pointed with clotted scarlet; and the stem was powerful, flexible, a slender column twisting itself slowly round among the crouching grasses, revolving upon the security of its roots like the ponderous gyring of some machine; it bore its heavy blossom balanced out at the sun as it pivoted steadily round under the weight of the flower, furred all over with a covering of fine silver hairs, shining, delicate, like the silvery invisible shagginess downing the body of a child. The workman, smiling and detached, forgetting in his pleasure his death and his burial, sat up to look at it twisting towards the morning sun. He put out his fingers towards it and saw suddenly the broad backs of his hands thicketed with veins, waxy where there was no coal-dust as the hands of the dead in the sun, and when, instantly remembering everything, he drew them back to his breast he saw the centres of both his palms worn into holes, the flesh gone through into a hole like the thin sole of a shoe. It was terrible to look at, but he felt no pain now, and he was holding the sun hot in his lap. He looked no more over his body. He fell back again and soon he was dreaming of acceptance, seeing the pouring rain falling on to the skin of his shoulders and his arms while he received it through into the inward thirsting parts of his body. And then it seemed he stood alone under the dark glare of a bruise-blue desert sky, while a brilliant cactus growing before him like a green divided fruit on the sand sent a new fleshy shoot growing upward, curving towards him from the cleft where it opened out bright green on a pool of sand the sun turned white as salt. And when the sharp spine of the cactus shoot touched his breast he wondered whether he should trample on its fresh green brilliancy or accept it and allow it to penetrate past the protection of his skin into his body. He looked down and gazed with absorption at the spine that had moved upward with such rapid growth and saw it enter his breast-skin like a spear-head; he watched it without resistance slowly thrusting its green blade upward as it grew right into him, tearing off its vivid juicy flesh as it entered. But what the cactus-point found when it had broken into his heart he did not know because it stabbed him wide awake and he opened his eyes to find the daisy with its petals shut into a point and the lovely evening star flickering over the dark valley.

IV

Just outside the village a big square house stood by itself with every window darkened. The night wind rushed at it up the valley with a sound like harsh water, savaging the hedge-bushes and the dishevelled branches of the sumac trees surrounding the garden. Suddenly the door of the house opened and a man ran out bewildered into the night. He ran into the middle of the garden and stood with the light of the open door shining upon him, looking around in a dazed way, bareheaded, bewildered by the darkness, and the wind in the bushes deafening him. A voice from the house shouted that many roads lead out of hell.

The man shivered with the wind and walked slowly out at the gate without looking round. He went in dejection down the road that led towards the village nursing the large bandage of his hand, looking around at the dark valley stretching away on both sides of the road and up at the black slope of the sky ahead with its disorder of stars. When he was beyond the sheltering trees and the house, he found it hard to walk because of the wind, and his hand began to ache although he protected it under his coat from the cold, and soon he was forced to make for shelter towards the roadside where a black lonely tree roared up like a fire in the darkness. But before he reached it the tree spun him a leaf out of the struggle of its empty branches, and as he stooped to pick it up the wind pushed him over as it pushes a candle-flame over on to its back. He lay still in the road unable to move.

V

The workman walked down the slope making for home. As he went along the mountain path, the wind began to rise and the night got colder, the sky quickly filling up with stars. Below him was the valley flooded under soft liquid darkness, black like water, and, above, the body of the mountain out of which he had broken sloped into the night holding up a breast with both hands against the rubbing sky. He came at last to the bows of the hill where the broad valley ahead forked into two and from there he could see a group of shuttering lights, the floating house-lamps of the village for which he was making. The wind was blowing hard, wincing up through the bracken. He hurried down the hill into the darkness, trying to keep his wounded body warm because the wind was flowing so cold, washing low over the curvature of the earth, penetrating his clothes and keeping him back, but even when he got down into the valley it was hardly any quieter. Along one side of the road leading down to the village was a line of naked poplars all shoved sideways, swaying to one side like the long hair of earth blown up erect.

Ahead the white moon laboured slowly out of the ground.

The workman longed to speak again, longed to see the bodies of men and women moving once again with passionate or even commonplace movements as the restless urgency used them, hungered and thirsted to taste with his mouth, longed to smell living bread, to feel fire. If only he could exist to touch flesh with his healed hands, never increasing suffering, in the ignorance of the touched flesh, if only he could give his body to be burnt. At his feet a man lay face downwards on the road clutching a dead leaf in his hand. Over him a charcoal tree screamed spreading its branches like a menacing bird come down on savage wings at the roadside. The workman turned him over, feeling his breath beautifully warm on his pierced flesh, going among the hairs of his cold hands like an insect and his heart knocking very slowly with the tapping of a knuckle under his breast.

The cautious moon was scattering light, going up the sky like a firework, and the workman recognized his brother.

VI

All actions seemed pitiful, like a cruel fraud. Her passionate body once had been the grave of her child and she had suffered because of it, but when she herself was buried flesh her anguish would mean nothing at all, a wastage of feeling and creation. She felt cheated, bitter and rebellious that enjoyment and suffering were both a fraud.

A stone struck the kitchen door like the peck of a hard beak. The old woman got up and opened it quickly, and stood staring out into the darkness of the garden. The wind rushed past her into the house but she could see nothing in the night outside except the tip of a tree-branch above the skyline and the stars looking hard into her eyes. A voice came out of the darkness saying tenderly:

'Mother, don't be afraid, we have come back.'

The old woman recognized the dead voice of her son. A hand struck an aching blow at her throat and she leaned against the open door weak with emotion.

'Don't light the lamps, mother,' the voice went on gently. 'I am carrying my brother. Make the fire up for him; he is ill.'

The old woman turned back into the house wailing softly to herself:

'My son, my son.'

VII

The village bell struck, starting off another day.

Inside the cottage the mother and her two sons sat down around the table in the darkness while the fire tongued into the chimney and the spittles of the little chewing clock were loud in the darkness. The workman was happy, warm and reposing inwardly, very near tears although the pain had left his flesh. Presently he said to his brother quietly:

'Show me your hand.'

Their mother got up at once when he said it, agitated, her voice protesting in the darkness.

'No, no,' she cried, almost hysterically, 'don't undo those bandages again. You mustn't do it. It is terrible. It is terrible.'

'If my brother is willing I will see it,' the workman said gently. 'Fetch me a candle, mother. And don't be afraid of an action for healing.'

She turned away and went slowly out of the room beginning to sob, defeated by him, her resistance broken at once, but presently she returned bearing two brass candlesticks which she placed submissively on the table before the two men. Her face was in shadow but they could hear her sobbing bitterly in the darkness, and they knew she was too wounded to say more in protest now. Then, her hands trembling, she struck the matches for them with great weariness, whimpering like a hurt child, and when the candles were lit she turned to the fire with a helpless gesture of resignation and sat with her face averted, renouncing everything, weeping helplessly to herself without hope or remission.

The brother looked pityingly at her for a moment and then as the workman signed to him, he lifted his heavy arm out of its sling and placed the bandaged hand between the candles on the table. It was huge and ugly, shapeless. The workman, bending forward, his eyes showing up very white, shining moist in the candlelight out of the dull coal-dust still covering his face, and his small fibrous beard sharpened from his chin, stared at it with a fascination of pity, the dark hollow mask of his face unrelaxed, intense, close to the two vivid flames and low against the table-board. He stared for a long time as though he were unable to assert himself, not looking at his brother at all and heedless of his mother and her suffering, only gazing at the shapeless wrappings grey on the table with living eyes from the earthy skin of his face. Then very slowly he began untying the bandages. He fingered them with his large hands as though his ministration were sacred, laying them gently aside with slow priestlike tenderness and deliberation while the big shadows twitched behind them on the walls of the room. At first the bandages were clean and unwound easily but when he had taken off the outer layers they began to be patched darkly at intervals with black blood where the bleeding had oozed through and dried, and at these places they began to stick so that he had to ease them gently apart before he could get them off. Love slowed his hands, and the distresses of his brother. But gradually the pile of tangled bandages grew beside the candlestick with the steady unspooling of the hand and then as its flesh was slowly revealed to the air it began to stink into the room.

'Don't undo it,' said the mother, in anguish, her first weeping spent.

But the workman went on steadily unwinding, tender-fingered as a mother in spite of the wounds hindering his blunt hands, taking up the weight of his brother's arm on his hand and twisting the bandages off continually with great care and tenderness. His love-acts were skilful, and soothing to his brother, tender and reverential, and his calm absorption in this eucharistic task seemed child-like and complete. And as he worked steadily at the sticking length of cloth it became blacker and blacker, completely soaked at last with rotten blood, and with the gradual laying bare of the upper hand the stink of putrefaction issuing from it became worse, oppressive, almost unbearable. But the workman went on untwisting in spite of everything although his movements were tiring, and presently after many pauses for his brother's exhaustion, all the bandages were uncoiled into a tangled pile on the table; and, when the soaking undercloths were unwrapped as well and pushed aside, the whole hand lay naked on the table in the candlelight. It was terrible to see, pitiful beyond anything the workman had imagined, and at the horror of it he felt numb, he could only bow his head and remain silent. It was a great heavy mass of black flesh, soft and thick, swollen up with black spongy decay and larger than twice its normal size, showing no trace anywhere of veins or knuckles or the pink shine of fingernails or even of the shapes and divisions of fingers. Beginning from the wholesome pale wrist-flesh and spreading to the farthest tip, it was a shapeless black mass of stinking flesh like some bad inward part cut from an animal, warm and soft throughout, not divided up into fingers at all and with only a small bud of foul black flesh sticking out at the side where the thumb should have been growing. The workman, used to sights of the body diseased and lacerated, had never seen anything so terrible or so pitiful. Beside this putrid rottenness gradually claiming the flesh the wounds he had known were clean, nothing, and looking up at his brother's face his compassion for him was perfect. But there were no tears in his eyes as he looked down again, trying hopelessly to discern in this raw stinking corruption perhaps the ridges of sinews, or the jointed bones of his brother's fingers, or even the three divisions separating them from each other. But it was hopeless. And as he glanced up with emotion, and looked over to where his mother was sitting, he saw she had fallen back across the arm of her chair in a faint with a swallowing vein prominent along her neck; she had fainted without his noticing it, and she lay in her chair before the fire with her face inverted and her hair hanging out of her head like a soft root and a vein gulping uneasily along her throat.

Very tenderly, with tears running down his face, he bent forward and kissed the putrid flesh of his brother's hand.

Knowledge

❧

I

On the top of Ystrad Pit three men were repairing the winding rope. It was a lovely sunny morning, blue and fresh, and they worked with the thick black criss-cross shadows of the steel winding-gear falling across them over the sparkling ground, and their fire looking pale because of the strong sunlight, as though it were going out. One of the men was the colliery smith, a grey priestlike old man with a serious, almost mournful, expression, gentle, having the face of one possessing himself completely, claiming nothing. He was grey and clean-shaven, dressed in an old cotton boiler suit of navy blue, and he wore a soiled cap with the peak broken in the middle above his eyes. But although he was old, and his eyes were weary, his body was slim and upright, and the grip of his hands on the stubborn rope was vigorous, as assured and masterful as the handling of a young man; but his face wasn't masterful at all, only kindly and gentle with knowledge. The three of them, the two men and the boy, were working at the pithead and not speaking much, with the cage hitched up in safety above them near the sheaves and the thick steel rope lying coiled over the dusty ground at their feet. They had the stiff brush of strands from its ravelled end fixed securely up like spiky hairs through the bottom of a sort of deep iron cup or inverted bell held in a bench-vice into which the second man was pouring molten lead out of a long metal ladle. The boy apprentice, very dirty with grease and coal-dust, was blowing the fire-bucket from time to time with a foot-bellows to keep the iron crucible of lead hanging over it molten. The man pouring out the liquid metal was the pitman, being responsible for the ropes, and the cages, and the shaft of the pit generally, a big handsome youngish man, with grace in him and restraint, doing his delicate job easily and with perfection. He was using a lipped ladle with a long flat metal handle that he gripped with squares of soft leather, tipping the lead out like water, waiting for it to sink a bit on cooling and then filling it up again to the brim; and he never spilt any, he had done it so often, although once or twice it swelled up like a bubble with the scum cracking on the blister-like curve. He had taken off the oilskins he usually wore for his job and was working in a thin white shirt with his sleeves rolled up almost to his shoulders, and his trousers fastened low about his loins by means of a thick leather belt buckled with two tongues of brass. He was big and powerful, his flesh like most pit workers as white as a girl's in the sunlight, and his arms large and white, and solid, but smooth, not lumped into muscle although they looked capable and were firm with power. He wore a wide strap on his wrist and his hands were big too and soiled, with blunt fingers. He was much younger than the smith but he effaced him with his huge shapely body and his energy. His face was pale and smooth, rounded, and his soft dark hair was cropped short, not moving in the breeze; he was very big, his thin shirt tight on him, and yet he seemed shy, his light eyes troubled a bit from time to time as though he feared being hurt, although not through the body, and his handsome edgy lips were too ready for kindness. He had none of the smith's gentle stoicism and endurance. He knew he could be hurt and he feared it.

The smith was his father-in-law.

Finally the bell-shaped container was completely filled and the pitman lighted a cigarette waiting for the metal to cool before fixing the rope to the top of the cage. It was Sunday and there were no workmen about the colliery, only one or two officials and the lamp man. The boy, who had not long left school, was trying to pitch his cap over the sparrows.

'When are you coming up?' asked the pitman, speaking to his father-in-law.

'I'll come up some night this week, Penn,' he said, stretching out his hand towards the cooling metal. 'Is Gwyn all right?'

'She's all right,' the pitman answered, 'only wondering when you're coming up.'

The old smith smiled; there was sympathy between the two men.

Gwyn was Penn's wife, being eight or ten years younger than himself, a kind of stranger people didn't know very easily, a bit awkward and distant with anyone she didn't care about. People liked her, she was so pretty, narrow, with long straight yellow hair almost golden, cut in a long bob at the back nearly to her shoulders, and growing cropped in a line across her forehead; and she had white skin and spotted blue eyes. But there was something in her people missed, as though she kept something back purposely for herself from everybody. She wasn't easy in her intercourse with people and she flushed readily as though speaking to anyone unfamiliar was a strain, a good bit of a hardship. But inwardly she had the steady unassuming assurance of the old smith, her father. She had no real fear of being hurt at all; she disliked irritating little contacts with people and she avoided them, being at times almost panicky, but she was passionate and she knew she could fight although she never wanted to. Penn understood this somehow and he relied on her, feeling safe with her at his back; she put such spunk into him.

When the metal was cool through and through, Penn got up the iron ladder on to a platform in the winding-gear high above the open mouth of the shaft that tapered below him like a huge inverted fool's-cap, and clamped the rope on to the cage with two long strips of reddened steel. He watched the spokes of the big wheels above him beginning slowly to move round in answer to his signal, and the thick steel rope dithering like a harp-string as it took the weight of the big iron cage; and then he tested his job himself by getting into his yellow oilskins and being wound down the shaft standing on the roof of the cage. Everything was in order. He called to his father-in-law and started up his motor-bike for home.

II

Penn and Gwyn lived in a pleasant old house belonging to her father, a good way from the pit, right out in the country beyond the edge of the coalfield, with the khaki mountains beginning close behind it. In some ways living there was inconvenient for them because if there was something wrong at the pit Penn had to go out at once, often in the middle of the night and in all weathers, to get to his job somehow. But he had his motor-bike and they thought it was worth it to be out of the dreary shabby town and the smoke and the endless noise. The house was pretty with the bright-coloured painting Penn had done to the outside woodwork, and all the flowers and the trellises; it stood the other side of a brook with a wooden bridge over it, and it had a big garden at the back with fruit trees and roses. Penn spent most of his time growing flowers, particularly roses, and in summer he gave away dozens of bunches to his friends. It was queer to watch him in the rose-garden; he had a large number of little white linen tents, that he could adjust against the sun, clipped on to the supporting stakes of his most valuable rose-trees, and when he looked at the blooms under them he became intent, as though his eyes were seeing past every curled rose-petal, touching the small inner quick and earth-urge that thrust up the stalk and pushed out the shallow petal wrapping from the tiny yellow attachment to the stem; he looked as though he were seeing all over the flower and into the heart of it, right down the thin trunk-stem, knowing the action of its threaded roots, and his big hands went delicately into the thick of a rose bush feeling their way round a flower to pull it back for the loose rose-whorl of its petals, or to scissor it off low down on the stalk. When Gwyn saw him stooping to handle the roses, peering into the tangled bushes at them in his intense absorbed way, so quiet, she felt excluded, strangely out of it. She couldn't see she came in there anywhere, but she loved him for it, shearing himself off like that from time and place, caring about nothing, existing only with the rose between his hands and at peace with it. She was filled with tenderness for him almost to tears, seeing all the latent feeling and power of his magnificent body fused down to this intense observation of an unbudding flower, giving himself up without any reserve of doubt or fear. But she could see there was nothing scientific or curious in his expression; he seemed as though he understood pretty well already, and his look wasn't of inquiry at all, or speculation or even wonder, but just acceptance, and slightly puzzled knowledge. When she saw him like that she was at once filled with pity and tenderness, and she was a bit awestruck as well at the completeness of his withdrawal from everything. She used to say nothing at those times with this awe upon her, but just go back to her house-work again.

It wasn't often she asked him to go to chapel with her. She was religious like her father and went pretty regularly although she didn't like the concerts and the tea-parties; she went and hurried back home again as quick as she could, not very sociable. But the evening her father came up after work as he had promised she said, 'Penn, dada and I are going to chapel. Will you come?'

He made a face. 'Oh, I don't know,' he said uneasily. He didn't like to refuse outright because of the old smith.

'Come on,' she said, 'this once. You always like the meetings in the weeknights.'

'Oh all right,' he answered. 'I've got nothing much to do, I don't mind really.'

So the three of them started out, walking.

III

It was still daylight when they crossed the wooden bridge outside the house, but the chapel was in the town and by the time they got there it had become quite dark and the lights were lit in the streets. They went through the wooden door into the warm silent little schoolroom behind the chapel and separated, Gwyn going on to sit with the other women near the fire the far side of the aisle between the benches, and the two men finding seats in the recess at the side of the wooden door porch. They were early and there was hardly anybody there, only half a dozen women and two or three men on the benches near Penn and his father-in-law, and when they sat down there was dead silence except for the gas coming hoarse through the rusty brackets sticking out of the walls and the tack-tack of the clock over the fireplace swinging its quick pendulum behind the little glass window. Apart from these noises and the sound of the slipping fire there was a drowsy silence that sank into him throughout the room, very warm and peaceful, and comfortable. Penn had been once or twice before but it was always a bit strange to him, the shabby schoolroom and the few motionless people waiting absorbed in utter silence for the meeting to begin, because his family was English really and church, and he had gone there when he was younger. He watched the people coming in, one or two at a time, short people nearly all of them, undistinguished, the majority of the men colliers dressed almost invariably in black suits with their skin pale and shining, looking tight and a bit sickly in the green gaslight. He watched them creaking awkwardly over the bare knotted floor-boards into the shabby vestry and sitting round him, crooked and a bit misshapen some of them, with blue scars tattooed across their hands and their tight shiny faces, not picturesque at all, commonplace, but it was a satisfaction to him somehow to be there touching them, with their rich earthiness warming him through. They sat around him in quiet until they were a good number waiting for the meeting to start, motionless most of the time, some with their eyes shut, solid and finished, wanting nothing; they had been hurt often and had suffered, and they looked uncouth, almost monolithic, with no desire in them, only the warm look of knowledge and understanding. They sat so calm Penn envied them, seeing no bitterness in their easy hands and so much acceptance in the look of their bodies and their clean shining faces. And around them all was the still warm atmosphere, rich and getting drowsy, and the gaslight coming green off the distempered walls.

The meeting started with the young minister reading out a hymn. There was a good number of people present for a weeknight, perhaps thirty, and Penn enjoyed the meeting, especially the hymn-singing; the voices were rich and the words and music moving. He was glad he had come. Usually he didn't like any religious service, it seemed to be about something else, nothing to do with him at all. But he never said anything to Gwyn; he wanted her to go if she liked it.

Then several people prayed and quoted scripture, and one or two spoke describing their experiences and temptations, a sort of confessional. They were good too, some of them, natural actors and story tellers, humorous even, and full of drama and vivid speech. Penn was filled with admiration for them, and contented. But near the end the young minister asked Gwyn to pray. He was a nice young chap, very earnest and hard-working, and Penn liked him, but he was unwilling at once, and apprehensive. He wanted to stop her from doing it, it wasn't fair. It was wrong because Gwyn was passionate and would say things to give herself away kneeling on the floor before them all. But her father just bowed his face slowly and waited in silence with his eyes closed, calm and tender-looking, quite unmoved. Penn didn't know really why he was so mad and unwilling, resisting it so much, except that he was afraid of what she would say to hurt herself before them, and for a moment he hated all these people sitting round her waiting to hear her reveal herself; it was ugly to him to see them watching the grace of her kneeling body, secretly triumphing over her, hoping to see how her passion would give her away. She began softly, Penn didn't really know what she was saying. She was kneeling with her head bowed at an empty seat, her long yellow hair hanging down from under her blue cap so that no one could see her face at all. Her words were muffled, and from time to time she stopped, and there was silence letting in the sound of the gases buzzing and the eating of the fire and the awkward little coughs breaking from the other women. Penn was white, watching her over his hands, pale and strained-looking with his lips dry. As long as he was watching her he felt he could defend her and justify her, and hold her somehow in his protective control against all these other people. He was afraid to stop looking at her and thinking about her, willing her passionately to hold out against the bitter strength of her emotion and the words surging in her blood, lending her his strength. He was mad against the women near her and his mouth was like fire. He knew how unfair it was to let her kneel down like this; it was cruelty, but he wouldn't let anything happen to her. He could feel rage and strength filling him like a sap rising at the thought of her giving way; he was in a sort of fury, but quiet, knowing she must resist the concentration of so many wills, and he didn't want any longer to stop her; she had to go on and complete her prayer in spite of them while he lent her all his strength. He glanced round feeling powerful with anger and protective tenderness. Then suddenly her body went slack and she began to sob. She faltered in her prayer a bit and finally stopped, her head jerking slowly over the chair. And then her body shuddered with fierce weeping. She couldn't say anything any more and she just knelt and wept helplessly with her fingers spread out over her face and her hanging hair rocking to and fro from under her cap. She was shaking right through her body before them all with uncontrollable weeping, making hardly any sound except little choking cries from time to time that broke loose from the strife of her throat. Penn was helpless, feeling nothing clearly, bewildered and helpless. Slowly she got up and sat on the bench, her face bowed over her lap, her shoulders hunched and the sobs still jerking through her like stabs. The silence and the tension were awful and interminable to Penn, who sat on defeated and hopeless, not even wondering how it was going to end, completely empty. Then slowly the young minister got up and gave out a hymn and they sang with spirit as though Gwyn's crying had released purity into the room. But she sat throughout the singing slowly coming back from her prayer with the subsidence of her passion, and by the time they had finished she was calm again, flushed and red-eyed, but composed, gathering her things together to leave. Penn was dazed, it was all so sudden and so hateful. After the meeting he found himself walking home with her through the streets, shining after the rain, and saying good night to her father; not one of them had spoken a word of what had happened. In the lane that led up to their house he stopped her and said:

'Gwyn, what was the matter?'

She laughed and lifted up his hand and kissed the knuckles of his fingers clasping hers. He sounded so sad and bewildered she had to comfort him. She went close up to him not being able to stop laughing, he sounded so tragic.

'It was nothing, Penn,' she said, 'only I love our people and I so seldom show it. Smell the gillies in the garden after the rain. I am so busy fighting.'

She ran on ahead dragging him by the hand. It all seemed so strange to Penn.

Wil Thomas

❦

At the top of a disused incline running up the mountain stood a lonely row of ironworkers' cottages. In front of them were fields and rough heathland, but behind, the big black tips rose up into the height of perpendicular cliffs, crested and streaked with white clinker like the droppings of gigantic birds. On the doorstep of the end cottage a man called Wil Thomas stood looking down the incline towards the town in the valley, and watching the sun beginning to set in the clouds beyond as though it were going down behind yellow celluloid. He had a bottle in his hand and he was waiting for his wife to come home from the prayer meeting.

Wil was an ordinary-enough chap to look at, being heavy and thick-set with short legs, wearing a greenish suit and a white muffler. His body was egg-shaped, set diagonally from back to front, with the heavy end of the egg swelling out full behind the lower end of his tight waistcoat and the fly-buttons of his trousers, stretching them apart, and the small end rising in a low hump between his shoulder-blades, lifting out his coat a bit. He had no neck and his head fitted plumb on to his body. His hair was white and cut short, and for a nose he had a hook like a large soft beak, big and fleshy, constellated all over with small, equally-spaced blue black-heads like pencil dots. His heavy jaw, wanting a shave, was like white velvet and his eyes were noticeable, being khaki – his eye, more like, because he had only one. The place where the other had been looked sore, the raw lids hanging loose, the flesh all round red as though the eye-hole had been cut in his skin with a scissors. Usually he wore a false eye but he hadn't had it in for the last fortnight because he had been home from work with a clout on the back, so that he hadn't been able to leave the house at all.

After watching for a bit he grinned to himself because he was able to make out his wife struggling up the incline road with her breath in her fist. As she got nearer he could tell by the explosive kind of way she was walking, jerky, automatic, scattering her feet and kicking her skirts out, that she wasn't very sweet, and she wasn't either, although she had been to the prayer meeting. Before going she put her coms through the mangle and broke the buttons, and that had upset her, and now her feet were beginning to ache and her back-comb was sticking hard into her head under her heavy best hat and giving her jip every yard of the way. And she knew what Wil would be after with his clowning as soon as she got to the house. But she wasn't going until she'd had a rest. He'd have to wait for his beer for once, that was all about it.

When she got up to the doorstep Wil stopped her and pointed towards the sunset with the flagon, 'Mari,' he said, gazing before him, 'what other hand than His?'

She pushed past him into the kitchen. 'I know what you want,' she snapped, 'as long as you can bathe your gums that's all you care about.'

Wil shrugged his shoulders, grinning to himself. He was a bit of a comic and he thought he would be able to humour her saying something like that. But she was a queer plant. She could be awkward when she wanted to, Wil knew that, turning very spiteful and touchy at times. She was a little woman dressed in a big heavy hat of black velvet and a dark costume with long wide skirts, and she had little steel glasses on only just big enough to cover her eyes, with black wool wound round the nose-piece. She was always full of quick mechanical energy, her movements were always a bit sudden and automatic-looking, and now because of her boots and her heavy hat she was filled up with spite and malice, vindictive, as fierce and quarrelsome as a little bullfinch. Her face was a bit purpler than usual, and her small tidy little features looked snappish, disgusted with everything, and her lips were tight too, and hard as a couple of pebbles, evil-looking. But Wil wasn't a bit frightened by her nasty little darting eyes or the dirty look she kept on giving him as he followed her about carrying the bottle. He only grinned behind her back and after a lot of coaxing he got her to go for him. She put some steak and onions in the oven and then went out wearing comfortable things, houseshoes and a shawl and one of his old caps on her head. She wasn't willing but she couldn't refuse somehow.

'Well done little Mari,' he said, and he came with her to the doorstep. 'You'll think of this in years to come. Long after I have joined my eye, my little pelican.'

He grinned after her as she went down the pavement.

Soon it began to get dark in the house so Wil lit the oil lamp and put it on the table by the window. Then he pulled the blind down and sat by the fire feeling pretty good, taking an occasional look at Mari's medicine bottle that was standing on the window-sill, and enjoying the warmth and the steak-smell, listening from time to time to the wind outside beginning to rise over the mountains, moving uneasily in the belly of the darkness. His back was comfortable too, and he was enjoying himself fine by the fire in his low little kitchen, dreaming about his eye which had dropped out like a pop-alley when he was born or had been eaten by a rat that time he was dull enough to work underground, he couldn't remember which, he had told so many different tales about it. No, that was sure to be wrong though, he wasn't any rat's leavings, he was sure of that. He had dug a fork into it when the woman next door ran out of the lavatory on fire, that was more like it. Yes, that was it, she was Lissa Richards, number two, who used to smoke her husband's long-ends in the lavatory, but what she'd done was set her drawers on fire by accident, the wicked bitch, and made Wil stick an old fork in his eye with excitement. But he felt pretty good waiting for Mari to come home with the beer.

Then the preacher knocked at the door.

'Cokes of hell,' said Wil, 'who can be there now?'

He got up and went to have a look, taking the lamp off the table with him because it had become quite dark outside. When he saw it was Evans he brought him in at once. 'Come on in, come on in,' he said, glad of company now that he had been feeling so shabby. 'Damn it all, little Evans, come on in at once.' The preacher stepped from the pavement into the kitchen, ducking as he came, thanking Wil in his big preaching voice.

'May the thumbs of the dragon never lift the latch of William Thomas,' he said in his big voice, stopping just inside the door, towering above Wil with his hand aloft. 'How do you feel, William?'

'Blessèd, little Evans,' said Wil, 'blessèd. Come right in and sit your little bottom down on the stool over by here.'

Evans was a queer-looking chap, tall and dark, dressed from head to foot in black clothes, having his mouth half-way up his face and filled with big false teeth that were broken in the plate and rattled when he was talking like a pocketful of taws. He had big nostrils too with tufts of black hairs sticking out of them, hooked and black like little bunches of candlewicks. He always wore very thick glasses that made his black boot-button eyes look small and queer, with the glass in them as thick as a pop bottle, and his eyebrows were heavy and black, curving upwards, the shape of nail-parings.

'Come right over here by the fire,' said Wil, noticing his funny strong smell. And when he had got him sitting he took his black hat off for him so that his ears sprang upright, and then he hung it on his knee. The preacher's forehead was the width of a good garter and his hair was like astrakhan.

Wil never went to chapel himself; he pretended he was too dense, but he wasn't embarrassed at all because of that. He was glad to have Evans in the house, hoping to be able to tease him a bit, because the preacher was supposed to be a bit simple and once he had cocked his leg over the pulpit to show the people Balaam riding on the donkey. But he wanted to make him feel at home as well.

'Have a cup of tea?' he said.

'No tea,' said Evans, shaking his face.

'Small beer then?' said Will.

'No small beer,' said Evans.

'Whisky and water?' said Wil, moving towards the window sill.

'No water,' said Evans, and he sucked a line of fluid like a macaroni pipe back up into his nose.

Wil was glad he had shown willing anyway. He got down two cups and poured out some of the whisky Mari kept on the window-sill for her heartburn, and they enjoyed themselves nice and tidy. They sat at the table in the low comfortable little kitchen, one each side of the lamp, with Wil's nose throwing a huge shadow shaped like a rudder across his face and Evans turning his eyes up and muttering as the whisky was coming out of the bottle. Wil did most of the talking at first; he was glad to, living in that back-crack up the incline and not being able to go out at all, but he was watching Evans all the time, trying to draw him out. He started to talk about the compo doctor not asking him how he felt but how soon he was going to start work again. He clowned a lot, imitating the doctor's classy English, and then he spat in the fire with disgust.

'There is none to hold up the arms of the needy, William,' said Evans, solemn and important, and he drew through his nose again so that he could have a drink. His big face near the lamp-globe was full of edges under his thin skin and heavy-looking with a lot of bone in it like a horse.

'There's no two ways about that,' said Wil, convinced. 'How are you shaping? Aren't you empty yet?'

Evans glanced down into his cup. 'The lord giveth and the lord taketh away,' he said, gazing at the ceiling boards as Wil poured out again.

And with a new drink in front of him and Wil encouraging him he cleared his throat and started to talk, letting Wil have one of his old sermons, the one about Samson and Delilah and the Dragon. 'Like me,' said Wil, interrupting him for devilment and wiping his eye with his coat-sleeve, 'I dug a fork in mine.'

Evans swallowed with a lot of noise, a bit impatient, wanting to get on. 'The scratches of the Dragon are stripes in the army of the lord,' he said, heavy and dramatic, starting off again.

'Quite right, quite right, little Evans,' Wil broke out showing he was convinced, and nearly upsetting his whisky. 'And when I'm in the bar of the Angel and I want to pass water, Evans, I haven't got to spit in my beer before I go out, see?' Evans nodded slowly, not very interested, anxious to have his own say. 'I've only got to take my glass eye out,' Wil went on acting the part, 'and put it on the counter by my pint and everything is fine. I only say "Watch here a bit little one", and it's as good as if I was there myself.' He picked up his cup and held it to his lips grinning. 'That's quite right what you said, little Evans.'

Wil took a sip. But Evans waved his big hands before his face, eager to have another go. He looked cunning and while Wil was swallowing his drink he took his chance and started off again.

'It is better to have one eye, William,' he said, 'than two and hell fire . . .'

Wil brought his cup down smartly. 'There was hell fire when I lost mine all right,' he broke out in a hurry, and then he went on describing and acting how he had been on the back doorstep getting a cork out of a bottle with a fork when the woman next door ran out into the garden on fire.

'The roots of the tobacco tree are suckled in hell below,' said Evans, poking his finger out at Wil with his thumb up like a trigger, determined to be listened to, 'but I have come to speak comfort, William, if my arm is long enough. I ought to have said my tongue, that was a mistake.' He boomed at Wil and lifted the lamp towards him. 'I have brattice, William, against the blowings of the Dragon. I can make you a whole man again.'

Wil grinned at him, thinking he'd got him well started now. 'That's how you chaps are when you wear your collars arse-frontwards,' he said, 'you'll say anything.' He just leaned back and let Evans have his say, preparing to enjoy himself. But what fascinated him after a bit was the preacher's nose. He was so interested he couldn't take his eyes off it. One of the huge black nostrils had dried up in the heat and left a narrow glistening line like a snail-track along his upper lip between his nostril and his mouth, but the other side was exciting to watch because it was still active, and a thin tube of whitish liquid was all the time creeping slyly out of his nose and advancing towards his mouth as he was talking. At times Wil got so excited he could hardly hear what he was saying, thinking it would tap him on the knee or the back of the hand, but always at the last minute Evans would sniff it up again out of sight. Then Wil would listen in comfort for a bit until it began to signal once more, wet and shiny among the growth of black hairs. He was so excited and amused, most of what Evans was getting on about was going right over his head and he didn't notice how he was working himself up. The chap was talking like the river, his broken teeth chattering as though there was a horse-bit in his mouth and his arms were exercising in front of his face like mad. Then he stood up suddenly, still talking in his double bass, and his hat fell off his knee to the rag rug, but he took no notice of it at all. Instead he stood towering above Wil in his black clothes with his glove-back hair up against the planks of the ceiling and his huge shadow flapping about on the wall like a big bat's umbrellas or the wings of a goodyhoo. Wil was a bit surprised at first, thinking it funny that the medicine was making him talk like this, but wishing all the same he'd go off the boil a bit and take it easy now before Mari got back. 'Little Evans, little Evans,' he said trying to soothe him, 'sit down and be comfortable and don't stand up there, boy, bending like a black bluebell.' But he took no notice and because of something or other he'd said he started emptying his tail pocket, babbling all the time about the dragon and taking things out of his pocket by the fistful, piling them on the table in the round pool of lamplight. 'Well, God knows,' Wil grinned to himself, 'there was supposed to be everything in the ark but there's sure to be more in this.' Evans went on talking as fast as he could with his pointed Adam's apple working like a piston, but he wasn't getting any change out of Wil although he continued being dramatic, pulling things out of his pocket, string and papers and pins and camphor balls. 'No doubt that's why he always smells like the cathedral,' thought Wil wondering what was coming out next. And because the preacher looked as though he was going to tread on it, he picked up his hat off the rug for him and put it under the lamp where it looked, because of the dent across the top, like the round head of a big black screw driven into the table.

When he looked up again he had brought a human eye out of his pocket.

'Wonderful man,' cried Wil jumping up, forgetting all his clowning, 'what's that you've got there?'

It was a real eye, fresh and glistening in the lamplight, with threads of thin steam rising from it and the nerve-roots hanging out between the preacher's fingers. It lay solid and big as a fine peeled egg, shining among the camphor balls on his shaking palm, polished like china in the lamplight with the pupil and the khaki iris gazing up at Wil in a fixed way he didn't like at all. There were no lids on it and it stared wickedly up at him all the time so that he couldn't avoid it whichever way he looked, fixing its clear shining pupil on his good eye, making him feel very uneasy, and, although there was no face round it, it seemed to be jeering at him all the time. He had seen plenty of scraps of bodies about after accidents in work, and when he was a boy he had carried the top of the lodger's finger about in a matchbox until it stunk too bad, but he had never seen anything like the eye before. He couldn't have touched it for a fortune although Evans was holding it out to him, asking him to take it, his arm going up and down under Wil's face like a pump handle. And he began to look so fierce, he was turning so curly that Wil thought he'd better take it into his hand to save trouble. It was cold and wet underneath, slimy like a peeled plum, heavy and moist as an egg-plum with the skin pulled off as the juices of the chilly wet flesh touched his unwilling palm.

Wil shivered from head to foot, and outside the loud wind stumbled over the house.

As Mari was coming up the dark lonely incline in the wind, carrying the beer, she said good night to some man she wasn't sure of. He reminded her of Evans the minister. 'Poor fellow,' she thought, 'a year today he swam the Jordan.' When she got back to the house the lamp had burnt out, and when she relit it she saw Wil lying on the sofa fast asleep on his back and looking pretty rough. She went through a little door that looked like a cupboard into the pantry to put the beer on the stone and when she came out she noticed her whisky bottle empty on the window sill. That settled her. Without stopping to take off her things she pulled Wil's steak and onions out of the oven and ate them up with relish while Wil still lay fast asleep with his mouth open on the sofa behind her. Then she drank his beer. The gravy that was left over from the steak she spread around his mouth where it stuck well because he hadn't shaved for a few days. Then she took out a book called the *Grapes of Canaan* and adjusting her little steel glasses sat by the fire reading. Her face was innocent, white, round as a little coin.

At last Wil woke up. He wanted his beer. 'Mari,' he said, 'let me have my supper.'

'Supper,' she snapped at him, 'how many suppers do you want you, belly-dog?' She snatched the looking-glass off the wall and held it before him.

Wil clapped his hand to his empty eye.

Eben Isaac

❦

Pentrebach was a little farming village in the hills behind the Sidan bay, a couple of rows of whitewashed cottages in a street sloping up to the top of a hill where there was a square with a pump in it. From here you could see the cut fields on the hills all round like sheets of green blotting paper among the tangled cables of the hedges, and on a clear day you could make out the sea, smooth as a slab of blue bag-leather in the distance. The village baker was a mean old chap called Eben Isaac Evans, a slow-moving silent old creature who was always grousing and belching about in the darkness of his little bakehouse. In appearance he was a bit of a peasant, heavy and thick in the body, full-shouldered, but with legs so short you couldn't stand a two-foot rule upright between them to the fork of his trousers. His bald head was shiny and tight as a plum skin, and he had a noticeable turn in his left eye which looked like a horse-ball because the coloured iris was tucked up almost out of sight in the corner; then swelling full out of the middle of his pale shrunken face was a thick fleshy nose, inflamed and veiny, like the rubber bulb of a water pistol or a barber's spray bottle. Often you could see him standing motionless by the bakehouse oven with a brine-bead hanging under it. He wasn't very handsome, what with his bad eye and his drooping moustache that was like a scarce fringe of yellow cottons hanging out of his lip, but he was married all the same. He lived with his wife Keziah, a loud-mouthed blowzy woman, next door to the bakehouse, right on the main village road, and it was on this road that Keziah spent most of her time watching the funerals coming down the street on their way to the graveyard outside the village. Every time one of these processions came in sight she made Eben Isaac come out of the bakehouse with his bowler hat on so that he could take it off as the body passed the door; and she always used to shout to the men carrying the bier to find out who was being buried even when she knew all about it already. Sometimes the mourners who knew about her would tease her, and once, as Eben Isaac was standing beside her in his shirt-sleeves, hat in hand, he heard her call out, 'Dafy Etwart, whose corpse have you got there?'

'Shadrach,' answered the bearer, 'the husband of Mari the Bag.'

'Oh, he's a heavy one. Have you carried him all the way?'

'No indeed little Keziah, he walked for us as far as the pump.'

She grunted as the other bearers laughed, and spat a spider on to the dusty road.

It was funny she had to ask so many questions because according to her she used to see the ghost-candles in the street at night, the spirit-funerals meaning somebody was going to pass out pretty soon. But nobody took much notice of her with her noise and her shouting. She was fat and dirty, tent-like, with her black clothes sloping out all round from her neck-band, and because she never wore her stays her breasts hung down inside her thin black blouses like a pair of huge buttons hanging off, drooping loosely right over the tapes of her swelling sack apron. She never had her false teeth in, and she wore her hair on top of her head in a loose bun, balanced there in the shape of a horse-tod. She was always worth seeing standing on the top step of the bakehouse in her dirty white canvas slippers, cleaning the dirt out of her nails with a hairpin, or coming untidy out of the house before breakfast, scratching her jaw and showing all her empty red gums as she yawned at the morning.

One day in the summer Griff Penclawdd was killing a bull in his farmyard just outside the village, and everybody from Pentrebach had gone down to see it. It was a lovely sunny day, the fresh whitewash on the cottages was bright and flat as marble in the brilliant sunshine, and the tree growing out of the top of Eben Isaac's chimney was throwing a black basketwork of shadow down on to the road. But the street itself was deserted, and the white pigeons were down like clockwork after grain and the indian corn. Keziah had gone with the others, but she had made Eben Isaac stay behind to work in the black sweltering bakehouse. He stood for a long time after she had gone without moving, patiently waiting near the iron oven-door for the bread to do, his shrunken face lit up beside the elbowed bat's-wing burner that was the only bit of light in the black bakehouse; he was in his shirt-sleeve, covered right down to the eye-holes of his boots with flour, and in his hand he held the tall wooden oar he used for shovelling the bread-tins out of the oven. From time to time his hollow cheeks filled out with wind like puffy sails as he belched gently to himself, but apart from that he did not move at all. He stood still there so long the arm he was holding the bread-pole with began to go to sleep and he thought drowsily to himself, 'No, my arm is wide awake, I can feel it, it's the rest of me must be going to sleep.' He was always a bit dull and while he was puzzling which it was, he heard the sound of gritty cartwheels rumbling down the road in the distance, crunching over the small stones of the street with a noise at last like the hissing sound of a scissors scissoring through a cut of thick hair. He walked over to the little square window, lifted the flour sack off the rusty nail and looked out blinking into the sunny street. His chin behind the glass, because the bakehouse had been built sunk below the roadway, was about on a level with the pavement pebbles. As he crossed the flagstones of the bakehouse floor he noticed from the thumping noise that the tip of his left boot was missing. There was nobody in the street when he put his face against the pane, but in a minute or two Steffan the Smelly came into sight wheeling his fish-cart. And on the top of it he had an elm coffin with white metal handles like door-knockers. Eben Isaac lifted his dusty bowler slowly and without thinking from the hook behind the door, put it on and went up blinking to the top step, carrying his long oven-oar with him. He watched Steffan hanging back on the shafts of the cart, and got ready to call out to him. 'Steffan,' he said when the cart was opposite the door, 'whose body have you got there?'

Steffan spent most of his time tramping about the country, being always on somebody's knocker for the end of the loaf or a slice of bacon fat, but sometimes he sold fish among the hills from a cart or a basket. He had three bowler hats on, and two beards. One of the beards was a thick little tuft of hair stuck in the middle under his lower lip like a hairy beech-nut that moved independently when he was talking, and the other was a thick, coconut, lion's-mane of bull's wool wrapped round his neck and half his face. The skin of his broad nose was about the only bit of face-flesh he had in sight, and that, curving out into the sunshine from beneath the shadow of his hats, was full of small holes like a piece of orange peel. Then at the base of his nose, just where the nostril joined on to the cheek, he had a small yellow growth like a shrivelled green pea that he used to play with when he was thinking. He had on a long black overcoat of some curly stuff reaching almost to his heels and fastened in the middle with a six-inch safety-pin. His right boot had no tongue, and was cut from the lace-holes half-way across the toe-cap, showing his green woollen stockings. The other boot fitted better because it came from a different pair.

He took no notice the first time Eben Isaac shouted. So with his hat still on his chest he shouted again, 'Steffan, who have you got there?'

'Eben Isaac Evans,' Steffan answered, looking puzzled up at the houses, 'the baker of Pentrebach.'

That brought Eben Isaac's eye out of the corner and the water-drop under his nose began to swing like a sign-board in the wind with the jerk it gave him. But just then, before he could say anything, the front door of the pink house opposite opened and old Harri Hir, a tall white figure, ran out of the shadows into the sunlight shouting, 'Steffan, Steffan, a nice meaty one, Steffan,' filling the silent street with his noise and frightening the pigeons, who slapped their little sides with their wings and rose to the roofs. He was a very long, narrow old man with a white beard down to his middle, thin, and so bloodless three fleas could have sucked him dry. He was not wearing any of his top-clothes when he ran out into the street and he was dressed only in a cream flannel vest and knee-drawers with black knitted stockings on his legs with scarlet toes and heels. He was a queer old man who used to act as a midwife when he was younger, but he was a bit cracked now and one of his favourite games during full moon was to stand for hours behind his front door with his fingers hanging out through the letter-box. Steffan stopped and old Harri trotted up to the cart, chuckling to himself as he came and stroking his beard with his large cracked hand as though he had an animal on his chest. 'One with a hard belly, Steffan,' he said as he got alongside the wheels, but Steffan shook his head at him. 'No fish today, little Harri,' he said smoothing the coffin, 'I only tickled up a dead-head this time.' Eben Isaac could only watch them from the bakehouse step with the sun in his eyes; and just then Harri's ginger kitten ran out of the pink-washed house after him and started to reach up against his leg, playing with the tapes of his drawers that dangled for tying at the knees; but Harri took no notice of it and began running his nose along the grooves and joins of the coffin, asking Steffan whose body it could be then. 'Eben Isaac Evans,' he answered, pushing his growth up with his thumb, 'the baker of Pentrebach.' Eben Isaac heard it again, but he only stood dejected on the top step with his head in his feathers just looking at them, wondering what he had better do. 'The baker?' said Harri, standing upright again and looking surprised. 'He will be straight at last then. But he will have the burns on his knuckles under the lid of his coffin all the same.' With that he tucked his kitten up under his armpit and ran back into the house on his heels with his legs stiff, chuckling to himself and shutting the door with a bang behind him.

Steffan looked after him and shrugged his shoulders, and turned back his coat sleeves that had come down over the backs of his hands. He kicked away the stone he had guided before the cart-wheel and went on, taking no notice of Eben Isaac who began to follow him without thinking down the empty sunlit street. Eben Isaac remembered the burns on the backs of his hands. When he was small and his father had the bakehouse, the boys who were older than him used to put ha'pennies in the hot bread-tins for him to snatch out because they knew how much he liked a bit of money even then. His father used to tell him what a good boy he was for doing it.

Presently they left the village and were out on the road leading to the cemetery. The grass on the hedge-banks on both sides was shining like tin in the clear sunlight, and Eben Isaac noticed the big shadow of a bird drop solid as a black stone down the sloping bank on one side, skid slowly across the flat road and bolt suddenly up the opposite slope like something plucked quickly upwards with a string. It was a big white gull battering the upper wind, her wings bent like bike-bars. He looked all round on the red road but he found he had no shadow at all in any direction. He belched a bit at that and put his bowler hat on, changing the pole over to the other shoulder. He began to wish his legs were a bit longer because every now and then he had to break into a little trot to keep up with the cart which was making a noise ahead of him like grit between the teeth except when it went rubber-tyred over a drying trail of brown cow-stars.

But presently they came round the bend upon Griff Penclawdd's farm, where the road was so narrow you could spit across, and the crowd from the village was making plenty of noise there. On the left-hand side rose the high stone wall of Griff's orchard, and on the top of it a row of farm-boys were sitting to have a good view of the slaughter, mimicking people in the crowd the other side of the road and shouting out rude things to them all the time like, 'Maggie, what did you leave you husband for? To have a drop of titty off your mother?' or 'Two ounces of cheese please, Hannah the Gwalia, and my mother said to cut it with the bacon knife.' The farmyard where Griff was going to kill the bull was on the other side of the road and here the crowd was gathered, mostly women in shawls and aprons, talking out loud together and looking over the low farm wall into the yard, hiding from view almost everything that was inside except the top of Griff's bald head, orange-coloured, shining with sweat like a piece of brass in the sunlight. Keziah was there for one, on the edge of the road, a black cone with her arms folded over her chest and her bun coming down. And the crowd was spread out into the road so much Eben Isaac was forced to pass near the wall on the other side, and looking up he could see the soles of the farm-boys' boots right above him, the square-headed nails of their big working boots polished as their feet dangled in a row along the wall and threw a wide fringe of shadow sideways across the stonework. One of the boys had a glittering shadow-glass in his lap that he was using to tease Griff with, flashing the sunlight, Eben Isaac could tell by the shouting, right across the road into the bull's eyes, and then blazing it bang into Griff's own eyes as he turned round swearing at him at the top of his voice for doing it. Eben Isaac could see the long firm beam of bright light coming through the faint dust Steffan's frayed trousers were making, hanging over the backs of his heels as he walked along; and just as they passed below the wall the boy swivelled the light shaft off the mirror in Eben Isaac's direction and he saw it pass right through him, through the tweed and the buttons of his dusty waistcoat and straight through his body as though he weren't there at all. But nobody took any notice of him with his missing tip thumping along the road and the twelve-foot bread-shovel sloped over his shoulder.

Some of the boys shouted to Steffan though, 'Steffan, who have you got there on the fishcart?'

'Eben Isaac,' he answered, 'the baker of Pentrebach. He's dead at last.'

They started shouting at that, 'He didn't have much work dying, he didn't,' and 'There they go again those haystacks,' because that's how Eben Isaac used to grumble at his apprentice when he loaded his teaspoon with sugar and everybody in the village knew about it. And some of them started belching as loud as they could, because the baker was famous for that too; he would do it even when someone quite respectable was in the bakehouse, like Mrs Thomas the Bank who had a piano and two fireplaces in the parlour. Then, just as the coffin passed the spot where the bull was fastened inside the yard, Eben Isaac could hear him beginning to plunge and bellow, rattling at his chains so that the women scattered a bit, and he could see his tail tossed into the air like a bit of old rope. But Keziah, standing there like a drab, took no notice. 'Strike now, little Griff,' she shouted, 'you'll have a foot more beef,' and all the people laughed, seeing what was happening inside the yard.

Soon they were on their way to the cemetery once more, the cart-rims making a noise in front like a horse tearing grass off a field with his teeth. As they went along Eben Isaac was looking at the rip lengthening the vent of Steffan's overcoat half-way up his back when suddenly a swallow came lurching swiftly towards him in the dazzle of the sun, licking out its wings along the middle of the road. He ducked when the white breast was flung up near his face but the bird-beak hit him straight between the eyes and went on through his brains without stopping. He sweated, but after a bit he got used to it, and he didn't even jump when the blackbirds hurdled the hedges together and went into him like a broadside. Then they came in sight of a ploughed field looking like a piece of a big rasp between the hedges, and it was here they had to turn into the little round cemetery. It was neglected, full of tall grass and gravestones, with a day's washing hanging out to dry on a rope across it. Steffan went in and drew the cart up right out in the middle beside a deep open grave, and then he took off his overcoat and laid it across a flat tombstone. Underneath there was a wide space between the top of his trousers and the bottom of his waistcoat, and his right arm was naked because he had ripped out his shirt-sleeve at the shoulder so that he could tickle for trout. For a bit he sat down on his overcoat playing with the growth at the side of his nose and drawing his fingers like a comb through his beard, talking to himself all the time about how he was going to get the coffin down into the hole single-handed. For the first time Eben Isaac was near enough to notice the strong fish-smell coming from the cart, and he was staring at the coffin, thinking how much like tin and cardboard it looked, when he heard Steffan call out, 'Lewsin, Lewsin, come and give us a hand will you?' Lewsin Parc-y-lan was going by on the other side of the low graveyard wall with a lemon handkerchief round his neck and a double-barrelled shot-gun under his arm. He was a tall thin chap with huge lumpy shoulders and long slender legs, bandy as a pair of cart-shafts, that looked thinner because of his tight black corduroy trousers and the big naily boots he always wore. He had gold ear-rings, a huge bunch of grey curls under the peak of his cap and a chin like a rock-cake with smallpox. He got a living by poaching and liming the river. He was a bad character, drinking and fighting about the place, and once he had been living in tally with a gipsy. He got over the stone stile that was on that side of the graveyard when Steffan called him, making a lot of squeaking noises with his naily boots.

'Give us a hand to get this coffin underground will you, Lewsin,' Steffan said again, his beech-nut bobbing about, 'it's Eben Isaac, the baker of Pentrebach.'

'Eben Isaac is it?' said Lewsin, leaning his gun against an angel. 'I don't mind helping to bury a kite like that, I don't. When did he die with you then?'

'Stop you a bit now,' said Steffan pondering, 'if he had lived till next Thursday he'd have been dead a fortnight.' Lewsin grinned; his face was the colour of a flowerpot and he showed his long wet teeth, brown as if he had been drinking iodine. He knocked upwards at the coffin bottom with his knuckles where it stuck out over the edge of the cart.

'Jeez, his behind will soon be out of this,' he said. 'He was too mean to give himself a good coffin was he?'

'Aye, he was,' said Steffan, 'and him with plenty, never giving so much as a red penny to a man and cutting the dough off the edges of the tins for Keziah to make loaves out of it, so they are saying about him in the village, then.' They took up the tapes that were ready on a grave near by and after spitting on their hands they twisted them through the tin door-knockers and lifted the coffin with difficulty off the cart. They carried it to the mouth of the grave and then rested it on the grass, surprised at the weight.

'He's heavier than he looked for such a little runt as him,' said Lewsin, stooping down to read the big medal on the coffin-lid with a frown, and rubbing his hands on the seat of his corduroys. 'It doesn't say he was a deacon with them, Steffan,' he said.

'No indeed,' Steffan answered, 'his wife is such a slut she never brushes his bowler hat and there is flour in the brim every Sunday on the chapel hat-rack. They are telling that is why he is not a deacon.'

They lifted the coffin once again together and started lowering it into the grave, Lewsin standing on one side and Steffan on the other. It was heavy and they had a big struggle with it, the muscles on Steffan's bare white arm standing out like ropes. And, as it descended by jerks and bumps out of the sunshine, Eben Isaac, standing unnoticed near the head of the hole, could see Steffan's pile of hats slipping forward gradually over his forehead, sliding gently down over the sweat of his forehead as the coffin got lower and lower into the rich red earth. Steffan himself could feel it too, and he tried to jerk it back, but that only made it worse, and the three hats went on creeping up at the back of his head and down over his eyes, threatening to overbalance into the grave. Just as they were nearing his nose, almost on the brink of falling, Steffan flicked off the tapes with a yell and clutched at the brims with both hands, forcing them back on his head again. The coffin fell crashing down into the grave and Lewsin, his hands still twisted in the tapes, dived in after it and disappeared completely out of sight, thundering down on top of the coffin with a roar like the sound of blind-linen suddenly rolled up. But he was all right because presently Eben Isaac could hear him cursing out of the deep earth and Steffan, standing on the lip of the grave, began pointing down and cursing back at him; but when Lewsin climbed out, dirty and capless, and ran to the angel's thigh where the blue barrels of his gun were shining, Steffan backed off and suddenly turned and dashed away, howling among the long grass and the tombstones; he fled screaming for cover behind the line of washing, making for the gate, sheltered at last by the sheets and the blankets, a large patch like a pale butterfly prominent on the behind of his trousers. Eben Isaac was always afraid of guns so he ran too, the opposite way, towards the stile, dropping his bread-oar on the graveyard grass. After trotting through a good number of fields, he came at last to the garden behind the bake-house, and here he put back the stones he had kicked out that morning so that his hens could run through and scratch in Griff's field the other side. Then he climbed over the wall and went up towards the kitchen door. As he was coming into the house this back way he could see Keziah the other end of the dark passage standing like a pouter pigeon on the doorstep with a black woollen shawl over her shoulders.

'My uncle Niclas,' she was shouting, 'whose body have you got there then?'

'Richard Top of the Cross,' a voice answered from the street, and just then Eben Isaac could see the funeral procession passing the front door.

'Is he dead then?' asked Keziah.

'No indeed my girl,' her uncle answered, 'today is only the rehearsal.'

Eben heard the people laughing as he crept upstairs quietly and went to bed, examining first the heel of his boot where the tip was missing. Then he fell asleep almost at once. When he woke up it was dark in the bedroom except for two candles, one burning on a green cake-plate each side of his head; and he could see a little pane smashed in the window and a poker leaning upright on the sill. But he wasn't surprised at that at all, nor at the white bed-sheets hung all round the walls of the room. He was feeling pretty shabby now, his head was sore as a boil and his mouth tasted as though he had a penny on his tongue. Then presently he heard Keziah answering the front door and bringing someone into the house. 'I knew it would be somebody before long,' she was saying in her loud voice. 'The street was full of lights last night, it was. Come up, the corpse is on the planks in the bedroom.'

Cadi Hughes

~

Upstairs in number one Colliers' Row, Ifan Cariad was dying by inches. People often say 'dying by inches' without really meaning it, but as a description of Ifan it was almost literally true, because his left leg was gangrenous to the knee, and every day for the last week when Cadi his wife went upstairs to dress it and clean it out she found a new hole sometimes the size of the palm of her hand in a different part of his leg or the flesh of his foot. Then yesterday two of his toes had come off into the cottonwool. The disease had started as a small piece of bad skin under the ball of the big toe, and it would soon pass upwards over the knee into his thigh; and then, when his whole leg had become putrid it would separate from the rest of his body at the hip and lie discarded in the bed beside him. But Ifan would probably be dead before then, poor chap, unless a miracle happened.

Most of the time he was lying sog after the dope the doctor was giving him daily to ease his pain. His face in a short time had become yellow as clay and tiny, hardly bigger than a hand, with his nose rising up tight in the middle like a hen's breastbone. They had cut his hair short for comfort, and it looked like the pile on black velvet or plush and fitted like a cap on top of his little monkey-face. And he had become so thin that his body lifted up the bedclothes hardly at all. He never was very much but he had shrunk to nothing. For days he hadn't eaten a bite, and all that had passed his lips was the water that Cadi fed him with out of a teapot. The smell of cooking nearly made his inside jump out of his belly, but one day near the end he whispered, 'Cadi, give me something to eat.'

'Of course, little Ifan,' she said, humouring him, 'what will you have?'

'I'd like some of that dinner I can smell cooking.'

'Oh, you can't have that, little Ifan,' she said, 'that's the ham boiling for the funeral.'

She was like that, always planning and scheming. She did everything possible for him; it suited her. She wouldn't let the district nurse come near, and when she wasn't actually fussing round him she would pray, or sing hymns in the voice she used when there were strangers in the chapel; not the nice modern hymns about Jesus and harps and rest beyond Jordan, but savage old-time stanzas by cracked Welsh poets preoccupied with punishment and corruption. She was wonderful the way she waited on him. But she had nearly killed him with her bossiness during the twenty years of their married life. When Ifan married her she was worth looking at; she wasn't just pretty like so many of the dark little women with heavy bottoms living in the mining villages, she was a beauty, big and straight, with blue eyes and hair the colour of a new penny. Ifan himself was small and dark; he looked wicked, a handful for any boss, the sort that always smells foul air and sees too much water quicker than anybody else and makes trouble among the men generally. He was all there; and he knew the *Mabinogion* backwards. As for her, she had no idea of her own beauty. All she wanted was for things to go on smoothly as she planned them. Anything odd, strange, eccentric, she hated like poison. And Ifan was a bit odd, what with his politics and his vegetarianism. He was a pretty hot socialist, of course, but if he went on the stump she held herself off from him and gave him hell. And she didn't just stop with her tongue either. Poor Ifan wasn't much of an agitator in his own house; he had to draw his horns in at number one Colliers' Row or he could look out. She was a holy terror, bossing everybody and making arrangements all round, and turning out such a fuss-arse, and so trivial. And yet Ifan couldn't do without her; he was always a bit soft on her, imagining her, because of her hair, like Rhiannon or Blodeuwedd, or goodness knows who. And he could always think with pleasure of their courting days when the village boys going about in groups used to sing after the courting couples strolling up towards the lonelier roads:

> Red are the shivvies and red are the hips,
>   Hazel nuts are brown;
> Two of us climb up the Pandy tips
>   And three of us come down.
> Hoo!

There were more verses.

It was then he got his nickname. He was really Ifan Hughes, although everybody called him Ifan Cariad, which signifies Ifan the Lover, or Ifan the Sweetheart. He used to tap at the window of her house at night when he was calling for her, and her mother would call out from inside, 'Who is there?'

'Ifan,' he would answer.

'Which Ifan?'

'Ifan the lover of Cadi.'

The neighbours heard, and of course such a chance for a nickname

seemed like a godsend. He became known as Ifan Cariad Cadi, Ifan the
lover of Cadi, or Ifan Cariad. But such a name in the village was never
taken as a sign of disrespect. Everybody else had a nickname anyway.

Sunday morning, just as it was getting light, Cadi came into the
bedroom to see if he was still alive. It was a bitter raw morning with no
sun and thick clouds *crêped* like slab rubber over the sky. He was all
right, but just as she was going back to bed someone started knocking
hard at the front door. Cadi was surprised, it was so early. She leaned
over the banister and saw someone standing outside the figured glass
panel she had had put in the middle of the door, like her sister-in-law.
It was just a dark shape, she couldn't tell who, although she stood there
guessing instead of going to see. She got into a jacket of Ifan's and
slipped a petticoat over her head shouting, 'Who's there?' There was no
answer but the knocking started again, louder this time as though it
wasn't going to stop in a hurry.

She opened the door.

It was God.

He was dressed in a dirty green tweed suit with patch pockets and
leather buttons but not much better than rags. There was a sack pinned
round his shoulders, and on his head was a cloth slouch hat with a
brim turned down over his eyes. His clothes were so disreputable, and
yet he looked splendid somehow. His left leg finished at the knee and
he hugged a rough wooden crutch as thick as a bedpost, with some of
the bark still on it, not padded at all, and spreading out like petals at
the end. His grey beard was long but rather thin, and much of his skin
was covered with red blind boils like rivet heads. His face was
handsome though; patriarchal and grand, but a bit seedy, and his hair
was on his collar. She knew him all right.

'Let me in, Cadi,' he said. He was her boss.

She did so, and upstairs he went sprightly enough and straight into
Ifan's room. There was chaff on his back and horse-dung on the heel of
his boot.

'What do you want with us, little God?' she asked upstairs rather
anxious. He and Ifan were smiling at one another, knowing, as though
they had something good up their sleeve.

'I've come for Ifan,' he said, still smiling and hardly looking at her.

Although she half expected it, it was a good bit of a shock to hear
him say it straight out like that. 'O little God,' she began, sobbing,
'don't take Ifan; I can't live with my brother, his wife quarrels with me,
and I'm too respectable to be a washerwoman or go to the Big House.'

Ifan grinned. He was a bit pinker than he had been, and more
arrogant already.

'I must take him all the same,' said God.

He stood his crutch against the commode and sat on the edge of the bed, quite at home like a preacher. His eyes were cunning and very bright, with the skin drawn in all round as though his visit were a bit of a lark. He took very little notice of Cadi except to glance at her sometimes with his spotted eyes. She had more or less gone to pieces; all her bossiness and importance had got flat. She snivelled and started to whimper again.

'Take my daughter, Esther Cariad,' she moaned, 'she's unemployed and hard for us to keep.'

'A cup of tea before we go, please,' said God. 'No fear,' he continued, 'it's not I'll be coming for her, Cadi.'

Ifan nodded and looked serious.

She hung about whimpering for a bit and then went downstairs almost gladly to make the tea, and when she returned Ifan was sitting on the side of the bed dressing, with his huge bandaged leg hanging over the edge. She set the tray down hurriedly and started off on another tack. 'Little Ifan,' she pleaded going up to him, 'don't go and leave me, and me so good to you always.'

Ifan looked at God, one leg in his trousers.

'Not so good, Cadi,' he said, putting his saucer down.

'Indeed I have, little God,' she answered reddening, 'you don't know. I've nursed him hand and foot in illnesses and accidents and pinched myself in the strikes for him and Esther.'

'Ay I know,' he said, 'but what about having the bile on Labour Day and throwing his Cheap Editions on the fire and hiding the pennies for the gas so that he couldn't read, and keeping him home from the summer school to do the garden. You're a bitch, Cadi.'

She smiled hoping to humour him. 'It was only a bit of fun,' she said; and seeing Ifan in difficulties over some vital buttons she was bound to go and help him.

'Very humorous,' said God. 'Anyway, come on Ifan, get on my back. Cadi, thanks for the nice tea. We must be shifting.'

She could see they were going in good earnest. She was red and serious again and desperate. 'Don't go,' she cried. 'Ifan, stop. Let me get you a clean nightshirt first, then.'

'Lay off,' said God, 'you'll tip us.'

'Plenty of nightshirts where I'm going,' said Ifan grinning. 'Good-bye, Cadi.'

Downstairs they went, not too badly. When they were in the passage, seeing them going for good and all, Cadi shouted down over the banister, 'Ifan, have you got your handkerchief?'

God put him down quickly in the oak chair Cadi had in the passage for fashion and came headlong back upstairs. He swung at her with his crutch and hit her into the corner by the chest of drawers. She lay there in a heap without a sound, her mop of hair half down and her false teeth hanging out of her mouth.

God and Ifan hurried out of the house as fast as they could go, shutting the glass-panelled door with a bang behind them.

Eden Tree

❧

The workman stood in the long grass and the dog daisies that pelted the tilted sides of the railway cutting, watching the night trains come hastily like jointed rods round the coloured bend. Each train as it passed him, holding down with difficulty swift flexible squares of light on the side of the cutting, seemed an exact symbol of his life until that moment when he found himself standing there in the darkness with the moon only a phosphorescent smudge like a roof hole, and his feet beginning to send antennae down among the dry cracks of the earth clay. The coaches holloed by in carefully-cut blocks of compressed light, and between them fluffed the rush of darkness with steady darkness whooping behind the shackles of the last vacuum brake, just as his mechanical days and nights had gone over him. Rooted there he could feel the sap coming up over his feet out of the subearth below the scales of clay that covered them like a crust, mounting as the return of new blood over his knees, and spilling into the cold of his loins. In his body it was like the morning sun warming his skin through a thin shirt. The soles of his feet gulped steadily at the yielding earth, and the tiny veins swarming over their upper parts ran on down carrying their mouths open towards a waiting pabulum. And he could feel down to the end of each of these roots, its gentle sucking at the hidden rains, and the terrible mouthing of a stone.

The workman spat and thought yes, you were more like this when you were young. You shovelled your hands into the chilly dirt of the garden and then bit your nails; and bathed in the canal where they drowned dogs; and blew up a pig's bladder with your mouth to play football with. But bit by bit they got you clean – leave that alone, come away from there, don't dirty yourself. The workman began to wonder at one time if to keep clean wasn't the Cosmic Ultimate, as though soap and water and petrol were not known. But gradually he saw that was all bunk. Utterly pure water isn't even wet, and utterly pure salt is no good for potatoes. He had inherited enough horse-sense from his father, a grinning peasant off the Black Mountains, to realize that he ought to regard what is impossible as undesirable. And one summer, just when he was at his most untouchable, a foreign countess came to stay at the Plas, the squire's big house outside the village. He was as romantic as you please, and refined and handsome, and he secretly thought of becoming her lover after the manner of those astral relationships he was so fond of thinking about. So much tripe and cowheels! When he saw her maid he forgot all about the countess and his daft uppishness. She was a tall, fair, strapping girl with a lovely rounded backside, breasts like dumb-bells and nipples standing out through her dress like push buttons. One night he went to her window meaning to throw gravel up because that was how the lads about there found out if a girl was willing to be courted in bed. Well, if there wasn't a ladder there already, with someone then actually coming slowly down it. He hid in the bushes for a bit and then recognized the figure with a shock of delight. It was his father. They laughed and clung to one another until both of them were in tears. The next night the old man helped him to get the ladder into position.

But what was worse than touch me not was machinery. One day in summer when he was back home because of a spell of unemployment in the valleys, he went over to his uncle's place to help with the corn a bit. He was dead tired when it was all over, what with the noisy reaper and the sun, and he could feel the cut stumps of the corn straw thrusting up through his boots as he walked back to the farm. He came down the shady apple orchard and the herb garden, and saw his two little cousins sitting on a piece of sacking at the doorstep eating their porridge in their nightshirts. They were pretty little boys with yellow hair and sunburnt patterns on their bare feet through wearing sandals; but he was too tired to play with them, and he went and sat in the big open fireplace looking up the hollow cone of the chimney at the circular piece of sky, like a blue coin at the top of it, and watching the white light striking down on the lumps of soot that encrusted the pebbly sides. From time to time the fibres of a cloud like the long white skeleton of a leaf would float over, and it was enough excitement for a tired man to wait for the moments when everything was clear again. But he began gradually to wonder whether he was really looking up a chimney at sky, or down a well at blue water. There seemed to be a head on the smooth lid of the chimney, but that was most likely because he was looking down at his own reflection on the water at the bottom of the well. Such uncertainty and confusion made him feel ashamed and desperate. But as he went on looking the mirror assumed the image not so much of his face, but his working heart, because his breast had become transparent like a sheet of glass. He was horrified at what he saw. His heart was not what he imagined it to be, a small soft pointed thing beautifully throwing his blood in silence through the dark tunnels of his arteries and gathering it again from the tough mouths of his veins; there was nothing living about it, no flesh, no juices or pulsation; it was a huge and intricate machine working under dials with the precision of care and maturity, but making a deafening sound that shuddered everything. Flat-fingered cogs spun dryly into one another like dead catherine wheels; long polished steel rods slid accurately on and back through oily collars fitting tightly as sea to the sides of fishes, and in the middle of it four brass-elbowed pistons tupped determinedly down into a steamy square of darkness, working on grimly but seeming to produce at each clank and jerk nothing but a teethy hiss and clouds of thin steam. But as bad as anything to be seen was the dull shuddering vibration of everything that made the workman want to pitch something in to stop it.

He was so shocked by it all that tears of shame and rage fell to his hands as hot as candle-grease, and taking off his working boot he shied it at the water mirror with the fruitful curses of a haulier. Everything disappeared.

He felt much better after that. But he knew he wasn't whole yet. He still wanted to find something definite and positive and not go on with an endless catharsis. And in the country one day he watched where the sea heron planted her webs in secret on the gums of a pond-bottom, with the black water close about her elegant leg stems to the knees; he watched her until she put out thoughtfully the stiff slate of both her handsome wings and lifted herself with easy effort off the water, elbowing her way over the low air with her lovely feet dragging after her, and then he ran down and started to dig at the spot with his hands. He tore up in agony the stalks of pink lilies just then putting out their blossoms like a hand coming through the sleeve of a dress, and the endless roots of the water weeds holding the mud like a bag, and fast as an old mattress in the sand, trying with his finger-nails to reach the roots of the strata. The water closed over him as he dug deeper in the warm pap and the puffy mud, getting beyond shells and roots and the bones of fishes, down below the dry rock pitted like a thimble and the colour of fire. There he found tears.

And one Sunday as he passed the colliery where he worked he looked over the iron grating at the pit head and saw the hard steel rope groping down into the blackness beneath him, and heard the heavy splash of water drops falling plumb on to the hard hollow pit water at the bottom of the shaft. He knocked for the cage, went down, and hurried along the road until he came to the coal face several miles in. The seam was narrow there, about two feet six and he had to crawl in under the rock top to reach it. He started digging furiously, not bothering to timber and not caring what came out under his pick, muck or coal. He couldn't tell how long he went on digging, it might

have been years. The top came down into his back but he dug himself
out wiping sweat off his face and leaving blood there. It was agony, but
at last he came to a spot which he thought must be beneath the highest
mountain in the range above the coal measures. He had often been up
there in the wind with his girl and had sat up to watch the
mountainous edge of the earth tilting up against the face of the sun at
nightfall. The thought pleased him. He dug round in a circle, and there
he found a cross.

He sometimes thought he hadn't got much, but it made a lot of
difference, he noticed, if you found out something for yourself. You can
understand the meaning of almost any wise saw, or dogma or
proposition pretty well, but it's abstract, in the metaphysical air. It is
only when some accident or circumstance works it under your skin like
an inoculation bubble that it has any effect on you. Take any common
saying such as 'God was the Word' – well, you can write brilliant books
and answers about that, but only when something happens like
childbirth, or a lot of suffering, and it wades into the middle of you and
squats there giving orders that you begin to put your clothes on the
beggars or run away into the woods. And when you've found
something it's time to stand round for a bit seeing how things work
out. So here he was with a robin redbreast come out of the shoving
morning by way of being friendly and standing with his flap tail on the
peel of the workman's index finger fast turning into twigs. He was a
dandy bird, not a bit fat, but with his feathers all nice and tidy down
his back and the grainy sides of his wings, and the white bits where his
legs came out, and towards his tail, creamy and sweet-looking. He was
funny and important with those rings of eyes, but, goodness, you had
to respect him. He hopped higher on to the workman's knuckle and
squinted about from his nice brown head and held on there swaying a
bit by his marvellous claws, hooked almost into black half circles like
an airship's anchor and so sharp they hurt. He was quite a weight too.
He bowed, and then did a little white watery streak of mess on the
back of the workman's hand.

The workman laughed.

'I expect I'll get well doused before I drop,' he said.

He spat for the last time.

The Blue Bed

❦

The gardener looked out of the window into the green evening,
seeing with hatred the deep light green as lock-water heaped high
above the garden, pressing against his fragile window-glass, drowning
the house and the tallest dove-leaves. Somewhere the setting sun was
green, letting in this heavy flood of unstaunched light that filled up the
high walls of the garden; and the flowers and the trees rose stunted into
it as from a level sea-bed, rocking low among the tall waters, breathing
the cold tides. No one was in sight, and a blackbird swam three times
round his bush. But the gardener saw that if he laid an axe into the
stems of the laurel bush it would not fall to the lawn but rise spinning
slowly upwards through the light-flood like a bubble or a wrenched-off
sea-weed branch, thrusting its hissing bough-leaves upwards through
the light to float on the shining surface of the evening.

He hated the peaceful mockery of the garden, the meaningless cold
perfection of the roses unfolding into death, the tall tiger-lilies
trumpeting perfume among the honey flowers, and the pink tulips and
the branches of the apricots, all drawing an eager death out of the
deadly earth. It was senseless, and yet the garden was coldly beautiful,
and would be lovelier later with the syringas in full bloom on the lawns
and the flower-beds tall with flowers. Looking at the lawns, he
remembered a woman walking there in the sunlight, watching a bee
put his head and shoulders into a campion-pot, clinging round the lip
of the down-drawn flower with both black hands, drinking the wet
sugar, and himself nearby tapping the cottage wall with a stick whose
crooked shadow zigzagged upwards over the uneven stones of the
sunny wall to meet unfailingly the tapping point; and at the bitter
remembrance of this he went out into the garden and snapped a
slender cane of laurel thick with leaves from low on the blackbird's
bush. He carried it into the house and into the empty bedroom, and
stood at the door looking with hatred at the blue bed the woman had
slept in. Then suddenly releasing himself he broke forward and
swinging up the branch in one hand struck the bed heavily with it
again and again, bringing it crashing down with fury upon the wooden
bars and the soft blue covering, crushing the broken leaves, slashing
deep weals across the blue silk like crossing whip-marks, with the
frenzied weight of his blows. The leaves hissed through the air above

his muttering as he swung the branch downwards with all his strength and power, furious, battering the blue silk, bending his powerful huge body fiercely to the flogging, and at last, when the black branch was stripped clean as a whip, and the bed was strewn and stained with shattered leaves, he fell exhausted to the cold floor, his frenzy out of him, ready for tears.

The gardener got up and went shivering out of his cottage into the cold greenness of the evening, walking eye-deep among the blooms, smelling the hated dead scent of under-sea. He looked back along a grass alley at his cottage, soon to be a ruin, and saw the long crack in the rough grey stonework marked like a zigzag scar or a vein of black lightning pouring from the vivid eaves into the foundations under the earth. He was glad of it, and though he hated everything in the garden, he watched the blackbird for a moment with pleasure, smiling as it jumped round and bit the grass that the second before was under his tail; then he saw him curve from the lawn upwards into the thick boughs of his laurel tree, blown back in a lovely bird-curve like a returning leaf. He walked on among the howling flowers and the rose-rain, poisoning a dahlia and a deep scarlet bell, deep as his finger, with a dumb rigid tongue broken like a bone against the rim, and at last he came to the door in the wall leading out into the hills. He went through and looked down shivering over the bare steep slope of the hill into the bottom of the valley. The sun had gone out and it was colder, beginning to get dark, the lights in the villages far below starting to come out, glowing into a pattern of rows deep among the mountains, reddish like the edges of black burnt paper with the glow still hot along it. And over the sharp ridge of the opposite hill he watched the struggles of the first star, soon seeing her in the green clear sky bright as a lovely woman, her hair brass-clad; her shoulders shone like ice and she carried a shimmering flame between her fingers, a flame with a long slender stem like the green stalk of a flower, opening out above her fingers into the cup of a golden crocus bloom, but not stiff like any flower, quivering, transparent, gold-green, changing its shape and its clear golden colour, a real flame with shivering fire-petals growing on a thin stalk of threaded flame.

She offered it to him, saying gently: 'To kindle under-flame for the cold point of a heart.'

He could laugh at that, his belly shook with laughter at the star, at the woman with her flower who should do what she had said. He turned laughing towards the blackbird balanced on an overhanging damson bough and saw the wind blow a feather out of his shoulder; he picked a snail off the garden wall and flung it at him, watching him fly off back into the garden, a red worm writhing in his beak.

To go down out of the mountains was to gather identity at every step, to feel the warm limbs full, the heart hot in the body like a coal. The gardener walked down the hill through a short summer night that hardly stretched across the sky, making for the point of the valley. He went on until he reached the river bank where a boat was suckled and from there he could see a cottage ahead of him built up above the roadway. It was a square lonely cottage fastened into a socket of the hill, with a square bright light cut in the side of it, a clear light shining out from the bare window, and as he stood watching it he saw the door open for a moment in a click of light, and a woman in a cloak come down towards the road, carrying a lantern out of the cottage into the darkness. He stood still on the grass verge and watched her as she came walking soft-foot along the road towards him, shadowy, almost invisible in the darkness, the lantern a warm star splashed across her knee, and when she came to the river on the other side of the road near to the plugging boat, he saw her lower the lantern to the ground and then kneel down slowly beside it at the edge of the slow-running water. The lantern threw a yellow wheel of light around upon the grass, spoked out with bars of shadow, and the gardener saw her slowly bend forward and with great care begin to wash the blood from her hands into the dark water. He watched her with excitement, the tired movements of her hands, the water glossy on them, but he could not see her face for the shadow and the high collar of her cloak. She took no notice of him standing there in the darkness beside her although he was so close he could hear between the gnawing of the boat-rope the water from her hands splash drop by drop into the river, and when he passed her, walking near her on the grass, she took no notice but went on stooping forward towards the slow flow of the river, languidly lifting the water up with a mechanical movement over her hands and her wrists and smoothing the blood off back into the river. He passed by in the darkness without disturbing her and went up to the cottage window, standing beside a cherry tree that pointed its stiff boughs sleeved with leaves towards the light. Putting his face close to the glass he looked in. The room was bare, but a lamp bowled with orange glass and covered with a round black shade hung low from a roof-hook, forming a cone of clear light built into the darkness. And underneath it, in the middle of the room, stood a bare wooden table with a new-

born child lying naked upon it. The gardener watched it lying quietly
there close under the warm-coloured light of the lamp, so still it might
have been dead, the small legs crooked upwards, the red hands feebly
half-clasping the slender body, and the face with a pointed shadow of
hair sharp on the forehead turned towards the window. The child's
body, except for the hands and the feet, was very white, and it seemed
small in the middle of the table, warm-looking, lying soft and limp on
its shadow, slack, completely inert and tensionless. The gardener
looked at it for a long time, feeling with his eyes the soft limbs and the
flesh-weight, and then he lifted the latch and went quietly into the
room. It was cold and empty inside, deserted. Standing near the bare
table he looked about him into the dark corners, and at last he took
both feet of the unmoving child separately into his hands. They were
soft, blade-cold, so cold the sharp chill passed at once like a current
into the hot palms of his hands and his arms as he held them, the small
icy feet, firm-soft, shod huge with his warm earthy hands. But it was
the touch of flesh and when he picked up the child into his arms, the
chill weight of his small slack flesh touching him went cold as the dash
of morning leaves into his warm breast, as he held him close for
warmth; he shivered at it but his heated body began to suck out the
outer cold like a poison from the child, receiving the chill of his limbs
and his heavy shell-cold head into the burning warmth of his body.
And soon under the cold nipple and his thumb, he could feel the small
heart beating steadily, pushing the tiny blood among the flesh. He went
out at that into the garden, holding the naked child against his skin for
warmth, and watched the lantern floating low along the road in the
direction of the house, feeling the small foot still glass-cold beneath his
arm and his working body drinking out the coldness of death like an
unfreezing fire from the child; he was giving up the great heat of his
fiery body to him, pouring out his animal blood-warmth through the
contacts of his flesh into the heat-parched inner body of the child.

   He looked around him and saw that the rose bushes had snowed
heavily during the night; and over the darkness of the valley he could
see a new moon, bright as he had never seen it before, a solitary silver
hoof-print brilliant on the night.

   He waited, seeing the lantern already at the gate.

Porth-y-Rhyd

❧

I

Machludiad

Tudur was going in the sunshine down the steep little road from his cottage to the bay. It was so hot there was nothing out, no creatures and hardly any birds, only a dusty snake rowing his way across the path, and the baggy cormorants. The coast there was lovely in parts, and then lonely again, and a bit terrifying; and the bay itself was a curve of tigered sand between the headland and the line of pitch cliffs that the water shawled, bubbled with woods behind, whose brambles mixed with the sea-pinks and the blue thistles.

There was nobody to be seen, not on the beach nor in the fields on the sunny headland; Tudur was disappointed; this endless desolation was making him miserable and desperate. He seemed to be losing touch with everybody, living by himself in that little cottage of his overlooking the bay, as though he were out in the thin air between suns fighting to land on the dark earth again. For a long time he hadn't seen anybody; and there wasn't a soul he could speak to, that was about the truth of it. He stood under the last oak tree shading his eyes, feeling frightened and heartsick. He was slight and dark, rather delicately made for a workman, with black curly hair and red cheeks tanned over with his neck and the rest of his skin, a descendant most likely of the first men to light their fires in the coast caves there, with other blood mixed in him making him a bit taller. He had on a blue knitted jersey with the collar cut off, grey trousers rolled up to his knees, and heavy laced boots with salt in the stitching. For convenience he had no stockings on, so that his legs were bare; and he carried a deep narrow box made of wood on his back, slung across his chest by means of a thick leather strap fixed to the ends of the box with big nails. It was for holding fish. As he came down the slope towards the beach he could see the tide had gone out a long way, right beyond the big rock headland that bore loaded fields on its back and the leaning ruin of cliffs on the left, leaving the sand thicketed with weed, and his line of netted stakes high and dry far off on the sandbank. He wondered if he would have any luck out there this time; the day before it had been hot too, and sunny, but not a fish was gilled in his nets and his four-mile walk had been for nothing.

But he thought bitterly there would be no one to sell his fish to anyway. He couldn't tell exactly what was happening. He had always lived near the bay, and his father and mother before him, and when he was a child he had known plenty of people about there and in the village beyond the headland, and once he had loved a woman living in one of the cottages along the road, but he seemed to be getting more isolated, remote from everything. He looked up and saw a raven sitting in the stony branches of this cracked oak tree stretching down the fingers of his wing feathers out of his shoulder, with his leg underneath like a weapon, and he thought instinctively to learn something he didn't know or had forgotten. That polished wing was lovely too, in the fire of the sun, like the smooth grain in black wood, and the dark blade of each of its flat feathers a finely-split layer of long thin stone, black and slender, and polished, like a book-knife; but he shut his wing again on his secret and pulled his skin lids down his flat eyes for the sun and made himself finished and entire. Tudur's heart sank; he was excluded, with no connection anywhere. And he heard in dismay his blood shouting the tide had gone out for the last time.

He flung down his box and pulled his boots off, and started running across the sands trying to catch sight of the tide before it slid back over the horizon for the last time. He ran shouting towards the sun over the hard sand rippled like the rib muscles of a stretched torso that jarred his feet, but he hardly noticed it, and at last he came to a stream running rapidly away between the sandbanks, that shoved him like a crowd and pulled with a strong tug at the two loops of his sinking ankles, nearly dragging him down. He ran up the bank the other side and there he came to long beds of black seaweed growing like rubber on the stones where the sand had been swilled away, leaving them raw and exposed for the weed-grain. He had to go slowly over this, it was so slippery, like long strips of shiny leather, wet, with bunches of black hollow swellings clustering on it that exploded with a snap as he trod on them, and below it was a sort of thick mucus making it full of peril. His feet began to bleed and several times he fell, cutting his hands on the rough crests of small cone shells encrusting the stones, but at last he reached the muddy sand, soft as paste on the other side. Here he tried to run again, but the mud was too soft and slippery, and it came oozing up between his toes in thick ribbons, and the shells buried in it bit his feet cruelly. He ploughed on, sobbing in his throat, with the burning sun-ovens at the horizon opened full against his face and breast, and the sweat itching in his hair, but nowhere could he see the tide.

Then suddenly he stopped, and gave up shouting; he knew with horror that he was alone on the earth. In front of him was nothing except a laddered sea-sun on the sand, and the stones shagged black and green with weed, and stretching over him a thin white sky-skin with a crazy sun in it; when he turned to the shore, that too was empty in the distance and completely desolate, with the sloped shadow of the headland ruled to the beach, nibbling its way across the sand. The headland itself was lovely as ever, plated up with slabs of flat brown rock against the sun, and on the far side of the flush of the rock-prow, where before the blue river had come out from among the hills and advanced slowly over the plain, there was no water, nothing between the fields, only the tall muddy banks still wet, glistening in the sun, full of ruts and folds like crumpled brown paper.

He stood in a warm pool and wept, with his hands bloody over his face and the bleeding wounds of his feet sending out red growths into the water. It was bitter, knowing no man and being entirely alone on the earth. His life crumpled up and went dry and shrivelled, like a membrane. And then he felt the heat getting more than he could bear, and his tongue became like an earthy pebble in his mouth. He came out of the pool and hurried back frightened from the beach, afraid of the yellow bones and the fungus he might see among the fringed stones, and crossed again the awful black beds of seaweed growing thick like coarse dead hair with bunches of edgy shells clinging among it, and came to the foot of the headland. He climbed over the rocks and went up through the fields to the highest point but he saw no one; only from the distance there came the gurgling of the sea-water gathered in a huge ring for swirling down into the hidden hole of some pit or crater of the earth, polished and heaped up at the edges with a smooth circular hollow sloping down to the pointed bottom, spinning round this open column that tapered shining in a cone down like the silver throat of a trumpet into the suck of the pit, swaying on its axis like the tall bell of some flower.

He could see under the sun the cracking ground where the sea was sucked off, and farther back the rocks, green with soaking weed, with the stranded life beneath them seething like a rockpool, so until the baking sun dried out the grip of every root, and caked the earth up like the dusty ocean beds of a cold planet, where nothing would be moving, except the shadow of a cormorant or a big gull crawling like a bug over the shouldered weed-crop. So he hurried back in fresh terror through the woods towards his cottage, listening for the sound of a match or an axe, but he could only hear the hissing wind beginning to rise, and the sap running over the joints of the branches, out of the trunks of all trees, pouring back into the earth again; and he could feel the roots loosening their hold under him on the drying ground, and although it was high midsummer the leaves tossed down to him were shrivelled up like bits of dead skin. Soon he knew everything would be dead, every bird pouch emptied of fish and insects, and all flowers hauled back to earth like struck flags. As the sun slid on to the horizon, the air became chill and the sky let in a hooting wind that came like a cold jet across the sand, hitting it so that it sent up dust like the spurt of a bullet, and bucking under the crooked gulls that tried to ride it. Tudur crawled into his cottage and watched the sun dousing from the window facing the bay. It went down big, and close to the earth, and the air turned cold as water. He stared at it, helpless, knowing that it was smashed and that it would never rise again, until it was only a lip of fire, and at last it ducked out of sight like something frightened. His head fell on his arms and he sobbed with the bitterness of a child. Soon it was very cold and completely dark, and he was alone on the sick earth. Only there was a fire in the grate and his heart was still beating.

II

Codiad

Tudur saw from the window without stirring the pale light like a thin bending flame blown over the sky. It had happened so often before, as he imagined, from the big fins of a meteor hovering outside the darkness that he took no notice of it, and his bitterness was the same. Darkness had passed right into him, entering through the ports of his body and through his skin, and had filled him up continuous through and through with the outer darkness around him. Only there was still a fire in the grate, that was important, antlered all the time with flame and warming the air a bit. That was as much as he could expect and he was satisfied. But gradually he could see unmistakably things outside wet and getting solid. Around the edges of the window were big black leaves that had gone shiny in the rain tapping the panes all the time like a thimble or a finger-nail. The darkness was slowly lifting like hands off the outside of the sky, he was bound to believe it, and there were grey clouds with pale edges like water marks over the bay.

Slowly the light smoked up between the clouds, and Tudur saw with excitement the bay full of water between the headland plastered with irregular fields and the sliced cliffs on the left, black and grooved like whalebone, sloping down into the water. It was lovely, a thing for praise, although the air was dull and filled with small rain cold as dust, and there were no waves, only the sea with light floating on it like a wafer, heaving gently, and the skin of the water never broken. He rose to run down to the beach, but as he lifted the latch he saw a quiet woman in the room, holding out her long hair to dry it like a net before his fire. He flushed and was shy at once, a bit unwilling, but he didn't say anything. He went slowly back to her, diffident and awkward, and saw in the dim light that she was lovely, big, with heavy black hair and smooth cheeks, and her gown loaded with her lovely breasts. To see her first was wonderful, yet he was disappointed somehow, displeased that she was standing there like that before his fire as though he were nothing, ignoring him. But she was wet with rain, her hair and her dress.

'So there is a woman on the earth,' he said, trying to please her. 'I am glad. Where have you come from? Who are you?'

He thought she said, 'Yourself,' but he wasn't sure.

'How can you be myself?' he asked gently. 'You are a woman with breasts. I am Tudur Porth-y-Rhyd, a working man.'

He was troubled, anxious to know what she meant, but she didn't answer; she only took her hand out of her bodice and opened it. Tudur held her wrist, wet, and cold as iron, and drew her to the window, and on her palm lay the small frail skull of a seagull, white, and complete as a pebble. It was lovely, all the bones pure white and dry, and chalky, but perfect without a crack or a flaw anywhere. At the back, rising out of the beak were twin domes like bubbles of thin bone, almost transparent, where the brain had been that fixed the tilt of the wings, with the contour of the delicate sutures inked in a crinkled line across the skull, and where the brow-bone sloped down into the beak were two dark holes like goggles where the eyes had shown out of the feathers. The beak itself, pierced with the slanted ports of the nostrils, was smooth and curved beautifully, and all its yellowness had gone with the tide; and lacing the weight of the beak upward to the skull were struts of slender bone, long and delicate, and taut as a hawser, the white hair-bones of the face and the cheeks. Tudur felt how lovely it was, fragile, and yet having prevailed against so much.

'They are beautiful,' he said. 'I often see them between the stones.'

'You only see them as beautiful,' she answered, looking at him like a woman meaning to teach something. 'Would you kneel down and feed a snake out of your hand?'

Tudur looked at her, trying to understand. He was puzzled, and moved, she was so strange. He forgot all about the light plumping the things outside his window and the tide pulled like a cloth over the seaweed. He knitted his brows at her, not understanding at all, expecting something to happen, and then she pointed over his shoulder out of the window to where at the thin edge of the tide a little sailing ship had floated in with her mast lamp still burning, a small black ship with her sails down and her mast writing endlessly against the sky. A young man with yellow hair was sitting in the rain bareheaded near the stern, and his father was looping up a rope on the bow thwarts. Tudur looked back to her. She was smiling, pleased at the little sight, but he felt bewildered, almost ready for tears with the strange puzzled excitement within him. There were men on the earth again, and he was thankful, but he was so eager to understand her. He knew what she was telling him was vital, although he was only beginning to understand.

'How could I feed a snake?' he asked.

She pulled her hair hanging behind her over her shoulder and began plaiting it slowly. 'I will tell you,' she answered. 'I had a child huddled in my body whom I carried with heaviness and terror; but when he came from me he was small, only crumpled flesh, and warm. When I felt his weight, and when he gulped suck out of me, I knew I had never seen anything before. I knew I had never looked at anybody properly before.'

She stopped, and Tudur looked at her, waiting for her to go on. The man in the bows of the boat could be seen clearly now near the cordage, chucking his anchor out. He felt a strange excitement, as though something vital he had forgotten was about to return to him from the tip of his brain, the imminence of some important discovery. He had not forgotten the bitterness of the sun going down upon him, his isolation and his complete loneliness on the earth, but he accepted it now, and when the woman spoke a sort of warmth overflowed from his belly like happiness; although he was moved to more than happiness. Dimly he could discern what she was telling him as she went on describing the son of man to him, and he wanted to cry out in his emotion. She came to the end of her plait and finished it with a bow of ribbon. 'A man opens womb and grave together,' she said, 'and it's a bitter place where the snake gives up his breath.' The fire stirred like a rat, and he saw what she meant. 'I know,' he said quietly, and with excitement. 'I loved a woman who died, and at her burial I saw blood in the bottom of every man's cup. I know the men who have come in from sea.' He turned away from her and ran down the little road in the rain, shouting greeting to the father and son waiting for him in the boat.

The Apple-Tree

❧

Two brilliant hills stood on the coast, with the river swollen between them carefully swallowing the sea. Over the fields of one were spread the shadows of the clouds with the slow wind peeling at them, skinning slowly back off the grasses their dark membrane of shadow, but the sea-thorns were plastered flat and brown in a bush-crust against the round rock of the other, caking its bareness, although a red tree grew on the curve of its only field. A burning sun poured out of the sky on the thick liquid of the sea, and on the ripples of the eating river, and on the shore-pool with its darn of groundwind, and on the sea-sand, and the timber, and the flesh.

Down at the foot of the field-bearing hill stood a grey cottage. Three children lived there, and the eldest was called Sibli. She wore a bright blue dress, sleeveless, and fastened with gay buttons of scarlet bone; she had rock-black hair and blue eyes, she was tall and narrow, the sunlight hanging tiny cups of shadow under the little shallows of her breasts. She stood among the flowerbeds, the sharp sun pouring over her body, biting into her flesh like the sting of an acid as she watched the full sea flat beyond the garden with a dark flaw running the length of it, and the distant swimming arm of rock, and the few white-wearing clouds. She walked to Robyn's little apple-tree and stood in its openwork of shadow, looking for the infant fruit among the dark leaves. But she found nothing, and through the branches she watched Trystan take a fish out of the sea and pass it in through the window, and Robyn upstairs letting a thick lemon thread of wool in a curve down into the garden, brilliant against the grey roughness of the wall. And when her two brothers saw her searching they too came into the garden and helped her, the three children stood together under the tattered shadow of the tree, the black hair, the orange hair and the gold, gently pulling back the leaves, heedless of what the sun was writing in shadow upon them.

Trystan wore tall boots and a black jersey; he floated his scarlet boat across the bay, and, having emptied them, spread his new and creamy nets upon the hillside grass to dry. He loved a night with a scholarly moon and a day with the soft sea flowering upon the stones. He wrote in a book for Sibli and for little Robyn, who broke the water with his curl-cap and his golden skin, or came down a tree with an egg in his mouth, or waited daily for the apple-packed tree to spread its curving blush.

Saying 'Little boy with the bird's name,' Sibli went back into the dim cottage to watch her baking bread. There, in the half-darkness, she saw with delight the rigid white arm of the sunlight, thrust in through the little window, kindling the red roses and the glistening lip of the glass jar on the sill. She took a heavy book, like a block of gold with black covers, off the table and placed it between the glass candlesticks on the mantelpiece, and she laid the table in blue for three.

Soon Trystan and Robyn came in and sat by the table. When Sibli returned to the kitchen she carried an egg in each pocket of her dress and a plate of slices in her hand. She gave an egg to each of her brothers, and Robyn's was dyed scarlet for his holiday and he kissed Sibli for it. As the children ate, the smell of baked bread was strong and sweet. Sibli went to the fireplace from time to time and knocked at the bottoms of her three loaves with her knuckles, listening to the voice of the bread and to the voice of Trystan reciting his poem to her. 'Listen to the wind in the village, Sibli,' he said.

> 'Clouds go grey for snow or sleet,
> The gulls are blown about our street
> Where the lad I'd love to wed
> Paints his black boat black and red –
> I hope my mop of hair will lie
> Tidy till I've passed him by.'

Sibli laughed at that, thinking of her lover. Then she put the loaves in a bag with a rope to it, and Trystan, seeing her do that, left the table smiling and took his bucketful of fish off the sill and poured it into his lidded basket. Robyn wanted a poem then and before he left the house Trystan said, imitating the children:

> 'The Little Boy: That's the lonely wind
>   That little one at the door,
>   Crying to come in.
> The Little Girl: What's he crying for?
> The Little Boy: The night is so dark and cold,
>   And ah! he heard when we laughed:
>   He has for company
>   Only the dead and the daft!'

Then loaded with his bread and fish he kissed his brother and sister and started off from the cottage for the city, hoping to sell what had been caught and made. Sibli and Robyn watched him go through the mob of flowers from the doorstep, and heard him shout back, because of his load, 'I wish God had put a ring in my elbow.' He went out through the gate and up the hill, waving to his brother and sister until he was out of sight.

When he was gone Sibli and Robyn sat in the garden. Sibli looked round at the hills for the coming of her lover and Robyn made a long daisy chain and hung it like a ribbon round and round the trunk and the branches of his little apple-tree.

Trystan came back in the pitch darkness along the road to the cottage. The symbol of his mind after a day in the city burned like the blazing bush, the dark-endangering tree, sentient and unconsumed in bud and branch, the burnt birds tonguing its endured agony of fire. He longed for Sibli, to tell her of his suffering, the phoenix-torture of his mind. As he came into the garden in the pitch darkness, the lamplight from the window shone upon the lonely apple-tree. But it did not seem a golden kitchen shine, it was greenish, a cold transparent citrus light filling up the room like a bitter liquid and gleaming out into the garden through the green panes like a chill liquor held before a candle-flame. He stood and watched it in anguish, this evil light shining coldly on the little tree, burning it up in its icy fire, the acid glowing of the leaves, the chill smouldering of the puckered bark braided with its withered daisy chain. He shivered before it, feeling the cold bandage of the wind about him, and lifting the latch he went into the kitchen.

Sibli was sitting alone, a coat thrown over her shoulders for her bare arms, her breadfire out and Robyn's clothes ungathered on the floor. The cottage was dim and comfortless. She sat staring at the lamp before her, her face white and her blue dress unbuttoned at the neck, and when she saw her brother she lifted her head and said, 'Trystan, my lover is dead.'

Trystan had been about to speak of the anguish he had himself borne out of the city, but when he heard her say this he stopped and leaned his back against the door. He stood and watched her, longing to be comforted by her as she sat at the table suffering, her elbows before her and her fingers sunk in the black runners of her hair.

'Sibli, tell me about it,' said Trystan.

'All the afternoon I waited for him,' she answered in a colourless even voice, still staring at the lamp. 'All the afternoon I wandered in the sun of the kind garden. I looked at the shadows but I did not know what time it was; I looked from the full-blooded petal and the long golden globe of the unbroken tulip, and my eyes went up again and again and gathered the roads strapped over the hills, awaiting his coming. I searched for the coming apple-blush in the cool-hearted tree, wondering when he would come. I went out at the water-gate and watched the tide swill its thin silks over the sand. I stood forgetful, remembering his body with delight and suffering, knowing how the ecstasy of love is short and its agony long. A bird dived into the back of the sea and I looked. I saw in the distance, at the place where the last tawn of the pointed sandbar always drowns, a small black figure; it might have been a dog or even a cormorant breaking like a black Venus out of the water. I put my scarlet hand to my eyes. The figure seemed to stand up, it stood with its wings uplifted like a tree or a floating bird. I could tell it was a drowning man already wearing the water around his waist. There was no sound, out of my throat came no voice, only a gull-scream. As I watched I could see the flat tide rising, halving the small black figure with blue from the waist to the breast, from the breast to the shoulders. I turned my eyes away towards the disturbed feathers of the sea upon the water, and when I looked back again the silent arms were still held up like the frozen branches of a tree, black and motionless in the water as the tide lapped the chin of the severed head. Then the hair set and the stiff sloping arms, still rigid, disappeared quickly under the sea.'

Trystan listened in agony, and then, seating himself by the cold hearth, he dropped his head forward and the collapsed flame of his hair fell over his hands. He heard Sibli go on with her speaking, the steady anguish of her voice as she held her face close to the yellow lamplight.

'My spirit ached, I heard the creak of the well-rope. I could not speak, my mouth was dust like the blackened flower-tongue, my eyes dry as the barren finger-nail. And I saw my hands were orchards fruited with grief. I wished for thick darkness, for this day to drain like sand back into the sun, or for the bright hand of the rain around me. I saw the torn mouth of the poppy mouth my knee and the stumps of the fractured bridge sticking out of the sides of the hills. The waterbirds cried, the arum's frosted gold was snapped, the lily-bell showed the blood-veins red in her aching throat. I was naked in a bleak island of spotted thistles and my heart was broken like a heart in a picture. I saw on the coasts a drowned body wrapped in red rock under the hawk-hang of my heart – Christ send a night angel to stand by my candle – and the sea was a vivid ruffian that roared over it, gathering his freckled shoulder into the rock. I turned for comfort to the friendly flowers and saw only the nod and windy denial of the rose, while the beech released her leaves upon me like a down of snow or tears. I was heavy, the yarn of gossamer bore down my heart. I saw my grave with the sea pouring into it, and the sun and the flowers and the stars. I prayed the homing angels to stay with me, to fill my arms in the coming darkness.'

As she spoke Sibli's breasts moved beneath her dress like the working of a yeast. When she had finished speaking the children sat in silence, heedless of the room around them and the night outside and the soft sea-thunder beginning to blow in over the water. At last Trystan got up and opened the large black book upon the table and started to write in it. The little nib went swiftly over the pages, making a breathless sound.

'Trystan,' said Sibli at last, 'tell me quickly about our bread and fishes in the city – the thought of his mouth is like fire that first night with the air and the rain between us.'

'I went up towards the city,' he told her. 'The trees moved round me, each standing in a separate pond of shadow. The thrush was heavy in the hedge. The blackbird hurried along the horizon. The poplar made its fuss and the little hawthorn was heavy with the milks of her bloom. A blue-eyed weed grew in the bank. The hills were pollened with the gold smudge of the ragwort. From the hilltop I saw the white moon blown on before me over the city, transparent, clad in her thinnest flesh. I saw the jaws of the city close round the bottoms of the hill. I saw the brick buildings under the moon, the cock and the arrows and the copper foxes leaping the domes, and the sun poured heavily into the city from the blue bubble of the sky.'

Sibli seemed not to hear him; her knuckles were white in her hair, but she said, 'It was a lovely morning, Trystan.'

Then her brother looked down at his book and read by the lamplight what he had written there.

' "Where the roads forked for the city I found a man alone with a broken heart beneath the derision of branches.

' "On the outskirts I saw the gay confetti of a crowd among the scarlet and the music and the twisted brass, and the dead lying in rows along the indifferent roadside.

' "I entered the primrose chasms of the city and saw the incurable disease called life. I saw the endless flesh flow over the pavements with its symbols, the imbecile with his thistle, the beggar's violin-string, the black-bottomed cloud above the dwarf and the cripple, the lunatic guiding his shooting canoe.

' "I saw the multi-eyed bridge weep out the river from under her hard brows. I saw the sick girl drown unheeded in the city water, the phlegm-slide of her body. I saw the irony of the she-dwarf's breasts. I saw the bitter man put his hand in his coat and finger his pride. I saw the queue hang out into the street like a measuring tape for the doom of the city, and the skeleton in the sky.

' "I saw the agony under forgotten gravestones, and the cemetery tree eating the mourning child. I saw birth buried and the unearthing of death like treasure, the worm working at his thigh and the sovereign yellow in his teeth.

' "I saw the great roots grab the rain. I passed the pearly turnstiles of the market-place and saw the bunches of snakes and the corners heavily catkinned with serpents. I heard from the stringcourse the chant of the bitter-speaking corbels, gold, coal, iron and diamonds. I saw the eyes of the changers scrape the facts off my face before they answered my question – and I knew the brutality of a smile. When I brought out my bread, I saw the swallowed cornfields in the full belly of the few, and the army of beggars empty and carved out of driftwood. I found the blush rare as the winter bee, and commanded back to the heart. I saw the heartless tasker explain, an unheeded creature counter-speaking truth from his wrist, and the elbow-brained merchant unmoved at his life recounted to an audience of angels.

' "I saw the martyr's candle, and the fool who would seek out the springs of the whirlwind to destroy them with the truth slit out of his throat.

' "I saw the lights come out over the town like a uniform and the elastic reflections in the river, whose tide slid out smooth as the steel withdrawal of a blade. I returned in the dark through the crowds of fabulous faces gazing from the fairground at the crawl of the god-searching rockets. Around me were the flares and the steamy music and the coloured dragons. I saw the bare elbow and the blood ruby, the harelip and the thin-skinned beauty covering the skull" . . . I can't go on, Sibli,' he said looking up. 'I can't go on. In my basket my fishes were serpents and my bread stones.'

His eyes lost their tears upon the open page.

The brother and sister sat hand in hand before the lamp comforting each other, Trystan looking along the thin blade-edges of the twin flames, and Sibli seeing only the flat yellow side of the flame nearest to her. From time to time they heard the pour and tumble of the sea-thunder, and Trystan said, 'Sibli, turn out the light.'

The little apple-tree outside the window disappeared and the whole house and the garden were in darkness. The sky was as dark as the earth, the pit of darkness had been swung above their heads and over the world. Only down near the low water someone had set down his lantern to tie two ropes together, and the little bead of flame gleamed on the stones like a coppered star.

But the noise of the thunder gathered upon the roof of the house. It was like the blowing of a big wind or the metal throb of a great struck pipe humming in the darkness. Then sometimes, with the house shaking, the children heard it drop heavily among the garden beds with the crackle of a cold star falling down.

The children, sitting hand in hand, stared out into the darkness and saw for a moment the pale purple of the sky, the lightning flickering its purple wing along the edges of the sea or the curtain bottoms of the darkness blown back, letting in the outer brilliance above the dark horizon.

Trystan could feel the blood full in Sibli's hand. They sat close together because the lightning was ready to swing his flashing blade over their heads.

Then, of a sudden the earth heaved out of the heavy darkness as though out of black water, it burst up into the glare where the stringy lightning was playing with waved yellow, the world was a brief bubble candled a moment in the daffodil brilliance of the flash flickering over it. The little light down by the water went out as though it had been kicked into the sea. The black trees leaped out of the garden to their full height and stood for a moment palpable and violent in the brass and radiant ague of the sky. Then the whole world dropped suddenly like a stone out of the purple-yellow light and the darkness swallowed it down again. And the little lamp reappeared, it was to be seen once more boring its tiny red hole in the darkness. The children waited, and the crash came upon the shaking house, loud and heavy like the dropped burden of a big wave.

'Sibli, Sibli,' cried Robyn, 'I'm on fire.'

Sibli ran into the other room and carried Robyn shawled into the kitchen. On the edge of his nightmare grew a bare golden tree gleaming in the darkness and bearing large scarlet fruit. A boy and a bird shared the branches. The smooth gold put on leaves like candle-flames and the burning bird flew into Robyn's breast.

'Sibli, Sibli,' he screamed, 'I'm on fire.'

Then, as the brother and sister comforted the child, stroking his honeyed hair, the lightning dropped into the garden again, it spread its brilliant roots over the little apple-tree, it seemed to shake the loosened gold of its pulsing hair over the branches, and they received the burden with uplifted arms, the tree reached up and sucked at the fluid tresses, gulping the lightning eagerly out of the sky like a sucked poison. And then, after a silence, the crash of the thunder came, there was a loud crack as though a huge bone had broken, a long-drawn-out breaking noise as though one of the great bones of the night was cracking slowly from end to end, slowly splitting under some terrific pressure.

The children clung together as the house trembled.

'Robyn's tree won't bear any more,' whispered Trystan.

The Saviour

❧

The tall swaying girl crouched with her left hand cupped on her lap, digging frantically into the palm of it with the huge fingers of her right hand and blabbing in a husky voice – 'Jesus let it stop, O Jesus Jesus let it stop!'

Outside the sun burned the ground like a famine. The girl felt upon her heart the suffocation of his power, she found no sanctuary for the flesh against his blunted stroke. She bowed her head as it were beneath a scourge, acknowledging his mastery, feeling his ponderous blood-throb pounding heavily like a pulse against the walls of the airless room in which she suffered. Then looking up again into the unfaltering heat with her bulging eyes she began once more to mutter loudly, 'Christ, let it stop, let it stop. O Jesus let it stop.'

The room where she sat tortured by the outer presences was hung with an inescapable swarm of small and distracting objects, it was confined, oppressive and motionless. She gazed from time to time, her face twisted in growing frenzy, at the uneven wallpaper, drab and plastered with zigzags of eggs and minute flowers, and as her frantic white eyes leapt along the bulges of the walls she felt a sort of anguish, a restless hatred at the sight of the familiar tranquil implements hanging upon their pins and nails, the clothes-brushes and the button-hook, the yawning scissors and the plush pincushion, the gaudy almanacs, the woollen kettle-holder, the circular looking-glass and the little blue book on its loop of twine. She hated them, their constant presence and their incessant signalling to her, she wanted the fiery throb or the thunders of this annihilating sun to consume them at one clap, she felt a demoniac hunger with her own hands to shatter them in fragments. And then, as her frenzy crested to its peak and her anguished hands cracked against each other, she closed her eyes, seeking a refuge from them in the stupor of the afternoon and her unrest died within her.

The girl's mother sat rigid outside the house in the vertical pour of the sunlight, gazing with fixed lids at the workman toiling in her little field. As she sat with her red stick across her knees, the dust of the road leading down the naked hill was about her clogged feet. She was tall and heavy, the dusky burden of her flesh borne unstooping upon her loaded bones. Her savage face, the brown skin of it dinted with shallow

pockmarks, although peevish and masterful, was beginning to slobber
and to lose its formal solidity, the lower half of it sagged like softening
brown rock gone flabby to the touch. The erect brow was firm still and
the small black eyes brutal and active but the skin of the cheeks and
the puffed underlids had begun to pucker and to decay, and the hung
leathers of the jaw-flesh drooped in folds like an unfixed curtain over
the bones of the face and upon the baggy throat. Yet her hair was sleek
and black, coiled round and round her large and orderly head in long
thin plaits glistening in the sun like jet, and she wore unmoved in the
silent deluge of erect sunshine a thick black skirt and bodice and a
black shawl crossed upon her breast. She began to beat with her heavy
red hollystick upon the ground.

As she watched the young man mowing in her field, she heard again
from the kitchen the rising hysteria of her daughter's voice imploring
Christ to let it stop, beseeching Jesus to let it stop. She fidgeted,
striking the glittering dust with her stick, enraged at the raucous
distress of the voice and the endlessly repeated prayer that became
louder and louder as she listened; she felt the tension increase like the
unbearable slow opening of a furnace door, and at last she rose in
anger, crying out in a loud voice as she powdered her way forward,
blaming her daughter and taunting her, bearing her merciless dark
flesh up towards the black door of the house with hulking stateliness.
She left her stool and trampled through the dust as it were in fetters,
and reaching the house began to curse the afflicted voice of her child
and her endless prayers, shouting aloud and hammering with despotic
fists for respite and silence upon the door. But in spite of the blows and
the menacing words the imbecile chant was repeated – 'O Jesus let it
stop, O Jesus let it stop,' the girl screamed out, and the old woman
began battering at the bolted door with the polished hollystick that
shook out violent flashes like the spokes of a spun wheel; she clutched
her heavy red stick with both her powerful hands, the repellent skin of
her brown face lifted from her teeth like lunacy and her lip in her
mouth, she struck again and again at the sounding woodwork, insane
with hatred, using the maniacal energy of her joints to plaster the
rowdy boards with a heavy machine-like weight of blows, trying to
overwhelm the screamed gibberish of prayers. Then suddenly the
savage noise of hammering was over and in the silence the old woman
leaned flushed and hunch-shouldered towards the door, she held her
brooding sullen face close to the smouldering door, breathing heavily
upon it, listening for her daughter's voice, her ponderous ungainly
flesh relaxed as though the insane puppet-strings which jerked energy
through her erect stature dangled for a moment slack upon her joints.

But the crying voice was mute and a tingling silence spread itself out over the dust of the hot slope. The old woman lowered her stick and turned, awkward as a hobbled animal, away, pushing in the dishevelled corner of her shawl and twisting the snake-like tail of a jetty plait back into the coils of her hair. She looked out frowning and panting towards the sunny field, and there the lemon-haired workman had lowered the scythe, and shading his eyes was gazing up towards the house in puzzlement at the unhidden scandal of the shouted curses and the beaten door. Instantly she screamed at him, incoherent again with fury, waving her fiery stick and beating the ground in clownish frenzy, she laughed, her teeth set and showing and a convulsive grimace on her swarthy face as the young man began to slave once more at his mowing.

Inside the house the yellowish heat of the room was oppressive and motionless. A scalding yellow shawl drawn like a curtain across the window dimmed the air and tried to withhold the strong sunlight from the red hump of fire smouldering in the grate. Flies laboured in a ring before an indistinguishable picture hung above the tarred chimney-piece. After the uproar of the hammering upon the door, the grey girl rocked herself from side to side, dim and unreal as a phantom in the shadows of a settle, babbling to herself and fretfully boring with her large fingers into the palms of her hands. She was a tall grey-clad figure, very angular and a hunchback, dressed in clothes similar to her mother's but the shapeless and baggy garments were pale grey, the heavy skirt and the thick-fringed shawl folded around her humped shoulders were of silvery greyish wool. She wore a sort of soiled handkerchief spread out on top of the plentiful and fluffy hair of her head. Her small bony face was thin and undeveloped and apart from her eyes, large, abject and gentle, she was hideous. A sickly greyish skin moist with grease covered her watchful sharp-edged features and a pair of taut sinews strained in unrelaxed and ugly prominence across her sunken cheeks. But as she sat with the yellow gloom falling upon her glistening skin and her pallid clothes she looked dim and unsubstantial, her pale face and her uncoloured fluffy hair and the nacrous bulges of her red-rimmed eyes made her appear spectral and shadowy, her figure seemed almost transparent in its greyish coverings. In the stupefying heat she no longer prayed but jabbered about the trees and the primroses and the buds.

Spring had come, daily her uneasy heart had watched it through its bars. Morning after morning she had heard the throaty lecherous whistle of the thrush and looking out into a raw dawn she saw the sky glow dull and red as the back of a mirror. She went down into the misty field when the vast shadows lying upon the earth were still white with hoarfrost and sat crouching in the hedge fearing the long flock of starlings that wavered low overhead like the skin of a spotted serpent. She gazed with her bulging whitish eyes at the small dewdrops on the faces of the pale primroses, the minute drops of moisture like a tiny perspiration spread out upon the yellow petals, and when the curve of birds writhed by again she hurried home fearfully, high-shouldered and with long strides. Each morning she escaped to the field and at last the buds of the little horse-chestnut in the hedge began to crack open upon their branches. She stood gazing in ecstasy at the fine white velvet of the breaking buds, the delicate grey-green birth-fur covering the infant leaves as they unfolded from their husky glues. She stood forgetful, watching the static gesticulation of those little grey-gloved hands, the grey-green herringbone of the leaves standing up crumpled from the splitting buds. And then suddenly she heard a shout. She looked round, it was the radiance of broad daylight and the great trees were drying in the sun. Her heart seemed to leave her body and return again burning like a hot spark to her breast. Up the gritty path she ran, avoiding the demented old woman who waited massive and wine-faced with fury at the roadside, striking a convulsive blow at her with her red stick as she passed. She reached the house and, flinging herself with prayers into the kitchen settle, waited in agony to see the loutish figure fill the door.

The young man worked the slow circuit of the field, his feet in their heavy boots crawling one after the other in the stubble and the scythe-blade flashing through the packed stems in an arc of which his body was the liquid axle. There was a buttercup growing out of his faintly-bearded mouth and his hair was short and bright yellow, almost the colour of a clump of stonecrop, standing up with the vigour of young wheat upon his head. He wore the dress of a travelling labourer, a dark blue flannel shirt, cream corduroy trousers belted at the waist and heavy hobnailed boots. His sleeves were rolled up to the shoulders baring his large tawnied arms, and his blue shirt, open to the waist, hung in a hollow bladder from his coloured body as he crouched with solicitude and absorption over his scythe. The heat of the unsheltered field was burdensome but he continued to prowl intently through the golden-haired grass, the liquid action of his body appeared easy and graceful, he seemed easily to skid the cutting blade over the roots of the grasses severing the crowded stalks in armfuls as he crept forward. Although he was not tall he bent over the scythe and diminished it with his skill and the grace and fluid sweetness of his stroke; he huddled his body over it protectively, and it became light and almost toylike in his hands. From the corner of the field where the grass rose to his belt he could see the old woman sitting with the rigid inactivity of a puppet outside the house, her red varnished stick across her knees and the metal toes of her clogs glistening in the sun. Then, when he was out of sight of the path, he stopped and leaned back under the young horse-chestnut tree, where the hay rope was that he wound round his scythe blade, and his bottle and his food basket sheltered under his black coat from the sun.

As he chewed his bread, he looked up at the scene around him, the desert hills and the mountains above, the bare squalid peaks smouldering in a dung-brown row, porous and pitted with large sponge-holes, the parched earth giving up its heat like an oven. He saw around him outside the field the stunted scrub tortured on the unslaked dust of the mountain, but down in the bottom of the valley were the trees and the fields swimming in a flood of green verdure.

There was silence now on the sun-sodden slope, and remembering the old woman's attack upon the door he looked up at the house clinging low to the side of the bare mountain at the end of the field. It was whitewashed and stone-roofed; it looked dead in the glare of the afternoon like the incrustation covering some torpid creature motionless under its shell on the barren rock. He smiled to himself, thinking of the frightened inmate, wondering at the raving hatred of the old woman. He finished his food and pulling the petals in bunches from the purple clover blooms he bit the sweetness out of the ends of them with his front teeth.

The girl slept with her long body stretched across the table and her rigid arms pushed out before her. A line of spittle hung from the corner of her twitching mouth on to the boards. She wore over her face and over her whole body a protective membrane of greyness, almost like an obscuring moss; she was enveloped in a grey film like a natural silvery-greyish down. She lay stiffened across the table and when at last she began to awaken, her spirit bruised and uneasy, she lifted up her head from the board and her large lustrous eyes went round the walls in anguish and bitter recognition. The tap sounded again and she rose to her feet, her glance bounding round the room towards the door and back again to the window. She stood restlessly twisting together her huge fingers, feeling the little streams of hot sweat trickling over her body and the strong blows of her heart rocking her tall flesh upon her naked feet.

And then, trying to prevail against her terror, she began anxiously to wade like a gawky flightless bird towards the window, she dipped forward with excitement and apprehension, bony and deformed, her head thrust out and nodding before her and her bare soles whispering warily on the flags. At the window she drew back the warm shawl and confronting her the other side of the glass were the wet head and wide shoulders of the young workman, a smile upon his tanned and tranquil face. At the sight of him standing so close to the window she was startled and afraid, the dizzy walls slid round her and went black with the heavy plodding of her heart. Mechanically she hooked back the curtain, and then she began fiddling feverishly with the twisted fringes of her grey shawl. In the fierce sunlight his dense short hair shone clear yellow, almost lemon-coloured, and his eyebrows appeared in a pale and fluffy line with the intense blue eyes contracted beneath them. As he grinned out of his faint yellow beard a bubble burst over his mouth and he showed in his sunburnt face an unbroken shelf of white teeth.

The girl felt powerless under his long-lashed gaze, the bewildered flesh of her limbs was numb, heavy and fatigued. He began to perform the action of raising a bowl from the sill, and although she understood him she remained bulge-eyed and immovable, staring out in panic through the shut window at the vivid and miniature scene behind him the thick blue sky and the moulted hills and the block of uncut grass in the middle of the field. She was conscious of the cupped hands raised to the white-smiling mouth and the golden-crested head beady with sweat tilted backwards in the sun, but she could not budge to grasp the window-bolt, she felt helpless and lazy in his presence, she stood bewildered by the obstinacy of her heavy limbs. She knew she must open the window but before his bearded smile and his mimicry her will was dried up with terror and her indolent long arms hung down beside her as though in great weariness, loaded with ungoverned bunches of heavy fingers. And all the while as her heavily-beating heart plundered blood and her desire out of her limbs, the tranquil brown face beyond the glass continued to smile and the bewildering hands journeyed again patiently to and from the mouth.

The flesh of the girl's feet clave to the flagstones, she could not open to him, she shrank in anguish from laying her languid hands upon the blazing fabric before her, the fiery doorway of that single window pane. Her body resisted and remained inactive with distress and bewilderment, seeing the glint of the thick golden hairs on the man's bare arms and the smile of entreaty and gentle mockery on his wet face. She glanced round at the door and then moved in a sudden reversal of her agony; she dropped sideways as though she had been cut down and crouching beside the water jar dipped the hanging tin cup into it. This she bore splashing to the window, and when she had drawn back the bolt, she placed the spilling tin in the waiting hands of the workman.

Outside the white butterflies blew sparkling over the grass and a jittering blackbird scissored his startled way across the field. As the workman swallowed his drink the girl turned round and stared with the goggling eyes of a victim at the kitchen door, her huge wet eyes started out bulbous with terror from their red lids and the glazed skin of her greasy face shone. Half consciously through her panic she heard the thunderous cracking of the heated timbers above her head and the gulping of the workman's throat as he swallowed the water out of the tin cup. In spite of her trembling body she flooded her desperate will into the room, trying with her resistance to seal up between its lintel and its threshold the bolted door through which her mother might enter. She stood fiercely facing the wall, her face gleaming with the lustre of perspiration spread over it and her woollen clothes grey and rough against the incandescent rod of sunlight leaning into the room, as though they were hoary with a felt of mist or minute rain. Over the skin of her back and her flanks ran the sweat in long wet lines and her body was becoming limp and exhausted, the uncontrollable blood seemed to be retreating from her knocking head and climbing up out of her bare feet. Then suddenly she heard the workman's voice at her back thanking her for the water. Her fists opened and the thin cords pulled out across the cheeks subsided. Stepping forward through the glowing probe of sunlight and without raising her eyes to the man's smile, she snatched back the tin and slammed the window against him. Then when she had unhooked the curtain the place became dim again and in her relief she began whimpering and clapping her large frenzied hands in the four corners of the room, catching the flies. 'Jesus, Jesus,' she muttered to herself, slapping her palms together, but all the time she remembered the crack which appeared like a white head-scar across the pane when she slammed the window.

Everything around the workman on the dusty hillside was silent and motionless, the earth endured her senseless load of heat and brilliance. On the green and lawny floor of the *cwm* below him grew the bladdery groves and a flat pool of corn was yellowing amongst the green fields. Leaning with his gathered things against the little horse-chestnut trunk, he remembered the black door of the cottage with its dented boards and its beads of rosin and the heavy iron bolt on each side of it; he thought of the heavy old woman waiting outside, her full stiff body immobile like the black hulk of some stuffed and crucified scarecrow and her hands blackish as she counted out the silver coins of his payment. And he thought too of the terrorized head of the girl looking through the window, the small pale face with the prominent tendons across the cheeks, the eyes pale as though they were staring out over a snowfall and the huge mop of fluffy hair damp at the roots, his spirit began to bleed in the evening remembering the glitter of alarm and revulsion that spread over her greasy and tremulous features when she saw him at the window.

Then suddenly as he leaned forward in the shadow of the slim young tree he felt her move against him, and he looked up with excitement. Her branches were swaying gently above him, almost he could hear her heart beating as she swayed forward against his breast and softly withdrew herself again, lapsing to and fro with timid grace. He stepped out into the finished field and the winds dived at him. Everything had changed in shape and colour, the sun was sealed up now behind the storm clouds and alone striking obliquely down into the valley on his left was the huge nail of a sunbeam. He felt the wind come in powerful cold puffs, racing past him with the speed of a hip-deep sluice and distantly he heard the muted cackle of thunder like a flexible cane clicking across a fence. Gathering up his belongings he ran across the field and reached the road, and as he watched the disorder of the darkening sky increase, a large black cloud like the roots of an entire uptorn forest crept nearer spreading its soils and its dangling tendrils low over the whole sky and from its edges shaking out its shower over the back of the hill. Large bright drops splashed heavy as spilt lead on the gritty road, and the thunder, standing nearer, blurted out its protest with increasing frequency. Changing his mind in this heavy rain, he ran hot and breathless up the slope through the mud and the young wrinkled brooks forming on the hillside, his basket under his arm and the bandaged blade of his scythe clawing the air. Reaching the house again he bounced his fist impatiently upon the black door and the bawling inside stopped. There was a brief silence except for the distinct rain that spat like scattered lead against the warm-blooded wall, and then he heard the voice of the old woman shouting out sharply in her bitter and vindictive tones asking who was there.

'Let me in, let me in,' the workman replied, with the rain already through his coat. A sleety squall of lightning glittered with the swagger and impermanence of sunlight flashed on flung water as the voice of the old woman began frantically to curse his return, but her words were drowned by the uproar of many thunders summoned muttering and yelling through the explosive doorways. The dark sky from end to end boiled with smoke the bruised slaty shade of a blue leaf, and the white rain-rods beat into the earth at a steeper angle. Although the sun had a two-hour drop before it, the daylight was almost gone; the dark muslin of rain dragged in long veils over the annihilated floor of the valley and only the golden lightning illuminated the dimness, flashing its stutter upon the gloomy door.

'Let me in, let me in,' the workman shouted again with impatience, ignoring the refusal of the old woman and beating with both fists on the warm woodwork. The thunder rippled and crashed above the house and he heard the daft voice of the girl yelling out in terror, saying 'Let him in mother, let him in. O Jesus, Jesus, Jesus.' Then when the bragging old woman had bawled out brutally in reply there was a sound like a blow and a tumble, and the gurgling idiocy of the girl's voice sank to a whisper in the small silence. The workman smiled standing in the unprotected doorway with the diagonal rain pouring over him as it were from a nozzle; he felt a little laugh being born in his belly as he ran the rain off the back of his head. Lifting up his heavy boot he kicked hard at the flimsy plank door and with quick blows smashed the bolt out of the doorpost on the inside. The wood splintered easily and the door flew into the room with a bang, crashing into a little table that shattered itself on the flagged floor. In the dim room the grey figure of the girl, her face buried in her hands, was just visible as she sat sobbing on the floor in the shadows of the settle. Beside her on the hearth rug stood her mother, powerful and ugly in her black baggish clothes, the flies buzzing before her brown-skinned leather-loaded face and circling the surly and arrogant head with the ornate plaits carefully harpooned round it. The room looked dim as underwater brickwork, it was like a tarnished and flowerless interior viewed through a gloom of coloured glass. But the yellow curtain had been torn back from the window and there the dissolving landscape poured melting down the cracked pane.

'Why do you refuse me?' the workman asked, the pale palms of his hands facing into the room. He smiled gently from the doorway, his golden hair dark with rain and the bright finery of the water running off his jacket and the lobes of his ears and the point of his beard on to the kitchen stones.

As they stepped out of the house the storm roared its welcome, the winds passed each other, they overleapt each other yelling over the mountain. The girl and the workman ran soaking down the hill and sheltered under the horse-chestnut tree whose bark streamed with rain as though it had waded the river. She wore her mother's clogs but she had lost her grey shawl and the cloth from her fluffy hair. She crouched hunch-shouldered beside the workman wiping her face and her sticking lids, her heart beating in her throat like the blood of a handled bird. Her mind was ablaze with the glaring remembrance of the brandished thicket of lightning burning at the window. 'Leave us alone,' the old woman had cried to the workman in her jarring voice, 'what have we got to do with you? What have we got to do with you?'

The workman under the tree took off his soaking jacket and put it over the girl's head.

The powerful tendrils of the storm had dragged at the house, the mother's anger was elaborate and fanatical, the daughter remembered her flushed face and her lifted lip and the heaving of her stiffened and sluggish bulk.

And now the pity of the workman's hand glowed like a hot glass on the girl's wet arm.

At the window there had been the rustle of the pouring rain, packing, above entreaty and abuse, its silks against the pane of glass. In the wet and sunburnt grip the daughter's voice was raucous with uncontrollable anguish, it was a tearing of the chained flesh to be sundered from the hug and comfort of that tyrannical body. The workman's pleading tone to the mother was decent and unraised, but she in a spurious voice thirsted for the solace of her child; she was an old woman with her weight on her stick, and she bit into the hand firmly bungled upon her wrist. The girl screamed at the workman's blow and the sight of her mother's falling figure, she heard the thunder crash over the stone roof like the waves smashed open upon the rocks. In the light of the scribbled lightning the blood spouted out of her mother's divided face in a loop of heavy drops. The girl's bulging eyes saw the brink and the depths always black, her husky voice cried upon the help and forgiveness of Jesus, her meagre body twisted up like a device.

The rain was flooding down the road in broad pure streams, the sides and foundations of the solid hills were melting together and pouring away in floods of water. Blood from her mother's body splashed her bare feet, the powerful black hulk with its foreign flabby face hooded under the metallic hair. The hill was dark, but presently there came a vivid flash, the girl and the workman saw the whole of heaven's lightning driven sprawling out of the sky; it crashed out and landed in outspread splendour upon the little clinging house. The walls split open and the stone roof smashed like a clay pan. The girl cried out, her feverish fingers twisted in the workman's hands. 'She's dead,' she yelled. 'O Jesus, Jesus, she's dead.'

The Wanderer

❦

Beams of the sun were strong on the waves, and on the beach where the sea uncovered her bones, and on the side of the skinned hills and a scarecrow's slumber under a screaming white wheel of gulls. The hideous figure lay in profound sleep at the bottom of its darkness with the bone of its arm across its face, wearing a large grass hat in the dense heat and a fur-collared overcoat, and a split carpet-slipper covering the corruption of its swollen foot. All around it sloped the sore earth and the ring of gulls sailed flat over it, crying as above carrion, but sleep was its hiding-place, for there were talons to the daylight; in through the blue birdhole of sleep a sea-dove flew bringing its dreams like a beakful of infinity.

A loud bell rang under the figure's mask and the eye bared on the blazing sun. Here, with the parting of the glow and shadow-patterned lids, was the agony of the hewn rock, to recognize the daily light was to be dragged out again from darkness for the world to feed upon. Slowly he sat up and saw with groaning and anguish the glitter of the sea in the distance like a glass knife, the purity and innocence of this and each withdrawn tide put a fresh hook into his heart. 'Over the sea are the silver doves,' he said, beginning to weep, 'golden-eyed, crowned in the branched and blossomed purple of the trees. Over the sea is the green-glittering grass in gardens shapely as a harp where round me rings of angels were singing and their curls together. Over the sea are all virtues and the tender people, the sighs of my heart float over the sea to my father, the remembrance of whose love is in my heart every minute of the day.'

On the red ground he heard the voices of poverty and sickness tempting him to tryst with worm or fish, justifying his great pride. 'My cheeks have dropped in,' he said, 'my eyes burn deeper in the cups of my skull, my nose is sharp as a ripping claw. I wade through my shame plump-footed on the bone legs of a water-bird. Under this heavy growth of hay-like hair my hands are thin bone and my pockets tunnels guiding them towards bandages or my corrupt body. The birds shall hop through my skeleton before I return unsummoned for the pollution of my native land.'

And at the sight of the distant glitter of the tide again like a gutter of silver, he remembered his father's headland house and the sea outside where the light of dawn made a low purring sound as the morning poured in softly over the water. With a gold bar ablaze in his window he left his bed at his father's morning call to watch the boat departing in answer to the ferry bell, the white-bladed oars dipping gently in the blue water like cotton-gloved hands, and then the dawn sun on the green-lit grass and among the glassy lime leaves, green as a climbing figure in the emerald-glowing tree. He remembered at night, with welcome footsteps at the door, how he watched the glow of the kitchen fire, seeing the twigs of a small nest built there among the flamy branches of a little bush, with a pretty scarlet bird sitting patiently upon it and all made out of fire; or standing at the threshold waiting for the returning boat, the moon's snows brilliant in the darkness, bright over the water as the milky neck of the galloping unicorn.

Beneath him now was the village, tranquil beneath the seeming innocence of her breathing. With the dark flow of the evening air, he left gulls and weeping and foxglove ground, and limped sadly down the sunk road under the trees into the dirt and clamour of his whitewashed sea-slum. In a passage between two windowless houses a daft negress danced with her back to him, howling over the sea-muds and the yellow fields brilliant under buttercups, keeping the stumbling pigeons in the air with her ape-like hands. A sick hag had tarred the stump of her arm to destroy the white worms eating the meat of it and now in the ash and nettles of her unweeded yard she tried feebly to chop a block into firewood with a woodcutter's axe. He hurried past her down the narrow grass-grown street and met the imbecile barefooted dwarf with the gigantic brass head and the fouled work-suit, who screamed at the sight of him and ran gibbering to the door of his wooden shed where he stood in the squalor, spitting and pointing to his boots and the obscene words he had printed in large tar letters on the wood. The son in his wide hat and his rumpled overcoat hurried along the passage-like street, avoiding the animal dirt and the nibbled lifebuoy, and the stinking fish-heads with dung-flies eating the eyes of them; and kicking his toe on the ground to dislodge a pebble beneath the ball of his foot, he averted his face from the heat of the blazing table lamp flung into the street and burning itself out on the grass and sea shells of the confined roadway. Then he went on past the whore with stiff yellow hair cut in a bob like starched tow, who lounged on the carved abortion of a fallen log feeding her twins at her naked breasts, past the pig-faced drunkard whose eyes went over her like a hand as he bore a blood-soaked calf's head into her hovel by the lip, past the dirty tree in the corner like an old broom scratching arcs on the whitewash where the man with marble bones sat in his wicker chair, swinging the scabs

and slobber of his head, cursing his daughter as she scraped a tin into
the roadway, wishing to be carried into the house. At the door of his
dark dwelling he stood aside to let the green-shaded beggar-woman
pass, and the three children bestriding the sty roof opposite shouted
after him, jeering at his poverty. 'Here's the dreaming scarecrow,' called
the one with a hoarse voice, 'his hayload hair sprouts out through the
holes of his grass hat.' – 'The bunchy straws of his beard,' shouted
another, pulling the petals out of the face of his sunflower, 'is more
than enough for the badger's bedding.' – 'A family of toes stands naked
at the open doorway of his boot,' cried the third, throwing a loose wall-
stone which struck his showing elbow.

The son hurried along the dim passage and climbed a ladder to the
gloom and rat-reek of his bare chamber where beside the dead rabbit
on his table a bead of golden light soon floated on the wick of his oil-
lamp. Throwing off his grass hat he stood in weariness and despair,
listening to the floor-rats on the boards where the clamour of curses
and blaspheming streamed up nightly past his bed from the idolatrous
rooms of the house below, and looking round at the scabby walls with
the large cheeses of fungus growing out of the corners and the lumps
kicked in agony out of the plaster by the boots of the romping suicide
repentant before his rope had strangled him. He gazed up at the clay
tiles of the roof through which no prayers but his had ever steamed out
into the stars, for a long time his eyes rested willingly on the hanging
rope and the hook in the roof timber, and climbing with difficulty on
the rags of his bed he fingered it eagerly and blew out the light.

Outside the small window, against the angry sun, the black branches
of a dead tree swept past the glass like magnified hair. In the field below
him he could see a mangy-skinned horse doped among ragged bushes,
and the digging of a garden grave, and the heavily blood-stained
bedclothes spread out to dry. With the rope in his fingers his eyes closed
as he remembered himself again a child with the gold-wearing hair who,
hearing the ferry bell, ran through sunlit flowers and silver-seed rain to
the blue-oared boat; he saw forgotten the homely tongue that warned
how the world had cheesed her traps among the nightly orders of her
illuminations, he heard the song sweeten from his young man's heart on
its bough at the rumour of the paradisal city and the murmur of her lies
and her oppression rising over her moon-mottled marble as from the
lips of the sea. He saw the constellated glitter of her milk-white
thoroughfares, her debauchery, her bare-bubbed harlots with sweet-
tasting hair, her mockery, gold the glue in the kiss of her lovers, his
pocketed field pearling the neck of a whore. He fled from her flower-
filled streets turned bloody as the butcher's sawdust, the massed angels

of her miraculous citizens imbeciles, merciless dwarfs, insane drinkers of crimson and purple, lecherous, self-mutilators. He saw himself now a grown man in his guilt, with the remembrance of the city like a hair shirt about him, tortured, lacerated, a prowler of sea-slums, a familiar of the decaying and the dead, homesick for the remembering fields of his innocent country and the assurance of his father's morning call, sweet as the dawn dream of the condemned.

He opened his eyes again and night had come black to the window, he cried out above the riot of the room beneath, it was the darkness that no candle can or any light lift. Then groping with his fingers for the rope and arranging it carefully around his neck, he hung down rigid as the gong of a giant bell.

'Oh dead in sin who lay at my side,' said the preacher, 'among the stones and rat-holes of the wilderness, dark after dark with starlight on our bones, I heard the voice of prophecy and rose in the darkness from the roots and shadow of my palm; walking the rocks in the glare of a moon on fire, I came at last to the shining sea and a slit of dawn like a lid lifting and the flat glass of daylight floating green on the water. Here with dawn-dew thick as lamb's-wool on my bones I watched the work of the Lord and the breaking of His day, until the voice of prophecy called me like a bell across that blue, that leopard-sided sea. Oh burning sands, oh green burn of the foreign leaves, oh blowing sun hot on my fleshless bones, oh young she-swallow, sliding before her shadow from the shore, I salute you and enter the paths of the sea. Now my feet tread the muds of the ocean and the turns of a coral road, and the heavy flesh of great fish glides over my skull. I wade the deep grass and the growing grain, I pass the pink harvests of sea-corn, I see the soft-branched trees with blossoms and sea-leaves swaying in eternal twilight, disturbed by the clear green winds of the waters. I come through the silence and the oblivion of the sea until streams and springwater from my native country flow cold around my bones. I arise from the ocean and see in the sunlight the emerald hills of my heavenly homeland with the mansions of my Father before me dazzling white in the blaze of His eternal day, and the fields around them and the fruit trees loaded with blossom in undecaying clouds. White birds flock over the sands to greet me, up the golden beach towards my homeland go my gull-bearing bones.'

The preacher paused and peered ahead from the lamp-lit prow of his pulpit into the small dim chapel where the few upturned faces floated like foam on the gloom of the evening. Behind him a wide red ribbon was painted on the cream wall with DUW CARIAD YW done in gold letters across it. On top of the upright bars of iron, black and twisted, that were placed one each side of him, was the copper bowl of an oil-lamp with a little flame burning inside the glass chimney. The preacher's great flesh in its heavy black clothes filled up the little boat of a pulpit. His neck was full, his jaw shone black, his black hair, thick on the flanks of his head was brushed back in a stiff slope above his shining brow, leaning in a rigid mass like a bush pushed backwards in the wind. In the dangerous valleys he had taken the curved layers of coal out of the hill, and by the amber blush of the lamplight, bright blue veins ran in all directions through the flesh of his large smashed face.

As he went on with his sermon, the ferryman glanced round at the handful of listening people, their faces like the foam of a yarrow-bordered sea, and as he looked at them he recalled a life that seemed all mornings under the green benediction of branch and bough, concentrating with ecstasy one moment upon the soft, faintly-freckled skin over the curve of a youthful cheek-bone, and then remembering the horror of his boy's abandoned bed, wondering with anguish what the future had poured into that lovely face, innocent beneath its growing gold. Believing in the swords and ministers of prayer, and the protection of angry angels with burning wings, the thoughts of love and death could not meet in his breast; his rebellious fatherly heart rejected death and the golden curls in clay among the buried agony of the world.

Ready for the tolling of the bell and his task, he sat in his seat wearing black jersey and sea-boots. He was an old man, grey-bearded and heavily-lined, but powerful still, gull-winged across the brows and deep blue-eyed, his firm crinkled hair dinted and folded upon itself, thick and comely as the pleats of the walnut kernel. Hearing the tide of trees in the graveyard, he looked out of the narrow chapel window fringed with web-fingered ivy-hands beating the glass, and watched the sunset take shelter among the rocks. From where he sat he could see across the red ferry to the little bell-house on the opposite shore from which he received his summons. The land there was bleak and a wilderness. Soon everything would be dark. The glancing rain, hair by hair, began to put a bright pelt of water on the window panes.

'The love of God is like the tolling of a bell,' the preacher was saying from his lighted boat, ringing his vast arm like a clapper. 'When first I heard it in that foreign wilderness where the stars looked into my bones, it was a beam of sound striking as upon my heart alone, a shaft of pure light shot into the darkness from a tower. Then when I knew saints and my brothers heard its call, in a vision I saw the love of God as a great wheel of sound turning about a tower, the beating of a tower-bell which swung its peals around until they touched our hearts like spokes of blessed sound. Now my soul knows God's love is not a beam for me alone or the turning wheel of the few elect, the love of God envelopes like a vast sphere of sound, the tower fills the world with music every heart can hear. The souls abandoned by all, and the souls abandoned by all but their enemies, the Father remembers. Amen.'

The old ferryman heard the back of the wind squeezing past the rough walls of the chapel and the split rain hard against the glass. Not waiting to be blessed he got up and went out into the dark and the rain. He hurried among the tufted graves and on to the road leading down to his house, under the cliff, at the water's edge. Here, where a little wave, grey and white-striped, slid again and again its goose-wing over the rock, he pushed his small white boat off its platform into the water and began rowing eagerly across the ferry with the blue white-bladed oars. The black air was troubled and once he was out of the shelter of the cliff the wind leapt from its hole, tearing back the tide from beneath the boat, tilting it on rough discs of tarry sea, bobbing it like a cork over the big wind-ribs curved in massive ridges across the water. The ferryman was blind in the darkness, and the rain poured like a waterfall into the creaking boat, but he welcomed the cold of that stinging fringe drawn heavily across his hands and face, he wished in spite of his soaking sea-jersey and his pouring head for green leaves wet from the morning to cool his brow and breast. And once out in the middle of the roaring ferry the sea was deeply curled, towering crystals of wind ploughed out of the darkness over the water, rapidly thundering after one another, grooving the sea, curving a slab of bended transparent water like foot-thick glass or bent ice over the bulwark of the little half-drowned boat as they passed, smashing themselves to pieces upon the thunderous rocks behind.

But the boatman sang; the heavy body of the fallen wind could crash and destroy itself upon the unstiffened waters, the quaking waters themselves sway like the upper jungle, he thought only of the little chapel-like building ahead on the abandoned shore into which the rope of the ferry bell hung down. And when, after leaving his boat on the beach among the anguished arms of the sea, he was grasping it, he began to pull with eager hands and the bell inside its little stone hood started its steady tolling, he stood tugging the rope at the gable door of the tiny stone house that bristled with water, wearing the heavy rain like a fine fell around it, so that he could see in the gloom and the pouring rain the awkward ape-rock of the black bell in the gable sending its loud notes out into the darkness from the roof. The blows of the iron tongue seemed to be falling upon his naked brain, stunning him with its clamour, but he pulled and pulled, his heart blazing like a broken fire-coal as his bell sent out its penetrating notes, and from the darkness the long lip of the water gathered the beach.

The beggar, who, paid to scare the gulls, had slept at his task under their fluid flying, now lay crumpled in the darkness, fallen down with his rope on the floor of the room. Slowly he awoke in the silent house with the fragrance of heavenly presences momentarily like perfume upon him. He lay in his rags as the dream ebbed out, sobbing on the boards at the horror of what had happened, at the memory of the hanging and the broken rope, at the agony of his bandaged foot and his leg wounded from hip to heel and bursting with pain. And then, as waiting slowly pared away the suffering, his mind turned again, hearing what the heart was always watchful for. He lay still, his fearful ear sucking at the darkness, because above the blowing of the wind, and the rain on the tight window, he could hear an intermittent noise in the darkness terrifying and joyful, solemn to him as the sound of the opening of graves, he heard the tolling of a bell that beat faintly in the distance or strode up to the window and struck.

Many times had he imagined the happiness of this salvation, even in the rhythm of unholy music, many times heard this bell ring in his bird-disturbed dreams, but now it was sounding upon the flesh of his living and awakened ear. He rose with difficulty from the floor, loosening the rope about his neck, and struggled noisily down the ladder and out past the cursing doorways into the narrow street, through which the rain ran like a river. At the sound of the summoning bell his unskilful and uncertain soul wished to sing with the faith of a loud lark over hopeless country, but it raised in its hoarseness at the sound only the raucous morning rook-row of a heart long unfamiliar with such blessedness. He hobbled joyfully and ankle-deep in water down the road in the blackness and the rain past the ruins of the charred lamp which he kicked from his path, laughing at the wooden shed where he knew the bare-footed idiot had nailed his boots to the wall. He passed the last house of the village where a woman came out with lamplight painted yellow on her back, and went along the road in the pouring rain until his solid coat was like lead and his useless grass hat pulp and abandoned in the soaked bushes. And as he went further from his sea-slum, his wound, once the centre and unconcealable hill-city of his flesh to which his whole consciousness endlessly turned, was ignored and forgotten; in his eagerness and his dread that the bell should cease to guide him with its nourishing stroke, he no longer heeded the agony that had once been the hub round which day and night his body had painfully turned.

Soon he was clear of the valley and climbing the hung skin loose on the hillsides, but he cared nothing for the difficulty of a climb where flowers were heaved through the earth and where he felt set stars rise up to see in the blackness as he sought the path like a rope-groove through the hills. Still the bell rang and many times he mended his direction to keep the sound ahead of him, limping through the towering forest of fishbones and nut bushes whose trees were almost overturned one by one in the wind, and over the top of the pass where he heard the ringing coming clearly from the sea. There the rain fell on him, the wind blew his arm from his side, there was no light to be seen anywhere, although perhaps ships were on the sea ahead and the rushcutters' cottages lay near him on the shore. With the broken rope hanging down his back he hobbled in increasing excitement through the wood and over the soft marsh like the six-winged fire-bearing bird through darkness, and the drench of joy glowed warmly round him as though he closely pursued through heaven the blazing rags of a shooting star. And once on the flat shore he could mistake it no longer, the sound of the bell-peal was near, pounding from the direction of the swollen sea. He crossed the rocks, and then the seaweed like a soft squash of flesh was under his feet; he entered the brambles of the sea with his hung heart in a blaze that for radiance would outstar the sun; because the ringing bell was near at hand, his flesh felt clearly the iron blows and through the darkness came the thundering vibrations of the tolling mouth.

The wind had fastened in the tide far up the beach; as he waded eagerly forward, a wave came down upon him like teeth and he went under the tide, but rising again he struggled on and soon he saw before him through the jumping water the roof of the little drowned bell-house rising from the waves, with his father up to his breast in water still pulling at the bell-rope, at last he saw the bell swinging on the roof sending out its endless throb like the glow of a blood-ruby in unconsuming fire, and his father faithfully tolling at the rope, his tired body streaming with water from rain and sea. And near him, where wave after wave was hurled struggling into a corner of the rocks, the little boat floated high, rising and dropping as the cloven water met and parted under its keel.

The old man saw the soaked figure from the shore struggling out towards him through the broken water and the floating loaves of foam, the clothes drenched and the long wet hair plastered over the transfigured face. His heart was filled with joy and a great tenderness for even in the darkness he knew the call of his bell was answered.

The Four-Loaded Man

୬

The little girl sat in the cottage kitchen drawing a fire like a rose-bunch, and a wine-cup, and a shooting star. Except for the two chalk dogs on the mantelpiece she was by herself, but she wasn't frightened although the house was lonely and the owlish snow was swimming among the tips outside the window. In the middle of the table top lay the long black iron house-key, and she had the red-haired fire with his frosty parable for a friend.

The clipped hair was a dark vee in the groove of the little girl's neck-nape as she bent at her chalice and her flashing star. Her large bright eyes were china brown and shiny by the blown mop of fire, and at the apple-lipped corner of her mouth grew the small brown crust of a sore the round size of a daisy-centre. She wore a warm apricot dress of wool, all lily-worked on the sleeves, and in her hair she had a crimson feather.

She heard the wind go file-screeching from the beech boughs over the shabby mountains, and she thought of her grannie saying 'Rhys y Mynydd.' So she took in her tongue to look at the brass-handed clock throbbing on the wall. It was time to make food, but as she passed the window she saw a man coming slowly down the tips through the thick, wrapping snowflakes. She peered out over the sulk of the window daffodils, and then she forgot about the old man in the weather and the cold kettle lid in her hand. The torn snowflakes came swarming out at the end of the valley, the first grey crayon-work of snow was already smooth over the roundness of the tips. Her grannie's garden bramble was furred like the milky tangle of a woolball, and the tufted hedge-grass in the garden bank was bear-fur rough with snow. A small robin, an eggcupful, flicked brick-breasted among the swirling flakes.

When the old man knocked, the little girl took up the key and opened the door after she had jumped. Flakes curved past her into the kitchen like three white flies as she held the door wide open, and the cold breeze began bee-buzzing at the firm bird's feather in her hair.

'Is your mam in?' asked the old man.

'I haven't got a mam,' answered the little girl.

She could see the stranger was a glazier-man with large squares of glass strapped like a big window on his back. He made the little girl laugh because his bowler hat and his long black coat were sheeted all down the front with cracked snow as though he wore a coating of thick white-lime. He was short and small, very old, not much taller than the little girl herself although he had thick clogs of snow caked under the soles of his boots. His shrunken face was yellow, wrinkled, the skin sagging under his eyes and seeming to pull down the lower lids so that they showed the bloodshot inside flesh to the little girl. His nose was narrow and bony, a thin pink claw, sharp-hooked like a rose-thorn, and his heavy bottom lip hung down the bright purple-black of tracing paper. His scarce beard grew in a small grey tangle, brushing over his buttoned coat-collar with the tremble of his head. When the little girl had got him sitting in her grannie's wicker in his shaken hat and coat, she noticed that his resting hands were high-veined down the backs like the underside of a rhubarb leaf, only very hairy.

But the old man's small shaking face under the bowler brim made the little girl unhappy; it had a fume of pain always hovering over it, and she began to wonder who the visitor was. Because he looked so sad she thought he might be Rhys y Mynydd, the wind-man who moaned over the mountains. So she told him to put on his glasses to look at the drawing of the fire-coals, and the love-cup and the swift-prowed star. He held the paper close up under the pink hook of his nose, bending over and shaking so much the girl thought his eyes would drop into his glasses, and that made her laugh again.

He said nothing about the drawing, but when he looked up he asked:

'What is that *'smotyn* in the corner of your mouth, *cariad*?'

The little girl put her tongue on her lip-sore. 'My grannie calls it a *cusan bwbach*, a goblin's kiss,' she told him. 'And now I can ask you a thing. Why do you shiver by the fire and have leaf-lines on your face, then?'

He looked up at her, shaking. One of the eyes of his little glasses was cracked across the middle.

'It is because of the four-pointed load I have to carry,' he said, spreading his fingers before the fire.

'But not now,' said the little girl, puzzled. 'Your glass pack is leaning in the garden.'

The old man parted his purple lips, smiling feebly.

'I carry the four quarters of a heavier load than that,' he answered.

'Show me your load, tell me about the four quarters of your heavy load,' cried the little girl.

The old man's top lip twitched like an eyelid. He put his glasses in his pocket and wiped his wet eyes with his cocoa-coloured handkerchief.

'My first is called my poverty,' he said.

The little girl went into the pantry and brought out some bread in her frock.

'I will cut you the kissing-crust of my little milk-loaf,' she said.

'No crust will heal my second, called my loneliness,' he answered.

The little girl went to the door and pulled the big key out of the lock.

'I will give you the key of my grannie's kitchen,' she said.

'No key will heal my third, called my sickness,' he answered.

The little girl remembered her grannie would jump off the armchair to jerk a bean through her swallow and make herself well again.

'I will help you on to the wicker and catch you when you jump to the mat,' she said.

'No jump will heal my fourth, called my old age,' he answered.

The little girl thought of her grannie saying the clock brings birthdays in his hands.

'I will cut the card out of the clock-face and my fire will burn it,' she said.

A big snow-load jumped off the roof into the garden and the old man got up and slowly opened the door. It had stopped snowing and the wind had almost gone, leaving only a fingerprint crumpled on half a path-pool. Everything in the garden was still and covered with smooth snow, a cherry like a white growing bone and the beech boughs, where the glass was, weighted down with their burden of whiteness, the big branches snow-snaked and each tiny twig perhaps no wider than an eyelash, with its little load of snow. The leaning pack was covered thick with a sheet of square snow, and the little girl, with the flat of her crooked finger pressed deep through touching the cold glass, cut a big upright cross in the middle of it; she spread a dark glass cross with her wiping finger wide in the middle of the sheet of snow.

'Remember the bread, *cariad,* and the key, and the jump, and the clock face,' said the old man, and he turned slowly away out of the garden. The little girl said 'Good-bye, Rhys y Mynydd,' feeling sad to see him going so feebly down the path. She watched him climbing like a cripple over the tips towards the milky mountains, the big black cross bold in the white square on his back.

When he was out of sight she went into the kitchen, putting her tongue like a bud into the corner of her lip. She tasted the sore had dropped off. So she lit a candle and hunted for it under the table.

The Little Grave

❧

In this weather the world was silent and without her scents, and yet the cold stillness of the earth was beautiful because a tranquil covering of new snow lay over her odourless fields and hung upon the baskets of her bare bushes. There was no wind and no motion in any of the large fields on the hill, only a little black sparrow pushing his crust of bread through the still air, clinging with his beak to his little lump of dry bread as he swung himself eagerly over the snow.

A child dawdling out of the wood and crossing the bended field left behind him the first tracks in the deep sheet of that white pasture. He wore scarlet mittens and a scarlet shawl around his head, but he felt the afternoon too cold and too unhappy for play. He thought of her soon to lie out under the earth and under the deep snow of the cemetery at the bottom of the field, and shivers went through him because of it. And then he forgot her again, seeing how the small birds had made their faint footprints in the snow, how, when they had hopped forward, the middle toe of their little claws did not quite clear the surface of the snow, so that there were little parallel lines leading over the field, like the tracks of a tiny cart pulled this way and that over the snow.

This snowfall had descended everywhere straight out of heaven, there had been no wind to blow it sideways and the flakes had spread themselves out flat over everything in an equal covering. So that when the child reached the cemetery he found the slabs of the flat tombs covered with a thick slice of snow, the many crosses bearing cushions of pure white upon their outspread arms, and a grey Jesus above the grave, whose stone gown was furred with snow pith, wearing a large soft cap upon his marble curls. And near the wall there stood the tangle of a drooping willow, its downward-bending branches decked with snow like some great sea-crag overgrown with white weed, and beside it, cold and lonely, was her little open grave. The boy, looking down from the snow-covered pile of earth, saw the pick-marks on the chill sides, and at the bottom a mat of snow to lay her coffin on. His breast throbbed at the thought of her resting there, cold and alone, with no one to warm her. Everything around him was chill, silent and motionless. There were no flower-scents, no bird-notes and no blooms, and only the long lock of his breath moved, floating upwards from his mouth. Yet at the foot of the willow grew a frail crocus-cup, two, three of them, a little group of early white crocuses, thin and papery and with dark leaves, the faint purple veins in the fragile petals inflamed and purple as they rested among the roots of the tree.

The child hurried on until he came to a field with a house in the middle wearing a thick cape of snow over its eaves and snowy kneeling-cushions upon all its windowsills. He walked towards it and heard his grandfather chopping up a fallen tree with a hatchet. The old man was simple, but this was a job he could do even when the moon was full. It was the tall birch from the middle of a little snowy plot that the old man was feebly cutting and it lay beside a heap of chopped firewood with a little cupful of snow upon the stumps of all its sawn-off arms.

The child went into the garden and kissed his grandfather, who was short and bent, wearing yellow rib trousers and a sack pinned round his shoulders. But he was so old he did not remember who the little boy was, he stared open-mouthed at him with his pale snow-blue eyes, losing his spittle from the ends of his mouth, and then he began to cry. He had a face the colour of the long goblin watching from the side of the copper kettle, with light watery eyes to it, and a long white beard brown with spittle on the chin. He laid down his axe on the chopping block and when the little boy had comforted him and used the sweeping brush on his boots, they went into the kitchen together. It was cosy there, with a clay fire glowing hot behind the bars, and a shepherd's crook on the chimney and a little blue book hanging up on the wall with a loop of string tied to its corner. And on the table near the window lay her coffin with a plush cloth over it. The old man, the tears still wet upon his copper cheeks, gently pulled back the cloth, and there underneath lay the boy's grandmother. She was sleeping comfortably on the table with her mouth not quite shut; she seemed warm and cosy, her smooth cheeks the colour of the pink silk under her head, and her narrow shoulders a good fit for her wooden box. She was a small woman, wearing a lace cap and a long white gown fastened with blackberry buttons, and in her little hand with its golden ring, crooked over like the arm of a stiff-jointed doll, the old man had placed a large rose of red paper. The child kissed her, and then his grandfather covered her up again with the plush tablecloth.

The little boy stared out from between the curtains, thinking of the cold grave he had seen under the snowy willow. Outside the window his grandfather was at work again, slowly chopping up the tree, his spittle running down his beard and his body humped as though

something sat under the sack between his shoulders. The child heard
the wind rising and saw a tree in the field with its load of snow bend
over suddenly as though something had landed upon it, and then
spring upright again, black and empty. As the dusk began to gather he
thought of this cold wind sweeping into her grave. He saw a black
heavy bird drift down like a dark anchor out of the sky and flounder
heavily across the field, up to its breast in snow, collapsing sideways as
the wind raked the level field and shoved him over with his long wings
outspread over the snow. He heard the crack of the fire behind him and
thought of her going down alone under the coldness of the thick
snowfall.

It was beginning to get dark so he went out and led his grandfather
into the warm kitchen.

When the child woke up his bedroom was full of light and the moon
shining in had made a window upon his floor. Hearing outside the
noisy tide of trees roaring he left his warm bed and looked out into the
blue cube of the world. The sky, which had been grey all day, was now
a deep blue, and moonlit, and only a few broken clouds swept swiftly
across the stars. Most of the velvet trees around the house had tumbled
their snow into the wind, and the skin of the slim fish-bodied birch
lying before the door gleamed silver in the moonlight. Silently the child
dressed and went down the stairs that led into the kitchen.

There the fire had gone out and the moon shone in coldly upon the
still and silent furniture, and the little blue book on the nail, and the
hands of his grandfather who sat in the armchair asleep by the
fireplace. The child went up to the coffin on the table and drew back
the thick cloth from his grandmother's face. There she lay, pale and
chill now, she seemed to shrink in her coffin as the moon drew a wet
finger across her little face. With that the child made up his mind.
Slipping some matches into his pocket he softly unlocked the kitchen
door and went out into the bright moonlit garden. There he gathered
many great armfuls of the sticks his grandfather had chopped from the
fallen birch, and tying them together with a straw rope, flung them
over his shoulder. Then he set off for the grave, struggling in the wind,
across the white fields with the milky silver of the moon above him
washing the world.

Under the willow by the edge of the grave the child kindled his fire,
burning first the straw rope and then the little twigs. The bladed wind

swept round the tombs spreading the flames, and soon a tall bonfire, taller than himself, pushed up its orange horns towards the sea-sounding branches overhead; the bright scarlet flames roared upwards warmly, lighting up the auburn boughs in the cold blue light of the flying moon. The child felt the glow go through him, he smiled with pleasure as the golden light flickered upon his burning cheeks. Each time he threw on more firewood the blaze sparked loudly like thousands of clocks beginning to tick together, and threw up its shovelful of golden grain through the blazing sheets of fire. The snow around, on the tombs and the smooth paths striped black with the wavering shadows of the crosses, blushed a deep flesh-pink as the bonfire roared hotter and the ruddy light deepened upon the bloodshot snowfall. The child knew that this golden upward-pouring liquid would warm the grave because he could feel the heat of it tingling on his wind-chilled flesh, and the bare-toed Jesus above the blaze glowed warmly in his thin gown as he held out his hands and gazed down in surprise and pleasure at the flames. Then when the heat was at its greatest, the boy took his remaining branch and with it swept the blazing fire down over the brink into the open grave.

But he was disappointed because everything was cold again at once and the fire began to go out instead of blazing upwards out of the grave. As soon as the last spitting stick had disappeared, the child felt the bitter cold upon him and he could see the grave had swallowed up his lovely fire. The snow around lost its ruddy flush, it became pallid again in the moonlight now that the flames no longer bled their warmth upon it, and a chill of disappointment ran through him as the icy wind lifted his hair above his ears. The round moon sailed her glittering snow across the sky and, starry-coated, Orion stood vast above him in the heavens with his foot upon the hill, but all the warmth and brightness had gone, only the dying fire burning in the cold underworld threw up its column of black smoke and flickered feebly upon the sides of the grave. The cold wind leapt up from the snow again, licking his face like a cold flame, and the little boy sat down beside the crocuses, weeping because his swallowed fire had gone out at once in the belly of the earth and he had failed with his bonfire to warm his grandmother's grave.

The old man woke up from his sleep with the back door banging, and the chill wind sweeping into the moonlit kitchen. He got up and lit a candle, and the moon plucked back her bright light out of the room. He called the child at the foot of the stairs and searched through the house for him with the candle, but he could not find him anywhere, and there was a heavy stone at the bottom of his heart. Finally he lifted his crook off the chimney, wrapped his sack around him and went out into the garden, leaving the candle alight in the saucer beside the coffin.

There in the moonlight he saw the tracks of the little boy, the footprints and the sweeping hair-lines of the hanging birch twigs in the snow. He followed the marks across the fields under the wide-open sky, feeling the wind rough as water upon his beard, and hearing it in the distance choiring its high-pitched music behind the snowy hills. From time to time he stopped for breath, while the snow stretched out flat in all directions around him, and he watched with open mouth the milky bull-charge of the moon across the vast blue sky above.

At length he reached the cemetery and there on the root of the willow, weeping and blowing his red-mittened fingers, he found the little boy. The fire was out in the grave and as the sobbing child described to the old man what he had done, the moon flew down the throat of a wide cloud and disappeared and the cemetery became darker. The little boy cried with cold and disappointment as he and his grandfather clung together for warmth against the tree trunk, and he told how the coldness of the grave was so great that it had overcome the flames of the bonfire he had lit to warm it. The old man opened his sack and wrapped it round the boy. He noticed the little crocuses beside him closed up for the night and the dim Jesus in the shadows with deep eyes and bony arms. His memories stirred as he thought of a way to comfort the weeping child, they sprang up in his mind and went out again like the violent shadows flung round from a jangled lantern. And as he stared in front of him with his watery eyes, trying to remember, the moon escaped again and suddenly shone out full of new power, scattering her wild brightness about the heavens and the world with its snowfall and its tombs, she rushed whole out of her imprisoning cloud and suddenly poured her glory over the upright figure with the bowed head and the blessing hands before him. The swung lantern came to rest in the old man's mind as he watched the stone-gowned form that dazzled white against the blackness of the sky, he recalled at last what he had been thinking of, and lifting up his crook he pointed with it in the brightness of the moon.

'Don't cry, little one, don't cry,' he said, comforting the child. 'He has warmed the grave for her.'

The child's sobbing stopped and he raised his head. He saw the radiant figure glowing warm as a sunbeam above him, and the end of his grandfather's crook gently touching the outstretched hand.

Explosion

❦

Iam late going to school because I have stopped on the tramroad to watch some night-shift collier-boys playing catty-and-doggy in their pit-clothes. It is a frosty morning, the sun only a few cold cinders glowing among the clouds and all the cart-tracks frozen, with a little slate of white ice roofing them over. And the workers' circle round the firebucket has contracted. As I am watching, the market bell strikes nine, landing like a mother's thump between my shoulder-blades, and I run up the hill to the school. My marble-bottle jerks in my trousers pocket and by my side runs the red lid of my polish tin tinkling loudly on its string along the horny road.

Outside the slaughterhouse I meet Danny Davies crying to himself, his face cream with cold and his little red nose wet as a leaking nipple. He is dawdling along playing alleys by himself, a piece of torn-off wallpaper folded in his hand. He says this is a note telling teacher he is late because the cupboard door has cut his head open. He has a dirty white scarf going under his chin and tied into a big knot on top of his head, the fringes hanging down to the levels of his ears, and on top of the knot he is wearing his blue school cap with the back burnt into a scorchy hole. He is dressed in his sister's high-heeled laced boots and a long check overcoat trimmed with braid. In his pocket he carries a little saucepan he found when he was crossing the brickyard, and he is taking it to school to have a game with it under the desk.

As we are on the pavement passing our classroom window we know by the school-hum coming from it that our teacher isn't there, and that makes us glad. And when we get inside we see a big boy who has been put back into our class looking after the boys. The walls of our classroom are painted dark brown, cow-colour, and our floor is boarded with wooden planks full of rowdy knots and splinters. On one side of the room there is a glass partition where teacher has pinned a long red, white and green decoration for Christmas. We have two pictures on the wall, one of the claws of birds and a coloured one of an apple growing on a twig, and over the glass partition there is a map showing how the world is oval and covered with lines like an egg in a cage. A long gas-pipe hangs out of the middle of the ceiling, and where it divides into four burners our teacher has tied a purple balloon with some printing on it. In front of the class we have a board and easel, a desk for teacher and a blazing fire with a guard round it.

Danny has stopped crying when we come into school, so we sit down in our desk together and watch the big boy trying to make the class say their prayers with teacher's cane in his hand. This boy, whose name is Gogger Roberts, chews tobacco and never prays himself. He is big and heavy, as big as any of our teachers, and he wears long black corduroy trousers that don't reach his boots and a broad belt holding them up covered with brass army badges like a piece of harness. And on both the lapels of his coat he has a shiny line of metal bottle-tops in an upright row. His heavy face with its big bottom jaw is always sprayed with little boils, and a dust of moustache grows round the ends of his upper lip. Then he has one pure white eyebrow, and a bunch of white curls in front like a splash of bird-dirt among the tangled black ones covering his heavy head. Master has put him back because he only gets three marks out of a hundred in his own class, and that makes the boys tease him. If you cheek him, or say 'Parting your hair in the middle now, Gogger?' he begins to curse and swear, but if you give him a ha'penny he will bake you a little dough mouse by the next day with currants for eyes and a wool tail. He can do this because he greases the cake-tins in the bakery after school.

Danny rolls his wallpaper note into a ball and throws it into the fire, and then he starts to play with his loose tooth. Soon there comes a tap at the frosted window. Gogger pushes it open and our teacher hands his hat and coat in from the street so that Master won't know he is late again. Our teacher must have a bowlerful of hair, because when he takes his hat off you can see it swollen up in a fluffy bunch on top of his head, enough to fill the whole hollow of his tall bowler hat. In a few minutes he comes red-nosed into the room and spreads out his fingers like wheel-spokes before the fire, showing the bald spot at the back of his head surrounded by his black fuzzy hair like the pink spot of flesh under a dog's tail. When he turns round he notices Danny's bandage. He stares at him for a long time with nibmarks between his eyes, and then he asks him what he is wearing it for. He is from the North and the way he speaks makes the boys smile, it is all hisses and explosions like a damp stick on the fire. Danny doesn't hear him properly, he is playing with his saucepan as quiet as a flea laying his little egg, so I give him a nudge and he gets up and says without thinking:

'My father threw his boot at me, sir.'

The boys start to laugh at that. Danny's eyes fill with tears and his upper lip with the snail-slime down it twitches as though it is on a piece of elastic. But our teacher makes him tell everything, how his brother changed his prunes when he was saying grace the night before and how his father threw a working boot at them because they spilt the tea quarrelling. Danny is crying by the end, and he can hardly finish. Our teacher tells him to sit down and he does it, wiping his eyes with the back of his coat-sleeve. Our teacher stares medicine-mouthed round the class from his bulgy glasses to see who is smiling. He is tall and thin, very narrow, with thin plum-coloured lips and a pale face wrinkled as a map of rivers. His glasses swell outwards, shining like the round owl's eyes of a tall bird, and on his head, black and thick, is the bunchy parsley of his hair. He always wears a black suit, short brown leggings and a tall winged collar with gold notes at the sides to keep his tie down.

When he has finished warming himself he goes to the blackboard and pushes up his glasses to read the names of the six boys Gogger has written there for shouting or throwing chalk. But Gogger's scribble is crooked as the coalman's signature, and he has to bring the boys out himself. Then our teacher raises a big rib on their cold behinds with a cane-cut, and sends them back to their places holding the seats of their trousers. After that he gives us bibles to read so that he can mark the register, and while we are reading he sits like a hunger-striker staring in front of him, pulling hairs out of his big pink nose until his eyes are full of tears.

When all the bibles are out, Gogger sits behind us and shows us a small round rusty thing shaped like a covered-in watch or a tin of boot polish. He carries it in a blue sugar-bag all wrapped up in a sheet of paper with writing on it. He lets us feel it and it is very heavy, but when he asks us to read the paper wrapped round it we can't because it is in real writing and full of long words. Then he tells us the message says that if we throw the iron thing into the night watchman's fire-bucket we will see something magic we haven't seen before. He says he is going to do it on the way home from the bakehouse that night. Danny offers him his saucepan for it, and the alleys he has with his tooth in the pen-groove, but Gogger won't.

Soon the second lesson comes and our teacher gets up and brings sheets of sum paper round for us. Danny is always lucky in school and he has the middle page with the shiny bit of wire fastened in it. But although he tries he doesn't get the pen with the bright red handle because Gogger is giving them out and he keeps it for himself. The first sum our teacher writes on the blackboard is one about five and sixpence for a hat multiplied by two, and we can hear Gogger behind us saying, 'Crimes, I'll have to rattle my brains over this.' But he can't do it, and in a minute or two he puts his hand up and asks if he can run across the yard.

Before he answers our teacher stares at him without saying a word. Then he puts his long thin bony tongue out of his mouth like a finger, bends it round to the side, and starts scratching his cheek with it. Then he pulls it in again and tells Gogger to fetch the bible.

Gogger knows what he wants. When he puts the open book on the desk he places one hand on the pages, cups the other over his left bottle-tops as though he is hiding a wet sum, and says he swears on the bible he wants to go badly. Our teacher nods and Gogger goes out to the lavatory. But he is chewing his tobacco before he leaves the room and as he passes behind the easel we see him drop something that looks like his sugar-bag on the back of the fire.

As soon as he is gone we hear another tap at the window. Our teacher opens it, and outside stands Lisa Rhydderch wearing a hat like a parlour-pot with black feathers growing out of the top of it. She is smiling, showing her long pink gums with small yellow teeth on the end of them like bits of indian corn, and although she is thin she has a sort of soft double chin hanging under her shiny face, lined and wrinkled as a lump of porridge skin. Sometimes you could see her drunk in town with her boots open and her hair out of the pins. She used to tap at the window sometimes to try our teacher for the price of a pint, but now when he looks at her she says, 'There's awful news isn't it, Mr. Owens?'

Our teacher stares out of the window at her, the curving watch-glasses of his spectacles shining and the skinfolds on his face like a piece of wrinkled wallpaper. We all stop our sum because Lisa is daft and we have some fun out of her.

'There's a awful explosion in the Graig, Mr. Owens,' she goes on, shaking her chin and her feathers. 'If I was to drop down dead by here I'm not joking. They're bringing some of the men up in the ambulance now, poor dabs.'

'You're drunk,' our teacher tells her. He bangs down the sash and then hurries out of the room. At that all the boys crowd to the window and stand on the desks and the inside sill to watch the ambulances coming up the street. But we can't see much except a man wheeling a mangle on a truck, and Gogger's boss kicking the bread pony under the belly, and Lisa hurrying away among the people with so much movement in her long black coat she looks as though her legs are divided up to her collar-bones. Then in a minute or two we hear our teacher's big boots in the passage, so we all get on with our sum again. He calls Danny out and stares down at him, stroking the pink blotting paper of his nose. Danny looks small in front of him, his little face peeping out of its bandage no bigger than a policeman's pap.

'Don't go home to your dinner today,' he says at last. 'Go to your auntie's in Quarry Row. You,' he says to me, 'you go with him. Go now.'

Danny looks up at teacher. Our teacher looks back down at him as though even dipping his sugar in syrup wouldn't sweeten him.

'Your father has been hurt in the explosion,' he says at last. 'Your mother has gone to see him so she can't make your dinner. Now go home to your auntie's.'

Danny goes back to his place for his saucepan, but before we can get out of the room we hear a terrible explosion. It is like the bang of a thick squib bursting, sending out a flash and a loud roar. Clouds of smoke blow out of the chimney, rolling into the room, and the Christmas decoration floats down on to the boys sitting under it. And one or two pieces of whiting off the ceiling drop with a smack from round the gas-pipe. At first there is a wide silence, the faces of the boys pale and blank as the back of a gravestone with surprise and fright, and then one of them begins to cough like a cow. Gogger sits fingering his white curls, red-faced, his head steaming like a dinner and the puzzled Chinese letter of a wrinkle twisted over his eyes; and our teacher is red too, the pipy veins standing out on his forehead like plumbing. Danny starts to cry, but our teacher turns and pushes us through the door as quickly as we can.

As we are outside on the pavement passing the classroom our teacher flings open the window to let the smoke out. He notices us, and when he sees that Danny is still crying he shouts, 'What are you crying for? Hurry home out of the cold. Your father isn't bad. He's only had the edges of his ears burnt off.'

Danny stops crying and I let him run my polish tin all the way to Quarry Row.

An Afternoon at Ewa Shad's

✺

Em was my friend. He lived with my Ewa Shad and my Bopa Lloyd in a lonely row of whitewashed cottages on the side of the hill. It was a lovely sunny afternoon when I went up there carrying a brown paper parcel, and my mother had put my blue print trousers on me. These were real trousers with a button fly and a patch pocket for my handkerchief on my behind.

Em lived in the end cottage in the row. There was a pavement in front with gutters crossing it half-filled with soapy water from the colliers' bath-tubs. In front of the pavement again stretched a flat patch of rusty ground, a sort of little platform in the side of the hill where the sagging drying-lines stood and a chickens' *cwtch* built of orange-boxes. At the back of the row, beyond the colliers' gardens, the steep tips of pit-rubbish sloped smoothly up into the sky, and it was on these tips the men who were out of work used to scratch for coal. Em's father, my Ewa Shad, had made a fence round his garden out of old pit-rope and sheets of rusty corrugated zinc, but the bottom part was formed of the two end frames of a black iron bedstead, with the bright knobs and the brasswork still shining in the sun upon them.

I went into the back garden, and there I found Em playing with his fish. He had a big zinc bath half-filled with water sunk to the level of the ground to keep it in. He took his finger out of his nose to wave to me. It was a good garden for playing in because only about a quarter of it was set, and the earth of the rest had been trodden hard as the flags of a kitchen. There was a sycamore tree growing in the middle, and a whitewashed lavatory stood like a sentry-box in the far corner. Em's father was lying on his back between the lettuce beds, his boots off and his cap over his face. He was dirty and in his working clothes, and every now and then he would take hold of his shirt and start scratching his chest with his fist.

'It's our Mam's birthday today,' said Em, as I went up to him. His jersey was navy blue with a new light blue sleeve to one arm and half a sleeve, from the elbow down, to the other. He was sunburnt, his nose dotted with black freckles like the spots on a bird's egg, and his ginger hair was cut very short and in a notchy way, looking as though something had been nibbling at it. I could see he had a red bloodshot blot in his eye that afternoon, and I thought I would like to have one of those, too. We played with the fish, which was about as big as my middle finger and which had a bright scarlet line all around the gulping edge of its mouth.

Presently Bopa Lloyd came out of the kitchen to throw some potato peelings over the fence. When she saw me she looked glad, and when I gave her the parcel for her birthday she patted my face like a pony. She was a fat woman wearing a black flannel bodice with grey pin-stripes and a wet sack apron that hurt you when she wiped your nose with it. On her forehead she had lines across like you use for music, and her grey hair was coming down out of her combs like the feathers of an untidy hen. Her nostrils were black and big enough for her to put her thumbs up them, and there were three or four little round lumps of shiny purplish skin growing on her face, each very smooth and tight-looking and with a high polish on it. And one of these lumps, the glossy plum-coloured one on her chin, had a long brown hair curling out of the top of it. 'Shad,' she shouted, 'come from by there now and wash yourself for dinner.'

Just then a big drop of rain fell into the middle of the pan. The sycamore opened and let out a bird. Loads of dark clouds with torn wispy edges like black heavy hay were blown across the sky, soon leaving no blue. It became dark and cold, and big pieces of white water began falling heavily out of the sky and dropping cold as lead right through my thin blouse, wetting my skin. Bopa Lloyd hurried towards the kitchen door with her parcel like a hen off her nest, shouting to us: 'Go and shelter in the dubs while I get your dinner or you'll get wet soaking.' Em and I ran into the W.C. and Ewa Shad got up too and trotted down the garden, the peak of his cap on his neck and his working boots under his armpits. 'I been with the angels,' he muttered as he passed us, and we sat and watched him till the kitchen door had gulped him through.

Soon it was raining like tapwater and we heard the bumming of the thunderclap, but it was a long way off. From where we were we could see a big rain-stream pouring along a gutter the coal pickers had worn down the side of the steep tip outside the garden, and half-way down, where it met a big lump of orange shale, it spouted up into the air, curving high out like a fountain. We sat on the wooden seat of the lavatory watching the inky tips through the open door. Then when Em peeped out he said the pipe from the troughing next door was pouring rain into the garden. I could see it was broken off halfway down, and it swung loose against the wall like the empty coat-sleeve of a man with one arm, making a big rusty tobacco-stain on the white-lime of the wall. Em ran out into the rain, picked up the piece of piping that had fallen into the garden, and sloped it from the wall to the edge of his zinc bath sunk into the earth. Then he ran back again, and we waited for the pan to fill with water.

We could see the earth spitting hard with rain, and hear it hissing like poured sugar or a cockle-bed. Grey rain-fur grew round the pit-ropes of the fence and the iron bedstead and over the sheets of rusty zinc. The surface of the water in the bath swarmed with tall rain, each heavy drop as it fell bouncing up again like the bobbing rod of a sewing machine. Then two of Bopa Lloyd's hens, a white one and a ginger one, struggled through the hedge into the garden, their feathers stuck to them with rain. 'Shoo,' said Em, and the white one fell into the bath. Em laughed, but the chicken made so much noise Bopa Lloyd came out to the door of the kitchen drying her hands on her sack apron. When she saw what had happened she pushed Ewa Shad back, and swinging a towel over her head she ran round the side of the house and got a big shovel out of the coal-house. It was a collier's shovel, an old one of Ewa Shad's, shaped like a heart-shaped shield. With this she shovelled the chicken up out of the pan while the water ran out of the tool-bar hole in the corner. She kicked the piping down from the wall and shouted, 'Come on in now, boys, and have a meal of food.'

It was dark inside Bopa Lloyd's kitchen, but I could smell the fried onions and herrings cooking for dinner in the big fireplace where the row of bright candlesticks was and the brass horses in the hearth. The ceiling was brown wood with beams across, and the stairs curved down into the far corner. Some sheets of newspaper and two pieces of sacking covered the parts of the floor you walked on. When the back door opened it banged against the mangle which had a couch alongside with a bike on it. The wallpaper was brownish with purple birds and upright daisy chains of black roses, but Ewa Shad hadn't put it on well near the curve in the wall made by the stairs, and all along that side the stripes were diagonal. Our Mam said Ewa Shad must have two left hands.

'Emlyn,' said Bopa Lloyd, 'go and fetch your father's slaps.'

Four of us sat down to dinner, Bopa Lloyd, Ewa Shad, Em, and myself. Ewa Shad had washed a bit now, the middle of his face and the palms of his hands. He was a funny-looking man, pale, with a big oval face and round popping eyes, whitish grey and very shiny and wet-looking. On his head he had a brown covering of my father's armpit hair, and now that he had taken off his red flannel muffler I could see the swelling wen hung in his neck like a little udder, half of it grimy and half of it clean and white. When I went into the kitchen he was rubbing his back up and down against the edge of the open pantry door to scratch himself. He didn't say anything to me, he just rubbed and showed his teeth with the dirty dough on them. Then he sat down and read the tablecloth with his head twisted round on one side.

Bopa Lloyd sat on a chair without a back nearest the fire with her false teeth on the table in front of her. 'There's pretty trousers you've got on,' she said, as she served me half a herring. 'Let me see, a pocket and a coppish and all.'

Ewa Shad ate his potatoes and onions without saying a word, but he looked over all his food before he ate it, and sometimes he gave a loud wet belch. And every now and then he would start scratching himself, putting his arm inside his shirt and rubbing his chest, working around under his armpit to his back, and at last letting his fingers come back up through his open collar-band on to his wen. I was looking most of the time at the little purple potatoes sprinkled on Bopa Lloyd's face; they were so tight they looked inflamed, like little bladders ready to burst. Then I heard Ewa Shad and Bopa Lloyd talking loudly. Suddenly my Ewa stopped and stared before him with his mouth open. I could see the spittles stretched like thin wires from his top teeth to his bottom ones in an upright row.

'You'll be sorry,' he growled at Bopa Lloyd at last. 'You'll be sorry,' and he left the table and went up the stairs out of sight.

'What's the matter with him now, our Mam,' said Em, as though he was going to cry. 'What's he gone to bed without washing for?'

'Because he's gone dull,' said Bopa Lloyd, running her finger round her gums, her face very red. 'Since he's lost his job he's not a-willing to eat his fried onions if they're not all in proper rings. He's going daft, that's what's the matter with him.' Then she went quieter. 'Have you had enough of food, *bach*?' she said to me, putting her teeth back in her mouth. 'Don't take no notice of him. Try a bit of teeshun lap, will you?'

When she had sharpened her knife on the doorstep, Em and I sat down there, eating our cake and playing dixstones. We could hear Ewa Shad thudding about in his stocking-feet upstairs. The rain was slackening and by the time we had reached fivesy, it had stopped.

'Can we go out now, our Mam?' said Em.

Bopa Lloyd was sitting on the couch by the bike, sewing Ewa Shad's coat up under the armpit, and she said we could. We went into the garden. The heavy rain had made the place look different, there was gravel about and dirty pools with small-coal in them like mushroom-gravy. And the earth smelt strong as an animal. But the sky was clearing again, although the sunshine seemed weak after the rain. Then after a bit, as Em was pulling up a long worm to give to his fish, we heard someone throwing the upstairs window open, the one with the blue blouse across for a curtain, and Bopa Lloyd, her face very red, leaned her body far out of it with her hands on the sill. 'Stay where you are,' she shouted, waving her arm, and then, clapping her hand to her teeth, she disappeared suddenly like a sloped nail driven out of sight into a piece of wood with one blow. And then we saw a big heap of bedclothes like a large white cauliflower bulging out through the open window, with smoke oozing upwards in thin grey hairs from it as Bopa Lloyd pushed it out; and almost as soon as she had dropped it into the garden she came running out of the kitchen door. She began dragging the smoking bundle of sheets and blankets across the wet garden towards the bath of water. 'The silly flamer,' she kept on saying, 'the silly flamer. Matches with blue heads again. Every time he sees those flaming things he does something dull.' She piled the smoking bedclothes into the bath and at that Em began to cry.

'What are you grizzling at?' she asked, turning her red face towards him as she stooped.

'My fish,' he answered, pulling a little Union Jack out of his pocket. 'You'll kill it, our Mam; it's in the bath.'

'Fish *myn uffern i*,' she cried. 'Your father sets the feather bed on fire and you grunt about your fish. Get out of the road or I'll brain you.'

She stirred the bedclothes and spat on the garden. Em and I moved away and climbed over the wet bedstead. As we went slowly up the tip, Em wiping his eyes with his flag, we could see her standing in the garden striking a boxful of matches one by one, while Ewa Shad's two big staring eyes watched her without moving over the blue blouse in the bedroom window.

We wandered about on the flat top of the tips for a long time, afraid of Bopa Lloyd. Em showed me the hole where Ewa Shad had been scratching for coal. At last we came in sight of the old air-shaft in the distance, and Em said, 'Let's go right up to it.' The shaft was a pale yellow tower shaped like a lighthouse standing far up on the lonely side of the mountain. To get at it we had to go through a lot of brambles and tall bracken with snakes in it, but we didn't get very wet because we kept to the path. There had been a lean rainbow, but as we went towards the tower the sun blazed again, and the tips steamed like a train in a cutting. The shaft was very tall and built out of some cracking yellowish brick like shortbread. Some of the bricks were missing here and there, and right down near the ground we found a good-sized hole in the side. Em put his notchy head in and said, '*Brain*, look down there.' I lay down beside him on the steaming stones and looked into the dim hole. Every small sound resounded there, it was like putting your head into the hollow between the two skins of a drum. The shaft inside was huge, like a vast empty hall, like some shabby ruin with the floor gone through, very cold and bleak, the walls disappearing below us into the blackness, making you feel giddy and sick. And the spiders hung their webs there, round like a gramophone record or strong and dusty as sacking. Then, Em picked up a piece of brick and pitched it into the darkness. It plunged down out of sight like a diving bird and we could hear it striking the sides of the shaft from time to time with a note like the loud pong of a pitchfork and a stone howling over the ice. Then when we had waited and waited, staring down with our heads hanging over the cold blackness, we heard a terrible splash and roar like a train in a tunnel as the stone at last exploded on the water at the bottom of the shaft. The hollow pit broke out at once into an uproar, it was filled with a storm of echoes and the splashing noises of the water, and when at last all the sounds had died away the darkness was as still and silent as before. I felt sick and frightened, and we ran away together, a long loose patch across the behind of Em's trousers flapping like a letter-box in the breeze.

At last we climbed the warm bedstead and Em made straight for the bath to look for his fish. 'Go and ask Mam for a jam-jar,' he said to me, 'she'll give it to you.' I went up to the kitchen door and opened it. It was dim inside at first, but I could see Ewa Shad sitting on the bottom step of the stairs that curved down into the kitchen. He had his shirt and trousers on, but although he was wearing his cap he had no boots on his stockinged feet. And his waistcoat was open, the front of it like a looking-glass with grease. He was catching hold of the long curved knife, the carving knife Bopa Lloyd had cut our cake with, and he was sticking the point of it as hard as he could into the side of his neck. He was using both his hands to push the knife in, and it was going through the skin just below his ear. When I saw him cutting himself like that I went cold between my legs. Every time he stabbed he jerked his head sideways to meet the knifeblade, keeping his head stiff, so that the baggy wen on the other side gave a little shiver each time the point of the knife went out of sight into the side of his neck. There was blood all round his chin and his throat and down the front of his shirt, red and thick like jam. When I had watched him give two or three slow hard stabs like this, showing his teeth out of the froth round his lips, he stopped and stared at me with his swollen white eyes. Then he pulled up the leg of his trousers and started to scratch the back of his calf as hard as he could. His scratching seemed to go on a long time and then, just as he was about to start using the knife again, Em screamed behind me and Bopa Lloyd came down the stairs, her nostril-holes like thimbles as I looked up into them. When she saw what was happening, she pushed past Ewa Shad, snatched the knife from his hand and threw it on the fire. His eyes were like big, white, milk-bubbles staring up at her, and the lining was showing at the back of his cap. Gradually he slipped sideways on his step as though he was going to fall to the ground. Then with a shout Bopa Lloyd pushed Em and me out into the yard, turning the lock behind us. Em stood crying by the kitchen door, rattling the clothes-peg latch, and sometimes going to the window to look in over the cardboard mending the bottom panes. In a few minutes Bopa Lloyd unlocked the door and peeped out, and I had a whiff of the handle of the knife smouldering in the grate. Her red face glowed, it was the colour of a low fire, and the grey feathers of her hair were nearly all out of her combs. 'Go home now, there's a good boy,' she said to me, 'and tell your mother, thank you for the parcel and will she come up as soon as she can.'

'What's the matter with our Dad?' asked Em, making a face and crying all over his mouth.

'He's better now,' she answered. 'Go and play with your fish, there's a good boy.'

As I went home down the road I could see the bloodshot mark like a little smudge of red ink on Em's eye, and I thought again how lucky he was to have that. I told my mother how Bopa Lloyd's chicken had fallen into the bath, and how Ewa Shad had stuck a knife in his neck and made it bleed. And every time I went into the pantry in the dark or when I closed my eyes I could see the inside of the air-shaft with the big drop below me, and that made me feel sick and giddy. As my mother was dressing to go up to Ewa Shad's, she said, 'The fool couldn't even cut his throat tidy.'

Wat Pantathro

❧

I got the crockery and the bloater out of the cupboard for my father before going to bed. He would often cook a fish when he came in at night, using the kitchen poker to balance it on because we didn't have a gridiron. Then I lit my candle in the tin stick, and when I had blown out the oil-lamp I went upstairs to bed. My father was a horse-trainer, and on the handrail at the top of the stairs he kept three riding saddles, one of them very old, with leather handles in front curved upwards like the horns of a cow. We slept in the same bedroom, which was low and large, containing a big bed made of black iron tubes with brass knobs on the corner posts. Behind our thin plank door we had a cow's-horn coat-hook on which hung a trainer's bridle, one with a massive bit and a heavy cluster of metal fingers like a bunch of keys, to daunt the young horses. There were no pictures or ornaments in our bedroom, only a green glass walking stick over the fireplace and my father's gun licence pinned into the bladdery wallpaper. When I had undressed I said my prayers against the patchwork quilt which my mother had finished the winter she died. Then I climbed up into the high bed and blew the candle out.

But I couldn't sleep at first, thinking of my father taking me down to the autumn horse fair the next day. I lay awake in the rough blankets hearing the squeak of a nightbird, and Flower uneasy in her stall, and the hollow dribble of the dry plaster trickling down behind the wallpaper on to the wooden floor of the bedroom. I dozed, and when I awoke in the pitch darkness I could see narrow slits of light like scattered straws shining up through the floorboards from the oil-lamp in the kitchen beneath me, and by that I knew my father was home. And soon I was glad to see the light go out and to hear him groping his way up the bare stairs, muttering his prayers to himself and at last lifting the latch of our bedroom door. I didn't want him to think he had wakened me because that would worry him, so I pretended to be asleep. He came in softly, lit the candle at the bedside and then finished the undressing and praying he had started on his way upstairs.

My father was very tall and slender, his hard bony body was straight and pole-like. At home he always wore a long check riding jacket, fawn breeches and buttoned corduroy gaiters. He had an upright rubber collar which he used to wash with his red pocket handkerchief under the pump, but because he had not been to town there was no necktie round it. His face was long and bony, dull red or rather purplish all over, the same colour as the underside of your tongue, and covered with a mass of tiny little wormy veins. He had thick grey hair and rich brown eyebrows that were curved upwards and as bushy as a pair of silkworms. And when he pushed back his brick-coloured lips, baring his gums to get rid of the bits of food, his long brown teeth with the wide spaces between them showed in his mouth like a row of flat and upright bars.

He stood beside the bed for a moment wiping the greasy marks off his face with his scarlet handkerchief. He did this because when he balanced his fish over the fire it often tumbled off into the flames and became, by the time it was cooked, as black and burnt as a cinder. Then when he had done he blessed me with tobacco-smelling hands and laid down his warm body with care in the bed beside me. I listened, but I knew he had not been drinking because I could not smell him or hear the argument of the beer rolling round in his belly.

The next morning we went down to the fair in the spring body. This was a high black bouncy cart with very tall thin wheels painted a glittering daffodil yellow. It had a seat with a back to it across the middle and a tiger rug for our knees. Flower, my father's beautiful black riding mare, was between the shafts in her new brown harness, her glossy coat shining in the sun with grooming until she looked as though she had been polished all over with hair oil. As I sat high above her in the springy cart, I could see her carrying her small head in its brown bridle a little on one side as she trotted sweetly along. I loved her, she was quiet and pretty, and I could manage her, but I was afraid my father would sell her in the fair and buy a younger horse for training.

The hedges that morning were full of birds and berries. The autumn sun was strong after the rain and the long tree shadows in the fields were so dark that the grass seemed burnt black with fire. The wheels of the light cart gritted loudly on the road and the steel tyre came turning up under my elbow as it rested on the narrow leather mudguard. We sat with the tiger-skin rug over us, my father beside me holding the brown reins loosely and resting the whip across them, his hands yellow with nicotine almost to his wrists. He looked fresh and handsome in the bright morning, wearing his new black riding coat and his best whipcord breeches, and his soft black hat with the little blue jay's feather in it tilted on the side of his head. And round his upright collar he had a thick scarlet scarf-tie smelling of camphor, with small white horseshoes sprinkled all over it.

I said to him, 'We are not going to sell Flower are we, my father?'

'No, little one,' he answered, teasing me, 'not unless we get a bargain, a biter or a kicker, something light in the behind that no one can manage.' And then, with his tusky grin on his face, he asked me to take the reins while he struck a match on the palm of his hand and lit another cigarette.

It was six miles down to town and all the way my father waved his whip to people or drew rein to talk to them. Harri Parcglas, taking his snow-white nanny for a walk on the end of a thirty-foot chain, stopped to ask my father a cure for the warts spreading on the belly of his entire; the vicar under his black sunshade put his hand from which two fingers were missing on Flower's new collar of plaited straw and reminded my father he was due to toll the funeral bell the next day; and Lewsin Penylan the poacher, coming from his shed, brought a ferret whose mouth he had sewn up out of his inside pocket and offered us a rabbit that night if my father would throw him a coin for the shot. It was on the hill outside Lewsin's shed a month or two ago that I had been sheltering from the pelting storm after school when I had seen my father, soaking wet from head to foot, passing on his way home to Pantathro. He was riding a brisk little bay pony up from town, his long legs hanging straight down and nearly touching the road. He had no overcoat on and the heavy summer rain was sheeting over him from the cloudburst and running off his clothes as though from little spouts and gutters on to the streaming road. But although he was drenched to the skin and there wasn't a dry hair on the little brown pony, he was singing a hymn about the blood of Jesus Christ loudly to himself as the rain deluged over him. When he saw me he didn't stop the pony, he only grinned and shouted that it looked devilish like a shower. The boys who were with me laughed and pointed at him and I blushed with shame because they knew he was drunk again.

We came down into the town at a sharp trot and I could see the long narrow street before us crowded with people and animals. There were horses of every size and colour packed there, most of them un-harnessed and with tar shining in the sun on their black hoofs, and yellow, red and blue braids plaited into their manes and tails. And there was a lot of noise there too, men shouting and horses neighing and clattering about. The horses were all over the roads of the town and over the pavements as well, standing about in bunches or being led by rope halters up and down the street, or disappearing through the front doors of the public houses behind their masters. I hardly ever came to town and I loved it. From the high position in the cart where we sat, the crowd of bare backs before us seemed packed together as close as cobblestones, so that I thought we should never be able to get through. But my father governed our mare with his clever hands. He kept her going, waving his whip gaily to people he knew, even sometimes urging her into a little trot, easily steering his zigzag way among the mixed crowds of men and horses around us. And as we passed along he had often to shout 'No,' with a grin on his face to a dealer who asked him if Flower was for sale or called out naming a price for her. Because our mare was pretty and as black as jet and many people wanted her.

But just when we were taking the sharp turn out of Heol Wen at the White Hart corner, breaking into a trot again, suddenly, without any warning, we came upon Tal y Fedw's big grey mare, a hulking hairy cart-horse standing out at right angles from the pavement, with her thick hind legs well forward into the narrow street. Without hesitating for a moment my father leaned over and took the turn, and the axle-hub struck the big mare a stinger across her massive haunches as we passed, sending her bounding forward and then in a twist up into the air on her hind legs with pain and fright. The Tal y Fedw brothers, two short black little men, ran out at once cursing and swearing into the road to get hold of her head which she had torn loose from them. I was shocked and excited and I clung to the mudguard because the light trap with all the leathers wheezing rocked over on its springs as though it was going to capsize with the suddenness of the blow. And Flower, frightened by the shouting and by the unexpected shudder of the cart behind her, threw back her head and tried to swerve away across the road. I looked up anxiously at my father. He was grinning happily, showing the big boards of his teeth in his reddish face. He didn't stop at all when Tal y Fedw swore and shouted at him, he only whipped the mare up instead.

My father sold Flower after all to a man he met in the bar of the Three Horseshoes, the inn where we put up. Then, after the business was over, we went across to the large flat field which the farmers used for the horse fair. We wandered about for a time talking to many people and listening to the jokes of the auctioneers but I was downhearted because I wouldn't see Flower any more. And in the end my father bought a lovely slender mare with a pale golden coat to her shining like the wing-gloss of a bird and a thick flaky cream-coloured tail reaching almost to the grass. She was shod but she seemed wild, only half-broken, with wide-open black nostrils, and a thick-haired creamy mane and large dark eyes curving and shining like the balls of black marble on a gravestone. In a nearby field a fun fair was opening and each time the loud roundabout siren hooted the tall filly started as though she had received a slash with a cutting whip, her large black nostrils opened wide with fear at the sound, and she began dancing up her long slender legs off the grass as though a current of terror were shooting through her fetlocks. She edged warily out of my father's reach too as long as she could, keeping at the far end of the halter-rope, and when he put out his hand towards her dark muzzle she shied away in a panic, peeling open the terrified whites of her eyes as they stood out black and solid from her golden head. But he wouldn't have that from any horse and after a time she became quiet and docile, fawning upon him and allowing him to smooth, with hands that were almost the same colour, the glossy amber of her flanks. Then telling me to fetch her over to the 'Shoes, he handed me the halter-rope and walked off laughing with the man who had owned her before.

It was hot and sunny in the open field then, so bright that if a man threw up his hand it glowed crimson like a burning torch in the sunlight. The great golden mare trod heavily behind me, a thick forelock of creamy mane hanging tangled over her eyes, and her frightened ears pricked up sharply on her high head like rigid moonpoints. I didn't want to lead her, perhaps she was an animal nobody could manage, but I was ashamed to show my father I was afraid. I was almost in a panic going in the heat among the tall and awkward horses that crowded in the field, I was afraid of being trampled down, or of having a kick in the face from the hoof of a frightened horse. And most of all I dreaded that the fairground hooter would begin its howling again and scare this wild creature up on to her hind legs once more with terror and surprise. It became more and more frightening leading her across the crowded field with the hot-blast of her breath upon my flesh, I was sweating and in agony expecting her to shy at any moment or to rear without warning and begin a sudden stampede among the horses that crowded around us. My panic and helplessness as the tall blonde mare came marching behind me, large and ominous and with heavy breath, were like the remembered terror rippling hotly over my flesh one night as I sat alone in our kitchen through the thunderstorm, waiting for the endless tension of the storm to break.

But all the time my father, using long and eager strides, went ahead with the other man, waving his cigarette about, enjoying himself among the crowds and slapping the horses recklessly across the haunches with his yellow hand if they were in his way. 'Indeed to God,

Dafydd,' he shouted, jeering at a sallow man with a fresh black eye, 'you're getting handsomer every day.'

At last the gate came in sight, my hopes began to rise that I should get out of the field before the siren blared into the sky again. To leave the fairground we had to cross a shallow ditch which had a little stream in it because of the rain, and over which someone had dropped a disused oaken house-door to act as a footbridge. As soon as the young mare heard her front hoofs resounding on the wood panels she recoiled powerfully with fright and flung herself back against the rope, she began plunging and shying away from the ditch with great violence, her nostrils huge in her rigid head with surprise and terror and the fiery metals of her shining hoofs flashing their menace in the sun above my upturned face. I was taken unawares, but I didn't think of letting go. The halter-rope became rigid as a bar of iron in my hands but in spite of the dismay I felt at her maddened plunging and the sight of her lathered mouth I didn't give in to her. I clutched hard with both hands at the rod-like rope, using all my weight against her as she jerked and tugged back wildly from the terror of the ditch, her flashing forefeet pawing the air and her butter-coloured belly swelling huge above me. My father, hearing the noise and seeing the furious startled way she was still bucking and rearing on the halter-rope, ran back shouting across the wooden door, and quickly managed to soothe her again. Meanwhile I stood ashamed and frightened on the edge of the ditch. I was trembling and I knew by the chill of my flesh that my face was as white as the sun on a post. But although I was so shaken, almost in tears with shame and humiliation at failing to bring the mare in by myself, my father only laughed, he made nothing of it. He put his hand down in his breeches pocket and promised me sixpence to spend in the shows after dinner. But I didn't want to go to the shows, I wanted to stay with my father all the afternoon.

After the meal I had the money I had been promised and I spent the afternoon by myself wandering about in the fairground eating peppermints and ginger snaps. I was unhappy because my father had been getting noisier during dinner, and when I asked him if I could go with him for the afternoon he said, 'No, don't wait for me, I've got to let my tailboard down first.' I was ashamed, I felt miserable because he never spoke to me that way or told me a falsehood. In the fair-field the farm servants were beginning to come in, trying the hooplas and the shooting standings and squirting water over the maids from their ladies' teasers. I stood about watching them and when it was tea-time I went back to the inn to meet my father as we had arranged. My heart sank with foreboding when they told me he wasn't there. At first I waited in the Commercial, hungry and homesick, pretending to read the cattle-cake calendar, and then I went out and searched the darkening streets and the muddy fairground, heavy-hearted and almost in tears, but I couldn't find him anywhere. And after many hours of searching I heard with dismay a tune spreading its notes above the buildings and I saw it was ten by the moon-faced market clock. The public houses were emptying, so that the badly-lighted town was becoming packed with people, the fair-night streets were filled with uproar, and drunken men were lurching past, being sick and quarrelling loudly. I stood aside from them, near the fishes of the monumental lamp, weary with loneliness and hunger, glimpsing through my tears the ugly faces of the men who crowded swearing and singing through the green gaslight, wondering what I should do. And then, suddenly I realized I could hear someone singing a hymn aloud in the distance above the noise of the town. I knew it was my father and all my fears dropped from me like a heavy load as I hurried away because at last I had found him.

I ran along the dark and crowded street until I came to the open square outside the market entrance where the two lamps on the gate pillars had IN painted on them, and there I saw a lot of people gathering into a thick circle. I failed to get through the crowd of men, so I climbed on to the bars of the market wall at the back where the children had chalked words and looked over the bowlers and the cloth caps of the people. There was my father, his black hat sitting on the back of his head, standing upright beneath the bright gas-lamps in an open space in the middle of the crowd, singing 'Gwaed dy Groes' loudly and beautifully and conducting himself with his two outspread arms. But although he was singing so well all the people were laughing and making fun of him. They stood around in their best clothes or with axle-grease on their boots, laughing and pointing, and telling one another that Pantathro had had a bellyful again. By the clear green light of the pillar globes above the gates I could see that my father had fallen, because his breeches and his black riding coat were soiled with street dirt and horse-dung, and when he turned his head round a large raw graze was to be seen bleeding on his cheekbone. I felt myself hot with love and thankfulness when I saw him, my throat seemed as though it were tightly barred up, but I couldn't cry any more. He soon finished his hymn and the people began cheering and laughing as he bowed and wiped the sweat off his glistening head with his red handkerchief. And soon the serving men were shouting, 'Come on

Wat, the "Loss of the Gwladys", Watcyn,' but I could see now they only wanted to make fun of him while he was saying that sad poem. I couldn't understand them because my father was so clever, a better actor and reciter than any of them. He cleared away one or two dogs from the open space with his hat and held up his arms for silence until all the shouting had died down; he stood dark and upright in the centre of the circle, taller than anyone around him, his double shadow thrown on the cobbles by the market lamps pointing out towards the ring of people like the black hands of a large clock. Then he spat on the road and started slowly in his rich voice to recite one of the long poems he used to make up, while I muttered the verses from the wall to help his memory. As he recited in his chanting way he acted as well, gliding gracefully to and fro in the bright light of the ring to describe the pretty schooner shooting over the water. Or he held his tall, pole-like body rigid and erect until something came sailing at him over the mocking crowd, a paper bag or a handful of orange peel, and at that he cursed the people and threatened not to go on. When I saw them do that I went hot with shame and anger, because my father was doing his best for them. Then suddenly he stood bent in a tense position, shading his eyes, still as a fastened image with a peg under its foot, his eyes glittering under their thick brows and the big bars of his teeth making the gape of his mouth like a cage as he stared through the storm at the rocks ahead. Rousing himself he shouted an order they use at sea, mimicking a captain, and began steering the schooner this way and that among the dangerous crags, pointing his brown finger to the thunderous heavens, burying his face in his hands, embracing himself and wiping away his tears with his coat sleeves. Every time he did something dramatic like this, although he imitated it so well that I could see the mothers kissing the little children for the last time, all the people listening laughed and made fun of him. I didn't know why they couldn't leave him alone, they were not giving him fair play, shouting out and jeering all the time at his good acting. When the ship struck in the imitated howling of the wind he shrieked in a way that made my blood run cold, and began chasing about the open space with his arms outspread and a frightening look of terror and despair on his face. He was acting better than ever he had done for me in our kitchen, the sweat was pouring from him now because he was doing all the parts and yet the people were still mocking at him. Sinking his head resignedly into his hands and dropping on one knee in the middle of the circle he sang a few bars of the pitiful death hymn 'Daeth yr awr im' ddianc adre', in his beautiful bass voice. It was so sweet and sad I was almost breaking my heart to hear him. Some of the farm-boys took up the tune, but he stopped them with an angry wave of his hand, which made them laugh again. And then suddenly he gave up singing and as the sinking decks of the ship slid under the water and the mothers and the little children began drowning in the tempest he crouched down low on the cobbles with his hands clenched in agony before him, asking with the sweat boiling out of his face that the great eternal hand should be under him and under us all now and for ever. He forgot he was a drunken actor reciting before a jeering ring of people, he ignored the laughs of the crowd and behaved like a man drowning in the deep waters. He wept and prayed aloud to the King of Heaven for forgiveness, sobbing out his words of love and repentance, and when the ship with her little flags disappeared under the waves he dropped forward and rolled helplessly over with a stunning sound, his face flat downwards on the cobbled road and his limp arms outspread in exhaustion and despair. Just then, as he sprawled still and insensible on the cobbles like a flimsy scarecrow the wind had blown over, one of the spaniels ran up again with his tail wagging and lifted his leg against the black hat which had fallen off and lay on the road beside my father's head. The crowd laughed and cheered more than ever when they saw that and I could feel the scalding tears trickling down my face. I jumped down from the market wall and started to hurry the six miles home with angry sobs burning my throat, because the people had laughed at my father's poem and made him a gazing-stock and the fool of the fair.

All the afternoon I had dreaded this, and in the dark street before finding my father I had wept with alarm and foreboding at the thought of it. I knew I should never be able to manage the golden mare alone and bring her in the night all the way up to Pantathro. And now I was doing it, holding the whip across the reins like my father, and the tall indignant creature with her high-arched neck was before me in the shafts, walking along as quietly as our Flower and obeying the rein as though my father himself were driving her. I had prayed for help to God, who always smelt of tobacco when I knelt to him, and I was comforted with strength and happiness and a quiet horse. The men at the Three Horseshoes who had altered the brown harness for the mare said when I went back that if I was Wat Pantathro's son I ought to be able to drive anything. I had felt happy at that and ever since I had been warm and full of light inside as though someone had hung a lantern in the middle of my belly. At first I wished for the heavy bridle from the horn hanger behind our bedroom door for the mare's head, but now I didn't care, I felt sure I could manage her and bring her home alone. There was no one else on the road, it was too late, and no dogs would bark or guns go off to frighten her. And beside, it was uphill nearly all the way. Only, about a hundred yards from the railway I pulled up to listen if there was a train on the line, because I didn't want to be on the bridge when the engine was going under, but there was not a sound spreading anywhere in the silent night.

And what made me all the happier was that my father was with me, he was lying fast asleep under the tiger rug on the floorboards of the spring body. His pretty horseshoe tie was like a gunrag and the blue jay's feather was hanging torn from his wet hat beside me on the seat, but he was safe and sleeping soundly. When the men at the 'Shoes lifted him still unconscious into the spring body they examined him first, holding his head up near the light of the cart lamp. I saw then the whole side of his face like beef, and when they pushed back his eyelids with their thumbs the whites showed thick and yellow as though they were covered with matter. And on the inside of his best breeches, too, there was a dark stain where he had wet himself, but I didn't care about that, I was driving him home myself with the young mare between the shafts and I was safe on the hill outside Lewsin Penylan's already.

The night was warm, the moon up behind me and the stars burning in front bright and clear like little flames with their wicks newly trimmed. And in the quietness of the country the yellow trap-wheels made a pleasant gritty noise on the lonely road and from time to time the mare struck out bright red sparks with her hoofs. We passed the vicarage where one light was still lit, and came to Parcglas where Harri's snow-white nanny pegged on her chain chuckled at us like a seagull from the bank. I thought the mare would be frightened at this, so I spoke soothingly to her to distract her attention. She just pointed her sharp ears round and then went on smoothly nodding her high-crested head, her golden toffee-coloured haunches working in the light of the candle flame thrown from the two cart-lamps stuck in the front of the spring body.

The sloping hedges slipped by me on both sides of the white road. I wanted more than anything else to please my father after what they had done to him, shouting he had dirtied on the swingle-tree again and was as helpless as a load of peas, I wanted to bring him home safely by myself with the golden mare, and I knew now I should do it. Because at last I saw a star shining over our valley, a keyholeful of light, telling me I was home, and I turned into the drive of Pantathro without touching the gateposts with the hubs on either side.

The Last Will

❧

'Six golden sovereigns and that's another hundred,' muttered my little grandfather, his face red in the great blush of sunset.

That year was so dry our water-cask split and the rusty pump only gurgled gug-gug-gug when you worked the handle. And it was so hot your flannin shirt made you feel as though something terrible was going to happen. Then one week-night our preacher called a special meeting to pray for rain, and when my grandfather didn't trot back to his coffin after food, I thought he was going to chapel for once. I watched him lathered and in his grey-stockinged feet before the kitchen mirror – a gin advertisement it was, hanging in the open doorway – scowling like a fat-nosed Jew and scraping the growth of three days off his jowl with a cut-throat. 'Don't forget the little book, Mari *fach*, don't forget the little book,' he muttered out of a round hole in the end of his mouth to my grandmother, who was getting his black coat and waistcoat out of the mothballs, and the rubber collar with the breast attached he wore for his funerals. When he mentioned the exercise book I knew he was going to do another will.

My grandfather was the parish carpenter and undertaker. He was a very swarthy man, squat and stout, small in the head and feet but fat around the belly where the bulk of his weight bulged his trousers out like a giant poultice. He had only his grey flannel shirt and his baggy black-ribbed trousers on now, but when he crossed the road to our zinc shed to work at the coffins he always wore a coat braided with red piping and a velvet smoking cap with blue forget-me-nots worked round the edge of it. I liked to see him push his cap off to scratch his scalp because the top of his tiny head was as flat as a board, and from the back he looked as though two or three slices had been cut off the top of him. But this round platform wasn't bald or smooth, it was planted with tufts of thick rough hair like little trees and shrubs, it was like a little garden with plants and bushes growing out of the top of his head. As he stood there wiping the soap from his hairy ears in the doorway, and watching the sun glowing like a big red egg in the crimson sky, he was a bit Jewish-looking, with black eyes and a big baggy nose that used to bladder out when he blew it, and a soft bristly pouch of fat sagging between his chin and the neckband of his flannel shirt. He often used to laugh when he thought of his money, opening his big black mouth, and although his gums seemed vacant, the few teeth that remained there were fine upstanding ivories, a bit yellowish and slimy-looking perhaps, but still gaunt and majestic in their loneliness.

But my grandfather wasn't only a carpenter and undertaker, he was a lawyer as well. If you showed him a book, he would lower one black lid and squint along the edges of it with his carpenter's eye, because that was the only way he knew of finding out if it was a good one or not, but for all that he could read like a parson. And because he could write as well he used to draw up wills for the farmers around us who had plenty of means and who were anxious to save a few pounds lawyer's fee that way. Usually he took me with him, and when the neighbours wanted to know how much he was asking for his trouble he would refuse anything for himself and, with a hand black as a chimney brick on my hair, answer, 'Two pounds for the little boy,' or 'Ten pounds for the grandson,' according to the amount of money the people had. And whatever he said they had to pay because they were afraid he would hand them the dirty end of the stick with a shabby coffin or a dear funeral.

'Come to chapel for once tonight, Dafydd Penry,' pleaded my religious grandmother as we went out of the house in our best clothes.

'Not tonight, Mari *fach*,' he answered, 'not tonight. Six little pounds and we've got another hundred salted away.'

'Beware of covetousness,' she shouted after us as we went down the road, but my grandfather, who was wicked, only grinned, showing a single round white tooth like an ivory peg plugged into his upper gum.

Soon the meaty sunset was over and as we crossed the quiet fields it began to get dark. 'Whose will are you going to make, Dadcu?' I asked, going *lincyn loncyn* beside him.

'William Nantygors's at last,' he answered. 'And six of his sovereigns on to our ninety-four will make us another hundred.'

I was disappointed, it put pounds on my heart when he said where we were going, because William was a savage old creature, a widowerman everybody was afraid of, one who was always shouting out, 'Hook it, hook it,' if you went near the fences of his land. 'They say he's a miser, Dadcu,' I said.

'He is so mean that if he had two watches he wouldn't tell you the time by one of them,' he answered.

Although I was only nine or ten, my grandfather and I were about the same height, except for his high bowler hat. He always walked with little prancing steps, gliding up and down with his knees sagging in the way we used to play at trotting like a show pony. As he bobbed alongside me with his camphor smell, I watched the slow loll of his belly and listened to his ripe corduroys rubbing together, wheep-wheep-wheep, at every step. Because, although he had his bowler hat on and his best coat and waistcoat, he hadn't changed his working trousers or his hobnailed boots. He said he never would any more after Didi Gai's burial, where the sexton cut the grave too narrow and he spoilt his funeral trousers digging it big enough to get the coffin in.

'Six sovereigns for another hundred,' he muttered again, lifting up his bowler and scratching among the little herbs of his head.

As we were coming down a field on the steep breast we could see Nantygors where William lived alone below us, a dirty ruin of a house with a yellow window lighted up in the pine end and a big claw of ivy going up one side and over the roof like a birthmark growing on the side of a head. Although it was almost dark now, we could make out the bog all round, the marshland that had crept closer and closer to the farm as William's sons had quarrelled with him and left the nest for good and all.

'Nantygors,' said my grandfather, grinning and gliding, 'where we will soon be finishing another hundred, Joseph *bach*.' He trotted on, using the little tripping steps that years ago had caused the quarrel between him and William Nantygors. William, when he was sick in bed, asked my grandfather to pace out the distance round his rickyard for him so that he could buy some of the galvanized wire for it my grandfather was selling cheap. My grandfather did it and William bought the number of yards my grandfather said, but when he went to fix it, it wouldn't come to answer, he found he had about twice as much as he wanted because of my grandfather's short legs and little steps. They had words about their bargain and there hadn't been much Welsh between them for many years after that.

But before we got to the house we met Phylip Mawr Wernddu crossing the stile on his way to chapel. 'Good night, children,' he said to us in the dusk, but when he saw who we were he cried, 'Hallo, Dafydd, you are going the wrong way. Supplication service tonight.'

'No, no,' answered my grandfather, still bobbing up and down but not moving forward, 'I am going to visit the sick.'

Everybody loved Phylip Mawr, he was a big heavy old man dressed all in black, with a smell of red soap and a beard like a pointing trowel. And now because he was going to pray for rain he had his umbrella under his arm. But my grandfather didn't like him at all because he was always asking him to come to chapel and to put his shoulder under the ark. And once he knocked at the door of our shed, where my grandfather had our heights, my own and my grandmother's, pencilled up on the wall so that he could build our coffins for us if we died away from home. When my grandfather opened the door, old Phylip began talking about money, stroking his beard and saying he knew where plenty of it was to be found. 'Oh, where is it to be found, Phylip *bach*,' pleaded my grandfather in great excitement, reaching for his cap and his red-piped jacket, and nearly cutting his hand in two with the chisel. 'Where is it to be found in plenty, as you say?' – 'It's a pity you don't come to chapel oftener, Dafydd Penry, and then you'd know,' said Phylip, moving off. 'On the banks of the Jordan, man, everyone must leave his riches there!"

My grandfather never liked him after that, but he had to say he was going to visit William Nantygors, who was in a very bad condition.

'Indeed,' said old Phylip, 'he is a skeleton, that's all he is, a skeleton. If you want to make his will, Dafydd Penry, you had better hurry, because he will close his eyes at any time now, poor dab.'

'I didn't say anything about making his will,' answered my grandfather, offended, dancing up and down like a cock in the snow. 'And if I am going there to do it, you remember, Phylip Thomas, I am not like the men with the quills – I never take a ha'penny for my trouble.'

'Of course you don't, Dafydd *bach*,' said old Phylip, patting me on the head, 'of course you don't. But still the chick picks where the cock scratches. Good night, Joseph *bach*,' he said to me. 'Good night, Dafydd,' and off he went up the field to chapel, with his umbrella under his arm.

I was frightened to death, I could feel my mop standing up like knapweed on my scalp. I was sure that behind that yellow window pane I was going to see a real bone skeleton propped up white and chalky out of the bedclothes, with a skull like a large eggshell, and bare horse-teeth, and empty eye sockets, and no flesh on its bones to stop them rattling together when it moved about. I wasn't usually frightened by things like that, I was used to them. When my grandfather was busy in a hard winter, with his shed full, he would often varnish the coffins on the chairs in our kitchen, and at night if I came downstairs for a tin of water I would pass amongst them in the firelight, just as though they were pieces of furniture. And one night Rhoda Tyllwyd, who lived two miles up the road, carried the corpse of her dead baby to our house in her shawl, almost before it was cold, to have it measured for a coffin. I saw the little bare body lying pink under the lamplight on our kitchen table with Rhoda's big glassy tears on it like rain on cabbage, and as I helped my grandfather to run his inch-tape over it I thought nothing of it. But the picture of the old miser turned into a skeleton in that lonely house frightened the life out of me. I clung close to my grandfather in the darkness, afraid of William's washing spread out on the bushes, and nearly jumping out of my skin when his old white cow breathed hard in the hedge beside me. I would have given anything if my grandfather had said he would go back to chapel with old Phylip Mawr Wernddu.

But soon we were outside the back door of the farmhouse. 'Only six more pounds and I'll be lying on the little feathers,' I heard my grandfather mumbling against the brickwork as he rattled the latch. In a minute or two we saw the door opening and a woman's voice said, 'Who's there?' out of the darkness.

'It's me, Dafydd Penry,' answered my grandfather, 'come to see about the will of William Nantygors.'

'Come inside,' said the woman, and we went into the house where the upper half of a skeleton with no ears and only a black hole for a nose sat upright behind the yellow window.

The woman was William's daughter, Lwisa, who had come back from off to look after him, and because she had been pulling a fowl I could smell her long before I could see her in the dim passage. She and my grandfather stood whispering together a long time, they seemed to be plotting something, while I held tight to his tail with my heart thumping and the skin on my whole body gone too tight for me to breathe.

'Do you think he will last long now, Lwisa?' my grandfather asked her in a whisper. 'No, no,' she answered, 'that old owl was hooting outside again last night and today two pictures fell off the wall.' – 'Fair play,' said my grandfather, 'and how will he take it, do you think, me coming over the doorstep of Nantygors again after all these years?' – 'Don't you worry, Dafydd *bach*,' she answered, 'you and he were raised together and it's easy to light a fire on an old hearth when the grave is close by. We'll humour him and your six pounds will soon be safe in your pocket.' My grandfather seemed to brighten up at that. 'Lwisa *fach*,' he said, dangling his bowler behind his back, 'there's see you changed I do. You are getting too fat to get in your coffin, girl,' and he butted her towards the door with his big belly. They both laughed and we all went together into the back-kitchen, a small room lit by a miserable half candle standing in its own grease on the bible and the ready-reckoner by the window. The air in the room was thick with the smell of soot and sickness, you could cut it and it would open like liver. There was a wooden four-poster bed without any frill or curtains to it in one corner of the room and as I went forward in the gloomy half-light I fell over the branch of a tree lying right across the bare flags with one end of it smouldering in the bottom of the grate, where there were a few cinders glowing like a widow's fire. The whole place was thick with grey dust and full of heavy cobwebs, the room was everywhere festooned with them like a disused cowshed, they were like hangings of grey cheesecloth draped from the ceiling and fastening all the furniture to the walls. The only clear place in the room was the track from the door to the fireplace and the shiny armchair that old William had kept clear with his daily movements when he still had his legs under him. Everywhere else, over the pictures, and the dresser, and the fox in the case on the mantelpiece, were spread the grimy muslins of the cobwebs, thick with dust. The only bit of light in the room, too, was from that stump of candle stuck in front of the paper blind; the part nearest the window and the head of the bed was light – that was all; the rest of the room was gloomy and the spanish-brown walls were deep in shadow. You could tell how mean old William was by that, and by his working boots under the bed, tied up with white binder-twine instead of leather laces.

At first I was too terrified to look into the bed; I glanced everywhere with my heart thumping, around at the dusty grandfather's clock with the stopped hands dividing the face at six, and up at the bunches of bogbean and the sides of fat bacon thick with dust hanging out of the cobwebs from the butcher's hooks in the ceiling. I was afraid if I looked I was going to see the bone ribs like ladder-rungs and the chalky skull on top of them with the bare teeth chattering, the upper half of a skeleton sticking out of the bedclothes in the candlelight. But soon I saw William wasn't a real skeleton after all, although he was very skinny. He didn't say anything when we went in, he just lay there very drowsy, wearing a nightgown made out of a dark brown flour sack with a hole slit in the bottom for his head to come through and the corners cut off for his arms; he was propped up stiff against the pillows of his four-poster with his eyes shut and his long arms, bare and bony, spread out over the dark bedclothes. His fierce face was thin and whitish in the candle-light and hung with sagging festoons of loose skin; there was no meat on his bones and the loose folds and wrinkles of skin draped under his eyes and over his cheek-bones were caught back like window curtains each side of his toothless mouth, and his long neck was thin and skinny like the neck of a cock turkey. He was quite bald and his head was shiny, and climbing up across his white temple was a prominent zigzag vein, a bluish twisting tube looking as though a buried blue-bodied worm had burrowed its way under his glistening skin already. He had no hair and no moustache, but his eyebrows were stiff and heavy and because he hadn't shaved there was a faint sparkle to his jaws and his chin. He had changed a lot since I saw him last and he was for the worms now, I could see, but I couldn't take my eyes away after looking at him. I was fascinated by the hanging skin of his savage face and the thick blue blood-vein going zigzag up over his shiny temple.

William's short daughter brought the polished armchair to the bedside for my grandfather. Then she got another chair for herself, dusted it and sat down on it, lifting me on to her canvas apron. I didn't like her doing that, I wanted to be the other side of the bed by my grandfather. And besides, she had such a big swollen bust and a shallow lap that I kept sliding off her knees all the time, and my trousers were soon cutting me hot between my legs like cheese-wire. She was a short stout woman, bosomy, with small feathers in her hair and on her black flannel blouse from plucking the chicken, and all the time her face was a dull glowing red as though she had just come upright from a bending position. But the funniest thing about her was her mouth, because her wide-spaced teeth were set at right angles to her gums and splayed out between her rubbery lips like the stubbs of a banana bunch.

For a long time we all sat there in dead silence, the skeleton in the bed, my grandfather with his belly in his lap and a holy expression on his face, and Lwisa on the border of her chair, nearly pushing me off her apron with her heavy breathing. She didn't so much sit as hook the spare fat of her rump on to the edge of the seat and every now and then her rough hands would begin searching in my hair. Because the clock had stopped, the room was as silent as the grave, except that somewhere a watch was beating like a small heart, and from time to time the grit in the candle wick would splutter like a pinch of toenails thrown on the fire.

Then at last old William began as it were to chew the insides of his dry cheeks, altering the folds of skin upon his toothless face like the wrinkles moving on a pig's bladder when you begin to blow it up with a straw. And slowly lifting his thin lids he turned his face on the pillows to Lwisa and spoke in his heavy bass voice. His eyes under their stiff straw-like eyebrows were black and fierce, but bright, they shone like a shop-lamp from his dead face and I jumped to hear such a deep voice come out of the sitting bones.

'Lwisa,' he said, 'is there a drop of cold water in that cup by your elbow?'

'Yes, father,' she answered, very religious, 'will you have some now?'

She pushed me off her lap to help the old man to drink the water, as fussy as a hen with one chick, but closing his eyes again he said, 'No, I don't want it, but your tongue is sure to be dry with all the talking you've done to me this evening.'

Her hot face went red as a toasting fire and she smiled sheepishly, showing her teeth like a bit of machinery; she took the hint and began to explain she had brought her father's old friend and neighbour to help him make his will.

'Who is it?' he asked. 'Dafydd Penry the carpenter,' she answered, winking at my grandfather.

The old man opened his eyes and shot her an angry glance that missed her and went right through my shirt and into my heart. 'Dafydd Penry,' he growled. 'I'd see him coke first. A man who could jew a neighbour out of fifty yards of galvanized wire! If he is here, he had better put his foot to the earth fast, or I will get off my deathbed and turn him over the threshold of Nantygors myself.'

There was a lot of wrangling then between Lwisa and William, with my grandfather joining in now and then trying to keep the dish steady between them, with his little herbal head steaming. I couldn't understand all of it, but in the end they got the old man to agree to draw a line under their quarrel and to let my grandfather make his will. 'You must learn to forgive, my father,' Lwisa kept on saying, pulling me back on to her knees again, 'you must learn to forgive.'

'All right,' he answered, 'I'll forgive him because I'll soon have the big stone over me, but there's no need for you to forgive him, mind, Lwisa. If I thought you had forgiven him I wouldn't leave you a red penny, remember.'

'No, no, of course not,' she answered as she nodded and winked at my grandfather, who was sitting the opposite side of the bed again, glazed after shaving and like a dark toby jug with the top off.

Then old William began saying what he wanted done.

'The elbow, Dafydd Penry,' he said, 'is nearer than the wrist, and although the children have quarrelled with me I don't want a lot of old strangers who speak English and wear rubber heels to handle my money. So put it down that the money is to be shared between the children.'

'Very good,' said my grandfather, bladdering the long pod of his nose into his handkerchief and then writing in the little book. 'Very good indeed. But, William, don't you think Lwisa ought to have a little bit more than the others? She is the one who has come back to you in the days of your tribulation.'

The old man looked steadily at him with his hooded eyes and then began scratching at his knee-bones as though a worm was already eating its way in there. 'All right,' he said, in his gruff voice, 'she shall have the gold watch and guard off the dresser there, instead of Johnny Emlyn. He is not a quarter right, poor dab, and he doesn't know how to use one yet.'

'Not a quarter right!' said my grandfather with a crafty look, soaping the old man up as fast as he could. 'Not a quarter right! He's not a half right, and from the way he has treated you he doesn't deserve anything, the scamp. Why don't you leave his share to Lwisa altogether?'

The old man sat nibbling at this for a bit, casting suspicious glances at Lwisa and my grandfather all the time, and looking every now and then as though he was going to come to the boil again. But after a bit of arguing and coaxing they got him to agree to it, and then they went on in the same way for a long time, saying not to leave anything to Thomas Henry because he had a curl in his tail; and giving to William Francis would be like carrying water over the river, because he had any amount already; and since Marged Elin went in with the bread and came out with the buns it was best not to trust her with money now, poor thing; until the old man seemed to be leaving nearly everything he had to Lwisa.

But I was dead tired by this; every time I moved my eyes bobbed to and fro in my head with weariness and bad air and at last, in spite of my cutting trousers, I began to doze. I didn't want any rocking that night and soon I was fast asleep on Lwisa's lap.

I don't know how long I slept there on those short thighs, but I woke up abruptly when Lwisa threw me into the foot of the four-poster. There was a riot in the room and I saw her springing forward to hold old William down in bed. 'I've had a bellyful of this. No cup will hold more than a cupful,' he was shouting, trying to get at my grandfather with his claws and shaking the loose skin and pouches of his face. 'I'll do what I like with the money, Dafydd Penry,' he yelled. 'Leave you six pounds for the grandson, indeed! I'll settle who's to have the money. Who's dying, me or you, you scoundrel.' He struggled so hard his eyes went into a bad squint and the blue blood-vein in his head swelled up to such a size I thought it was going to burst. He seemed to lose all his weakness, he was shouting and tossing his scarecrow arms about so that Lwisa and then my grandfather had to hold him down fast by the nightshirt and the ankle, while the bedclothes overflowed on to the flagstones. 'But fair play, father, fair play,' Lwisa pleaded. 'Dafydd Penry must have something for his trouble. He must live, like all of us.' – 'Live,' the old man howled back at her. 'Live, did you say? Dafydd Penry will live where the crows will die, so don't you worry about him living.' 'Leave upsetting him, Lwisa *fach*, leave upsetting him,' said my grandfather, pulling the bedclothes back over old William's feet. 'Always best to pat the head of a wicked dog. Die now, little William,' he went on soothingly, 'everything is settled, so die now tidy for me and Lwisa, there's a good boy.' Gradually the old man became exhausted again, and soon the uproar was over. While Lwisa dried the sweat off his head, I fell fast asleep again, seeing first my grandfather winking and tucking his rubber front back into his waistcoat after the struggle.

When I awoke the second time everything seemed different. The fire had gone out and there wasn't a sound in the room. I looked up towards the top of the bed and there was Lwisa tying her father's jaw up with a piece of pudding-cloth and in the corner shadows by the dresser was my grandfather in his shirtsleeves trying on a new pair of trousers over his corduroys. I saw him take his eyes out of the corners. 'Do you think he's gone, Lwisa?' he whispered.

'He ought to be,' she answered, 'I've held his mouth closed long enough. But I can't get this cloth to stay round his head.' As she tried her teeth-ends showed out through the mound of her lips.

My grandfather came prancing into the candle-light, wearing the brand-new pair of trousers, too long in the leg and too tight round the middle. He drank up the brandy and the jug of bogbean off the table and then, sidling up to Lwisa with his white fang grinning and giving her a dig with his elbow, he said, 'What about the six pounds, Lwisa?'

'Very good, Dafydd,' she whispered, 'you tie him up and I'll feel under the mattress for the stocking.'

I knew old William was dead but I was too tired to care. I lay half dozing in the foot of the four-poster and saw my grandfather go to William's hard bald skull that was shining in the candle-light smooth and hard as a bubble of glass, with the blue tube still to be seen in it. I saw him tying his jaw up with the grey rag and bragging to Lwisa that he could always tell at once if a customer was dead or not by the feel of the gums, even Didi Gai, who was fat as a breeding-sow and still warm three days before the funeral when he went to deliver her coffin, because the hot weather and her feather bed had kept her heat in under her.

Then as he was finishing his job Lwisa groped out a long black woollen stocking with a white toe from under the mattress and held it up while the two of them grinned at each other, one each side of the bed, showing their different teeth. The next moment they were in the shadows by the dresser with their backs to me, my grandfather's little head so queer it looked as though a heavy blow had hammered it flat. They were there a long time, whispering and laughing quietly, and at last I heard my grandfather dropping coins into his hand, counting out his sovereigns 'two – three – four – five – six.' But the moment he finished there was a tremendous crash of thunder that shook the house from its foundations to its eaves and gutters, the yellow spire of flame on the candle cowered with the shock, and the whole dusty room trembled violently on its foundations, as though it had been almost bumped over by the charge of a powerful row of bulls. Lwisa and my grandfather stood stock still waiting for silence again in the quaking house, but before they could move the grandfather's clock in the corner began slowly striking as though it would never stop, it crashed out the strokes at the top of its hoarse voice, retching and making dry noises among the wheels and chainwork of its unoiled inside, and finishing the sixth stroke with a deafening crash that sounded as though it had smashed its inside to pieces, beginning with the broken bell. Strike – strike – strike – strike – strike – strike – and outside the pouring rain hissed down suddenly in tons around the hollow house. Lwisa and my grandfather looked at each other and then turned together towards the head of the bed. The way they stared, as though they had seen a roaring ghost, Lwisa with the whites of her eyes showing and my grandfather with his fat black underlip hanging out of his face like a windowsill, made me look, too, in the same direction. For a cold second I saw William with the pudding-cloth hanging in a loop on his chest and his black eyes wide open; he was staring straight before him at Lwisa and my grandfather, holding on to their stocking by the dresser. His white face seemed all skin against the rough brown sacking of his nightgown, his eyelids and his cheekbones were hung with sagging skin and his scraggy chicken's throat had enough loose flesh for two necks hanging around it. But he was breathing, and his two black eyes under their thick thatch of eyebrows were wide open, watching the fat little figures by the dresser. Then his wattles began to move, but before he could say anything my grandfather, the sweat like glass beads buried in his face, jumped with a loud yell out of the shadows and snatching me off the foot of the bed dragged me towards the door of the kitchen. But in his hurry he forgot the tree-branch lying across the floor and it tumbled him over with a heavy thud so that he lay kicking like a black beetle on his back, and before we could get out of the room we saw Lwisa in the armchair with her eyes going round and round in her head and William sitting down on the floor in his nightshirt pulling his boots on with his claws.

When we opened the back door we heard the loud roar of the rain like rooks rising and the night was pitch black before us, it was like looking into a dark cupboard, but we dashed without stopping out into the yard in the pouring weather. As we splashed our way forward through the deep mud, the thunder would pound the heavens above us and big sheets of lightning would drop out of the sky in one piece, lighting up the pouring rain. But we didn't wait to shelter although we were soon soaking wet, all we wanted was to get away from Nantygors as fast as we could. We hurried forward, my grandfather in his bowler hat and his shirt-sleeves, stopping his trot every few yards to hitch up William's trousers that were dragging in the mud. We splashed our way on, passing close to old Phylip Wernddu, who was singing a hymn under his umbrella on his way home from chapel. But the night was black as a bull's belly and he didn't see us, and soon we reached the stone stile. There, just as we were crossing over, we saw William Nantygors by a flash of lightning, standing outside the house on the edge of the bog in his boots and his boiled night-bag. He was tall and narrow, like a long-legged scarecrow in the pouring rain, with his thin head and his skinny arms showing out of the corners of his black nightgown. In his hand was the long stocking and by the next flash of lightning we saw it sailing out over the bog, the golden coins from it in a shower in the lightning as they scattered flashing over the muddy land.

I looked at my little grandfather and he was crying steadily in the darkness beside me, he was sitting on top of the stone stile in his shirt-sleeves and his bowler hat, crying, with the rain pouring over him.

'What's the matter, Dadcu?' I asked him. 'What are you crying for?'

'It's my six sovereigns and my little book,' he sobbed aloud. 'I left them on the dresser and William has thrown them into the bog.'

'Never mind,' I said, trying to comfort him, 'we'll make another will somewhere else soon. Perhaps for Mari Cyn Adda – she isn't looking very healthy these days.'

'Never again,' he said, 'never again. I have finished, and my fiddle is in the thatch. I ought to have seen that I could never get the better twice of William Nantygors. Everybody knows that even if the devil was on the other side of the broth-bowl William would get the bread. Joseph *bach*, I ought to have known better.'

He sat there crying in the thunder and lightning and I couldn't get him to budge, until at last the hailstones tapping at his bowler hat and a wind like the cold coming under the door made him start trotting home again.

It rained hard all night and the next morning we heard that with the flooding of the stream, Nantygors and everything in it had gone under the mud.

Price-Parry

෧

Snow and darkness lay thick over Llanifor Fechan and all the boots in the village were under the beds. Suddenly night came off the sky like a shirt, and a vast red orb of sun rose up intolerant and masterful above the earth, watching the world from the back of the mountain. It glared down upon the sweep of snowy landscape, upon the ring of hills black with stiff trees like wooden hairs and on the pan-shaped hollow in the middle of the white fields where the village chimneys began to steam up into the morning. The earth turned colour under the ruddy gaze and the houses caked in the bottom of the pan were transfigured. The panes of the hillside vicarage blazed like slabs of pure copper; Glandwr's unsoiled roof was pink and on the sills of the little windows were wedges of pinkish snow; and the tumbledown cottage of Mati Tŷ-unnos blushed in the glare of the sunrise, its low and scabby walls bulging outwards like the wallow of a bitch in heavy whelp.

And when the whole land was lighted another orb rose in counter arrogance to the west of the village, as majestic and domineering as the first, and almost as all-seeing; it too exalted itself and looked out in rival possessiveness and mastery over the snow-clad scene. It was the blue eye, cold and blue as ice-water, of the Reverend Roderick Pari Pryce Price-Parry, son of the sons of Rhodri Fawr, Vicar of Llanifor Fechan, surmounting at daybreak the shawl-fringe of his four-poster to find if this were burial weather. Seeing the snow still thick it stopped. The hillside graveyard would be bitter cold. With grandeur in its sweep the icy eyeball and its blue fellow blazed at the silver watch hung on a horse-nail hammered into the wooden bedpost. It was time to rise. As the tall vicar put on his dark clothes he saw the village below him steam like a vomit and the black reaping-hooks of his eyebrows contracted. He turned away, thinking of his tree and the paintings fastened upon his parlour wall.

On the boards of Geta Glandwr's bedroom hung a little mirror framed with plush and cockleshells, and as she woke with her mother's shout she saw the risen sun's reflection glowing in the glass like a ball of molten bronze. She sat up in her nightdress watching, and heard a gambo-wheel crack, a dog and a cock bark and crow together, and then the ring of the thick milk belling into the pail. She scrambled out of bed, said her prayers and looked from the window into the farmyard below. There was interlacing snow on the orchard boughs like a shawl of thick knitting laid over the trees in one piece. The cart-shed, left open all night, had a strip of snow along the top of the door and leaning against the white-thatched rick was a ladder with snow on every rung. It would be cold leading the vicar's horse to the graveyard. Geta shivered at the thought of it, as though a snowflake had fallen into her ear.

The hanging blood-ball showed itself hot too at the one-pane window of old Mati Tŷ-unnos. But she did not look at it, or rise, or care a scratch how chill the day was going to be. She was lying cold and still. She was lying dead.

The vicar stood with his back to the empty fireplace, staring about at his bare kitchen, small, cold and comfortless in the gloom. It was half underground, built like a kind of stone cellar into the hill at the back of the vicarage and the small window was up near the ceiling. Moisture ran down the unwiped walls as though they were the sides of a vault. Large thick slabs of blue slate with black warts growing out of them paved the floor. There was a shelf for boots over the back door where a pair of waders hung from a cup-hook, and a thick wooden peg was driven into the chimney wall to hold the pony's harness. On the bare plank table beneath the dim light of the window lay a broad-brimmed clerical hat, and a large black cloak was piled on the seat of the armchair alongside it. The hat had a round disc of grease on the top as though all the fat of the vicar's body was slowly oozing out through the top of his head.

Large and ominous in the gloom Price-Parry shivered on the hearthstone in his ancient clothes. Even the back of his tongue felt cold and he was rubbing his hands together to try to warm them. His fingers were large and knuckly, the big nails flat and yellow like sheets of thin horn. He was a very tall bony man, bow-backed and eagle-beaked, his out-thrust face ecclesiastical brass and his white hair, parted in the middle, drooping in a curve on each side of his head like the pages of a bible open at the 97th Psalm. His yellow features were covered with smooth book-skin and bending from his jawbone down into his collar were two or three ribs of loose flesh like the curved vaulting of a church roof. As he waited for Geta, he saw the mocking face of Mati Tŷ-unnos before him, refusing to call him 'sir', and his fierce blue eyes blazed round in indignation at the boot-rack and the wood of the armchair like streaky bacon, and the rusty duck-gun leaning against the streaming wall.

Soon there came a knock at the kitchen door, and when Price-Parry had shouted 'Come in,' he heard a kicking noise outside as Geta knocked the snow off her clogs before entering the house. When she came in the waders swung to and fro in the dimness behind the door and at once she remembered how the first time she entered the gloomy kitchen she ran out again screaming because the sight of those feet not reaching the slate slabs made her think the vicar had hanged himself from the bacon hooks.

As she stood demurely before the towering vicar she was small and dainty, she seemed light and birdlike as though she might at any moment begin hopping or pecking under her armpits. She had a small white face as compact as the face of a watch and two curved hair-slabs of gold met along the middle of her head. She wore a thick grey overcoat made prettily out of a blanket with a belt and bright stripes on it as blue as grass. She had her thick black working stockings on and her canvas apron showed below the hem of her overcoat.

Geta was a kind-hearted girl and for months she had gone daily into Mati's cottage to look after her in her last illness. As she stood before the black and yellow vicar, looking so handsome to her now because he was cold, she said 'Good day, if you please, sir,' and dropped him a curtsey. He swung his fierce bird-head from side to side before replying and then pulled the skin back off his yellow teeth. They were large and three-cornered, the points fastened up in the gums. 'Good day, good day,' he said, staring down hard at her in his overbearing fashion. When the vicar stared, Geta noticed, he did not so much slide back his lids as push his eyeballs farther out of the bones of his face. But he hardly saw her, thinking how Mati Tŷ-unnos who had thwarted and provoked him so long was now lying dead, and within an hour or two would be buried for ever. The thought pleased him. He smiled again. He would show this child his tree. 'Margaretta,' he shouted down at her, 'have you heard about my tree?' – 'Yes, if you please, sir,' she answered curtseying once more. 'Everybody has heard about your tree, sir.' Price-Parry dropped his lip back over his teeth. 'Would you like to see it?' he threatened. 'Yes, if you please, sir,' said Geta.

Leaving the dim cellar, he led the way through the passage to the front of the house and Geta slipped off her clogs to follow him. In the darkened parlour his boots creaked about as though they had been by the fire, but at last he divided the curtains a bit and let a thin sheet of icy white sunlight into the room. Geta stood like spoon-food outside the busy mouth, waiting patiently to be invited into the shadowy room, making out the desk in the darkness and the books with shields on them lining the walls and the long narrow picture covered with sacking that reached almost from the floor to the ceiling.

'Come in and stand here,' he commanded, pointing with the stiff twigs of big fingers to a bald spot in the carpet well back from the picture. Geta crept in on feet soft as rabbit-pads and stood on it. Price-Parry had a bright seat to his serge as he bent down in the sunshine and rolled the long piece of canvas up off the picture.

Near the bottom of the thick frame Geta saw a stiff man very much like the vicar lying on the ground wearing an overcoat but no trousers. There was a hole in the breast of his coat and into this disappeared the bark-covered roots of a tree. The rest of the picture was packed with leafy branches on which hung names and little paintings like square fruit. The vicar told Geta the man lying down on the ground was Rhodri Fawr, King of the Kymry, and the little pictures showed the gold-gowned fathers of Price-Parry marrying, ruling and killing one another. He smiled and rubbed his hands together, a little warmer now even in a house where the crack of a fire was never heard, as the slice of sunlight made the little paintings glisten.

Geta stood, not looking at the tree, watching the vicar, with her coat open and her hands under her canvas apron. 'Do you like it?' he said, creaking like upholstery as he moved about in his stiffness. 'Look, this is Griffith Frith, lord of the top half of our parish. And here on the lowest branches, where the tree divides, are the six sons of Rhodri Fawr. Can you see them from there?'

'Not very well, if you please, sir,' she said.

He came back and stood close to her, his peering face out-thrust and the skin of it yellow over the bird-bones.

'Twti down a bit,' he said doubtfully.

She twtied.

Then with loud cracks he bent low himself until his head was nearly resting on the floor. She could see his flannel shirt inside his gaping collar and the crop of warts on the front of his neck, each with a little bow of cotton tied round it.

'This one here,' he went on, getting up again and going back to the picture, 'is Griffith Benfras. This one is Ifor ap Cynan ap Maredydd ap Rhisiart. And here at the very top of the tree,' he cried, getting on to a chair and pointing triumphantly to a name near the ceiling, 'is Meurig ap Rhys Goch, my great-great-great-great-grandfather.' He sneezed like glass smashing and then turned round. 'What are you twti-ing down for?' he asked. 'If you please, sir, you told me to sir,' she replied, looking up at him. He scowled, coughed and took out his silver watch. 'Harness the pony,' he commanded. 'I shall be with you in two minutes.' He got down off the chair frowning. Geta straightened herself and crept silently out of the room to harness the pony.

The vicar sat upright in his high-wheeled cart, wearing his waders, his black hat and his big cloak, gazing out over the snow-clad country with the glance of a bird of prey. His breath floated about, blown over his face like fine powder as his stare dominated the white fields and the weak sun that was now dissolving above them like a lump of pale butter. Before him marched the stiff-limbed gingerbread horse, his thick unclipped hair standing out at right-angles to his skin and his frozen legs unbending at the knee-joints. Geta trudged through the snow holding his bridle. 'A little child shall lead them,' murmured Price-Parry as he spread out his cloaked arms like a king on the seat each side of him.

Geta too looked about her as she went along at the pony's head, seeing the starlings hopping like flocks of rabbits on the white slopes, and a bramble-bush rising low off the field as though it were the bones of a snow-buried skeleton. She thought of old Mati Tŷ-unnos, soon to be buried, and cried a little to herself with cold and grief. She pondered on the walk she had done every morning to Mati's tiny cottage which had a curved red horn of a chimney, and scabby white-washed walls like flesh with a poultice just taken off, and an overgrown thatched roof gay as a garden in summer with foxglove and willow herb and dandelion. Morning after morning old Mati had lain in bed until she got there, her foot cold as though it had stood in the river, watching the black stump of her bandages take shape against the glow or primrose of her one-pane window. Under the thick blankets she was a swollen load, heavy, a bedful, a big spreading old woman with a long egg-like face showing over the quilt-edge, her skin covered with a tangle of little lines and cracks like the cheek of an old broth basin. She wore a couple of firm grey plaits wool-wound at the ends over the bedclothes, and on the top of her head was a greasy black felt hat with crimson pork-scorings down the crown and a glass-headed hatpin stuck through it, glistening white as a glassy eyeball fixed unblinking on the morning. She had learnt to keep dead still at night because every time she shifted the four brass balls fell off the bedposts into the bed.

As Geta cleaned and fed her, they talked of her repentance and of the time before that when Mati had a little grey donkey and a flat two-wheeled cart and earned her living by carrying the farmers' eggs and rabbits up to market. Shâms Bach was so small his four little shoes wouldn't cover your hand and the people used to say that when he fell down ill in the field, poor dab, Mati carried him into the kitchen in her apron to give him a cup of small beer. And they used to say, too, that once when Mati had had a skinful she rolled to the back of the cart and her weight hoisted the little animal right up off the road. But she was loath to tell Geta that, or that a few times she had stood before her betters in the court, or that once or twice a low-flying baby had happened to fall into her lap. She was only a repentant and balloon-legged old woman now whose toes every morning were cold as icicles until the passing sun shone into her cottage and warmed her bandaged foot so that it began to smoke like a steam pudding before the window.

'Geta,' she said, when she knew she could not last much longer, 'I am not afraid to cross the Jordan now after what you have told me and read to me. On the other side there are not only black marks against us in the big book, there is a big ginger-rubber there too to rub them out, isn't there?'

'That's right, Mati,' said Geta. 'If we repent we will be forgiven everything.'

Mati considered a bit, wearing on the long egg of her face her little glasses with brass frames.

'It won't matter if I can't speak much of that old English there, will it, Geta? Indeed now.'

'No, no, not at all,' Geta told her. 'But go to sleep there's a good girl or you won't feel worth a roast potato.'

'I will do whatever you tell me, and I thank providence fifty times a day for you, my sweetheart,' she answered.

In the mind of the vicar too ran the thoughts of old Mati. He sat brooding in his cart, his head outstretched on a long bony neck that looked as though it had lost its feathers and the wind splitting against the edginess of his beaked nose as the river divides at the sharp arches of the village bridge. He recalled how she had always jeered at him and made sport of him, and the thought of it knitted the black sickles of his meeting brows. One blazing hot day he remembered he had caught her up driving Shâms Bach to market wearing a grey shawl and a hat with a new red ribbon. On the cart was a butter tub with the unprotected butter running like water in the heat and leaking out all over the cart. As he passed she called after him. 'Vicar,' she shouted, sounding as though she had stopped often after leaving Llanifor Fechan. 'Vicar, there's proud you are. Where are you going to?'

'I'm walking to market,' he said shortly. 'The pony has cast a shoe.'

'For the sake of everything, jump up here,' she shouted, patting the box she was sitting on.

He looked down from his great height at Shâms Bach but he did not reply. Every night as he put his head to the pillow of his four-poster he heard the blue blood of Rhodri Fawr march past his ears. Soon his long legs had carried him ahead. 'Are you ashamed of the little donkey?' she shouted after him. 'There's no need for you to be. Your Master rode on the back of one of these.'

The vicar took off his hat and shook his lion-locks at the remembrance of it. Mati Ty-unnos, the by-blow, the bush-begotten, the chance-child and the mother of chance-children. Even now on his way to bury her the thought of her transgressions against his pride tasted bitter as bogbean in his belly. When her second child came he went to the little cottage to speak to her about the baptism. There was the thatched roof in full bloom, and the little shaggy rick in the yard looking as though it wanted to scratch itself against the wall, and Shâms Bach to be seen through the window in the field outside with a tremendous crow standing outspread on his little back. Mati was sitting by the fire giving suck to the child because Wil Saer was there putting a new leg in the stool.

'William,' bawled Price-Parry coming down the path. 'Leave off your hammering. I want to talk to Mati Rees.'

'Yes, sir; at once, sir,' said Will. He touched his cap and went out the back way. He was a heavy man with thick fluffy moustaches that covered his mouth and had taken root in his cheeks.

'So you've got a new baby again,' said Price-Parry standing at the low doorway, the fierce bird-bones of his head hung forward into the kitchen. Mati smiled up at him. 'That's how it is,' she said. But although the kite-eyes were masterful upon her she was cool, she didn't alter a feather.

'Is it a boy or a girl?' he thundered.

'Give a guess,' she answered at once. He was taken aback. He frowned. He saw Wil Saer safe outside grinning in through the back window.

'A boy, a boy,' he guessed impatiently.

'No!' she replied. 'Give another guess.'

'Well, a girl,' he shouted back at her.

'Ay, how did you know then? You must be a wiseman, or somebody told you.' She smiled up at him again with her long-fleshed face.

He warned and denounced her with all the power of his mouth, crying woe from the doorway upon her fornication and debauchery until the baby began to howl. 'Put that child back on the breast,' he shouted, coming at last to Rhodri Fawr, his little pictures and his tree. But at that she lost her temper. 'It's a pity you haven't got a photo of your Uncle Roderick on your old tree, getting out of his carriage to throw my grandfather and all us children out of Parcau Bach on to the road, the endless tyrant. Get out of here, get out, get out, Price-Parry,' she shouted, 'or I'll break your back with a pole.'

But today Mati Tŷ-unnos lay quiet in her coffin, the body that had known the sweat of lechery was at last at rest, having reaped in reward for its sinfulness, corruption and a leaking foot and death. In half an hour it would be all over. He saw the church spire over the snowy hedges close ahead with the green cock still crowing into the east.

Snow lay all over the grass and the tombstones and the daylight was beginning to fail on the countryside. In the middle of the graveyard rose the little church with a light burning in the vestry window and around it stood a grove of bare trees like the picked black bones of a monster.

Geta crouched holding the pony's head and watching the burial over the low cemetery wall. She saw the vicar reading the service at the graveside while a small group of people in gloves and overcoats stood beside him listening. She was too far off to hear what he was saying, but as he spoke he huddled down low on the earth, pointing into the hole, and then rose like a great white bird to his full height. Would he take off, Geta wondered, would wings leap from his shoulders and bear him out of sight over the church and the trees? He fluttered down to his normal size again. Soon he turned away and strode back to the little church to change while the handful of mourners touching their hats moved off towards the graveyard gate. Mati Tŷ-unnos was buried.

Geta crouched from the cold against the stonework, hoping the vicar would not be long. The daylight was becoming dim and when she peeped over the wall to see if he was coming the vestry light seemed brighter, more intense. The red pony began plucking grass out of the mortar and while she waited she played idly with some pale snail-shells striped like peppermint humbugs that she found in a hole in the wall. Suddenly she awoke with a start. The vicar in his black clothes, wearing around his neck a wide collar of his own breath, was bending down and shaking her by the shoulder. 'Margaretta, Margaretta,' he was shouting. 'Get up into that cart at once. God forgive me, I mean will you please get up into the cart my child?' He pushed her up the iron step and guided her gently into her place and then flicking the reins sat down on the seat beside her. The pony moved off willingly down the lane. The vicar's blue eyes glittered, his bare skin gleamed like backing-silk. He looked very queer to Geta, warmer than he had ever looked before. Had he been drinking in the vestry, she wondered, or was he saved? He drove the red horse along the snowy lane laughing and murmuring to himself.

' "Repeat or repent," she said to me, Geta,' he muttered, spreading his great baggy cloak out over her shoulders. ' "Repeat or repent,

Roderick," she said to me. "You are an old man, your time is short now. Do not drown three inches from the shore. Show you have gathered wisdom and not only warts on your skin." ' He laughed like a narrow bottle filling up with water.

Geta was afraid to ask him whom he was speaking about. Why was he laughing and sitting up here beside her with his arm around her when, like a mangy king, as Mati called him, he always wanted to be led about the roads to every marriage and burial in the parish? From the narrow of her eye he looked thin, flushed and handsome to Geta. Perhaps he was ill or beginning to be queer. At last she said to him – 'Please tell me who you are talking about, sir.'

He turned his narrow face towards her. His nose under the broad-brimmed hat was a blade, a curved out-bending blade with a sharp edge to it. 'As I was taking off my surplice by the candle,' he said, 'she oozed steadily through the vestry door like the fog through a bare bush, she stood before me in the guise of a great queen. "Mati," I said to her in my overbearing way, for which heaven forgive me, "Mati," I said, "beware, beware. I have just buried you legally, with reverence and holy writ. What do you want with me? Get back into your coffin at once, my girl." But I could see Geta *fach* she was not the same Mati as I had put safely under the ground. When I look out among the countenances of our short-legged peasantry, no, I mean among the faces of my countrymen, seldom do I encounter eyes on a level with my own. But this new Mati was a head taller than I am, she gleamed, she was pearlish with grandeur and her form was phosphorescent in the yellow candle-light. She with her dripping foot, and teeth in only the left-hand half of her mouth and the big eyebrows of her long face up near her hair, you remember her, Geta, as she was, that body had shed its corruption and shone with glory, like the radiant cloths of the fuller.'

The repentance of Mati Tŷ-unnos was real then, and she after all had reached paradise. Had she a golden plate behind her head, Geta wondered. And had the vicar really spoken to her and she uprisen from her grave?

'Please, sir,' she said with great happiness, 'did you see Mati Tŷ-unnos in the vestry and did she really speak to you?' The vicar nodded, showing his three-cornered teeth and squeezing her with his arm. 'Don't you believe me, Geta *fach*?' he asked.

'Oh yes, sir,' said Geta. 'She said that if ever by great grace and repentance she once managed to get her fingers up through the floorboards of heaven she would let me know somehow about it. And praise be she has.'

'She repented then, did she, Geta? That's why she said to me, "Vicar, repeat or repent." – "Your time is drawing near," she said. "Perhaps in a dozen spins of this old world from now the earth will be trickling on to your face through a crack in your coffin lid. So repent while there is yet time." But kicking against the pricks my stony heart spoke and may heaven forgive me for it. "What do you know of repentance, Mati Rees?" I asked her. "I don't suppose you could even spell the word." She only smiled at me, Geta, she didn't shout, "I wouldn't give a hair from my nose to spell it," or some other rudeness as she would have done but for grace. "Vicar *bach*," she said to me patiently, "you don't understand not even rule one. Believe what I tell you. I am not just breaking words but trying to save you from your pride. When Geta read to me, struggling with me day after day, as you should have done, at last I felt I was forgiven; once it was as though a wing touched me and I soared. And now by this victory I, Mati Tŷ-unnos, know all secrets and mysteries, I have seen the nest of the stirring thunder, the eyes that watch the nether sinks of hell, the knuckles that wring out the showers and the storm of falling stars." Those were her very words, Geta, she spoke them in a deep voice like an organ-chord, towering above me in her shawl and poppy hat, filling the vestry with her bean-field fragrance and her glow.'

By now the cart was out of the cemetery lane and on the road back to the village. The frozen pony went easier, bending his knees a bit because he knew he was heading for his oats. Geta felt happy, in her heart the sun was on the hill. 'Let me get out now and lead the pony, sir,' she said, 'and if you please, sir, tell me what else she said.'

'You lead the pony? No, indeed,' said the vicar. 'I will lead the pony.' He slipped off his cloak and wrapped it warmly round her. Then with loud cracks he got out of the cart and took the bridle, turning round and talking to Geta as he walked the road towards the village.

'Her eyes, Geta,' he said, 'that were small and cunning, like the black beady eyes of the bat, you remember, were open wide and shining brightly in her face. "I will tell you a secret I have heard," she said to me. "I, whom you despised so much, I, Mati Tŷ-unnos was also a daughter of Rhodri Fawr, his blood flowed in my veins too, I had as much right to be on your tree as Griffith Benfras or Ifor ap Cynan. And what is more, Geta *fach* Glandwr, she too is a child of the Great King; we are all related, Vicar, and not in the ninth degree, neither."' The vicar stopped the cart. 'When I heard that, Geta, that she whom I had hated so much was related to me, at first I couldn't breathe, my bones felt heavy as though they were going to fall out of my skin. But she was slowly melting out my frozen heart, may heaven be praised.'

He lifted his hat off his white locks and started the pony again.
' "Beware of pride, Roderick Price-Parry," she said. "Beware of the
vanity of that tree of yours. It is nothing Vicar *bach,* only a bit of a
show-on-a-shelf, remember. Pluck out those roots that are eating into
your heart." I knew what she said was true, Geta; I knew it was the
truth, but I had to deny it. "Pride!" I said to her. "Pride! I have no
pride. When I heard of the heathen knocking his forehead on the
ground before his god, I, Roderick Pari Pryce Price-Parry, of the line
of Rhodri Fawr, the very next Sunday got down full length before my
God in this very church." You remember me doing that, Geta?' he
asked turning round.

'Yes, sir,' said Geta, her hair protruding around her face like a
curved golden shell, 'I remember you lying down flat in front of the
altar to pray. Please won't you have your cloak on, sir?'

'No, indeed, Geta,' he said. 'I feel warmer leading this pony than I
have been for years. Wrap it round you well, my child, to keep out the
cold. Mati only smiled at my excuse. "Speak the truth, Vicar," she said,
"and shame the devil; send a blush all over him right down to the spike
of his tail. You know that as you lay there your heart was as cold as the
stone of the steps beneath you." And what she said again was true,
Geta.'

They had reached the cottage of Wil Saer by the roadside. Wil was
coming out of the gate of his little garden with a new white cart-shaft
over his shoulder. Seeing the vicar in his waders leading the pony down
the road and Geta sitting up there in the cart wrapped up in the black
cloak, he dropped the shaft in the snow and clapped his hands to his
furry face. He was just going to dodge back into the house when the
vicar left the pony's head and ran down upon him shouting at the top
of his voice so that the rooks smoked out of their trees crying and
floating about like bits of burnt paper from a chimney on fire.
'William, William,' he cried holding him fast in his powerful eagle's
claws, 'forgive me, forgive me. Will you forgive me, William? In my
heart of hearts I despised you for years for being a carpenter and the
son of a carpenter. If you can forgive me I shall be forgiven in heaven
for forgetting my Master was a carpenter. Can you forgive me,
William?' the vicar shouted, gripping Wil's overcoat by the collar and
shaking him with his crooked yellow talons until Wil's red tongue shot
out the length of a hand from among his plentiful moustaches. 'Yes, sir;
yes, sir,' he gasped, frightened out of his life, crouching down with his
elbows over his ears as though he was going to have a beating. 'Yes, sir,
I'll forgive you anything, sir.' He fought himself loose and ran terrified
through the tiny garden to the house. 'Don't call me sir,' the vicar

roared after him. But Wil was safe inside the house, and when he slammed the door all the snow fell off the roof on the vicar. Price-Parry was too happy to notice. As he came back to the trap, tears gushed from his eyes. 'Geta,' he said, standing again at the gingerbread's bridle, 'Mati once said I never had any fires in my house because I was too high-nosed and proud to burn anything less grand than stars in my grate. Look out of your window tonight, my girl, and you will see smoke from every hearth in the vicarage. My uprooted tree and its pictures and its frame and every book about my tree and its pictures shall go up this night in smoke. Look out of your window, Geta *fach*, and see the flames.'

'Yes, sir," said Geta, who sat watching wide-eyed from the cart with her mouth like a ball-hole. 'Thank you, sir. And please, sir, what became of Mati in the end?'

'I cannot tell you all she told me, Geta, you would not understand it. But I heard a line of music,' he said, 'something whistled as it whizzed past me, the vestry candle went out and she was gone.'

Through the darkness the deserted cottage of Mati Tŷ-unnos seemed more dilapidated than ever, its bulging walls crouching low in the snow. In the farmhouse of Glandwr, Geta had climbed out of bed to stand at the landing window, staring in the direction of the vicarage. Presently in the pitch night she saw volumes of thick smoke pouring out of the chimney-stacks with a fiery glow glaring on it as though all the chimneys of the house were on fire. Once or twice as she watched glove-fingers of flame showed themselves for a moment from the chimneypots. Geta turned away smiling and crept back to her bedroom. Snow and darkness lay thick over Llanifor Fechan, and soon all the boots in the village were under the beds.

Bowen, Morgan and Williams

❧

After what I had done the night before I couldn't very well refuse. Benja Bowen and I had come home from Imperato's about nine o'clock and I had gone straight into the front room to slip my canvas boots into the window flowerpot with my school cap on top of them because my father didn't like me going boxing. (I used to keep Benja's boots there too, because his people were very strict and religious, much narrower than mine – his father tried to start a sect that believed there were thirteen Persons in the Trinity, and he made Benja go to chapel on Saturdays.) There in the parlour my mother was sitting with our new electric light on full-float, talking to two visitors from our chapel – Miss Philips (M'Liza, William the Rates's sister), and Mrs. Rees the Come-inside, who had heard about her tumble. My mother was in her oil talking to them, she looked beautiful with her crinkly auburny hair and the summerspots on her eyelids, but she made me blush because she had her dress on backwards. Mrs. Rees was a sour, knowing-looking woman, red and stoutish, with a sultry expression on her face as though she was having bad heartburn. She had untidy grey hair like the stuff that comes out of a rip in the sofa, and clothes that seemed, but for the heavy brooches with which she bolted them on, as though they were going to slide off her body. She had on now her husband's panama hat with a barricade of hen's feathers stuck upright into the ribbon, and a gnawed fur coat hanging half-way down her back the way our masters wore their gowns. She kept an ironmongery shop and everybody called her the Come-inside, because if you stood looking in at her window for a few seconds she would waddle out on to the pavement in her mangy coat and whisper, 'Come inside, come inside.' She had a long stocking but she was stingy with her money, and she and her husband lived in a little shed at the top of the garden behind their mansion.

Miss Philips, William's sister, was very genteel and polite, but poor-looking as well and very old-fashioned and dowdy. Summer and winter she wore a long voluminous greenish-black skirt, a riding coat of the same colour trimmed with wide braid like flat spanish, and a squashed velvet hat that looked as though she had found it under the cushion. I used to make fun of her with her elastic boots and tall umbrella, and then be ashamed because really she was fine and I liked her very much.

Her thin face was refined and white as ivory, very genteel, with a prim expression on it, because before William's leg got bad she used to be a governess.

I wanted to back out directly I had got inside the room, both because I had the boxing boots under my arm and because I remembered in a flash that the mouthy Come-inside had seen Benja and me from her shed smoking up the mountain where we used to go to shave one another, but it was too late.

'How do you do, Mr. Williams?' said Miss Philips, holding out her thin white hand to me. (She was so polite she used to say 'Yes'm' and 'No'm' to my mother and she started to call me mister as soon as I got into the county school.) I told her I was all right and I asked her how she was, of course.

'Thank you for your kind enquiry,' she answered. 'If you mean my physical health, I am very well indeed. And now will you allow me to take this opportunity of congratulating you upon your recent success?'

I was taken aback for the moment, this speech seemed so elegant after Imperato's, but I realized she meant my passing senior at last. I blushed again and thanked her, but I was relieved to see the Come-inside looking as though her water-brash was a bit easier on her as she too wished me well. After a bit more handshaking amongst us and dropping the boxing boots all over the floor, I got out into the cool passage.

I went into the kitchen avoiding the puddles and there Mam Evans, my mother's washerwoman, was crouching, eating toasted cheese out of a tin plate by the glow of the fire because she was afraid to turn the electric light on. I did it for her and then I sat down on the couch and began pumping her about the time she went to the seaside and about her mother when she was a shindry girl. She was a big fleshy old woman now with a bun at the back of her head and a hot smell to her blouse. She had a soft shapeless face looking as though there were no bones in it, the flabby flesh beginning to hang into her goitrous neck, which was really a good bit wider than her head. There were no teeth or lips to her mouth, it was only a pleat in her skin right under her nose. She couldn't see much with her pale watery eyes so that my mother often had to wash the clothes over after her, and when she had scrubbed our kitchen floor she used to leave it swimming with puddles with small heaps of brown snuff, like little molehills, scattered all over it. When she had finished her cheese, she took off her sack apron with the holes in the knees and wrapped it in newspaper, asking me what time it was. I told her it was nine o'clock, and she swore in her faulty old-fashioned way because she would be too late to buy twist for her poor mother alone in the dark house with an empty clay-pipe in her head. She hurried out the back way in her cap and shawl, and then I began to tease the canary a bit, hoping M'Liza and the Come-inside would go so that I could have my supper, but he was too sleepy to respond. Then alongside my father's trombone in the corner I saw my mother's new vacuum cleaner and I began examining that. I fixed a sort of plug with a wire on it into the wall, and then I turned on the current by means of a button I found under the handle. The engine started to hum but almost at once there was a loud snap and a blue flash and the electric light went out in the kitchen. I dropped the handle in my fright and then when I had recovered a bit I tried to put the light on at the switch, but nothing happened. I crept out of the kitchen in the darkness and tried the light in the middle room, but nothing happened there either. Just then my mother opened the door of the parlour, which I could see was also in complete darkness, and shouted out, 'Evan, Evan, now stop that nonsense. Put the lights on at once, will you!'

The next morning my mother's foot was a lot better and she said, 'Ev, take these roses up to your Uncle Sam's and ask how his asthma is, will you?' (She was holding the canary under the tap to revive him as she said this because she had turned on the gas-ring and forgotten to light it and the poor little dab had fallen off his perch in a faint.) The roses were all right, some of my father's best, each bloom bursting out like a coloured cabbage and bound together into a huge bouquet nearly three feet in girth. But remembering the night before, and not being able to think of an excuse, I said I would go. So I heaved up the flowers off the table and started out the lane way to see my Uncle Sam, who lived the other end of the town. Before I got to the main street I passed the Come-inside's husband on the prowl for back-rents, and the half-grin I fancied I saw on his face made me blush a bit. But I soon remembered seeing him looking silly in the big seat in chapel with a white price-ticket, four inches by five, still sewn on the tail of his new frock coat, and that cheered me up again. Before crossing over High Street I hung the flowers negligently half-way behind my legs to conceal them a bit and hurried over towards the tramroad, not looking to right or left. This tramroad ran parallel with the main street almost all the way to my uncle's house, and it wasn't bad walking there with no one about and the sun yellow as electric light on the walls, although the place itself was shabby and dusty. The only thing that made me really uncomfortable was that my mother had been darning my socks again, and my right foot felt as though I had a poultice on it. My mother was lovely, with freckles and auburn hair, but it was wonderful my brother and I were alive with all the things she had done to us. When our Rhysie was a baby, so she said, and she was tidying the dresser, she slipped him in the knife-drawer to answer Watcyn the milk and when she came back into the kitchen she began to search all over the place, behind the blower and in the boot cupboard, because she couldn't remember where she had put him.

At the back of the Temperance Hall I met Madame Jones-Edwards (Llinos Cwm Du, the majestic ex-singer) who had married three husbands, all of them little men about half her weight, each one before the last was cold. She was a tall stately woman leaning on an ebony walking stick, wearing a starched collar and a tie like a man, a costume of crimson plush and a cartwheel hat with red seagulls skewered on to it. She rolled over slowly from side to side as she walked like a boy riding a bike too big for him. She was so sparkling and highly-coloured she looked a bit out of place on the grimy tramroad which was only a narrow lane for the colliers' train with the backs of shops and houses on each side of it. Her hands were covered with rings, there was a gold chain looped many times over her chest and a long pair of droppers shaped like golden indian clubs swung on chains from the lobes of her ears. When she saw the roses she came slowly to rest upright, and asked me with an elegant sort of bow if she might smell them. She had a soft-skinned creamy face covered with fine lines as thin as hairs, and black bossy eyes, very glittering and watchful. The smell of the roses seemed to give her great raptures, she kept her face buried a long time in the massive bunch, closing her eyelids and letting her head loll on one side. She asked me where I had got them from and I thought she wanted to find out who I was too, but I didn't tell her much because she was so gushing and I didn't know what she would do if she discovered my father played the trombone. At last I got away, leaving even her scent behind, but I felt better after meeting her because these roses were silver bowl-winners after all, something to be proud of. My father grew about the best blooms in town, in the whole valley perhaps, and Llinos Cwm Du had liked them and she had been all over the world singing in her young days and had received bouquets too, no doubt, like the actresses Arthur and I saw in the Theatre Royal. She wasn't bad at all except that she was too dramatic in everything she did, but you could see she was a good judge of roses, so that was nothing. But when I came round the next bend I saw Arthur Vaughan Morgan crossing the tramroad on the way up from High Street with his bull-terrier on the lead beside him. I dodged and marked time but it was no good, Arthur had seen me and he was waiting with a faint smile on his face, looking at me as though I was something that had crawled out of the long grass. It was the same sort of look as he had for the kid who tagged on to us when we were small the first day we were in the county school. 'Which way are you going?' he said to him. 'We're going the other way.' He greeted me now with his lids half down over his deep blue eyes. 'Hullo, Williams,' he said, 'going to a wedding?'

When I told him I was on my way up to my Uncle Sam's, he said he would come with me after he had slipped home to give a message to his father. So for a start I had to carry my roses up to Arthur's house.

The first time I ever saw Arthur was when we were little boys and there was a coronation fête and gala on in town. I was with my father going among the crowds after the procession and we met Arthur doing the same with *his* father, a well-known character the people called Tommy White-hat. The first thing I noticed about Arthur was that he had a much better Union Jack than I did, with a real gilded wooden point on the end of his flag-stick and not a bit of pointed cardboard like mine. He was dressed in a sailor suit with long trousers and a thick whistle-cord hanging out of his pocket.

His father was a tall big man wearing pale spats, a white felt hat pushed on the side of his head and a thin grey suit with a collar to the waistcoat and a scarlet carnation in the buttonhole. He was smoking a thin cigar like a pencil which he was using to point with, and which he kept passing from hand to hand as he made jokes and explained things to Arthur and me, bending down with his bright eyes close to mine and his breath smelling of scented cachous. He had a gold band on one of his fingers with a little hailstone in it, and he laughed and talked all the time in a rich-sounding way, showing a lot of gold in his big teeth. I thought him lovely then, more beautiful than a mermaid, with his mannish smell, and his handsome pink cheeks, and his thick curly hair like grey tobacco.

When Arthur and I got to the county school, Mr. Vaughan Morgan always talked to me in a grown-up way and asked about my mother and father in his rich throaty voice, very cheerful and friendly. I always thought then he came right off the top shelf, but whenever I mentioned him at home my mother would turn on me and say, 'Hark at him, he likes Tommy Vaughan Morgan who feeds the children on bread and spit and works poor Annie's hands into holes so that he can live among the *crachach. Ach y fi.*' I couldn't believe it at first when my mother said the Morgans didn't have tuppence to put in the gas at the same time and we could easily buy them up, because although I knew the wolf was a long way from our door we seemed to live pretty close to the ground compared with them – my father came home from work dirty and never wore a gold ring on his tie and smoked cigars like Mr. Vaughan Morgan, and we didn't have a big house like theirs, either, with red tilings on the roof and a white flagstaff in the garden. (Although when I thought about it, I saw it was true their place was battered about by the children, and whenever you went there you might find a bucket on the piano and perhaps nearly break your neck with the holes in the carpet. And upstairs you would see the marks of running water in streaks down all the bedroom wallpaper from the winter the Vaughan Morgans had a big hole in the roof where the gutters joined and they tied a zinc bath with rope to the rafters to catch the rain coming in through it. Because when the bath was full and Cuckoo and his father went up the manhole to fetch it down they upset it between them in getting it off the ropes and the bathful of water poured in gallons through all the ceilings and down the bedroom walls.) And once my father came in from practice laughing, saying he had just met Tommy White-hat and then acting what had happened for my mother, exaggerating everything as he always did. Mr. Vaughan Morgan had seemed as gay as usual when they had met, but when my father asked him how Annie was he changed altogether and looked very downhearted. His blue eyes filled up with tears and he could hardly speak as he said he had just come from the hospital where they told him she had coughed up one of her lungs that very morning, poor girl. Likely enough she had coughed up the other by now he said, throwing away his cigar and taking his bandanna out of his breast pocket to mop his eyes with. He spoke for a long time, crying salt and describing how all his life he had lived under the showers and how Annie had been his only comfort, so no wonder he was shedding the tears nearest his heart. My father sympathized with him and invited him down to our house for a meal of food. He thanked my father again and again for this with his hand on his shoulder, and wiping his eyes and shaking hands, he said, 'Thank you, Rhys, for your kindness in my trouble. Poor Annie, poor girl. How she's suffered – years and years of it. Nobody knows.' Here he gave a deep sigh and a final blow to his nose, and putting his spotted handkerchief away took out his gold half-hunter. 'I don't think I'll come down today, Rhys, my boy,' he said, 'if you don't mind. Thank you all the same. You see, I must hurry off to catch the special – I want to see the final between the Wanderers and the Thursdays.' My father watched him swaggering down the road with his white hat on the side of his head lighting another cigar.

'The dirt,' said my mother. 'No *dal* on the White-hat.'

But Arthur was always distant with people; he wasn't much like his father, friends with everybody, except that he was handsome too, and always wore smart clothes, with a bit of handkerchief showing at his breast pocket. (I noticed his nice suits because my mother used to try to make my school clothes herself until I refused to wear them after she put the two sleeves of my jacket in backwards so that I looked like a cripple.) He was a tall slim boy with black wavy hair, pale skin and red lips, and a habit of lowering his long-lashed lids over his eyes when he was talking to you. His dog was a classy-looking bull terrier, shapely and milk-white, called Tiger, and when he saw me and my roses he winked his pink eyes and wagged his tail in an indifferent way. He was a dog who had fits and didn't seem quite right in the head by the way he behaved off the lead. Everybody hated him except the Vaughan Morgans, and once or twice they had found him laid out flat in the gutter a long way from home.

Arthur's house was in a row of big villas, where the people lived on bloaters and were in debt. We squeezed in through the swollen door that had a bulged knob, a broken fanlight and a panel the dog had scratched into a hole with his claws, and went through to the large sunny dining-room overlooking the lawn at the back. Here Arthur left me, saying he wouldn't be long, and went upstairs with Tiger to look for Mr. Vaughan Morgan.

In this big bare room, where the white ceiling paper hung down at the corners like the flaps of a huge envelope, Nicholas y Glo, one of the lodgers, was sitting on a broken-backed chair reading the paper and eating his breakfast off dishes that were all of different colours, sizes and designs. He had a bad stomach and before him, holding up the newspaper on a bit of tablecloth, were a lot of medicines – some peppermint ovals, a cup of bicarbonate of soda, and a bottle of wind and water pills. I said good morning to him, lifting a heap of washing on to the sewing machine so that I could get into the armchair, which had a hollow arm and all its springs on the floor. As I sat there carefully, with the championship roses across my knees, I noticed on the table the blue sugar-bag and the loaf started at both ends as usual, and the tin alarm clock ticking upside down on the sideboard and the crack in the big mirror that Mostyn, Arthur's younger brother, had made in walking across the mantelpiece with the coal hammer in his hand. And on the wall below the American clock, whose pendulum and workings had all fallen into the glass case at the bottom, were a lot

of drawings of actresses in pencil and the huge purplish splash caused
by the blackcurrant wine bottle exploding against the wall-paper four
or five Christmases ago.

The sun's rays were pouring in so strongly upon Nicholas's waxy
little head that it glistened under his thin hair and the yellow skin
looked as though it had started melting. 'Good morning,' he said to
me, and then he became so bashful he blushed and started whistling
the bass part of the 'Men of Harlech' to himself. One reason he never
said much was that he had a high falsetto voice coming out through his
nose so that whenever he spoke he sounded as though he was trying to
imitate somebody. He was very nervous and he always acted queer
when there were visitors about, cracking his fingers and playing with
his watch-chains and tapping the table with the dishes. He was as
flustered now as a fly caught in a glass of water because he knew I was
watching him, and in his embarrassment he picked up his silver
serviette ring and screwed it into his right eye, staring round at the
cobwebs and the ceiling flies through the hole with a deep blush on his
face. But I didn't take much notice of him; my mother said he was
never the same after he fell through the trapdoor outside the 'Ship and
Castle.' All the boys thought him a bit queer because if there was a
window rattling in chapel, or the sun was disturbing the preacher, he
would pull off his boots, blushing like a girl, and creep about the
gallery in his black stockings, full of big holes, to fasten the catch or
pull the curtains, the joints of his feet giving off loud snaps on the
floorboards at every step. He was a very tall thin man with legs like
whips, wearing a black coat and striped trousers, a cream flannel
waistcoat with a bunch of gold chains across it, and a very high white
collar which looked as though he had stepped into it and slid it up his
body into its position under his head. He had a small square face, very
thin and wrinkled, and all the time he was whistling and beating on the
table with his alphabet plate, and glaring at the newspaper like a one-
eyed spider, I was afraid that if his jawbone lost contact with the top
edge of the massive collar on which it was supported, his whole head
would disappear inside and perhaps shave off his gristly ears as it did
so. The moustache on his long upper lip was perfect, neatly trimmed
and waxed out, but minute, a tiny coloured model, hardly visible at all
in the shadow of his nose, and yet perfect in every detail like a tiny
grub or a fly seen under a microscope. His hair was long and dry-
looking, but not very plentiful; it was pressed lifeless and wiglike on to
the wax of his bony scalp. But it wasn't its shape or its texture that used
to attract my attention, but its colour, because it was a deep and
sombre green.

There was always a lot of noise in Arthur's house, people were always coming in and out of rooms and banging doors and shouting, and all the time I watched Mr. Nicholas as he squirmed and blushed on his broken-backed chair that creaked like an unoiled ratchet at every move, I could hear the bump-bumping noise from the other side of the wall that Mostyn was making riding round the drawing-room on his bike. Then someone started pounding on the piano, and one of Arthur's sisters thundered up the stairs two at a time shouting out to stop it, and a fierce argument started on the landing with 'By Babylon's Wave' coming louder and louder out of the piano all the time. I hoped neither of the elder girls would burst into the dining-room and catch me with my flowers because they were very smart and witty. They had always heard everything before and they used to use French words, like *blasé* and *à la mode,* that I wasn't sure of the meaning of.

At last there was a deafening crash as the hallstand fell over in the passage and Mostyn came skirmishing into the room fighting with Tiger.

'Hullo, Williams,' he said, staring hard at my flowers, and I only said 'Hullo, Cuckoo,' because I didn't want to see him. He had yellow curls and blue eyes like a girl, but he was dirty and objectionable, always smashing things and getting into a mess, and Arthur ignored him, he didn't like him at all. If one of the masters at school said, 'Arthur, is your brother present this morning?' he would answer, 'I don't know, I'll find out for you if you wish me to.' And if we happened to pass Mostyn on the other side of the street, perhaps with his thumb to his nose on the top of a lamp-post or showing off on his yellow racer and I said 'Arthur, there's Cuckoo over there,' he would reply, 'I've seen him before,' without troubling to look across. And when we had passed him he would start quoting dirty Latin.

Mostyn started pulling Tiger across the room by the ears, and then tried to get him to jump on to the table where he knelt with his knee in the butter. He was giggling all the time and whispering something to the dog about my roses, and I could feel myself colouring because of it. He was always a nuisance, doing silly things that made Arthur sneer at him, like putting a handful of the black beetles that were always running about the house into Nicholas's cup of tea, or tying Crumpy's front door-knocker to the lamp-post. And he was the boy with a face like an angel who had five rulers stuck down his neck as soon as the master left the classroom, and his shirt pulled up over his belly and a tin box of instruments pushed into the front of his trousers.

'That will keep, Cuckoo,' I said, showing him I had heard.

At that Mr. Nicholas's blush became so plentiful it looked as though it would pass into his hair and collar and dye those scarlet too. And in his embarrassment he screwed Mr. Morgan's serviette ring into his other eye and glared hard at the newspaper before him like a goggle-eyed insect, bending his fingers so far back I was afraid they would snap off and squirt blood at the knuckles. But he was too nervous to say anything and Mostyn only laughed.

For a bit there was complete silence in the house and in the quiet I heard the tin alarm clock stop, change gear and then begin ticking again with a deeper and more important note. But the noises started almost at once. There were two heavy bumps right above us like a couple of people falling out of bed and in a moment or two Mr. Vaughan Morgan came into the room with a gale behind him, rubbing his gold-ringed hands and lowering the full skin-bags of his lids over his deep blue eyes against the sunglare. 'Hullo, hullo, hullo,' he said smiling, the glitter of his rings and his golden corner teeth bright like brass in the sunshine. 'Your father's roses, Evan?' he said. 'How is the old pilgrim? Don't move my boy.' Without asking he took a little folding cigar cutter from his waistcoat pocket, snipped off the best bud he could see and put the crimson flower in his buttonhole. His skin looked fresh, as though he had just come from the bath; he was wearing a pale pair of spats, a thin light grey suit with sharp creases down his trousers and a spotted bow-tie round his wing collar. His handsome face was as pink as lint, it was clean-looking and faintly powdered after shaving, and there was some sweet-smelling oil rubbed into his thick grey hair.

He went round the table patting Nicholas on the back and putting a thin cigar out beside his plate. 'How do you feel today, Nat?' he said to him.

'Common,' said Mr. Nicholas in a falsetto voice like the sound squeezed out of a conjurer's dummy. The sun shone bright as a burning glass on the green back of his head and on his collar, swelling out and narrowing as he gulped his bicarbonate of soda, as though someone were pumping air through it. Then, feeling embarrassed, he got up and stood reading the news before the huge marble fireplace and the cracked mirror, his big ears burning scarlet like a pair of cart-lamps hung one each side of his head. Mr. Vaughan Morgan was tall but Mr. Nicholas was taller. When I glanced at him standing there on the hearthrug, long and narrow as a vinegar-drinker, the flushes all the time coming up out of his collar and disappearing into his green hair, I thought he had his boots on the wrong feet, but when I looked again I saw his long legs were crossed behind the paper.

Everybody knew that being in the same room as Tommy Vaughan Morgan was like living at the foot of the waterfall because he could talk by the hour. His bass voice was rich and resonant, he seemed to have three or four throats when he was speaking with a deep note bubbling out of each of them, making his voice into a harmony like a handful of keys sounded together on an organ. 'What are you trying to do Mostyn?' he asked, ruffling his curls. But Mostyn pushed his hand away; although he was from the bottom of the nest, he was always cheeky to his father. 'Like this look,' Mr. Morgan went on. He got up from the table again and began calling the bull-terrier to entice him towards the casement window, which he managed to open after a lot of tugging which made the handle come off in his hand. (It was through this window that I once saw him throwing out the dinner when Mrs. Morgan was alive. Arthur and I were below near the flagstaff on the lawn when we saw Mr. Morgan through the open window coming into the dining-room. He had been at 'The Bull', potting, by the look of him, because his white felt was low down on his ears like a comedian's bowler, his pincenez were hanging out of his pocket and his face was sulky and flushed purple. 'Annie,' we heard him shout in his high-class way, 'what's for dinner today?' Arthur's mother was a quiet little woman always pattering about the house in silence, she never went out except to meet the trains in when Tommy had been away. 'Ham, my love,' she said meekly, holding before him a dish with a big piece of ham on it. 'Damn the ham,' said Tommy, and he threw the meat out of the window.

'My father,' said Arthur, 'under the influence of words or liquor, exhibits a strange vehemence of behaviour.'

He began fondling the dog and when he had got him near the wall he shouted, '"Cats, Tiger! Cats!' The dog gave a growl and with a clever spring disappeared through the window on to the lawn, but when he found he had been fooled he dived back into the room again. Tommy laughed and, taking the bread-saw off the table, started to comb him with it.

'This is the most wonderful dog in the valley, Evan,' he went on, going over to the sideboard that had a row of cigar burns across the edge. 'Now where are those snaps of him, Mostyn?' He took the cigar from the table and Mostyn lit it for him with a match. With his spring pincenez on he began searching about first in the bulgy tea caddy and then in the shallow drawers, piling the contents on to the table, a dog's bone, a gym shoe, some gas mantle cases, two or three pigeon rings, a mass of clockwork, a toffee hammer and a cigar-box holding a wad of letters and a handful of watch-wheels. He couldn't find the photographs but among the letters was a telegram which he handed to me. 'Read that, Evan,' he said. 'From our Arthur when he matriculated.'

(There was one word in the telegram – *Undergraduate*.) 'This is what I was going to say. You know Mam Evans, Evan?'

'My mother's washerwoman,' I said, and Mr. Nicholas put his newspaper behind him to listen.

'On the tramroad yesterday,' he went on, 'I saw her with Sian her mother in a pair of chairs outside the house. I got my watch ready because she always wants to know the time. And it's a trick to tell her the time, you know. Have you tried it, Evan?'

'Stick to your story, Tommy,' said Mostyn.

Mr. Morgan laughed. 'Mostyn *bach*,' he said pulling at his cigar. 'The lamb teaching the sheep to graze.' Then he began again, imitating the impediment of the old woman. 'If ever she asks you, tell her to the nearest quarter of an hour – she's got no looks on minutes. "Thomas Vaughan," she says to me. "Thomas Vaughan, have you got the right time, please?" So I take out my watch to tell her.'

Here Mr. Morgan opened his half-hunter, but the belly fell out on the table. He pushed it back in again and stared at it down the side of his pink Roman nose, but before he could say anything Mr. Nicholas made his middle finger go off snap behind his back with a crack like a pistol shot. Tommy was startled by the noise and Nicholas went red and looked as though he would like to fold the big flaps of his ears over his face to hide his blushes but he didn't dare open his beak. Then, as he was getting behind the paper again, Arthur came into the room and motioned me out. I got off the armchair, which gave out a long chorus of pings like a number of pitchforks struck in a cluster as the springs worked up one by one through the plush again, and Mr. Morgan recovered himself at the noise.

' "Well, Mam Evans," I say,' he went on, mocking the way she said s and r, ' "it's now precisely eleven minutes past five." That won't do for her at all. Not at all. "Eleven minutes past five, indeed," she says, rubbing that old scab on her chin. "What sort of time is that? Tell us the right time now, boy." I don't know what in the world to tell her, so I say, "Well, I *have* told you the right time, Mam Evans, it's now nearly twelve minutes past five." – "There's funny you are getting, Thomas Vaughan," she complains, disgusted with me, "tell us the right time now tidy and don't be so dull, boy." We go on like this until it's quarter past, and then she's satisfied.'

Tommy was in a *hwyl* by now with a story to act and an audience to listen, his blue eyes were glittering like stars and his mouth was full of spit. When he was like this he seemed overflowing with energy and I had seen him posting a letter in the middle of a tale as though he was going to stuff his arm up to the elbow into the pillar box, and turning the kitchen tap on so that the word COLD went round and round and the water splashed all over the kitchen.

Slowly I edged round to the door, Tommy talking like the pit of the sea, telling us how the old women had walked out of the house because Tiger had come in and was lying fast asleep by the fire in the kitchen. I stumbled over the hymn-book holding up the leg of the table, but at last I stood by Arthur near the door, ready to slip out. Before us in the liquidy sunshine of the room I could see the others as though they were in a play, Mostyn smoothing the dog with the match-box, Tommy pink with acting his story, a trellis of lines clear on the soft bags under his blue eyes, and Nicholas y Glo in an upright coil on the mat, his hair green as seaweed and his collar like a white legging rising above the paper. And then our chance came, because we saw Mostyn setting fire with a match to the bottom edge of the paper Nicholas was again holding spread out before him. The sheets kindled at once, they flared up like celluloid, divided into two by the flames, and when Nicholas saw he held a blazing mass in each hand his face went crimson, he let out a terrified shriek in his high-pitched voice and began waving the burning sheets around his head so that I was afraid his hair would catch fire, he danced up and down on the mat shouting out 'I'm on fire, I'm on fire! Holy water! Holy water!' loudly through his nose. Mostyn laughed, the dog set up a howl and dived out through the window and Tommy stopped with his cigar up, his golden fangs and the flat band on his finger flashing like signals in the sun. Arthur and I bolted out into the passage, but as we were coming on to the path through the front door it stuck fast, and Arthur pulled it after him with such a bang that six feet of iron down-pipe dropped off the wall and nearly knocked me cold.

When we got to the end of the road Tiger was waiting for us, wagging his tail and blinking.

As soon as we got back on to the tramroad we met Benja Bowen on his way home. It was a Tuesday in the holidays, but he said he had been to chapel. I didn't feel much like taking him to my Uncle Sam's house because he was such a clown and you couldn't trust him. (Once when he came with me to my Mamgu Williams's he tried to creep into her sleeve by showing her a balancing trick with some of her cut-glass tumblers, and he smashed them all.) But he said, 'Going towards up?' and when we told him we were he said he would be with us as soon as he had changed his clothes. I couldn't think of anything to say so we went back with him to the shop.

Benja was a bit mis-shapen, he was short, thick-set and bull-necked with arms hanging down to his knees like an ape. His short powerful legs were rather bandy because he had broken both of them and he had a great wrinkled cone of ginger hair piled up on top of his huge head like stiff coconut matting. His bottom jaw, covered with blond unshaved cub-fur, stuck out beyond his top and his cheeks were red, but if you called him Rosie or Cochyn he would punch you on the muscles. He had his best clothes on, an Eton collar, a black coat and vest and striped trousers stinking of tobacco, and a pair of button boots that someone had ordered from his father and never called for. His father was a bootmaker and you could always see the top of him showing above the green-painted win-dow of their shop, his bald head very shiny and dirty as though he had polished it a bit with the heel-ball. He was an evangelist too and you had to keep your hat straight when you were talking to him. One night my mother called round at his house to look for our groceries and when he said they hadn't been left there, my mother thought he was teasing and said, 'Go on, Mr. Bowen, aren't they here indeed?' – 'Mrs. Williams,' said Benja's father, 'my yea is yea, and my nay is nay,' and he slammed the door and bolted it after him. My mother said *wfft* to him, she had no looks on Bowen the bootmaker after that.

But he was very strict with his children too, and sometimes Benja would turn up to play for the school wearing his ordinary clothes and only one football boot, because that was all he had been able to smuggle out of the house. And perhaps even then he had jumped out of the upstairs window. He was stupid in school, he didn't have much under his hair except for games (once when the Welsh master asked him if his home was bi-lingual, he said, 'No, sir, by the Ship and Castle'), and on the morning the school reports came out Benja would be seen skulking in the shop doorway asking people if they had seen the postman.

We thought Benja would be quicker if we didn't go inside his house so we sat on a box in the little backyard with Tiger between us. Benja's father was a queer man and before he tried to start his own religion he used to come to our chapel and disturb the meetings by shouting out 'Amen', and beating his breast and groaning when the minister mentioned Judas Iscariot. You never knew what he would do next and once when it was nearly midnight we heard from our house a great crash, and Mrs. Bowen ran down to my mother in a fright asking if she could come in. She said her husband had got up out of bed and suddenly started sweeping the soot out of the flues, and with a mighty heave of the brush he had pushed the back kitchen chimney over into the glass house next door.

But whatever he did himself, he always sat very tight on the tails of the children, and one Sunday at tea-time he asked Benja if he had been that afternoon to the *gymanfa ganu* rehearsal at Bethel, a chapel a couple miles up the valley. Benja said yes he had, and he enjoyed the singing too. 'Where were you sitting?' asked his father. 'Behind the clock on the gallery,' said Benja. His father landed him a stinger with his heavy stitching hand on the side of the head, and chased him with a walking stick from the table up into the bedroom. Benja was startled out of his wits up there, hearing his father roaring about downstairs and the furniture smashing, and after a couple of hours, as he sat bewildered on the bed with a kettle boiling in his hot ear, he heard his sister at the keyhole whispering his name. 'What's all that noise down there?' he asked, 'what's happening?' – 'It's our dad,' she answered, 'he's gone mad and he's attacking the back of the piano with the hatchet.' – 'What's the matter with him?' asked Benja, 'what did he hit me across the ear like that for?' – 'There's no gallery in Bethel,' she said. 'I was there.'

But that was a long time ago, when Benja used to spend the time he wasn't in chapel swimming in the canal where the hot water poured out of the boiler-house and teasing the pawnbroker by spitting on his crossed fingers outside the shop window.

After a bit Benja came out dressed in his holiday clothes instead of his dark suit and Eton collar. He was wearing over his pile of ginger hair a man's tweed cap with the broken peak pointing skywards, and his grey suit so shrunken with boiling that the tight bandy trousers were above his boots and the cuffs almost up to the elbows of his monkey arms. And under his jacket he had a white cycling sweater tied with waxed thread round his waist to stop it hanging down to his knees like a shirt.

The three of us started out again for my uncle's with Tiger trotting behind us like a pack sergeant, and as we passed the front of Benja's shop we could see the dirty top of his father's head showing above the green paint, it was bald and shining as though he had held it hard against the spinning brushes he kept for polishing the leather in the shop. We turned into the tramroad once more, just where I had met the crimson singer, passing Dai Ben-tip nursing the baby with the shawl wrapped all round him, and M'Liza's brother, William the Rates, resting his bad leg on a window sill. He had a big black beard and hair all over him, and he growled all day long like a big dog who wants you to spit on a stone and throw it for him. As we passed by, Benja said something cheeky and the old man hit him across the behind with his walking stick. But Benja only laughed and soon he began smoking a cigarette nip, pulling hard at it, grimacing, hollowing his ginger-haired cheeks and wrinkling up his eyes as though it was a hard job to suck any smoke out of it.

After a while he began telling us again about the time he went abroad to play for the country against the French schoolboys (his father didn't know till after, he thought he was bad with the bile in his Auntie Blod's in the next valley) and how they gave him so much brandy over there they couldn't keep him in his seat at the banquet and before he was sick he wanted to fight the Mayor of Paris. He always made me laugh with this story, but Arthur didn't take any notice of him.

Then, to annoy me and Benja, Arthur started talking about Horace and Catullus, and we didn't know anything about those poets because he had got up into a form above us now. We were sorry they had separated us because you could get fun out of the cool way Arthur always spoke to the masters, like when he cheeked Crumpy in the Latin lesson and told him of course he had a crib and he found he couldn't do without it. Besides, Benja didn't have anyone to copy off now. Benja never had much time to do his homework because he was always in chapel or boxing over Imperato's, so he used to scribble Arthur's lessons out behind the fives court during dinnertime, fetching a pen and an inkwell stuffed with paper out of school for the job. He was always in such a hurry that he used to make a broth of it with blots and smudges, and when he had finished he used to throw the inkwell away into the bushes and hurry down town without us for a smoke and a game of billiards. (I wouldn't go with him now, because the only time I went I found a couple of yellow snooker balls in my schoolbag when I got home.)

Very soon he had had a bellyful of Horace and Catullus, and he started talking about the footwork of Maxy Imperato, because that was the only thing he knew more about than Arthur. I didn't much care what they talked about as long as it wasn't my bunch of roses, but presently Arthur said, 'What did you say was the matter with your uncle, Williams?'

'Asthma,' I said. 'Chronic.'

'Asthma,' he said, 'and you're taking him flowers. Don't you know things like that plastered with pollen will bring on an attack for him?'

I was angry with him and I said that was old-fashioned talk, fly-me, like spitting on warts and having a potato for rheumatism, but I knew for sure somehow he was right. I felt cross with my mother, it was just like her to do this to me. (I couldn't help remembering the time my cousins were coming for Christmas when I was small, and she gave me and Rhysie a sleeping draught to stop us getting excited. But she gave us so much we slept fast for three days and never saw our cousins at all.)

'I've never seen anyone having an attack of asthma,' said Benja in a thoughtful way, grinning and picking at his bad teeth. So I was feeling worried when at last we got outside my uncle's house, and all I wanted to do was to get away as soon as I could.

My Uncle Sam's stone house was very small and so full of furniture that there were only narrow passages in between the hulking dressers and the chests of drawers for you to move about in. Every shelf and flat space had a big bible on it, or a collier's lamp, or a crowd of photographs and china mementos, and you could hardly see the wallpaper anywhere because of the family enlargements, and the Rechabites' calendars and the massive furniture big enough for a palace or a castle. My Auntie Maggie was very clean and always smelling of carbolic, she was for ever smoothing the table oilcloth with her apron, and using her goose's wing on the curtains and scouring the handles of her sweeping brushes with red sand to keep them white. And though it was misty in her kitchen now, as dim as the inside of a bottle, still every piece of wood and every strip of metal shone like polished glass in the smoky gloom, especially the heavy brass airing rail, and the steel stand and fender, and the gleaming fringe of brass around the mantelpiece. My uncle and auntie always lived in this little box of a kitchen, which had a bosh in the corner smelling of soap, and white stoning swirls on the floor, and a square of drying wires on the ceiling, and a chimney that was always blowing down clouds of stife into the room in winter. They had a nice parlour too, but my auntie only used that to let the jellies set in, and whenever you went in there your feet stuck to the oilcloth and all the ornaments trembled.

I liked my Uncle Sam ever since I was small and he taught me corkwork. He used to draw a flag for me then, and the *gwdihŵ*, and harlequin, or swallow his watch on the end of a string and let me hear it ticking in his belly. He was my favourite uncle, although I knew he was a born liar. When he was a young man he had run away because my Mamgu Thomas used to beat him for buying bottle beer with the money from his drapery round. But he was old now and bald, and a bit deaf, he looked very respectable drowsing in the rocking chair by the fire with a snowy shawl round his shoulders and a jug of herb beer in his hand. He was wearing a washed suit after my father and a pair of old carpet slaps, and round his neck there was a black knitted tie but no collar. And although he hadn't done a tap for years now, you could tell it was true he had once been working underground because there was a jagged blue mark running like quartz across his forehead and continuing in a thick blue vein down his cheek. He had yellow eyeballs, a red nose as bright as a berry and brown bamboo marks mottling the skin of his long hanging cheeks. His moustache was small now (when he was on his wanderings it had been a huge one shaped like a steer's horns or the badge of the Buffs) and because he hadn't shaved his bristling chin glittered like a stubble of hoar-frost. He had been ailing so long he smiled with pleasure when he saw us, showing his bad teeth under his moustache. All my uncle's teeth were of different colours and sizes. Some were brown, some yellow and some slatish, and one buff-coloured tooth would be twice the height of the little black stump standing next to it.

My Auntie Maggie made us go inside the kitchen, dog and all, to talk to Uncle Sam. She was always dressed in baggy black, and she was fat and soft all over with a lap like a feather-bed. Her face was clean and handsome, she had a lot of grey horse-hair, a big curved nose and a lovely smile, but there was something the matter with one of her eyes – the right ball was fixed and pitch black, it stood bulging out of her head and shining with the polish of the big black-leaded pebble that kept the back door open and it never slid about into the corners at all. Sometimes after chapel on Sunday nights my uncle and auntie used to come down our house to sing hymns round the parlour harmonium while my father accompanied us on the trombone. My auntie had a lovely soprano voice but her favourite Sunday night solo was called ''Tis Heaven or Hell with you and me', and she used to frighten the life out of me with that song because the great polished knob of her stuck eye was fixed fast upon me the whole time she was singing it, making me remember all the times I had smoked and told lies and even gone up the woods miching. I knew where I was going, and in the dead silence after her song, with only the gas shade ringing, I could feel my hair creeping about on my head.

But all that was years ago and I knew now my auntie was innocent, she would believe anything. And she waited on my uncle hand, foot and finger, saying, 'You'll come, come you,' to him all the time to cheer him up a bit. She was a lovely woman and she put the roses out the back where Mam Evans was getting the washing ready, without hurting my feelings, although Benja wanted to take them in the kitchen for my uncle to have a good smell.

Although I was so anxious to get away we had a tidy little time talking to my Uncle Sam. We could hear the two women banging about among the buckets outside the window behind us, my auntie using the canebrush like mad on the back, and every now and then popping the big black knob of her horse-eye up against the pane and staring through the geranium leaves to see how we were getting on. The three of us sat in a row on the couch opposite my uncle and he told us interesting lies with gusto about America and Woolangong and other places, but none of us believed him; we had the yarn about the man who worked in the airways and the tale of how my uncle found that week's *Football Echo* in the middle of the Australian bush when he was a lost man out there. (Benja grinned at that, his teeth like barnacles on his gums. 'And now tell us the one about the three bears,' he said.)

At times my uncle would get so excited he would have to stop his tale for a bit of puff, or to take a swig out of his herb jug, sucking his soaking moustaches into his mouth after he had done it. 'The old bellows,' he would mutter pointing to his chest and smiling. With the fire lit, the door closed and the sun shining hot outside, the boxy little room was becoming warmer and warmer and I would move to go while my uncle was drinking, but Benja would say, 'Take a blow, Evan, I think he's got an attack coming on,' although he was hot in his white sweater. But nothing happened and I would have to sit down again while my uncle hooked his hand like the skinny yellow claw of a boiling fowl around his ear trying to catch what Benja was saying.

When we made my uncle understand who Arthur was, he rolled his amber eyeballs with pleasure and laughed, shaking his hanging mottled cheeks; he knew Tommy Morgan well, and his father, the Gentleman Miner, before him, and he began telling stories about him when he was a young cutter, before he got his tail into the mud. Arthur smiled, very polite, hanging on to Tiger's collar, but he didn't say much, he was too indolent to shout although really he was a fine conversationalist; he used to talk very far back and use phrases you couldn't understand like 'the perihelion of Mercury', and 'the pucelage and virginity of women.' But Benja didn't mind shouting and he began showing off like a red-headed ape, telling my uncle fairy tales about his family, and turning round to show the scar on the back of his ginger head that he said his mother had done when she crowned him with the frying-pan because he couldn't remember the three headings of a sermon on charity. (Arthur and I knew that really he had bolted some secondhand spring expanders up in the attic on the sly and when he went to use them the hook had pulled out of the wood and nearly brained him.) He had started his clowning as soon as he had come in, shaking hands with my uncle and auntie with the wrong hand like a big-headed gnome, and grinning at them as though he were an idiot, the gaps in his teeth showing like book-backs missing from a shelf. He was daft now and his nonsense made me hotter than ever, although I had to laugh when he rolled up his tight trousers and showed the birthmark on his bandy leg shaped like the Caspian Sea that he said had made him top of the class when he copied it on his geography paper. 'Come on, Benja,' I said standing up, wanting to peg him back a bit because my uncle was laughing and sweating at the same time; his snowy shawl was down behind him in the bars of the rocker and he was holding his chest with his bright yellow fist, his eyes shut tight, his cheeks puffed out and his puce tongue showing under his moustache with a fit of coughing. But before I could get him to move my auntie padded smiling and bulge-eyed into the kitchen, sidling with her tin tray among the massive mahogany, and gave us a slice of apple-tart each, and a fork to get it up with. Then she went over to my uncle and tidied him up a bit, wiping his ripe red nose and dusting his face with her apron as though he were a piece of furniture, persuading him to have another dose of Cough-no-more as she draped the shawl around his shoulders. Then when we had started eating Mam Evans came in with some of the things *she* liked, bread and cheese and a jampot of pickle cabbage which she put down on the table for us. They never had anything with vinegar in it in Benja's, because Bowen the bootmaker had found out the word meant 'sour wine', so when no one was looking Benja threw his piece of tart under the couch and started enjoying the pickle cabbage.

'Bowen,' said Arthur, 'why do you catch your fork so low down?'

I didn't notice that Benja held his fork low down, but I always used to look at his finger with the top off.

Mam Evans, who stood by the table as we were eating, dipping now and then into the pickle cabbage with a spoon and a piece of bread, had a face like rubber or fresh putty. She had no teeth and because her mouth was right up under her nose she seemed to be chewing with her nostrils. And her flabby head with the watery blue eyes in it and the toe-nail growing out of her chin seemed narrow compared with her neck because on each side she had a smooth and solid wen. She was wearing a pair of clogs, her black flannel working clothes with a canvas apron round her and a man's cap fastened with a hat-pin through her bun. She listened to my uncle telling Arthur and Benja the old story of how he fell down and kissed the railway line in *hiraeth* when he was abroad because he saw by the stamp on it it was rolled not fifty yards from my Mamgu's house, and then she interrupted him, chewing all over her face. 'Sam Thomas,' she said loudly, 'you won't laugh at me will you?'

My uncle stopped his story and we all looked at her.

'Laugh at you, Mam Evans?' he said, when he understood her broken English. 'What do you mean? Laugh at you?'

'Well, if I ask you a question you won't laugh at me will you?' She had big baggy hands like coal-gloves and she played with her scabby chin.

'Of course not,' said my Uncle Sam, all his different-coloured teeth showing like a street skyline. 'What do you want to know?'

'Well, you've been to America abroad, haven't you?'

'Yes I have, Mam Evans,' my uncle answered, his yellow talon hung on his ear.

'And you know the sun and the moon?'

My uncle nodded. 'Yes I do, of course.'

'You won't laugh at me will you?'

'No no, I won't laugh, go on.'

'Well, do they have the same sun and moon in America as we do have here?'

We all laughed at that, my uncle and all, and Benja threw his feet in their button boots into the air. My uncle said yes they had the same sun and moon, and at that Mam Evans clumped back to her work chewing and grumbling at us and taking snuff, her skirts down at the sides and up at the back.

My auntie stood by smiling too as we were eating, landed that we were enjoying ourselves, and then she began questioning me about Rhysie and my mother. Anybody else would see I didn't want to talk about our mam just then, but my auntie was so innocent she didn't notice. Our door-knocker was a solid brass hand with a palmed brass ball in it, and when I couldn't hold her off any longer I had to blurt out my mother's foot was bad because when she was going to chapel she pulled the front door after her and the knocker came away as she did it. She came a cropper down our five steps and landed up with her leg under the gate, and she had to go to chapel with the brass knocker weighing three or four pounds in her overcoat pocket. I was ashamed to say what had happened because everyone would say it was just like my mother, so I ended by turning to Benja and saying, 'Don't start on that culff, Benja, let's go home.'

He shook his big head, his cheeks full of bread and his bad teeth quarrying the cheese. 'Take a blow, mun,' he growled like a prompter, 'the bloke that made time made plenty of it.'

Arthur had let go his hold on Tiger to eat his tart, and the dog had his paws up on the couch, hoping for a bit of it. Suddenly he growled and quivered all over, and without any more warning jumped on to the couch alongside us and then bolted straight out through the window from between the geraniums; he took a header clean through the glass as

though it were not there at all and disappeared out of sight. The pane
shattered into fragments, leaving only a fringe of jagged pieces like a
paper hoop around the edges, and there was the deafening clatter of an
accident with trays among the buckets in the backyard. We all jumped up
and stared out of the window, feeling the cool air at once on our faces,
my uncle behind us gripping our arms and wheezing with excitement.
Arthur began whistling through the broken pane after the dog, which
had galloped up the path and was now standing rigid near the garden
wall on which the next door's tabby was sitting, and gradually getting
smaller in safety. 'Tiger, Tiger,' he called coolly. 'Come here, boy. Come
here, boy.' And at last Tiger turned round and came bounding and diving
back down the garden path towards the kitchen again. He saw Arthur
standing by the broken glass of the window and without any hesitation
he plunged back into the room through the other pane, bursting it like a
water-bubble and bringing all the geraniums down on to the couch
behind him as he tumbled over on to the mat. Arthur gripped him by the
collar and began slapping him about the head, his black hair hanging in
curves like the claws of a pair of callipers over his face.

My auntie, who used to pick my uncle up at the doorstep when it
was raining and battle her way through the passage with him on her
back to keep the oilcloth clean, didn't know what to do, she just sat
down on the stool and said, '*O wel ta wir*,' with her face in a twist and
her glued eye staring at the mess on the floor. Because it was a sad
sight to her, as bad as a pig's breakfast spoiling the stoning on her
lovely hearth. There were pieces of glass scattered all over her spotless
kitchen and the geranium pots, in falling, had split open and the earth
lay spread in dollops all over the hearthrug mixed with fragments of
cheese and red cabbage and flakes of pastry. And the dog, who had
opened his bowels with fright on the mat when he crashed like a
cannon-ball back into the room, made my uncle fall over backwards
into the rocker, overturning the little table behind him and sending all
the crockery to the floor including the Mabon milk-jug, and splashing
the herb beer all over the wall and the cupboard and the black-leaded
fireplace, where it ran down the oven in long tears.

Just then Mam Evans put her head on the end of her wide wenny
neck around the door, a snuff stain on her nose and her bottom lip
fitted up over her top like the flap of a bandage.

'Maggie Thomas,' she said, not noticing anything with her pale half-
liquid eyes, 'I want a bit of soda. Have you got a bit of soda?'

But my auntie took no notice of her, she sat glaring downwards with
her black ornamental eye and muttering to herself, '*O wel ta wir. O wel
ta wir.*'

Suddenly, in the middle of all the mess, I noticed Benja's face. He wasn't paying any attention to my auntie, or to Mam Evans squinting round the corner, or to Arthur slapping the dog; he was gaping at my Uncle Sam's bald head starting to simmer, and his blue wound growing brilliant on his forehead, and his boiling chest beginning to bubble like a kettle as his shoulders heaved up under his ears. He sat fascinated with his short finger in his nose, his lower jaw hung out like a balcony and a daft smile of satisfaction on his face as the attack began to develop.

The Water Music

❧

Shall I dive, shall I dive? Behind me the patterns of the coloured town I left lie spread out in the green valley like a carpet taken out on the grass for beating, and I race down the sunny slope out of sight of it. I am a flier with the wind rushing under the bony arches of my wings, I am a white gull, I am two-hundred gulls, I am the gull-shower of snow in sunshine, and the whirled flakes of summer whitening the world. I turn my beaked face and out of a bright eye I see beside my head, rigid and purposeful, my crooked wing with its piled-up foam-crest of feathers broken wave-white along its ridge in the speed-created wind, I see the few cricketing children dwarfed in the tree-surrounded meadow and the grannie in black who minds their picnic fire, and the column of wood-smoke upright in the odorous air of the field. Beyond the curtain of foliage surrounding the oval meadow glitters the curve of the river in silver patches, poured like a flat snake among the trees, sundering the rooted feet that crowd upon its bank. And beside the river's biggest pool rises the grey diving-rock, the stone in the sunshine pale as coltsfoot leaf but felt-smooth and smouldering warm to the fingers. Shall I dive, shall I dive?

As I stood by the little sherbet shop at the cornfield gate and looked over the wheat, a large broken-hearted bird came crying inland on long transparent wings like knives, radiant as fine sailcloth or sunlit snow. He was a beautiful gull, and after circling he came to rest on one leg like a wineglass upon the gatepost beside me. He had a lovely white neck and the sun-kindled curve of his swelling breast gleamed white as the milky dazzle of coconut kernel in the sunshine which he faced. Over his powerful boxer's back was spread a mantle of smooth dove-grey feathers, and below the glitter of his theatrically darkened eye-disc he had a brilliant broom-yellow bill, long, curved and tigerish, with a blob of blood-orange red painted near the nostrils.

'Gull,' I said in bad Latin, 'why have you left your green egg?' – 'Wha, wha, wha,' was his reply, as he folded up his webs and flew off rapidly up the valley ahead of us. Shall I dive?

Now I am across the scented meadow and through the partition of trees, I climb the high grey diving-rock and see the bathers undressing on the cliff-shelves opposite or already swimming in pure water. I greet twenty boys from my crocketed pinnacle, waving towel and black triangular slip, hailing red-tied Thomas as comrade, a ginger boy with freckles and the blue eyes of a black kitten as neighbour Williams, and having to cry 'Gracias' to the pale and orphaned Scabbo Ball, who, wishing me well, addresses me with a bow as señor. The water beneath is limpid, the pebbles and the sandy bottom waver under it, smoothly it flows over them like flawed glass. Shall I dive with the speed of the gull or like the capering swallow who plunges with shut wings?

Below me among the rocks is the perfectly fitting pool, large and circular, with the sun shattered upon its surface; there is the voluminous river cataracting down the grey limestone steps in crystal fans and ferns and luminous ice-sheets and floods of clear rock-varnish, and bunches of glass bananas; there is the dim tunnel that receives the sliding river in a long sealskin volute out of the dazzling floor of the pool, the down-drench of birch-boughs and the green masses of beech-leaves sleek under the smooth glove of the sunshine are arched over the glossy water. The broad scarlet towel-stripe glows unbearable as ruby on the grey rock, the black-slipped boys in naked groups lounge white and delicate in midday moon-flesh, and warm, on the sunlit shelves of the little cliff. Rosie Bowen the bootmaker's boy, begotten of mild mother and boxing-glove burning sire, ignoramus, *victor ludorum*, stands in the water severed at the knees, with half-revealed distaste upon a dunce's countenance of endearing and transcendental ugliness. As he ponders, somebody throws a pebble into the water, and his back is splashed.

'Ay Scabbo,' he shouts without looking round. 'I'll dig you in the chin.'

And then he slowly advances over the velvet-growing stones like a thief among snares or a sufferer from foot-warts; with the pool-water chilling his bandy legs he is hesitant as Dic Dywyll, reluctant and maladroit now, no reckless Christmas morning plunger to be met with an ice-hammer in his pocket on the track to the frozen tarn. He toes the slippery pool-stones in his path, each bearded with a long phlegm of green weed, into water as clear as crystal he peers with the intensity of a louse-hunting mother examining the hair of her dirtiest. By spreading to the sun his boxer's ape-arms, powerful and muscular under their gleaming ginger fell, he achieves for a moment the unstable balance of the tightrope artiste. He is an indifferent concealer of his dislike of this element in its icy mountain freshness, unwarmed by equatorial current or outpoured boiler-water from the pit-head engine-room, but gradually he sinks into the depths of the pool, the blackish Caspian birthmark on his leg is submerged, the rings spread from his hairy thighs, and finding with his soles a rock-slab in the river bed when the water is around his waist, he crosses his arms in respite on his chest, and tucks into his armpits his yellow iron-mold hands – because he would smoke tea-leaves, or seaweed or even india rubber. His abnormal homeliness in the pool is as rare as great villainy or genius. Upon his giant head is sewn a dense fibrous hump of coconut hair; his cheeks even now are tomato-red, and his protrusive lower jawbone with the liquorice stumps of disordered black teeth gapes open like a half-shut bottom drawer. Were I to dive and come up beside him, before punching he would stare with the incredulity of Gerallt's soldier voiding a calf. Dare I dive into this huge water?

Under a tree with the curving tail of a branch hanging down over the water stands Arthur Vaughan Morgan, Rosie's friend, tall and lovely-limbed, forgetting now the humiliation of battered teaspoons and the charred cork for a knob in the broken teapot lid; he leans garlanded and naked in a dance-dress of sunlight flimsily-patterned with transparent foliage. And Evan Williams, the third of The Three, his hair corrugated like biscuit-paper, surreptitiously unrobes behind a jut of rock, concealing thus the unique and resourceful fastenings of his broken underwear. He removes last a sort of check bodice with a frilled waistline. He has orange-golden hair and orange-golden freckles you couldn't put a pin between. He does not wear the black school bathing triangle but a scalene slip of his own devising fashioned from a pair of bootlaces and a folded red handkerchief covered with white polka dots. That Sterne-visaged grammarian, our English master, who annihilates me with sarcasm when I audibly praise heaven for prose-writers who use two words where one will do, yet reads aloud with approval to the assembled form my essay upon the virtues of our native land. 'Glory be to the Isle of the Mighty for her ponds and the pools of all her rivers,' he sneers, 'for Pwll Wat, and Pwll Taf and Pwll Tydfil. And for her lakes, for Llangorse and Llyn y Fan, and for Llyn Syfaddon lovely under Dafydd's swan.'

'Let there be praise also for the pools of the Po and for the waters of Lake Titicaca,' Evan whispers behind my blushing ear.

'Praise her for her towns and villages and her ancient divisions, praise her for Gwynedd and Powys and Dyfed and Morgannwg. Praise her for her lovely names, for Llanrhidian, Afon Sawdde, Fan Girhirych, Dyffryn Clwyd. Praise her for Rhosllanerchrugog – "

'And for Llanfairpwllgwyngyllgogerychwyrndrobwllandysiliogogo-goch,' softly intones Williams to a mutilated version of 'Hen Wlad fy Nhadau'.

'Let us praise her for Lleyn and Llanelly, for Dinas Mawddwy and Dinas Powis, for Cwm Elan and Cwm Rhondda, let us praise Tresaith equally with Treorky and Penrhyn Gŵyr equally with Pengarnddu.'

'Let us praise Moscow equally with Little Moscow,' growls Evan, 'and Llantwit Major equally with Asia Minor,' and the only thing to do is to cough.

Now Bolo Jones the overman's boy, togaed in many towels, wishing to show Arthur little Dai Badger denounced as Catiline and indignantly interrogated as to when he shall cease oppressing the people, shouts down, 'Acker, Acker, look at this.'

Arthur, dappled under his hanging bough, ignores him.

'Acker Morgan,' shouts undaunted Bolo again from his proscenium, a grey ledge of rock six feet above the water, his arm outstretched in indignation towards the singing Catiline.

Arthur frowns, examining his nails. He is a cock with a high comb. His three sisters are knowing and fashionable, they have haughty expressions but short legs.

'Ack–er,' shouts Bolo once more, loud above the cries and the chorus singing and the low roar of the river rushing into the pool with the splash of water washing itself all over.

Arthur turns towards him. 'My name is Arthur,' he says testily. 'Arthur – heroic and European. Arthur Trevelyan Vaughan Morgan."

Bolo Jones drops his towels, claps his hand to his head and collapses backwards into the pool.

And dare I dive from this height into the water?

Rosie Bowen is swimming. He has waded up to the foot of the cataract and now, using a breast-stroke, proceeds kicking with the help of the current down the middle of the water. His swimming is laborious and convulsive, like a frog who has swallowed a handful of lead-shot, but everyone remembers Imperato's and his head is not pushed under. On the lowest ledge of the cliff opposite, Phil and Sinky swing a grinning Dai Badger to and fro by the wrists and ankles, while Scabbo, his body white as pipeclay, gives them his orders. 'Away with him,' he cries, 'cast the perjured caitiff into the roaring torrent of the river.' – 'The traitor says he cannot swim, my lord,' says Sinky. 'Clearly,' answers Scabbo, 'here is a fine chance for him to learn.' Dai bounds outwards, he enters the water in the button of a ragged bloom of spray. Bleddyn Beavan who has just climbed out to watch crouches smiling in a sleek skin with his toes gripping the rock brink, his hands on his knees and a thread of water running back into the pool off his chin. All of us in our form have a firm and scientifically accurate knowledge of our physical genesis because his father is Doctor Gomer and Bleddyn will lend you his medical books at tuppence a week. Shall I dive?

When I was small and dirty, with a quilted bottom to my trousers, I wanted only to learn swimming. Out of my big brother's book I spelled this sentence: 'The action of the frog should be studied and imitated.' On washing day I mitched and went up Cwm Ffrwd, croaking about by the river like a frog. At last I found a big green one weighing a quarter of a pound. I put him in my cap to bring him home and he didn't like that because my cat used to sleep in it every night. My mother had two tubs of clothes-water in our back and I put him in the one for the flannels. I made him swim about in the warm water among the shirts and the nightgowns, and soon I could swim lovely. When I heard my mother coming I put him down the lavatory and poured a bucket of water on top of him.

That evening I went up the pit-pond on the tips where the collier-boys used to swim dirty. I climbed on to the timber balks and dived in. When I woke up a big crowd of men was carrying me home across the fields on a stretcher. I thought I had been punished for drowning the frog who had taught me to swim. At home the doctor said, 'And last week he pulled the coping of the Methodist Chapel wall on his chest.'

The same summer my mother took us to the Wells for our holidays. I borrowed tuppence off my brother and went for a swim in the open-air baths. I had never been to a baths before. The water was black and crowded with people. I dived in at the shallow end. This time when I came to I was stretched out on the mohair couch in our lodgings with my skin cold as glass and a big smooth lump like a teacup on the front of my head.

And now dare I dive?

Behind me across the meadow, I see through the trees the luminous green slope where I was a rugger-running gull, tilted to the sunglare, the grass seething in the summer sunbeams vivid and crystalline, the brightness glowing over the kindled surface with a teeming lustre of intense emerald as though the grassy fabric were a sheet of transparent crystal evenly illuminated with rays of pure greenish fire from beneath. And over it goes my gull, rigid and ravenous, crying 'Wah, wah, wah'. He is beautiful enough to be addressed by the wandering scholar who said, 'Lovely gull, snow-white and moon-white, immaculate sun-patch and sea-glove, swift-proud fish-eater, let us fly off hand-in-hand, you are light on the waves as a sea-lily. My grey nun among sea-crests, you shall be my glossy letter, go and carry a *billet* to my girl for me and win distant praise by making for her fortress. You shall see her, Eigr-coloured, on her castle, gull. Carry her my note, my chosen, go girl-wards. If she is alone do not be shy of talking to her, but be tactful in the presence of so much fastidiousness. Tell her I shall die without her and look, gull, tell her I am over head and ears in love with her, that not even Merddin or Taliesin desired her superior in beauty. Gull, under her tangled crop of copper you shall behold Christendom's loveliest lovely – but she'll be the death of me if you bring no for an answer.'

'Take my boots off when I die, when I die,' sings Dai Badger, shaped like a ship's anchor floating on the surface of the pool.

'Take my boots off when I die.'

The butcher's cart and bill-heads of Dai's father bear the slogan, 'Let Badger be your Butcher,' which seven-syllabled line in the opinion of that erratic but pithy critic Evan Williams, contains more poetry and *cynghanedd* than the similarly hortatory but more famous words of the High Priest of Lakery urging us to take Nature for our Teacher. For Evan, who always hears of such things, has solved the riddle of Hamlet. The clue lies, he maintains, with the hidden character called Pat, addressed directly only once and that in the tortured reflection of young Denmark – 'Now might I do it, Pat, now he is praying,' but whose machinations and subtle influence have confounded three hundred years of criticism. Shall I dive now like a glider of the boughs?

Dai Badger is again on the shelf, juicy-nosed, counting his tail-feathers after his ducking and the bravado of his song. He spots me watching him across the pool and wants to know if I will come over the mountain with him tomorrow. 'To where?' I ask cautiously. 'One A one b one e one r one d one a one r one e,' he cries at breathless speed. 'Will you?' He is a fabulist and claims to be in love with the vicar's Swiss maid there, who is indeed a nicely shaped young woman but twice his size. I make an excuse and he sings a wicked ballad describing his passion for her foreign body. He feels no *pudeur* at our natural out-curves and tuberosities and his naked belly now is tight as a bagpipe with lyricism. But Rosie Bowen, hearing him, spits into the water; he has coconut hair, an undershot jaw, and, to a god's-eye view, a hump like a high bosom on his back; he spits copiously and without displaying muscular action, projecting a large and heavy gob down-stream without a twitch of his face, sending it flying in a sweet curve from his immobile face.

And now shall I dive?

Arthur leaves the shelter of his tail-shaped tree and stands among the swimmers on the soaking ledge like a patrician candidate heroically facing the malodorous citizens. Flicker, our mathematics master, who declares so-and-so to be an outstanding this, that and the other, if he would only more frequently 'duck his nut,' is despised by Arthur, the inelegant phrasing, bad breath and linoleum waistcoat of this unpleasant sciolist deeply offend him. 'Here is a clever chap,' sneers Flicker, distributing the marked examination papers after his terminal test, 'Arthur Morgan, the famous mathematical genius. He can solve a quadratic equation in one line! Stand up Morgan! You cooked the answer!'

'I didn't,' says Arthur with dignity.

'You did,' shouts Flicker, reddening and bulge-eyed. 'I didn't,' says Arthur.

'You did,' shouts Flicker.

'Oh, all right,' says Arthur sitting down. 'I'll give you the benefit of the doubt.'

But he is teased because Bolo Jones has his photograph taken in his first long-trousered sailor-suit, with a cane whistle on a cord and a fouled anchor worked on his front.

Below me where the water is quiet, foam in clusters of pappus and pints of cuckoo-spit and fine meshes of foam thin as beer-froth float on the dark water; under the overhanging boughs of the boy-bodied beeches and the cataracting birches, a broken mesh of reflected gold is thrown up in the gloom, the network of uneasy golden light on the under-branches is torn apart and joined up again as the green liquid glass of the water is splashed and the sunlight scattered. A breeze starts, the wind is handed on from tree to tree, I hear near me the first soft clatter of the poplar leaves. Soon the swimming will be over and I dawdle and have not dived. Rosie retires shivering in the hot sunshine, cold beyond the reach of wine or smith's fire. Evan says a swig would be welcome as hail in hell and Dai Badger shouts, 'I feel poppish too.' They dress and leave together for the widow's shop at the cornfield gate where on a piece of torn cardboard, for the information of picnickers, is chalked the message – 'Hot water sold here. Pop round the corner.' I must dive.

Shooting down the silky chasm of my plunge, with my soles to the brilliant county blue and the cortex of that highly convolved and dazzling cloud, I shall be the gull off her olive egg, the diving gull from the covey dawn, the herring-gull or blackback falling like large snow off the roof of the world. Rosie is a powerful land-animal, Evan charming and unawakened, Arthur learned in Latin, beautiful as Sande or some musk-scented princess; but I am the finest swimmer in this water and the only person who knows what a *vidame* is. My lungs are full, with hirundine screamings I hurdle hedges, I plunge performing the devil-dive of a star. I bomb the water blind and all images are shattered in my head. I sink and soon it is silent there, the dark beards of the stones wave as though in the breeze and the small grains of sand bowl in the current along the bottom of the pool. My breath rises like anchor-bubbles through the water green as glass edges, I lie like sand-eel, water-snake, or Welsh Shelley under the ten-foot slab of transparent green, watching it reach the world of my God whom I continue to praise, whom I praise for the waters, the little balls of dew and the great wave shooting out its tassel; I praise him for the big boy-bodied beeches and all trees velvet in sunshine and shying like mad when the grass is flat under the wind; I praise him for the blooms of the horned lilac, for the blossomed hawthorn with the thick milks of spring rising over her and the blood-drop of the ladycow bled on the white lily. I praise him for the curving gull, the brown coat of the sparrow and the plover with wings like blown hair.

I praise him for words and sentences, I praise him for Flicker Wilkins and for Arthur Vaughan Morgan and his sisters in fashionable hats like low buckets; I praise him for Bolo Jones and Dai Badger and Scabbo Ball, and for Scabbo Ball's auntie who keeps the weighing machine and has green glasses and one hand. I praise him for the golden freckles of Evan Williams as much as for Rosie Bowen who suffers a traumatic malformation of the jaw.

I praise him for the things for which I have not praised him and for the things praised only in the pleats of my meaning.

I praise him for his endless fertility and inventiveness, that he stripes, shades, patches and stipples every surface of his creation in his inexhaustible designing, leaves no stretch of water unmarked, no sand or snow-plain without the relief of interfering stripe, shadow or cross-hatch, no spread of pure sky but he deepens it from the pallor of its edges to its vivid zenith. I praise him that he is never baulked, never sterile, never repetitious.

There is praise for him in my heart and in my flesh pulled over my heart, there is praise for him in my pain and in my enjoying. I show my praise for him in the unnecessary skip of my walk, in my excessive and delighted staring, in the exuberance of my over-praise.

And when I dive I shall feel the ice of speed and praise him, the shock and tingle of the gold-laced pool and praise him, the chrism of golden sunshine poured on my drenching head again and praise him.

I dive into the engulfing water, praising him.

Jordan

❧

I am worried. Today when I cut my chin with my white-handled razor I didn't bleed. That was the way Danny's shaving went. Danny was my friend. Together we had a spell working the fairs and markets out there in that country where there are nothing but farms and chapels. It was a sort of uncivilized place. I had invented a good line, a special cube guaranteed to keep the flies off the meat, and Danny had his little round boxes of toothpaste. This toothpaste he scraped off a big lump of wet batter, a few pounds of it, greenish in colour and with a bad smell; it stood on a tin plate and sometimes Danny would sell it as corn cure. So as to gather a crowd around his trestle he used to strip down to his black tights and walk about with a fifty-six-pound solid iron weight hanging by a short strap from his teeth. This was to show what wonderful teeth you would have if you used Danny's toothpaste. It was only when he was doing this that you ever saw any colour in Danny's face. The colour came because he did the walking about upside down; he was on his hands doing it with his black stockings in the air.

Danny was thin and undersized. If I made a joke about his skinny legs he would lower his lids offended and say, 'Don't be so personal.' He was very touchy. His tights were coms dyed black and they looked half empty, as though large slices had been cut off from inside them. He had a fine, half-starved face, very thin and leathery, like a sad cow. There was only one thing wrong with his face and that was the ears. Danny's ears were big and yellow, and they stood out at right angles to his head. From the front they looked as though they had been screwed into his skull, and one had been screwed in a lot further than the other. His straight carrot hair was very long and thick and brushed back over his head. When he scuffled about on his bandy arms with that half hundredweight dangling from his teeth, his mop opened downwards off his scalp as though it was on a hinge, and bumped along the cobble-stones. He was very proud of his teeth. He thought so much of them he never showed them to anyone. Nobody ever saw Danny grinning.

My own line was that special cube I had invented to keep the flies off the meat. I used to soften down a few candles and shape the grease into dices with my fingers. Then I put one or two of these white dices on a cut of meat on my trestle in the middle of the market crowds. There were always plenty of fat flies and bluebottles buzzing about in those markets, what with the boiled sweet stalls and the horse-droppings, but you never saw one perching on my meat with the white cubes on it. This wasn't because the flies didn't like candle-grease but because under the meat-plate I had a saucer of paraffin oil.

One night Danny and I were sitting on the bed in our lodging house. The place was filthy and lousy and we were catching bugs on our needles off the walls and roasting them to death one by one in the candle flame. Danny was bitter. The fair had finished but the farmers had kept their hands on their ha'pennies. And the weather was bad, very wet and gusty and cold all the time. Danny said we were pioneers. He said these farmers were savages, they didn't care about having filthy teeth, or eating their food fly-blown. He was very down-hearted. He hadn't had much to eat for a few days and between the noisy bursting of the bugs his empty belly crowed. I was down-hearted too. We had to get money from somewhere to pay for our lodgings and a seat in the horsebrake drawing out of town the next morning. I asked Danny to come out into the town to see what we could pick up but he wouldn't. At first he said it was too cold. Then he said he had got to darn his tights and his stockings. In the end I went by myself.

The town had been newly wetted with another downpour and Danny was right about the cold. As I walked up the dark empty main street I could feel the wind blowing into the holes in my boots. Everywhere was closed up and silent and deserted. I looked in at 'The Bell' and 'The Feathers' and 'The Glyndŵr', but they were all empty. Then from the swing door of 'The Black Horse' I saw inside a big broad-shouldered man sitting down by himself in the bar. Apart from him the bar was deserted. He was by the fire and his back was towards me. I knew bumming a drink out of him would be as easy as putting one hand in the other. I knew this because he had a red wig on coming down over the collar of his coat, and a man who wears a wig is lonely.

On the table in front of the man I could see a glass of whisky and in his hand was a little black book. He was singing a hymn out of it in Welsh. It was sad, a funeral hymn, but very determined. I stood by the door of the empty bar and listened. The 'Horse' was small and gloomy inside. I wondered if I would go in. The man seemed huge in the neck and across the shoulders, and every time he moved all the flesh on him seemed to begin to tremble. If he kept dead still he stopped trembling. I went in past him and stood the other side of the table by the fire.

When I got round to the front of this man something snapped like a carrot inside me. His face was hideous. The flesh of it looked as though it had been torn apart into ribbons and shoved together again anyhow back on to the bones. Long white scars ran glistening through the purple skin like ridges of gristle. Only his nose had escaped. This was huge and dark and full of holes, it curved out like a big black lump of wood with the worm in it. He was swarthy, as though he was sitting in a bar of shadow, and I looked up to see if perhaps a roof-beam had come between him and the hanging oil-lamp lighting the bar. There wasn't a hair on him, no moustache or eyebrows, but his wig was like the bright feathers of a red hen. It started a long way back, half way up his scalp, and the gristly scars streamed down over his forehead and cheekbones from under it. He had a tidy black suit on and a good thick-soled boot with grease rubbed in. The other leg was what looked like a massive iron pipe blocked up at the end with a solid wooden plug. It came out on to the hearth from the turn-up of his trousers.

It is best to tell the tale when you haven't got any cash to put on the counter. When I began to talk to him by the fire, I tucked my feet under the settle and said I was a salesman. Although Danny and I could put all our belongings in a tobacco-box, I soon had a fine range of second-hand goods for sale. The man closed his little book to listen. He told me he was Jordan, man-servant to the old doctor of the town. I took a polished piece of a rabbit's backbone out of my waistcoat pocket and passed it over to him. It looked like a small cow's skull, complete with horns. He examined it slowly, trembling all the time. He had huge soft hands and his finger-nails were as green as grass. I told him he could keep it. He called for whisky for both of us.

As I drank my whisky I enjoyed thinking what I had for sale. I had a little harmonium, portable, very good for Welsh hymns, perfect except for a rip in the bellows; a new invention that would get a cork out of a bottle – like that!; a nice line in leather purses, a free gift presented with each one – a brass watch-key, number eight, or a row of glass-headed pins; a pair of solid leather knee-boots, just the thing for him because they were both for the same leg. The man's eyes were small, they looked half closed up, and he watched me hard without moving them all the time. In the heat of the fire a strong smell came off him. It was a damp clinging smell, clammy, like the mildewed corner of some old church, up there behind the organ where they keep the bier. At last he bent forward and held his smashed face close to mine. I stopped talking. He trembled and said softly, 'I am interested in buying only one thing.'

Somehow I felt mesmerized, I couldn't say anything. I am not often like that. I lifted my eyebrows.

Jordan didn't answer. His little eyes slid round the empty bar. Then he moved his lips into a word that staggered me. I stared at him. For a minute by the blazing bar fire I went cold as clay. He nodded his head and made the same mouthing of his smashed face as before. The word he shaped out was, 'Corpses'.

There was dead silence between us. The clock in the bar echoed loudly, like a long-legged horse trotting down an empty street. But I let my face go into a twist and I squeezed a tear into the end of my eye. I crossed myself and offered the serving man the body of my brother. I had buried him, I remembered, a week ago come tomorrow.

Jordan took his hat and stick out of the corner. The stick was heavy, with a lot of rope wound round it, and the black hat had a wide brim. When he stood up he was like a giant rising above me. He was much bigger even than I thought. He looked down hard at the little bone I had given him and then threw it on the back of the fire. We went out into the street. As we walked along, his iron leg bumped on the pavement and made a click-clicking noise like a carried bucket. He would show me where to bring the corpse and I was to come between midnight and daybreak.

We walked together out of the town into the country. It was pitch dark and soon the way was through wet fields. It was still cold but I didn't feel it any more. Jordan had this peg leg but he was big, and I sweated keeping up with him. He trembled all the time as he walked but his shaking didn't make you think he was weak. He was like a powerful machine going full force and making the whole throbbing engine-house tremble to the foundations with its power. I trotted behind him breathless. He was so busy singing the Welsh burial hymn that he didn't drop a word to me all the way.

At last we came to a gate across the lane we were following. There was a farm-house beyond it, all in darkness. Jordan stopped singing and shouted, twice. There was no reply. He started singing again. He poised himself on his iron leg and his walking stick and gave the gate a great kick with his good foot. It fell flat. We found ourselves going at full speed across a farmyard. A heavy sheepdog ran out of the shadows barking and showing a fringe of teeth. He looked huge and fierce enough to tear us in pieces. Jordan didn't pause and I kept close behind him. The dog changed his gallop into a stiff-legged prowl, and he filled his throat with a terrible snarl. Then suddenly he sprang straight at Jordan's throat. As he rose in the air Jordan hit him a ringing crack on the head with his stick. He used both hands to bring it down. The dog dropped to the pebbles of the yard passing a contented sigh. He didn't move again. Jordan put his good foot on him and brought the stick down on his head again and again. He went on doing this, his sad hymn getting louder and louder, until the dog's brains came out. I

went cold in my sweat to hear him. At last he wiped the handle of the
stick in the grass of the hedge and went on down the lane, singing.

We came in sight of the lights of a big house. 'That's the place,' he
said. 'Bring it round to the back door. Good night.'

He went off into the darkness like a giant in his broad-brimmed hat.
I wiped the sweat off my head. After he had disappeared I could hear
his hymn and his leg clicking for a long time. His hymn was slow and
sad, but it didn't make me unhappy at all. It frightened the life out of
me.

On the way back to the town I kicked the dead dog into the ditch.

Danny never let his job slide off his back. As I climbed up the stairs of
our lodging house I came face to face with two eyes watching me
through the upright bars of the top-landing banister. It was Danny
dawdling about on his hands, practising. I had a lot of trouble
persuading him to be a corpse. All he had to do was pretend to be dead
and to let me and the blackman on the landing below carry him out to
the doctor's house. Then when we were paid and everybody in the
house was asleep he could get out of one of the downstairs windows.
We would be waiting for him. We could leave the town by the first
brake in the morning. It was safe as houses. Nothing could go wrong.
At last Danny agreed.

At midnight the three of us set out for Jordan's house. We were me,
Danny and Marky. Marky was a half-caste cheapjack, a long thin shiny
man the colour of gunmetal, selling fire-damaged remnants and
bankrupt stock and that. He used to dribble and paw you at close
quarters but he would do anything you asked him for tuppence or
thruppence. We walked through the fields carrying a rolled-up sack
and my trestle until we came in sight of the house Jordan had shown
me. Danny stripped to his coms under a tree and hid his clothes. He
put on an old cream-flannel nightgown Marky had brought out of
stock. Then we sewed him in the sack and put him on the planks of my
trestle. It was pitch dark and cold, with the small rain drizzling down
again as fine as pepper.

The doctor's house was all in darkness. We went round to the little
pointed wooden door at the back of the garden. I whispered to Danny
to ask if he was all right. There were two answers, Danny's teeth
chattering and the uproar of dogs howling and barking inside the
garden. I had never thought about dogs. What were we going to do?

At once I heard the click of the leg the other side of the wall and
Jordan's voice speaking. 'Down, Farw. Down, Angau,' he growled. The

narrow pointed door was thrown open, and suddenly we saw Jordan. He was stripped naked to the half and he had left off his wig. He looked so huge, so powerful and ugly in the doorway, with his swelling nose and his fleshy body all slashed, I almost let go of our load with fright. And behind him the hounds, three of them, black and shaggy and big as ponies, yelped and bayed and struggled to get past him to attack us. Jordan spoke sharply to them and at last we were able to carry Danny into the garden. He was as light on the boards as a bag of hay. Jordan spoke only to the dogs. He made a sign and led us hobbling along the pebble path across the yard towards some dark out-houses. The three hounds paced whining beside us, sniffing all the time at the sack and spilling their dribble.

The room we went into smelt like a stable. It was dim and empty but there was an oil lamp hanging from a nail in a low beam. We laid Danny across some feed-boxes under this lamp. Jordan stood back by the stable door with the whimpering dogs while we were doing it, watching us all the time. I could feel his eyes burning into my back. His skin was very dark and his chest bulged up into big paps resting above his powerful folded arms. But all his body was torn with terrible wounds like his face. Long shining scars like the glistening veins you see running through the rocks of a cliff-face spread in all directions over his flesh. His bald head had a large dome on it and that was covered with scars too. His whole body gleamed down to his waist, the drizzle had given him a high shine like the gloss of varnish.

We left Danny lying on the boards across the feed-boxes and came back up to the door to ask for our money. Jordan didn't reply. Instead he took a large clasp-knife out of the pocket in the front of his trousers and opened it. Then, ordering the dogs to stay, he went past us and bumped over to where Danny was lying in his sack. He seemed to take a long time to get there. There was dead silence. As he went from us we could see a black hole in his back you could put your fist into. My skin prickled. Marky's eyes rolled with the dogs sniffing him and he began to paw the air. I looked round and saw a hay-fork with a stumpy leg in the corner. Jordan turned round under the lamp and looked back at us. The blade of the open knife trembled in his hand. He turned again and cut open the sewing in the sack above Danny's face. I could hardly breathe. Danny was so white under the hanging lamp I thought he was really dead. My hair stirred. Danny's teeth showed shining in his open mouth, and in the lamplight falling right down upon them the whites of his half-opened eyes glistened. He was pale and stiff, as if he had already begun to rot. Jordan bent over, gazing down at him with the knife in his hand, the lamp spreading a shine over the skin of his wet back. I was frightened, but if Danny's teeth chattered or his belly crowed I was willing to use that pitchfork to get us out. At last Jordan turned. He spoke for the first time.

'He is a good corpse,' he said.

'He is my brother,' I told him.

'Where did you get him from?'

'I dug him up.'

He nodded. He left the knife open on the feed-box and came over to us. Putting his hand again into his front pocket he brought out a large lump of wadding. This he opened and in the middle lay three gold sovereigns. He passed the coins over to me with his huge trembling hands and motioned us out roughly. He went back and blew out the oil lamp and we left Danny alone there in the darkness. Jordan locked the stable door and the hounds trotted round us growling as we left the garden through the little door.

'Good night,' said Jordan.

'Good night, brother,' I said.

We walked about in the fields, trying to keep warm, waiting for the time to go back to get Danny out. Marky had gone icy cold. I was worried, especially about those dogs. I wished I had a drop of drink inside me. When we thought everything would be quiet again we went back to see if it was safe to give Danny the whistle. I threw my coat over the bottle-glass stuck on top of the garden wall and climbed up. I could see a candle lit in a downstairs window of the doctor's house and by its light Jordan moved about inside the room in his nightshirt and nightcap. Presently his light disappeared and all was in darkness.

An owl in a tree close by started screeching. Marky was frightened and climbed up on to the garden wall to be near me. There was no sign of Jordan's dogs in the garden. It was bitterly cold up there on top of the wall without our coats on. The wind was lazy, it went right through us instead of going round. It had stopped raining again. There was a moon now but it was small and a long way off, very high up in the sky, and shrunken enough to go into your cap.

We waited a long time shivering and afraid to talk. Marky's eyes were like glass marbles. At last I saw something moving in the shadows by the stable. My heart shot up hot into my throat. Marky caught hold of me trembling like a leaf. A figure in white began to creep along the wall. It was Danny. He must have got out through one of the stable windows. I whistled softly to him and at that there was uproar. The three hounds came bounding across the yard from nowhere, making straight for Danny, baying and snarling like mad. I didn't know what to do for the moment with fright. The dogs were almost on top of him.

Danny sprang on to his hands and began trotting towards them. His black legs waved in the air and his night-shirt fell forward and hung down to the ground over his head. The dogs stopped dead when they saw him. Then they turned together and galloped away into the shadows howling with fright. When Danny reached the wall we grabbed him firmly by the ankles and pulled him up out of the garden at one pluck. We were not long getting back to our lodging-house. The next morning we paid our landlord and the brake driver with one of the sovereigns we had had off Jordan.

I didn't have any luck. All the rest of the summer it was still wet and there were hardly any flies. I tried selling elephant charms, very lucky, guaranteed, but the harvest failed and in the end I couldn't even give them away. Danny got thinner and thinner and more quiet. He was like a rush. He had nothing to say. There never was much in his head except the roots of his hair. Having been a corpse was on his mind. And he was like a real corpse to sleep with, as cold as ice and all bones. He lost interest even in standing on his hands.

We visited a lot of the towns that held fairs but without much luck. One market day we were sitting in a coffee tavern. It was a ramshackle place built of wooden planks put up for the market day in a field behind the main street. The floor was only grass and the tables and benches stood on it. You could get a plate of peas and a cup of tea there cheap. Danny didn't care about food now even when we had it. Because it was market day this coffee tavern was crowded. It was very close inside, enough to make you faint, and the wasps were buzzing everywhere. All the people around us were jabbering Welsh and eating food out of newspapers.

Presently, above the noise, I heard a bumping and clicking sound in the passage. I felt as though a bath-full of icy water had shot over me inside my clothes. I looked round but there was no way of escape. Then I heard the funeral hymn. In a minute Jordan was standing in the entrance of the coffee tavern. He was huge, bigger than ever, a doorful. In one hand was his roped-up stick and in the other his black hymn-book. His broad-brimmed hat was on his head, but instead of his wig he had a yellow silk handkerchief under it with the corners knotted. He stopped singing and stood in the doorway looking round for an empty seat. A man from our table just then finished his peas and went out. Jordan saw the empty place and hobbled in. We couldn't escape him. He came clicking through the eating crowd like an earthquake and sat down at our table opposite us.

At first I didn't know what to do. Danny had never seen Jordan and was staring down at the grease floating on his tea. I tried to go on leading the peas up to my mouth on my spoon but I could hardly do it. Jordan was opposite, watching me. He could see I was shaking. I pretended to fight the wasps. I could feel his bright bunged-up eyes on me all the time. He put his arms in a ring on the table and leaned over towards me. I was spilling the peas in my fright. I couldn't go on any longer. I lowered my spoon and looked at him. He was so hideous at close quarters I almost threw up. The big black block of his nose reached out at me, full of worm-holes, and the rest of his face looked as though it had been dragged open with hooks. But he was smiling.

'Jordan,' I said, although my tongue was like a lump of cork. 'Mr. Jordan.'

He nodded. 'You've come back,' he said. 'Where have you been keeping?'

The whole coffee tavern seemed to be trembling with his movements. I felt as though I was in the stifling loft of some huge pipe-organ, with the din coming out full blast and all the hot woodwork in a shudder. His question had me stammering. I told him I had been busy. My business kept me moving, I travelled about a lot. The wooden building around me felt suffocating, airless as a glasshouse. I glanced at Danny. He looked as though he had been tapped and all his blood run off. Even his yellow ears had turned chalky.

Jordan nodded again, grinning his terrible grin. 'The chick born in hell returns to the burning,' he said. All the time he watched me from under the front knot of his yellow handkerchief. He ignored Danny altogether. His eyes were small, but they looked as though each one had had a good polish before being put into his head.

'Our bargain was a good one,' he went on, still smiling. 'Very good. It turned out well.'

I was afraid he would hear my swallow at work, it sounded loud even above the jabbering. 'I am glad,' I said, 'I did my best. I always do my best.'

'My master was pleased,' he said. He leaned further forward and beckoned me towards him. I bent my head to listen and his wooden nose was up touching my ear. 'A splendid corpse,' he whispered. 'Inside, a mass of corruption. Tumours and malignant growths. Exactly what my master needed. Cut up beautifully, it did.'

There was a loud sigh from Danny. When I turned to look at him he wasn't there. He had gone down off his bench in a heap on the grass. People all round got up from their tables and crowded round. Some of them waved their arms and shouted. 'Give him air,' they said, 'he's fainted. Give him air.' For a minute I forgot all about Jordan. I told the people Danny was my friend. They carried him out of the coffee tavern and laid him on the grass at the side of the road. 'Loosen his neck,' somebody said, and his rubber breast and collar were snatched off showing his black coms underneath. The crowd came on like flies round jam. At last Danny opened his eyes. Someone brought him a glass of water out of the coffee tavern. He sat up, bowed his shoulders and put his hands over his face as though he was crying. I spotted something then I had never noticed before. There was a big bald hole in his red hair at the top of his head. He looked sickly. But before long he could stand again. I pushed his breast and collar into my pocket and took him back to our lodging house. I looked round but I couldn't see Jordan at all in the crowd. Danny was in bed for a week. He was never the same again. For one thing if he cut himself shaving he didn't bleed. The only thing that came out of the cut was a kind of yellow water.

Before the year was out I had buried Danny. It was wild weather and he caught a cold standing about half-naked in his tights in the fairs and markets. He took to his bed in our lodgings. Soon he was light-headed and then unconscious. Every night I sat by him in our bedroom under the roof with the candle lit, listening to his breathing.

One night I dropped off to sleep in the chair and he woke me up screaming. He dreamt Jordan was trying to chop his hands off to make him walk on the stumps. I was terrified at the noise he made. The candle went out and the roar of the wind sawing at the roof of the house was deafening. My heart was thumping like a drum as I tried to relight the candle. I couldn't stop Danny screaming. A few minutes later he died with a yell. Poor Danny. Being a corpse was too much for him. He never struggled out from under the paws of his memories.

The next night the man from the parish came. He asked me if I wasn't ashamed to bury my friend like that. He meant that Danny hadn't had a shave for a week. In the candle-light he had a bright copper beard and he wasn't quite so much like a cow. When the man had gone I started to shave the corpse. It was hard doing it by candle light. High up on the cheek-bone I must have done something wrong, I must have cut him, because he opened one of his eyes and looked hard at me with it. I was more careful after that. I didn't want to open that vein they say is full of lice.

The morning of the funeral I borrowed a black tie off our landlord. I bummed a wreath on strap. It was very pretty. It was a lot of white flowers on wires made into the shape of a little armchair. In the bars of the back was a card with the word 'Rest' on it done in forget-me-nots. Danny always liked something religious like that.

There was nobody in the funeral except the parson and me and two gravediggers. It was a bad day in autumn and very stormy. The long grass in the graveyard was lying down smooth under the flow of the wind. There were some willow trees around the wall all blown bare except for a few leaves sticking to the thin twigs like hair-nits. The parson in his robes was a thin man but he looked fat in the wind. As he gabbled the service, the big dried-up leaves blown along the path scratched at the gravel with webbed fingers, like cut-off hands. I wanted to run away. When Danny was in the earth, the gravediggers left. The parson and I sang a funeral hymn. The wind was roaring. As we were singing I heard another voice joining in in the distance. It was faint. I had been waiting for it. I didn't need to look round. I knew the sound of the voice and the clicking leg. They came closer and closer. Soon the voice was deafening, the sad hymn roaring like a waterfall beside me. Jordan came right up and stood between me and the parson, touching me. For shaking he was like a giant tree hurling off the storm. His little black book was in his hand. Even in the wind I could smell the strong mouldiness that came off him, clammy as grave-clay. He was bigger than ever. The brim of his black hat was spread out like a roof over my head. As he stood beside me he seemed to be absorbing me. He put his arm with the night-stick in his hand around my shoulders. I felt as though I was gradually disappearing inside his huge body. The ground all around me melted, the path began to flow faster and faster past my feet like a rushing river. I tried to shout out in my terror. I fainted.

When I came round the parson was beside me. We were sitting on the heap of earth beside Danny's open grave. I was as wet as the bed of the river with fright. When I spoke to the parson about Jordan he humoured me. That was a fortnight ago. Yesterday when I cut myself shaving I didn't bleed. All that came out of the cut was a drop or two of yellow water. I won't be long now. I am finished. I wouldn't advise anybody to try crossing Jordan.

The Boy in the Bucket

৯

Dockery-crick – dockery crick, went the clock in the silence. Outside the chapel windows the Sabbath-silent sun deluged morning over the valley. Only a few clouds, woolly puffs of sunlit willowherb, floated by on the blue. On the opposite side of the *cwm* a great whale-browed mountain rose up bedecked and glittering into the sunlight. It had the fascination for Ceri of a vast velvet monster risen green from the lumber-room of sea-bottom, bearing upon its brow grove-growths and out-cropping rocks and rows of cottages. Sunday after Sunday, morning and evening, he watched it from his seat, in silence as now, or with the shameless shouting of the rooks in his ears. But today he was not able to pay so much attention to it as usual. He was afraid Roderick the policeman was going to call at his house with a Blue Paper.

The service was bound to start soon now. The six black-clad daughters of Penffordd were already in, they had swept up the aisle in their silk-swishing mourning and, like one man, stuck their foreheads to the hymn book ledge. Richards the Stoning in the side-seats was getting restless. He was an old man with white hair and beard, but the thick hairs in his ears were brown as though he had been smoking through them. He stretched his legs in impatience and the splitting timber of his pew-back crack-cracked sharp as pistol shots in the silence. Mrs. Rees the Bank in her fox furs was worried by a fly. From the little gallery behind came a loud cackle like trucks shunting, and Ceri knew without looking back that old Bara-chaws the roadman was up there, clearing the metallic phlegm out of his throat for the singing.

Ceri always loved the sunshine to fill up the chapel. The walls, washed in a buttercup light, looked so clean, and the bright green paint on the gas brackets glistened with such freshness that they appeared wet. On the wall behind the pulpit a large curved ribbon with '*Duw cariad yw*' on it was painted in salmon-tin gold – 'God is love.' And as Ceri was admiring the gleam of it the door beside the pulpit opened and Jones the schoolteacher led the deacons into the Big Seat. Jones was Ceri's dayschool teacher, he had scabs in his hair and he used to go behind the blackboard to pick them off. Then the preacher, a very narrow man in black and glasses, entered and went up into the pulpit. His hairless head was lacquered a heavy brown, it always took the reflection of the chapel lights on its polish, and now there was a nice ring of windows gleaming all around it. He gave out the hymn, the harmonium started and all the people stood on their feet to sing.

Ceri's mother used to sit in the front of the chapel to see that the little children gathered together there behaved themselves during the service. Because of that Ceri felt it was safe to look around a bit. Right in front of him was Hughes the *Vulcan*, old dome head, the back of his neck glowing like a ploughed sunset. You could always rely on Hughes to sigh out loud, bored, if the sermon was poor, and this helped Ceri to know what to tell his mother about it when she questioned him after chapel. Across the aisle Mair Morgans was wearing a new lot of best clothes. Her straw hat had a ring of juicy cherries around it and on her crimson coat were large wooden buttons, round and yellow, with plaited edges like tartlets. The pew door hid the rest of her but most likely she had new shoes on too, because every now and then she would stop singing, move her hymn book sideways and have a good peep down at her feet.

But one thought kept on worrying Ceri; what would his mother say when Roderick the policeman knocked at the front door with the summons in his hand? It drove him desperate to think of it. She made everything out to be so serious, such as being kept in after school, or swearing by accident, or breaking down in the psalm he was supposed to have learnt for the *gymanfa*. He didn't mean any harm, but she always made him feel that whatever he did was wicked. Only the other day, when they all had their heads bowed over their baked potatoes and she was asking a blessing, he and his little sister couldn't stop giggling and his mother said that was an *insult* to *Iesu Grist*. What would she say when she knew he had been playing with the O'Driscolls again and had broken the street lamp through throwing stones? He felt a sultry flush soaking his face, and just then he caught her large varnished eye full upon him, she had turned it back over her shoulder in a frown because Ceri was dreaming and had forgotten he was supposed to be singing the hymn.

When the sermon came Ceri was afraid to make sketches of the deacons so he settled down against the door of the pew to have a good worry. On the mountain opposite he could see the overhead wires that carried the bucketed colliery dirt away, and the diminishing row of trellis masts supporting them. The O'Driscolls would be on their way up the mountain now, most likely, and he wished he could be with them again. Ceri's mother preached day after day against playing with them – knowing their mother, she always called them 'Ceridwen's boys' – because they were rough and bad swearers. But Ceri could see nothing wrong with them except that they never had pocket handkerchiefs. They pinched their noses with their fingers and shot it into the gutter. But they were all kind boys. Aneirin, the youngest, would take a lump of chewing gum from behind his ear where he always kept it stuck and bite a half of it for you; Ginger Irfon would give you a go on the bar of his pink bike that had such soft tyres you felt you were riding on jubes; and Taliesin, the big one, would let you come in their gymnasium shed in the backyard any time and have a bang at the punching-ball. But Ceri's mother said he wasn't to have anything to do with them. Their mother was Welsh but their father was an Irishman, and they never went to chapel properly, only to the mission sometimes just before there was going to be a tea-party.

There was a patch of ground at the end of the O'Driscolls' row where you could kick a ball about, but you had to stop for horses and carts to pass. While they were playing football there one of the boys from down by the canal drove his horse and cart by; his job was to collect the small coal the colliers didn't want and left heaped in the lanes outside their houses. This boy was black as a sweep and dressed like a scarecrow, and his cart was falling to bits, it even had a big piece out of the rim of one of the wheels. The poor nag could hardly creep along, his back sagged like a drying-line and his harness was tied together with cord and wire.

Taliesin had picked up the ball they were playing with, a soccer case stuffed with newspaper, but the horse was so long creeping across the patch that he became impatient. 'Come on, Small-coal,' he shouted. 'Get a move on.'

'Shut your blower, snobby-nose,' the boy on the cart answered.

'Shut your blower yourself,' Tally shouted back, 'or I'll come and shut it for you.'

The boy snatched up a handful of small coal off the cart behind him and flung it point-blank in Tally's face. Then the stone-throwing began. Ceri's stone went right through the street lamp they used as a goal-post and they all ran away. They had a last glimpse of the small-coal boy; he had fallen off the cart and was being dragged across the ground on his back with his heel caught in the harness.

Ceri was terrified with the memory of it. What was going to happen? Up there in the pulpit, behind the golden edges of the Bible, the minister was preaching a sermon that kept the *Vulcan* silent. The light was coming through from the windows behind the preacher, it filled one of the thick pebbles of his glasses and swelled it up into the size of an enormous glowing eye. Oh dear, oh dear, what could he do?

Outside, across the valley, the bright sunlight poured down on the monstrous velvet scalp of the mountain, with the file of dressmakers' dummies going up over it, and the overhead wires sagging across it between them like pulled-out chewing-gum. Because it was Sunday the buckets were empty and stationary. It was almost time now for Miss Rees to tap Ceri on the shoulder from the seat behind and for him to put his hand carelessly on the back of the pew to receive his peppermint.

Life seemed so dangerous to him, like a large black savage dog in the road, and all he wanted was to creep by unnoticed. Oh, how he wished he was away. How lovely to go up over the mountain now, to be up there in the air and the sunlight for ever. To be a stander in a Sunday-still muck-bucket, to hang over the *cwm*, a trapezist, two hundred feet above the river. Over his head, not very far off, he imagined the blue sky with a limpid bloom of illumination upon it, and the snowy cushions and pillowings floating there, the silken bulgings of the sunlit shadow-casters, the radiant clouds. Grasping tightly the thick bars going overhead to the wheels, he looked over the edge of the bucket. Everything below was placid and motionless. The whole valley lay green beneath him like an apron held out for catching. There was the river in the middle, glittering, from so high above, in a silvery vein. There on either side of it the slopes of the mountains glowed in the sunlight, the great whale-headed promontory was dimmed as the cloud shadows passed over it, and its grass blazed bright green again in the sun when their darkness had gone, like a heap of embers with the bellows blowing them. Further down the valley, where the pits were, a long solitary bow of black smoke curved out of a pitstack. Right beneath him he could see his village, standing to attention in fourteen rows of yellow brick and whitewash; and his own tidy little street, Ugain Tŷ, remote in the hillside trees, its chimneys all boiling fast into the morning like the spouts of a row of kettles. The chapel gleamed beautiful on the slope, snow-white and long-windowed. Nothing moved except Griffith's coal-black mare, a speck stirring on the bright green slope. And then, just beneath him, a flock of small birds went by in the breeze, their wings were shut, and they swam like a swarm of fish through the clear air.

He felt with surprise the nudge of Miss Rees. Sliding his hand along the back of the pew he received his peppermint.

A martin shot up to the chapel window and fell abruptly away, its wing tearing the morning with a lateral stab. The wheels overhead squealed. The bucket began to move. A little engine, under a mop of steam, burst round the curve of the valley. Ceri climbed with a rapture of increasing speed the slope of the mountain. Great lights seemed to fall upon him, as though he stood upon a vast stage. He was away. He heard his departure heralded by hooters and birdsong, his bucket swayed in delight, sailing rapidly like a great bird over the belfries of the trees.

'Goodbye, cottages,' he called. 'Goodbye over-tidy Ugain Tŷ; goodbye little valley; goodbye spreading fan of valleys; goodbye little chapel; goodbye Mam, Dad and obligation, I give you all farewell and a big kiss. In my bucket of salmon-tin gold I leave you, it is my saviour. I have enhanced it with poppies and elder blooms, badged it bolder than diplomats, I have decorated its edges with paper lace. Goodbye Roderick, goodbye Blue Paper, up the mountain I go in the shaken-down showers of light and the hullabaloo of birdsong. My troubles I leave behind, my heart has a long wing on each side of her, her feathery breast is breeze-borne, she is buoyant in her iron bucket. I am the lord of the bucket, and I have a lung full of laughing. I am the bucket-borne boy, I am the boy in the bucket, I am bucketed boy. I am on the heights, the world is blotted out, the sun, the all-seer, sees only me; all the valley, all the world below is hidden under the long rhomboids of smokes. The radiance of upper air enveloping my bucket is bright, but pale, like bedroom gaslight. The great swans of joy and illumination beat up around me, Oh, milky majestic thunder, Oh, rhythmic throbbing snow, Oh, compounded flakes and plumage of snowstorms of brightness. Lead me on. Lead me on to my dirty auntie – somewhere I have her – and my cousins of chaos, unreproved; to the houseful of children spotted like wallpaper, to the white mice in swarms and the great flocks of pigeons, to the house of indifference and joy. Lead me on to the wise, the wished-for and the wonderful.

'One of my cousins is the same age as I am, but he never gets out of bed to go to school in the morning. When the teachers scold him, my auntie goes up to school and shouts at them, striking them on the behind with her umbrella. My cousin smells of stale tobacco. He has long corduroy trousers with baggy knees and brass railway-buttons everywhere. His face is enchanting and completely covered with warts, it has a crust of yellow warts laid all over it, each one no bigger than a pinhead. All day long we are down the beach in the beautiful weather, we spend our time rolling a heavyweight gambo-wheel about in the fine sand. My cousin knows many dirty songs which he sings sweetly. We find a heap of cherries swept into the roadside and we eat them instead of going home to dinner. My cousin spits and if it falls on the knees of his corduroys he doesn't wipe it off. I sleep with him the first night, and the second night, and by the third night I am lousy.

'It is just after teatime when I arrive. My auntie is kind and she gives me a cup of port to drink. She is a stout woman. Her fat arms are the inflamed shiny colour of rhubarb, but her nails are black. Her hair is coming down. She smiles all the time, and all the time she smiles she draws a lip down over a bunch of black teeth. Her blouse comes out around her waist. She never takes her apron off in the afternoon. After dinner she piles the dirty dishes back in the cupboard, and goes out to talk over the wall with the woman next door from the steps of the *dubliw.*

'The old granny sits by the fire every day with her chin on her stick. She is very old and hairy everywhere. If you speak to her she parts the hair hanging over her eyes with her fingers to see who it is. She is in her second childhood and my cousin asks me to come and watch him teasing her.

'"How old are you now, Mamgu?" he says to her. "Tell us now, honestly, when will you be two hundred?"

'"I am not old," she cackles, "I am not old, I tell you."

'"Come on, Mamgu, tell us about the battle of Waterloo. You can remember that, can't you?"

'"I am not old," she shrieks at him, "I am not old." She puts the yellow claws of her hands on her chest. "Feel me, if you don't believe, feel me by here, I am like a girl." My cousin looks at me and laughs. She waves her walking stick at him in temper. "Go away," she says, "or I'll go home to my father and mother. You naughty boy, you."

'Just then my auntie comes in from the backyard. "Now then," she says, "stop teasing your grannie. And wipe your nose." My cousin draws his sleeve across it.

'On Sunday afternoon my auntie goes to bed with my uncle. My cousin and I don't go to Sunday school. We play ludo on the mat in the middle room where my uncle has left his flannel shirt on a coat-hanger. Suddenly there is a loud crash and the leg of the bed comes through the ceiling.

'My uncle is a tall man and very jolly. He hardly ever wears a jacket or a collar and tie, he is about the house in broken boots and an open waistcoat. There is a clear green stud-stain on the front of his neck. His face is like frayed fibre because he always wants a shave, and he has an oily quiff buttered down on his forehead. He does light hauling. His cart is painted all over a light purple, shafts and wheels and all. My cousin says you could tell he had pinched the paint for it, because nobody would *buy* paint that colour. His horse has prominent bones, and such a bent back you feel you want to pull his tail hard to straighten it. My uncle keeps a stub of a pencil behind his ear and writes notes on his matchbox. To save money he smokes ferns and then all the children go out to play coughing. He is the best everything where they live. He was the one who fired the very last bullet before the hooters put a stop to the war. When he hasn't been to the pub, he sits downhearted opposite the grannie by the fire, and then my auntie gives him beer-money to get drunk.

'One night we are all having supper in the kitchen. The oil lamp is lit and the six spotty children are around the table. It has been too wet for light hauling and my uncle has been in "The Beehive" all day. He is happy and he makes us all laugh. Suddenly we see a big black rat running across the shelf of the dresser, and everybody is excited. My uncle dashes from the table and is just in time to hold the rat fast behind a big willow-pattern meat-dish. The creature struggles but he cannot get away. My uncle holds him with one hand, and with the other fumbles the two-pronged carving-fork out of the knife drawer. We all sit fascinated, wondering what he will do. Gradually he allows the rat to squeeze out from behind the dish, and then with a sudden jab pins him to the wall with the fork. The fork goes right through the rat's body and into the soft plaster. The rat screams loudly for a bit and then dies. My uncle takes him by the tail and throws him on the fire.

'Every night my cousin and I go to bed in our shirts and we do not clean our teeth. In the kitchen, behind the old grannie, there is a smoky mirror. It must have come from somewhere else, because it has a keyhole in it. I clean the corner with my elbow and examine myself. My face is covered with a mass of rough skin like breadcrumbs, and my teeth are coloured in bands – black near the gums, then khaki, then grass-green, and a thin fringe of white at the sharp edges.

'My auntie is going to have a washing day and the kitchen is full up to the door with steam. We can just see the grannie by the fire through the swirling mists, eating gruel out of a basin with a wooden spoon and spitting the hard bits all over the floor. My auntie sits down at the table with us, tugging the bacon rinds through her broken teeth.

'Suddenly there is a sharp knock at the back door. When my auntie opens it we see Roderick the policeman there with the Blue Paper in his hand. It is a perishing day and his face is the crimson of a fire bucket. But he is cosy, the thick soles of his boots hold him up off the cold floor, his long heavy overcoat wraps his body from the wind, and even his ears are plugged up with cotton wool against the weather. The steam from the kitchen blows out around him as he scowls in the doorway and points in my direction with a white woollen glove. I am terrified. I have been so happy and indifferent I have forgotten all about the Blue Paper. Roderick shouts it is for me. My auntie snatches it off him and comes back with it through the steam to the table. I begin to sob.

'"Don't you worry, *bach*," she says to me. "I'll show you what I think of Roderick the policeman and his summonses."

'She looks angry. She takes two slices of bread and dripping off the table, puts the Blue Paper between them and starts to chew the sandwich. Her face is red.

'"Don't you worry, *bach*," she says again between chewing, "it was this Roderick that booked our Dada for carrying a bit of coal from the sidings. And for being after hours in 'The Beehive.'"

'But I am frightened. Roderick the policeman has found me. He comes angry and crimson across the kitchen. I hide in the steams and rush past him into the open.

'Oh bucket, bear me to a distance, bear me away, I cry. Oh, solid beneath me and the steamy earth far below. Oh, respite, Oh, flight, Oh, escape. I glide again over the mountain with the speed of a gliding gull, the dashing brass-clad sun accompanies me, flashing for hours across the sky. At last in the dusk I am heralded with hooters; as I go down into the valley the sun has set, the purple sunset is a long flood of plum-juice. With the stopping of the hooters my bucket comes to rest. The men far below me in the valley are going home from work. Hundreds of pit-black men begin to pour homeward along the roads of the valley. How shall I go home? I shall be suspended all night, for ever, for all eternity, above the valley, in the darkness, in the chill of the winds. I shout, I bawl, but I am too far away, no one pays any heed, all the crowds beneath me are busy with their own thoughts and homeward bound.

'I must jump. I look over the edge of my bucket and call and wave, I strip off my poppies and orders of elderboughs and cast them over the edge, but it is of no avail. Darkness comes. My tears are deep and icy cold on the floor of my bucket. I lie down in them and weep. I long for my mother and her comfort, I will return to her, I will creep under the shadows of her harsh wing.

'I throw my legs over the bucket, hang myself down by my hands over the darkening valley. The weight of my body on the rim of the bucket tips it up sideways above me. I hang in the breeze, my heart throbs. My fingers slide over the edge. When I drop where shall I land? In the trees? In Griffiths's field? Shall I be borne by the breeze to the graveyard of the chapel? I let go and fall screaming through the darkness, the trees rush past me roaring like riff-raff. . .'

The catch on the pew door flew open under Ceri's weight and he fell with a loud crash out into the aisle. He was scarcely awake before his mother was beside him, kneeling. How beautiful she looked to his startled eyes, her black hair so lovely clustering about her ears, her large straw-brimmed hat letting the sunlight through with a new winsomeness on to her face. Never before had he smelt so sweetly the faint perfume of her, the breathed-in freshness of her presence. How lovely the chapel was, too, around her, so clean, so purified in the sun, filled up with the clear buttercup water of the sunlight.

Sitting outside in the porch, Ceri told his mother about breaking the street lamp and the Blue Paper. 'Ah,' she said, 'I dare say you couldn't help it.'

From the chapel behind them came the singing of the last hymn. The sun fell over the great headland opposite, and the houses on it, white-limed, looked unreal in their whiteness. Ceri went out on to the hot grass and had a good look at the valley.

It's not by his Beak you can
Judge a Woodcock

୬

It was nearly midnight. There was a frosty stare to the big stars and the full moon above the farmhouse gleamed like a splash of whitewash. Not a blade or a twig moved in the frozen Nantwig fields, and the only sound was the grass cracking like cake under a pair of heavy boots. In the distance the Reverend Gwilym Nanney was coming down to the farmhouse for the second time.

Gwilym was a simple man. He spoke little. He was good at making fishing-flies from the hackles of a cock. Sometimes he mixed up the points of his sermon, but he would carry a can of milk every day to a drunkard like Jim Saer and pray with him until the beer was overcome. He gave his money away. He gave away his jacket to Theo the tramp who came cuckooing through the parish in the spring. People marvelled at their vicar's big naily boots, and at his grey flannel shirt, just like their own, when he took off his coat to help with the hay of a widow, or a farmer gone into the decline. Gwilym was tall, but on his large bones no flesh had ever found a resting-place. He had the long chin, the bulging chest and the lifted shoulders of the asthmatic. From the middle of his white face the cold gristle of his nose pointed sharply up, the tip of it nibbled at the air all the time he was speaking. To visit Nantwig in the freezing weather he was wearing his round hat and his black overcoat down to his boots.

He tramped over the crust of the field and there at last, in a bowl full of trees, the light of the farmhouse shone. The whole glitter of a lake came flooding into Gwilym's moon-wet eyes. His hump of a chest wheezed, but his long and knock-kneed legs moved faster. During the last three weeks an idea had entered his mind like something green brought by a far off pigeon. When he reached the middle of the farmyard he stood a moment under the oak tree, watching the smoke coiling out of the farmhouse chimney like a brandished rope, and thinking of what had happened in that house on his last visit. But he was clear now as to what he should do, and he would do it.

It was three weeks since the last time Gwilym had been called to Nantwig. That night, when he went into the house, he saw that the big iron double bed had been moved down into the middle of the kitchen and a great furnace of a fire stoked up in the chimney. An oil-lamp, the flame turned low in the frosted globe, was placed on the window-sill, and by its light he caught a glimpse of Phoebe Harris, the saffron-faced wife of Nantwig, peeping out at the doorway that led into the parlour. But at the sound of his boots on the kitchen flags she disappeared, and soon her stockinged feet could be heard on the ceiling boards low above his head. Gwilym took off his round hat and placed it on the brass bed knob, where a pair of cord breeches were hung up by the braces. Then he stood gripping the bars at the foot of the bed and slowly recovering his breath.

There facing him, propped up by the pillows, a sullen look on his big red face, was Ahab Harris, Nantwig, wearing a frayed nightshirt of red flannel. Ahab, a heavy man, had pitched into the stack-yard off the roof of the stable and was dying in full flesh. But Gwilym could still feel blazing through the bedrails the bullying furnace of Ahab's strength, the power that comes from a gigantic frame, a bull's bellow and a bulging nose-bone. Ahab's fleshy face, through which whisky had driven a mass of crimson pathways, was still fiery red, the skin looked hot enough to crack open and let the flames inside blaze out. The front of his head was bald, but half way up the scalp a torrent of thick black hair gushed out and fell behind him. He watched Gwilym with close-together eyes, too small for his huge head, while his black eyebrows, a pair of thick furry wings, shot up and down all the time like the brows of a monkey. As Gwilym watched him in silence a purring sound came out of him like the buzz of a huge cat snoring.

What was in the heart of this Ahab, Gwilym wondered, this mocker, this flagrant adulterer, this drinker for whom there was often not room enough on the roads? Ahab was as worldly a man as any between heaven and floor, carnal and violent, never would he put his shoulder under the ark, never ponder the unsearchable riches, never once of a Sunday had he sought the lake-bank of the Means. What could he want? When Gwilym had got enough breath into his lungs the tip of his nose began its restless scribble against the air of the kitchen as he spoke.

'Good night, Ahab Harris,' he said. 'You wanted me.'

Ahab blinked out at him.

'Yes,' he answered in his arrogant voice. 'That's right. I want to talk to you.'

'What's the matter?' Gwilym asked.

'I was fastening some loose tiles on the stable roof and I fell into the yard. Nothing serious.'

Gwilym nodded and the heavy, cunning, brick-skinned face stared back at him. 'You look well,' Gwilym said.

'Why not?' Ahab answered. He grinned. 'In a week from now I'll be in town with the chestnut mare under my thighs again.'

There was a pause. Ahab spat at the fire and it boiled on the bars. Suddenly he scowled at Gwilym.

'Don't you think now, Nanney,' he said, sullen and threatening, 'from what I am going to tell you, that I am moving out of Nantwig stiff in a few days with my feet in front of me. No, no. I will stand on the graves of a good many yet, yours included. But I want you to do something for me.'

Gwilym said nothing. Then Ahab spoke about his will. He said what Phoebe and the children were to receive. They were a judgment on him and it was little. But there were some things he did not wish to put down in black and white. And he wanted Gwilym to promise that he would see these things carried out. He paused and then dropped his voice. 'Come here,' he whispered, glancing up at the ceiling, 'I want to explain to you.'

Gwilym took his hands off the sweating bars and went round to the bedside.

'You have been with religion these thirty years now, Nanney,' he said, 'and I know you are like a gunbarrel. Now listen. Although I am not clothed, yet I am in my right mind. Remember that. Across the *nant* I have five fields. You know them. Good fields. No rushes. No stones. No need to cut thistles. The best of Nantwig. They are on Twm Tircoch's side of the brook. And Twm wants to buy them. But I won't sell them to him. Do you understand, Nanney? I wouldn't give a hair of my nose to Twm Tircoch. And I refuse to sell him my fields. If I am under the big stones before Phoebe she is not to sell them to him. Now remember.'

'Thomas is a faithful churchman,' said Gwilym, 'and a good neighbour.'

'You are right,' Ahab answered, 'Twm is a faithful churchman and a good neighbour. There's nothing wrong with Twm. Only the air still goes in and out of him. Only he feels the stroke of the blood in his veins. And he sings hymns! *Yr argian fawr*, that little voice! I would sooner listen to a bandsaw. That is all. He wants my fields. I don't know why. Perhaps he thinks the railway will wish to come through them some time. Perhaps he likes the look of them under heavy hay. I won't sell them to him. I won't. But I want them sold. *Yr Israel*, yes, I want them sold. Do you understand? And do you know why? To provide for a widow. No, no, not Phoebe. Not her. My real widow. The one in Hills Terrace in town. Mrs. Watkins forty-two.'

Gwilym remembered her. He had seen her one mart day, a big purple pigeon of a woman with a mop of red hair, standing the other side of the street under the arch that leads into Hills Terrace. 'That's Ahab Nantwig's fancy,' someone said. She saw Gwilym looking at her, standing with her big hip out and her hand on it like a trollop. 'What the hell are you staring at?' she shouted across at him.

'Stoke the fire if you are cold,' Ahab called out, 'stoke the fire, man.'

Gwilym was sweating with heat and anger. His bleak nose looked warm. He picked up the big iron poker and with one blow broke the back of the fire so that it roared up the chimney. Then he came back to the bed.

'Listen,' Ahab went on. 'I want those five fields sold, and the money paid over to Mrs. Watkins. They are good fields. They will fetch a good price.'

A long and thick silence followed. Gwilym was too angry to speak. His big ears had become bright red and stiff, they shone like slices of lacquered wood. He looked up at the black ceiling near his head. It was so hot the hung bacon was sweating. What words was he to use in protest against giving to a red-haired harlot the best of Nantwig, the undercut and all the thigh slices? Five fields of ungathered hay velvet under the breeze, or ploughed red with the gulls like white pebbles upon them. All for a hard whore who wouldn't shed a tear even of gratitude. In his distress the long grey hairs brushed over his bald head fell down in a bunch, and hung tangled at the side of his face like a mass of creeper the wind has clawed by the roots off a ruin.

The bed creaked. 'Answer me,' Ahab shouted, with temper red in the webwork of veins netting his face. 'Answer me, Nanney. It's like drawing teeth to get you to speak. Do you promise or not?'

Gwilym bent his head to one side as though before the blows of a big wind. He heard the glass globe of the oil-lamp ringing at the loudness of Ahab's Welsh. How could he lay the seal of his blessing on this? But would he do more than blue himself if he fought against a hard man like Ahab? And dimly he knew what might happen to Phoebe and the children if he refused. He saw himself putting his head into a beehive but for the sake of Phoebe he nodded. 'I promise,' he said.

Ahab grunted. 'Put the belly of your hand here on my heart and swear it,' he said.

Gwilym bent forward. He placed his hand on Ahab's breast, and felt the heat blazing out through the red nightshirt as though his palm were laid against a furnace door. Ahab's huge hot hand then covered his own, glowing like a poultice, while he swore he would see the five fields were sold, but not to Twm Tircoch, and the money received for them paid over to Mrs. Watkins.

He finished, and Ahab's great, red, upholstered face was no longer sullen. He grinned. 'Good,' he said, 'and now that we've got the gambo over the hill, what about you, Nanney, what will you take as your share of the whitemeat?'

Gwilym shook his head. 'The church, Ahab Harris,' he said. 'Give something to the church.'

Ahab laughed. The bald front of his head shone like a coal-shute in the lamplight. 'The church?' he said. 'What does the church want with money? I always thought the gospel was free.'

With considering Gwilym considered this. With his bony bare hands he picked up some of the glowing coals fallen on to the hearth and put them back on the fire. 'The gospel,' he answered at last, 'is free. But we have to pay for the paraffin oil and the sweeping brushes.'

A sound boiled up into Ahab's throat like a huge bubbling of porridge. He opened his great mouth and laughed. It was a laugh that filled the house and had in it the note of a roof-cock triumphant over many hens. Nanney the harmless, the dull as a bullock, had promised. All was well.

Nanney came out from under the oak-tree which stood in its gaiter of whitewash and went towards the farmhouse. He had finished considering. A light shone from the kitchen window. He tapped at the back door, lifted the latch and went in.

There was silence in the room. Phoebe was sitting one side of the fire and Twm Tircoch the other. The big bed had gone back upstairs and the table, with the lamp standing on it, had been returned to the middle of the room, for Ahab had been dead a fortnight. Gwilym took a stool and sat wheezing between Phoebe and Twm with his hat on his knee. Before him was a nice kitchen fire on which grew a good crop of flames like yellow bristles.

'It's a bitter night,' he gasped.

'You are right, Mr. Nanney,' said Twm in his thin voice. 'Bitter. And me thinking it was going to rain because the cat was so playful.' When Twm realized what he had done he stopped short, blushed and fell silent.

Phoebe nodded. She was a small and thin woman, her wrinkled skin seemed to be in a yellow light, as though it were catching a powerful reflection from a sheet of brass. Because of Ahab's death she was wearing a black dress but her canvas apron was still on, steaming in the heat of the fire. On her head was a gold hair-net like a soft birdcage. Gwilym could see the snow was heavy on her heart. Her face was sad and her eyes were red with weeping.

For a time the three sat in silence. Phoebe wished to ask a question but she did not know how to begin. In her embarrassment she bent forward and brushed off Nanney's shoulder a patch of brown cow hairs left there when he had milked the cross-bred for Elin Tŷ-fri that afternoon. 'Mr. Nanney,' she said at last. 'What were his wishes?'

Gwilym paused for wind before answering. Would he be able to explain? He turned to Twm Tircoch sitting at the other side of the fire. 'Thomas,' he said, 'you wanted to buy Ahab's fields on your side of the brook. Is that right?'

Taken unawares, Twm looked startled, and the colour went up his plump face to the roots of his hair. He was a big blusher of a man with a thin voice, he was shy, and he used to tell the neighbours that although he was all right with the dog he didn't know what to say to the baby. He wore a suit of bulging corduroy and the laces of his boots and all his buttons were under heavy strain. He had no collar and tie on and his stud was a brass cuff link. Gradually his blush passed, but all over his head his untidy hair stood up, as though his scalp had been glued and he had passed through a heavy shower of craneflies.

'Yes, yes,' he said. 'And I do now. That's why I came over tonight. I hope Phoebe will give me the first chance. I will pay her a good price.'

'Ahab's wishes, Thomas,' said Gwilym, 'were that his fields on the Tircoch side of the brook were to be sold.' He paused again and looked at Phoebe. 'Phoebe,' he said, 'the night I came here to see Ahab three weeks ago, do you know what I promised Ahab?'

Phoebe shook her head. 'He never told me his business,' she said.

'I promised,' Gwilym went on, 'that I would see the five fields were sold, as the will says, but I also promised to see you did not sell them to Thomas here.'

For a moment Twm looked up in a vague way, like one suddenly conscious of a draught. Then he went red from the tight of his neckband to the roots of his hair. 'What wrong did I ever do to Ahab?' he said.

Phoebe sighed. 'When they are sold,' she said, 'what is to become of the money? I suppose it is not to come to me and the children?'

Again Gwilym looked about, thinking of words to use so that Nantwig should not fall to the dogs and the ravens. 'Phoebe,' he said, 'have you heard of Mrs. Watkins forty-two?'

Phoebe began to cry.

'She,' said Gwilym, 'is to have what is received for the five fields. I have promised it.'

There was silence in the room, except for the sobbing of Phoebe.

Twm got up to go.

'Sit down, Thomas,' said Gwilym. 'Phoebe, you must sell the fields. It is in the will.'

Phoebe nodded.

'Who will buy them?' Gwilym asked.

Phoebe raised her head. She shrugged her shoulders. 'Anyone,' she said. 'Plenty will be ready to buy them. They are good fields, as good as any in the parish.'

'Well then,' said Gwilym, wondering if this was where his plan would go under the water. 'Now listen Phoebe. Will you sell those fields to me?'

Phoebe stared. 'To you, Mr. Nanney?' she said. 'But the fields are large. And very good. And what will you be wanting five fields like that for?'

'Phoebe,' Gwilym repeated, 'will you sell them to me? All right. That is settled. I will buy the fields from you and I will give you a shilling each for them.'

'A shilling . . .' said Phoebe, and Twm began, 'But Mr. Nanney . . .'

'Will you agree?' said Gwilym. 'I will give you a shilling each for them. Remember, what you receive for the fields goes to Mrs. Watkins forty-two. If I give you a shilling each for them, that is what Mrs. Watkins will get – five shillings.'

Phoebe sat with her mouth open. Gwilym turned to Twm. Slowly he was unhooking the three-weeks-old load from his heart. 'Thomas,' he said, 'you were not allowed to buy the fields off Phoebe. Will you buy them off me? For a good price?'

Twm nodded. 'And what will you do with the money, Mr. Nanney?' he asked.

'All but five shillings I shall give to Phoebe,' he said. 'Do you agree?'

Twm nodded.

'And now,' said Gwilym, wheezing suddenly, 'let us pray.'

The three stood up. Gwilym thanked God that He had made some as cunning as serpents and as harmless as doves, that out of the mouths of babes and sucklings should come forth wisdom. As he prayed he felt his legs so cold he could have sat for an hour before the fire with his feet stuffed in between the bars. He brought his prayer to a close. 'The Lord giveth and the Lord taketh away,' said Gwilym. 'Blessed be the name of the Lord.'

'Amen,' said Phoebe.

'Amen,' said Twm.

Four Tales

❧

Robert Jeffreys

When I first came to live in the Ystrad valley I was bewildered by the number and the variety of the shocks to which the assumptions of my upbringing had made me subject. But in one matter I was extremely fortunate. My first landlord was a Mr. Robert Jeffreys, a voluble ex-collier, eloquent in two languages. He spoke English copiously, but in his sustained story-telling he used Welsh, so it seemed to me, like a poet, like those uninhibited natures we read of whose work flows, who produce poems as naturally, as abundantly, and as effortlessly as a great tree puts out its foliage. He lived with his wife and his unmarried son, Gareth, in Morlais Road, a pleasant street not far from St. Teilo's church where I served as curate. There was another child, a married daughter, Myra Powell, who, with her husband and two children, occupied a house on the hillside overlooking the town, a house Mr. and Mrs. Jeffreys had themselves once lived in, early in their marriage.

'Mr. Herbert,' Mr. Jeffreys said to me at one of our early meetings, wagging before my face his mutilated index with a thick bunch of black hairs sprouting like a little brush out of the first knuckle, where it ended, 'Mr. Herbert, you leave it to me. I am the Bobby Greencoat in these parts and I know it all. My job takes me everywhere. I see everything. You don't know what a Bobby Greencoat is? Well, I am the Whipper-in. No? The school attendance officer then, and if the children are absent, or late, or miching, I am the one to hunt them up and summons them. If you want to know anything about this valley, Mr. Herbert, you leave it to me. I have heard who is expecting sooner than the midwife and who stole the chickens long before the sergeant. Talking about chickens, I was in one of those cottages – they're more like ruins – down there by the canal side this afternoon looking for a micher – a rum lot they are down there I can tell you – and do you know what they were up to? They had stretched wire netting round the legs of the kitchen table and they were trying to raise a brood of Buff Orpingtons under it. Now what do you think of that? You leave it to me, Mr. Herbert because I see it all.'

A stocky man, he grinned up at me, his spectacles twinkling and the pair of eff-shaped cello-marks deepening on his swarthy cheeks.

After completing my course at the theological college, I came to this mining valley curacy from mixed proselitizing zeal and a kind of romantic or sentimental interest in, to me, so enigmatical a region. My father, although most of his life had been spent in incumbencies in the more genteel parishes of outer London, was a native of North Wales. In consequence the languages of the various English vicarages in which I was brought up were Welsh and German – German because my mother came from Heidelberg where my father had been a student at the university. I found many of the characteristics of the valley there-fore, the universal dissent, the pervading egalitarianism, the powerful sense of community and of clan, at first strange and disturbing in their intensity. For one of our poorer parishioners, I remember, a young Mrs. Richards, I secured a regular supply of paid sewing from a patroness of my father devoted to charitable works. Mrs. Richards received a large roll of towel-cloth every month which she undertook to make up into diapers for use in some orphanage Lady Harriet was interested in. But after a while I found that Mrs. Richards was not returning all the articles she had cut out and stitched, and that several of her neighbours were benefiting by this dereliction. I was angry, but when I remonstrated with her she treated the matter coolly and laughed. 'Don't you worry about it, Mr. Herbert,' she said cheerfully, *'God understands me.'*

I was completely baffled by this reply and when I returned to my lodgings I mentioned to Mr. Jeffreys what had happened. He heard me with nodded understanding, but proved to me, with more theology than I could then counter, that her attitude was really unexceptionable, that she was benefiting herself not at all, that she was giving up her time to sewing for her poorer neighbours, that the diapers were in any case intended for the needy, and so on and so on, the sophisms delivered in a torrent of unanswerable Welsh eloquence. I realized then I had to deal with a race of strange and powerful loyalties, of dangerous persuasiveness in the justification of alien modes of thought and feeling.

It was my habit from the beginning to take a stroll every night after supper a little way along the road which led up the side of the mountain and eventually over into the next valley, and sometimes on my walk Mr. Jeffreys came with me. One night, as we were setting out in the dark, rather later than usual, through the deserted streets of Ystrad, an event occurred which for me dispelled forever the easy assumptions of my youth and upbringing and brought me nearer than

I had ever been before to the life lived in those strange and perplexing valleys.

Although it was fine when we set out, the rain had been falling previously and had put a gleam over the dark wet streets like the sheen of steel in the lamplight. No one was about at that time of night and Mr. Jeffreys' theology was for long periods uninterrupted by acknowledgement or greeting. But as we were approaching the circle of brightness under one of the gas-lamps of the empty street I noticed the large uncertain figure of a man approaching us from the far side of the light, his clothes taking on the greenish brightness as he swayed forward out of the dark toward us. He was tall, wearing a bowler hat and a dark baggy overcoat that seemed to bang about his person as he came rocking forward. His advance into the light was crooked and prowling and I supposed at first that he must be drunk. But an observable regularity, an ordered rhythm in his uncertainty, suggested that some physical infirmity, rather, was perhaps the cause of this pitiful and ungainly shamble. We met directly under the street lamp and Mr. Jeffreys gave up his lengthy footnote abruptly to speak to him.

'Dafydd,' he said in Welsh. 'How are you? I haven't seen you a long time. Where have you been keeping yourself?'

The trance-like expression on the old man's face was replaced by a quick glance of apprehension. But as Mr. Jeffreys tumbled out questions and information he became calm again, he took off his hat and seemed to brood over us in silence, a look of profound sadness and humility upon his face.

And, as he stood in the clear gaslight, I studied him with some inexplicable fascination. He was a tall man but he stooped forward so that his shoulders were rounded and his chest hollowed. His head was large and beautiful, it seemed like heavy ivory become mellowed and yellowish, it was ponderous and comely, the eyes greatly overhung, the nose slender and delicate, the silvery hair thick and stiff and brushed forward carelessly in a fringe over the brow. The flesh of the clean-shaven face was everywhere firm and grooved; across the flat forehead, sloping outwards to the thick brows, rows of deep lines were immovably scored, each incision clean-cut and furrow-shaped; a bunch of wrinkles converged upon the outer corners of his eyes; fine grooves were present along the flanks of his nose; and upon his hollow cheeks one oblique and intricate meshwork seemed superimposed at an angle upon an earlier pattern, as though the sufferings of two different lives were recorded in that elaborate interweaving. The body beneath the massive head was proportionately bulky but as he stood listening to the talk it seemed shapeless, negligible, an appendage almost to the magnificence of the sorrowful features.

The old man was wearing a clumsy black overcoat, long, and reaching up to his throat, the buttons lost or dangling loose through the gaping buttonholes, the elbows patched with tweed. The bowler had lost its rigidity and seemed soft as a cloth hat in his fingers.

The one-sided conversation proceeded for a while and then abruptly it was all over. At the sound of working boots approaching along the pavement the old man glanced round anxiously and put on his hat. 'I must be going. Good-night, sir,' he said to me in his deep gentle voice. Then he turned to Mr. Jeffreys and took his hand. 'Good-night, Robert,' he said. 'Good-night. And God bless you for talking to me.' With that he lurched off into the darkness, his patched overcoat knocking against him as he went.

I felt strangely involved in this meeting although I had scarcely uttered a word during its brief duration. And I wished very much to learn more about the handsome and shabby old man whose blessing followed the simple act of speaking to him.

'Poor Dafydd,' Mr. Jeffreys said, looking back after him. 'There he goes again. Up to Bethesda, I feel sure of it. Let's watch him, indeed, Mr. Herbert. If we walk back a few yards we can see what he will be doing.'

Protesting, but not entirely unwilling, I went. From the corner of the next side street we could see the old man standing at the open door of one of the houses half-way along it with the light from the passage painted upon him. The by-street itself was deserted and unlighted. In a moment or two, as we watched, a little girl appeared on the doorstep and handed something out to him. Then the front door shut and the old man shambled away down the street into the darkness.

'There you are,' said Mr. Jeffreys. 'Did you see that? Thomas the Bethesda caretaker lives in that house. I thought it was the chapel key he was after. Dafydd can't leave the place alone. Every Wednesday night he's there, they say, sitting by himself in the gallery and the whole place in darkness. Some say he will rise and conduct an imaginary congregation, or the singing of an absent choir in an anthem or a chorus, but that is something I do not readily believe about him. Poor Dafydd.'

'Let me tell you then,' he went on, answering me. 'He is Dafydd Morris and he used to be a grocer in the valley here. At one time he kept the *Crown Stores,* that old-fashioned little place in Station Street, opposite the wall of the railway embankment. You know it. With the covered lane alongside and the bakehouse out at the back.'

I remembered the little shop, it was low and dark, I had seen many like it in the valley since my arrival. There was a large yellow crown painted on the wall between the windows of what seemed to be the living quarters upstairs. To get into the shop from the pavement one went down three or four stone steps. The floor was always covered with sawdust, and the gaslights were often on even in the daytime. When you passed the doorway, especially in hot weather, you noticed a very powerful smell of floor polish and lard.

I remembered these things as Mr. Jeffreys described for me Dafydd Morris conducting, Dafydd Morris singing, Dafydd Morris working underground, all in his torrential Welsh; climbing the mountain road in the darkness he recalled vividly what he had seen, heard and imagined of the old man's life, all that had led up to the knocking at the door in the side street and the handing out of the chapel key.

'Dafydd Morris bought the stock and goodwill of the *Crown Stores,* and the bakery behind it,' he told me, 'partly with the money collected for him by us, his fellow colliers, when it became clear his accident would make him say goodbye to the pit for ever. But he was always an indifferent man of business. I remember his telling me once that when he was out on his rounds delivering bread he would never *at the time* enter in his book how many loaves each customer had bought, he would rely on his memory and do it all when he got back to the shop at night. I have often seen him driving his bread cart up along this road we are on now. And on the cliff up there, Mr. Herbert, when he was the leader of our chapel singing, he used to stand looking down into the valley from the highest point of the road, I have seen him do it, wearing his shabby old clothes, unbrushed, covered from the brim of his bowler to the lace-holes of his boots with that film of grey flour from the bakehouse. He would take the tuning-fork out of his waistcoat pocket and sing softly in that beautiful voice of his, a disciplined baritone, magnificent, of great range and sweetness. Every week, whatever the weather, at that last bend in the road before it drops down into the next valley, he drew the cart into the side and hobbled across to look down into the *cwm* and over there at the hills on the far side. What he loved was to see the whole valley unobscured by rain or mist or darkness and lit by the bright sun of the morning. I heard him speak of it often in prayer meeting; he saw there, in the sunlight, the landscape of his favourite hymns, where his Saviour stood among myrtles, or strode out of Edom conquering, more lovely than the breaking of the dawn.

'But, humming to himself softly, his eyes shut, as I have seen him, he must often have forgotten the valley also, and its desolation; being a devout man, he was carried away by the poetry of our hymns and the splendour of the promises to us of divine forgiveness. He saw, in a blaze of lightning, a stander upon a lonely rock, as Ehedydd Iâl the poet says, his flesh grass and his bones clay, praising God for the forgiveness of sins while the rivers of blood froth round his crag and drink the hissing lightnings. In Dafydd Morris there was always a streak of unworldliness and dreaming, Mr. Herbert. I can imagine him, and indeed he has told us of it in the *seiat,* standing there alone above the valley in the sun, oblivious in a sort of holy trance, and being awakened by suddenly hearing the old horse behind him tearing grass out of the verge with his teeth. He opened his eyes then and recognized with a shock his dilapidated cart, with *D. Morris, Grocer and Baker* painted on it, and Captain, the big black funeral horse, awkward and ungroomed, between the shafts.

'But, as I have told you, Dafydd had not always earned his living as a grocer. Many years ago, when we worked in the mine together, he had loved music, and that, Mr. Herbert, seems the only interest in him which has survived from those youthful and unregenerate days. Music absorbed him. Arguing, as we squatted underground in the pit, eating our meal from our tin food boxes by the light of a ring of our safety lamps standing on the ground, he used to illustrate his points with the staves of old notation chalked on the pit timbers around us supporting the roof, or on the polished underneath of his steel curling box. I was only a boy then, but I remember it well. And he sang regularly in the public houses after work. At night people on this hillside left their kitchen doors open to hear Dafydd Morris singing at the crossroads after the public houses had been turned out. He was negligent of himself but never vicious, the passion of his life seemed to be for singing and comradeship and applause, and with the improvident and drunken among the miners he was popular. I remember when he carried off the baritone solo at Blaennant, an important *eisteddfod* at that time – I remember that a group of men of this rough drinking type collected among themselves to give him an additional prize and presented the money in the gaudy red velvet bag with ribbons on it, and embroidered with his initials, that was often used then in *eisteddfodau*. And if time allows, tonight, Mr. Herbert, I will perhaps have reason to mention that bag again.

'But now, about that time, that spirit – excuse me, Mr. Herbert, for some reason your own communion was untouched by it – that spirit, divine and incalculable, of religious revival, entered the valley. Dafydd Morris shared of course the universal curiosity and one night he went with his jeering friends to watch the scenes of seething emotionalism that took place night after night in the crowded chapels of Ystrad. There, I am told, he sat in silence. He did not weep, or beat his breast, or confess his sins aloud or kneel publicly in prayer as many did, but he came out into the crowd on the road outside the chapel changed and sobered. In work, and at home too, we were told, he became silent and absorbed. During the incessant discussions at the coal face of the triumphs and the follies of the revival he would say nothing. He did not visit any further meetings but his friends were quick to notice that singing appeared to be losing something of its domination over him.

'But this period was not all uncertainty and bewilderment. One evening when he came home dirty from his work in the pit, he prepared, as usual, for his bath on the hearth-rug before the kitchen fire. Stripped to the waist he lifted down the big iron saucepan off the hob and poured it out steaming on top of the cold water into the wooden tub. Then he knelt down absently and began with a cloth to swill the dirt off his arms and chest. Just then his wife came into the kitchen and began scolding him, poor soul, calling him a fool, not a quarter sane, and so on. And her anger, indeed, Mr. Herbert, was perhaps this time excusable; because what Dafydd had emptied into the bath tub was the broth for his dinner, and his washing water was still on the hob warming in another of the great saucepans.

'And then one evening he suffered the baptism of hatred and ignominy. As he was wandering, alone and unhappy, down there above the weir, he met half a dozen of his friends on their way back home from town. They had been drinking of course and they began their teasing at once, questioning him, jeering, with an undercurrent of malice and even drunken savagery in what they said. But to all their jibes Dafydd answered patiently, that was always his way, but he steadily refused to promise to sing for them again. Then they became angry, accusing him of ingratitude, desertion, the neglect of old friendships. Twm Gravell, the fitter, an amateur heavyweight he was, with the frame of a giant – Twm lost his temper at the calm and reasonableness of Dafydd's answers. "Boys," he said – excuse the language I am about to use, Mr. Herbert, if you please, it is Twm Gravell's and not my own, of course – "Boys," he said, "Mr. Bloody Morris have been converted. Here's the river by here, boys. Let's baptize the sod."

'Unresisting, they say, Dafydd was dragged down the steep bank, through the trees and thrown into the river. There, at the weir, the water is deep and he sank out of sight immediately. Rising again further down he clambered up the bank with difficulty and saw the gang running away into the darkness. He went home that night, he told

me, Mr. Herbert, in despair, his soul sickened by a sense of loathing at
the defilement of flesh and spirit he had endured.

'And then one day underground he had his accident. That was the
time I damaged this hand of mine working with the rescue party to free
the men who had been trapped – a late rock fell out of the roof and
crushed my finger here to a batter on my shovel handle. But that is by
the way.

'In spite of the jeers of Twm Gravell and his sort, Mr. Herbert,
Dafydd was not quite a convert yet, one of the "people of the
certainty," as we say; although, filled with remorse and a sense of
unworthiness, he was, as you will recognize, with his face in the
direction of the light. Then came the terrible accident. He was cutting
coal that day in the nine-foot seam, where we were working together at
the time – and I ought to tell you, Mr. Herbert, that Dafydd, a
powerful man, was a fine collier, and when he attacked the face the
coal came boiling out under his pick – as I say, working in the Rhas Las
nine-foot seam, he heard the top above him dribbling stones, a sign of
a coming roof fall, but before he could jump clear the whole ceiling,
twenty yards of rock, came down in dust and thunder around him. His
leap, although it failed to land him in safety, at least brought him to the
edge of the fall, so that, instead of finding him completely buried when
we at last groped our way to him, we saw him by our lamps pinned
down by masses of rock from chest to feet; he lay there unconscious,
the whole of his lower body held under an immovable burden, under
tons of rock and rubble.

'After working feverishly by the light of our colliers' lamps we at last
got him free and took him, crushed and bleeding profusely, to the
surface. He had regained consciousness by then. But from that
accident and the ordeal of the journey to the pit-shaft that followed it,
his shattered legs and feet never recovered. With one arm around my
shoulders and one round Jim Rice's, both of us shorter than he was,
Dafydd swung in agony between us as we made for the parting and the
pit bottom and the cage. He was conscious of the weight of his great
bulk upon us and he tried, from time to time, groaning, with sweat
pouring off him, to place his crushed feet on the ground to lessen our
burden. But the agony of it was unendurable. And I remember another
terrible thing during that journey. At intervals, in the darkness, his
dangling legs cracked against the steel rollers in between the tram-rails
over which the tram ropes ran; and with the agony of those blows he
screamed out loud and passed into unconsciousness again on our
shoulders. With the pain and throbbing of my own hand and the
memory of that journey I lay awake night after night, unable to sleep, I

used to hear in my bed those nightmare howls, Dafydd Morris's voice echoing in agony among the hollow headings as his smashed legs crashed into the unseen metal rollers.

'And Dafydd lay in bed too, month after month, in their little back bedroom, sometimes in great pain, sometimes in the merciful stupor of drugs. Both his legs were broken and his pelvis utterly smashed. It was evident that, even if he was to live at all, he would never work in the pit again. And in his physical agony and his mood of spiritual distress none of his visitors was more welcome than the vigorous old minister of his childhood's chapel, William Morgans, Bethesda, a grim old man, from whose presence as children at least, Mr. Herbert, we used to run away. He was short in figure and thickish, as I remember him, heavily, perhaps, some would say, even grossly built. His long pale face and the front of his neck were hung with plentiful loose skin and he had a shining skullcap of close-cropped silver hair. His nose, marked blue across the high crest with the scar of the coalminer, was arrogant, as was the glance of his large light eyes. His expression was always bold and authoritative, it had pride of mission and lofty dedication, and no church-prince, I used to think, could be more jealous than he was of the dignity and awesomeness of his calling. He worshipped the Saviour who blasted the fig-tree, and foretold for his followers the sword, who declared that the fruitless branch should be cast out into the fire, who drove out the money-changers from the Temple with the twisted cords. But Dafydd Morris found in the narrow pride and fearlessness of this upright old man some strange restoration and strength. Together they used to sit in the plain little bedroom watching through the window the scene in the valley below them and opposite them, the bare stretches of hillside grassland, the coloured gardens of the miners, the funnels of the anchored pit steaming into the sunlight.

'Sometimes, when Dafydd was well enough, they talked. Morgans cared nothing for the graces of conversation, he cared nothing for music either, or for discussions about it. Dafydd Morris's voice, the finest in five valleys then, he judged as the dust of scale-pans; and indeed he seemed almost insensitive, Dafydd often told me, to the suffering of that broken and emaciated body lying before him. His large glowing eyes were turned upon Dafydd in challenge rather than in tenderness and compassion. For him the big helpless man upon the bed was far more than flesh and bone in physical agony, he was the possessor of an immortal soul which might be saved and, with God's help, he, William Morgans, would defy all hell to save it.

'I was several times visiting in that little bedroom where Dafydd had to lie. It was clean and simple because Hannah Morris, with all her faults – and she had many, poor soul, as you shall hear, Mr. Herbert – Hannah was a good housewife then. There was a black iron bedstead in it, a red chair, a red washstand, a red door. The wallpaper had faded almost white, and a pink oilcloth patterned with bunches of red roses covered the floor. Later on, when Dafydd was recovering, we went there regularly to teach him to walk again, and we used those bunches of roses to mark his improvement from lesson to lesson – one week he would manage to totter on his crutches past two of the bunches, the next week past three, and so on.

'Always a little fire burned in the grate, and on the black iron mantelpiece above it stood three or four silver cups and a few plush-lined cases with the medals in them Dafydd had won singing at various *eisteddfodau* in the valleys. The red velvet pocket I spoke of earlier, presented by his public house friends, was also there, hanging above the trophies by its yellow ribbon from a glass-headed pin stuck into the wallpaper. And it was in that bedroom, as I have often heard him describe, that the events occurred which brought him for the time peace, and restored him to the community from which the heedlessness and irresponsibility of his youth, he felt deeply, had for a long time exiled him.

'It was a fine day in spring, the sun in panes of light on the white bed coverlet, a heavy fly buzzing against the window. Outside Dafydd could see his neglected garden full of willowherb, the wet fence steaming in the sun, the bare hills, and the blue sky. But for all its beauty the day was a bitter one for him. The doctor had that morning told him that amputation of one or both his legs might after all be necessary.

'As he lay in bed tears of bitterness and rebellion broke from his lids. The old preacher, on one of his visits, was seated in his thick black clothes with the braided edges beside the bed, the sun silvering the plush of his clipped skull-cap. He gazed down dour and unmoved at the weeping man, watching in silence the tears coursing down the scooped out cheeks. And then Dafydd caught sight of the velvet bag hanging from its glass-headed pin half-way up the chimney breast, and at the sight of it, he says, he felt some strange lightening of his grief, for the moment his heart was less heavy and in the middle of his tears a faint smile appeared on his lips.

'The old minister frowned and turned and followed the direction of Dafydd's gaze. His large beaming eyes fell upon the medals and the cups and the gaudy velvet bag hanging high above them with the letters *D.M.* worked crudely in gold thread upon it. Could it be this object which had brought remission to the face of the sufferer, the momentary respite and comfort? What was it? He left the red chair and went heavily across to the fireplace and took the crude red pocket in his hands.

' "What is this, Dafydd Morris?" he asked. "Your initials?"

' "It's a prize bag, a present given me long ago," Dafydd answered, pushing away his tears in shame with the back of his hand.

' "It was perhaps given you for singing?"

' "Yes. I had it for singing."

' "Where did you win it?"

' "In the next valley. In Blaennant."

' "That *eisteddfod*," said the old man, "is a big one. It surprises me they should present you with such a bag."

'He fingered the tawdry red object with his thick lower lip pushed out in contempt and distaste. "Shoddy. Unworthy," he muttered.

' "It was presented to me," Dafydd explained, "to acknowledge my win. Some of my friends gave it to me. My first big singing victory."

'The watchful eyes of the old man kindled, he lifted up his head with an affronted expression on his face.

' "What friends?" he asked.

'Dafydd hesitated and flushed. "Huw Reece," he said, "Twm Gravell, Steve Williams, Joe Phillips, those."

'Morgans tossed the bag on to the bed as though he had suffered defilement. "Friends, did you say?" he asked coming forward and standing above the bed. "Friends? Blasphemers who jeered at you, thwarted you, who cast you in your weakness into the river. Wantoners, fornicators. Evil livers who employed all the devices of Satan to drag you back from the circle of the promise, towards which, God be praised, you had turned your face. Friends, did you say? You can call them friends after the usages of this world, but answer me this, how many of them, since you have lain helpless in this bed, have had the grace to visit you?"

'Even in his unhappiness a half smile appeared on Dafydd's face. "Well, all of them," he answered. "They have all been here some time or another, shaking hands and hoping that everything was all right between us."

'The old man's eyes blazed. "It were to your advantage," he said flushed and in anger, "if they had never set foot over the threshold, if in shame and repentance they had stayed away." He glanced down at the bed. "This bag," he said, "it must be destroyed. Cast it from you as a symbol of a life you have repented of, which you have forsaken and abjured for ever."

' "No, no," Dafydd pleaded, the sweat thick on his forehead. "Don't let me destroy it. It was given to me in kindness. Don't let it be destroyed, wantonly."

' "Dafydd Morris," said the masterful old man, "it must be destroyed. Take hold of the evil thing. Cast it into the fire."

'He fixed his imperious hypnotic stare upon Dafydd's face. To him the fate of the gaudy little velvet bag had become of eternal moment, the tiny room was a battleground and around the beribboned pocket was being waged the final struggle for the soul of this dying collier. He gathered up all the authority and masterfulness of his powerful nature while the sick man hesitated.

' "Dafydd Morris," he said in the rich Welsh of his westward birthplace, "Dafydd Morris, I command you now, in the name of Almighty God, in the name of Christ our Lord and Saviour, in the name of the cloud of witnesses and the holy dead, I command you, in the name of everything sacred to you here upon earth and in heaven above, now, in this room, to renounce and abjure your life, I command you to come forth, I command you to burn, root out, destroy, every vestige of your sin. I command you, as the servant of the Eternal God I command you, to forsake sighing, backward glancing, the damnation of Lot's wife, and come away. And let this be the token and symbol of your submission and repentance."

'He picked up the red bag again off the bed and thrust it into the sick man's hands. Dafydd looked at it for a moment, glanced up desperately at the gross and menacing bulk of the old minister and tossed it weakly towards the fire. Through the feebleness of the throw it fell short but the old man picked it up off the rug and pitched it contemptuously on to the glowing coals. At once the dried-up velvet broke into a flame that went up the chimney like a golden rope. Dafydd's head fell back and he passed into the unconsciousness of exhaustion.'

Mr. Jeffreys stopped speaking and we halted a moment to look down from the mountain into the darkness of the valley now far below us. There we could see our town, well defined by the street lights clustered in handfuls and stretched out into long chains in the night. The weather was clearer now, the darkness was warm and soft about us and we stood side by side a few minutes in silence. Then somewhere in the town below an engine sighed and the metallic clink of shunted trucks came distinctly up to us, and we moved on again in the direction of the top of the mountain.

'I have not said much yet, Mr. Herbert,' Mr. Jeffreys went on, 'about Hannah Morris, the wife of Dafydd Morris, but now I ought to tell you one or two things about her because without her Dafydd's story would no doubt be very different from what it is. Dafydd always spoke of her to the end with tenderness and affection, especially of their life together before they came to the shop. And no doubt, with her glossy hair, and her flashing black eyes and her unhampered movements, she must have been a fascinating young woman to a man of Dafydd's temperament. But how difficult life is to foresee. Perhaps if her lap had felt the tread of children she would not have been so completely set upon money and possessions. She was, Mr. Herbert, without any doubt, the one with energy and decision, in her nature there was no room for the hesitancies of sentiment or any scruples. According to her own lights she was, no doubt, just, but her righteousness as time went on became grim and cold and unlovely.

'I remember Dafydd saying to me once, at the time I started visiting Lowri, "When I was courting Hannah, Robert, I used to go up to their house on a Saturday evening when her mother had gone out shopping, and watch her knitting or mending clothes by the table in the kitchen, or making apple tart for their tea on Sunday. She had a fine hand for pastry always, as you know. One thing especially I thought amusing and charming in her in those days, although I could never explain why. When she was cutting up the cooking apples to put them in the tart, she would never peel them, and when I saw her under the clear lamplight slicing apples on to the pastry covering the bottom of the plate, with the skin still bright green and shining like silk on them, the novelty was something magical to me, it used to give me a delightful sensation of enchantment almost, because I had never seen that done before." A strange thing for a man to speak about so long after. What do you think of it, Mr. Herbert?

'Undoubtedly the shop was the corruptor of her character, although I think the weakness of greed was within her before. Do you know that in the end she had become so grasping that Dafydd had to pay for every stick of barley sugar he took out with him on his rounds? And she used to charge herself too for the pinch of cloves taken into the kitchen for her apple tart? And for what, Mr. Herbert? For what?

'But let me try to tell you what she had become, from something I saw myself in the shop one day – greedy, sharp-tongued, suspicious, and yet with some attraction about her for Dafydd in spite of her faults. Let me piece together what I was a witness of and what I heard from Phoebe Francis and Willy her husband, and Maldwyn Edwards the assistant in the *Crown Stores*. And Dafydd himself also.

'Imagine Phoebe Francis, now, Mr. Herbert, a shabby old woman she was, coming slowly along the pavement of Station Street; she walks beside the high brick retaining wall of the railway embankment opposite the *Crown Stores*. She is dressed as she always was, all in black, wearing a man's cloth cap pinned on through the bun at the back of her head, a large woollen shawl, a heavy skirt, patched, and laced-up boots showing her poor bunions. Her name, Mr. Herbert, as I think I told you, was Phoebe Francis, and she would earn a few pence from her neighbours for washing their bedclothes or doing a bit of paper-hanging, or laying out a corpse, and some called her the Jews' Poker, because for a copper or two she would poke up the fires for the religious Jews on their Sabbath. Poor Phoebe, her face was always flabby and colourless, her nose swollen, covered with a network of red veins She was a bit simple-minded, really, I suppose, her expression; poor thing, was always harassed and resentful and, I must say, a bit crafty as well.

'I was in the *Crown Stores* when I saw her standing by the retaining brickwork on the opposite side of the street. She pulled her shawl around her and then started fingering the brooch at her throat. She crossed the road towards the shop and peeped in through the window; I could see her over the purple-stamped hams and dishes of bacon. Then, satisfied with her examination, she came down the steps into the shop where at the moment I was the only customer.

' "Where is *she?*" she whispered to the young man behind the bacon counter. *She,* of course, Mr. Herbert, could only be Mrs. Morris.

'The shop assistant was Maldwyn Edwards, tall and bald, in his white starched apron and jacket with the comb in the breast pocket. That was Maldwyn all over, Mr. Herbert, a real wag he was and a loss to this valley when he died. His blue eyes were brilliant, I can see them now, they used to flicker all the time with mischief. He bared the hard toothless gums he had, grinning, stripping off the wooden box from around the big fifty-six-pound butter block on the counter. "It's all right, Phoebe," he said. "She's gone into the warehouse. What can I do for you?"

'The old woman stood by one of the iron pillars holding up the roof beams. Dafydd always used to paper these pillars with coloured labels, so that the roof seemed to be supported by columns of salmon tins or tins of golden syrup. "Wanted to ask you, I did, to pin this brooch for me, Maldwyn *bach,*" she said. "It happened to come out jest as I was passing."

'Maldwyn leaned over the counter still grinning and fastened the big brooch back into the cross-over shawl. "There you are, Phoebe," he said. "Now, what next?"

' "Thank you indeed, Maldwyn," she said, patting her throat. "That's better. There's nothing else I wanted, thank you. I only wanted for you to fasten the brooch, because my hands are shaking so bad." She looked up at the green tea canisters on the shelves behind him for a moment. "I suppose you couldn't spare us a bit of firewood, like, could you?" she asked. "I haven't got a bit of anything I can put the chopper into in the house."

'Maldwyn stooped and pulled out a few strips of the white butter-box he had just thrown under the counter. "Will this do?" he said. "Put them under your shawl now before anybody comes. How is Willy there with you now?" he went on, grinning. "Is he any better these days?"

'Willy, as I told you, Mr. Herbert, was Phoebe's husband, a workshy if ever there was one. He was supposed to be suffering from nystagmus and you could often see him standing in the middle of the road shading his eyes and peering anxiously up at the town clock to see if it was getting near time for the pubs to open.

'"No indeed, Maldwyn *bach*," the old woman said. "When our Willy's legs are better, his arms are worse, and when he haven't got the earick, his bowels are upset or there's something the matter with his kidneys. I am daunted, indeed there." She took a sixpence out of her purse and very thoughtfully scooped a long groove up the side of the block of butter with it. "You couldn't let me have an ounce of shag on strap for him now, could you, Maldwyn? Only an ounce, like," she added, licking the butter off the sixpence.

'Maldwyn's blue eyes sparkled. "No indeed I couldn't, Phoebe," he said. "If the misses found out I'd given you anything on account the wagon would be in the ditch, I can tell you that. She's not a-willing, see."

'"She's a proper old screw, she is," Phoebe said. "I hope one day she'll be down on the bones of her behind worse than me and our Willy is. I suppose I better go now before I do see her, or I will be sure to give her the rough side of my tongue. So long now, Maldwyn *bach*, and thank you for the firewood. You don't mind me asking, like, do you?"

'"So long, Phoebe," Maldwyn answered, picking up the claw hatchet to go on with his stripping. "Come again."

'The old woman was pulling herself up the steps to reach the pavement when Hannah Morris came into the shop from the warehouse.

'"Phoebe Francis," she said, "stop a minute, will you?"

'Phoebe turned round on the middle step. Hannah was standing at the back of the shop with a ledger under her arm. She was by then a small jet-haired woman, juiceless and swarthy; she dressed in black, wore a long thin gold chain and seemed soured by everything she saw through her gold-rimmed glasses.

' "Hullo, Mrs. Morris," said Phoebe. "I didn't notice you by there. How are you keeping, girl?"

' "Never mind how I'm keeping," Mrs. Morris answered. "Listen here! Have you got a bit of salt with you?"

' "Salt?" said Phoebe, not moving, standing up there near the doorway. "Salt, Hannah Morris, did you say? How do you mean *salt*? What do you think I want salt for, say you?"

' "For this," Mrs. Morris said, holding the ledger out before her and tapping the cover with her finger-nail. "To rub into your account, Phoebe Francis. It's started stinking."

'The old woman stared down at her for a moment from the steps without saying a word. Then she turned and went on climbing in silence up out of the shop. When she reached the pavement, she turned again and kicked the sawdust off her boots against the doorpost. "Keep your flaming firewood," she shouted, taking the strips of butter-box from under her shawl and throwing them back down on to the floor of the shop. "Keep it. I'd rather freeze than use anything from this flaming place. Our Willy said the softest part of you is your teeth, and he's not far wrong neither. And I hope one day, when you put your hand down on the floor of your pocket you won't find nothing there, like me and our Willy. Keep your flaming firewood, you skingey old sow."

'She turned away and went off up the street, muttering and pulling her big shawl tighter around her. Before she had gone many yards she came face to face with Dafydd Morris hurrying out of the bakehouse next door and occupying most of the pavement as usual with his roll. They spoke and Phoebe went on her way calmer. "Don't be hard on Hannah, Phoebe *fach*, there's a good girl," Dafydd said in his gentle way. "I will bring an ounce of shag round tonight after closing. Say nothing. There is some fault on all of us, and a certain weakness for money is Hannah's, perhaps. Perhaps. Don't be hard on her, there's a good girl."

'Back in the shop Maldwyn expected the storm, I could see that, and he began humming *Crugybar* to himself. "None of that," Mrs. Morris snapped, glaring over her glasses. "And don't let me have to tell you again about handing firewood out. We've got to *sell* things in this shop, not *give* them away. You didn't give the slut any account, did you?"

'Maldwyn shook his bald head, silent and stubborn. She studied him a moment but he ignored her, he went on using the claw on the two stone of butter. She stepped across to the box with the tobacco in, on the counter, made up into tubular half-ounce packets. As she was examining them her husband appeared on the top step at the street door, large and awkward, dimming the shop.

'He spoke a word to me and then he asked where Harry was. Harry was his friend, Mr. Herbert, he called in at the *Crown Stores* for a chat every day and I will tell you more about him presently.

' "Where's Harry?" he said. "Hasn't he been in? I met him up the street and he said he was calling."

' "No," Hannah answered. "Not yet." Then she went on sharply, "I'm checking these half-ounces," she said. "They're still the same so far. I did wonder if Phoebe Francis was the one. I'll catch him though, whoever he is. I won't be bested by a thief, I'm telling you. A half-ounce packet every week for over a month now, sometimes two. But I'll catch him, you see if I don't."

'Dafydd looked down at her with troubled eyes. This was a hateful thing to him. "How will you do that, Hannah *fach*?" he asked soothingly, with a sort of pleading in his voice. "I expect you miscounted them."

' "No, I haven't miscounted them. I've made sure of that. I'll lay a trap for him, don't you worry. And if I catch him I'll prosecute him too, don't you fret now."

'Dafydd shuffled through the sawdust into the warehouse at the back and I saw the glance of understanding that passed between him and Maldwyn on his way.

'What I have been telling you now, Mr. Herbert, this last small episode, took place, let me see, about fifteen years ago, just before Dafydd Morris received from us what he considered high honour, the highest, even. His throwing into the fire of the little velvet bag, which I tried to describe to you just now, was for him the complete gesture of renunciation and conversion. Regularly after that, when he was able to walk again, I saw him towering among the baritones on the gallery of Bethesda, and then, when Thomas the Leader died, Dafydd became the conductor of the chapel choir. He performed this task faithfully for twenty years, he was beautiful at it, gentle and persuasive, and his only fault, in my opinion, was too great a leniency towards those who were indifferent and irregular in their attendance at singing school. But then Dafydd's purpose in this world, he had chosen it, was to be the long sufferer; the neck of Abel, as I heard that preacher saying, rather than the knife of Cain.

'And acknowledgement of his devotion during this time grew to be universal in the valley, and the stories of Dafydd's youth were forgotten or not believed. And as a mark of this regard for him the honour I mentioned just now was conferred upon him.

'I know you have learnt, Mr. Herbert, that the chapels in this valley hold at Easter an united religious singing festival, a *gymanfa ganu*. The conductor for this is customarily a guest from a distance, someone of acknowledged musical standing in our country. But about ten, fifteen, years ago, as I say, Dafydd Morris was invited to conduct this annual *gymanfa* in his own valley. At first, from feelings of unworthiness, he declined, but there were many persuasive tongues on that *gymanfa* committee and finally Dafydd consented.

'I remember very well the Easter Tuesday of the festival, a day of triumph for Dafydd Morris. The meetings were always held in Saron, the largest chapel in the Ystrad Valley, and that, in the evening, was crowded. I was recovering from my annual quinsy at the time and so I had to find a seat downstairs for once, and not with the choir on the gallery.

'While the chairman was speaking before the singing of the final chorus, I watched Dafydd Morris occupying the conductor's armchair up there in the high pulpit, prominent in the downbeam of the lamp hung just above his head; and it was plain to me that he sat there in fulfilment and blessedness, the expression on his face was one of complete serenity as he looked about at his choir in the chapel galleries to his right and left and before him. No clapping of hands is permitted in our chapels, of course, but during that packed-out meeting the conductor had other proofs and assurances of the regard of his audience. The people had sat in enthralled stillness during hymn after hymn, during anthem after anthem, although as I say the chapel was crowded. In fact the building was so full that chairs had to be carried into the aisles, and both the stairways leading up to the gallery were packed with a solid mass of people who had arrived too late to get a seat inside the building. There were even people sitting crowded together on the window-sills. But in spite of all this, the discomfort, the perspiring, the stifling air, the attention of the people to the end was strict and undiminished. And Dafydd Morris knew it was so.

'Dafydd was dressed, as I saw him under that glaring lamp, in his conducting clothes, the black suit of evening dress he wore for his engagements, with a bit of satin shining on the lapels of his jacket, a white collar attached to a breast, and a black tucked-under bow-tie. As he sat, with a sort of radiance upon him, under that downward light, I watched him, as I said, glancing round during the chairman's praises, fiddling with the buttons of his waistcoat; tin trouser buttons they were, Mr. Herbert, half of them, because when the cloth ones came off, Hannah was too mean, gone, to buy him new ones. After she went to the shop she cared nothing at all for the way Dafydd faced the world. She sent him out on his breadrounds looking like a scarecrow, only dusty with flour, and you could tell by a glance at his shirt collar that by then she hadn't much interest in the flat-iron. And yet, when he was underground, it was a pleasure to see him going to work, with tidy white duck patches on the knees of his pit-trousers, and the duck cap she had made for him, and the wide belt of duck for slinging his box-and-jack over his shoulder.

'But no matter for that now. The response of Dafydd's choir throughout the day, as I have said, had been warm and wholehearted, and his happiness in them was complete. He glanced round again and again with affection at the altos and sopranos seated in the wooden pews of the gallery above him, at the tenors and basses up against the green streaming walls of the chapel. He smiled and I smiled with him, at the earnestness of the singers, at Mrs. Rees Top-notes; at Clara Central Cottages who claimed she could only read her music in old notation and half her time held her copy upside down; at Bryn Chin stuttering the anthems out of his enormous jaw – "That sittetheth upon the thro-one, that sittetheth upon the throne"; at Lewis the Graig, the grumbler, complaining, as I remember him, every week in singing school, "Lev us rise, now will you, Dafydd Morris? Lev us rise. Us been sitting by 'ere now for two hours, aye, singing these pieces. Lev us rise a bit, like, now, will you?"

'Daylight had not left the sky when that evening part of the *gymanfa* began, and the crowded chapel was filled with golden light. It was pleasant to hear the black linen blinds that hung over the open windows making that clicking noise as the evening breeze puffed them forward into the chapel and then sucked them back again. But by the time the last chorus was to be sung all the lights in the building were lit and I could see stars shining through the curved uncovered fanlights above the window blinds.

'The chairman sat down at last and Dafydd, picking up the ivory baton the choir had presented to him, lifted his big clumsy bulk out of the pulpit armchair. The *gymanfa* was almost at an end. The organ commenced the vibrating introduction to the "Hallelujah Chorus", traditionally sung by us, Mr. Herbert, as perhaps you know, to terminate our Easter *cymanfaoedd*. The choir rose and the audience crowding the floor of the chapel rose also to join in, as was always done. Dafydd Morris conducted this singing like one inspired. His face there in the lamp's downbeam I shall never forget. "King of Kings, and Lords of Lords! And He shall reign for ever and ever!" The exultation of the music filled him, he seemed uplifted with a sense of the majesty of God, and the tenderness of His love, and with his own blissful identification with the singing around him.

'And then, in the middle of that chorus, an alarming and revealing thing happened. As everyone, choir and audience together, was singing the great *laus Deo*, the electric wire from the high chapel roof, from which the pulpit-light which shone down on Dafydd Morris hung, burst into flames, and the lamp with its large metal shade, narrowly missing him, crashed on to the table in the big seat below. There the flaring wire was quickly put out and no damage was done. But the strange thing was that so absorbed and uplifted was Dafydd Morris that he appeared not to notice at all what had happened, he remained unconscious in his ecstasy both of the great blue flare hissing down past his eyes and the loud crash which followed it. And the singing, in response to his triumphant mood, proceeded with unalterable movement and feeling. The only thing changed was this – during the latter part of the chorus, that expressive face was no longer illuminated from above to a bright transparency, Dafydd's conducting was carried on instead in the ordinary and equalized light of the chapel.

'After the *gymanfa* had finished, he told me later, he remembered little of what had happened, he had a sense of universal congratulation, of smiles and hand-claspings, but his feeling of triumph and identity and exaltation obliterated all particular impressions and he took to his house an inward illumination of peace and joy.'

Mr. Jeffreys and I had by this time reached the crossroads made by the intersection of the old Roman way running over the hill into the next valley. The wind was high and we stood for a minute or two again, looking down into the valley. From that height, nearly at the top of the mountain, we could see great distances. The risen moon, curved and glassy, sailed by in the glare of her own light. I felt a strange sense of fulfilment and elation.

'I ought to begin to tell you now, Mr. Herbert, Mr. Jeffreys said as we started our steep descent back into the town, about Harry the Boot, a very well-known and very engaging character in this valley at the time I am talking of. He was a littlish humped man, something like a hairless monkey to look at, but with big ears of a bright yellow colour, the lobes very fleshy, and hanging loose. His face was heavily wrinkled and covered with dark brown speckles but his bald head, on the other hand, had a tight polished look. He had no human dignity, or even self-respect, as the foolish eager sort of grin on his face showed plainly.

'Harry's real style was Jones, I think, but everybody called him by this other name because he had been brought up in a house that had once been a public house, the "Boot Inn". Some people held that Harry was just simple and amusing, others said there was real cunning hidden under his comicality. I don't know. It was hard to tell which.

'For instance now, when he was a lout of a boy he often used to come to our home on a Saturday afternoon to call for Emlyn, my eldest brother, to go to the football match together. One Saturday my mother said to him, "Em hasn't come home from work yet, Harry. Are you going to wait for him? You can sit down in there if you like." Harry said yes, he'd wait, so my mother put him in the middle room out of the way. "Would you like a cup of tea?" she said to him. "And there's a plate of rhubarb tart on the table if you want some." With that my mother, always busy with eight of us to bring up, went back to her work in the kitchen, leaving Harry on his own with an uncut plate of tart and a cup of tea before him. When she passed through the room a quarter of an hour later all that was left of that rhubarb tart was the tin plate and one thin slice no wider than your finger. My mother looked at him, flushed and very surprised, and Harry was quick to excuse himself. "I'm very sorry indeed, Mrs. Jeffreys," he said, "but I *couldn't* eat it all, I've done my best, but I *had* to leave that little piece behind." Was that simple-mindedness, Mr. Herbert, or cunning? I don't know which.

'But I do believe that after his accident any eccentricity or moral weakness or disorder in him was intensified. He used to work on top of the pit and one night as he was walking home along the railway line in pitch darkness, the colliers' train came up behind him, hit him flat between the rails and ran over him. Fortunately for him he was carrying a log of firewood over his shoulder at the time, so that his body did not receive the full impact of the engine; and also he fell, as I say, plumb in between the metals. But his head cracked heavily on the sleepers as he went down and he lay unconscious for several hours before he was found by the men coming on the day shift. He was, after that, I always felt, more unstable and unpredictable, in short, speaking with all charity, dafter than he was before, and as he grew older the differences between him and the rest of us became more and more marked.

'But his wrong-headedness, Mr. Herbert, please don't mistake me, was innocent and endearing, almost everyone looked upon him as a harmless droll and from one end of the valley to the other people welcomed him and teased him and laughed at him. "Why are you calling Tommy Carter your cousin, Harry?" I said to him once. "I didn't know Tommy was related to you." "Well no, Robert," he said with his puckered-up monkey-grin. "We're not related proper, like, but the wife had a child by him before we was married." That will show you, Mr. Herbert, the sort of world Harry inhabited.

'Dafydd Morris had a great liking for Harry. It was Harry, I might say, he always asked for when he came back into the shop after his bread round. Hardly a day passed but the two met. And there in the *Crown Stores* with Dafydd smiling at him and Maldwyn Edwards egging him on, poor Harry made some of his most famous jokes, the ones that people in the valley at one time used to pass on from one to another. But now, it was through him that tragedy came upon Dafydd Morris. I hinted, didn't I, some time back, that Hannah Morris was determined to set a trap to catch the thief who was stealing her half-ounce packets of tobacco? Harry the Boot turned out to be the thief. I am afraid, Mr. Herbert, as you shall hear, that there could be no question about his guilt, poor dab.

'Without telling anyone, Mrs. Morris carried out her threat. What she did was to cut about a yard of the white string they used for packing in the *Crown Stores* and tuck one end of it very firmly into one of the paper packets of tobacco. She put the packet back into the box on the counter with the others and hid the length of string underneath very cleverly, so that it could not be noticed. A day or two later Harry was in the shop as usual, Maldwyn was provoking him and he was talking with that comical wrong-headedness that people used to like so much to hear. But when it was all over and he was making his way up out of the shop, still laughing and joking, Mrs. Morris came in from the warehouse. She called him back in her abrupt way, exactly as she had done with Phoebe Francis. When he came down to the bottom step she said, "What is that string hanging out of your coat pocket, Harry? Come here, let me have a look. You don't happen to have half an ounce of tobacco on the other end of it, do you? Let's see!"

'She thrust her hand into Harry's coat pocket and pulled out half an ounce of tobacco with the string tied on to it.

'Harry, poor fellow, was terrified, he broke down, his face was white, like something peeled, he confessed and pleaded for mercy as though he was hysterical. All the instability and suppressed terror of his nature came out then; he was, so Maldwyn told me, like someone demented with fear, he cringed on the floor, he cried out loud, and sobbed in remorse, there was pandemonium in the shop as Hannah described in her cold mocking way what was soon to happen to him.

'Dafydd was out on his rounds at the time and Harry had been taken home a long time when he arrived at the shop again that night. He was greatly troubled at what had happened, all his concern was for the unhappiness of poor Harry. He assumed that nothing further was to happen to him. But Hannah – there was this strange hardness and malevolence about her, Mr. Herbert – Hannah told him that the matter was already in the hands of the police.

'It is painful for me, Mr. Herbert, even now, to speak of all the details of this episode, and I will not do it. But from what happened in the next week or two Dafydd Morris never recovered, nor ever will this side of the grave. For Harry did not make that appearance he so much dreaded before the police court. He shot himself. A day or two before the case was to be called, the poor frenzied creature went up to his brother-in-law's house, smuggled a shotgun out into the garden shed and destroyed himself with it. He was found sitting on the stool with the gun between his knees and nine inches of the barrel driven up into his head from under his chin with the kick of the discharge. Poor terrified mortal. And all for the sake of half an ounce of tobacco that Dafydd would have given him willingly for nothing. Why did he pilfer in this way, Mr. Herbert? He could have meant no harm to Dafydd, his friend, but did he, in some confused way, imagine that he was spiting Hannah for all her meanness? The workings of a mind like his are difficult to follow, I have found.

'But my concern is with Dafydd Morris. After the shooting his silence and absorption were pitiful. He went about like one haunted. In a short time he gave up his bread round and hired a man to do it for him; and soon he was seldom going beyond the warehouse at all. He withdrew into himself and on the road he passed his friends hurriedly with a dry nod, as though he feared that given the opportunity they might treat him in the same way. He didn't seek people out to repeat his story to them, or embarrass strangers with long protestations of his innocence, as I have seen many doing obsessed with grief or injury or injustice. There was something aloof and withdrawn about him always and I cannot think of him pouncing upon anyone like some, and diving into his inside pockets for documents to prove his case. His suffering was solitary and incommunicable. His resignation from his position as conductor of our chapel choir we accepted unwillingly, and with protest, but he continued to attend Bethesda on Sundays, slipping in after the service had commenced and leaving during the last hymn. And yet, during that whole time, I do not recall hearing a single word of blame or reproach spoken against Dafydd himself, but only expressions of sympathy rather.

'Feeling against Mrs. Morris, on the other hand, was naturally very strong in many quarters, as I shall show you, but for her to arouse antipathy and even hatred among her neighbours was not anything new. During the big stoppage in the coalfield that had only just come to an end at that time she gained many enemies by the bitter way she spoke about the strikers and, worse, her unwillingness to give "old account" to her customers. She grudged necessities like cheese and bread to decent, hard-working families who had bought their groceries at the *Crown Stores* for years, and who, before the strike, had never been a penny in her debt. She forgot that whatever prosperity she enjoyed had come from the generosity of the colliers who had set

Dafydd up in business after his accident. She said openly now that those who refused to work deserved to starve.

'In the circumstances Dafydd was able to lessen the harshness of her refusals by private gifts and other kindnesses, and I know that certain classes of people, large families, good singers, those who regularly attended prayer-meeting and so on, were well cared-for by him throughout the strike. But now he was helpless. Rapidly his hair seemed to whiten. His stoop became more marked. He shambled about the valley in his shabby old clothes alone, always silent and brooding, and the lines on his face appeared to deepen and multiply almost from day to day.

'And then, about a month after the shooting, something happened which completed the withdrawal into himself that Harry's death had begun.

'One sunny Monday morning, as he opened the shop door, he saw in huge letters something written in tar on the long station wall right opposite the *Crown Stores*. You will excuse me, Mr. Herbert, but I cannot lay my tongue to the malice and obscenity of the message that appeared there. The words were about Mrs. Morris and, as I said, they had been roughly printed there on the retaining brickwork with a brush-stump or a tarred stick, in letters two feet high; the whole sentence extended perhaps fifteen or twenty feet across the wall, and the sun shone on it.

The effect of this upon Dafydd was to turn him into a man no longer capable of speech or clear understanding of what was going on around him. Worse, he seemed unable to endure further emotion, he could no longer kindle because his heart was already a cinder. Before he read the tarred message he did attend Bethesda, sitting, as I said, in the backseat or in the "goats' pen", but now he did not go out at all on Sundays. Indeed, he was hardly ever to be seen abroad by daylight, he became a night walker, a prowler of the valleys. On two separate occasions at that time someone, late at night, still filled with a terrible unquenchable spirit of hatred and revenge, someone took a shotgun to the top of the station wall opposite the shop and used it to smash both the plate glass windows of the *Crown Stores*. But this seemed to have no effect on Dafydd now. Friends, neighbours, members of Bethesda, men who had worked underground with him, all of us tried to break through to him with words of comfort, but he could see himself only as an Ishmael, Mr. Herbert, exiled, forsaken, certain that God's love flowed now in different beds.

'A year or two later Mrs. Morris died, not of course of a broken heart but of some strange infection of the blood. She had, you may

depend, apart from Dafydd, a dry funeral. Dafydd gave up the shop at
once and went to live with a niece in the next valley. I thought he
would make straight for the grave then, but no, within a few months he
was back here and he went into the lodgings he now occupies. And vile
lodgings they are. I myself, from the street, have seen the rats inside
running across the window-sill of his room. And at night, as I told you,
he walks up to Bethesda and sits alone in the gallery, in darkness,
sometimes for an hour or two. What do you think, Mr. Herbert, could
have broken the heart of this good man? Is it remorse? But for what?
Or a sense of unworthiness, or the ache of being cast out from the
community of his fellows, or the agony of being abandoned by God?
What is it, do you think?'

He became silent and we walked on. We were back down in the
streets again now and the drizzle began to be dusted down cold on to
my face. And then, shambling over the uneven pavement with the
street light behind him, came again the tall stooping figure I had been
hearing about. We said no word to each other or to him as he passed in
the gloom, close enough for us to touch, and it was obvious from his
rapt and brooding air and bearing that he was quite unconscious of our
presence. We turned and watched him as he went at his laborious
shuffle along the pavement and saw him disappear in his swaying
overcoat in the direction of the poorer part of the town.

That night in Mr. Jeffreys' house I was haunted by the lined face of
the old musician, its sadness, its suffering; again and again at supper,
and afterwards in my room, making my preparations for the following
day, I pictured the scenes of his life as Mr. Jeffreys had described them
to me. His story, told in this way upon that mountain walk, greatly
moved me, stirred me to a tenderness and a compassion I did not
know to be in my heart. Love and illumination were upon me that
night. I wept over the lined face, on my knees I shed my tears into the
bosom of Christ at his suffering, and the suffering of the valleys, and
the suffering of all the world.

✌

Mrs. Jeffreys

I did not at first think that Mrs. Jeffreys was anything more than a
kindly motherly woman zealous for her family and her chapel. I was
often in the house alone with her and we frequently ate our midday
meal together in the kitchen; then it was that I found in her, beneath

her humour and her worldly concerns, a deep piety and an unexpected tenderness of conscience and a brooding awareness of a divine guidance in her life. She told me a great deal about herself, about her deeply-wronged mother and her own hideous childhood and the cruelty and viciousness of her father. One story, recounted over a succession of midday dinners, showed me how superficial my earliest judgement of her had been, and how much richer her experience was, and how much more complex and puzzling, than I in my ignorance and insensitiveness had at first estimated.

'Robert had come out of the pit early,' she said, 'because it was Christmas Eve. He was sitting in his shirt-sleeves under the light of the kitchen gas, clean and shining after his bath before the fire, the dinner I had taken out of the oven steaming on the table in front of him. Myra had been put to bed. Gari was only a baby then, he was lying fast asleep by the fire in the clothes basket we used as his cradle.

'I had almost finished putting up the Christmas decorations and the holly Robert had cut on his way home from work when I heard footsteps in our back yard. There was a knock at the kitchen door and when I opened it I found one of the neighbours standing in the darkness outside with a message for me. At the sight of my face when I came back into the kitchen and stood under the gas, Robert jumped up from his meal. "Lowri, what's the matter?" he asked, alarmed "What have you heard?"

' "It's my father," I answered. "Let me sit down. He's dying. In the *Court*. He wants me. What shall I do?"

' "I didn't know he was back in the valley," Robert said. "You must go. Shall I come with you? Or look after the children?"

'I hurried through the bright streets and the Christmas Eve crowds without Robert, carrying the baby in the woollen nursing shawl. Pity for my father, or fear that he would die had no part in the agony I felt at hearing that message brought by our neighbour. I had looked forward eagerly, as I always did, to Christmas Day, to spending the time happily at home together with my husband and my children, but now that suddenly was over, I was filled only with bitterness and resentment, haunted again by the thought of my father's waywardness and violence. Every memory I had of him was evil. At one time in childhood, whenever I closed my eyes, I had before me a horror I could not escape from. It tortured me. Out for a hillside picnic with other children during the summer holidays and wandering off alone I had seen a fight in a disused railway cutting up on the mountain. Two men were circling slowly round in the middle of a thick ring of excited colliers. They were naked to the waist, bare-fisted staring hard at each other with their heads down, crimson-faced, covered with sweat and breathing heavily like animals. One of the men I recognized as my father. As I watched, looking down in terror from the top of the cutting, I saw him suddenly rushing in at the other man, shouting out loud; he beat his opponent's fists down and struck him a heavy blow low down on the body, and then a heavier one right in the face. Even from where I stood I could hear the splashing noise of his bare knuckles against the man's mouth, and the gasp of the crowd as he staggered away and went down backwards on to the ground raising a cloud of dust. At the sight of the man crouching there kicking and screaming in agony I began to cry, but before I could move away I saw my father rush up to him and start to kick him fiercely about the chest and the face with his heavy pit boots. At that the ring broke up and the colliers swarmed towards the two fighters shouting. I ran away horrified and before I reached home I was sick. The only memories I had of my father were of his violence and cruelty, and ever since childhood I had hated and feared him. The lives of my mother and me had peace only when he left home, which he did from time to time, sometimes for weeks, sometimes for months on end.

'The *Court* was a workmen's lodging house, a big shabby building, one of a row in that old rough part of the town down there by the river where the navvies used to live. The ironworks' railway line ran along in front of it, and on the other side of the line rose a high and rusty cliff of furnace clinker. That part of the town was so dark that in winter the street lamps had to be kept burning day and night. I remember as I made my way along the railway line that Christmas Eve noticing the heavy drizzle drifting about as fine as flour in the light of the gas lamps.

'The front door of the *Court* stood wide open but the whole building was dark and silent. A strong smell of stale air and tobacco and sour clothes came out of the passage. There was no knocker so I shouted into the darkness and waited. This, I thought, my father's rejection and waywardness had brought him to, a deathbed in the squalor and loneliness of a common lodging house. But I felt no pity for him and I found forgiveness hard. Without the shedding of blood, I remembered with shame, Mr. Herbert, there is no forgiveness.

'It had been warm carrying the baby all that way in the wrap-around shawl and I was ready to sit down. "Hullo!" I shouted again, banging on the hollow-sounding door. "Is there anybody in?"

'After a time Keefe, the big old man who owned the *Court*, came shuffling slowly along the passage towards me in his shirt-sleeves and slippers, carrying a candle. I knew him by sight, he had been wild, a mountain fighter like my father when he was young, but now he had gone stout and feeble with drink. His big face was inflamed, a mass of red veins, and his eyes were glazed over and very prominent. He looked drunk and dazed, his grey hair on end, as though he had just woken up from a heavy sleep.

' "I have been asked to call," I said. "I am told my father is lying ill here. He's Edward Parry."

'Keefe swayed above me on the doorstep in those dirty shirt-sleeves, one of his puffy hands trembling as it shielded the candle flame. His heavy drunkard's face looked pear-shaped in the upward light, fattened out into a full neck and a bristling jowl and narrowing across the forehead.

' "Ay, he's here," he said in a drowsy indifferent voice. "You're his daughter, are you?"

'I nodded. He turned and shuffled back over the bare flags of the passage and I crossed the doorstep and followed him As I went I pictured the warmth and comfort of the room I had just left, my own kitchen, clean and brightly lit, with its coloured curtains and cushions and Robert's graining and varnishing on all the woodwork, and with the holly and the paper Christmas decorations everywhere and the fire burning brightly in the fireplace, and I felt a strong wish to hurry with my baby out of the bareness and the dark and the feeling of defilement around me. It was not love or forgiveness that took me along those flagstones, Mr. Herbert, only a wish to do not less for a father than was customary by a daughter in this valley.

'At the end of the passage we came to a wooden staircase leading off on the right. "Up there," Keefe said. "There's a turn in the stairs."

'I was just going to climb. "Is he very ill?" I asked him. "What's the matter with him?"

' "You go up and see," he answered. "He's got half his face blown off."

'He shuffled away and went on through a door at the end of the passage, taking the candle with him. I was left in total darkness. As I groped my way up the staircase I could feel my legs trembling. At the very top, after the turn, I found the bedroom door in front of me. I fumbled about for the latch and went in.

'There was very little light in the room but I could see there were three beds across it, two of them empty. In the one furthest from the window a heavily-bandaged figure was lying under a dirty sheet with a khaki greatcoat over it. A candle end stuck in the wrinkles of its own grease stood on the wooden bedpost and threw light down on him. The figure was motionless and very tall, extending the whole length of the bed. Although most of the head and the flesh of the face were under thick bandages I knew it must be my father. His mouth was wide open and his swarthy chin was bare and unshaved; his eyes, although not entirely covered, were in the shadow of the bandages. I could not tell whether he was asleep or not. I felt my heart shrink away from him in revulsion. I sat down on the tin travelling chest on the side of his bed furthest from the window and waited.

'This large shadowy room was an evil place, a sort of attic, the squalor and the stench worse than anything I had expected. Apart from the three beds and a battered chest-of-drawers there was no furniture. Under my boots the gritty boards were bare and the laths showed in large patches in the black walls where the plaster had fallen off. There was no ceiling, and above my head were only rafters, huge and very low, and then the roof-slates. A drying line went in loops across from rafter to rafter with scorched rags of clothing hung on it, and a gridiron, and a blood-stained woollen shirt.

'At the furthest end of the room, near the window, a fire was glowing in the grate and the blind man sat crouched beside it in his bowler hat and his long black overcoat. On his lap he held a small sack of cinders and these he fed with his mittened hands in handfuls on to the fire. He was ugly and wretched, a great drunkard, his black-blotched skin hanging slack about his face and down into his bare neck. I always had to overcome feelings of revulsion at the sight of him slouching close to the wall along the street, or sitting begging outside the big market doors, revulsion at his filthiness and at the horror of his large bloodshot eyeballs, staring out always it seemed to me in unseeing hate. He was wearing his high bowler hat and at the sides of his face the thick grey curls hung down in greasy tangles. When the crowds came into town on Saturday nights he sat cross-legged by the open doors of the market with a begging cup beside him and a great braille Bible open on the pavement in front of him; then, in a raucous, shouting voice, halting at every two or three words, he read his Bible aloud, his sightless eyeballs rolling and prominent in his swaying head and his large red claws creeping over the pages.

'When he heard me coming into the room he turned his face to me.

' "Woman," he said, in his harsh voice, "what's the weather doing?"

' "It's still raining," I answered. "Drizzling."

'He cursed the rain. He wanted to be out in the Christmas Eve crowds reading his Bible and collecting money for drink in his enamel cup.

'I sat perspiring on the tin trunk beside my father's bed. The blind man's fire was only a glow, but, carrying the baby, I was wrapped in his woollen shawl, and the window of the attic had been nailed up against the steady rain of grit blowing against it off the clinker tip beyond the railway line outside. I had made up my mind to be patient and to do all expected of me, I sat on quietly in the buzz of the baby's breathing, the raindrops on my lashes sparkling like glass beads in the candle-light.

'And I remembered in that attic the last time I had seen my father. We were living then, Robert and I, just after we were married, in a lonely cottage up there on the mountain, the one Myra my daughter lives in now. I was alone in the back kitchen one afternoon when I had the sensation of a cold blade suddenly being driven into my body heavily among my bones. Through the window I saw my father, tall and unkempt, coming up the mountain path towards the back of the house. I hadn't seen him for several years and I half believed, and hoped, may God forgive me, that he was dead. But there he was and with him was Hassan, the drunken half-caste who used to be his pub hanger-on, carrying a big fish-basket on his back.

'They were already at the garden gate before I roused myself to dash across the kitchen and close the back door. It was an old-fashioned door in those days, without a doorknob or a lock, and to open it from the outside you had to put your fingers in, about five feet up, through a round hole the size of half a crown and push up the wooden latch that was on the inside. The door had an iron bolt as well but I knew I would be unable to use it, it was stiff and noisy, and before I could shoot it the footsteps of the two men were sounding on the flagstones of the back-yard outside the kitchen. All I could do was to lean my full weight against the door with my heart pounding painfully. I had not come face to face with my father since my mother's death two years before. She had died of a breast cancer, the disease had spread from a blow he had given her when he was drunk, as he often was. I would have done anything then, or at any other time, anything, to escape the torment and humiliation of his presence.

'I heard the two men cross the yard and stand outside the house in silence. They whispered together and then one of them tapped very softly on the door. I did not move, I remained leaning my weight as heavily as I could against the middle of the door. Then two thin dark fingers came in through the round hole and the wooden latch was slowly lifted. The fingers of the half-caste were almost touching the sleeve of my bodice. I stared down at the smooth, strange-coloured fingernails so close to my shoulder pushing the wooden latch up and then letting it drop back into its socket again with a click. When the fingers were withdrawn there was complete quiet and in the stillness I could hear my heart beating like thunder on the boards at my back. The door started to creak under my weight. What should I do if the two began to force their way in? I heard my name called softly and quite close. "Lowri, Lowri," my father whispered outside. "Are you there, Lowri?"

'I held my breath. How was it they could not hear the door resounding under the heavy blows of my heart? My legs began to tremble. I knew I could not stay in this position much longer. Presently I saw the face of the half-caste at the kitchen window peering into the dimness of the room. But at that same moment, before he could see me, the pit hooters sounded in the valley, announcing the end of the day shift. The two muttered together, cursing as though they were beginning to quarrel, and then they went off across the yard. I shot the bolt and sank on my knees to the floor. Crouching there I wept bitterly, but I did not know why.

'I could hear the rats scuffling and squeaking in the attic walls as I sat beside my father's bed. The blind man put his bag of cinders down and groped his way to the window-sill. He took his big Bible off it, opened it across the bed and began to practise his reading. "And in the sixth month," he shouted, using his harsh market voice, his head on his bare neck swaying from side to side, "the angel Gabriel . . . was sent . . . from God . . . unto . . . a city . . . of Galilee . . . named Nazareth . . . to a virgin . . ."

'I saw my father stir and pass his tongue over his lips at the sound. "Lowri," he whispered. "Is Lowri there? Have you come?"

' "Yes," I answered. "Here I am. Can I do anything for you?"

'He rolled his head on the pillow. "I am dying, Lowri," he said. "Dying. Is your husband with you?"

'"No, only Gari. He's my baby. He's asleep in the shawl." Unwillingly I leaned forward towards him with the child. "Here," I said.

' "There's somebody else in the room, isn't there?" he asked.

'The blind man stopped reading and swaying and lifted up his pouched face. He had heard my father's whisper. "You don't expect me to go out in this blasted weather, do you?" he shouted across the attic. "Blast Christmas Eve, I say. Blast it."

'My father sighed. "I am dying, Lowri," he said again. "I have lost blood."

'The reading began to echo once more under the slates. My father was lying here because he had tried to poach the river by exploding a stolen shot in the water to kill the fish. These shots are powerful, Mr. Herbert, they are used by the colliers underground to blow out the stubborn coal. The thing had exploded in his face. I was able to understand so much. But his words were hard to follow. Soon his voice began to fail and his mouth fell open again. I thought he was dead.

"He shall be great," shouted the blind man, "and . . . shall be . . . called . . . the Son of . . . the Highest . . . and . . . the Lord God . . ."

' "'*Nhad*," I said, getting up frightened, "are you all right?"

'He lay there in silence, not answering, not breathing as far as I could see. Then he began clawing about on the greatcoat along the far edge of the bed, searching for my hand. "Where am I?" he said suddenly. "Lowri, listen. I want to tell you."

'I got up and went round to the other side of the bed with the baby and sat down on the edge. Reluctantly I let my father find my hand. "Shall I stop him reading?" I asked.

'"It was something I heard him reading from his Bible that made me send for you," he said. "He has to do with my forgiveness." He paused again in weakness and passed his dry tongue over his dry lips. He asked me weakly if I remembered Sergeant Probert. I nodded. I did. He was a good man and he had often been kind to my mother and me when we were being molested by my father, and were threatened and in trouble through him. My father hated him, for protecting us, among other things, and also because in spite of his terrible threats of violence the Sergeant was never intimidated by him, he never showed the slightest fear of my father at any time.

'He began to confess. He spoke about the time the Sergeant retired, and the night the whole village turned out in respect for the presentation to him. That same night my father went up to Ystrad cemetery on the side of the mountain and found the grave of Probert's son. Not much better than an imbecile that poor Probert boy had been but he had come late in life, an only child, and the old Sergeant had lived for him. When the son died, the father had himself carved the gravestone out of white marble, he had taken months over it, it was tall and beautiful. Everybody in the village had seen it, or knew about it. That night of the presentation in the Sergeant's honour my father smashed it to the ground. While the meeting was still being held down in the village he took a stolen sledge-hammer up to the graveyard and battered the marble headstone to pieces.

'His words were anguished and excited. He kept rolling his head on the bolster and weeping and asking God to forgive him. Of all the evil he had done why was it this that should disturb him so deeply? I did not understand. "And his mercy . . . is on them . . . that fear him . . ." came the voice of the blind man from the fireplace behind my back, raucous and discordant. "He hath shown . . . strength . . . with his arm . . . he hath . . . scattered . . . the proud . . . in the . . . imagination . . . of their hearts . . ."

'My father went on muttering, asking again and again the forgiveness of God. He wanted me to listen. He let a man die when he could have saved his life. It was Hassan. Hassan the half-caste. He was killed falling from the old viaduct across the valley. He wanted to know if I had heard of it. I was anxious to calm him but there was some great compulsion upon his heart. All I could do was sit beside him on the bed and listen, and feel unwillingly in mine the great bones of his hand.

'He and Hassan, he said, used to go down into the railway sidings at night to rob the goods trains. One night they were drunk. It was pitch black and blowing a gale. They left a candle alight in one of the vans while they hid what they had already stolen under the bushes on the river bank, and when they came back to the sidings they found the candle had fallen over into the straw. The inside of the van was ablaze in the wind. They hurried away. The shunters and the signalman up the line saw the fire and came running down the track. My father, with Hassan following him, ran up the bank towards the disused viaduct that went high across the river, it spanned the whole valley high up from mountain to mountain. Hardly any of the parapet stonework was left along its sides by then. The entrances to it were boarded up and barbed-wired and no one was allowed to use it. My father cared nothing for Hassan, all he wanted was to escape. He was not afraid to cross the viaduct even in pitch darkness, drunk, and in a high wind.

'He stopped speaking. Behind my back the loud voice of the blind man ran on and on. My father's head rocked on the pillow. I waited but he said nothing. Then he began to breathe more deeply, his breast rising and falling in great agitation under the greatcoat. "Up the bank, Hassan," he whispered in some terrible urgency. "Up the bank. Over the boardings. Chuck your coat over the barbed wire before you climb . . ." I could see he had become delirious. He no longer knew where he was, or who was listening to him, and he wasn't conscious of what he was saying. "Follow me, Hassan," he muttered in the compulsion of some terrible anguish. "Come on, you blasted fool. What are you afraid of? Stop screaming my name, damn you, do you want everybody to know who we are? Why don't you follow me, you half-caste bastard?" Suddenly he stopped and his voice in a moment trailed off into the silence of exhaustion. "O Christ, O God," he whispered, "what am I saying, what am I saying?"

'"And lo," shouted the blind man, "the . . . angel . . . of the Lord . . . came upon them . . . and the glory . . . of the Lord . . . shone round about them . . . and they . . . were sore afraid . . ."

'The candle flickered and went out, leaving the darkness smelling of burning grease. "Lowri," my father whispered, "there is forgiveness, isn't there? For me too there is forgiveness?"

'Even then I had no answer for him. I said nothing, not even a word of comfort. The reading stopped abruptly. The blind man rose from his place by the fire behind me and I heard him shuffle slowly across the gritty floorboards towards the door. Where was there forgiveness for my father if there was none for him in my own heart? I began to cry.

' "Lowri," he whispered again, hardly audible now. "Lowri. I am getting very near the river. Tell me there is forgiveness."

'In the darkness I dimly heard the blind man coming across the bare boards and standing behind me, but I took no notice of him as I tried, weeping, to make myself comfort my father. I was too confused, in too much anguish and conflict to feel my usual repulsion at the man's nearness. In his harsh voice he muttered something close behind me that I didn't catch. My father opened his eyes wide, staring over my shoulder, he struggled to rise up in the bed. I put my free arm round him to support him. His weakness was pitiful to see. "Lowri," he said again, desperately, "forgiveness. Your forgiveness. I am talking about your forgiveness." He was hardly able to speak at all now.

' "Yes, yes, *'nhad*," I said as best I could. "There is forgiveness, for you and for us all. 'Though your sins be as scarlet they shall be as white as snow.' " My heart was full. I wanted nothing but to tell him about the lost sheep, and the missing coin, and the younger son, and the forgiveness we have only to seek. I wept, knowing that this was what he had wanted all the time to hear, and that I, until this last moment, had with-held from him. As I looked down into his face his eyes were wide, fixed and staring from under the bandages into the darkness, and very bright.

'I heard the sound of the blind man shuffling off towards the attic door. My father's head rested heavily on my shoulder. The latch of the attic was lifted and I heard someone go down the stairs and leave the house. When everything was silent again my father turned his bandaged face up at me, sighed like a tired child and fell back more heavily against my arm. I knew he was dead. I went on my knees beside him and dropped my face upon the bed, weeping.

'Then a voice shouted out loud from the far end of the attic, and my flesh turned to water at the sound of it.

' "Lord . . . now lettest . . . thou . . . thy servant . . . depart . . . in peace . . ." the blind man cried out, "according to . . . thy . . . word."

'I raised my head, turned, and stared behind me. There he was with the glow of the fire still red upon him in the gloom, he was sitting with his Bible open on the bed before him, his head in its high bowler hat swinging from side to side and his black-mittened fingers still crabbing slowly across the pages.

'I do not understand even now what happened, what I heard and felt then. Our Lord said, "I have overcome the World." More than that, Mr. Herbert. The hardness of our hearts too. I know that with the death of my father, I, also, began to hope for forgiveness.'

๛

Myra Powell

'This suffering was a long time ago now, Mr. Herbert,' Myra Powell said to me. 'But nothing is lost. What was in the beginning, is now, and ever shall be. Suffering, I read, passes; having suffered does not pass.

'When I married Gwilym I gave up teaching. I had known Gwilym since we were children, we were in school together and his family belonged to Bethesda like ours. His father owned the timber-yard and Gwilym worked there, he did a bit of everything, from the accounts to driving one of the lorries. He liked this house, where my parents had once lived early in their marriage, it was so healthy up here on the mountain, he said, and he bought it from Uncle Evan, my father's brother. To me it seemed big enough, too big, and old and gloomy. So Gwilym began to alter it. He built those wooden porches round both the outside doors because we are exposed here, and the wind and the rain sweep down on us from the mountain. He put in a new damp-course, and the verandah, which is a great protection in summer and winter. He also changed the windows, and cut a completely new one in the kitchen. I first began to like the house myself when I put a clear glass water-jug, filled with white roses, on the new window-sill, and the sun came in and filled up the whole kitchen.

'Next door to us, about a hundred yards down the lane, lived my Uncle Evan and his wife, my Auntie Ren. Gwilym was often away from home overnight, driving the lorry, and they were good to me. Uncle Evan brought in my coal and locked me in for the night, he teased me about the alterations Gwilym was making to the house, especially about the bright paint we had on all our woodwork, and our doors, one electric blue and one daffodil yellow. But I was proud of everything Gwilym had done. Only one thing then disturbed my happiness in this house, but it passed.

'After four years Ann was born. I was overjoyed when I knew my prayers were to be answered. I hoped very much for a son. Gwilym said he wanted a son too, perhaps to please me. He was a hundred miles away with the timber lorry at the time of Ann's birth, and he did not know he had a daughter until he entered this dining room. From his very first glimpse he was enthralled by her. Very soon he had the telephone brought up here to the house so that he could speak to me about her when he was away. At home he was unwilling to leave the side of her cot. As long as she was small he hurried home here after each trip, he used to drive the lorry right up to the house, up the lane and into the field at the side, and then go straight to her room and gaze at her and put his present at her side – a painting book, say, or a doll with real hair. Anything. Things she was much too small to play with. And until he had nursed her he took very little notice of me. When I told him this his colour went up although I was only laughing at him.

'Then, when Ann was three, Alun came. His birth was a hard one, dangerous, the doctor said afterwards, wearisome for me, filled with darkness and misgivings. But I shall never forget the bliss of my first glimpse of him, my son. When my Auntie Ren showed him to me, I had the sensation that the whole bed of my heart suddenly overflowed with joy. I thought I had never seen such a lovely child in all my life. All parents think their own children wonderful, I suppose, but Alun in a day or two had skin like porcelain and his eyes, large and round, were the purest blue, they seemed to be filled always with a lovely radiance. I wanted to have him in bed with me all the time, of course, but I was forbidden; after the exhaustion of that birth, they said, I was not strong enough for a few days to look after him. And in a short time, to add to his loveliness, his head was covered with a mop of the most beautiful golden curls. But before that happened, his father and I had had our fill of suffering and bitterness.

'My auntie had looked after me during my confinement because this house is remote, not easy for my mother to get to from Morlais Road. She was wonderful to me, my aunt, my own mother could not have been kinder, but one thing about her began to puzzle me. I noticed she was very reserved when I spoke to her about Alun's prettiness. I felt hurt at that, that she did not seem to share our joy in what had happened, as I had expected she would. Each time I spoke about the baby she avoided my eyes. I began to be afraid, although I didn't know of what. And at last, one afternoon, I questioned her. Unwillingly and fearfully, she told me. Alun, my beautiful son, was sick. Soon I found out what she meant. His body was incurably deformed.

'I couldn't believe it. I had rejoiced so much in his loveliness that her words made me frantic. I half tore off his gown when she brought him in to me in the bedroom, and there I saw the truth of what she had said, I saw his poor deformed body, the beginning of the dwarf's hump on his back, the bulging chest, one of the frail little legs half the length of the other. Under his woollen cap the fontanelle had already closed up.

'I wept bitterly. But my chief emotion was not grief, or rebellion even, at first, but a fierce protectiveness. No one should take this little thing away from me, no one should pity him, or me, all should accept him, and rejoice in him, as if he were the most beautiful child ever born. I blessed my Uncle Evan when he brought the three half-crowns into the bedroom and put them into my hand. "An old custom now, Myra, *cariad*," he said. "For the child who is king."

'Later that day the doctor called. I could see he wished to say something. I thought he did not know my auntie had already told me about Alun. I did not wish to speak to him. Although he was a good man, I was stubborn and defiant towards him, I was sure he wanted to talk about Alun's deformity, and to sympathize with me. I asked for no sympathy. My child was still wonderful to me, in my heart I knew there was no virtue or loveliness not in his possession. But the doctor was determined to speak. He asked if Gwilym was at home, and when I said he was he brought him into the bedroom. What he had to say was not at all what I had expected. It was much more terrible. He told us that Alun was not only a cripple. He was also an incurable imbecile.

'What a life I led. I neglected Ann, I spent all my time attending to Alun. Ann went unchristened and, although she suffered with her throat, I was not interested enough in her needs to have her tonsils removed. All I could think of was my Alun. He used to lie out there on the verandah in his pram, in the sunshine, and when I went to see him his great blue eyes opened wide and looked up at me, they seemed filled with the lovely clear light of love and intelligence. The doctor must be wrong. These could never be the eyes of an imbecile. How I prayed the doctor might be wrong, how I prayed that Alun might grow up straight and sound, and his body be of use in the world, and a burden to no one. Often I persuaded myself he was becoming more normal, that the dangle of that pitiful little leg was less, and the hump under the pretty nape not so conspicuous. I pestered the doctor and my parents and my uncle and auntie with my questions. "He's getting all right, isn't he, Mam?" I used to say to my mother whenever she managed to get up here. "He's getting better, isn't he? Look, he's much stronger than he was this time last week. Look at him."

'And then Alun fell ill with pneumonia. I was frantic at the idea of losing him. The doctor tried to reconcile me to it, but his words made me angry and I turned on him. But I must confess he worked hard, he did everything he could to save him. This house is a long way up the mountain but he was here three or four times a day. At last it became more than he could do. Alun had to be taken away to hospital in Ystrad.

'I prayed day and night while he was there, not only that he would live but still more that he should grow up to be good and useful. I could not eat or sleep. Hour after hour I lay awake at night waiting for the morning. I can remember how I used to hear the branch of the elder tree in the garden rubbing against the kitchen wall in the wind, and how I used to long for the bedroom curtains to turn blue so that I could get up and prepare to go down to see him in Ystrad.

'And Alun recovered. I remember even now my senseless joy when the doctor told me he was out of danger. How I looked forward to having him home again, to carry him about, and to see his great long-lashed eyes looking up with love at me in the kitchen. I seemed to feel my arms full of work even at the thought of it. As soon as he was well enough, I told myself, I would take him out in the red plaid shawl into the garden in the sunlight. I would make him brown and healthy. I would buy him something, many things, to interest him, a clockwork engine, perhaps, that would whistle, or something alive, a bird or a dog. All the time his picture was before me, his curls and his clear blue eyes and the pale blue veins like faded handwriting, like some message written in a delicate ink under his skin.

'But my joy did not last long. Alun never came home from hospital. Within the week he had contracted pneumonia again. I prayed for him as I had done before, as wildly and as constantly, but I felt all the while he would not recover this time. In my heart I knew it, I felt it was all over. And I was filled with bitterness and rebellion at the certainty. Why could not my baby live and grow up? Why had he to be the condemned? Could he not live a little, a few years, until he was old enough for school, when all would be altered? I had seen this happen, and I begged that God might do it for me also. I threatened, may God forgive me for it, sometimes I came near to cursing. But Alun died. I was alone in the house when the hospital phoned me. And I was overwhelmed with rebellion and bitterness and despair. In my heart was chaos, and hatred for God who had deprived and tortured me, I felt all my love for Him was dead for ever.

'And then, almost as soon as I had had the message about Alun's death, the phone rang again. I thought it was Gwilym speaking, I thought he had received the message in his father's yard, but it was not. I heard the doctor's voice. I did not want to speak to him; in spite of his kindness and devotion, I didn't want to have anything to do with him, or with anyone connected with Alun's illness and death. He sympathized for a moment or two and then, just as I thought he was about to ring off, he asked me something that froze my whole flesh as though it were water. I could not believe my own ears. It was hideous. "Mrs. Powell," he said in his quiet voice. "Would you and your husband consent to our using Alun's eyes?"

' "Alun's eyes!" I shouted. "Alun's eyes! What do you mean, Alun's eyes?"

'And then, before he could answer, I remembered. I had often heard him speak of taking some part of the eyes of the dead for the use of the blind. And that was what he wanted now. But I could not think of it. Those lovely blue eyes to be taken away, the loveliest part of that poor twisted little body. "No, no," I shouted into the phone. "No, no, you mustn't touch him, you must leave him alone. Do you hear? Don't you dare to touch him!"

'I banged the receiver down. I could feel my heart hammering as though it would burst my chest open. In my anger and agitation I had not heard the lorry stopping in the lane, but now the sweet smell of timber in the room told me Gwilym was home from work and beside me. He knew Alun was dead. Instead of phoning me after his trip he had gone straight to the hospital. I wept against him as though my heart was breaking and it was.

'All that evening I could not rest. I told Gwilym what the doctor wanted us to do. And our decision was to be made soon, before midnight. I could not bring myself to consent. Since Alun was gone I cared nothing for the blind. What did it matter to me if they could see or not? I cared nothing about them, nothing, nothing. Why should I give to others when all that I loved had been taken away from me?

'Gwilym and I took Ann to my uncle and auntie's and left her there and then we went down to Morlais Road. Gwilym persuaded me to do it. But there in my mother's house I acted like someone demented. In the whole world I could see only one thing, that my baby was dead. On the way back we called for Ann and when we reached the house Gwilym left me and went upstairs with her.

'I could hear him above me in her room up there playing with her. I knew all the time what he wanted. But he said nothing to persuade me. When Ann was asleep he came downstairs and sat by the fire in silence. His gentleness was crueller than accusations. I wept then the bitterest tears of my life.

'As soon as I had made my decision I became calmer. A strange thing happened which at first I rebelled against. Comfort is hard to endure. I began to feel my prayers were answered. The glory of my child's body was alive, and had use and purpose, the blue eyes were not meaningless and without intention. Was I foolish to find healing in this? I found healing in it and my faith returned.

'We have Ann and our second boy now. Having suffered, Mr. Herbert, can never pass.'

❧

Gari

There were three people apart from myself living in my lodgings in Morlais Road, namely Mr. Jeffreys, Mrs. Jeffreys and their son Gareth.

Gareth was a colliery surveyor and he seemed to me, in contrast with his father, a very reserved and even taciturn man. He was a little older than I was, but he seldom spoke to me, and he seemed ready to avoid me always if he could do this without conspicuous rudeness. But one thing he *did* share with his father – a love of reading. Every evening after his bath – he usually came home grimy from work – he used to enter the front room which his parents had set aside for his use and stay there for two or three hours among his books. He seldom went out and he seemed to have very few friends in the valley. I understood from hints and compassionate allusions of his father, that he suffered from a sense of grievance, from some disappointment or frustration, but Mr. Jeffreys did not enlarge to me upon this. I felt ill at ease in Gareth's company, but I heard at last what lay behind his unhappiness.

He suffered, soon after I went to live at Morlais Road, a slight accident underground; a stone fell out of the roof of a hard-heading on to his foot and forced him to keep it off the floor for nearly a fortnight. During that time I spent part of every day in his room, and little by little he explained his position to me. He was, unlike his father, a dry rather than a dramatic narrator, and he spoke in English. I felt, when he *did* take me into his confidence, that there was something admirable in the candour and completeness of his story. What he had to say, as I have explained, I received from him a little at a time, with many breaks and interruptions, but what I write here is substantially the account he gave me of his misfortunes.

'When Nebo and I were together at the university in Dinas,' he said, 'and sharing digs at Mrs. Owen's, no two human beings could have been more unlike in appearance and in every other way than we were. But the funny thing was that many people, at a first acquaintance anyway, attributed my character to Nebo, and his, to some extent at least, to me. Mrs. Owen, our landlady, did. You can see from the photography on the mantelpiece what I looked like then – round-faced and plump, I had black hair, very thick and curly, and hard to keep in order. My clothes, out of regard to the sacrifices my parents were making for me, without being absolutely disreputable, always looked cheap and pretty shabby; and I spent so much of my time in the college library and out of doors on my geological fieldwork, that my times of returning to my digs were only moderately regular. If my scholarship grant from the Ystrad council was a bit late arriving, I failed to pay my monthly board and lodgings on time. The result of all this, the shabby clothes, the untidiness, the irregular hours, the frequent arrears in my rent – the result was that Mrs. Owen looked upon me with dislike and sour disapproval; she thought I was wild and heedless and unreliable. When Nebo was about she ignored me altogether. But him, on the other hand, with his know-all air, and his blarney, and his bald head, she treated like someone rich in experience, and of solid judgement. After the way he deflated her boil she came to credit him with skill and wisdom of the very rarest type.

'And yet the truth was, Mr. Herbert, that Nebo was so crazy, so idiotic in his behaviour, so completely deficient in even the most elementary common-sense that I sometimes wondered if he wasn't a bit demented. He hadn't the slightest concern for principle or morality; he was plausible, two-faced, heartless, untruthful and lecherous. You couldn't trust him within a hundred miles of loose cash, and no girl student in the university was safe from him either. No girl student, did I say? No woman lecturer or professor's wife even, if she happened to be young and the slightest bit attractive.

'Of course, nothing I could have said would have convinced Mrs. Owen then that this was true. And why? Because Nebo, even as a student, had that appearance, when he wanted to put it on, the appearance of a thoughtful and responsible citizen; his mature look, his suave understanding manner, his man-of-the-world charm, all this inspired respect and confidence wherever he went. In appearance he was tallish, probably six feet in height, and well filled-out, without being at all fat, or plump even. His face, I grant, was ugly, but it was very mobile and expressive, it was an actor's face, long and pale and heavily-lined, with furrows across the forehead and deep curved incisions down the cheeks. His lips were thick and hideous, wet and dark, like raw liver, his dense eyebrows very blond, white almost, and there were well-filled bags under his eyes. If he knew you were watching him, and if he thought it was worthwhile, he would try to impress you with a bit of thoughtful lip-biting, and head-nodding, and a scowl of heavy meditation. But by far his biggest asset in this farce of pretended earnestness and maturity was his bald head. The bareness of Nebo's scalp was that complete, highly polished and irremediable nudity that begins in early youth, all the bones and sutures of his skull were plainly visible under the hairless skin and the top of his head was bumpy and irregular, it looked like the battered cranium of a celluloid doll. It was better than the music-hall to hear Nebo talking about this head of his, describing the materials he had rubbed into it to restore the growth, from foreign urine to black pudding. But however much he made me laugh I worried about him. We were both from Ystrad of course, I had known Nebo all my life, and our families were friendly. At first, in Mrs. Owen's, I used to be foolish enough to lie awake at night resenting some sarcasm of his that had wounded me, or agonizing over what I ought to do about the indescribable lunacy of his behaviour. And there, as I lay fretting and worrying, I could hear Nebo snoring away in the other bed, sleeping the sleep of physical satisfaction and conscience undisturbed.

'In spite of what I have said, Mr. Herbert, my nature was then, on the whole, pretty placid and equable. But I suffered a mood of deep despondency, I can tell you, when I heard that Nebo was coming to the university and that I was expected to find lodgings for him. The letter I received from his mother asking me to do this I regarded as a kind of augury of disaster, because wherever Nebo went the result was upheaval and confusion. I found lodgings for him – at the other end of the city. But before the year was out I had him, the man I wanted to avoid more than anyone else in the university, sharing rooms with me at Mrs. Owen's lodgings. It came about like this.

'I had always regarded Nebo as a sort of lunatic, as I say. Although our parents were friends, I had never cared much to have anything to do with him, in school or anywhere else. He was amusing enough, that was one of the most dangerous things about him, but nobody in his senses wanted to be mixed up with the sort of lying and goatish maniac that he had become. We used to go to the same chapel when we were children and one of the very first things I can remember about him was the way he scared the life out of us other children one night on our way to Band of Hope by hoo-hooing about in the chapel graveyard with a white sheet over him. Then another thing. One day when we had passed into the Pencwm grammar school he slipped into the Head's room when there was nobody about, and tried to press a sheet of foolscap on to the jellygraph the Head was preparing our maths exam paper on, so that he would have a copy of the questions beforehand. I always remember the public belting he had for this. As the cane came down on his backside the Head noticed a very peculiar sound, most unusual, and he made Nebo take his trousers down before the whole school to see what was wrong. Outside four or five pairs of football knicks and three blackboard dusters, Nebo was wearing the rear half of a pair of home-made cardboard drawers, tied round his waist and thighs with football laces.

'Nebo's parents, I ought to say, were in much easier circumstances than mine; his father was a coal-merchant and his mother owned a row of houses of her own as well. In the end, sick and tired of the complaints from all quarters about Nebo's clowning and destructiveness, they decided to send him away to a public school, somewhere in Gloucestershire I think it was. Within the term he was back home. He had walked all the way. When he reached the house there was nobody in. He was dead tired so he turned their Airedale out of the kennel in the garden and went to sleep inside. His father found him there the next morning, still fast asleep and snoring loudly.

'He never went back to that school, they wouldn't have him, and some time later we heard he had had a call to the Baptist ministry. But when he was eighteen he eloped with their housemaid in his father's two-seater. People said that the old gentleman refused to have anything more to do with him after that, but whether this was true or not I don't know, because by this time I was in college. I ought to explain, though, that the elopement wasn't much of a success, because before Nebo had got out of the valley he had driven the car into a butcher shop through the plate-glass window.

'What I do know is that about this time he left home and was in lodgings at the other end of the valley. I found this out when I met him in Ystrad one day during the summer vac. We went to have a couple of games of billiards together and I just couldn't pot the balls for laughing. He had got a job selling paper doyleys from door to door. There wasn't much demand for this sort of thing in Ystrad then and he was short of cash. But I couldn't believe this, Mr. Herbert, he was dressed beautifully, as usual, he smoked the most expensive cigarettes one after the other and he wouldn't let me pay for our billiards. He told me he was so hungry, often, he would go down to his mother's house when she and his father were out in chapel and stretch his arm in through the pantry window for a long swig of milk or a slice out of the cake-tin. But his mother was worried to death over him, naturally, he was an only child and he had the name of having been a delicate baby.

She used to go up to his lodgings to see how he was getting on. He said
he had a card on the wall, hung up ready for her, with "What is home
without a mother?" printed on it. She used to cry, poor thing, at his
descriptions of his meals – a Welshcake and a cup of water for breakfast
and a bread faggot for his Sunday dinner.

'I lost touch with him about this time, as I say, because I was away
from the valley in college, but it seems *he* left the area too about then
and I heard occasionally that he had been seen in various parts of the
country by Ystrad people who knew him – sleeping in a bookie's car on
Epsom Downs, in a song and dance act on the variety stage in
Manchester, working as a wine-waiter in a West End Hotel, and so on.
I heard too that after some unpleasantness over a cheque he had gone
abroad.

'And then, towards the end of my third year in college, I had news of
him again in my weekly letter from my mother. "Who do you think is
back in Ystrad? Alcwyn Davies! (Alcwyn was Nebo's real name.) He's
been all over the world, they say. Looking very well, but old, and as
bald as a badger. There's improved he has, you wouldn't know him, so
attentive and sensible. Quite settled down. He was in chapel last
Sunday night with his mother and they asked him to say a few words in
second meeting. He spoke lovely. He said how everything he had learnt
in the Sunday school and the Band of Hope had kept him on the right
lines during his travels and brought him to what he was now. You ought
to have heard the 'Amens'! His poor mother was a proud woman, I can
tell you. Tears of course . . ."

'The only things I could remember Nebo taking real interest in in
the Band of Hope were his stink-bombs and his itching dust and his
sneezing powders, he used to nearly drive the poor women in charge of
the meetings mad with his cheek and clowning. But I felt perhaps it
was unkind to recall things like that after reading my mother's words.
Anyway, before long I had another letter, from Nebo's mother this
time, asking me if I could find rooms near me in Dinas for Alcwyn, as
he had been accepted at the medical school and was coming up to the
university the following term. My heart sank at this, as I said before, I
was filled with gloomy forebodings, but I did manage to get a place for
him to lodge, although, of course, not anywhere near me.

'I didn't meet him at all during the long vacation because he had
gone to some medical cram school in London, but when he came up to
the university the following term I used to see him fairly often in the
common room, with the card-playing gang usually, but I was always in
a hurry when we met. It was deadly to let Nebo work on you, Mr.
Herbert. He would get you laughing describing some fantastic

adventure that was supposed to have happened to him, and the next
thing you knew you had said goodbye to a ten bob note.

'And then one night, just when I was going to have my supper, I
heard a knock at the front door of my digs and who should be there
but Nebo. I had felt all the time, somehow, that this was going to
happen. He came into my room and began looking round and
admiring the place in a way I didn't like at all. He was wearing lovely
suede shoes that night, I remember, brogues, almost yellow in colour,
and a smart dark-brown suit with knife-pleated trousers. Nebo always
managed to have something in his clothes a bit different from the
ordinary and that time it was a sort of double-breasted waistcoat with
lapels, it had a sort of collar to it. He also wore a brown and white
spotted bow-tie. I often felt dislike and uneasiness in his presence, and
resentment, too, at the patronizing and insulting way he would
sometimes talk to me, but I had to admit that night that in spite of his
spongy lips and his pouched-up eyes he did look impressive; with the
fireplace gaslight falling on his face and his pink head, he did have that
distinguished air that's enough to inspire respect and confidence in so
many people.

'But there was another thing I didn't like about him that evening and
that was his affability. Except when he wanted something he didn't go
out of his way to be pleasant to me. When we met, knowing the state of
my finances, he was indifferent to me and often, as I say,
contemptuous and offensive. That evening he started trying to make
me laugh but I was wary and suspicious and I refused to respond. I
wondered what he was after, and at last it came out. He had been
turned out of the digs I had found for him. The opera company was in
Dinas that week and Nebo, so he claimed, had got a job with them for
a few of their performances, he was the silent Negro headsman in
Turandot. He wanted to do the part properly, he said, so he had
blackened himself all over, not only his face and hands, but when he
went to get the stuff off after the show he couldn't, he had to go to bed
with it on, and the landlady had thrown him out because of the mess
he had made on the sheets. Did I happen to know any other place
where he could stay?

'I felt sure all this about *Turandot* was only a lot of lies. Most likely he
hadn't paid the rent. I said no, impatiently, I didn't know of a place;
and I thought I was going to get rid of him because he gave up trying
to humour me and yawned and wiped his hands over his face with
boredom. But just then Mrs. Owen had to come in with my supper. I
could see in a flash from the sort of look she gave him that if he started
talking I was finished. He was sitting on the sofa when she came in but

he rose and cleared a chair out of her way so that she could put the tray of crockery on the sideboard. I cursed my luck but I had to introduce them, and then Nebo turned on his flood of blarney. First he agreed with her about the changeable weather we were having and it seemed to me in no time they were in absolute and complete accord no matter what subject they began talking about.

'Then Nebo started to be concerned about Mrs. Owen's health. At that time she had a big ugly boil on the side of her face, just in front of her ear, which, she soon began to tell Nebo, her doctor didn't seem able to cure at all. A look of interest and sympathy came over his face. He was practically a qualified physician and surgeon, he said, he wondered if he might have her permission to examine it. He was very diffident and hesitant saying this, as though it would be a great honour if she were willing. He touched her very respectfully, reluctantly, almost, the clown, he put her to sit by the fireplace with her head on one side under the gaslight. And then he began his examination.

'I have never before or since seen anything like what followed, or heard such utter guff spoken with so much absolute seriousness – solemnity, I ought to say. But I must say at the same time that I was, as usual, half mesmerized myself; I found myself succumbing to some extent to the idiotic and elaborate clowning. Nebo turned his sleeves back – heaven knows what for – and first delicately prodded the skin round the boil with his fingers. Mrs. Owen seemed to have gone off into some sort of trance, she didn't even wince. He moved her ear up and down very slowly, asking her in a soothing, purring sort of voice if this was giving her pain. She didn't answer. She sat absolutely motionless under the light with her lids down. He got her, still in her trance, to cross her legs and began tapping her knees with a dessert spoon. After a few minutes of this he apologized for not having his stethoscope with him and again, very respectfully, asking her permission, he knelt down by her side and pressed his ear against her chest. "Breathe deeply, please," he said. A half-smile of daft happiness appeared on her face.

'Then he returned to the boil. He put his heavily-rimmed glasses on and hovered over it without a word, he peered at it from all angles, frowning, screwing up the big jube of his face, biting his lips and nodding his bald bulgy head as though the big light had at last started breaking before him.

'Then he spoke. At that time he had hardly been in the medical school long enough to have tasted mother's milk in his tea, but to hear him jawing you could think his whole life had been spent in the study of boils, especially boils on the cheeks of middle-aged women just in front of the ear. I was used to him but, as I say, I was a bit impressed myself. He wasn't modest or diffident any more. He seemed to blaze with certainty and an urgent sense of mission. He got Mrs. Owen round out of her sock and told her he knew exactly what ought to be done. He was confident he could cure that boil in no time at all. No doubt her doctor was well enough but the trouble with the ordinary practitioner was that he was old-fashioned, he very soon lost touch with the latest researches of medical science. He, now, would prescribe a daily oil-massage. A little painful at first, perhaps, but nothing really. In a few days, he could guarantee, the boil would be no more than a memory.

'Mrs. Owen was a very vain and good-looking woman and this big, unsightly boil throbbing on her face must have worried her a good bit. She listened hard and took in everything Nebo said. The next thing I understood was that they were arranging for him to apply the treatment himself. And then, of course, the question of his digs came up. He was just leaving his present lodgings because the fleas were infesting the beds – well, that's what he hinted. Nebo knew exactly, Mr. Herbert, when the Queen of Spain has no legs. He pretended he was too squeamish to lay his tongue to a coarse word like "fleas" when speaking to a lady of Mrs. Owen's kidney. What he said, grinning, was that every night he was conscious of being only one of a very large number of occupants of his bed. Anyway, the clear solution was for him to come and stay at Mrs. Owen's, at any rate until the treatment was completed, and the very next night he was there, he and I had a single bed each in my own room.

'When Mrs. Owen had gone back to her kitchen that night I felt a very powerful sensation of anger against Nebo. I really was furious at having been completely ignored like this, at not having been consulted at all as to whether I would have Nebo as a co-digger. In my temper I said, "Now look here, Nebo, I'm not so stuck on this Mrs. Owen, but she can cook, she keeps this place comfortable and she doesn't try to rook me. So if you're coming here, no funny business, mind."

'When I said that Nebo looked shocked and hurt as though I had wounded him deeply. He couldn't understand what I was talking about. "Funny business? What do you mean 'funny business', Gari?" he said, absolutely bewildered. Well, to see him sitting there on the sofa fingering his beautiful clustery cufflinks and looking so innocent and hurt, I couldn't help myself, I had to grin at the absolute cheek and perfection of his act. And at that *he* grinned too and before we had finished supper, although my resentment and foreboding hadn't vanished by a long way, I was coughing and swallowing my food the wrong way, laughing at the fantastic craziness of his experiences.

'That was how I came to have the biggest liar and the most debauched and plausible lunatic in the university as my co-digger.

'The rest of the term passed with Nebo becoming more and more moody and unpredictable. He seemed, for a few weeks at least at the beginning, to have found a real interest in medicine, he was lively and buoyant all the time, and this, I felt, I ought not to hinder in any way. Many a night when he had come home very late, after I had gone to bed, he moithered me out of my warm blankets with his blarney and used me for elaborate physiological examination; he stood me naked and shivering on our bedroom oilcloth and passed his icy hands over me, he shook his head and looked serious when he said he couldn't find anywhere in my anatomy some process or other normal in the human frame. He was so plausible I often found myself the next day worrying over his words, fingering myself on the quiet, wondering if there was really some truth in what he had been telling me the night before.

'And by some miracle or other Mrs. Owen's boil was cured. He used to work on it for ages every day, very enthusiastic he seemed to be, massaging the inflamed lump lower and lower on her face until he had moved it into the soft flesh below the angle of the jaw. Here he lanced it and in a short time there was no trace of the thing to be seen, nothing at all except a small hidden scar.

'There were two results of this really staggering cure. From then Mrs. Owen's attitude to Nebo was almost idolatrous, she treated him as though he possessed some special, almost supernatural, skill and wisdom. And to Nebo himself the cure gave a very unhealthy interest in boils and pustules as such, for a few weeks nobody in the university with a few unsqueezed pimples could feel safe from Nebo's healing zeal.

'But none of this enthusiasm lasted. He began spending a lot of time in an expensive badminton club in the city, where the people, I heard, called him Dr. Bowen-Davies. It was here, I suppose, he met the girl he claimed to have run away with. I don't know. Lying had become to Nebo by then something more than a way of impressing strangers, or amusing his friends, or avoiding the consequences of some idiocy; it had evolved into a sort of grace, a refinement of existence, an activity of the spirit, as they say, to be indulged in entirely for its own sake without regard to purpose or advantage.

'I remember one instance of this very well. It happened after I had spent a day on the Bryngwyns carrying out a geological survey. I was tired and hungry when I got back to digs that night and I dare say I looked even rougher than usual, more crumpled and wind-blown. Presently, almost as soon as Mrs. Owen had brought supper in, Nebo appeared. He was wearing a black tie and a wide crêpe band round his arm. I was startled at this and I heard Mrs. Owen asking him what had happened. Very awed and sympathetic she sounded too. Nebo lifted his hand and shook his head, as though the subject was too painful for him to talk about. "My father," he murmured huskily, like somebody absolutely shattered with grief. "Dead. Telegram. Drowned at sea. Off Bloody Foreland. Body lost."

'I was stunned. I couldn't believe my ears. When I heard this absolutely idiotic and gratuitous lying I just stared, I couldn't say anything at all. But when Mrs. Owen had gone out I said, "What the devil did you say that for, Nebo?"

' "Say what, Gari?" he asked me. His blond eyebrows were still knitted after the act he had put on for Mrs. Owen and he looked hurt as well at my attack.

' "Say your father was dead, you fool," I answered, exasperated.

' "Well he is, isn't he?" he asked me cheerfully, and his big mouth went into a wide grin inside the brackets on his cheeks.

' "Yes," I said, "he is. But he died three years ago. And he wasn't drowned, anyway. Off Bloody Foreland, my eye."

' "Gari," he said, coming over to me and dropping his big face down almost on top of mine, "Gari," he said, "have you shaved today? You ought to stand much nearer to the razor, you know. Honestly, I'm worried about you, Gari. All you care about is giving your Mam the satisfaction of seeing 'B.Sc., Hons.' after your name. Nothing else matters at all. Look at you now in that suit, you're about as glamorous as a nun's umbrella." He caught sight of a letter on the mantelpiece behind me and reached over my shoulder for it.

' "Ah," he said, turning away, "from the old lady herself, God bless her, the one and only Emily Sarah Bowen-Davies."

'He held the letter in front of him for some time, staring at it. Then he opened it and took out a cheque which he placed very carefully in his pigskin wallet. The letter itself he pressed passionately again and again to his lips and then – I say this with shame, Mr. Herbert, even when I am speaking about Nebo Davies – and then he tore it up and threw it unread into the fire.

' "Don't get up in the bows, Gari," he said to me, seeing me scowling at him, I suppose, "and don't start pouting at what I tell you. Try to see yourself objectively, will you? That tie you've got on now. Honestly, is it home-made?" He ragged me like this for a time, he was in an expansive

sort of mood, and after supper we sat talking pleasantly enough by the
fire, going over the people we knew in the valley – the chapel deacons,
the neighbours, the grammar school masters and so on. He seemed
untroubled that night, quite at ease, he wanted to smoke a pipe for a
change and to do this in comfort he had to take his bottom teeth out
and put them in his trousers pocket.

'But he was less and less often so pleasant as the term went on.
Sometimes he came downstairs to breakfast sullen and baggy-eyed and
morose, and ate his porridge in silence. If I made a remark, he snapped
some obscenity back at me, or said something insulting, or just
twitched irritably and didn't answer at all. And then, the week before
his yearly exams, he began to appear with his right arm heavily
bandaged and carried in a sling across his chest. He had picked up an
infection from one of his patients, he told Mrs. Owen, although of
course he hadn't started to walk the wards then. He couldn't sit his
examination because he was unable to write. After the summer
vacation I heard that Nebo was not to return to the medical school.

'But that was not the end of his studies, unfortunately. By some
clever piece of manoeuvring, probably on his mother's part I should
think, he was allowed to begin his college career all over again the
following term, this time as an arts student. But he didn't tell Mrs.
Owen this because he wanted to stay out all hours drinking and
playing poker when she thought he was busy at the hospital.

'I ought to say, Mr. Herbert, that our landlady had never once to
wait even a day for her money for Nebo's board and lodging because
every week a cheque was sent directly to her from Mrs. Bowen-Davies,
and Nebo never had any chance at all of laying his hands on it.

'During my honours year I saw very little of Nebo. What he had said in
his jeering way about my wishing to please my parents was true and I
did work very hard so that I would leave college with a good degree. At
that time this was more important to me than anything else. I got
gradually more used to Nebo's moods and I learnt to ignore his insults
and his strange behaviour. I certainly did not allow myself to worry so
much about him as I had done when he first came to dig with me.

'When Nebo did his studying, if he did any, I don't know. Whenever
I spent a night at work in our lodgings, which was quite often that year,
he always had some appointment or other and had to go out. But one
evening towards the end of term, when I got my books out of the
cupboard after tea, I was surprised to see Nebo doing the same. He
seemed to read seriously and during a break for a smoke I asked him

how he was getting on with his course. He bulged his lips out, narrowed his eyes and made a fast cutting sweep in front of his face with the edge of his hand, which I took to mean that his work had been successful, and satisfactory to himself. And then his expression changed suddenly. "That reminds me, Gari," he said, with his thoughtful scowl, "I've got to turn up something. I heard somebody mentioning a book in our course this morning that I haven't read at all. In fact I've never even heard of it. And our exam starts in two days' time. *A Woman of Kilmer Kyness*. That's it. Have you ever come across it?"

'I said no, I hadn't, but then I knew very little about things like that. What was it, a poem, a play, a novel, or what?

'Nebo said that was part of the difficulty, he didn't know. He had overheard a group of men of his year talking about it that morning but he was too busy at the piano at the time to ask about it .

'With that he got up and fetched the comprehensive syllabus of university courses. We hunted up the section dealing with his faculty but *A Woman of Kilmer Kyness* did not appear there at all, not in the lists for general or detailed study. Twice or three times we went through those lists – Chaucer's *Prologue and Three Tales*; Shakespearean Comedies; Milton's *Comus*; *The Rape of the Lock and other Poems*; *Six Jacobean Plays*; *Lyrical Ballads*; *Longer Narrative Poems*; but we could find no trace of the mysterious title. I thought this was very strange because Nebo had a mind like a magnet, a rather weak one no doubt, that could and did pick up small unimportant objects that crossed its path, and picked them up whole. At last he got tired of searching and began making jokes, but I could see he was puzzled too. He couldn't start work again, he said, without finding out about the *Woman*, so he put his coat on and went up to Tonza Griffiths's to ask him about her. Tonza was a student living a few hundred yards up the road who was doing the same course as Nebo. He was an expert poker player, but he was debarred now from the students' hall for dropping a typewriter from an upstairs window into the lily-pond. From what I knew of him I wouldn't have guessed Nebo could have made reference very profitably to him on academic matters.

'When Nebo had gone I went back to my work and I had soon forgotten all about his problem; but the next morning, at breakfast time, he started talking about the book again. The funny thing was, he said, that when he asked Tonza about *A Woman of Kilmer Kyness* he found Tonza had never heard of her either. To me this did not seem remarkable since Tonza seldom read any printed matter apart from the sporting pages of the newspapers. But Nebo appeared puzzled, almost obsessed by this title, and he told me he was determined to get to the bottom of the mystery.

'What the result of his enquiries was I never found out because that night he didn't come back to digs at all. The next day, when I was out at the library, he called in to see Mrs. Owen. He apologized for his absence that night before and said he would be away from the lodgings indefinitely now between then and the end of term, because of pressure of work at the hospital. He had quite a chat with her apparently, blarneying as usual and trying to make her laugh. He had just come from examining a male patient, he said, an old-fashioned looking deaconish type of man dressed all in black, black suit, black boots, black hat, black tie – but when the old chap stripped off for Nebo to examine him – what a surprise! – all his underclothes were bright scarlet – socks, vest and drawers, all Welsh flannel and red as a pillar-box! That was Nebo all over, Mr. Herbert, always the tall story, the lies, the plausible yarn.

'Mrs. Owen reported all this to me, very pleased and flattered. I listened to her with great uneasiness and all my old fears and worries returned. A sort of gloomy foreboding settled on my mind just when, because my examinations were approaching, I wanted to be as free as possible from all anxiety. What was happening, I wondered; where was Nebo spending his time, what was the reason for his absences, what deceit, or worse, was behind his lies and his disappearances? All my latent dislike of his insincerity and hypocrisy returned.

'For a whole week I never saw him at all. And then, one evening, the day before I was to sit my first exam paper, something happened to bring us into contact with each other again.

'I had worked very hard all that term, as I said, and towards the end of it I began to feel physically the effects of too little sleep and too much application to books and to study. I was sitting that evening in my digs with a heavy volume dealing with the western coalfield on my lap, and when I opened my eyes and glanced sideways from it my head began to swim, I was puzzled to find the carpet only about eighteen inches from my eyes. I couldn't remember falling at all and I had not hurt myself, but I thought this sort of faint meant it was time I shut my books for an hour and took a stroll through the gardens opposite our lodgings – which was, at that time of the year, the length of my chain.

'It was a lovely June evening, the sky blue and the air warm and still, but my body seemed somehow inflated, and my mind was airy and weightless, I felt as though I was suffering pretty badly from the weakness of hunger although I did not want food. And through this sort of mental blankness I could hear snatches of the paragraphs I had been learning by heart buzzing about, classifications and locations of strata and so on, and every now and then the words of Nebo's mysterious title, *A Woman of Kilmer Kyness, A Woman of Kilmer Kyness*. I crossed the road feeling pretty unsteady and went into the park, but before I had gone many paces beyond the gates a young woman got up from her seat and began speaking to me.

'"Excuse me, please," she said. "I was sitting here and I saw you leave your house. I wonder if you know Mr. Bowen-Davies."

'I was in such a dizzy state that I found it hard to realize the girl was actually speaking to me, and I'm afraid I didn't answer her. For one thing, I hadn't often spoken to such an attractive girl before. Of course, I knew a fair number of women in college, but they all seemed to wear glasses and to smell, most of them, of the more penetrating chemicals. This girl was absolutely different, she was slim and tall and extremely pretty. What she was wearing I couldn't remember afterwards but I knew she had auburnish curls and a sort of emerald tam-o'-shanter. Her eyes looked green to me and I particularly noticed her skin, very fine-textured, and pallid. But my mind was only slowly recovering from its airiness and blankness; I was quite unable to take in details, and what I bore away from my meeting with this girl was only a general impression, prettiness and elegance, and lilac perfume, and a low resonant voice and a sense of refinement.

'I said nothing in reply to the girl at first, as I explained, and I saw her colour slightly. I made an effort of will and memory and answered yes, I did know Bowen-Davies.

'"I wonder if he still lives in the same place," she asked.

'I assured her he still had rooms in the house. She took her net-gloved hand out of her coat pocket and held out a letter towards me. "In that case," she said, "I wonder if you would be so good. Would you please hand him this note?" She smiled, said, "Thank you. Good-night," and hurried away.

'I sat down on the park bench with the letter in my hand and tried to think. What had I undertaken to do? I didn't know where on earth Nebo was. Should I keep the letter until he turned up? Or hand it to Mrs. Owen in case he called at the house when I was out? What if it was urgent? Ought I to spend some of my precious time trying to find him?

'I decided I would do this. I would go to Tonza's first. But I was puzzled and disturbed. Who was the girl I had spoken to? Why had she had anything at all to do with a flag like Nebo? The old refrain began to dance again through my mind, *A Woman of Kilmer Kyness, A Woman of Kilmer Kyness*. And then, suddenly, this sensation of dizziness and uncertainty vanished; like a thunderbolt came the realization that the unknown girl was going to have a baby.

'Tonza's lodgings were not very far away from ours. When I opened the door of his room, I saw Nebo at once, standing in his shirt-sleeves in the middle of the room with his back to me. There were three others present, Tonza himself, Inky Greening and Gunner. They were all smoking and the small room was thick with tobacco fumes. Tonza was squatting on the hearth-rug stripped to the waist examining his shirt and jabbering about his greyhound, Roxy. Gunner sat at a side-table near the window working at a piece of translation. Nebo had Inky Greening sitting on a chair in front of him swathed in the red plush tablecloth and he was doing something to his hair.

'I had no idea what to say to Nebo when I should find him, so I replied to the greetings and sat down hoping to think up some plan or other. To be with Nebo and his friends when they weren't silent over a card game I always found bewildering. It was like bedlam. Every one of them always seemed to be concerned only with working out his own pattern of talk and behaviour, and these patterns had no connection at all with each other as far as one could see. Their talk was a mad and baffling mixture of jokes, obscenities, private references and wild interjections, it was endless, but idiotically disjointed, there was no shape or coherence to it and I found it very hard to put up with. I never attempted to join in and I sat now near the door wondering how I could tell Nebo about the letter in my pocket. Was it confidential? Would he be angry if I explained before his friends how it had come into my hands? I had no experience at all of any sort of intrigue which would help me to determine how I should carry out my under-taking.

'Nebo seemed in high spirits. He was shaving the top of Inky Greening's head with an open razor. Inky, he explained to me, had begun to lose his hair at the crown; he was having four square inches of scalp shaved every day by Nebo to make the hair grow again. Inky, while being shaved, was guying their coming examinations in a string of mock questions. Gunner – I never knew what his real name was – Gunner, as I say, was surrounded with dictionaries, translating a piece of German prose, and smoking, and eating a banana dipped in a pot of blackcurrant jam. Tonza, on the mat, went through the examination of his shirt like a chattering monkey.

'"Well here's old Gari," Nebo shouted to them when I went in, "old small-sentence Jeffreys. How's things, Gari? You don't look too gay, *mon ami.* Rather down *danz la boosh,* as we say in Paris and the upper Ystrad valley." (He was still wearing the silver-barred tie of the medical school, I noticed.) "You know Tonza, don't you, Gari? And Gunner? And Inky here under this barber's sheet? Listen, all. Shut up with that German, Gunner, you're like a ha'penny book. Now listen, I've seen our Gari growing, we were kids in Ystrad, brought up together on the breast of the Sunday school. Honestly, we used to suck the same orange. Listen to what I was told; when Gari came to the university first – this is what I heard, I don't know if it's true of course – when he came here first he was a real Shoni, he used to take his cap off to go into the college bogs because it was all marble inside. I don't know if that's true mind, as I say, but one thing I can vouch for – he's got tougher since. Honestly, now he's no better than one of the wicked, his whole life is one long stagger from 'Boar's Head' to whore's bed . . ."

'Nebo could keep this sort of idiotic banter up indefinitely, so I just sat there by the door feeling rather numb again, and not saying anything. If I had been more wide-awake I think perhaps the undercurrent of sneering in Nebo's words would have hurt me, but what attention I was capable of in that chatter and thick tobacco smoke I gave to the problem of passing the letter over to Nebo.

' "Gari's mother," Nebo went on, wiping the razor, "used to buy her coal from the firm of D. Bowen Davies and Son, Ystrad Valley. That's the old man and me. Wonderful coal my old man used to sell; you could do everything with it except burn it. Keep still, Inky, you crawn, mind this razor or I'll be through to your brains. Where do you think I've been since I saw you last, Gari? Paris! *Ah, ma cherie, do you remember the moon rising and a leaf afloat on the river?* I spent two hundred quid in less than a fortnight. Never mind, I've got a motor-bike out of it. I lost the train from Paddington and I bought it to get back here before tomorrow. A Super. Twelve horse-power. Ninety-five miles per hour unpaced. Honestly, you must let me give you a ride, Gari. Listen, boys, I haven't told you this before. Do you know what happened when I was in Paris? My landlady was battered to death one night when I was where I shouldn't have been. Political thugs. Honestly. A Polish countess she was, four feet high and covered with tattoo. And talk about drink! I've seen her before breakfast pouring a whole bottle of hot sauce down her throat when she happened to be short of gin. She loved it. Oh, and one night at suppertime I was shaking the sauce bottle before pouring it out on my meat and the cork flew out. The stuff shot up into the air like a fountain and on the way down it landed splash on the top of my bald pate. And honestly, if I was to drop down dead here, do you know what she did? She climbed up on the rung of my chair and licked it all off, in a minute or two the top of my nut was as clean as if I had washed it."

' "Here's a dead certain question," Inky interrupted. "Absolute certainty! Listen! Quote. 'Oh that this too, too solid flesh would melt.' Discuss uses for liquid Hamlet. What do you think of that for a likely?"

'Nebo ignored him. "What was I talking about? Your humour gets right up my nose, Inky."

' "That the national pastime of Wales," Inky continued, "is nosepicking. Discuss this from your knowledge of the life and institutions of the country."

' "How does this strike you for Rilke, boys?" Gunner asked, laying down his banana. He swept his hair back with one hand like an actor and held the manuscript well out before him with the other. "And his scented locks were spread out over the young knight's neck like the hair of a woman."

' "*Honi soit qui mal y woollen pants,*" said Inky. "Give context of above, and comment upon it from . . ."

' "Talking about landladies," said Nebo, "how's Owen, Gari? God bless her. Honestly, since I cured her carbuncle she thinks the sun shines out of me."

' "Our landlady," Tonza said getting up and putting his shirt on, "old Ma Hartland, she's a witch if ever there was one I wonder which of us is *really* going to get married. That's the point. There's not much time left now. But if she says it – there's sure to be something in the wind."

' "She was in here just before you came, Gari," Nebo said to me. "She can read the tea cups and the cards. She said she wouldn't mention any names but one of us – she could touch him with a short stick – was going to get married in a few days' time. And she's always dead right. Isn't she, Tonza?"

' "Discuss either the action of music on steam," said Inky, "or the Thomist belief that Welsh goats breathe through their ears."

' "She's dead right," said Tonza. "Always. Last week me and Gunner enter our greyhound in a dizzy track up there in Pencwm. You never saw such a hole. They'd got a bike turned upside-down to wind the hare on and the track's so bumpy the rabbit-skin takes a flying leap six feet into the air every few yards. Ma Hartland tells us it's in the cards our Roxy's bound to win, but there are some good dogs against him, and in spite of her we don't think he will. So we lay heavy bets on another dog, everything we have, and to make sure we give our Roxy thirteen pies and a bucket of water. And even then the old witch is too much for us. Roxy gets home with three lengths to spare and me and Gunner are broke ever since."

' "Who or what are the following," said Inky, "Faithful Teat, Rosie Haas, the Woman of Kilmer Kyness . . ."

'In the smoke of that small room I could feel my light-headedness beginning to return. I saw Inky standing up before the mirror and I watched him in a confused way combing his dark crinkly mop back over the shaved spot at the top of his head. Nebo looked at his watch. I heard him saying he had promised to examine the fish-and-chip woman down the road who was complaining her rupture came down when she ate fresh bread. I got up to go with him but before I could open the door I felt myself becoming dizzy and I sat down again.

'When I came to, the first thing I set eyes on was Nebo's bald head. He was bending over me, and close to my face was the top of his hairless scalp with the shape of a large depression in it, as though all the hair roots had once been embedded in a sort of pink matrix. I was lying in the little tiled area in front of Ma Hartland's house, my head on Tonza's knees, while Inky knelt by my side with a glass of water in his hand. When I was on my feet again they arranged that I should go back to my lodgings on the pillion of Nebo's new bike, a rush through the fresh air would revive me completely, they said. I welcomed this because it would give me a chance to be alone with Nebo and to hand him the letter, so I agreed.

'Nebo went round the corner into the lane to fetch his machine and in a few minutes we were away. What a bike it was, huge and heavy, all scarlet and glittering with two large cylinders and long handlebars that came back to meet you. It went down the street with a deafening roar but we had only just taken the first corner when the engine sputtered and came to a standstill. This was my chance, I thought. As we stood side by side on the kerb examining the machine, I handed Nebo the letter, explaining how it had come into my hands.

'He looked at it a moment, grinned, said, "Oh glory," and put it carefully in his pocket.

' "Thank you, Gari," he went on. "I'm afraid our trip is *wedi popi*, boy. I'll give you a ride some other time, shall I? Honestly, I don't know what's gone wrong. She came down from London today like a two-year-old. Shall I come back to Owen's with you? I must wheel the old bus back to the garage first. . ."

'I told him not to bother. I had done what I set out to do and I was satisfied now. I walked back to my lodgings alone and went upstairs to the bedroom. I did not undress but lay down on the bed in my clothes. I meant to get up in an hour's time and go back to my books. But I fell fast asleep, Mr. Herbert, and when I woke up it was early morning.

'It was then I was taken for the ride Nebo had promised me. I slept heavily when I lay down on the bed, as I say, but some time after midnight I woke up. Work was out of the question at that time of night so I took off my clothes and went into bed. But I couldn't sleep, I tossed about thinking of the exam I would have to sit that afternoon. I must have dozed off for a time because the next thing I remember was, as I say, that it was beginning to get light.

'I rose and went downstairs to start some revision, feeling pretty common. I took some books out of the cupboard and drew back the curtains and opened the window a bit. I had the surprise of my life. Standing on the kerb outside the house was Nebo. He was dressed in a complete motoring get-up – mackintosh suit, leather helmet, goggles and gauntlet gloves. When he saw me he came in through the gate grinning, the ends of his lips disappearing into the sides of his helmet. I slid the window up a bit further and leaned out. He had only just arrived he said, how lucky, just when I opened the curtains. Yes, he had the bike, it was there at the corner. Could I hand him that book on the mantelpiece, the green one, *Six Jacobean Plays*? He was being examined in it that afternoon. Did I feel like a spin now? Come on. Do me good. The morning was balmy. I didn't want a coat or anything. Just round the block . . .

'I had only my thin pyjamas on and a pair of soft slippers, but I thought a short ride round the gardens might freshen me up and give me an appetite for the two or three hours work I meant to do before breakfast. This, Mr. Herbert, was the greatest mistake I could have made, and all my disappointments have arisen from it. It seems to me now impossible that, knowing Nebo as I did, I should yet agree to do this unbelievably foolish thing. But there, I did it.

'I slipped out through the window and hurried with Nebo along the pavement to the corner where he had left that dreadful scarlet motor-bike. It was only a little past daybreak then and there was not a soul to be seen, the whole suburb seemed absolutely silent and deserted. Nebo said he would ride me round the gardens and then bring me back to Mrs. Owen's so that I could start work. I didn't ask him what the motoring get-up meant. I knew he wouldn't tell me the truth about it anyway.

'The noisy cylinders burst into action at once. We circled the gardens quietly, at a slow pace, and then Nebo slipped his goggles over his eyes and we shot out on to the main road. We roared along it with tremendous acceleration out in the direction of the country, leaving the town behind us. At first, although I protested, I didn't really mind, the sensation of travelling at a high speed through the morning air I found exhilarating. There was no sign of life anywhere, not in houses or shops, we saw nobody at all except an occasional night-shift workman who stared at us.

'Soon we had left the streets behind us and were charging along between fields and hedges. The morning was brilliant by now, very bright and sunny, but although I had the protection of Nebo's body I began to feel cold. Nebo took all the corners like a maniac, he never seemed to slacken his speed at all, he relied for our safety on the emptiness of the roads. In spite of my shouts and threats he showed no sign of returning. We left the main road and went deeper and deeper into a part of the country I had never been in before, an endless area of narrow twisted lanes and high hedges. I became more and more angry and alarmed, and as well I suffered very much now from the cold and the terrible jolting of the bike on the rough roads. "Hold on, Nebo," I shouted with my teeth rattling in my head. "Let's go back, shall we? I want to do some reading before breakfast, you know."

' "It's all right," he yelled sideways at me. "So do I. We'll turn round now in a minute. By the crossroads up there."

'I looked forward over his shoulder, my body pressed close against his mackintosh for warmth, my eyes pouring water all the same. I began to feel rain on my face. In the mirror I could see the road pouring away behind us like a by-product. We shot over the crossroads without even slowing down.

'Suddenly an old jibe of Nebo's flashed through my mind. "You're such a terrible sucker, Gari," he had jeered at me. "You must have been hard to wean." That was it. When I realized my own gullibility suddenly like that I became almost frantic with resentment. Nebo wasn't merely giving me a motor-bike ride, how could I ever have believed that even for a moment? I was part, of course, of some considered plan of his, I was being used as everyone who came in contact with him was used. But how? What was his scheme? I could not even guess.

' "Nebo," I shouted at him, really angry, "slow down, will you? If you don't, I'll lean over and get us both into the hedge."

'Just as I said this the engine began to sputter exactly as it had done the day before, making a noise like a blade on a grindstone, and within a few yards the uproar and the jolting were over. We had come to rest at the roadside. What a relief. We dismounted and Nebo stood the bike on its rest. He took off his gauntlets and pushed up his goggles and stooped to examine the cylinders. The rain was falling although not heavily.

' "Now what's the matter?" he said, his face going into extraordinary grimaces. I looked down angrily at him as he knelt there fiddling with plugs and cables, but although we were in this pickle, stranded in a country lane miles from my lodgings, I couldn't help being relieved and thankful to have my feet on firm ground again. In spite of feeling bitterly cold too, my teeth chattering and my eyes and nose watering freely in the cold air. In my relief at getting off the back of that awful bike I had forgotten for the moment my suspicions of Nebo. The sun had gone in and the rain was soon falling steadily. I knew nothing about motor-bikes so I began trotting up and down the deserted road trying to restore my heat. But the rain drove me for shelter under a tree near him after only two or three turns.

'At last he said to me, "I'm awfully sorry about this, Gari. Were you enjoying it too? Honestly, I've no idea what's the matter. But I know what we can do if you'll help me. You remember that long hill we came up just now? Let's shove her back there and let her run down and then perhaps she'll start. Shall we try?"

'"Why the devil did you bring me up here, Nebo?" I said to him. "I told you plenty not to. If I come out from under this tree, I'll get soaked. Look at the rain."

'But in the end I went. There was nothing else to do. Together we pushed the heavy machine back a few hundred yards along the flat until we came to the top of the long slope. Here Nebo tried again to kick the thing into action but it was still quite lifeless. The rain was falling in a heavy downpour by now, it was through my pyjamas of course and I was soaked to the skin.

'He got astride and gave me my instructions. I was to run behind him pushing, and the moment I heard the engine starting I was to give up at once and jump back on to my place behind him on the pillion. Never mind about the rain, he knew a short cut that would get us back to Mrs. Owen's in no time, in a matter of minutes. Everything would be fine.

'I did exactly as I was told. I ran and pushed, the machine rolled pretty easily down the hill and within nine or ten yards the engine started with a tremendous roar. I was excited at this but I remembered what Nebo had said and ran along at the side of the bike and tried to climb on to the pillion. I received a violent blow on the chest from Nebo's side-swung arm. I stumbled and nearly went down on to the road. In a second or two I had recovered but the big bike had very rapid acceleration and before I could do anything it was roaring down the slope and in a minute or two it had disappeared round the bend.

'It was breakfast time, nearly eight o'clock, when I reached Mrs. Owen's house.

'After Nebo and the bike had disappeared it continued to rain heavily, a sort of silent thunderstorm with straight, icy thunder-rain. Down the road I could see a wooden platform with some milk churns on it, so I went along and crept in under it for shelter. I had given up trying to stop myself shivering. In about half an hour's time a milk lorry drove up and took the churns aboard. And the driver gave me a lift in it to right outside Mrs. Owen's door.

'I felt very ill. Even in the warm cabin of the lorry I seemed to be hot and feverish and yet clammy and shivering at the same time. When Mrs. Owen answered the door to me she just stood staring, she couldn't believe her eyes. "Well, where have you come from?" she said. "I thought you were upstairs in bed." It didn't seem to occur to her to do something, she just stood in the doorway and gazed. And there was I trembling violently from head to foot, and soaking wet, and dressed only in my pyjamas. "Mr. Davies has been here," she went on. "He told me not to disturb you. What happened?"

'By then I couldn't answer. I staggered forward and I would have collapsed on the floor of the hall but for her quickness. She half carried me into her kitchen where there was a good fire and got me to lie on the sofa. She loaded me with coats and bedclothes until I began to steam while she carried some hot-water bottles up to my bed. In a few minutes I dragged myself into the bedroom.

'Mr. Herbert, I found the place in confusion. Although I was hungry for warmth and rest, I began to examine the open drawers and cupboards and my clothes lying about the room in disorder. All my loose change was missing, the two pounds my mother had sent me to last the rest of the term, every shilling that was left of my scholarship grant, my watch, my cufflinks, my fountain pen, some of my books, all were gone. But Nebo hadn't taken all this trouble for the few pounds he could steal off me personally. He knew I had a good bit of money not my own in the room, it was the fifty odd pounds I was holding as treasurer of our honours class text-book fund. That too was gone. I sat down shivering on the edge of the bed and I'm afraid I wept.

'Mrs. Owen was good to me then, I must agree. She gave me some tablets and when I had dried myself in the bathroom she got me to bed and piled clothes on me and drew the curtains against the daylight. After a time I went to sleep.

'It was lunchtime when I awoke. Fortunately my exam didn't take place until the afternoon. I was feeling very ill, quite weak and feverish, but I got up, dressed and went downstairs.

'There Mrs. Owen told me what had happened. She was sheepish doing it. Early that morning, she told me, when she was still in bed, she heard a knock at the front door. She found Nebo on the doorstep dressed in his motoring kit, something she had never seen him wearing before. He told her some yarn about his having been selected by the medical college to make a dash to Scotland with a rare drug. To save the life of a dying child. An only child. He was going on his motorbike. Non-stop. Speed was everything. Could she lend him a fiver? He would like to get one or two things from his room. He would not disturb Mr. Jeffreys. He went upstairs and returned with a full case that he strapped on the back of his bike.

'Mrs. Owen confessed she had lent Nebo "over five pounds", but her pride, no doubt, wouldn't allow her to be more exact. She was shocked and humiliated at what had happened, at Nebo's lying, and his calculation and his cold-hearted duplicity. To think he could cheat and rob a man he had shared a room with, and whom he had known since childhood. My own emotions now were different. I found hard to bear the plain fact that, knowing Nebo intimately, I had accepted so readily the part he had laid out for me in this scheme of deceit and lying and theft. And I knew that the full result of my incredible foolishness was not yet to be seen. I still had my exams to sit and I felt less ready for them physically than I had ever done before.

'One more thing happened that morning. When Mrs. Owen was bringing in my lunch, she took a plate out of the cupboard with a couple of slices of bread on it I had forgotten about. Pinned on to the bread was a letter in Nebo's handwriting addressed to me. "Dear Gari," it said, "Ma Hartland was dead right. It caught up with me. By the time you read this I will be a married man. You have already met my wife. A charming girl, but frail. Almost, one might say, bracken was her downfall. Wish me luck. Excuse my writing – there's a tear in my eye."

'It was signed "Nebo" and there were two postscripts. One said, "Best of luck in your exams. I hope your Mam soon has a first-class honours son." The second, "Talking about exams. It's dawned on me who the *Woman of Kilmer Kyness* is. A Jacobean play by one Thomas Heywood. *A Woman Kilde with Kindness*. I must have got the name wrong. What a thought to guide a married man."

'I have never seen Nebo since, Mr. Herbert. I struggled to attend all my exams although I was ill the whole time. At last, when I was back here in Ystrad, in hospital, recovering from pneumonia, I heard I had come out with a third. I knew this degree would be useless to me. I gave up all thought of an academic career and decided to return to this valley permanently. Through the influence of my father and his friends I was taken on at the colliery as a sort of apprentice mining engineer. I find the work interesting and I am less unhappy here now and less disappointed than I once was.

'I don't know what has happened to Nebo, Mr. Herbert. His mother is dead now and nothing has been heard of him in the valley for many years. Whether he married that young woman or not, or whether he ever even intended to, I don't know. But I wouldn't be at all surprised to meet him back here in Ystrad some day. Nebo is quite shameless.

'I remember once, though, when I was in London on a holiday, meeting Shenk Lewis, one of the men who had been at the university with Nebo and me. He had been very friendly with Nebo at one time, in fact, when his digs were next door to Tonza Griffiths's. Shenk was married and with a young family by the time I bumped into him; he was teaching German in South London, somewhere near Croydon, I think it was, and it was pleasant chatting to him about college friends that we hadn't seen for a few years. We had coffee together and during our talk I mentioned Nebo of course, and made one or two remarks about him. The name seemed to throw Shenk into a sort of frenzy, a misunderstanding of what I had said really. "Where did you see him, Gari?" he said across the table in a kind of anguish. *"Where* did you see him? Oh God, I hope I don't have to fall into his clutches again. I'll move. I'll leave London. Was it today you saw him?"

'I was astonished at the outburst. "I haven't seen Nebo, Shenk," I said. "Not since I left college. How did you think I had seen him?"

'I could see Shenk was making an effort of will to control himself. "I thought you said you had seen him," he said. "Didn't you say a minute ago you had been talking to him?"

'I reassured him and gradually he became calmer. But the charm of our meeting was gone. Shenk left me in a short time greatly disturbed, I could see, filled with forebodings and agonizing memories.

'I sometimes wonder, Mr. Herbert, what I should do if I *were* to meet Nebo again. Should I try to revenge myself on him in any way, I wonder? Or should I start laughing again at some fresh piece of lunacy he had become involved in. I hope I should have enough of my father's grace to do neither.'

The Tower of Loss

৬৯

It was a big surprise to Gronow and me when we recognized Loss Llewellyn rowing the boat.

The summer evening had turned out very placid and beautiful and as we came over the stepping stones set in the mud down to the edge of the ferry, I was struck by the silence of the place, the absolute desolation all round us. The river was getting very wide there; it was like a broad lake, because its mouth and the open sea were only round the next curve of the hills, and a full tide was in it, the water moved slowly down past us in one solid mass, the surface flat and shiny, smooth as a mirror. The hills all round and the blue sky above were reflected in that glass, the slopes vivid green or eaten red with what looked like the rust of enormous sheets of tin or under big untidy fir plantations growing over the baldness, black and ragged like vast patches of buffalo wool right down to the water. There was no sound at all anywhere, only a gull sliding past us up the river every now and then, letting loose an occasional croak like a hinge-creak.

I stood by Gronow on the last of the stone slabs sunk to the level of the mud, right at the edge of the water, and bawled across the river for the ferry boat, which we had been told was kept on the far bank. My shouts carried pretty well in that stillness and before long we saw a man opening the door of a sort of stumpy lighthouse or low tower on the opposite bank and waving across to us. This tower was painted in broad prominent bands of black and white, you were bound to notice it because it was the only bit of masonry to be seen anywhere in the whole landscape. We watched the man hurrying along a little jetty in front of the tower, getting into his boat and starting to row across the river towards us.

Gronow and I were on a walking tour through this wild country of West Wales. Gronow was my friend, a broad plump man in a sort of tussore suit, a heavy figure with a belly and thick tight thighs. He had a large black head so solid his neck had disappeared under it, it looked as though it had been squashed down into his trunk under the heavy weight resting on it. That belly started behind his shirt collar, it sloped gradually out towards you, flat as a drawing board, and swelled up the tussore into a sort of rubbery pregnancy. His fat face was swarthy and shapeless, always under a thick film of oil, and the fight he had had when young over a slighting review hadn't improved it. His nose was broken. Between his bouts of laughing, his big mouth brought the swelling bulk of his lips together over a massive balcony of white teeth. As well as his yellow suit he was wearing heavy black boots and a fitter's blue shirt with pearly buttons; also he carried his panama in his hand, showing his black hair sticking up stumpy on his head like something in the garden cut back for the winter. I watched him gazing out across the river at the black and white tower on the far bank, his little eyes glittering behind the horn-rimmed glasses.

I read somewhere or other that the muses love the warty boys. Gronow was at the time a rent collector in London and also a high-class Welsh poet. I had hardly read a line he'd written and we were friends because we came from the same mining valley, we had been at the grammar school together. But I had always studied the notices of his books with interest and they seemed to make him out to be some sort of literary freak, a bit of a monster almost, it seemed to me, a mixture, one of the critics said, of poetic toryism, dandyism and exoticism. Something like that. I wasn't a poet and I couldn't understand it properly. But as I watched him standing there beside me on that bottom slab by the water I thought what they said meant the whole scene before us, every image and sparkle of it, most likely, was being tucked away, blink by blink, through those black-rimmed glasses and into the beady little eyes glittering away non-stop behind them.

Because in spite of the desolation all round us this was a pretty impressive sort of scene to be mixed up in. Half the blue sky in front of us above the river was filled up with one massive cloud, a great white mass like a complete mountain range of ballooned-out ivory; every glade and cliff and summit of it was delicately silvered, it had its own clouds hiding its own peaks, and the whole radiant mass moved majestically up the valley above the water like some range of fancy mountains towed inland from the sea. And at the same time, at the edge of the wood we had just come through, a thrush was singing, sending his summer passion down my spine like slow ice. I glanced at Gronow again to see how he was taking it. His face was almost expressionless under the shine of grease but his nostrils were fluttering, I could see his belly rising and falling in a rapid kicking rhythm he was trying hard to control. He pointed out across the ferry, his laugh very quiet, making a soft hooting noise with a bit of a hiss in it.

The boat we had seen the man on the opposite bank row out from the jetty had reached mid-stream by now, but it wasn't coming across in our direction any more. It looked like some demented beetle performing a series of idiotic tacking motions in the middle of the river. At the same time it was drifting further downstream at a good speed, it looked as though before long it would disappear round the bend and float out helpless into the open sea. As we watched, the boatman seemed to realize this danger himself because he began to pull on the oars like mad, for twenty yards he came up the middle of the river rowing like a maniac. But when he was once more right opposite our stepping stones, travelling at a good speed, suddenly the boat stopped absolutely dead; it came to a halt with such a jerk the stern reared up out of the water with the shock of it. And at the same moment we had a lightning glimpse of the boatman pitching over backwards on to the floorboards with his seaboots in the air. Both his oars rose up helplessly as though they were washing their hands of the whole business and floated slowly away on the water looking exhausted and despondent.

Then every single hair on my head was driven like pins and needles into my scalp with fright. The boatman scrambled to his feet and, without hesitating for a second, sprang overboard fully clothed with a big splash right in the middle of the river. I shouted out with excitement, but the water didn't rise above his calves. He paddled down on the hidden sandbank after the oars and when he'd put them back on board he leaned forward and began pushing the boat towards us from the stern; he didn't get back in, he came calmly through the water leaning against the back end rather like someone wheeling a railway tea-wagon in front of him up the station platform.

Gronow had retired to a log at the edge of the wood. He sat there speechless beside our knapsacks, his heavy cropped head propped between his hands, and his shoulders shaking as though he was shedding a heavy drench of laughing. He was helpless.

The boatman came on, pushing, until he was within about twenty yards of the stepping stones. Then, seeming to want to round off his lunacy – or perhaps the water got much deeper again there – he jumped back aboard and rowed in to the shore. And then I recognized him, I could see that the erratic ferryman, the lunatic in the navy jersey and the sea-boots, was Loss Llewellyn with his beard shaved off.

Before the war I used to meet Loss very often in the flat of a man I lodged with when I was working in London selling typewriters.

This man's name was Hoverington. He was supposed to be a bit of a yogi or something, and he wrote a very philosophic type of poetry, it had no rhymes and was very spaced out on the pages. He and his wife Tessa, a nice red-headed slut she was, lived in an enormous attic flat, a great green barn of a place with wooden walls about three feet high and all the windows in the roof. They were always in heavy debt and having deadborn babies. In some ways lodging with them was pretty inconvenient. The door of my bedroom, for instance, would never close properly, the room was so small that the foot of the bed came out permanently on to the landing. Then every single thing that Tessa cooked tasted queer; her meals made you think of sweet timber in slices or else a cut off a cold poultice. They hadn't got one complete set of crockery in the place or even a knife that didn't turn sideways in the handle when you pressed on it. Often you had to use your shaving-stick to bath with because there was no soap, and in the jakes you'd only find a few sheets of cardboard, or perhaps a blue sugar-bag or a lump of wadding from inside the baby's teddybear. Once, stubbed out round the handbasin in the bathroom, I counted thirty-five cigarette ends – and two slices of beetroot.

But Hoverington was a wonderful character, he was always serene and quite willing for everything. When I talked to Gronow about him he only jeered. 'Hoverington's a spineless slug,' he said. 'Hoverington!'

'You can't see anything good in poise and magnanimity, can you, you rude ape,' I answered, a bit rattled.

'Anybody can be like Hoverington who's had the cheesy life he's had,' Gronow grinned. 'He wasn't brought up in the Valleys. He knows nothing. He lives on top of the hedge and blows about with every breeze. Has he ever put one foot past the other to help anybody at all? Shitten Hoverington!'

I remember the first night I brought Gronow up to my lodgings, it was to a party by invitation of Hoverington who always wanted to meet poets and painters and that. Gronow, poor dab, was speechless after fetching his big bulk up the half dozen flights of stairs leading to the Hoveringtons' flat. When we got inside, the whole place was in darkness, apart from a candle burning on a saucer, that is, and the glow of the gas fire. As usual there was a powerful smell of babies. By the light of the fire I could make out Tessa beside it smoking a cigarette, she was stripped to the waist and giving suck to a baby that had managed somehow, so far anyway, to survive her good nature. Hoverington himself was only a cigarette-glow in the gloom and when he heard us coming in he called us towards him, welcoming us in the sort of posh soothing voice he had. I felt pretty certain he would be flat out on the settee wearing his ragged green tweeds and his black polo-neck pullover and the gilded sandals some Indian disciple of his had given him. And I guessed too that he and Tessa had run out of shillings for the electric light again. I put a couple of bob in the meter behind

the landing door and the powerful glare pounced into the room from
the two unshaded bulbs hung from the rafters.

I could see Gronow blinking behind his glasses. But he took it all in,
the big resounding attic as bare as a barn and much shabbier, the drab
three-feet-high wall-boards painted committee-room green, the cracky
skylights, the silk stockings drying on the candle-brackets of the piano,
the parrot-cage hanging from the tie-beam with a half-dead rabbit in
it. He took Tessa in too. 'She's a nice sort of girl, Tessa,' he used to say
about her after. 'It's a pity she can't understand the baby's bottom is
more important than its face. But she's very nice is Tessa, poor little
sod.'

'I'm glad you've been able to come,' Hoverington said, waving his
cigarette to us from the settee. 'Dewi has told me a lot about you. My
wife, Tessa. Gronow Lloyd the Welsh poet. Please do sit down, won't
you?'

I saw Gronow bowing and, still pretty blown, looking round, anxious
to sit down anywhere after that climb. But the orange-box furniture
and the three chairs were all heavily under books, papers, magazines,
used crockery and Tessa's underclothes. So to give him a lead I did
what Hoverington always expected his guests to do when he was lying
comfortable on his settee. I sat down on the floor. But I was careful to
go down on one of the home-made rope mats they had about the
place. I had been in Hoverington's flat long enough to know that half
his friends suffered from crippling rheumatic pains in the hams
through sitting in the fresh air that came whistling up through the
cracks between his bare floorboards.

'Don't bother about me,' Gronow panted, 'I'll lean.'

In his tight black coat and striped trousers and his nailbrush hair he
looked a bit out of it; he reminded me somehow in his working clothes
of a low-grade football tout, or still more of a shady faith-healer. As he
rolled off to take up his position leaning in the corner, I saw him
breaking into a little trot; something had happened to the flooring in
that part of the attic and the boards dipped downhill into the wall at a
big angle.

'We've got another countryman of yours coming along in a few
minutes,' Hoverington said to Gronow. 'A painter. Carlos Llewellyn.
Do you know him?'

I had met Loss many times of course but Gronow shook his head
and lumbered back up the slope again to open the door to let Tessa
out. What the devil was he grinning at, I wondered. I hoped it was only
at his little trot when he ran downhill into the wall, or rather the
ceiling.

In appearance this Hoverington was pretty unremarkable. His body was long, thin and limp, he lay now stretched out flat on the settee in his terrible old patched-up suit and his black ganzy. When you saw his head like this, from a point near the floor, it looked thin and supple, soft, a bit like a snake's, hardly more than a thickened-out extension of his long thin neck. His hair was thin and puffy, very unsubstantial, unattached to his scalp somehow, like a cloud floating about around the summit of a high mountain. His profile always looked to me slightly adenoidal. Hoverington had that half-strangled look you see on those side-faces the phoneticians use on their charts, when they want to show you the proper way to manage the larynx and the vocal cords. And, of course, he had completely swallowed his chin. Only Hoverington's eye, I always felt, set in a skin the colour of old dough, saved him from looking absolutely wet. But even this eye never seemed quite normal, not an object that sensation was passing into; more like it was something itself steadily pouring out a powerful beam of dotty good nature.

Soon the other guests began to arrive. A lot of the Hoveringtons' friends seemed to be cranks of some sort, or maniacs almost, and I was connected with their world really only through my lodgings and the typewriters and stuff I sometimes managed to sell them. One of the visitors that night again was Max, a sculptor who never seemed to sculpt anything, a chap who always came with a couple of bottles of gin in his pockets and sometimes bellowed about the attic like a stung bull. Another was an unpublished novelist, baring his teeth all the time in a way that made you think of an intelligent horse drinking. Another was an Indian poet who was always getting caught scratching dirt on the walls of the public dubliws. The dirt was in Greek but that didn't stop the poor chap getting convicted.

All these, and the others, Hoverington called over the boards in turn to meet Gronow and I watched the ones who were seeing him for the first time whispering to one another after the meeting and looking puzzled.

Because Gronow that night, as I say, was wearing his working clothes, his tight black coat and vest and striped trousers. He had brought his rent-collecting ledgers with him, stuffed into the special pockets inside his jacket, and these gave his trunk several large flat planes with upright edges, there were smooth surfaces round his body that made him look a bit like the stump of a six-sided pencil. With his oily skin and his big mouth and his broken nose he didn't make you think much of the dazzling sort of figure the reviewers made him out to be. He was a real puzzle. And his laugh as well didn't help, it had something very unsettling and jeering in it.

People kept on arriving until between twenty and thirty squatted down on the floor or stood about smoking and drinking and jawing at the tops of their voices. Tessa was soon back in the room wearing a green quilted dressing gown, she looked very picturesque as usual under her auburn halo of hair; and Hoverington still lay stretched out comfortably on the settee, listening. He didn't say much, he just idled there under the light of the naked bulb, smoking a cigarette with a big bend in it, swivelling his huge pale eyes slowly around the room like the benevolent beams of a lighthouse.

And at last Loss Llewellyn came into the tobacco smoke, hand in hand with the girl he was living with, the one everybody called Jersey. He was in his colours, wearing a salmon-pink shirt, a thick purple tie, a sky blue jacket and sandals. He had small gold ear-rings in his ears. His beard was black and silky and so was his hair, but in spite of this, and in spite of his tall figure too, Loss never managed to look dashing at all, or piratical, or anything like that. For one thing his eyes had a bleached look and the outlines of his skin and jaw, which you could see clearly through his thin beard, looked pretty meagre, and his pink nose wasn't much help to him or his top teeth hanging out as though he was giving them an airing all the time he wasn't talking. But the people who came to Hoverington's flat always treated Loss with a lot of respect. For one thing he had money, and for another he was always telling everybody he had dedicated his whole life absolutely and irrevocably to painting.

I think they called Loss's girl Jersey because she was supposed to be like that actress who was the fancy of one of the kings. To me, what with the band she always wore round her forehead and her long, loose, sack-like dresses hung everywhere with long fringes, she looked more like a stage Red Indian. But she wasn't dark, she had a mass of light golden hair which billowed below her head-band all round her pink high-class face. She was easily the most beautiful girl that came to the Hoveringtons', very tall and slender and elegant, more beautiful than Tessa even, or anyway more superior-looking. She never said a word to anybody. All she wanted was for everybody to take notice of her all the time. One night very late when half a dozen of us, Hoverington's friends, were walking along the empty street arguing like mad about something or other we forgot she was with us, for four or five minutes nobody said a word to her. She walked on ahead of us and fell in a heap on the pavement. We all ran up to her but we saw soon enough there was nothing much the matter with her. After we petted her a bit she was all right – but she made Loss call a taxi and take her home in it all the same.

Hoverington waved Loss and Jersey forward and introduced Gronow to them. Loss squeezed down on the floor beside me under the roof of Gronow's belly and Jersey sat beside him. At first all Loss did was frown in the middle of all the talking; he was quiet and reserved, very moody, he went on turning one of his ear-rings round and round in the lobe of his ear and fiddling with his beard. But after a few swigs from the sculptor's bottle he found his tongue and he began to explain some theory or other he had about poetry, for Gronow's benefit I thought; he brought Shakespeare into it when he was a homosexual, and Byron sleeping with his sister, and John Ruskin because he was impotent and mad. And that poet Swinburne was mixed up in it too after a bit, somehow, because he was forty before he knew where his bladder was; and some writer I'd never heard of who lost his nose through an attack of the pox. That was one of the best things about Hoverington's lodgings, I always used to think, you would never hear any talk there except about culture. Anyway, when this was going on, Gronow, behind us, got cornered by a couple of young women, a pair of poetic twins who often came to the Hoveringtons', real tuft-hunters they were, 'intense, tow-haired and titless' Gronow said after; they were trying to get him to discuss some theory or other they had, but he wasn't interested, I could hear him saying, 'Yes, yes, yes,' indifferent, most likely bored.

After a bit the bedlam in the room began to die down, the hush seemed to be spreading from somewhere round about the settee where Hoverington was lying; he was holding a very thick sort of magazine in his hand and reading out of it in that thrilling organy voice that was really the poshest thing about him. He had put his glasses on and because of that he could only read with one eye. He had accidentally snapped off the right-hand side-piece of his specs a couple of months before and to use them now he had to tie a length of red darning wool round the nose-piece, pull it taut across his eyeball and use his right ear as a cleat to twist it round and round.

The first words I actually heard Hoverington read out began with, 'For sex is the over-riding problem of our generation, as faith was that of our grandfathers'.

Loss stopped talking at once at this. Hoverington gave out the sentences very slow and solemn, his voice rose and fell in a real parsonish singsong, you could swear he was reading some extra heavy bit out of one of those eastern books of religious meditation he was so fond of, or even one of his own poems. Everybody in the attic sat absolutely absorbed and silent in no time, after a few more of Hoverington's sentences the jabbering stopped altogether, the cups and bottles were lowered to the boards and on the faces of all the listeners around me I could see the serious expressions, very grave and solemn, and sort of devotional.

I glanced round at Gronow. He had shaken off the twins and had been talking to the rabbit in the bird-cage with his back to us. I could see his shoulders were shaking. Gronow had two laughs. One was a sort of outburst of coarse guffaws, very startling and upsetting, he was speechless when this struck him, and helpless, all he could do was sit down until the fat on him stopped quaking a bit and the convulsions quietened down to normal. His other laugh was usually a sort of overture to this, it was almost silent, only a long hoarse sound came out of his throat, it sounded a bit like the brassy hiss of a bugle when somebody blows into it without enough wind to make the proper note. I was pretty well attuned to Gronow in those days and it was this hoarse hissing sound that I began to hear now coming out of him.

In the meantime Hoverington's sentences went on. The atmosphere in the attic seemed very religious and devotional, you could think you were in a real prayer-meeting. Heads were nodding reverentially all round, one or two of the listeners even started hear-hearing – only it was so much like a meeting house you felt they ought to be saying 'amen'. And then the writer reached the high spot of his article, he began maintaining, in what I thought was a pretty eloquent and convincing way, that the dimensions of the male organ *can* under suitable treatment, with diet and exercise, be greatly increased.

Fair play, that brought the religious atmosphere to its most intense, I could feel it in the silence like a revival. But Gronow failed to hold in any longer, his awful guffawing laugh and the echoes it made everywhere resounded through the hushed attic, he began moving across the room looking clumsy and loutish, and signalling me to the door.

Hoverington stopped reading and waited. He was still serene and unmoved on the settee, all he did was pass his hand through the thin cloud-cap of his locks in slight embarrassment and jerk his golden sandal up and down a bit. But his guests looked bewildered, some of them, others red and angry; the sculptor glared towards the door and the poetic twins hunched together like moping poultry, they raised up identical eyebrows, indignant and severe.

Gronow waited for me with his hand on the door-knob. He couldn't say a word. He stood with his big white teeth bulging out of his face and his skin drenched with grease. He was managing by now not to make any sound although his belly kicked up and down all the time under the ledgers. When I got to him he flashed his glasses round at everybody, waved his hand and went down the stairs.

Out in the street he clung to my arm. All the time the laughs were
rising in his throat. When he was a bit calmer, he outlined a poem he
was going to write for chanting, with a chorus denouncing religion,
justice, peace, philosophy and that, and proclaiming the primacy of the
external genitalia. I saw him on to his bus and then went back to my
lodgings.

All the guests had gone. Hoverington was still calm and unmoved on
his sofa; I searched him but I couldn't see the smallest dot of
resentment in his eye. All he did was ask me if I could spare him a few
cigarettes until the morning.

Loss Llewellyn always liked to be on the jeering side, I knew that, and I
never saw him at any of Hoverington's parties after that night. But
Gronow and I used to bump into him often in other people's places
and he began to surprise us by taking an interest in our background,
the sort of way we had been brought up and that, so different from his
own childhood in a mansion in some posh Sussex village. Then one
day when we hadn't seen him for two or three months, we got a long
letter from him telling us about a new religion he'd found and asking
us down to his place to hear more about it. He told us he'd given up
painting altogether, he had sold his studio and returned to his native
country, to Wales, to live there among the workers of one of the Dinas
dockland slums. The letter was full of Loss's usual big talk and up-to-
date jargon, so modern you could hardly understand it. What was the
use, he asked us, of applying paint to canvas in a world free-wheeling
to disaster? Only political action was logical and satisfying; the inflated
ego of the artist was an anachronism; Loss was determined, a
dedicated soul, to march forward in the van of the class which had
history on its side. Did we realize the conditions in which millions still
lived? Mrs. Moncrieff on the floor of the tenement below him was so
poor she had swallowed a bottle of disinfectant when she knew her
tenth was on the road; and the Johnsons next door had tried to bury
their baby in some garden when it died of malnutrition, because they
couldn't raise the price of a funeral . . .

Gronow and I knew all about this, we had known it all our lives. To
us Loss sounded as though he'd gone a bit odd, but we decided to pay
him a visit the next time we were in Wales; it would be interesting
hearing this stuff straight from the lips of somebody so unlikely as Loss
Llewellyn.

It was early evening when our bus got into the Dinas dockland area
where Loss lived then; the sky was transparent yellow, like a long glass

dish of lemonade. From the rise in the road over the railway bridge we could see the whole steaming mass of dockland brickwork below us, grey and shapeless, like something the city had had back on the foreshore.

The area Loss told us he lived in was called Tiger Bay, it was mostly made up of shabby houses and cafes and ships' chandlers and shops selling oilskins and groceries and engine valves and boiler piping. Groups of seamen, many of them coloured, lounged idle at every corner and coloured children ran about screaming or chalking their games on the pavements. Every building seemed old and shabby and run-down. In the bare front windows of the cafés we could see an aspidistra perhaps, and a plate of fly-blown rock-cakes, and inside a few drabs with pimples and untidy hair sitting round the fire.

We found Loss's street and went in to his address through a dark passage alongside a barber's shop. 'If I know anything about this sort of place,' Gronow said, 'we'd better light a couple of pipes before we go any further.' We went up the pitch-black wooden stairs, several flights of them, to a small landing surrounded by doors and with a skylight overhead. Here the smell of stale fish was strong in spite of our pipes, but Gronow only grinned as he looked round, his face gleaming as though it had been basted.

On one of the doors on the landing we found Loss's number, seventeen, tacked on in tin figures, but the door was fastened with a padlock and a galvanized chain that went in through a hole burnt in the panel and out through another between the doorpost and the wall. There was no answer when we knocked. We tried next door where we could hear a melodeon playing 'Jack o' Diamonds' but we had no luck there either; nor at the next door where a kid was grizzling, nor the next where a man and woman were having a knock-about quarrel. That left us only one more door on that landing to knock at. When Gronow failed to get an answer he quietly turned the knob and looked in.

It was dim and bare inside and the room was lit only by a bats-wing burner with a wire ball around it. It stank of bloaters. Here and there big pieces of plaster had dropped off the wet walls showing the lath ribs. A man sat at a table with his back to us reading a newspaper.

'Excuse me, please,' Gronow said, leaning in, his hand still on the door-knob, 'I wonder if you could help us.'

The man turned round in time, got up from his chair and very slowly padded over the floor towards us, bringing his paper with him.

He was a very peculiar sort of chap, he must have been the greyest man in dockland. He was short but he seemed to loom up towards us

like some ancient mud-monster with this powerful fishy smell about
him and dried-hard sludge making up his flesh and everything he wore
on it. He came on at a sort of slow boxer's crouch, his knees bent, his
long arms dangling, his feet in their slippers dragging on the floor as
though they didn't want to come apart from their native slime. He was
wearing grey corduroy trousers and a dark grey flannel shirt, both of
them dirty and shapeless, and a colourless muffler went round his neck
instead of a collar and tie. His waistcoat shone like oilskin and hung
open, the two sides anchored together by a big brass watch-chain. He
was a good bit undersized as to height but very heavy, and very bulky
in the trunk. All his baggy old skin was grey, and wrinkled as dried-out
mud-banks, his big stupid face was unshaven and covered with a mass
of muddy puckers. A grey fringe went round his bald head above his
thick quilted-looking ears and he had a grey walrus moustache.

I saw Gronow twinkling down at this sort of mud-made prodigy, his
nostrils fluttered and his mouth seemed ready to fly open any minute
and let his teeth come through.

'Oh, ah!' the man said, coming to rest from his clumsy shamble and
shooing us off with his paper. 'Ah'm not signing, mister, Ah'm not
signing. Ah'll take my oath on that.'

His voice was very hoarse and sudden, but resonant, he sounded a
bit like those ball-balancing sea-lions giving out in their excitement a
series of asthmatic barks.

Gronow took no notice of the shooing off. 'We are trying to find a
friend of ours called Llewellyn,' he said. 'I wonder if you could help us.'

The man scowled up at us, from Gronow to me and back again, and
his lower jaw began a slow sideways chewing action. He looked
bewildered.

'Liwellian,' he said, 'Liwellian, did you say? Oh, ah! No, Ah don't
know no Liwellian round here.'

'No?' said Gronow. 'The address we were given was in this building.
Number seventeen. Tall and dark. With gold ear-rings.'

'With gold ear-rings, mister?' the man repeated. 'With gold ear-
rings? No, there's no Mrs. Liwellian in this house, no Mrs. Liwellian
here, mister.'

Every time he stopped talking, his mouth began this slow cud-
chewing motion; his bristly bottom jaw went meditatively from side to
side under the big moustache like the mouth of a cow.

'No, no,' Gronow said, grinning. 'It's a man. With a black beard. Tall,
dark. *Mr.* Llewellyn.'

'*Mr.* Liwellian,' he replied. '*Mr.* Liwellian. With gold ear-rings.' He
stopped and scowled again from Gronow to me and back again, very

suspicious. And then the idea seemed to amuse him a bit, for a second or two there was a break in the dense mud-like cakings of the skin of his face. 'No,' he went on, sober again, 'there's no Mr. Liwellian in this house, Ah'll take my oath on that now. Never was a Mr. Liwellian in this house, mister.'

'Is this the man with history on his side?' Gronow said to me in Welsh, grinning. 'Shall we give him the bullet or try him again? I feel sure there used to be a Mr. Llewellyn here,' he said to the man. 'Tall, dark, with ear-rings and a beard.'

'Tell him about the workers,' I suggested. 'A great one for the workers,' I said to the man. 'A leader.'

He folded up his newspaper. His grey shirt-sleeves were rolled up to the elbows and the outsides of both his arms were covered with a mass of dull blue and red tattoos, and so was his chest. After a bit of pondering a faint gleam shot out of the wrinkles.

'Oh, ah!' he barked hoarsely. 'Mr. Liwellian did you say, mister? Ah though you said Liwellian. Ah know Mr. Liwellian right well now.'

Gronow looked at me and grinned.

'Well,' he said, 'can you tell us where Mr. Liwellian might be?' 'Honestly,' he said to me, 'I meant to say Llewellyn.'

'No,' he replied, nodding. 'No, Ah don't know where he might be now, mister.'

There was a pause for a bit again and the three of us stood without saying a word. The cud-chewing under the big hairy mainsail of the moustache began again and every now and then we were belched at with bloatery breath. Gronow sucked his pipe hard and began to explain, very patient he was, what it was all about and what we wanted to do.

'It would,' the man said at last, 'Mr. Liwellian's door would be locked now. Mr. Liwellian went into hospital these ten days gone, they say.'

'Into hospital,' we said together. 'What's the matter with him?'

'Mr. Liwellian's in hospital now,' he said, 'because he was hit over the head with a bottle.'

'Hit over the head!' said Gronow. 'With a bottle? How did that happen?'

'Was it a riot or something' I asked. 'Police and the workers? A clash?'

Again that look of faint amusement broke through the wrinkles. 'Oh, ah! No!' he said, and the barks sounded a bit brighter. 'He wasn't with the workers when he got hit, Ah'll take my oath on that now.' He puckered his face up at us. 'Mister,' he said to Gronow, 'it was a worker what hit him with the bottle.'

'A worker hit him?' said Gronow. 'Why? Was there a fight or something?'

'A fight! No! There weren't no fight now.'

'Well what then?'

'Mr. Liwellian was met coming out of the Owens' room.'

'Yes?'

'And Owens was coming ashore earlier than expected.'

'And Owens is a married man?'

'Oh, ah ! Ah'll take my oath on that – Owens is a married man.'

'And big?' I asked.

'Oh, ah, mister,' he answered. 'And black. Big and black, that's Ali Owens.'

I could feel Gronow's belly at my elbow beginning to fluctuate and the sort of soft hooting began to blow past my ear. He turned away without saying any more and went back out on to the landing. I thanked our man but he didn't seem willing to let us go now.

'Mister,' he said to me, padding out on to the landing after us, 'Ah thought you was from the shipping. That's what Ah thought you was, mister.'

'You're a seaman, are you?' I asked him, beginning to follow Gronow down the stairs.

'Ah'm a donkeyman. That's what I am, mister, a donkeyman.'

My head was level with his slippers. I asked him what hospital Loss had been taken to. Gronow had gone down into the darkness but his pipe-smoke floated back up the staircase. 'Oh, ah! No! Ah don't know which hospital he was took to,' he barked at me. 'Ah thought you was the company, mister.'

I took another few steps down. I couldn't see the old man any more. 'Ah thought you two was the company,' he barked down after us. 'And Ah'm not going to sea in the flat-racing season, Ah'll take my oath on that.'

Gronow heard. His laugh went past me up the stairs, it sounded like the crazy uproar of a brick howling down a disused airshaft.

We heard later that Loss had retired to the country but we never set eyes on him again until after the war when we met him at the ferry that lovely evening during our walking tour in West Wales.

In spite of everything, the journey over the river in the evening sunlight was very pleasant.

I sat on the stern thwart of Loss's little rowing boat with our knapsacks beside me and Gronow got up in the bows. Loss didn't look

much of a ferryman to me. The inside of the boat was swimming with
water and it wasn't easy finding a decent bit of dry seat to sit down on.
Loss was facing me and as he rowed I could see he was trying to look
very intent all the time, as though he was absorbed in some heavy
private business or other, very solemn and important. But he was
nervous or clumsy or something. Every time the boat wobbled a bit or
the oars jerked out of the rowlocks he had to shoot me a very self-
conscious look from under the brim of his sou'wester to see if I had
noticed.

Without his beard his face looked meagre, childish, I thought, and
the cold pink hump of his nose seemed to be all over it. The holes in
the lobes of his ears were empty and he had clipped back his eyebrows
like moustaches. The expression he tried to keep on his face was
humble, he looked meek and long-suffering; he seemed to be trying to
give us the idea his mind was busy milling very pure thoughts all the
time and there was an expression of patience and understanding in his
silver eyes when he turned them up to the sky.

The evening was lovely, very cool and dead silent on the water.
Ahead of the boat the brown cliff on the far side of the river was
receiving the full blaze of the setting sun, it seemed to glow like a wall
of dusty bronze. The sky by now was almost everywhere blue and clear,
very radiant, and only a few clouds were floating there, as transparent
as steam. I could see a heron sunning himself on his little beach below
the cliff, parading the sand as slow and dignified as a cigar-smoker. As
Loss pulled at the oars the water bulged up before the bows of the boat
and spread out when we cut through, frilly and tinkling on both sides
of us. The breeze was delicate coming off the sea, it went over the skin
as smooth as milk. In his tight tussore suit, looking like two cushions
stuffed into one cover, Gronow sat facing the light, he was bareheaded
and grinning, his glasses flashing and the shiny lubrication coming out
all over his face.

We still had three or four miles to walk after getting out of the boat,
Loss told us, before we reached the village we meant to spend the night
at. When we asked him about the road he stood up to point, we were in
midstream at the time and the boat began rocking like mad and the
water from the oars added to what was already slopping about in the
bottom. He showed us our road curving over the hills like a flat snake
and dangling its tail down into a near-by plantation. He was very sorry
he couldn't have us to stay with him, but there was only room in his
tower for himself, worse luck. He was practically a hermit, he lived
absolutely alone, he saw nobody now except the few local people he
ferried over the river. He had cut himself off completely from his old

life, from politics, from art, from painting, with another ex-artist he could say, 'Je ne m'occupe plus de cela.' Did we still know Hovering-ton, with his pathetic concern for art, and his theories, and his parties? What was his latest craze, was it brewing herbs? Or mat-making? Or bottling that ghastly home-made carrot wine, or what?

I told him I didn't live with the Hoveringtons any more, my territory had been changed, but I still saw them from time to time. Gronow sat grinning up there in the bows behind Loss, his glasses signalling like twin heliographs in the sun. He wanted to know how Loss came to be in this no-man's-land. What about the workers? Had their cause triumphed at last, or what?

Loss bared his hanging teeth at me in a slow smile, full of calm and patience and understanding. As he spoke he made out he'd learnt some deeper wisdom among his own people, here amid the remote solitude and grandeur of his native hills. As long as his tower stood and gave him shelter he would continue to live in this place and serve the people. With a soppy sort of look he sketched out his conversion. During his illness, brought about as a result of living in slum conditions, he had had a vision of what life for him should be from then on. He knew for a certainty that he had been called and chosen, that his days were to be spent exclusively in service, and what he called expiation.

These words coming from Loss made me feel pretty uncomfortable, especially as Gronow's grin, instead of getting less with respect and understanding, was taking in wider areas of his face-fat. He was very interested to hear that, he said, speaking into the back of Loss's neck. He had often wished the flow of his own thoughts could change its bed somehow, and that he could inhabit such exalted planes of experience himself. But having to work for a living, he always felt, tended to coarsen one, and to bring one all the time into contact with what was cheapest and crudest and most sordid in life. Didn't Loss agree with him?

Loss had never done a day's work in his life but he did agree and he also said we must never forget there was always compensation in the dignity and nobility of labour.

For instance, Gronow went on, ignoring him, how was it possible to devote oneself to the real problems of existence when one was subject to the experiences encountered in rent-collecting? Only the week before our tour started, he said, he had gone into a substantial sort of villa in suburban London and asked for the rent. A big hard-faced bossy-looking woman showed him in, she put him in a large front room, dim and very raffish, her huge soft bosom quaked when she was doing it as though she had loaded a couple of gallons of upright jelly into her dressing-gown. She told him to sit down, if he would excuse her she wouldn't be long getting the money. After a bit of delay and whispering in the passage the door opened and a beautiful girl walked into the room grinning, wearing a man's long dressing-gown. She came round and stood on the carpet in front of Gronow. Then she slipped her dressing-gown off and underneath she was naked, she didn't have a stitch of clothing on apart from a pair of fishnet stockings.

By this time Loss had stopped rowing and was turning his head sideways so that he could hear better. Gronow grinned over at me.

'Yes, yes,' said Loss, 'go on. What happened then?'

Gronow laughed. 'Nothing,' he said. 'I had fifty quid of rents in my pocket. But how disturbing for me.'

Loss saw he had been hoaxed and began to row again. The slum-dwellers, he told us, he found brutish and unresponsive, indifferent to sacrifice and the generosity of disinterested action. But now, he felt, his life, however remote and obscure, was one of serene contemplation and service and fulfilment.

Bit by bit, as we got nearer the jetty below the black and white tower, Loss told us the story of the place we were in. An ancestor of his, a landowner in these parts a century ago, had promised the farmers he would build a bridge across the river for their use – he had put twenty thousand pounds aside for it – if they would return him to parliament as their member when the time came. He lost the contest by about twenty votes and to spite the electors what the old chap did was to build a huge folly at the river's edge just where the bridge ought to have been; he spent the twenty thousand pounds on a lot of useless roofless buildings and miles and miles of walls with nothing inside them. As time went on the folly gradually disappeared, the farmers all round began to use it as a quarry, they carted whole buildings away stone by stone to patch up their homes and extend their outhouses; and now, after more than a hundred years, almost everything had disappeared, only the tower Loss lived in was still in one piece. Lying sick in hospital he had determined to dedicate his life to, as he said, the expiation of this act of ancestral vindictiveness; since he couldn't afford to build the bridge himself he meant to devote the remainder of his days, an inglorious Welsh Christopher perhaps, to ferrying the people of the neighbourhood and their goods across the river. In this remote spot, once the home of his fathers, forgotten by the world, he was passing his days now alone in service and contemplation and renunciation.

I got my eyes away from Gronow's grinning face. We were rapidly approaching the shore and I could see the details of the stumpy tower.

It had a low pointed slate roof and one or two tiny windows, and those alternate bands of what looked like white lime and tar around it which we had seen from the other bank. Surely I could make out a head at the middle window – or was it a flowerpot? On the jetty where we were going to land two young women were standing in the sunlight waiting to cross. In a few minutes Loss got the boat somehow alongside the wooden landing stage.

The two girls were young and pretty, one dark and one auburn, they looked like farm girls coming back from the village where we hoped to stop for the night. One of them carried a big empty butter basket and the other was in trouble with a new pair of heavy hobnailed farm-boots, the backs threaded together with twine. They giggled a lot and the colour rose in their cheeks as Loss handed them into the boat in our places after we got out; he was tall and solemn doing it in his sou'wester and blue jersey and we could see he was enjoying it, especially pocketing the fare. They went to the dry places we had left, the auburn sat in Gronow's seat in the front and the dark one went back to the stern, and we passed the square basket and the boots in after them. They seemed to be enjoying themselves too, they laughed and blushed and giggled all the time, but they didn't say much. When they spoke it was in Welsh. Loss apologized for having to leave us at once in this way, but he hoped we would forgive him. We would be certain to reach the village before nightfall now. Goodbye. He was glad to have seen us again. No, no. No charge of course. Goodbye. Goodbye.

We pushed him off and waved to the girls as he paddled out into the river and then we walked up the jetty towards the shore. The tower was at the far end of a little path that sloped up from the jetty to its tarred door. It must have been a head I had seen at the window because it wasn't there any longer. We passed close to the glistening door and I couldn't help noticing that the doorstep under it was well-worn and hollowed out; it looked a bit like a bottom lip in a kind of wry grin.

After leaving the path we went over some beds of bladderwrack that Gronow didn't enjoy, he said it was like treading on a squash of bowels, but we were soon on the hard sand where I had seen the heron, and I found it pleasant walking there in the sunlight at the side of the river. Gronow sloped along beside me, to balance the mass of heavy flesh he carried in front of him he always moved along leaning slightly backwards, the angle of his body to the earth made him look rakish like the masts of a schooner.

From this little beach below the cliff we could see the woods opposite across the water and the line of the stepping stones we had used coming down from them to the edge of the river. There was a ploughed field on the hill behind the woods, the furrows rigid as harp strings, and the blue mountains were like a batter in the distance all around. As we looked, a full blackbird flew past us quite close with his chin up, making a loud clinking noise, and he drew our attention back to the water.

Loss's boat was by now a fair distance out in the river; it was broadside on to us and at a standstill. The two girls looked as if they were trying to change places, they were both on their feet, the auburn-haired boot-carrier was struggling towards the stern and the dark one was groping her way towards the bows at a crouch. When they met in the middle where Loss was sitting they clung together giggling and the boat began to rock violently. Loss, as though he meant to steady them, got up on his feet. The next minute both the girls gave out loud screams and fell overboard into the water.

Loss at once sprang on the thwarts with his back to us; he threw off his sou'wester, shot out his arms, poised himself a second or two and then went into the river with a terrible gutser. There was a lot of spray rising from the water beyond the boat, we could see it splashing up as though a tremendous struggle was going on, but as the boat drifted on down we saw three figures rising into view dripping wet, they were standing in a line on the sandbank in the middle of the river, almost up to their knees in water.

We saw Loss getting the water out of his eyes and then wading down after the boat. As the two girls climbed back in, soaking wet, the door of the tower behind us flew open and a dark buxom young woman ran out pulling a red jumper on over her head.

'Carl, Carl,' she shouted, in a very posh English voice. 'Carl, are you all right, darling, are you all right?' She ran like mad to the end of the jetty, taking no notice at all of Gronow and me.

Gronow looked inflated; although he was standing still, his flesh seemed to be convulsed, it was making those jerky swelling leaps you see in the curtains when there's a breezy window open behind them. 'Saint Christopher,' he hooted, pointing out at Loss. 'Saint Christopher, induced by a blow on the head with a bottle. The Christophero Sly of the mountains.' He went his length on the rocks at the foot of the cliff and lay there in uproar.

The young woman in the red jumper heard him, she turned and shook her fist fiercely in our direction.

Rhysie at Auntie Kezia's

❧

I had noticed a lot of whispering in our house that Christmas and there was something the matter with our Mam. But I didn't know what it was. Then one night, when he was finishing his bath by the fire, Dada said to me, 'Evan, you are going to your Auntie Kezia's for a bit tomorrow. Over Christmas. Your Mam isn't very well. You see you behave yourself, now.'

'Is our Rhysie coming?' I asked him at once.

My father's head was coming through his flannel shirt just as I said it, and he shook it very slowly without saying a word. There was a very cunning sort of expression on his face.

Still, it wasn't bad in my Auntie Kezia's, out there in the country. Sometimes you would find a square of thick grass growing under the bed in her cottage, and every time the trains passed by, her piano played by itself, the keys tinkled a little tune from one end to the other.

Early the next morning Mrs. Richards next-door took me to the station with my little cardboard week-end case in my hand. It had been snowing a lot in the night and the gatepost outside our house had been given a white brow and a big snout. As I looked back at the house from the pavement, I could see two or three of my little sisters waving goodbye in the parlour window, but my brother Rhysie was still upstairs, I could see him up there in his nightshirt, his big ugly face pressed against the attic window scowling down at me. He couldn't come down to see me off because my father had hidden his shirt and trousers before he went to work; he didn't trust Rhysie and he wanted to make sure he wouldn't dodge out and come to my auntie's with me.

Mrs. Richards hurried me up town to the station but the snow was thick in the streets and we didn't get on to the platform until the guard was getting his whistle out and his green flag unrolled ready. I got into a compartment at the back end of the train and then, just as our neighbour was saying goodbye to me, I spotted a funny-looking girl running down the empty platform towards us; she was in a big hurry, limping and waving her coat about above her head and shouting at the top of her voice. As she came nearer, I recognized her. It was our Rhysie. He had gone down into the girls' bedroom, I could see that, and he was wearing a white satin party dress with ribbons belonging to our Mari, sleeveless, too tight for him everywhere, and on his feet he had our Mam's lace-up boots with the high heels. He had put a couple of bangles on his bare arms too and on his head was Gwennie's big pink sunbonnet, tied under his chin with the ribbons.

Mrs. Richards didn't know what to do. Rhysie jumped into the compartment and before she could make up her mind the guard blew his whistle and waved his flag and the train started off. As he sat opposite me, scowling as usual, his bare arms and his face purple with cold, I had to admit he looked a pretty ugly sight; his upper lip was thick and long, it bulged out over his teeth as though he had his tongue always stuffed under it, and he had the biggest nose of any boy I have ever seen, bent and bony and twisted on one side, and always very red and sore-looking. Anyway, when our auntie met us at the other end and saw that tough-looking face glaring up at her from under the sunbonnet, I thought she was going to have a turn.

Nobody who knew Rhysie seemed to trust him, and that night we had to sleep in the same room as our auntie. She had hung a white bed-sheet across the middle and we could see her shadow undressing on it by the light of her candle. In the morning Rhysie woke up first and because he didn't have anything to do he started to cut my hair with our auntie's scissors. He had a row for that when he got into the kitchen but he was used to it.

Our auntie put him into the spare clothes my mother had packed for me in my cardboard case and bundled us both off to school in the village. Everything was still thick with snow, the scene on the way was pretty, but we were cold. The school was small with only two teachers, and the headmaster was giving the children their Christmas examination. He was a very thick short man with little arms and legs, and over his big bald head he had a few tails of wavy bright yellow hair like flat unravelled rope. Rhysie and I sat in the same desk in the front row and he asked us questions about Saint Nicholas in a big voice. We couldn't answer any of them but he didn't give us a row. Instead he started to sing 'While shepherds watched' loud enough to deafen you, banging like mad on the school piano at the same time. When he finished all the children clapped.

In the playground a boy called Bazzo shouted, 'Dunce' after Rhysie. Rhysie punched him in the chest and the ribs and clipped him across the side of the head. The boy tried to kick him on the thigh and Rhysie closed with him. They fell to the ground struggling and rolling about in the wet snow and soon the boy began to cry because Rhysie was beating him. When I pulled Rhysie off, there were two purple sets of teeth marks in his cheeks, perfect, where Bazzo had bitten him twice. That night after tea, when our auntie was doing a bit of extra washing, a woman called at the back door and complained that Rhysie had nearly murdered her boy. Auntie Kezia believed her and Rhysie went to bed without any supper.

Rhysie didn't like exams so the next day he got me to mich. We went down the main road and spent our time throwing snowballs at the white stone-ginger bottles holding the wires on the telegraph poles. There were stones inside the snowballs. That night Pugh the policeman called in at our auntie's about it and she began to look more worried than ever. She was a small woman, her face yellow as a canary, and she had pale blue eyes always swimming about in a lot of water; she looked as though her eyeballs were slowly dissolving with anxiety.

Rhysie and I didn't like this Pugh at all. He was the shortest policeman we had ever seen, and the fattest, and he couldn't see properly without his glasses. If you watched him from the side standing on the front doorstep in his street, you would notice that a lot of him was hanging out over the pavement. He had a big curving moustache and a red face the colour of an old roof, with the nose-part varnished, and half a dozen bottom teeth that stood up brown and rotten like a few old clay pipes in the fair ground shooting gallery. He was very bossy and if he saw you kicking your cap up the street he would shout at you to stop it. And even if the village people left their ash-boxes outside a bit too long in the morning he would knock at the door and tell them to take them in.

The third day was the Christmas party in the church vestry for the village children. Rhysie coaxed our auntie to let us go, although I didn't want to much because of the mess Rhysie had made of my hair. The vestry was a very small low building built all of dark brown wood. For the party it was decorated with streamers and balloons, and crowds of kids from the village were screaming and running about the place in their best clothes. Rhysie and I had a good tea by ourselves after all the others had finished and as we were eating it a tall man came and talked to us. We thought he must be the vicar. His thick loaf-coloured hair was parted deep down the middle, it looked like the cut in a crust of bread. He asked us who we were and when we told him he shot up one of his eyebrows into his hair, pulled it down quickly, and then went away.

After tea all the gaslights in the vestry were turned out and the place was in darkness except for the little candles alight on the Christmas tree. The vicar told us all to be quiet and to look up at the roof at the place he was pointing to, just above the tree. We saw the wooden manhole in the ceiling taken away and a face, with glasses on and a big white beard, showed in the square hole, looking down at us. It was

Santa Claus. A ladder was fetched and after a big struggle he began to
climb down into the vestry in his hood and his red robes. Some of the
little children screamed when they saw him, but Rhysie and I knew
him by his boots and his big bum, we could see it was old Pugh the
policeman.

Pugh stood short and fat in his red gown and his wadding beard by
the Christmas tree and after blowing a bit he started to unhook the
presents off it and give them to the children. I was standing in the crowd
with my elbow against Rhysie's jersey and the funny thing was I could
feel his chest bumping like mad with excitement. I suppose he had set
his mind on something on that tree, a knife with a spiker was what he
liked, or a box of caps for his cowboy gun or a mouth organ. But by the
time the gases were lit again everybody had a present except Rhysie and
me. I suppose they forgot about us because we didn't live there.

While the children were laughing and shouting and running about
the vestry with their presents Pugh suddenly called us all around him
again, we had to stop whatever we were doing and listen to him. He
pushed back his hood, unhooked his beard off his moustache and gave
us all a good row. It would be the worst for us if any of us went into the
graveyard to play snowballs, he told us, looking over his glasses. We
could look out, or he'd give us snowballs. The children went very quiet,
and after that we all got our clothes and went home.

The next day was Sunday and I knew Rhysie was up to something
but he didn't tell me what it was. He couldn't come to church again
after tea, he said, because the shaking of the organ had given him the
bellyache in the morning. But when our auntie and I got home after
the evening service we couldn't find him in the cottage. I thought
perhaps he had gone to meet us and had missed us in the dark so I
went back towards the church to look for him by myself. When I got to
the church lane somebody called me in a whisper and I found Rhysie
hiding in the hedge. He wanted me to go and play snowballs in the
graveyard.

'Don't be so dull,' I said. 'You know what old Pugh said last night.
He'd screw us.'

'Him?' said Rhysie. 'Old Pugh? Come on, I'll show you something.'

We went over the stone stile into the snow-covered churchyard and
started dodging about among the graves, pelting each other with
snowballs. Every time I hit him Rhysie let out a loud yell. I couldn't
make out what had come over him, he seemed as though he had gone
daft.

All of a sudden he stopped shying and said, 'Look out, here he
comes.'

We dodged behind a big gravestone and twtied down there out of sight. In a minute the moon came out full again and I could see Rhysie had a candle there in a jamjar and a white nightshirt, it looked to me like one of our auntie's. He got a box of matches out of his pocket and lit the candle. He slipped the nightshirt on, but the neck part had been tied so that it wouldn't come over his head. 'What are you going to do, our Rhysie?' I asked him, but he didn't answer.

As we crouched in the snow we could hear somebody climbing over the stone stile, coming into the graveyard with a lot of noise.

'That's him,' Rhysie whispered from inside the shirt. 'It's Pugh. I saw the back door of his house opening just now. Listen to this.'

He let out a loud moan.

'Who's there?' Pugh shouted. 'Drat you, I'll give you playing snowballs in the graveyard. Who's there?'

Rhysie waited a bit and then moaned again, louder this time but more creepy. Pugh seemed to be hesitating near the stile but in a minute we heard him crunching slowly up the path in the snow.

'Who's there?' he said again, trying to sound brave. 'Who's there?'

I peeped out from behind our stone. There he was, fat and short, not twenty yards away down the path, holding on to a headstone. The moonlight was strong and I could see everything about him, his shiny buttons and the badge on his helmet and his big moustache. But he didn't have his glasses on. That was a funny thing.

Rhysie moaned the third time and as he did it the moon suddenly backed into the clouds and the whole graveyard went black as pitch. In the darkness Rhysie slipped on to the flat tombstone behind us, I saw him kneeling upright on it; his head was gone, he was glowing like a huge gas-mantle, holding the nightshirt away from his body with the candle in the jamjar under it.

There was another loud moan, but Rhysie didn't make it. I looked out at Pugh clutching at the headstone. He wasn't there. I looked again. He was splodged down on the snow, spread out on the path, tipped out helpless as a cart-load of mortar. He had fainted.

We left everything and ran home to our auntie, terrified out of our lives. Rhysie began to cry.

The next day she sent us packing. But we had been away just long enough. When we got home we had a new little brother and our Mam had named him Christmas.

Lias Lewis

❦

The forest glowed like a forge in the setting sun as the unbrushed and dilapidated remains of a fat man walked his three geese among the trees.

The man's name was Lias Lewis, and his tall gaunt body moved through the sunset beams in a greenish-black jacket that fell in grooves about his bony figure, and a shabby pair of greenish-black trousers with a hanging seat. The only place where he carried any weight now was in his heavy nose, and that shot out broad and purple from the wanness of his face with the bulky curve of a waterfall. He had bushy eyebrows, pure white eyeballs, and a beard of two reds.

As Lias saw the radiant trees prowling round him, silent and incandescent, he recalled with pride the blazing bush and Nebo's patriarchal bones, he thought of unburied Enoch, the seventh from Adam, and of that Baal-baiting, bullock-burning Tishbite whose name he bore. In that golden afterflush, remembering the miraculous uprapping into paradise of prophets who had never tasted death, he thumped the forest grass with his thumbstick again and again, and cried aloud in rapture like the holy jumpers; his blazing white eyes sent their powerful glare even through the skin of his shut lids at the thought of the whirlwind, and the flaring stallions, and the Israelitish charioteers.

Then, with the roar and the red-hot glow of a sky-bound angel, Lias himself went thunder-bolting up through the forest branches, hearing ahead the thrilling roll of majestic thunder, the deafening welcome of silver trumpets and of tenor drums; as he trailed the flames of his whirl-blast over the village house-tiles and the chimney-pots, he saw Rachie Pritchard gazing upwards, dumb with alarm on her dirty doorstep; and the staring horse-teeth of Maesypiod prominent in the open cut of his mouth; there beneath him he caught a glimpse of the dyed hair of Cadi Bryncoed, and of Lonso drunk at the roadside, with his head lolling half-way down his spine. And further on in the sawcut of the village street he could see a howling swarm of children, and on the red road Maddox the Minister, the unfaithful, the servant-soured, beetling his way with his little basket to visit the sick after evening chapel.

Lias opened his eyes suddenly on geese and grass and glowing timber, he groaned aloud and banged his thumbstick on the path, because he was back on earth again among the thieves, and the bulls, and the blasphemers of Pwllybaw.

It was a Thursday as the gaunt and dusty old man dreamed of his apotheosis, the night of the prayer-meeting, but all chapel as soup without salt to Lias now. He bitterly remembered his last visit a few weeks ago, and, 'Shame, shame,' he muttered to himself at the recollection of it. Maddox the Minister had raised the text that Sunday out of the book of Jonah, holding up in his *hwyl* his short arms that didn't reach above the top of his head, preaching the prophet was swallowed, not by the whale, but by Babylon the Great City. Lias went into a ferment at the words. His head glowed like an oven, he felt his heart thundering against the hollow back of the pew, and his blood beat so hard in his feet that his tight best boots tapped out loud like clocks. And this was not the first time; Lias remembered the preacher saying Elias his namesake was fed by the *natives* beside Kerith, and the word *ravens* was somebody's mistake.

After the meeting he ran home through the darkened village in a fever of resentment and offended pride, banging his bony head as he ran. All Sunday night he groaned in a frenzy, wrestling on the bed with Maddox the Minister, forgetting to lock up the geese and water the shorthorn. At daybreak he was on the preacher's doorstep with his massive brass-bound Bible opened across his chest at the book of Jonah. But it was no use, no use, however adamant was Lias and zealous for the belly of the whale.

'Lias *bach*,' said Maddox still in his nightshirt, his white teeth chattering inside the doorway, 'if you want to believe Jonah went into the creature, you believe it.'

'If I want to believe it!' said Lias, feeling the furnace again and the pumping blood. 'Why shouldn't I believe it? If it said it here I would believe the whole ship went into the creature and came out again the other end without striking a sail.'

He left raving. Sunday or week-night, he would never frequent the meeting again.

And yet during those few weeks he had already begun to feel homesick for chapel, for the clean reek of the oilcloth on the aisles on a warm summer's morning, and the sound of the varnished woodwork of the pews creaking in the stillness with a sticky crack as the people sat down heavily in them and prayed.

But these thoughts were vanity, his pride hounded them back into the corner, remembering hungry-for-money Maesypiod with a lot of neck at the back of his head, sucking during communion the sacramental wine through his teeth like a thirsty horse; and black browed Cadi Bryncoed who never gave an egg to the cause in her life, bulging in her print frock and heaving the flowery garden of her back as she howled the hymns. The dregs. Between them and their potch. He was proud he had no more to do with them. He was better than any of them if they would only see it. How many of them would have sold their only milker as he had done, and she suffering from udder-warts, because she haunted the darkness every time he closed his eyes to meditate on the wickedness of Pwllybaw? How many of them, although he was everywhere known as one lazy to wrath, would have used the lump-hammer on the neighbour who tempted him to drop a pill into the ailing sow on the Sabbath? How many would have taken his own wife's gold and silver, her chest-chain, her sinful brooches, her devil's earrings, and handed them all over to his sister?

At the remembrance of these things a scalding blush of pride spread over his whole head, and to cool it he took off his plaid cap with the tied-up ear-flaps. The skull of Lias was brown and very bald, it had a knobbly ridge running the length of it as though his backbone was coming up over the top of his head.

On his way back home Lias trod the high path above the sunken road that ran through the forest. His three white geese as he walked plucked at the gay green mane of the grasses, and above his head the silent evening sky, blue and clear, was lit with long frills of sunset fire.

Hearing a footstep on the road below him he peeped through the trees down into the cutting, and saw a short plump man dressed in black walking lightly along the red road. It was Maddox the Minister, a man with a large bare head, powerful glasses, and cheerful rosy cheeks, carrying his black hat on top of his little basket. As he passed along below, underneath the pale eyes of Lias, the old man saw the preacher's stiff black hair sticking out round his scalp like a bird's nest, and the large white egg of his bald-spot laid in the middle of it.

Lias glared down in scorn. The minister stopped on the road right below him and began to nod his head in time as a little tune tinkled into the evening silence; nod, nod, went his head, as the delicate little melody, sweet and clear as a peal of tiny bells, floated up to Lias out of the sunken road. The old man frowned, puzzled and angry, before he knew the music came from the little clock chiming under the black hat in the little preacher's basket. He shook his fist as the tune stopped and the minister moved on again, he shook his fist again and again in outraged dignity at the thought of this clock-cleaning minister, until the small big-headed figure had disappeared joyfully round the bend. Then, beating the grass with his thumbstick, he started his way angrily for home.

Farther on Lias himself entered the sunken road where the air was dim and the crimson earth of the cutting covered by an exposed basket-work of tree roots.

All of a sudden Lonso trampled at a slow trot round the bend, with his hulking lurcher following behind him the size of a black pony. He was narrow and shorter than Lias, a blackguard and a poacher, his blaspheming tongue and his unshaved goat-skin face made people afraid of him. He was sweating through running. He had been fighting again and he had one eye buried in black. His broken clay, soaked with dribbles, was cackling upside down on the black brink of his crinkled teeth. On his head he had a whole felt hat with a piece of golden thatching-twine going up over the top and under his chin to hold it on. He was wearing wet hobnailed boots, sopping corduroys tied under the knees, and a long black overcoat almost reaching the road, ragged, ticketed all over with fluttering edge-tears and with a new six-inch nail skewered through the middle buttonhole to hold it together. One sleeve of this coat was empty, because years ago, poaching, he had blown his left arm off with a shotgun. His flea-marked neck was bare and Lias could see inside his flannel shirt the dirty string on which he hung his lucky lump of bacon fat.

'The only good I know of this creature,' said Lias angrily to himself as Lonso approached, 'is this. Once I saw him drive away from outside the chapel vestry those noisy children playing by the river and disturbing the prayer-meeting with their shouting. Now he is hurrying to reach the "Black Horse" before the tap is turned off. I have no call to talk to such a blackguard as he is.'

Lonso continued his trot until he came right up to Lias. When their clothes were nearly touching, he stopped, took his pipe out of his mouth and put it under the armpit of his stump. Then he dived into his inside pocket and brought out a fat fish about ten inches long with a green twig through its gills.

'How much, deacon?' he said to Lias, sticking up his hairy face. His good eye was pink and fierce, the headstrong eyeball greasy. The dog, a black long-haired lurcher with webbed feet, lay down across the roadway and showed his fangs to the hissing geese.

'I am not a deacon,' Lias shouted, the anger powerful within him at the touch and the evil smell of this thief and drunkard, this ragged fish-stinking Ishmael. The thumbstick in his hand seemed to come alive like the rod of Aaron, he wanted to use it as the hairy, animal face pushed up into his own, and the poached fish dangled silver on its willow twig. 'Thou shalt not covet and thou shalt not steal,' he cried out in temper, trying to push on past the snarling lurcher.

'What about a groat for it?' asked Lonso grinning, taking no notice of the uproar. 'What about one little groat?'

'A groat will buy a pint of the tavern liquor. Wine is a mocker,' Lias shouted again, 'strong drink is raging.'

Lonso lowered the fish. 'Thruppence then,' he said. 'A thruppenny bit for a twelve-ounce sewin.'

Lias could feel the anger bursting his boots and thundering under his plaid cap. 'I wouldn't give you a penny for it,' he bawled back. 'Not a penny.' But when he moved the lurcher bared his tusks.

'A penny? Let's cut the apple in half and call it tuppence,' Lonso said, wheedling, showing the black of his teeth in a bad-smelling smile.

Lias's eyes filled up with tears of rage. He began to stammer. 'I said I would give you nothing for it,' he shouted. 'Nothing at all.'

'You want it for nothing?' Lonso grumbled. 'Are you trying to milk me? What is the matter with you, Lias?'

'Lonso,' said Lias, sighing loudly, trying to cool down. 'The tighter the string the nearer to snapping, so I had better say no more than this now: I don't want the sewin. And for why? To poach is unlawful. To sell what is stolen is unlawful. And I will not part with silver that you will put into the drawers of the "Black Horse" before ten minutes are over.'

'Me?' said Lonso, baring his pink gums. 'The "Black Horse"? I'm soaking up to the knees, and I'm going straight home to have my supper.'

'I thought,' said Lias, 'you were sweating to reach the "Black Horse" before they stop the tap.' Then suddenly an idea ran glittering round inside the old man's skull like a ball of quicksilver. What if he, Lias Lewis, could convert this unchastened outcast, what if he could subdue the defiance of his corrupted heart and bring him over Jordan contrite and with his flesh healthy? What if he were seen some Sunday morning by Maddox the Minister and his followers – O, moment sweeter than the suck of honeycomb – walking the village with Lonso and Elisabetta, well-clothed, well-washed, and wed beside him? What a triumph over the saints that would be!

'Lonso,' he said softly, 'listen to me. When wilt thou and all thy house return to the commonwealth of Israel? Answer me. When wilt thou marry Elisabetta and step within the circle of the promise? Through the windows of Ramah I saw thee during the meeting, one working-night, driving away the noisy imps who played *talu pump* by the river outside the chapel and disturbed our meditations. Thou showedst there, Lonso, thou hadst reverence for the sanctuary. When wilt thou leave the wilderness and like Joshua possess the land?'

Lonso's pink eye blazed, he laughed, showing the charred stumps stuck round his salmon gums. A powerful fish-and-stable stink surged up to Lias off him. 'Why don't you try washing the feet of the ducks,' he said, pocketing the fish, 'instead of preaching to me? Do you know why I put my finger in the chapel broth and drove the children away? I had spotted a ten-pound salmon under the river bank further down the water and I was afraid the children would disturb it with their riot. When they were all gone I landed it and Dafis gave me a dozen pints for it in the "Black Horse". Goodnight now, Lias. If Elisabetta hasn't got my supper ready I'll break her arm. And if she has I won't eat it. Come on, Fan,' he said, and the two of them trampled on down the road, Lonso with his pipe-smoke hurdling his shoulder and his empty coat-sleeve blowing back behind him.

The sun was almost setting as Lias and his three geese skirted the edge of the huge open field in the middle of the forest. The last low beams thrust themselves in between the trunks of the beech trees and lay in bright yellow stripes across the path like light issuing from many half-opened doors.

Two cottages, grimily limed and dilapidated, squatted close together before him, and the more sluttish one belonged to Rachie Pritchard. He could see her zinc roof tarred and whitewashed in broad stripes, and her two long chimney-pots like a stiff pair of khaki trouser-legs sticking up into the air through her roof. Across the window, with two tomatoes ripening in it, hung a square of lace curtain sagging with dust, and the bottom of her front door was repaired with pieces of soiled unpainted timber, shaped like the teeth of a gigantic saw. On the doorstep stood a tipped dish of grey dog-slop and there were peelings and ashes in the large pools of muddy grey water before her door.

'Poor Matthew,' said Lias as he approached, thinking of Rachie's little husband, and of Rachie herself, with her body like the parish stallion. 'Poor Matthew,' he said, 'he went through the wood and picked up a rotten branch.'

People said Matthew had to keep his dog in the bedroom to save himself from Rachie. And once when she had emptied the teapot out through the front door she saw a little crowd of the village children searching among the tea-leaves. She stood puzzled on the doorstep for a minute, and then she shouted, 'Children, what are you looking for?' 'Only to see, Rachie,' they answered, running away, 'if you have thrown Matthew out with the tea-leaves.'

But Matthew had been separated from her since then, and now he was living in the other cottage next door. And Rachie by this time was going wild as a bullock after the big-bodied roadman with the hook hand.

O to be delivered from the iniquity of this village, O to rise blazing on angelic wings as on that whirlwind of revenge that once blew all the cabbages out of the ground, O to be tied as it were to the tail of a shooting star, leaving behind all those village brats bold enough to have called Elisha bald-head, and the fornicators bedded behind black-berries, and the fish-poachers and the lewd adulterers, the swill-bellies and the beer-bibbers, and Maddox the Minister the blasphemer, the setter-forth of strange gods, and the servant of all.

Lias drove the three geese in anger past Rachie's rag-spread hedge, which had a lot of bottles flung into it, and a rusty rat-trap, and a tin enamel plate.

But before he reached the cottages themselves he stopped. Matthew, he knew, was off somewhere, away in the next parish burying his mother, but somebody was picking fruit in his apple tree. As Lias watched, he saw the heavy aproned body of Rachie beginning laboriously to descend the ladder out of the branches. She had fat legs bulging over her ankles, she looked as though she had a pair of leggings on under her black woollen stockings. In the middle of her face there was a large oval depression where her mouth and her eyes were set and out of the middle of which rose two soft red nostrils and a flattened shapeless nose, pale like the underside of a strawberry where the little green seeds grow in it. Seeing Lias approaching she grinned, showing in her wide open mouth her jaws packed with crowds of unweeded little teeth.

'Lias,' she shouted, as common as grass, 'come here, come here. Like to buy a few of these apples? Eaters! Draw water from your teeth!'

Lias felt many words to denounce her thieving and her adulteries rising within him, and a deep religious flush, purple in colour, heating his face. But what was the use of rebuking her? The more you tread on mud, the muddier it gets. After his talk with Lonso he would more than ever use his teeth to hold his tongue and go by without answering.

'Look at these indeed, Lias,' she shouted from the ladder, showing him Matthew's rosy apples in her apron as he came on without a word.

'It would benefit you to put a few of these down you. They will wet the root of your tongue. What's the matter with you, Lias?' she shouted, seeing him so close there on the path and still not opening his mouth. 'There's proud you are. Why don't you answer? Can't you understand Welsh any more? Or are you too big to talk because you go to the satin chapel?'

Lias felt his flush thicken. She was laughing at him and the words of denunciation boiled up into his mouth. But it is wiser to shelter from a shower than try to stop it, so he hurried the geese towards her. Soon he would be past her, and past the apple tree, and the whole of her garden and Matthew's next door would be behind him.

'Old Lias Lewis,' she jeered as he came opposite her in silence, 'the front horse of the satin chapel and a power on his knees.' Every time she shouted a word the fat cushion of her belly gave a kick upwards jerking up her clothes, and all the time her eyes glittered at him like hanging drops of water. 'Don't you be dull, Lias *bach*,' she went on, changing her tone a bit, 'you jack that old chapel up and enjoy yourself instead. What are you starving yourself to death for? Are you so eager to bang the golden harp? By the look of you another two clean shirts will see you out, and when you are in your box there won't be a wheel the less on the road, remember. Have a bit of fun, boy, and taste a cut of the whitemeat now and then. What odds that you are sixty – there's many a good tune to be had from an old fiddle. Why don't you try wetting your beak for a change? And have you thought of courting Cadi Bryncoed? She would be a good one for you – if she hadn't dipped her head in the tar bucket. Let it out, let it out, Lias *bach,* and don't churn it round inside you. Why don't you answer? Have you got a thick tongue or what? All right, don't listen, have it your own way; no fools no fun is what I think. No, I won't throw my slops against the wind for you. You'll be old before I talk to you again, Lias Lewis. Go on, go on, they say the back is the best of the goose. And eat a bit more of food when you get home and then you won't have room for a loaf of bread in the seat of your trousers.'

The words drenched heavily over Lias's back like rain before the wind, but at last he was out of hearing. O, the Jezebel, to tempt and despise him. O earthy, sensual and devilish. Would that she could be cast down there among her whorish poppies, to be devoured by the dogs and only her palms and footsoles left uneaten.

Then, just at that moment, as Lias came out into the field from a gap in the hedge, he saw ahead of him at the top of the grassy slope the shining dead tree that stood before his house. It had lost nearly all its bark, and in the last blazing beams of the setting sun its weather-polished trunk and branches gleamed as though they were made, not of white timber, but of pure silvery metal, brightly burnished and massive and solid. Lias stopped to look at it. Was this a portent, was this tree of glowing silver, burning and unconsumed, a sign? Were these the blazing branches from which he was to take fire and launch himself in splendour over Pwllybaw? O to be justified, O to be exalted thus in righteousness above Maesypiod and Cadi Bryncoed, and Maddox the Minister, and all the false saints of Ramah. Until that should happen, Lias said to himself, he would swallow his existence and find it tasteless, he would gulp down his unprofitable life ravenously, like a dog with the worms.

Lias stood upright at the top of his dead tree, waiting for the moon to rise. Darkness, lit only by a few diminished stars, was everywhere about him, and from the choral forest below surged up the sound of the baffled winds boiling among the boughs. This was the night for which he had waited, starved himself and importuned providence; at the uprising of the moon this gusty wind should waft his fleshless body in terrorizing circulations over Pwllybaw.

'I will show them,' he muttered to himself, smoothing the six goose-wings before him. 'At last I will show them.'

These wings, chopped from the shoulders of his own slaughtered geese, he had nailed fast in a row to the flat of an old swingle-tree, and as the full moon climbed up the darkness he would launch himself upon them like a new Elias and, with denunciations, circle the chimney-pots of the village. 'I will show them,' he muttered again, 'I will show them, every one.'

On his high swaying perch he waited. To lighten himself he wore no boots and his long bony body was clad only in a white flannel nightshirt. On his head he had his cloth cap with the flaps tied down over his ears. The wind streamed his beard out from his face like a two-coloured flag, and although the chilling winds blew round his body, ballooning his baggy nightshirt, he did not notice the cold. Watching alone in the tall black air he felt fulfilled and exalted. As he gazed up at the black sky, stretched out and glittering like a frosty cloth with stars, his flesh blew out and was magnified again and again, his body seemed to multiply itself, extending towards those distant glimmerings above him. And expanding downwards at the same time it engulfed the massive boniness of the dead tree, the rigid branches seemed completely enveloped within him like the refleshing of a gigantic skeleton. But yet he swayed, he was still light as a breastfeather, the towering fabric of his bulk felt through its airy cells and interstices the cold flow of the night air. O to be among the mighty, O to rise, to float, a holy migrant, through the encompassing firmament, O to be majestic swan or paradisal firebird.

As Lias rocked gently to and fro he lost himself in this forgetful ecstasy, the passage of time increased in speed like a gale around him. Suddenly, without any warning, the whole moon rushed lit into the sky, flinging the shining paint of her illumination over all the sheeted roofs of the village below. Lias's gaze swept up towards the salt glitter of the stars with a prayer for his exaltation, and then, the swingle-tree clasped tightly across his breast, he dived off the dead branches in the direction of Pwllybaw.

Tack-tick, tack-tick, tack-tick, tack-tick.

A lantern was hanging from a hook in the rafters of a small square barn. Beneath it, in the yellow light, Maddox the Minister, his chopped hair sticking out all round his head like untidy twigs, was sitting on an upturned wooden bucket, and unconscious on a thick bed of hay before him, under a covering of sacks, lay Lias Lewis. There were rings in the thick glass of the minister's spectacles, and from his rosy grin was thrust his outstanding china tooth with the corner chipped off. The clothes covering his plump body were all black, and his black hat and hymn-book lay on top of the clock in the basket beside him.

Tack-tick, tack-tick, tack-tick, tack-tick, went the little clock.

There was perfect silence in the barn but for breathing and clock-ticks, and then Rachie Pritchard, weeping as she knelt in the hay at the minister's feet, started to whisper in an empty-chapel voice. 'I was sitting down in the kitchen,' she whimpered, 'when I heard an awful scream – as though somebody had a knife at his throat. I went weak at the knees, but you will have to tie me up to stop me, Mr. Maddox, when somebody is wanting my help, so I put my foot to the earth . . .'

'Poetry, poetry, Rachie Pritchard,' said Lonso, cross and in low tones. 'I love her sort like a row of neckboils,' he growled to the minister. 'Bragging, always bragging, sir.' He was kneeling the other side of Lias from Rachie and in his hat and mangy overcoat he stank like a dead horse.

'You leave me alone, Lonso,' Rachie answered, using her flannel apron on her scooped-out face. 'I'm big enough to say my piece myself I am.'

'The cow is big enough to catch the rabbit,' he said, 'but nobody has ever seen her doing it. I was going for a walk in the moonlight, Mr. Maddox, sir,' he whispered, saluting his tied-on hat, 'when I heard that scream. I ran to the roots of the dead tree, and there I found the old man lying on the grass, groaning, with his leg folded in half under him and his ripped nightshirt wrapped round his head. I straightened him out and when Rachie came we got him in here. That's the middle and both ends of it, sir.'

He looked down. 'I must drink more of water,' he thought to himself. 'I must from now on. Bull's beer. Better for me than swilling bottle-ale. What if I was to die like Lias? Poor old dab,' he went on aloud, 'he looks to me, Mr. Maddox, as though he is knocking at the gate already.'

The gaunt and broken body of Lias lay outstretched between him and Rachie, dressed in his cap and rumpled nightshirt still. They had made the thick bed of hay under him and piled the sacks on his body to keep him warm. His leg was broken, his face torn, and tears were tearing out of his lids and along his cheeks, making for his red beard. While the three gazed down he bared his marble eyeballs. 'Pray for me, Mr. Maddox,' he whimpered feebly, 'pray for me. I have fallen, somebody is thumping me on the head, and I have cut the forehead of my knee.' Then closing his eyes again he clasped his hands upon his chest in readiness for prayer. They were thin and hairy, like a heavy crop of red hairs growing on bare bones.

'Yes, yes, I will pray for you, Lias,' the rosy minister answered. 'But tell us how it happened, Lias *bach*. Tell us how it happened.'

Tack-tick, tack-tick, tack-tick, tack-tick went the unseen clock as the old man rocked his head on the hay from side to side. But at last he opened his eyes again and spoke between the sobs.

'I fell out of the tree, Mr. Maddox,' he said, 'I fell out of the tree. In my pride I climbed up into the tree, and I had my fall. The goose-wings were powerless, my nightgown opened like an umbrella and tipped me upside down.' He groaned in remembrance, and hearing him Rachie sobbed to herself. 'I must chase the dust in that parlour tomorrow,' she muttered. 'What if I died like poor Lias?'

'Through a rip in my nightshirt,' Lias went on, 'I could see the blinding moon going bump, bump, bump, it was wheeled round the horizon on a broken-wheeled wheelbarrow. The next thing I knew was I opened my eyes on the dung-fork and the wooden rake there in the corner. I am black,' he cried aloud in anguish, 'I am black, black, and my pride has killed me. In my pride I sold the shorthorn and the golden chains, in my pride I abandoned the chapel of my fathers. In my pride I climbed the tree and prayed to be exalted above my neighbours. I shall never be forgiven, never, never, and I will now draw in my feet and die.'

He looked tearfully up at the minister. His swollen nose was black and soft, pulpy, like a lump of burning wool bubbling on the fire, and his scratched face had turned colour as though he were blushing green.

'No, no, Lias,' said the minister, 'repentance, repentance. Have you forgotten about repentance? God is good, remember.'

Rachie bent over the old man, weeping, her greasy bobbed hair hanging out of her head like leather laces. 'I must give up courting that Roberts the roadman too,' she was thinking. 'That's right, Lias,' she whispered, showing her unthinned crop of teeth in a crying grin. 'Raise your heart, raise your heart, boy. God is good, and the devil is not so bad.' She looked up at the minister for encouragement, with massive tears bulging out of her eyes. 'It breaks my heart to see him so low in his spirits, Mr. Maddox,' she said. 'I'll take this tight old cap off, for him to have his agony out in comfort.' As she sat on the hay her nose was scarlet with weeping, and her stockings were so fat she looked as though she had her feet on the wrong legs.

The old man groaned aloud as she bared the battered backbone running the length of his bald head, he cried out as though he were giving up the ghost.

'Every one of us needs forgiveness, Lias,' said the minister. 'Evil is the portion of all flesh, our iniquities and transgressions are manifold and numbered with the morning dew. You answer him too, Rachie. And you, Lonso. Why don't you answer him?'

'I don't know, Mr. Maddox, sir,' said Lonso, 'I don't know about forgiveness, sir, myself. But I won't argue with you, sir. I know my weight. I must give up that poaching,' he was thinking. 'No if-and-half about it, I must give it up altogether. What if I died like Lias Lewis?'

'Don't know indeed,' said Rachie, wiping her cheeks and glaring at Lonso. 'Ask him, Mr. Maddox, what he was doing out in the field tonight. Him going for a walk in the moonlight!'

Lonso glared back across at her in one-eyed resentment. 'You stop your blowing, Rachie,' he growled.

'Going to see his night-lines, that's what he was doing,' she said. 'He's always poaching. Going for a walk indeed! And he's swaying every day by dinner time when he can afford it. And what about that Elisabetta he's living with?' She folded her bare fat arms in defiance but she was so stout they would hardly meet over her bosom.

Lonso shook his stump in her face across the groaning old man. 'She's on my back every chance she gets. And only tonight I saw Roberts the roadman coming out of her garden. What did he call to see you for at nearly midnight, Rachie?' he jeered. 'Was it to show you the muscles of his back?'

Rachie coloured and tears began to pour out of her again. She buried her face in her hands, and as her man-shaped shoulders shook with weeping, the water sprang out between her fingers. For a moment there was silence in the room. Then the minister spoke quietly with a grin on his face.

'You see, Lias *bach*,' he said, 'we are all, every one of us, in need of forgiveness.'

Lonso glared and then he too dropped his head.

'Let us do what Lias asks us,' Maddox went on. 'Let us have a little prayer. Lonso, take your hat off, if you please.'

'I know my manners, Mr. Maddox, sir,' Lonso muttered, talking down into the neck of his shirt. 'I was raised on the breast of religion.' He pulled off the golden string round his hat, and his head was thick with fur like a thatched roof; it sloped up sharply from above his ears like the roof of a house with grass sides. Lonso, holding his hat under his arm-stump, Rachie, fingering her wet apron, and Maddox the Minister, the yellow lamplight like a halo in his hair, knelt down around the hay bed of Lias, and the minister prayed for grace and the forgiveness of sins.

'Blessed is forgiveness,' he said, 'blessed is the clean day-star of repentance after the night, and the dawn of innocence like the rising of the sun. Then to the sinless heart is the world renewed, the trees of the field shout and wave their green arms, the bright waters shout, branchy among the rocks of the river. The small flowers of the grasses burst open in the sun, and every moment a wave of perfume leaves the earth. The little roof-birds twitter in gladness, the blackbird sings a sweet song, he sings to his Maker a song of praise. Then is the contrite soul exalted, it floats over the dewy fields with the sun of forgiveness smoothing its wings. O to see the night slouch from our hearts and the dayspring of forgiveness shine upon us. Amen.'

Tack-tick, tack-tick, tack-tick went the clock, and Rachie and Lonso said their amens in silence. All three opened their eyes and looked down at Lias. He lay pale and quiet among them under the sacking, and the stillness of death was like a light upon him. Seeing that a big hole had opened in his beard where his mouth was, and the hairy bones of his hands were still clasped immovably upon his breast, the eyes of the three signalled to each other. The minister nodded and began to get up off his knees.

But suddenly the sacks fell away from Lias as he sat up on the hay. 'Amen!' he shouted. 'Hallelujah! How beautiful, how beautiful! My heart is hot with forgiveness, and in a soft place, it is like putting the frozen hand under the sitting hen. And for why? At last I am exalted, I am exalted, but in forgiveness, in my forgiveness I shall lead Rachie and Lonso like Israel to repentance.'

His blazing, colourless eyes flashed from one to the other, and the two fell back in terror before the prophetic flashings of his beard.

'Rachie,' he cried, pointing a bony hand at her, 'you put the wool on the pins and begin by forgiving Lonso. And you, Lonso, you take your claws out of Rachie's feathers. You must promise me, Lonso, before I go, you must promise me, Rachie, that you will repent. Promise me and I repose, I am refreshed, I die in peace. Promise me and I am forgiven, on the flat of my deathbed I am forgiven for my pride.'

Rachie looked up frightened at the minister, her tears pumping down her cheeks. 'Hallelujah,' she sobbed, broken-hearted. 'Yes, Lias, I know what you mean. I will go back to Matthew tomorrow.'

There was silence as a shower of drops hot as candle-grease fell on her bare arm. Then the bushy fire of the beard swung to the other side. 'Lonso!' Lias shouted.

'Amen,' said Lonso hurriedly, his eye bulging and a look of terror on his hairy face. 'Amen,' he gulped. 'Yes, all right, Lias, I will marry Elisabetta, Lias. I will marry Elisabetta in Ramah, Mr. Maddox, sir, for ever and ever, amen and amen.'

Lias smiled, drew his bushy brows down over his eyes and fell back, still, upon the hay.

'He is dead,' Rachie and Lonso gasped together.

The minister got up and opened the half-door of the barn to the night. As the sweet air entered, the hidden clock broke out into its delicate little tune, and the clouds, dividing outside in the darkness, showed three bright stars in a row.

Rhamant Drist

❧

The moon crossed the windy sky and the large clouds, meeting her, burst out into black smoke at her touch. On the earth below everything was under the deep snowfall. The hill, curving out from below its black cap of pine forest, was cut into gleaming fields of white velvet, and in the village all the houses wore the heavy fall of whiteness.

A child came toiling down the slope from the forest towards the village. His hair was beaten about his face and although he towed nothing behind him he bent forward into the wind as though he were roped to a heavy load. The cottage he saw before him was enchanting in the moonlight. Wild smoke twisted out of its chimney. The thatched roofs between the lattice windows came half-way down the walls, like the flaps of a cap pulled over the ears for warmth, and the straw was thatched again with a thicker thatch of snow. It had a low garden wall in front on which rested a snowy coping smooth as porcelain and each gatepost was surmounted by a little loaf of snow.

But loveliest of all, standing among the shrubs threshing in the wind, was a new snowman. His hat was a flowerpot, his eyes were two corks and he had a broken side-comb for teeth. He smoked a pipe made out of a sliced potato with a skewer stuck into it. Around his neck the children had tied a check duster for a scarf and there was an upright row of cinders intended for buttons down the front of his white overcoat. He had no feet and his hands were in his coat pockets so that he could hold the leg of the cane-brush under his arm.

The child stopped crying, his fears vanished as he gazed at the entrancing figure bright in the moonlit garden. He climbed over the low wall and as he did so he heard the laughter of the children sounding from the cottage. He crept through the shrubs until he came to the casement window, its sill thickly cushioned with the snowfall. The curtain was not closed and through the diamond panes he could see into the brightly-lighted room.

There the big fire pushed its bright horns up into the chimney and the ceiling was festooned with many paper chains and bells of coloured glass. Around the sparkling table some boys and girls were eating a little feast, laughing and talking to one another. The child longed to join them, he was filled with joy that this was the house at which he was to claim admittance. He was about to tap at the panes when he saw the mother open the door of the room and enter it smiling; she took out all the lamps and candles from the table and left the room in darkness so that all the children were rosy in the glow of the firelight. When she came in again she was carrying a large cake decorated with candles, a ring of slender little candles was burning round the edge, some rose-pink, some pale blue and some primrose yellow, each one standing in a little rosette of coloured sugar. The children, waiting in the warm gloom, cried out loud with delight when they saw the cake and the circle of bright and pure flames. 'If you please, if you please,' they began chanting, holding out their plates towards the mother.

The child no longer thought of drumming upon the window panes. Silently opening the front door he entered the cottage and sat down at the table. The other children talked to him excitedly in the candlelight as though he had been present from the beginning. He was expectant and enchanted, his heart glowed with happiness at their welcome.

Then, as the mother and her yellow-haired girl were preparing to cut the cake, bangs were heard at the door of the room and then a loud voice cursing. All the children became silent at once, they were pale and their eyes large with alarm. The mother, no longer smiling, turned from the table. There was another outburst of thundering at the door and it was pushed roughly open so that the paper festoons hissed loudly and the small pointed flames on the cake candles leaned back in a ring, tugging together at their little wicks, becoming clear and intense.

The child could see dimly at the door an evil-faced man standing with a lantern in his hand. He was short and heavily-built, wearing breeches and gaiters and a brass-buttoned coat. He had a large shining head like a new chestnut, it seemed round as a cannon-ball, too heavy to be moved in its cruelty. There was a patch over one of his eyes and his black teeth were twisted between his great lips. Under his arm he carried a heavy gun.

The little girl clung to her mother as the man trod angrily into the room. He clattered the lantern down on the table among the tea-things and stared around him. There was silence. Then baring his black tusks at the woman he pointed round fiercely at the children.

'Get them out,' he shouted, in a voice hoarse with rage. 'Get out, get out, all of you,' he screamed at the children, 'get out I tell you!'

He lifted his gun and brought the butt down with curses again and again on the large cake, smashing the sugar and filling the air with the reek of put-out candles. The children screamed and fled towards the door. The heart of the child was filled with protest. He could see the happiness of the boys and girls ended, he cried in anguish against it and jumped up to hold back the gun of the destroyer. The man crashed him with a sweep of his arm to the floor, he shook off the mother, slanted his heavy gun at the child and took aim. But before he could fire the nimble child had opened the casement window and was once more out in the night. As he dived through the bushes he saw that the snowman had been pushed over and smashed, it lay in broken pieces on the trampled garden.

He regained the road and trudged onward through the darkness. He sobbed with rage and disappointment. Then in his misery a strange sensation began to take possession of him; he felt as though the days of his childhood and their bitterness were over and that what lay before him was a different grief. He brushed away his last tear, clinging like a spark to his cheek in the moonlight.

Coming suddenly out of the dark cutting along which he had borne his misery, the lover halted and gazed down in wonder at the radiance of the vast plain before him. The big wind had died. The moon no longer hastened across a sky blue with cold, but stood mellow and assured, pouring out unstarched splendour over the world. The scattered stars trembled like a vast nursery of silver blooms. A broad river moved slowly through the snow, curving among the meadows, and its black waters, caught in a dragnet of silver radiance, glittered. At the foot of a distant hill covered with a forest of dark firs stood a castle, the dark curves of its towers whitened and its walls flecked with the great plumy snowfall.

As he gazed in silent gladness at the radiance and tranquillity of the scene at his feet, his heart was soothed and momentarily pacified. Then he heard a pounding sound in the forest close at hand. Poom-poom-poom, poom-poom-poom, on it came, and then out of the black wood broke a line of horsemen bearing torches; they swept out on to the clear slope of the moonlit hill and rode down at a fierce gallop in the direction of the castle, throwing up the snow in showers behind them. The lover saw them galloping away into the distance and plunging into the glittering river, where they flung their torches wildly into the current. Then, when they had reached the thickets on the further bank, snatches of a chorus reached him faintly, and the abrupted note of a horn, as they disappeared among the shadows of the castle. The lover's heart was troubled to its roots, stirred by the pride and glory of what he had seen. The leading rider, the one upon the large black stallion, plunging masterful through the breakers of his own breathing, had been a woman, her hair burning out behind her in a long blaze from her head.

When he looked at the sky again he could see a star, large and jewel-like, standing motionless above the flag of the castle.

The room of the castle in which he sat was lighted with two crystal chandeliers. It was an oval room, ornate and gilded, furnished with gold and crimson chairs of plush, and decorated settees. A crimson carpet covered the floor, and on the walls, worked with vivid coats of arms, were hangings of crimson velvet. Armfuls of fresh blond roses, relieved with green fronds, filled the porphyry jars on their pedestals. Several large mirrors, with bunches of candles branching from their gilded frames, were fixed to the walls, giving on every side great depth and brightness. A fire with a cat before it burned brightly in a white fireplace of chiselled roses.

A beautiful woman leaned forward to one of the gilded mirrors in the wall, her head on one side and both her jewelled hands fingering the lobe of an ear. The lover rose from his seat and she, seeing his reflection, his straight black brows and small pointed beard, smiled at him with moistened lips and turned towards the room. A faint blush was burning in the pallor of her cheeks.

She was wearing a white satin gown with a full sequined skirt and a bodice from the foam of which rose her gleaming shoulders. Bracelets sparkled at her wrists; in her ears were jewels and the base of her throat was ablaze with a deep collar of diamonds. As she stood facing the lover, the brightness from the hanging lights fell around her pale face and upon her gleaming hair, a flame mastered now into the formality of plait and curl. The edges of her full red lips were sharp, they looked as though they had burst apart with the ripeness of her scarlet mouth. From her body, from the movements of her dress, came off the cool fragrance of lilies.

She held out her hand to him and he led her, humming to herself, over the dumb carpet to her large black piano. Here she sat and began to sing softly, accompanying herself upon the instrument. The lover sat beside her, watching with enchantment the movement of her glittering lips, watching the planes of overhead brilliance falling about her head and shoulders, the light burning upon her flamy hair, smoothing a bright hand over the waterfall of fire. There was a thundering under his throat, his hair stirred involuntarily and his flesh seemed chilled to ice at her beauty and the incommunicable loveliness of her singing.

The black cat, ignoring the lovers, sat calmly before the fire licking his front paw, holding it up rigid to his red tongue and going over it with the delicacy and absorption of a craftsman.

Suddenly the fire slipped sideways and every coal put up its flag of flame. The woman, seeing the cat scurrying out of sight, left her singing and came over to mend it. She bent, coughed uncertainly and straightened herself, with the back of her hand to her mouth. She looked into the mirror and sobbed in alarm. At the same moment a hound somewhere in the castle began to bay loudly as though in terror, tearing in anguish at his heavy chain.

The lover sprang from his chair towards the woman. From the corner of her mouth poured a vivid line of scarlet. Her hand was covered with a glove of blood and the rosy drops were spread out over the front of her gown. He swung her off her feet and bore her still coughing to the settee. Here, muttering and pleading like one demented, he tried with his handkerchief to stop the blood oozing unstanched from her mouth, but he could not. The woman said no word and in a short time her long-lashed lids carried a darkness down her eyes; but even in her swoon her coughing continued and at every cough the bright red frothy flow increased. The blood was upon her breast, it had patterned the corsage of her gown with a scarlet lace. It was upon everything that had been touched, upon silk and carpet, upon her body and upon the hair and flesh of her lover.

Presently the scarlet hand with which, even during unconsciousness, she had fiercely gripped his sleeve, relaxed, and the long bangled arm fell away. The lover rose from his knees and stared down in stupefaction; with the perfume of her rising into the air about him a sensation of protest and unbelief took possession of him. To pass for ever, good and beautiful, under the dark lid of the centuries. But there were cries outside the room, the great ban-dog could be heard upright against the door howling in frenzy and beating and scratching on the panels with his paws. The lover bent down again, buried his hands up to his wrists in the collapsed flame of her hair and kissed again and again the bleeding mouth. Then, ignoring the clamour at the door, he made his way out through the curtains on to the snow-covered lawn.

The soldier went laboriously in the snow along the edge of the seacliff. His heart felt old and numb, so shrieked at, scorched, gashed and thundered upon that it seemed incapable again of being stirred to protest or compassion. He thought of his childhood, how he had defied the stroke of the armed destroyer, of his manhood when one glimpse of the flying riders could warm his heart like wine. Now he was old and wasted, haunted with memories, recalling a child kissing the cold cheek of a snowman, recalling a radiant face, spared, unlike his own, the elaborate and hideous make-up of grief.

Over the land lay a chill and pallid mist. Wearily the moon before him bleared and made downwards for the sea.

From the distance came the hollow sound of firing, as though muffled blows were falling on the soft outside surface of the night. Then there was silence, except for the faint splash of the waves below him.

He went on in the direction of the long lonely headland thrusting a great paw out into the misty sea. Then in the narrow pathway he halted. Approaching him over the crest of a rise he saw the light of a lantern. He had no trust in human-kind and his impulse had become always one of avoidance. There, at the side of the path, grew a wind-dwarfed thicket caked with snow and under this he huddled his bones for safety.

Presently nine or ten men came wearily out of the mist, following one another. They also were soldiers, each one dressed in a dark tattered uniform, some with rifles slung over their shoulders. The leader carried a lantern and his head and face were heavily bandaged. The lantern had one pane of red glass, it hung near his rag-bound feet, casting a jerked and distorted disc of light upon the snow. The soldiers approached the twisted bush in a profound hush, each one followed the steps of his comrade, absorbed in his own wretchedness, grave, quiet, moving through the moonlight as though under some enchantment of silence. Only one, coming at a little distance behind the others, uttered any sound. He, with the face of a schoolboy, limped on his way, sobbing bitterly to himself. Then, as the tattered and dejected figures were opposite the bush, a large dark bird loomed behind them out of the mist, he came on beset at first by a dreadful silence, but when he was above them he swooped down on rigid wings, he let out screech after screech of fury and malevolence; he traversed their file from end to end, menacing their heads with his massive wings and releasing upon them the shrieks of an insane hatred. The soldiers scarcely looked up, they went on in dejection and weariness, maintaining their silence, and presently even the light of their lantern was hidden in the mist.

The soldier rose and went on in the direction from which the file had come. A silver-haired star rested over the point of the headland.

Around the cabin a grove of dead pines rose into the mist, black and picked bare as fishbones. The moon, almost at the point of setting in the sea, looked distorted through the dividing vapours. The soldier knelt in the snow and in his hands were gripped two square iron bars set in a window frame. He had been in time to see an old man lift up his heavy burden from where it lay at the foot of the outside wall of the house, and to see him bear indoors, swaying under its weight, the dead body of his son.

The underground room into which the soldier peered was dim and bare as a cavern. It was lit by a single candle. Fishing nets hung drying from the rafters like enormous cobwebs. A clock with a motionless pendulum was fastened to the dark wall. A few cinders glowed on the hearthstone. In the middle of the cellar stood a table upon which was stretched the naked body of the young man. On this table the solitary candle burned, standing in its grease beside the head of the corpse, and casting its light upon the wild features.

This was a house into which he must gain admittance. As he watched he saw the old man coming very slowly into the cellar, his feet in heavy sea-boots dragging over the bare flags. He placed a large wooden bucket on a chair beside the table and poured water into it from an earthenware stane. He was a very old man, his black jersey rolled up to his elbows showing sun-blackened arms. On his head was a small black knitted skullcap and his white hair came out in a fringe from under it. In his ears were golden ear-rings. The skin of his wrinkled face also, like his arms, was burnt almost black, and against it his hair and his close beard gleamed silvery as cotton-grass in the candle-light.

For a time he stared in silence at the dead body of his son stretched on the table before him. He placed his palms to his cheeks and rocked his head slowly from side to side in weariness. The body was pitiful, black and emaciated, the belly scooped out and the curved bars of the ribs rising up from the table like a cage with the skin pulled tightly over them. The head was shaggy and unkempt, thickly bearded, the black animal-like hair furry on the neck and growing down over the brows into the eyes. The chest was torn with a row of bullet wounds and down the thigh, from hip to knee, a wound divided the flesh almost to the bone. Round the wrist nearest to the window was a broad strap of brass and a few links of a snapped-off chain attached to it hung over the edge of the table.

The father began to wash the body in the candle-light. He did not weep. As he bent over in absorption and gently sponged the blood away from breast and limbs, his lips seemed to be making a crooning sound. From head to foot he went over the glistening flesh, cleansing and swilling away the patches and cakings of blood, until the body was clean and dry; and then, dashing water upon the hair, he divided it with his fingers, taking it back from the eyes and smoothing it into order.

The moon sank and darkness lay over the snow-covered earth. Birds in a bare-headed birch beside the house began to grieve. The cheeks of the soldier had turned to water at the vision of the old man and his shot son but in his heart at the same time he found a strange emotion stirring. He recognized this stirring as hope.

The Golden Pony

ॐ

For the moment the child was at peace and in another world and the terrors of the island were forgotten.

The sun shone warm through the thick glass of the lattice window into the small schoolroom where the heads of the children were bowed over their work. The only sound was the dry creak of the teacher's chair. Then a bluebottle on the window diamonds let go his hold and tumbled droning off the panes about the shabby room. The teacher himself, a hot-skinned man with hob-nailed boots and hair like ginger wool, was drowsing in the airless heat with his chair tilted back and his huge hands locked across his belly. He would sometimes, when he had finished writing with them, lay down his things on the front desk where Rhodri sat, and now in the groove were a fresh stick of white chalk and a new red-ink pen, the wooden holder varnished brown.

Rhodri glanced round the desks. The dozen boys and girls who composed the school wrote round him in silence. He pushed the teacher's piece of chalk forward in the groove, so that the broader part, the white disc of its base, approached the domed end of the shining penholder. The sun poured powerfully on to the desk and the chalk emitted in its radiance a strong reflection, a powerful glow of white light beamed out of the flat disc and illuminated the rounded end of the varnished holder. As the child slowly withdrew the chalk back along the groove the shine on the pen was dimmed and as he slid it forward again the varnish lit up and glowed white in the beam of the oncoming radiance. Rhodri continued to slide the white stick slowly to and fro in grave ecstasy.

The sight called up for him the world which he inhabited with the golden pony, and his heart glowed. Whenever he was completely absorbed, whenever his eyes, his ears or his heart were filled and satisfied, he seemed to have fallen beneath the spell of that gentle golden-coated creature to whose world he attributed all loveliness and joy.

He meant to look up to see if the teacher was still drowsing but a thread of gossamer drifting out of the gloom of the schoolroom corner caught his eye; slowly it writhed from the shadows into the bright sunlight and suddenly hung burning there brilliant as a firework before floating out into the dimness again.

The edges of Rhodri's exercise book seemed hairy in the clear sunlight as a white cat. He picked up the teacher's pen. The nib was still
wet with red ink. He placed it vertically on its point right dead centre
of the dazzling clean page of his exercise book. There it cast a long
clear shadow across the bright blue lines of the page; and when he
tilted it towards him the shadow lengthened, it seemed to become
more slender and elegant, the nib tapering into a point of the greatest
fineness and delicacy. And the red ink in the slit glowed, both in the
nib and in the firm image of its shadow, it burned with a wet ruby
brilliance like a bead of scarlet wine. Rhodri was oblivious of
everything. Only the pen and its shadow on the dazzling page existed
for him, they absorbed his whole being, and the golden naked horse
moved round his mind in a glowing ring, casting upon it the radiance
of its strange loveliness.

To reassure himself that the varnish of the new pen tasted bitter as
his own usually did he placed the end of the holder between his teeth
and gently bit it. Small scales of varnish fell with a sharp taste on to his
tongue and he wiped them away with the back of his hand. Then he
erected the pen again on its nib and continued to slope it this way and
that, with his index finger firm on the domed end, watching with
complete absorption the altering shape and intensity of the shadow
and the jewel-like brilliance of the scarlet bead glowing on the sunlit
paper.

And then he stopped. A shadow had fallen on his desk, completely
darkening his sunny exercise book. He lifted his eyes, and close before
them was the guttered belly of the hot-faced teacher, a bone button
and a thick powdering of chalk in every groove of his waistcoat. The
other children must all have been watching Rhodri because when he
raised up his head and saw the teacher glaring down at him they all
began to laugh.

'Leave things alone,' shouted the teacher in his harsh voice, and
Rhodri felt a stinging blow fall on the side of his head.

The child had come to live in the island at the death of his parents. His
grannie had fetched him from the mainland and they had crossed the
sea in stormy weather. As they came down the path to the beach, his
heart was heavy, he could not keep his tears back with loneliness and
foreboding. His grannie walked beside him in her torn and shabby
cloak muttering to herself. Whenever she kicked against a stick on the
path she picked it up and put it under her cloak. The child had never
seen her before. She had a wild brown face and her hair was in

disorder. Her large flat eyes were staring and pale, they were fixed wide open and silverish in the darkness of her face. She said nothing to the child but muttered endlessly as she trod in sightless absorption along the path.

The air was heavy around them and utterly still, and the clouds over the whole sky had turned smoky with thunder. Above the sea's horizon a great raw patch was spread as though the outer skin of the heavens had been removed and the angry under-flesh laid bare, crimson, the sombre blood heavy behind it. Then a tree shivered and the sudden cold wind raised a fin of dust along the path. The old woman's cloak burst open. The cold lead-like rain began to fall, but she paid no heed to it. The child could see the ferryboat before them, low in the water, loaded down with people returning from the mainland. The two crossed the pebbles and found room in the stern. The people sat round them in silence and dejection expecting the storm, their dogs and their baskets at their feet.

In the gusty rain the whole air turned cold and dark as nightfall. Sea-birds flashed sideways through the wind. The boatman was drunk and his face hideous with a purple disease. He wore black oilskins and cursed the people as he pushed the heavy boat off the pebbles. The rain came in oblique gusts as though shooting out sideways from slits in the sky. The island lay smouldering in the distance, charred and sombre in the darkness, like a heaped fire gone out on the sea. Once the boat was out of the shelter of the land, the rain fell steadily upon it. The mast growled. The brown sail was out over the water and the rain poured off it into the sea. The sodden ropes, becoming taut, surrounded themselves with a mist of fine spray.

Out in the smoky channel the boat began to rise and fall, she shuddered from end to end as the waves exploded under her and the sea-wool boiled up on to the surface. The child, cold and wet, looked up in apprehension at his grandmother. She was heedless of the storm, she stared straight in front of her, her eyes hard and white and overlaid with an impenetrable glaze like mirrors. She muttered endlessly to herself. Her bonnet hung by its ribbon around her neck and her stiff disordered hair was being plastered down on to her head by the rain.

The people looked at one another in fear. They no longer tried to shield themselves from the pelting rain and their sodden clothes shone like black silk. They were silent. Some covered their faces with their wet hands. The dogs shivered and whimpered and were not reproved. Suddenly the boat banked steeply on its side as though it would turn over, and the sea smoked over it. Several voices cried out in terror. Rhodri's grandmother stopped muttering and looked about her. She left her seat. She knelt down in the water at the bottom of the boat and began a wild prayer. The boatman cursed her and pointed through the rain to the sea-plastered crags of the island. The child trembled with misery and fear. The woman sitting on the other side of him lifted her cloak and put it over him, covering his head. There, in the utter darkness, he could smell the sweat and camphor of her hard body. He could hear the quarrel above the storm, his grannie's voice screaming and the boatman shouting in reply. The boat plunged and shuddered and from time to time he heard a blow fall upon the taut cloak in a splashing thud as a wave came over the side. He drowsed. He could not remember landing. The next morning he woke up in his grannie's house.

A dog was yelling in unremitted agony. The child opened his eyes and heard some creature scampering rat-like across the hot roof sloping close above his head. Instantly he remembered and looked about in confusion. The grimy whitewashed bedroom was bare but filled up with sunlight. The window was a latched square of cobwebbed glass. He thought with a heavy heart of the meeting with his grandmother and the terrible crossing of the water. Hurriedly he got up from bed and looked out of the window. His eyes were on a level with a large vegetable garden where everything was green and glittering like tin in the sun. The dog was not to be seen but the cries continued in a high-pitched voice, the creature yelled hysterically and then sank into a series of agonized whimperings. The child, in deep distress, went down into the kitchen.

There it was dim and stifling, because a large piece of brown paper had been pinned over the window to keep the sun off the fire. He could not see his grannie. The room was bare but a great chained kettle hung boiling over the fire. His clothes were drying on a chair-back. He opened the kitchen door and looked out into the yard. The crying at once redoubled in intensity and he heard a drumming noise and the sound of a chain being rattled. The yard was a square of soft mud and dung with decaying outhouses surrounding it. In one corner was a barrow-load of dung overgrown with shoots of new grass. Near the kitchen door a great heap of his grannie's twigs leaned against a broken fragment of brickwork. He dressed.

It was an agony like a tearing of the flesh to hear the crying mount up again to a fresh climax of howls and yells. Soon it was plain the clamour came from an old outhouse on the far side of the yard, a broken-backed pigsty with a roof under heavy dock and feverfew. The door shook as it was thumped from the inside and the chain rattled.

An old man trudged into the yard at a stoop leading a hulking ginger horse. He was wearing corduroy trousers and a ragged black jacket. An old hat was pulled down over his eyes. The mare had been working in traces and her chains jingled as she placed her great hairy hooves down in the mud. The dog heard the jingling and his crying increased in anguish. The child closed his eyes, he felt utterly engulfed, quite overborne and annihilated.

When he looked again, the old man had begun to pile the mare's harness on the bank. The child could see the sweat dark on her naked coat the same shape as the harness. The old man gave no sign that he heard the dog. Slowly he leaned one hand against the mare's flank and with the other began to milk her. As he plucked beneath her a rigid stream of warm milk fell with a splashing sound upon the mud. The child felt a deep stirring of his bowels. The anguish of the dog's crying was unheard as the white milk flowed over the mud and dung of the yard. In a moment the old man gave up and crossed to unbolt the stable. His movements had the clumsy ungainliness of an aged animal. The door of the pigsty rattled under its battering as he trudged past, but he did not turn his head.

Out of the stable a beautiful golden foal bounded into the sunlight. The child's eyes opened with wonder and delight at the sight of her. She was the most beautiful thing he had ever seen and she was alive, she was moving and sunlit, and in his presence. Her coat was a pale limpid golden, a flamy honey-colour that seemed to flash off its fluid brilliance into the sunlight as she moved. Her mane and tail were already long and plentiful, to him they were as white as snow, but her muzzle had the dull smoky look of dark velvet. Her coming was a gap of ecstasy and pure silence. She trotted uncertainly into the middle of the yard, shying and prancing on her beautiful long legs, bewildered by the unsheltered brightness of the world. Then with a whinny she made for the great mare standing motionless and indifferent beside the bank and began to take suck. The child stared in blissful fascination. The marvel of the golden foal filled his heart, his delight ran through him like some great shaking draughts of ecstasy. Everything around him, while he gazed, fell under a spell of unassailable silence.

The old man, long-armed and high-shouldered, turned his back on the horses. Some cinders had been thrown down on the mud to form a path and he advanced over them with a stiff tread towards the house. His hoarse breath came with difficulty. He walked head down with a great hump-backed stoop, so that he was almost at the doorstep before he saw the child. Slowly he raised his eyes and Rhodri felt a sharp stab of anguish at the sight of them. They were dark as jet but the long lashes surrounding them were almost white, they were very thick and long, as dense as the hair of an animal, like a fringe of long yellow fur surrounding the edges of the dark lids. The face was rugged and bony, but the mouth hung open, the thick flesh of the lips seemed too slack and shapeless to cover up the hideous teeth. The old man said nothing, he stood and blinked at the child in morose suspicion, his great bony shoulders rising and falling as he gulped breath hoarsely through his wet mouth. Because of his stoop, the shining collar of his coat went out in a wide loop behind his neck and the sun shone on it in a half circle. He took off his hat and placed it on the sill. His long brown teeth showed and the broad back of his nose became loaded with a mass of wrinkles as he frowned into the dazzling sunlight. The child noticed the top of his head was hairless and not brown like his face, the dark skin ended abruptly where his hat had been and the pale scalp was thickly covered with beads of sweat. He lifted up his large bony hands and placed them with a clumsy action like a cap on the crown of his head. He held them there for a moment gasping for breath. Then he moved them slowly down over his soaking skin. The drench of sweat was squeezed forward along his scalp, it ran off his head before his hands and poured down over his face.

The child stared at him with the silent regard of complete fascination. Clogs clattered across the kitchen flags behind him and he could see his grandmother in the dimness beckoning with sud-gloved hands. Her stiff hair was wild and her eyes in that gloom seemed to have become completely sightless and transparent. The child went in towards her with fear. Behind him the explosive yelling of the dog broke out with unabated frenzy.

Soon the old man followed, bringing mud and dung into the kitchen. He sat down as though with exhaustion at the table. When he had replaced his sweat-sodden hat, he began to eat in stolid silence. His hands were large and stiff, like great rigid claws falling upon his food. The child, seated opposite him, tried to eat his own breakfast, but he could not. He was in fear, his soul filled with utter confusion and bewilderment. He saw the old man breathing heavily and turning his food round in his slack mouth; he saw the beautiful foal springing golden into the sunlit yard; and he heard the incessant yelling of the chained-up dog. He began to pray in silence that the agony might be remitted.

'Mamgu,' he said at last, looking round at his grandmother, 'Mamgu, why is the dog crying all the time?'

She came towards him with a look of puzzlement in her eyes. 'Crying?' she repeated, and turned to face the old man. She mumbled something which the child failed to catch. The old man shook his head slowly and resumed his chewing. The dog howled throughout the meal, and the chain rattled with agonizing repetition.

When he had finished, the old man got up and went out without speaking, a brown scum thick around his mouth. Rhodri said, 'Mamgu, is he my grandfather?'

She looked at him again in wide-eyed puzzlement. Then she nodded her head.

The child's cave, although it overlooked the sea, was not one of rock. It was a hollow under a grove of elders and, wearing only his ragged trousers, he sat at the mouth of it looking out over the water. The dog lay down panting at his feet and the golden pony, swishing her tail, cropped the green turf of the slope. The afternoon was still and silent, every leaf and blade of grass stood out brilliant and petrified in the intense heat. On an unsheltered rock cropping out of the turf the sun had kindled its uncoloured bonfire. The blue of the sky was flawless, it stretched out tranquil and unsoiled to the horizon and there was not a white cloud in it to cast the stain of a shadow upon the sea. From time to time, as the child watched, the breeze beat the water gently with ferns. At the foot of the slope, where the hill went into the sea in dark crags, the snowy gulls floated, they heaved gently upon a sea-swell that washed the black rocks in the milk of an endless caressing. The child had been bathing; before the tide was full he had ridden the golden pony naked along the lonely beach, splashing in the shallows of the sea.

The child came to his cave for safety and solitude. Every day now he was with the beautiful pony. At first he would stand by her when she was having suck and when she had finished she would come to him with milk on her mouth, blinking the dark globes of her eyes, black and lustrous. He was a little timid of her but she was gentle and gay and he soon learned not to fear her. He would put out his hand and stroke the soft sooty plush of her unquiet muzzle. When she had been weaned and placed in a field by herself, he used to go to the gate, before school and after, to speak to her. Directly she saw him she would throw up her head, point out her rigid ears and trot towards him with breeze-borne mane and outfloating tail. It was bliss to see her move rapidly over the grass with the grace of a great golden bird and the radiance of sunlight. She became more beautiful. Soon all the rough tufts of foal-fur had disappeared even from her long slender legs. Her white mane thickened, her creamy tail almost reached the ground. Her coat assumed a polish like brushed and smoothed silk, it was a golden orange colour, but in some lights paler, almost honey-yellow, or caramel, and then sometimes again the rich bronzy lustre of old gold.

Often when he came to the gate she was waiting for him, standing with her glowing flank against the bars. Then he would speak gently to her and give her sugar or an apple, and sit astride her back. Round and round the field they went, she placing down the pure white horn of her unshod hooves delicately upon the grass and tossing her dense and snowy mane off her neck at every step; he speaking gently to her her own praises, bending forwards to pat her neck with his hand beneath her mane. Her beauty and gentleness filled his imagination day and night. He loved the brown-eyed spaniel, but the mare was like a great flame of delight flaring up in the centre of his being. In his cave he crossed seas with her, climbed mountains, rode triumphantly through fallen cities. She accompanied him everywhere on the island. She dispelled the hauntings of the eyes, the animal stare of his long-lashed grandfather and the insane and transparent eyes of his grandmother.

One night the child had climbed out of his bedroom window into the moonlit garden. He found the dog, a little black spaniel, on a short chain in the ruined pigsty crying pitifully to himself. The whole floor was under an oozing mass of pigs' dung. He held the dog against his body to comfort him and the little creature leaned up against him, shivering and whimpering softly. His nose on the boy's cheek was cold and moist, like the touch of a snail. In a few moments he began gently to lick the child's face with his rough tongue. Every time Rhodri moved, the dog seemed to cling to him and his crying began again, but now it was only soft and plaintive. The child unfastened the chain and took the dog into his bedroom. They both slept. The next morning he tossed the chain into the nettles. Later he raked out all the stale dung off the floor of the pigsty, and was sick. His grannie came and watched him at work, she stood at the door of the kitchen, her great flat eyes fixed immovably upon him, but she said nothing.

Rhodri's grandfather spoke seldom and never to him. The island was rocky and he laboured in silence. Once, on the little beach below the farm, the child sat down and began building a model in sand. It was large and elaborate, part temple, part fortress, part palace, with courts, arches, and towers, all ornamented with cockle-shells and glittering chips of glass-like quartz. The weather was sunny and he worked for several hours with the spaniel panting beside him. He had built it beyond the reach of the tide, so that he could return to it. At last, when he looked up, he could see the sun was lying down close to the water, its great red eye glaring across the flat sands, and he knew he would not be able to complete his work until the next day. As he moved back to admire the square-built walls, and the pebble-studded windows, he saw his grandfather driving the cart across the sands. The hulking mare was in the shafts and she came out of the sunset at a smart trot. The old man was standing up stooping, his hat over his eyes, but Rhodri could feel he was looking at him. The great horse approached at a good pace, her hooves clacking and her harness jingling. His grandfather drove straight on towards him. The mare went heedless over the sand-building and kicked it to pieces. The child sat down and hung his head. His grandfather had not turned to look after him. The cart rolled on. The spaniel, seeing the child with his head bowed in misery, came up and began to lick his face; in his eagerness to bring comfort, he destroyed all that was left of the model.

The child's cave faced the sea. It was on the steep and barren side of the island where no one lived. He spent much of his time near it because the boys who persecuted him would never pursue him to this distance. To the cave he came to escape from his sense of solitariness and his unceasing desire to escape from the cruelty of the island. Here he forgot his fear of the brutal schoolmaster, and of the boys who hated him; here he was not haunted by the watchfulness of his grandfather and his grandmother's muttering and her screaming in the night. It was to the cave he came to eat the fruits he found on the island, the bilberries and the little wild strawberries and once or twice when he had fallen into the sea he had lit a fire there to dry his clothes. But he would not light a fire in it now. A robin had built a nest in the overhead boughs and her little brood had already hatched.

From time to time a swallow cut over the grass, capering around the heels of the grazing pony. The pony's coat was honey-yellow, and where the light fell upon her back it shone like a saddle of pure silver. She had been rolling and upon her shoulder was a pale grass-stain, like a green patch of the most delicate verdigris. With her head drooped forward on her arched-out neck, a thick lock of mane hung between her ears on to her brow the colour of the froth of meadowsweet. Her muzzle had a dusty look as though it had been thrust into dark pollen. Her wavy tail broadened out and then tapered irregularly to a point that almost touched the grass. The boy did everything for her now. One day he would ride her through the world and everyone would recognize her beauty. The crowds in the streets would see him astride her with his legs along her golden flanks and as she trotted by they would acclaim the fluttering of her mane, and the elegant alighting of her ivory hooves, and the soft swansdown floating of her tail. She had begun to cast her glow and enchantment upon everything that existed with her in his imagination, and objects and sensations were recreated for him in her image. When he opened his eyes in his bedroom, the morning was a great horse, green and naked, ravaging the world outside his window. Watching the snow alighting gracefully, flake by flake, curving in the wind towards him over the hedge, he saw the beautiful stepping of white ceremonial hooves, advancing with delicacy out of the weather. And each day he saw in her more clearly the symbol of his escape.

In the evening the weather became chilly. A gull, perching on a rock near by, recalled him with the screeches of the splayed nib of her beak. Inside the cave the little robins opened their beaks as he paid them his final visit. He watched the pony gracefully curving her front leg forward on the slope and rubbing her muzzle against the inside of it. He whistled and her head came up and her ears stood erect. Then he made for the house with the dog and the golden pony following him.

After school the child went to look at the nest. He had known of it from the beginning, when it was merely twigs and a bowl of smooth mud, like a large acorn-cup. He had seen the six warm-hued eggs laid in it and he had visited the young ones almost every day to watch them grow. Soon they would be fledged. On the way he noticed that three of the boys who persecuted him were coming at a distance behind him. The boys had one day chased the golden pony to annoy him by making her sweat. They cornered her in the field and as she broke out one of them ran behind her clutching at her tail. She cast up her hooves and at one kick the boy's arm snapped like a candle. Since then they had attacked him constantly.

To throw the boys off his track he hurried down the path leading towards the bay. In a little he glanced behind again and he found he was no longer being followed, so he turned up the cliff in the direction of the cave. He wondered if the little robins would have learnt to fly. They completely filled up the nest now, they seemed to repose quite motionless on top of one another, forming a dome of smoky-coloured fluff enriched with a gleam of jewel-like eyes and with six yellow mouths that opened wide whenever he approached.

Rhodri stooped and went into the cave. He looked into the recess between the boughs where the birds were. He found only a heap of twigs with moss and horsehair hanging from it. His heart went cold, he felt an iciness ripping over into every part of his body. He dropped to his knees and saw the robins lying dead on the floor. Some had their heads cut off and others had been squashed with heavy stones. He groped his way out of the cave bewildered with rage and anguish.

Standing on the path were the three boys who had followed him. They were stolid and old in their long, frayed trousers, their heavy faces dull and expressionless. One of them came up to him and gripped the front of his jacket. 'Robbing nests,' he said.

Rhodri tried to get away. He was afraid of the boys. They were bigger than he was, they worked on the land after school and were strong. The boy held him firmly by the coat, his face thrust close, heavy and repulsive. 'Let me go,' said Rhodri. 'I didn't rob the nest. It was my nest. It was you who robbed it. I know you robbed it.'

One of the boys came on to the path and spat on Rhodri's coat. Then he laughed. The child's heart thumped as though it had increased many times its normal size. He tried to wrench off the hand that was holding him, but the boy pushed him over backwards and bore him to the ground and lay heavily upon him.

At the pain of the fall the fear of his tormentors seemed to leave him and his flesh was possessed by an overwhelming frenzy of hatred. He writhed and struggled in the dust, trying to bite. He heard coming out of his own throat the scream of his demented hate, in its mastery he thought only of destroying the iron weight and the smell of the boy astride him. He lashed out savagely with his feet, he wanted to claw at the dull expressionless eyes, to smash into a pulp the bones and flesh of the stupid face. But he could not wrench his hands free, his wrists were held to the ground as firmly as with shackles. And gradually to his dismay he felt the great wave of lust and power ebbing from him. The knowledge that he had been impotent, even when nourished with this unaccustomed strength and ferocity, filled him with humiliation. He began to gasp for breath although all the time his lungs seemed full and bursting. He heaved his body up again convulsively and tried to squirm out from under the powerful unbudging body, but the passion had deserted him. Tears of dismay and frustration burned in his eyes. His body became limp. When he was quite still and the tears were running freely, the boy astride him leaned forward and struck him in the face. 'You pig,' he said, and slowly the immovable body was lifted.

Then the two other boys who had watched the struggle in silence and indifference came closer. One of them said, 'He's mad, like his grannie.' The other kicked the dust near Rhodri's head so that it fell over his face. The three then went away.

Rhodri crouched on the ground. His wrists burned like fire where he had been held down and he felt limp and weak, as though with long hunger. He made no attempt to rise. He sobbed bitterly on the path until his throat ached like a wound. No one came near. Presently a chill wind began to blow. He shivered. He had sweated during the struggle and now his bruised flesh seemed turning to ice. He felt sick and giddy. He crawled back along the path to the door of the cave and sat down in utter wretchedness, his face in his hands. His head throbbed. He would leave the island. He had no money but he would swim across to the mainland at low water and the golden pony should go with him. He wiped his face, and made his way back to the farm. His determination to escape filled his mind and his misery was overborne by it. Near the house he passed his grannie collecting sticks in her apron. She glanced at him from her staring eyes but did not stop or speak. He hurried on. The house was wide open and empty. He went upstairs and lay down on the bed, waiting for the darkness.

At midnight the child came down the beach with the pony behind him. In the distance, beyond the sea, was the dark mainland with a few lights sprinkled on the backs of the hills. A full moon glowed rosy in the sky as though an unseen fire were lit against her curve. The tide was like black glass. It had gone out a long way and as the child went over the wet sand the moon was fragmentary in the little water-filled grooves and depressions of the beach, rapidly its light splintered into bright fragments and as rapidly flashed together again into one shining disc as the brilliant image was momentarily whole in a wide pool.

The child stood at the edge of the sea, wearing only his shirt and trousers. The night was calm and silent and very warm. The water in the straits lay motionless before him except for a strip of tide near the mainland where the current was running out strongly. Down the shelving sand into the sea he waded and the pony came after him. The water rose over his bare feet, over his knees, over his loins. In spite of the mildness of the night the sea was cold. When he was over his shoulders, he heard the pony snort behind him and begin to swim. She came alongside with only her head out of the water. Her mane floated and her nostrils were wide, shaped out like the mouths of trumpets. The boy flung his arm over her back as she passed him and kicked out. Together they went along, swimming side by side through the silent water. The child's heart was filled with unutterable joy. He was no longer fearful. He was escaping and the golden pony would be with him, she was bearing him away in the moonlight for ever from the island. Before long they would touch together the sands of the mainland. Many times he had swum in this sea but never so tirelessly and with such elation as now. The moon gave them ample light. His arm lay in an easy grip over the back of the pony, her white mane floated and the water swished up against her body as she kicked out with her hooves. Calmly, in perfect unison, they approached the middle of the straits.

There the current became stronger, soon the child could feel it beginning to wash his body away from the flank of the pony. She too felt the strain and although her pace did not slacken her breathing became heavier. Presently he had to clutch fiercely at her neck and mane to prevent himself being swept away, and he feared this might bring her head under. The sea was no longer silent, it began to rush with the roar of a great river, deep ridges appeared along the current as though the water were being miraculously ploughed. His body was dandled about from wave to wave. He thought that if he could get to the other side of the pony then the current would drive him against her flank and not away from her as it was doing at present. They had drifted a long way below the nearest point to the island, the outward-jutting rock on which he had hoped to land, and the force of the current showed no sign of diminishing. And in spite of the powerful swimming of the pony they did not seem to be getting any nearer the land; instead they were being swept along parallel to it. The child feared that in this swift and rough water they would soon become separated. He determined to risk diving under the pony's head so that he could rest against her other flank. He was beginning to tire, but there all his energy could be used in swimming forward, not in holding on to the pony.

He drew himself up close to her, his arms around her neck. She went on swimming bravely, her wide-eyed head rising and falling as she went across the current. He whispered her praises and then dived. He tried with the ends of his fingers to maintain contact with her coat under water, but his hands were numb with cold and directly his head was submerged she was swept out of his reach. When he came to the surface, she was nowhere to be seen.

The glaring of the moon troubled him and the splashing of the moonlit torrent in his eyes. He found himself moving along faster than ever. The gutter-like current lifted him on to the crest of a ridge and he glanced rapidly over his shoulders. The pony was behind him. She was still swimming strongly in the direction of the land but she did not seem to have made any headway. She seemed rather to be further out from the rocks than when they had become separated. The child realized that when he had dived he had not gone beneath her head at all. The current had hurled him forward and now its force was separating them more widely every minute.

He tried hard to swim parallel to the pony's head but he made no progress, the powerful rush of the broken water bore him along past the land. Soon he would be swept out to sea. He struggled afresh, but he was cold and nearing exhaustion. His lungs seemed to be inflated all the time, and hard. His head went under constantly and the water roared in his ears. Each time he came to the surface the moon appeared to be held right against his eyes, dazzling bright and yellow as candle-flame. He spun round like a leaf on a cobweb. Rising suddenly out of the water, he glanced rapidly around again. In that hurried glimpse he saw the golden pony rising out of the sea; somehow she had reached the land and was slowly making her way up the beach, shining like silver in the moonlight. The golden pony was safe. What would she do alone on the shore? Would she wait for him? He had to reach the land, he was bound now to get ground under his feet again, so that they could be together.

And then gradually he felt the current diminish. He had been swept round into a small bay, behind which stretched out a large dark fan of land. The tide seemed to have run out completely and the waters to have become slack. With what strength he had left he struck out in the direction of the land. He had not gone far when he found his arms touching the floating fronds of seaweed. His feet sank to the rocks. He staggered forward, falling and slipping among the underwater boulders. He found he was naked. In utter exhaustion and wretchedness he climbed over the rocks and reached a cut field bordering the sea. There he pulled a haycock over himself and took sleep into his body like a drink.

When he awoke the sun was shining brightly. The loud morning rang like strings with birdsong. His body ached. He could scarcely move. But the thought of the pony gave him no rest. He dragged himself out of the hay and stood upright. There in the distance lay the island floating lightly upon the varnished sea, calm and beautiful in the morning sun. Far out in the channel was the ferryboat, making for the island under her brown sail. And behind the boat was a small black object moving along at the same pace. The child recognized it at once. It was the head of the golden pony. They were swimming her back to the island.

Notes

୨

At the head of the notes to each story, details of any surviving manuscript or type-script are given. This is followed by details of the story's magazine publication (if any), then a list of the volumes by Glyn Jones in which the story appeared (using the abbreviations listed below) and publication details of any subsequent antho-logies in which the story was reprinted.

Abbreviations

BB: *The Blue Bed and Other Stories* (London: Cape, 1937).
WM: *The Water Music and Other Stories* (London: Routledge, 1944).
SSS: *Selected Short Stories* (London: Dent, 1971).
WH: *Welsh Heirs* (Llandysul: Gomer, 1977).
GWWY: *Goodbye, What Were You?: Selected Writings* (Llandysul: Gomer, 1994).
DTT: *The Dragon has Two Tongues: Essays on Anglo-Welsh Writers and Writing* (London: Dent, 1968).
CP: *The Collected Poems of Glyn Jones*, ed. Meic Stephens (Cardiff: University of Wales Press, 1996).
MP: *Y Llwybrau Gynt* (1971), translated by Meic Stephens as 'The Making of a Poet: A Memoir', *Planet*, 112 (Aug./Sept. 1995) 68–79 (*MPi*) and *Planet*, 113 (Oct./Nov. 1995) 73–84 (*MPii*).
'Idioms' Notebook: a small exercise book in which, beginning in the 1930s, GJ noted down many south Walian idioms which he knew or had heard in use or idiosyncratic phrases which he had overheard.

Bevan: Tudor Bevan, *Glyn Jones: The Background to his Writings*, MA disserta-tion, University of Wales, Swansea, 1989.
Companion: *The Oxford Companion to the Literature of Wales*, ed. Meic Stephens (Oxford: OUP, 1986)
Partridge: Eric Partridge, *A Dictionary of Slang and Unconventional English*, ed. Paul Beale, 8th edn. (London: Routledge & Kegan Paul, 1984)

I Was Born in the Ystrad Valley

There is a holograph final draft of 'I Was Born in the Ystrad Valley' in the collection of MSS drafts and offprints of stories collected in *The Blue Bed* in NLW MS 20705B. The story's only publication was in *The Blue Bed*.

The precise date of composition is uncertain, but it is likely that it was after November 1935 (see Note to p.11 below). As *BB* was being prepared for publica-tion, Hamish Miles at Jonathan Cape wrote to GJ: 'The longest story in the bound-up notebook which begins "I was born in the Ystrad Valley" has no title. What would you like us to call it? Those opening words, as a matter of fact, would not be at all a bad title' (29 September 1936).

In a lecture to the Academi Gymreig on 'The Short Story' (7 March 1976), GJ expressed the view that what constitutes 'the authentic short story' is 'singleness of mood, [the] circling round the one character or the one situation . . . In my first book of short stories, I wrote one called, "I was Born in the Ystrad Valley" . . . I don't regard that now as a true short story, because it went beyond the one concept, or situation, and would have gone on into even more had I been much more experienced than I was at the time. The work was limited really, not by the requirements of the story itself, but by my own ignorance of how an armed rising could be carried out and what the emotions, reactions, even activities of those people involved in it would be likely to be. The work should undoubtedly have been a novel'. A revised version of the lecture was published as 'Duw, It's Hard: Notes on the Short Story', *Planet*, 35 (Dec. 1976): 6–8.

p.1 *Ystrad Valley*: Based on the Merthyr Valley, with 'Ystrad' being a fictionalized Merthyr Tydfil. The name is used frequently in Glyn Jones's fiction, including the 'Four Tales' published in *Welsh Heirs*.

p.1 *His people . . . from the west . . . my mother . . . unacknowledged love child*: GJ's paternal great-grandfather, William Jones, moved from a farm near Llanybri, Carmarthenshire, to Merthyr early in the nineteenth century (*DTT* 10). As Tudor Bevan (Bevan 27) has noted, there appear in Wyn's references to his family to be other echoes of GJ's own family history: William Jones's wife came from a family which claimed 'kinship with armigerous families in Carmarthenshire and Pembrokeshire' (*DTT* 11), while GJ's maternal great-grandfather 'married the daughter of a wealthy and well-connected Swansea doctor'. The daughter 'was, alas, illegitimate' (*DTT* 18). This couple brought up GJ's own mother who was in effect orphaned when her mother died in childbirth and her father, 'dandy, poet, calligrapher', emigrated to the USA (*DTT* 19).

p.4 *chalked trams*: The workers at a particular stall at the coal-face had their own number which they would chalk on the trams which they had filled, in order that the coal dug in the shift would be credited to them when weighed at the surface (their wages, of course, being based on the weight of coal produced).

p.4 *Jonah's gourd*: As Jonah sat outside the city of Nineveh, waiting to see if God would punish the people for their wickedness, 'the Lord God prepared a gourd, and made it to come up over Jonah, that it might be a shadow over his head, to deliver him from his grief. So Jonah was exceeding glad of the gourd' (Jonah 4.6).

p.5 *Paracelcus . . . Blessed Damozel*: 'Paracelsus', a dramatic poem by Robert Browning (1812-89); 'The Lady of Shalott' and 'The Lotus Eaters', poems by Alfred, Lord Tennyson (1809-92); 'The Blessed Damozel', a poem by D. G. Rossetti (1818-82). *Bells and Pomegranates* was a series of pamphlets containing plays and 'dramatic lyrics' by Robert Browning, which he published in the 1840s.

p.5 *Chartists at Kennington Common*: Chartism was the nineteenth-century movement for parliamentary reform, the Chartists' demands including universal male suffrage, payment of MPs, equal electoral districts and voting by ballot. In Nov. 1839, twenty-four Chartists were killed in a full-scale rising at Newport, Mon. Petitions were presented to parliament in 1839 and 1842. In 1848, the year of European revolutions, a third petition was presented following a large demonstration at Kennington Common, London. The movement declined afterwards.

p.6 *directly he begins to write . . . ideology of the middle classes*: Compare Wyn's comment here with GJ's comment in his journal (3 May 1936): 'Y mae pob artist yn enedigol o'r gwerin [*sic*] yn troi ei gefn ar ei ddosbarth trwy fod yn artist. Oherwydd nid yw'r werin, yn y mwyafrif, yn hidio dim am gelfyddid [*sic*]' (Every artist born of the folk/working class turns his back on his own class by being an artist. Because the people, for the most part, care nothing for art).

p.7 *I went to visit him*: In a conversation with the editor in 1994, GJ said that, like the protagonist of the story, he would in the 1930s, while a teacher at Wood Street School, Cardiff, visit the homes of pupils who were ill. In the same conversation GJ emphasized that the story arose directly out of such episodes and his concern for the squalid conditions in which many people in South Wales were living in the period. Cf. GJ's account of the condition of his pupils in *DTT* 29–30: 'what I witnessed on these visits, the squalor, the overcrowding, the degradation, the poverty, I have never forgotten'.

p.10 *going down to Merthyr Mawr in the summer*: a picturesque rural village near the Glamorgan coast, not far from Bridgend; still a popular area for camping.

p.11 *this upper chamber, love, and the cross, and the washing of feet*: In Luke 22, as the Passover and his own crucifixion approach, Christ and his disciples gather in 'a large upper room' in a house in Jerusalem. It is here that they share the Last Supper. In John 13, after the supper Christ 'laid aside his garments, and took a towel and girded himself . . . and began to wash the disciples' feet' (John 13.4–5). Already Wyn is experiencing the compassion and the impulse to sacrifice, imaged here in the religious terms with which he would be familiar from his upbringing in the chapel, which will later take a political form.

p.11 *the election results*: In a journal entry for 15 November 1935, GJ notes:

> Outside the City Hall today when they were giving the results out. Three Conservatives. One unemployed by me – I stood with crowd of them because I knew Ifor Jones – says 'Look at Lady Bennett, her fur coat cost more than I get a year.' Which was true. Sir E.W. looked ghastly and was hooted.
>
> One unemployed chap says to me 'Ramsey was bribed. They can all be bribed. The only one they couldn't bribe was Jesus Christ and they crucified him.' It was a real tough guy who said it , with a huge nose and teeth worn to black needles.
>
> One chap says 'Fair dooz for these, they give us a chicken every Christmas – pity it's in a shell.'
>
> They were bitter men when they knew the result and used foul language in a sort of desperation.
>
> Some women near me were nearly in tears, saying 'It's the damned upper classes have done it.'
>
> I should have said, 'No, it's us. If all working people voted Labour, Labour would govern.'

The General Election of November 1935 returned the National Government under Stanley Baldwin to power.

p.12 *means test*: a system introduced by Ramsay MacDonald's National Government in November 1931 whereby unemployment benefit could be drawn as of right for only twenty-six weeks. Those not entitled to benefit – that is, those longest out-of-work – had to submit to an examination of the family's financial means by the local Public Assistance Committee. The benefit allowed to an unemployed man and his family was reduced if the means test revealed any household income, such as income earned by a son or daughter, which could be set against benefit. The policy was designed to reduce overall Government expenditure on the unemployed. See, for example, Noreen Branson and Margot Heinemann, *Britain in the Nineteen Thirties* (London: Weidenfeld & Nicolson, 1983) and Walter Brierley's novel, *Means Test Man* (1935).

p.13 *city hall*: the 'ornate façade' described is clearly that of Cardiff City Hall. Cf. Note to p.11.

p.14 *reputation for gallantry*: 'reputation as a lady killer' in MS.

p.15 *a jubilee*: 1935 had seen widespread public celebration of King George V's Silver Jubilee.

p.15 *a long end*: unsmoked butt-end of a cigarette.

p.15 *keeping a cow when they can buy milk*: in a conversation with the editor in 1992, GJ recalled an episode that occurred when he was a teacher at Wood Street School, Cardiff. Prostitution was rife in the Temperance Town area, though the police took no action as long as the women's activities were restricted to that part of the city. A number of his pupils' mothers were prostitutes and GJ remembered one of them approaching him one day outside the school gate and enquiring if he were married. When he replied, 'No,' the woman said, 'That's right, isn't it, why keep a cow when you can always buy milk?'

p.17 *toric lenses*: heavily-curved convex lenses.

p.18 *Bute Road*: Bute Road is in Butetown, the dockland area of Cardiff. One of Britain's earliest multiracial communities, it was also in the 1930s an area of narrow streets and poor housing. Given its reputation for being both somewhat exotic and violent, the area was widely-known as 'Tiger Bay'. It has been largely redeveloped in recent years.

p.19 *Welsh Nationalists with their summer schools for spooners*: The Socialist Alun dismisses the summer schools held in the period by Plaid Cymru as being places where young people go more for romance than for political discussion; to 'spoon' is to pay court to, 'especially in a sentimental manner' (*OED*).

p.20 *jump into Etna*: The Greek philosopher Empedocles (*c*.495–*c*.435 BC) was born of an aristocratic family in Sicily, but was an ardent democrat, which resulted in a period of exile. He supposedly committed suicide by throwing himself into the crater of Mount Etna. Matthew Arnold based a dramatic poem, *Empedocles on Etna* (1852), on this episode.

p.21 *Italian refreshment bar*: From the turn of the century onwards, Italian immigrants opened a large number of ice-cream shops, cafés, and restaurants across south Wales. See Colin Hughes, *Lime, Lemon and Sasparilla: The Italian Community in South Wales, 1881–1945* (Bridgend: Seren, 1991).

p.25 *Welsh hymns about a victory in Canaan*: For these south Walian Socialists, to see their own ideal, post-revolutionary society in the registers of their chapel upbringing would have been wholly natural. GJ might have had a number of hymns in mind, to be found in the *Caniedydd* of the Welsh Independents (*Annibynwyr*), including the famous 'O! Iesu mawr, rho d'anian bur / I eiddil gwan mewn anial dir, / I'w nerthu drwy'r holl rwystrau sy / Ar ddyrys daith i'r Canaan fry,' sung to the great tune 'Llef' ('Oh, Almighty Jesus, give your pure nature / To the frail weakling in a desert land, / To strengthen him through all the obstacles

which / Hinder the journey to Canaan above') and the final stanza of 'Mi deithiaf
tua'r hyfryd wlad' ('I journey towards the beautiful land') would also have
appealed to these seekers of freedom: "N ôl cyrraeddd bryniau Canaan draw, /
A'm traed yn gwbwl rydd, / Fy melys waith fydd moli mwy, / Am nerth yn ôl y
dydd' ('After reaching the hills of Canaan yonder, / And my feet utterly free, / My
sweet task from now on will be / To praise for strength from day to day').

p.26   *blistered*: received a police court summons (Partridge).

p.29   *dole*: unemployment benefit; see Note to p.12.

p.29   *founded a university*: The quarrymen of north Wales contributed from their
wages towards the setting up of university colleges at Aberystwyth (1872) and
Bangor (1884).

p.30   *Sam Browne*: 'a belt, with supporting strap that passes over the right
shoulder, worn by commissioned officers in the British army' (*OED*). Named after
the nineteenth-century general who invented it.

p.31   *chamois leather*: 'shammy leather' in the MS.

p.32   *butcher blue*: her pants are the dark blue of the butcher's traditional blue-
and-white striped apron.

p.40   *Naked headed heavy birds . . . my bitten face*: When a speaker at a conference
in 1993 identified Wyn in these closing scenes with Prometheus, GJ later
commented in a letter: 'I don't think I had Prometheus in mind . . . At the time the
story was being written I think I was working on a radio programme with Prof. T. J.
Morgan on the Llywarch Hen poetry and in that poetry . . . are such images as 'A
head I hold wrapped in my shirt / Head of Urien, gentle chieftain in his own court.
/ And on his white breast, ravens eating his flesh'. The Heledd poems have more
such pictures of eagles eating the flesh killed in battle . . . No, definitely not
Prometheus' (letter to the editor, 26 March 1993). See James A. Davies, 'Bed,
Farm and Map: Three Responses to the Troubled 1930s', *Seeing Wales Whole: Essays
on the Literature of Wales*, ed. Sam Adams (Cardiff: University of Wales Press,
1998), 77–101, esp. 101.

In fact GJ's collaboration with Prof. T. J. Morgan was rather later, in 1952. The
poems, with a linking 'reconstruction' of the narrative, were broadcast on the
Welsh Home Service of the BBC on 22 November 1952, and were later published
in a limited edition, *The Saga of Llywarch the Old*, a reconstruction by Glyn Jones;
with the verse translated by T. J. Morgan (London: Golden Cockerel Press, 1955).
(GJ's adaptation of *The Misfortunes of Princess Heledd*, a further collaboration with
T. J. Morgan, was broadcast by the BBC on 23 March 1954 and a limited edition
of the translations was published by Gwasg Gregynog as *The Story of Heledd* in
1994.)

But the connection in GJ's mind between his story and the imagery of these
early Welsh poems is interesting, in that it was during the 1930s that GJ was
reading extensively in Welsh literature and, presumably, came upon the Llywarch
Hen and Heledd poems for the first time. Indeed, it was in 1935, the same year in
which 'I Was Born in the Ystrad Valley' seems to have been conceived, that *Canu
Llywarch Hen*, Sir Ifor Williams's major edition of the poems, was published,
complete with introduction and notes, and suggestions for the reconstruction of
the narrative links that once joined the poems

p.40   *marches of my loins*: 'marshes of my loins' in MS.

p.40   *gorcock*: male of the red grouse.

p.40 *sea-hawks*: 'shit hawks' in MS.

Textual note
For the most part, the text of 'I Was Born. . .' in *The Blue Bed* is that of the MS in NLW, though paragraph breaks have been inserted at various points. There are some minor variations, listed above. In addition, the rather more robust speech of the workers in the MS (although it is not altered in the MS) has been repeatedly toned down in the published version. Thus, although the published version has 'brainy buggers' (p.15) and 'bloody cuckoo' (p.29), 'The buggars [*sic*] gave us' becomes 'The board gave us' (p.12); 'sweating their bloody eyeballs out' becomes 'sweating their eyeballs out' (p.14); the capitalists who are 'cunning buggars' in the MS are 'cunning devils' in the published text (p.15). There are over a dozen such revisions.

The Kiss
There is a holograph final draft of 'The Kiss' in NLW MS 20705B. The story's only publication was in *The Blue Bed*.

p.41 *Lazarus*: Lazarus, having 'lain in the grave for days', was raised from the dead by Jesus and emerged from his grave, which was a cave with 'a stone upon it' (see John 11.1–46).
p.43 *reeving-string*: A reeving-string is one which gathers (e.g. other ropes) together, sometimes being passed through a block or hole.

Textual note
The text of 'The Kiss' in *The Blue Bed* is that of the holograph final draft.

Knowledge
'Knowledge' is the only story in *The Blue Bed* of which there is no MS or offprint in NLW MS 20705B. (There is an eighteen-page gap in GJ's numbering of the pages bound in MS 20705B at the point in the sequence where the story appears in the published version.)
BB, SSS.
An entry in GJ's diary for 30 November 1934 notes: 'Sent Pentrebach and Knowledge to "Story"'. The entry for 16 December 1934 lists 'Knowledge' as one of his works which is 'out this date', meaning apparently that it had been sent to an editor for consideration, since on 21 January 1935 he notes: 'Knowledge . . . back from Story'. ('Story' is presumably *English Story*, a series of collections edited by Woodrow Wyatt and published in the 1930s and 1940s by Collins. *English Story* later published 'Wat Pantathro' in 1941 and 'The Last Will' in 1943.)

p.49 *Ystrad Pit*: see Note to p.1.
p.49 *sheaves*: pulleys.
p.49 *pouring molten lead*: In March 1937, two months after the appearance of *BB*, GJ received a letter from a Mr. Jabez Thomas of Bynea, near Llanelli. Mr. Thomas congratulated the author on his 'beautiful collection of stories' and then went on to

indicate that he was a colliery smith and that lead could not be used for the task described in 'Knowledge': 'The Coal Mines Act states that the metal to be used should be six times equivalent to the load, therefore lead would be too soft, so that when it would take the strain it would pull the rope through the iron cup or "capel" as it is called in the Act. Besides, Sir, lead will not "wash", that is will not cling to the steel wires of the rope, the same as the special White Metal used.'

p.53   *blue scars*: the scars left after coal dust had entered a wound.

p.55   *gillies*: gillyflowers, which have the scent of cloves.

Wil Thomas

There is a holograph final draft of 'Wil Thomas', and an offprint of the *Welsh Short Stories* text, in NLW MS 20705B.

  BB, SSS.

  The story was collected in *Welsh Short Stories* (Faber, 1937), 213–25.

  Rayner Heppenstall's review of *The Blue Bed* (*Now and Then*, Spring 1937, 16) is very enthusiastic about the volume but notes: 'I groaned and cursed at the ending of "Wil Thomas", which is as near pure humour as Rabelais is all through, and then tails off.'

p.56   *her breath in her fist*: a literal translation of the Welsh idiom, *a'i gwynt yn ei dwrn*, to be breathless.

p.56   *coms*: combinations, a single undergarment for body and legs. (The buttons have been broken by the rollers of the mangle, used to squeeze out excess water after the clothes have been washed, before being hung out to dry.)

p.56   *giving her jip*: giving her pain, a south Walian idiom (also 'gip', 'gyp').

p.57   *tidy little features*: 'tidy' has wide usage in south Walian English. It can, as here, describe the appearance and behaviour of a person, with connotations not just of physical neatness but decency, respectability: 'he's a tidy fellow', 'she's a tidy woman' (of a housewife particularly, the opposite of *didoreth*, scruffy, feckless). It can also be used as an adverb, 'well, satisfactorily' (and can have connotations of friendliness and intimacy: 'Come and sit down by here nice and tidy.'). It can be used as an adjective of amount or degree: 'a tidy amount of money', 'a tidy distance' (a usage the *OED* records in standard English as early as *Nicholas Nickleby* in 1838); cf. pp.59, 157, 184.

p.57   *my little pelican*: In legend the female pelican is supposed to pierce her breast in order to provide sustenance for her young from her own blood; the pelican is thus an emblem of self-sacrifice. Wil is acknowledging what Mari is doing by going for his beer, albeit with a comically inelegant comparison.

p.57   *pop-alley*: a marble (a south Walian idiom, derived from the Welsh *ali bop*).

p.58   *long-ends*: the unsmoked butt-ends of cigarettes.

p.58   *little Evans*: Since Evans is described as 'tall', GJ is again translating literally from the Welsh: 'Evans bach', where *bach* means not 'little' or 'small', but is a term of familiarity or affection, something like 'My dear Evans'; cf. 'little God' in 'Cadi Hughes' (p.74).

p.58   *over by here*: a widely-used south Walian idiom, derived originally from the Welsh, *draw fan 'ma*; cf. 'If I was to drop down dead by here' in 'Explosion' (p.130).

p.58 *taws*: large playing marbles; the taw is the one which is aimed at the other marbles.

p.59 *Balaam riding on the donkey*: Balaam fails to see the angel of the Lord who appears before him, unlike his ass, who sees the angel and falls down before him. Balaam punishes the ass before 'the Lord opened the eyes of Balaam' and he sees the angel (see Numbers 22.22–34).

p.59 *enjoyed themselves nice and tidy*: see Note to p.57.

p.59 *compo doctor*: the doctor employed by the mining company to determine the extent of injuries incurred underground and therefore the extent of the company's liability for compensation.

p.59 *Sampson and Delilah and the Dragon*: After Sampson has been seduced by Delilah and his strength removed by having his hair cut off, he is blinded and bound by the Philistines, who offer up thanks to their god, Dagon [*sic*] who was part man, part fish. When Wil says 'Like me . . . I stuck a fork in mine,' he is remembering that 'The Philistines took [Samson] and put out his eyes' (see Judges 16.4–31).

p.60 *brattice*: stout tarred cloth, used in the pit to partition mine shafts, usually for the purpose of ventilation.

p.61 *wings of a goody-hoo*: from the (colloquial) Welsh *gwdihŵ*, an owl.

p.62 *swam the Jordan*: see Note to 'Jordan' (p.214).

p.62 *Grapes of Canaan*: See Numbers 13, where the spies sent into Canaan by Moses return with 'a cluster of grapes' which they bare 'between two on a staff' and report that the land 'floweth with milk and honey'. Presumably Mari's book tells of the rewards of a moral life.

Textual note

The text of 'Wil Thomas' in *The Blue Bed* is that of the holograph final draft and of *Welsh Short Stories*, the only variation being that 'like a bloody bluebell' in the draft becomes 'like a black bluebell' in *Welsh Short Stories* and *BB* (p.61 of present edition), and 'like a bluebell' in *SSS*.

Eben Isaac

There is a holograph final draft of 'Eben Isaac' in NLW MS 20705B.

BB, SSS.

The story was collected in *Welsh Short Stories*, ed. Gwyn Jones (Penguin, 1941), 69–79.

It is likely that the story which GJ refers to in his diary (30 November 1934) as 'Pentrebach' and as having been sent with 'Knowledge' to 'Story' was in fact 'Eben Isaac'.

After the publication of *BB*, Rayner Heppenstall sent his copy for GJ to sign. In his (undated) covering letter, Heppenstall says that he has just reviewed the book for *Now and Then* and that, while he admires the volume: 'I wish you'd not published the long story at all, as it stands, grand as it is in parts, but "Eben Isaac" I don't like either (it looks as if your death wish might get automatic)' (NLW).

p.63 *Pentrebach*: Welsh, 'a little village'.

p.63 *the hills behind the Sidan Bay*: Tudor Bevan points out that Pentrebach bears some similarity to Llansteffan: 'Cefn Sidan is the huge and notorious sand bar which almost completely blocks Carmarthen Bay', while 'Pentrebach, like Llansteffan . . . has "a square with a pump in it" (p.63) and its "red roads" (p.67) are carved through "the rich red earth" (p.70) of the surrounding hills' (Bevan 74-5). *Sidan* is the Welsh for 'silk'.

p.63 *horse-ball*: In the early years of the century, to administer a medicine which was in a powdered form to a horse, it would be rolled into a ball of bread, sometimes with treacle, and pushed into the horse's throat, often through a tube.

p.63 *little Keziah*: see Note to p.58.

p.64 *horse-tod*: lump of horse manure.

p.64 *indian corn*: maize, used to feed poultry.

p.64 *bat's wing burner*: a gas burner with a laterally spreading flame in the shape of a bat's wing.

p.65 *Harri Hir*: *hir* is the Welsh for 'long', hence 'Long Harry'.

p.66 *little Harri*: see Note to p.58.

p.66 *dead-head*: an individual who obtains free admission, transport, goods, etc., a cheap-skate or free-loader.

p.66 *with his head in his feathers*: a literal translation of the Welsh idiom *a'i ben yn ei blu*, thus looking miserable, like a dispirited hen.

p.67 *Hannah the Gwalia*: Hannah who kept the 'Gwalia' shop in the the village. 'Gwalia' (originally a Romantic revival of a medieval name for Wales) was a not uncommon name for such village shops in the latter part of the last century and the first half of this one. See, for example, S. Minwell Tibbott and Beth Donovan, *The Gwalia: The Story of a Valleys Shop* (Cardiff: National Museum of Wales, 1991).

p.68 *rasp*: a coarse file with raised teeth.

p.69 *Lewsin Parc-y-lan*: In Wales, in part because of the commonness of some surnames, other means of identifying individuals – within a small community where everyone knew everyone else – had to be found. One was by job: hence 'Jones the Milk' could immediately be distinguished from, say, 'Jones the Bread'. Another identifier was the place where the individual lived: the house, or terrace, or the geographical location. 'Lewsin Parc-y-lan' is thus 'Lewis of Parc-y-lan' (Bank/Shore Park), presumably the name of a local area or house. (Mrs Thomas the Bank (p.68) might live in an area called 'The Bank' or, more likely perhaps, is married to the local bank manager.)

p.69 *in tally*: to live out of wedlock. A 'tally' in English was a piece of wood kept in a shop to record the amount that a customer owed on credit, a version of 'a slate'. Thus to live with a partner 'in tally' or 'on tally' was to live with them without the cost of a wedding and with no legal financial commitment. A usage not limited to Wales, though see *byw tali* in Bedwyr Lewis Jones, *Yn Ei Elfen* (Llanrwst: Gwasg Carreg Gwalch, 1992), 99.

p.69 *kite*: 'a shark or sharper, or in general detestation' (Partridge).

p.69 *a red penny*: more usually, in Welsh, *dimau goch*, a red (i.e. copper) halfpenny. The English idiom would be 'a brass farthing'; cf. 'The Last Will' (p.156)

p.69 *cutting dough off the edges of the tins*: The village women would bring their bread and pies to the baker to put (for a price) in his oven; Eben has evidently been trimming the edges of the loaves brought to him and using the dough to make extra loaves for sale. (The baker in an untitled, unfinished fragment by GJ in NLW, written in the 1930s, is guilty of the same sharp practice: 'he used very carefully to cut off all the dough hanging over the edges of the tins [the women] had brought to make loaves for himself out of it'.)

Textual note
The text of 'Eben Isaac' in *The Blue Bed* is, with minor corrections, that of the holograph final draft.

Cadi Hughes

Adelphi, 10/2 (May 1935): 72-6; an offprint of the *Adelphi* version is included in NLW MS 20705B. No MS version of the story appears to be extant.

BB, SSS.

The story was collected in *Welsh Tales of Terror*, ed. R. Chetwind-Hayes (Collins, 1979), 135-40; *My Favourite Stories of Wales*, ed. Jan Morris (London: Lutterworth P., 1980), 113–18.

Cadi Hughes was accepted for publication in *The Adelphi* by Richard Rees in a letter to GJ on 14 December 1934 (NLW). GJ's diary indicates that the story had been completed some time before this, having been returned by the editor of *The Twentieth Century* on 24 October 1934.

p.72 *lying sog*: inattentive to or unconscious of his surroundings. 'In a soc' or 'in a sog' is a south Walian idiom; cf. 'sock' in 'Gari' (p.277).

p.72 *little Ifan*: see Note to p.58; cf. 'little God' on p.74.

p.73 *smells foul air . . . too much water*: i.e. in the colliery.

p.73 *Mabinogion*: the title, first used by Lady Charlotte Guest in her translation (1838-49), given to eleven stories preserved in the White Book of Rhydderch (written down *c.*1300–25) and the Red Book of Hergest (*c.*1375–1425). (Previously the title *Pedair Cainc y Mabinogi* had been given only to the first four stories: *Pwyll*, *Branwen*, *Manawydan* and *Math fab Mathonwy*.) See *The Mabinogion*, trans. Gwyn Jones and Thomas Jones (London: Everyman, 1949).

p.73 *his politics and his vegetarianism*: The date at which the story is set is unclear, but vegetarianism (along with, for example, antivivisectionism, pacifism and 'rational dress') represented a strand of 'ethical Socialism' which had been present in the Labour movement since the 1880s (see Edward Carpenter, *England's Ideal*, 1887, and *Civilisation: Its Cause and Cure*, 1889, as well as the writing of G. B. Shaw); such thinking was still sufficiently residual within the Left in the 1930s as to draw the scorn of George Orwell in *The Road to Wigan Pier* (1937), where he bemoaned the fact that Socialism seemed to attract 'every fruit-juice drinker, nudist, sandal-weaver, sex maniac, Quaker, nature-cure quack, pacifist and feminist in England'.

p.73 *fuss-arse*: a fussy person (Partridge); a mainly rural colloquialism, not restricted to south Wales.

p.73 *hair like Rhiannon or Blodeuwedd*: Rhiannon appears in the First and Third Branches of *Pedair Cainc y Mabinogi*. Pwyll, prince of Dyfed, 'thought that the countenance of every maiden and every lady he had ever seen was unlovely compared with her countenance'. In the Fourth Branch, Blodeuwedd is the beautiful wife of Lleu Llawgyffes; she is constructed of flowers by Math and Gwydion when Arianrhod swears that Lleu will never marry a mortal woman.

p.74   *little God*: see Note to p.58.

p.74   *go to the Big House*: the local workhouse.

p.75   *the summer school*: The Independent Labour Party held summer schools in the 1930s, as did the Fabian Society.

Textual note

The text of 'Cadi Hughes' in *The Blue Bed* is that which appeared in *The Adelphi*.

Eden Tree

New Stories, 2/1 (Feb.–March 1935): 30-4; an offprint of the *New Stories* version is included in NLW MS 20705B. No MS version of the story appears to be extant.
   BB.

'Eden Tree' was accepted for publication in *New Stories* by the editor, H. E. Bates in a letter to GJ on 23 August 1934: 'it is a first-rate piece of work' (NLW).

In a conversation with the present editor (February 1992), GJ noted that in this period he saw himself very much as an experimental writer, 'very interested' in Surrealism. He referred to 'The Apple-Tree' in this context, though he felt that none of his work was 'pure Surrealism'; he noted however, that 'Eden Tree', represented an experiment in the 'suspension of the cerebral' in which he, as writer, could not rationally account for everything.

p.77   *the Plas*: Welsh, a large (country) house, a mansion.

p.78   *tripe and cowheels*: rubbish (literally, offal).

p.78   *throw gravel . . . courted in bed*: An account of the nocturnal courting traditions of rural Wales, including the throwing of gravel at the girl's window and of 'courting in/on the bed' ('caru yn/ar y gwely'), is to be found in Catrin Stevens, *Welsh Courting Customs* (Llandysul: Gomer, 1993), esp. Ch. 3 and 4. While 'courting in/on the bed' – there would be, certainly in the depths of a Welsh winter, little other opportunity for privacy in a rural cottage or farmhouse – the couple supposedly kept on their clothes, removing only their shoes.

p.78   *touch me not*: that is, the fastidious cleanliness referred to above; a literal translation of the Latin, *noli me tangere*.

p.78   *really looking up a chimney at sky, or down a well at water . . . uncertainty and confusion*: The story appears to have had its origins in such moments of sensory uncertainty. In a conversation with the editor (February 1992), GJ described how 'Eden Tree' first came to him while walking on Garth Mountain, to the north of Cardiff, watching the sunset and finding himself uncertain as to whether the earth was rising up or the sun going down; cf. 'He had . . . often sat up to watch the mountainous edge of the earth tilting up against the face of the sun at nightfall' (p.80).

p.79   *tupped*: that is, moved like a ram copulating with a ewe.

p.79   *not bothering to timber*: not bothering to prop up the roof of where he is digging.

p.80   *God was the Word*: 'In the beginning was the Word, and the Word was with God, and the Word was God' (John 1.1).

Textual note
The text of 'Eden Tree' in *The Blue Bed* is that which appeared in *English Stories*.

The Blue Bed
There is a holograph final draft of *The Blue Bed* in NLW MS 20705B. The story's only publication was in *The Blue Bed*.

Textual note
The text of 'The Blue Bed' in *The Blue Bed* is that of the holograph final draft.

Porth-y-Rhyd
New Stories, 2/3 (June–July 1935): 168–74; an offprint of the *New Stories* version is included in NLW MS 20705B. No MS version of this story appears to be extant. BB.

An entry in GJ's diary for 16 December 1934 listing works 'out this date', i.e. under consideration by editors, includes 'Tudur – New Stories'. A diary entry for 8 January 1935 notes 'Porth-y-Rhyd accepted'.

p.85 *Machludiad*: Welsh, 'a going down, a setting (of the sun)'.
p.85 *the . . . headland*: Tudor Bevan points out that GJ's description of Wharley Point ('Y Werle') at Llansteffan, described in GJ's essay 'X = ?' in *Places: An Anthology of Britain*, ed. Ronald Blythe (Oxford: OUP, 1981) 97-103, 'is echoed in the menacing coastline of the first pages of "Porth-y-Rhyd"' (Bevan 55).
p.88 *Codiad*: Welsh, 'a getting up, an arising'.
p.89 *small frail skull of a seagull . . . fixed the tilt of the wings*: In 1964 it came to GJ's attention that this passage from 'Porth-y-Rhyd' had been reproduced, word-for-word except for the first line, in a poem by the Scottish poet Hugh MacDiarmid, entitled 'Perfect':

> I found a pigeon's skull on the machair,
> All the bones pure white and dry, and chalky
> But perfect,
> Without crack or flaw anywhere.
>
> At the back, rising out of the beak,
> Were twin domes like bubbles of thin bone,
> Almost transparent, where the brain had been
> That fixed the tilt of the wings.

The poem had originally been published in the Author's Note to MacDiarmid's *The Islands of Scotland* (London: Batsford, 1939) although not actually attributed to MacDiarmid. The reproduction of the poem in a study of MacDiarmid's work by Kenneth Buthlay (1964) and in the *Times Literary Supplement* review of that book (31 December 1964) provoked an exchange of letters between GJ, Lawrence Pollinger (his agent) and Oliver and Boyd, the publishers not only of Buthlay's book but also of MacDiarmid's *Collected Poems* (1962), in which, GJ discovered, the poem had also appeared. A lengthy correspondence on the matter also appeared in the *TLS*. A detailed account of the episode is given in Meic Stephens, 'Sad case of a "perfect" Welsh skull in a Scottish cupboard', *New Welsh Review*, no. 23 (Winter 1993-4): 37-42.

Tudor Bevan convincingly suggests that MacDiarmid's use of 'pigeon' rather than 'seagull' may have been the result of his seeing the passage not in *BB* but in a review of the collection in *Time and Tide* (6 February 1937), where the reviewer, John Brophy, mistakenly refers to 'pigeon's skull' rather than 'seagull's skull' before quoting the precise passage used in MacDiarmid's poem (Bevan 110).

Textual note

GJ has made a few minor revisions in his copy of the *New Stories* offprint in NLW MS 20705B and inserted paragraph breaks in 'Machludiad', which is not paragraphed in *New Stories*.

The Apple-Tree

Life and Letters To-day, 24/31 (March 1940): 288-98 (GJ included an offprint in the collection of *The Water Music* MSS and TSS, NLW); *The Best Stories, 1940: English and American*, ed. Edward J. O'Brien (London: Cape, 1940), 136-44.

WM.

'The Apple-Tree' was accepted for publication in *Life and Letters To-day* by the editor, Robert Herring, in a letter to GJ, 16 November 1939 (NLW). Edwin Muir, reviewing *The Best Short Stories, 1940* (a collection which included 'superb stories' by H. E. Bates, V. S. Pritchett and Ernest Hemingway), found 'The Apple-Tree' to be: 'In the vividness and beauty of the writing . . . by far the most remarkable story in the book' (*Listener*, 27 February 1941).

p.91 *Sibli*: Welsh version of Sibyl, Sibilla. Sibli is to be found in the medieval Welsh religious 'tale' *Proffwydolyaeth Sibli Doeth* ('The Prophecy of Sibli the Wise'), recorded in Llyfr Gwyn Rhydderch and Llyfr Gwyn Hergest; she also features in a triad as a stock character typifying wisdom:

> Three who received the Wisdom of Adam:
> Cato the Old,
> and Bede,
> and Sibli the Wise.
> They were, all three, as wise as Adam himself.

See *Trioedd Ynys Prydein: The Welsh Triads*, ed. Rachel Bromwich (Cardiff: University of Wales Press, 1961), 128, 508.

p.92 *Clouds go grey . . . passed him by*: a later version of this poem appeared as 'High Wind in the Village' in *The Dream of Jake Hopkins and Other Poems* (London: Fortune Press, 1954). See *CP* 47.

p.92 *The Little Boy . . . the dead and the daft*: this poem appeared as 'In the Kitchen' in *The Dream of Jake Hopkins and Other Poems*. See *CP* 48. The editor, Meic Stephens, notes that 'the dead and the daft' was 'a common expression among the people of Merthyr Tydfil: "Only the dead and the daft go to Cefn"', the reference being to 'Cefn-coed-y-cymmer, for long beyond the town's northern boundary, though now within it, where there is a large cemetery'.

p.93 *the blazing bush . . . agony of fire*: Trystan is conflating the account of the bush which 'burned with fire and . . . was not consumed' which Moses sees (Exodus 3.2–3) with the story of the phoenix, the mythical bird which arises anew from the ashes of the funeral pyre which consumes it.

p.94 *the back of the sea*: an echo of a literal translation of the Welsh *cefnfor*, the (deep of the) ocean (*cefn* = Welsh 'back').

p.94 *tawn*: apparently a GJ coinage: the last 'brown-ness' cf. 'tawny, tawniness'.

p.94 *like a black Venus*: Venus is the Roman goddess identified with the Greek Aphrodite, who was born from the sea. In Sandro Botticelli's painting of *The Birth of Venus*, Venus rises from the ocean.

pp.95–6 *I saw the endless flesh . . . beauty covering the skull*: in a conversation with the editor (February 1992), GJ referred to 'The Apple-Tree' as being a piece which manifested his interest in Surrealism in the 1930s.

p.96 *stringcourse*: 'a distinctive horizontal course [of bricks], projecting or flush, carried round a building . . . to mark roughly the division of a building into floors' (*OED*).

p.96 *corbels*: a projection of stone, brick or timber jutting out from the face of a wall, sometimes carved, to support weight.

Textual note
The text of 'The Apple-Tree' in *WM* is that of *Life and Letters To-day*.

The Saviour

Three pages of TS of the end of 'The Saviour', with holograph revisions by GJ, are contained in the collection of *The Water Music* MSS and TSS in NLW.

Life and Letters To-day, 32/53 (January 1942): 48-63. NLW contains an offprint of this version, with holograph revisions by GJ.

WM, SSS, GWWY.

p.100 *maniacal energy*: 'demoniacal energy' in *Life and Letters To-day* (*LLT*).

p.101 *a curtain . . . tried to withold the strong sunlight . . . fire smouldering in the grate*: refers to the belief that strong sunlight would put out a coal-fire. (Presumably originating in the fact that, if a domestic fire was in the sun, one would not be able to see that the flames had died down and that more coal was needed, and thus the fire might indeed go out.) Cf. 'The Golden Pony' (p.343), where 'a large piece of brown paper had been pinned over the window to keep the sun off the fire'.

p.104 *heavy limbs*: 'docile limbs' in *LLT*.

p.104 *her will was dried up*: 'the headwaters of her will were dried up' in *LLT*.

p.104 *remembering the glitter of alarm*: in his offprint of *LLT*, GJ has inserted after 'remembering': 'the indignity of that pariah look,'.

p.105 *cwm*: Welsh, 'valley'.

p.106 *move against him . . . looked up*: '. . . against him, her warm body came alive and she pressed herself forward into his arms. The workman looked up . . .' in *LLT*.

p.108 *she was an old woman . . . stick*: in his offprint of *LLT*, GJ has deleted this passage and inserted: 'she claimed the consideration of an old woman with her weight on her stick, and she . . .'

p.108 *like a device*: like an emblematic figure on a heraldic shield, perhaps 'couchant' (crouching, with the body horizontal but with the chest and head twisted upwards).

Textual note

All of GJ's holograph revisions in his offprint of the *Life and Letters To-day* text, some of which are given in the above notes, are included in the version of the story in *The Water Music*, with the exception of the passages referred to in the Notes to pp.104, 106 and 108.

The Wanderer

Wales, n.s. 2 (October 1943): 26-34.
WM.

Before its publication in *Wales*, 'The Wanderer' had been sent, with 'The Water Music', to *Life and Letters To-day*. The editor, Robert Herring, had written in August 1943: 'I am only able to keep *one* for, as you say, they are long and I am awfully harassed for space. But this is merely one of the miseries of war – not to be able to keep both. As it is, I've chosen "The Water Music", returning therefore "The Wanderer"' (letter to GJ, 11 August 1943, NLW).

p.110 *daily . . . for the world to feed on*: in the Greek legends of Prometheus, he is punished by Zeus, who has Prometheus chained to a rock and sends an eagle by day to eat his liver which, being as immortal as the rest of him, grows again at night, only for the eagle to devour it again next day. In Aeschylus's version, Prometheus is punished for giving humans the secret of fire; Prometheus of course is, somewhat like the protagonist of the story, a figure of self-assertiveness and disobedience.

p.111 *departing in answer to the ferry-bell*: the ferry in 'The Wanderer' is based on the ferry that ran to Laugharne from the Llansteffan side of the River Taf. A 'small empty stone house with a bell in its roof' stood beside the river on the Llansteffan side; those wishing to cross rang the bell to bring the ferryman across the estuary from his house. See *DTT* 193, where GJ describes the ferry and the ferryman, Jack Roberts, in the 1930s, as well as giving an account of taking the ferry to Laugharne with Dylan Thomas. The house in which Roberts and his family lived was at the water's edge, just below the Boat House which Dylan Thomas and his family later occupied. The ferry and Jack Roberts are again described in GJ's essay 'X = ?' in *Places: An Anthology of Britain*, ed. Ronald Blythe (Oxford: OUP, 1981), 97-103. A similar ferry and surrounding landscape appear in *The Tower of Loss* (see Note to p.294 below); Tudor Bevan describes the landscape of 'The Wanderer' as 'that of "The Tower of Loss" as experienced in a dream' (Bevan 75).

p.111 *a daft negress*: The passage which follows might be compared to the passage describing urban misery in 'The Apple-Tree', a story which GJ associated with his interest in Surrealism in the 1930s. See Note to pp.95-6.

p.114 *DUW CARIAD YW*: Welsh, 'God Is Love'.

p.114 *bright blue veins*: see Note to p.53.

p.117 *six-winged firebearing bird*: when Isaiah sees the six-winged seraphims praising the Lord, he cries 'Woe is me! for I am undone; because I am a man of unclean lips, and I dwell in the midst of a people of unclean lips'; one of the seraphims lays 'a live coal' from the altar on Isaiah's mouth and tells him 'thine iniquity is taken away' (Isaiah 6.2–7).

Textual note

Although 'The Wanderer' appears in GJ's handwritten list of the stories contained in the collection of *The Water Music* MSS and TSS in NLW, no MS or TS of the story appears to have survived. (In the list of stories, GJ originally wrote 'The Return' before crossing out 'Return' and substituting 'Wanderer'.) The text of 'The Wanderer' in *The Water Music* has undergone very minor revisions from that which appeared in *Wales*, mainly adjustments to the punctuation.

The Four-Loaded Man

A final MS draft of 'The Four-Loaded Man' is contained in the collection of *The Water Music* MSS and TSS in NLW. There is another holograph final draft and TS in Keidrych Rhys *Wales* Papers, NLW MS 22745D.

Wales, no.3 (Autumn 1937): 110-14; *The Best Short Stories, 1938: English and American*, ed. Edward J. O'Brien (London: Cape, 1938), 149–53.

WM, SSS, GWWY.

In an undated letter to GJ (?late 1930s), Rayner Heppenstall wrote: 'M[argaret] will send back "Water" etc. We both thought the 4-Loaded Man [*sic*] not so good as some – a bit Celtic and full of twilight . . . We think you must write more' (NLW).

p.119 *The little girl*: In a letter to Keidrych Rhys (?August/September 1937), GJ writes: 'About "the little girl" – I put it in often as a sort of refrain, the sort of thing I thought would appeal at Portland Place. No go. But let it stand now I think' (NLW MS 22745D). GJ had initially sent *The Four-Loaded Man* to the *Listener* (published by the BBC at Portland Place). However, GJ had reported to Keidrych Rhys in a previous letter (?August 1937): 'No story of mine will appear in The Listener. They took my story, accepted it, sent me the proofs, and then after about two months returned it and asked me for another instead! You bet.' (NLW MS 22745D).

p.119 *Rhys y Mynydd*: Presumably a parallel with 'Morys y Gwynt' (Morris the Wind) and 'Ifan y Glaw' (Evan the Rain) as a personification of natural phenomena. R. S. Loomis refers to Marie Trevelyan's accounts of Arawn, a figure of Winter, robed in grey, hunting with his hounds, the howling wind being the sound of the hounds. See R. S. Loomis, *Wales and the Arthurian Legend* (Cardiff: University of Wales Press, 1956), 81–2. Versions of the legend were extant in Glamorgan. In Welsh folklore, especially in west Wales, Rhys Ddwfn (Rhys the Deep, 'deep' in the sense of 'cunning') is the king of the faeries, who are known as 'Plant Rhys Ddwfn' (Children of Rhys Ddwfn). See, for example, John Rhŷs, *Studies in the Arthurian Legend* (Oxford: OUP, 1891), 271.

p.120 *'smotyn*: Welsh, 'a spot'.

p.120 *cariad*: Welsh, 'love'.

p.120 *cusan bwbach*: the Welsh version of the idiom does not appear in *Wales* nor in the holograph final draft.

p.120   *looked up at her, shaking*: 'looked sadly up at her, shaking' in *Wales* and in holograph final draft.

p.121   *kissing-crust of my little milk-loaf*: a kissing crust is the soft-baked surface on the side of a loaf where it has been in contact with the next loaf on the baker's tray.

Textual note
The text of 'The Four-Loaded Man' in *WM* is that which appeared in *Wales*, the only revisions being the two given in the notes above.

The Little Grave
Adelphi, 17/8 (May 1941): 273–8. NLW contains an offprint, with minor holograph revisions by GJ.
   WM.

p.123   *plush cloth*: 'a kind of cloth, of silk, cotton, wool or other material, having a nap longer and softer than that of velvet' (*OED*).

p.125   *Orion*: a large, brilliant star, to the south of the zodiac, figured as a hunter with belt and sword. (In Greek myth, Orion was the mighty hunter, slain by Artemis.)

Textual note
Although 'Little grave' [*sic*] appears in GJ's hand-written list of the stories contained in the collection of *The Water Music* MSS and TSS, no MS or TS of the story appears to have survived. GJ's revisions in his offprint of the *Adelphi* text are incorporated into the text which appears in *The Water Music*.

Explosion
A TS of 'Explosion', with holograph revisions by GJ, is contained in the collection of *The Water Music* MSS and TSS in NLW.
   Life and Letters To-day, 21/19 (March 1939): 70–7. NLW contains an offprint with holograph revisions by GJ.
   WM.
   Robert Herring, editor of *Life and Letters To-day*, wrote to Glyn Jones (26 January 1939): 'Well, I did like your story. Extremely. Has it a title? Or do I print it just as "Short Story"?' (NLW). The reference is presumably to 'Explosion', since that was the only story by GJ published in *Life and Letters To-day* in 1939.

p.127   *catty-and-doggy*: probably a version of 'Cat and Dog', 'a simple trial of endurance: which of two boys can longest support the pain of bearing a third boy, who has jumped up between them, and exerts his weight on a shoulder of each'. See Iona and Peter Opie, *Children's Games in Street and Playground* (Oxford: OUP, 1969), 233.

p.127   *playing alleys by himself*: 'alleys' is the colloquial term for marbles. (The narrator has his 'marble bottle' in his pocket.)

p.128   *upright row*: GJ has deleted the sentence which follows in *Life and Letters To-day* (*LLT*) and TS: 'He is no highness from the gilt-haired womb of a queen'.

p.128   *so that . . . late again*: the clause does not originally appear in *LLT* and TS.

p.128   *pink spot of flesh*: 'round flesh-coloured orifice' in *LLT* and TS.

p.128   *he is from the North*: the teacher is from north Wales and has a north Walian accent, very different from that of the south Wales valleys. He is 'from some other part' in *LLT* and TS.

p.129   *medicine-mouthed*: his mouth is wide open, as if about to take a spoonful of medicine.

p.129   *real writing*: the writing is in cursive script, the letters 'joined up', not printed separately, a way of writing the young boys have not yet learned. 'real' does not appear in *LLT* and TS.

p.129   *sum paper*: mathematical problems were worked out on squared paper rather than on the lined paper used for writing.

p.129   *Crimes*: 'Christ' in *LLT*.

p.130   *indian corn*: 'Communion bread' in *LLT* and TS. Initially, in his revisions to both GJ has 'chicken'. ('Indian corn', maize, would have been used to feed chickens.)

p.130   *try our teacher . . . pint*: 'ask our teacher the time' in *LLT*; the revision has been made in the TS.

p.130   *fun out of her*: in *LLT* and in the TS, GJ has deleted the sentence which follows: 'Put her on the decks of a shooting star and her Milky Way would sound like School Street.'

p.130   *the Graig*: the local colliery.

p.130   *poor dabs*: 'poor things' or 'poor creatures'; 'dab' is a widely used south Walian colloquialism in such contexts ('He's ever so ill, poor dab'), though it can certainly also be used more positively ('He's won the football pools, the lucky dab'). The phrase replaces *LLT*'s 'God help them'.

p.130   *terrible explosion*: the 'small round rusty thing' that Gogger throws onto the fire in the sugar bag is presumably a railway detonator; when railwaymen needed to stop a train in an emergency, these were placed on a railway line, usually in a spaced sequence of three, and the sound of the sequence of small explosions as the wheels went over them warned the driver to stop.

Textual note

The holograph revisions in the TS are also made in GJ's offprint of the *LLT* version and all of them are incorporated in the version in *WM*. Some of these are noted above.

An Afternoon at Ewa Shad's

A TS of 'An Afternoon at Ewa Shad's', with holograph revisions by GJ, is contained in the collection of *The Water Music* MSS and TSS in NLW.

Welsh Review, 1/1 (February 1939): 8-15 (as 'An Afternoon at Uncle Shad's'); *Writing Today*, ed. Denys Val Baker and Peter Ratazzi (London: Staples & Staples, 1943), 42–9.

WM, SSS.

The germ of the story appears in one of GJ's notebooks (?late1930s): 'The chap who goes potty through being unemployed. Puts on 2 pairs of trousers when he is in bed and disappears. Returns. Back in bed. Asks wife for a light. Sets mattress on fire, and runs from room. Wife throws it out of window into street. He downstairs on bottom step, sticking a carving knife in his throat, not once but time after time at the side. She jumps over his head and runs for police. They come and find him at the front door with his throat cut. They have to put him out and take him off, but he dies on the way to hospital' (NLW).

p.132   *Ewa Shad . . . Bopa Lloyd*: in south Wales, 'Ewa' is colloquial Welsh for 'Uncle' (from *ewythr*) and *Bopa* for 'Auntie'. 'Uncle' is used throughout the *Welsh Review* version.

p.132   *soapy water from the colliers' bath-tubs*: in the 1930s, the collier would, after his shift, bath himself in a (usually zinc) bath-tub in front of the fire; the bath-tub would then be emptied outside.

p.132   *cwtch*: A widely-used south Walian word with a variety of related meanings. The Welsh noun, *cwt* means 'a hut, or sty'; in south Walian English 'cwtch' takes on this meaning, as well as, here, 'hen-house', which is the word used in *Welsh Review*. The term is also used for a coal-house or the cupboard under the stairs (*cwts dan stâr*). (The Welsh verb, *cwtsio*, meaning 'to crouch down, to stoop, to hide', also contributes to the use of 'cwtch' in English as a verb – 'Cwtch down by here and hide'. The related notion of enclosure presumably gave the word its other meaning, to be cuddled lovingly; thus a mother might cwtch a child.)

p.132   *scratch for coal*: cf. 'coal-pickers' on p.133. In time of unemployment and when on strike, miners would search for lumps of coal which had been dumped with the colliery waste. The coal would be used by the family or sold. Such activity was illegal and also dangerous, as men burrowed into the tips. See, for example, Gareth Elwyn Jones, *People, Protest and Politics: Case Studies in Twentieth Century Wales* (Llandysul: Gomer, 1987), 80.

p.133   *from by there*: a south Walian idiom, derived originally from the Welsh, *o'r fan acw*.

p.133   *dubs*: a shortened form of the south Walian idiom, 'dubliw', an (outside) WC.

p.133   *wet soaking*: a south Walian idiom, the order of the adjective and the participle following Welsh syntax, cf. *gwlyb sopen, gwlyb botsh, gwlyb stecs*.

p.133   *troughing*: roof-guttering; the broken pipe is the downpipe from the guttering.

p.134   *meal of food*: a south Walian idiom, a literal translation of the Welsh, *pryd o fwyd*.

p.134   *slaps*: carpet slippers; cf. 'carpet slaps' in 'Bowen, Morgan and Williams' (p.189), ('slops' in *Welsh Review*).

p.135   *coppish*: trouser-flies, presumably derived from 'codpiece'.

p.135   *gone dull*: 'gone bloody dull' in *Welsh Review*.

p.135   *enough of food*: a south Walian idiom, a literal translation of the Welsh, *digon o fwyd*.

p.135   *bach*: see Note to p.58.

p.135   *teeshun lap*: a form of fruit-cake, from the Welsh, *teisen lap*.

p.135   *playing dix stones*: playing fivestones, a children's game in which the competitors pick up small stones or pebbles, while holding other pebbles in (or on the back of) the hand, in a set sequence; 'fivesy' is part of the game's scoring system.

p.136   *myn uffern i*: a Welsh expletive, 'hell' or 'bloody hell'.

p.136   *Brain*: a Welsh expletive, presumably an elision of 'Brenin' or 'Brenin Mawr' ('Great King', Christ). 'Good Chrish' [*sic*] in *Welsh Review*.

Textual note

The TS of the story in NLW contains various minor revisions in GJ's handwriting, including the change from 'Uncle' to 'Ewa' throughout. All of the revisions appear in the *Writing Today* version and in the text of the story in *WM*. Some of these revisions are noted above.

Wat Pantathro

A revised holograph draft of 'Wat Pantathro' is contained in the collection of *The Water Music* MSS and TSS in NLW.

English Story, second series, ed. Woodrow Wyatt and Susan Wyatt (London: Collins, 1941), 74–87.

WM, SSS, GWWY.

Collected in *Stories of the 1940s, vol. 1*, ed. Reginald Moore and Woodrow Wyatt (London: Nicholson & Watson, 1945), 233–43; *Welsh Short Stories*, ed. Gwyn Jones (London: OUP, 1956), 94–109; *New Penguin Book of Welsh Short Stories*, ed. Alun Richards (London: Viking, 1993), 146–58; and reprinted in *Welsh Books and Writers* (Welsh Arts Council: Autumn 1981), 8–10.

Tudor Bevan quotes a letter from GJ saying that 'Wat himself, in the story, is a (conscious) combination of two of my uncles'. Bevan continues: 'These were his uncle John [actually GJ's father's cousin, who lived on Y Lan farm] and John's younger brother Twmi, a horsebreaker, a good one, and a helper out at the cattle market in Carmarthen, insofar as he had a job at all. He was kicked to death in the stable behind his house, Y Battis, outside Llanybri [a fact given to Bevan by GJ himself]. That knowledge seems to lie behind "Wat Pantathro" . . . The boy . . . has a very clear sense that a spirited horse can kill.' GJ refers, in *Y Llwybrau Gynt* (*MPi* 77), to going with his uncle John in a 'spring body' to Carmarthen market; as Tudor Bevan points out, the setting of 'Wat Pantathro' is 'a recognisable Carmarthen, with its Autumn Horse Fair, its very wide Lammas Street, its market clock and pillars, and its public houses with passages wide enough to walk the horses through to the stables at the back' (Bevan 61). In a letter to Bevan, GJ writes: 'The rest of the story comes from the things, the sweepings perhaps, sucked up on my many visits to Llanstephan, Llanybri, Llangynog and Carmarthen' (Bevan 61). In a videotaped interview with the editor in the Arts Council of Wales *Writers in View* series, recorded in July 1994, GJ speaks of the autobiographical origins of the story and how the basic pattern of going in the trap to Carmarthen with his uncle and then returning became the 'magnet' around which other incidents and characters 'clung'.

p.139 *bloater*: a herring, cured by salting and smoking.

p.139 *rubber collar*: an artificial collar, which could be wiped clean, rather than one made of fabric, which would need washing or laundering; cf. p.213.

p.140 *brick-coloured lips*: 'plum-coloured lips' in *English Story*.

p.141 *Harri Parcglas . . . Lewsin Penylan*: Harri of Parcglas ('Greenpark'), Lewsin of Penylan ('Banktop'); cf. Note to p.69.

p.141 *his entire*: a male animal that has not been castrated, here presumably a stallion.

p.141 *ferret whose mouth he had sewn up*: The ferret would be put down a rabbit hole to chase out rabbits, but would not be able to kill or eat them.

p.142 *Heol Wen*: Welsh, White Road. 'Heol Ebrill' ('April Road') in *English Story*.

p.142 *Tal y Fedw's big grey mare . . . The Tal y Fedw brothers*: 'Trehuddion's big grey mare . . . The Trehuddion brothers' in *English Story*. The revision recurs throughout.

p.142 *the Three Horseshoes*: 'the Three Salmons' in *English Story*. The revision recurs throughout.

p.142 *a lovely slender mare with a pale golden coat*: GJ told Tudor Bevan that there was at Y Lan 'a magnificent golden pony' which GJ 'was enchanted by and which would come to him when he called' (Bevan 62). See the Note to 'The Golden Pony' (p.340).

p.144 *ladies' teasers*: early form of water pistol, sold at fairs, with which groups of boys used to tease girls. A regular feature of fairs across Wales.

p.145 *ugly faces of the men who crowded*: 'the heedless faces of the strangers who crowded' in *English Story*.

p.145 *Gwaed dy Groes*: 'Gwaed dy Groes, sy'n codi i fyny / 'R eiddil yn goncwerwr mawr' ('The Blood of your Cross, which raises / The weakling into a conqueror'), a well-known Welsh hymn by the great hymn-writer William Williams, Pantycelyn (1717-91).

p.146 *The Loss of the Gwladys*: Tudor Bevan notes: 'There was a tradition of marking by song or verse, death or dramatic rescue at sea, "The Women of Mumbles Head" being probably the best-known example with a South Wales setting . . . The technical detail of the schooner's manoeuvres echoes these kinds of disaster but the style was actually modelled on that of Bonny Lewis . . . who used to act out "The Wreck of the Titanic" on Llansteffan Square in a performance which included two songs, and in which he would burst into tears, and generally reproduce those emotions depicted by Wat' (Bevan 62). The identification was confirmed by GJ.

p.146 *Daeth yr awr im' ddianc adre*: 'The hour has come for me to escape homewards', the opening line of a well-known Welsh funeral hymn, 'Ar y Lan Arall' ('On the Other Shore') by Emrys (William Ambrose, Porthmadog, 1813-73).

p.148 *dirtied on the swingle tree*: 'in a plough [or] carriage, a crossbar pivoted at the middle to which the traces are fastened (giving freedom of movement to the shoulders of the horse)' (*OED*), here with a scatological implication. *English Story* has 'done dirt on the breeching' (the leather strap which passes round the breech of a shaft horse). 'Wedi cachu ar y gambren' appears in the *'Idioms'* Notebook.

Textual note

The text of 'Wat Pantathro' in *WM* is a revised version of that which appeared in *English Story*, although the narrative details and sequence are unaltered. Some of the revisions are noted above.

The Last Will

A TS of 'The Last Will', with holograph revisions by GJ, is contained in the collection of *The Water Music* MSS and TSS in NLW.

English Story, fourth series, ed. Woodrow Wyatt (London: Collins, 1943), 159–73.

WM, SSS.

p.149 *flannin*: colloquial form of 'flannel' (also 'flannen').

p.149 *Mari fach*: see Note to p.58. The initial consonant of an adjective following a feminine, singular noun in Welsh mutates, e.g b>f: 'dyn bach', a small man, but 'gwraig fach', a small woman.

p.149 *rubber collar*: see Note to p.139.

p.150 *Dadcu*: Welsh, 'Grandfather' (south Wales).

p.150 *lincyn loncyn*: Welsh, to walk in a leisurely fashion, dawdling.

p.150 *Hook it*: to leave hastily (as in 'sling your hook').

p.151 *wouldn't come to answer*: i.e. measure up (to judgement). (In Welsh, *mynd i'w ateb*, 'to go to answer', is to die and therefore to face judgement and answer for one's sins.)

p.151 *much Welsh*: a south Walian idiom, much conversation.

p.151 *William Nantygors . . . Phylip Mawr Wernddu*: cf. Note to p.69, William of Nantygors ('Stream of the Bog'), Big William of Wernddu ('Black Swamp').

p.151 *Good night, children*: In English, the usual greeting to someone at dusk would be, of course, 'Good evening'. Presumably we are meant to suppose that the characters are speaking in Welsh. Even so, the usual Welsh greeting would be *Noswaith da*, not *Nos da* ('Good night'), more usually used at parting or last thing at night. Again here we have a sense of GJ creating a sense of oddness or defamiliarization for the English-speaking reader.

p.151 *shoulder under the ark*: a literal translation of the Welsh idiom *ysgwydd dan yr arch*, to give aid to a serious enterprise, particularly of a religious nature, here to join the work of the chapel. See 1 Chronicles 15.15, where the Levites carry the ark of the Covenant, the symbol of God's presence among His people, on their shoulders according to Mosaic instruction. The phrase appears with several others used in 'The Last Will' in a list of idiomatic phrases and sayings in GJ's *'Idioms' Notebook*.

p.152 *on the banks of the Jordan*: cf. Note to p.214.

p.152 *poor dab*: see Note to 130.

p.152 *Rhoda Tyllwyd*: cf. Note to p.69, Rhoda of Tyllwyd ('Greyhouse').

p.153 *lying on the little feathers*: in the lap of luxury, a mattress filled with little feathers presumably being the softest and also the most expensive in *'Idioms' Notebook*.

p.153 *come back from off*: a literal translation of the Welsh idiom *dod yn ôl o ffwrdd* or (in the south) *dod yn ôl o bant*, to come back from having been (living) away.

p.153 *light a fire in an old hearth*: The phrase was also collected in GJ's *'Idioms' Notebook*; it is a literal translation of the Welsh idiom *cynnau tân ar hen aelwyd*, to renew an old affection.

p.153 *there's see you changed I do*: idiomatic south Walian English; the syntax, with the verb earlier in the sentence than in standard English, is based on the Welsh word-order.

p.153 *a miserable half candle standing in its own grease on the bible and the ready reckoner by the window*: Compare GJ's account in *Y Llwybrau Gynt* of life at Y Lan, his uncle's farm in Carmarthenshire: 'Yet every year I would come to Y Lan with a paint-box and brushes and paper and books; there was nothing to read there . . .

except the Bible, the Ready Reckoner, and the pretty almanac that advertised cattle-feed' (*MPi* 77; cf. *DTT* 76: 'the only books I ever saw were the Bible and the ready reckoner, and the second of these was in use much oftener than the first'). Tudor Bevan (Bevan 64) points out how GJ takes these remembered incidental details that represent 'an aspect, and only an aspect, of his relatives' lives', their apparent cultural impoverishment, and makes these details symbolize the central, materialistic values of the characters in the story.

p.154   *spanish-brown*: liquorice-brown.

p.154   *bogbean*: a herb (buckbean or marsh trefoil).

p.156   *put his foot to the earth*: a literal translation of the Welsh idiom *rhoi troed ar y tir*, to get going, to run away.

p.156   *trying to keep the dish steady*: a literal translation of the common Welsh idiom, *trio cadw'r ddysgl yn wastad*.

p.156   *a red penny*: see Note to p.69.

p.156   *toby jug*: 'a jug or mug (formerly common) in the form of a stout old man wearing a long and full-skirted coat and a three-cornered hat (18c. costume)' (*OED*).

p.156   *the elbow is nearer than the wrist*: a literal translation of the Welsh idiom, *nes penelin nag arddwrn*; an English equivalent would be 'blood is thicker than water'.

p.156   *wear rubber heels*: Presumably people who wore rubber heels were people from the town or city who wore shoes, with a connotation of moving stealthily, not the nailed boots of the countryside. (*Sgidia dal adar*, bird-catching shoes, were the antithesis of *sgidia hoelion mawr*, shoes with big nails, which is what the *gwerinwr*, the man of the Welsh countryside, would wear.)

p.156   *poor dab*: see Note to p.130.

p.157   *a curl in his tail*: a literal translation of the Welsh idiom *tro yn ei gynffon* (or, in south Wales, *tro yn ei gwt*), describing a sly or underhand person.

p.157   *like carrying water over the river*: a literal translation of the Welsh idiom, *cyrchu dŵr dros afon*; an English equivalent would be 'to carry coals to Newcastle'.

p.157   *in with the bread . . . out with the buns*: of limited intelligence; bread takes longer to bake and would thus remain in the baker's oven after the buns, containing sugar, would be cooked and removed. A loaf removed at this point would be underdone, 'half-baked'.

p.157   *little William*: see Note to p.58.

p.157   *tidy*: see Note to p.57.

p.158   *pudding-cloth*: see Note to p.166.

p.160   *my fiddle is in the thatch*: a literal translation of the Welsh idiom *rhoi'r ffidil yn y to*, to give up doing something and to put the tools/instruments in the attic.

Textual note

The text of 'The Last Will' in *WM* is that which appeared in *English Story*, except that while William is 'scratching at his thigh' in *English Story* he is 'scratching his knee-bones' in *WM* (p.156).

Price-Parry

Welsh Review, 3/4 (December 1944): 236–46.

   WM, SSS.

   Collected in *Stories of the Forties, vol. 2*, ed. Woodrow Wyatt (London: Nicholson

& Watson, 1947); *Welsh Short Stories*, ed. Gwyn Jones (London: OUP, 1956) 109–27.

There is no draft of 'Price-Parry' with the other *Water Music* MSS and TSS in NLW; 'Price-Parry' was added to *WM* after the volume had been accepted by Routledge, GJ sending it to the publisher's director, T. M. Ragg, along with GJ's signed agreement to Routledge's terms It was placed immediately after *The Last Will* at GJ's request (T. M. Ragg, letters to GJ, 28 February 1944 and 3 March 1944, NLW).

The story was accepted by Gwyn Jones in February 1944 for publication in *Welsh Review*: 'Mind you, the *real* time for it would be the Xmas number wouldn't it? In that context it would surely be appreciated by all lovers of your stories, by all lovers of happy endings, and by all whose hearts beat on the right side of their chest' (letter to GJ, 27 February 1944, NLW). The story was ultimately published in the Christmas issue, 1944.

p.161 *Mati Tŷ-unnos*: Her name is in fact Mati Rees (p.167). Again, cf. Note to p.69, the name by which she is known in the community is derived from the house where she lives: *Tŷ-unnos*, 'one-night house', with a possible reference to Mati's sexual morality.

p.161 *Rhodri Fawr*: Rhodri Mawr became King of Gwynedd in 844, of Powys in 855 and of Seisyllwg in 872. He successfully defended his lands against the Danes and the English, dying in battle against the latter in 877. 'His subsequent reputation was such that to be of the line of Rhodri Mawr was, in succeeding centuries, the first qualification for rulers in both north and south Wales' (*Companion* 514). He was the grandfather of Hywel Dda (d.950) who gained power over most of Wales by the time of his death and under whose authority the native laws of Wales were codified.

p.161 *gambo-wheel*: cart-wheel. A 'gambo' in south-west Wales was a hay cart.

p.162 *eagle-beaked, his out-thrust face ecclesiastical brass*: Price-Parry's physiognomy, emphasized throughout the story, resembles the eagle, carved in wood or cast in brass, which forms the main lectern in many Anglican churches.

p.162 *97th Psalm*: A Bible opened at Psalm 97 would be open at its mid-point, equal numbers of pages falling open on either side of the spine, like the vicar's centrally-parted hair. The psalm itself asserts and celebrates the power of the Lord in tones which Price-Parry, given his own sense of pride and power, would find sympathetic, although the imagery of the psalm is in contrast to the icy coldness which is associated with the vicar's egotism until the end of the story: 'A fire goeth before him, and burneth up his enemies round about . . . The hills melted like wax in the presence of the Lord, at the presence of the Lord of the whole earth' (verses 3, 5).

p.164 *twti down*: to crouch or squat down. A widely-used south Walian idiom (perhaps from the colloquial Welsh, 'twt', a little person or child, thus 'twti', to crouch and make oneself small; 'coopy / cwpi down' is a parallel usage, perhaps from 'coop', as in 'cooped up').

p.164 *warts . . . each with a little bow of cotton*: to tie cotton around a wart was a folk remedy for removing them.

p.165 *A little child shall lead them*: see Isaiah 11.6: 'The wolf also shall dwell with the lamb, and the leopard shall lie down with the kid . . . and a little child shall lead them.' There is clearly an ironic contrast between Isaiah's vision of harmony and peaceful equality and Price-Parry's pride, as he sits in his cart 'like a king', while the 'little child' trudges through the snow.

p.165   *poor dab*: see Note to p.130.

p.166   *Shâms*: a Welsh version of James (also 'Jâms', 'Siâms')

p.166   *like a steam pudding*: Steam puddings were wrapped in cloth to be cooked.

p.166   *cross the Jordan*: See Note to p.214.

p.166   *ginger-rubber*: 'India-rubber' often became 'inja-rubber' (d>j, as in 'diawl'>jawl), then 'ginger-rubber', an attempt at rationalization.

p.166   *that old English*: Presumably we are meant to understand that Mati and Geta are conversing in Welsh; this is one of the few points in GJ's stories at which the issue of the actual language spoken by his village characters is raised; cf. Notes to pp.227 and 325.

p.166   *won't feel worth a roast potato*: a literal translation of the Welsh idiom *[dim] gwerth taten bob*, used to express the feeling of being drained of energy, tired out.

p.166   *for the sake of everything*: a literal translation of the common Welsh idiom, *er mwyn popeth*.

p.167   *Your Master rode . . . these*: Christ entered Jerusalem on an ass, shortly before His arrest (John 12.14–15).

p.167   *bitter as bogbean*: see Note to 154.

p.167   *Wil Saer*: *Saer* = Welsh, 'carpenter'; 'Wil Saer' is thus the name by which he is known in the community.

p.167   *give another guess*: GJ is translating the Welsh idiom, *rhoi cynnig ar*, 'to give a guess' (rather than the Standard English, take/have a guess).

p.167   *with all the power of his mouth*: a literal translation of the Welsh idiom, *â holl nerth ei geg* or *holl nerth ei enau* or *holl nerth 'i ben* (*pen* = lit. 'head' but also colloquially 'mouth', as in *llond pen*, a mouthful, and *ca' dy ben*, shut your mouth).

p.167   *an endless tyrant*: a version of a Welsh idiom which exists in various forms, including *bwli diddiwedd*, an endless bully, still used in areas of Carmarthenshire.

p.169   *radiant cloths of the fuller*: To full cloth was to beat or tread it in order to clean it; the fuller used 'fuller's earth', a hydrous silicate of alumina. (*OED* gives a relevant metaphorical usage from 1670: 'The blots of sin will be easily taken out by the soap of sorrow and the fuller's earth of contrition.')

p.170   *I wouldn't give a hair from my nose*: a literal translation of the Welsh idiom, *rown i ddim blewyn o'n nhrwyn*, 'I wouldn't lift a finger to help him'.

p.170   *breaking words*: a translation of the Welsh idiom *torri gair* (or *torri geiriau*), lit. to break a word (or words), to speak, to break the silence (e.g. *Nid wyf wedi torri gair â neb ers dyddiau*, 'I haven't spoken a word to anybody for days').

Textual Note
The text of *Price-Parry* in *WM* is that which appeared in *Welsh Review*.

Bowen, Morgan and Williams

A holograph MS draft of part of 'Bowen, Morgan and Williams' and a TS of the whole story, with substantial holograph revisions by GJ, is contained in the collection of *The Water Music* MSS and TSS in NLW.

WM, SSS, GWWY.

Collected in *Penguin Parade, No. 11*, ed. D. Kilham Roberts (London: Penguin, 1945), 145–84. Denys Kilham Roberts wrote to GJ on 11 March 1937, indicating that Penguin planned to issue each quarter 'a collection of stories and sketch-stories of a high literary standard and of what is usually considered from the publisher's and editor's point of view a difficult length – 3000–10000 words', and asking if GJ had 'anything that has not previously been printed in this country that you would care to send along for me to see?' It is not clear when GJ sent *Bowen, Morgan and Williams*, but Roberts wrote to GJ on 12 February 1943: 'I have had your story *Bowen, Morgan and Williams* on the *Penguin Parade* short list, and I am hopeful of being able to find a place for it in *Penguin Parade 11* which, with any luck the publishers should be able to bring out some time in the course of 1943.' Further delays followed until GJ wrote to tell Roberts in March 1944 that the story would be in GJ's new collection. Roberts acknowledged GJ's return of proofs of the story in December, noting that 'if Routledge get the book out before *Penguin Parade 11* appears, it just can't be helped' (correspondence in NLW).

Bowen, Morgan and Williams was subsequently translated into French by Raymonde Asselin and published in Paris in *Fontaine*, 59 (April 1949): 77–100, an issue which included work by Raymond Queneau and Jean Cocteau. The story, unfortunately, was published over the name of *Gwyn* Jones. (See correspondence in NLW, which also contains a TS of the translation.)

The story was collected in *Components of the Scene*, ed. Ronald Blythe (London: Penguin, 1966), 313–39, an anthology of literature written during the Second World War.

p.173 *my father didn't like me going boxing*: GJ is remembering the fact that his mother did not like him playing with a rather scruffy neighbouring family in Merthyr, the O'Driscolls, who had a gymnasium 'which was a good place to practise boxing – one of their sons was a champion at this sport' (*MPi* 73). Cf. Note to p.216.

p.173 *in her oil*: a south Walian idiom, 'in her element'.

p.173 *she had a long stocking*: a translation of a Welsh idiom, which exists in several variations: e.g. *Mae ganddi hi hosan dda* ('She has a good stocking') or *Mae hosan fach gyda hi* ('She has a little stocking'), meaning that the woman had a nest-egg, 'a little money put by', at one time literally saved in a stocking in a drawer or under the mattress. Presumably the idiom was more usually used of a young woman before marriage.

p.173 *flat spanish*: flat strip of liquorice; cf. Note to p.154.

p.174 *passing senior*: passing the examination for admission into the senior school.

p.174 *water brash*: acid indigestion, belching of fluid.

p.174 *shindry girl*: a household maid, one who cleared up the cinders from the fires (from south Walian Welsh, *sindrins*, cinders). An idiom which was current in the Merthyr area.

p.175 *poor little dab*: see Note to p.130.

p.175 *the big seat*: the pew at the front of the chapel where the deacons sit, from the Welsh, *Y Sêt Fawr*.

p.176 *Llinos Cwm Du*: cf. Note to p.69, Llinos of Cwm Du ('Black Valley').

p.177 *handsome pink cheeks*: 'cheeks pink as blotting paper' (*Penguin Parade*).

p.177   *crachach*: Welsh, the minor gentry or the well-heeled, with a connotation of self-conscious gentility or snobbery. The term is still current, in both languages.

p.177   *ach y fi*: Welsh, an expression of disgust, also frequently used by English-speakers in south Wales.

p.178   *crying salt*: a literal translation of the Welsh idiom, *wylo dagrau hallt*, to cry bitterly. In the *'Idioms' Notebook* GJ records, 'A lovely ham funeral. She was crying salt after 'im.'

p.178   *lived under the showers*: a literal translation of the Welsh idiom, *byw dan gawod*.

p.178   *meal of food*: a south Walian idiom, a literal translation of the Welsh idiom, *pryd o fwyd*.

p.179   *No dal on the White-hat*: in Welsh, *dim dal (ar rhywun)* means someone not able to be depended upon or trusted.

p.179   *bloaters*: herrings, cured by salting and smoking.

p.181   *that will keep*: a literal translation of the Welsh idiom, *mi/fe gadwith*, we needn't go into that now, it'll keep for another day.

p.182   *living at the foot of the waterfall*: possibly a play on the Welsh idiom *siarad fel pwll y môr*; cf. Note to p.185.

p.183   *from the bottom of the nest*: a literal translation of the Welsh idiom, *cyw gwaelod y nyth*, 'the chick at the bottom of the nest', the last or youngest child of the family.

p.183   *potting*: drinking (beer or ale).

p.184   *the lamb teaching the sheep to graze*: a literal translation of the Welsh idiom, *yr oen yn dysgu i'r ddafad bori*, an equivalent to the English idiom, 'teaching one's grandmother to suck eggs'.

p.184   *got no looks on*: got no regard for, a south Walian idiom, a literal translation of the Welsh, *'doedd gyda hi ddim golwg ar*.

p.184   *tidy*: see Note to p.57.

p.184   *hwyl*: Welsh, 'in a fervour, zest, high spirits'. (The *hwyl*, relatedly, was the musically-cadenced, chanting delivery at the emotional climax or peroration of some Nonconformist ministers' sermons; some ministers were renowned for this emotionally dramatic, or operatic, style of preaching to a congregation.)

p.185   *talking like the pit of the sea*: to talk incessantly, a literal translation of the Welsh idiom, *siarad/clebran fel pwll y môr*.

p.185   *Mamgu*: Welsh, 'Grandmother' (south Wales).

p.185   *to creep into her sleeve*: to ingratiate himself with her, a literal translation of the Welsh idiom, *mynd i'w llawes*.

p.185   *going towards up*: a literal translation of the Welsh idiom *mynd am i fyny*.

p.186   *beyond his top*: in Welsh *pen* translates both 'head' and 'top'.

p.186   *Cochyn*: Welsh, 'Ginger', a red-headed person.

p.186   *heelball*: 'a polishing substance composed principally of hard wax and lamp-black used by shoe-makers to give a shining black surface to the sole edges of new boots and shoes' (*OED*).

p.186   *keep your hat straight*: a Carmarthenshire idiom (also in Welsh, *cadw eich cap [het] yn strêt [syth]*), to act respectably when it is in one's interests to do so. (Though there is also a south Walian idiom *cadw ei gap yn gymwys*, keep his hat straight, an equivalent of 'keep on the right side of him'.)

p.186   *she had no looks on*: see Note to p.184.

p.187   *gymanfa ganu*: Welsh, hymn-singing festival.

p.187 *spitting on his crossed fingers*: There are many childhood rituals relating to crossing fingers and spitting, most of them with a relation to oath-taking and usually to God or Christ. (The only Welsh rituals recorded by Iona and Peter Opie, in Anglesey and Aberystwyth, involve a rhyme, 'Cris croes, tan poeth, byddaf farw ar y groes' (Criss cross, hot fire, I will die on the cross), with the child moistening a finger and making the sign of the cross on forehead and neck. See *The Lore and Language of Schoolchildren* (Oxford: OUP, 1959), 124-5.) Presumably, in the story, the jibe at the expense of the pawnbroker is a reference to his Jewishness.

p.187 *a pack sergeant*: a servant, responsible for carrying luggage, who walked behind his employer.

p.188 *fives court*: fives is a game in which a ball is struck (by the hand) against the front wall of a three-sided court.

p.188 *make a broth of it*: a literal translation of the Welsh idiom, *gwneud cawl (o rywbeth)*, to make a mess (of something).

p.188 *fly-me*: Eric Partridge gives 'flymy' (to rhyme with 'slimy'), 'knowing, artful, roguish' ('fly' as in 'he's a fly one'). See Eric Partridge, *Penguin Dictionary of Historical Slang* (Harmondsworth: Penguin, 1972).

p.189 *Rechabites*: The Independent Order of Rechabites, a benefit society, founded in 1835. (The Rechabites were originally associated with abstinence from alcohol, cf. Jeremiah 35.2–19.)

p.189 *bosh*: a kitchen sink (a south Walian idiom).

p.189 *stoning swirls*: stoning = rubbing or scouring (flagstones) with an abrasive stone to clean them. Here the repeated cleaning has left white/bleached curves or swirls on the flagstones, comparable to the pale semicircle one used to see on the pavement outside terraced houses, the circumference being the reach of the housewife's arm as she knelt on the doorstep, facing outwards.

p.189 *stife*: 'a suffocating fume or vapour' (*OED*).

p.189 *let the jellies set in*: because the unused parlour would be unheated and thus the coldest place on the ground floor of the house.

p.189 *gwdihŵ*: Welsh, colloquial term for an owl.

p.189 *carpet slaps*: see Note to p.134.

p.190 *hadn't done a tap*: a south Walian idiom, 'he hadn't done any work'.

p.190 *jagged blue mark*: characteristic blue scars of the miner, caused by coal-dust entering a wound while the man was working underground; cf. Note to p.53.

p.190 *the Buffs*: an infantry regiment (originally the Third Regiment of Foot); their regimental facings were buff-coloured.

p.190 *miching*: playing truant (a south Walian idiom); also 'mitching'.

p.191 *take a blow*: 'take a breath', 'take it easy' (cf. p.193).

p.191 *talk very far back*: to affect a polished (English) middle- or upper-class accent, with rather glottal vowels and limited lip-movement.

p.191 *perihelion*: 'that point in a planet's orbit at which it is closest to the sun' (*OED*).

p.191 *pucelage*: 'the state . . . of being a "pucelle" or girl; maidenhead, virginity' (*OED*).

p.192 *hiraeth*: Welsh, 'longing, wistfulness, homesickness'.

p.193 *landed*: contented, in her element (idiomatic in parts of south Wales); also in Welsh, 'Mae hi wedi landio', especially after a success, 'she's all right', 'she doesn't have to worry any more'. Still current in Welsh in Carmarthenshire.

p.193   *culff:* probably from the Welsh 'cwlff', a hunk or chunk or large slice of something, especially bread. ('Culff' is used in English in some areas of south Wales with this meaning.)

p.194   *O wel ta wir:* Welsh, 'Oh, well, there we are then' (usually at the conclusion of a conversation or discussion).

p.194   *Mabon milk-jug:* A jug commemorating 'Mabon' (William Abraham, 1842–1922), first President of the South Wales Miners' Federation (founded 1898). He became MP for the Rhondda as a Radical in 1885.

Textual notes
The text of 'Bowen, Morgan and Williams' in *WM* is that which appeared in *Penguin Parade*, with only minor revisions.

The Water Music

Two holograph drafts of 'The Water Music' are contained in the collection of *The Water Music* MSS and TSS in NLW.

   Life and Letters To-day, 39/75 (Nov. 1943): 109–20.

   WM, SSS.

   'The Water Music' was accepted for publication in *Life and Letters To-day* by the editor, Robert Herring, in a letter to GJ, dated 11 August 1943, NLW. See Note to 'The Wanderer'.

p.196   *crocketed:* in architecture, a crocket is 'one of the curled leaves or similar ornaments up the side of a pinnacle' (*OED*). The narrator, as much a word-fancier as his creator, demonstrates his knowledge of, and love for, unusual words throughout the story.

p.197   *volute:* a twisted turn.

p.197   *boxing-glove burning sire:* see Mr. Bowen's rigid attitudes and religious beliefs in 'Bowen, Morgan and Williams' (pp.173, 186). At the same time Benja is '*victor ludorum*', winner of most events in his school sports.

p.197   *Dic Dywyll:* Richard Williams (*c*.1790–1862), a writer of comic and satirical ballads; he was blind, as well as being short and fat.

p.197   *Caspian birthmark:* see p.192

p.198   *Gerallt's soldier voiding a calf:* In *Itinerary Through Wales* by Giraldus Cambrensis (Gerallt Cymro): 'A soldier, whose name was Gilbert Hagernel, after an illness of nearly three years, and the severe pains as of a woman in labour, in the presence of many people, voided a calf. A portent of some new and unusual event, or rather the punishment attendant on some atrocious crime.' See Giraldus Cambrenis, *'Itinerary Through Wales' and 'Description of Wales'*, trans. R. C. Hoare (1908; London: Dent, 1976), 25.

p.198   *scalene:* 'unequal-sided (esp. scalene triangle, with no sides equal)' (*OED*).

p.198   *Sterne-visaged:* The best-known portraits of Laurence Sterne (1713–68) show him as having a hard, angular face. Sterne, however, with his love of wit and word-play, might have been more in sympathy with the narrator than his teacher is.

p.198   *Llangorse . . . Llyn y Fan . . . Llyn Syfaddon:* Llangorse Lake is in Breconshire; Llyn y Fan is near Llanddeusant in Carmarthenshire (it is the site of the legend of the young man who falls in love with a maiden who lives in the lake;

she agrees to marry him but warns she will leave him if he strikes her 'three causeless blows' and she returns to the lake when three blows are accidentally struck. GJ wrote a short, unpublished version of this story); Llyn Syfaddon is also in Breconshire (it is the site of two legends: in one a town is drowned because of the wickedness of a prince and his subjects and, in the other, the birds of the lake will sing only at the behest of the true prince of south Wales). On the legends, see *Companion*.

p.198 *lovely under Dafydd's swan*: The swan at 'Llyn Yfaddon' [*sic*] appears in fact in a poem by an unknown author; see 'Yr Alarch', *Barddoniaeth yr Uchelwyr*, ed. D. J. Bowen (Cardiff: University of Wales, 1959), 69-70, translated as 'The Swan', *Medieval Welsh Lyrics*, trans. Joseph P. Clancy (London: Macmillan, 1965), 156-7.

p.198 *Llanrhidian . . . Llantwit Major*: Llanrhidian, a village on the Gower Peninsula in south Wales; Afon Sawdde, a river in Carmarthenshire, near Llanddeusant (it also appears in Revd Eli Jenkins's morning hymn in *Under Milk Wood*); Fan Gihirych, a peak in the Brecon Beacons, referred to in GJ's poem 'Merthyr'; Dyffryn Clwyd or the Vale of Clwyd in north-east Wales, is celebrated in some of Hopkins's verse (see Note to p.203); Rhosllanerchrugog, a town near Wrexham, Denbighshire; Llanfairpwll . . ., supposedly, one of the longest place-names in the world, a village in the south-east of Anglesey; the Lleyn, or Llŷn, Peninsula, the north-west arm of Wales, jutting out into the Irish Sea; Llanelly, now Llanelli, a town in Carmarthenshire, to the west of Swansea; Dinas Mawddwy, a town in Merionethshire; Dinas Powis, once a separate village, now a suburb of Cardiff; Cwm Elan, a scenic valley in mid Wales, near Rhayader; Cwm Rhondda, the Rhondda Valley in Glamorgan; Tresaith, a village on the Cardiganshire coast; Treorky, usually Treorchy, a town in the Rhondda Valley; Penrhyn Gŵyr, the Gower peninsula, to the south-west of Swansea; Llantwit Major, a village in the Vale of Glamorgan, not far from Cardiff.

p.198 *Hen Wlad fy Nhadau*: the Welsh national anthem (lit. 'The old/dear land of my fathers').

p.199 *little Moscow*: The name is usually identified with Mardy, in the Rhondda Valley, because of the radical nature of its Socialism between the wars.

p.199 *denounced as Catiline*: Catiline, in 64 BC, conspired to raise an armed rebellion against the elected consuls of Rome. The boys' play-acting – 'perjured caitiff . . .' – suggests that they have in mind the best-known version of the story: Ben Jonson's tragedy, *Catiline* (1611), which they have presumably studied at school. (*WM* has 'Cataline'.)

p.199 *Imperato's*: the gym in 'Bowen, Morgan and Williams'. Bowen is a good boxer; cf. note to p.173.

p.200 *mitched*: see Note to p.190.

p.200 *the wandering scholar*: Dafydd ap Gwilym. The passage which follows is a translation of his poem 'Yr Wylan' ('The Seagull'). See *Gwaith Dafydd ap Gwilym*, 313-14. The poem is a *llatai*, the Welsh poetic convention by which a poet sends a bird or animal with a message to his sweetheart. See also GJ's verse translation of the poem in *Collected Poems* (*CP* 52-3) and 'Dafydd's Seagull and the West Wind' (*CP* 73-4).

p.200 *billet*: *billet-doux*, a love-letter

p.200 *Eigr-coloured*: in his verse translation of 'The Seagull' (*CP* 52-3) GJ has 'Eigr-complexioned'. Eigr was a legendary heroine and, supposedly, the mother of

Arthur. She is referred to as a measure of female beauty in a number of poems by Dafydd ap Gwilym.

p.200 *Merddin*: a version of Myrddin or Merlin, fictional poet and prophet, associated with the Arthurian legends.

p.200 *Taliesin*: a poet (*fl.* late 6th century), named with Aneirin in Nennius's *Historia Brittonum*, in a passage which lists the poets who flourished in the 'Old North' of Britain (i.e. what is today the south of Scotland).

p.201 *cynghanedd*: the intricate system of alliteration and internal rhyme used in Welsh poetry. Cf. GJ's reference in *DTT* to the motto on the billhead of a coalman in Cardiff: '"Dyma'r boi i dwymo'r byd"', which means, "Here's the bloke to warm the world". . . this line could, from a technical point of view, appear in a classical *cywydd* or an *englyn*, since it has seven syllables and contains *cynghanedd groes* . . .' (*DTT* 131–2).

p.201 *High Priest of Lakery*: William Wordsworth, who was born and lived much of his life in the Lake District, in his poetry expressed a belief in the educative and ameliorative powers of Nature; in his poem 'The Tables Turned' (*Lyrical Ballads*, 1798), the narrator urges: 'Come forth into the light of things, / Let Nature be your teacher'.

p.201 *Hamlet* : The reference is to Act 3 Scene 3, where Hamlet is wrestling with the dilemma of whether to kill the king, Claudius, who is also his uncle ('pat' here, of course, means 'immediately, without hesitation').

p.201 *pudeur*: sense of shame or embarrassment, especially about sexual matters.

p.201 *sciolist*: 'a superficial pretender to knowledge, a conceited smatterer' (*OED*).

p.202 *pappus*: the downy growth on the seeds of certain plants, e.g. the dandelion.

p.202 *Sande*: in the list of Arthur's court in *Culhwch ac Olwen*, Sandde Bryd Angel is, with Morfran son of Tegid and Cynwyl the Saint, part of the triad who escaped from the battle of Camlan: 'Sandde Angel-face (no-one placed his spear in him at Camlan, so exceedingly fair was he; all thought he was an angel helping)'. See *The Mabinogion*, trans. Gwyn Jones and Thomas Jones, revised edition (London: Dent, 1976), 102. ('Sandef' and 'Sande' are the forms in the MSS – d = dd – with modern orthography giving 'Sanddef' and 'Sandde'.)

p.202 *vidame*: 'formerly in France, one who held lands from a bishop as his representative and defender in temporal matters' (*OED*).

p.202 *hirundine*: 'of or pertaining to a swallow' (*OED*).

p.203 *Welsh Shelley*: The poet Shelley was drowned in the Bay of Spezia, Italy, in 1822. Shelley, above all the Romantics a poet of fancy and logomancy and idealism, would seem to be an entirely appropriate idol for the young narrator.

p.203 *I praise him for his endless fertility* . . .: The celebratory tones and the occasional alliteration in the final movement of the story ('I praise him for the big boy-bodied beeches') would seem to echo the sprung-rhythm poetry of Gerard Manley Hopkins (1844–89) in praise of God's creation. The present paragraph in particular is reminscent of the thought and mood of Hopkins's 'Pied Beauty':

> Glory be to God for dappled things –
>   For skies of couple-colour as a brinded cow;
>   For rose, moles all in stipple upon trout that swim . . .

> Whatever is fickle, freckled (who knows how?)
> With swift, slow; sweet, sour; adazzle, dim;
> He fathers-forth whose beauty is past change:
> Praise him

Hopkins studied Welsh *cynghanedd*, and attempted some strict-metre poetry in Welsh, during his three years of theological training at St Beuno's College, near St Asaph, Flintshire, 1874–7. GJ published an essay on 'Hopkins and Welsh Prosody' in *Life and Letters To-day*, 21 (1939), 50-4, and also gave a radio talk on Hopkins's poetry in Welsh on the BBC Welsh Home Service on 27 August 1945. See also Tony Conran, 'Gerard Hopkins as an Anglo-Welsh Poet', *The Welsh Connection*, ed. William Tydeman (Llandysul: Gomer, 1986), 111–29.

p.203 *chrism*: 'oil mixed with balm consecrated for use as an unguent in the administration of certain sacraments' (*OED*).

Textual note

The text of 'The Water Music' in *WM* is that of *Life and Letters To-day*.

Jordan

A TS of 'Jordan', with minor holograph emendations, forms part of the collection of TSS collected together by GJ as *The Golden Pony*, apparently intended for a volume of that name: 'Jordan', 'The Boy in the Bucket', 'It's Not By His Beak . . .' and the stories ultimately published in *Welsh Heirs. The Golden Pony* TSS are in the Glyn Jones collection in the Library of Trinity College, Carmarthen (Box File 5).

SSS, GWWY.

Collected in *Welsh Tales of Terror*, ed. R. Chetwynd-Hynes (London: Fontana, 1973), 13–26; *The Green Bridge*, ed. John Davies (Bridgend: Seren, 1988), 93–105.

p.204 *fairs and markets . . . in that country*: GJ based the figures of Danny and the narrator on 'the cheapjacks who used to come to Carmarthen market' (conversation with the editor, 22 February 1992). In the same conversation, GJ said that he had 'no idea' what the origins were of the grotesque figure of Jordan.

p.204 *coms*: see Note to p.56.

p.206 *Jordan*: In a conversation with the editor (10 April 1994), GJ remembered that the name was that of a local funeral director in Whitchurch, Cardiff. The aptness of a funeral director being called 'Jordan' – to cross the River Jordan being to die, a verbal play with which the story ends – thus contributed to the germination of the story.

p.208 *Farw . . . Angau*: Both words translate from the Welsh as 'death', *angau* being a more literary usage. (In the TS the dogs are called 'Fan' and 'Tango'.)

p.212 *the chick born in hell returns to the burning*: a translation of the Welsh idiom 'Cyw a fegir yn uffern, yn uffern y myn e fod', 'A chick brought up in [lit.] hell, hell is where he will wish to be'. *Uffern* in this context is the ashpan or fire-grate, the allusion being to the weakling chick, reared on the in heat of the the kitchen range, as near as possible to the fire.

p.213 *rubber breast and collar*: see Note to p.139

p.213 *on strap*: on credit.

p.214   *crossing Jordan*: see note to p.206. The image of crossing the Jordan at death, perhaps to reach The Promised Land on the other side (cf. Joshua 4), is widespread in anglophone cultures – as in the spiritual 'Swing low, sweet chariot' – as well as in Welsh-language hymns like that of Ieuan Glan Geirionydd (Evan Evans, 1795–1855): 'Ar lan Iorddonen ddofn / 'Rwy'n oedi'n nychlyd, / Mewn blys mynd trwy, ac ofn / Ei stormydd enbyd: / O! na bai modd i mi / Osgoi ei hymchwydd hi, / A hedfan uwch ei lli / I'r Ganaan hyfryd' ('On the shore of Jordan deep / I linger feebly, / Longing to go through, and fearing / Its perilous storms: Oh! if there were only a way for me / To avoid its surge, / And fly above the flow / To beautiful Canaan').

Textual note
The TS has a few minor holograph revisions by GJ. However, a comparison of the TS with the version published in *SSS* indicates that the story underwent a further stage of revision before publication, although the events and sequence of the narrative remain unaltered.

The Boy in the Bucket

A TS of 'The Boy in the Bucket', with minor holograph emendations by GJ, is included in *The Golden Pony* TSS at Trinity College, Carmarthen.
Anglo-Welsh Review, 12/30 (1962): 22–9.
SSS, GWWY.
Collected in *The Shining Pyramid*, ed. Sam Adams and Roland Mathias (Llandysul: Gomer, 1970), 123–33.

p.215   *cwm*: see Note to p.105.
p.215   *a Blue Paper*: a summons.
p.215   *Richards the Stoning . . . Mrs. Rees the Bank . . . old Bara-chaws the roadman*: cf. Note to p.69. Richards is presumably the supplier of abrasives for scrubbing (cf. Note to p.189); Mrs. Rees is the wife of the local bank manager; 'bara-chaws'=Welsh, bread and cheese, which is presumably what the old roadman habitually eats in his meal breaks.
p.215   *The Big Seat*: see Note to p.175.
p.216   *gymanfa*: Welsh, *gymanfa ganu*, hymn-singing festival.
p.216   *Iesu Grist*: Welsh, 'Jesus Christ'.
p.216   *playing with the O'Driscolls*: Ceri's mother's dislike of his playing with the non-respectable O'Driscolls is clearly based on GJ's own mother's antipathy to his playing with a neighbouring family in Merthyr: '. . . although I was fond of these funny, feckless people, my mother wasn't keen for me to be too friendly with them – they used to curse and swear, play football on a Sunday, and wipe their noses on their sleeves' (*MPi* 73). This Merthyr family also kept a gymnasium; the O'Driscolls have 'a gymnasium shed in the backyard'; cf Note to p.173.
p.217   *jubes*: fruit pastilles.
p.217   *small coal . . . outside their houses*: miners' families received coal at a reduced price, delivered to their door.
p.218   *Ugain Tŷ*: Welsh, 'Twenty Houses'.
p.219   *gambo-wheel*: cart wheel. See Note to p.161.

p.220 *down over a bunch of black teeth*: 'down over a black tooth' (*Anglo-Welsh Review* and TS).

p.220 *dubliw*: see Note to p.133.

p.220 *Mamgu*: see Note to p.185.

p.221 *through her broken teeth*: 'through her teeth' (*Anglo-Welsh Review* and TS).

p.222 *bach*: see Note to p.58.

p.222 *riff-raff*: 'rabble, disreputable persons' (*OED*). (Ceri is now fleeing back to maternal respectability.)

Textual note
Although only minor holograph textual revisions appear in the TS of the story, from a comparison of the text with the versions in *Anglo-Welsh Review* and in *SSS*, it is evident that the TS version underwent further revision before publication and the *Anglo-Welsh Review* text was slightly revised again before inclusion in *SSS*, although the events and the sequence of the narrative remain the same in all three versions.

It's Not By His Beak You Can Judge a Woodcock

Although the TS of the story is listed by GJ on the Contents page of *The Golden Pony* TSS at Trinity College, Carmarthen, the actual TS of the story is missing from the collection.

Stand, 7 (1954): 5–12; *Welsh Short Stories*, ed. G. Ewart Evans, 2nd ed. (London: Faber, 1959), 42–51.

SSS, GWWY.

Collected in *Twenty-Five Welsh Short Stories*, ed. Gwyn Jones and Islwyn Ffowc Elis (Oxford: OUP, 1971), reissued as *Classic Welsh Short Stories* (Oxford: OUP, 1992), 105-13.

The first outline of the story appears in a diary entry in July 1952: 'Farmer has 3 fields across the river – won't sell to his enemy – has mistress – (one day railway will go over them?) – dying – minister in house – makes wife swear she will sell fields and give money to mistress – in the will – she sells them for a few shillings and gives money to mistress'.

Glyn Jones read the entire story and commented on it as part of a videotaped interview on his fiction, with Tony Curtis and Michael Parnell, at the Centre for the Study of Welsh Writing in English at the Polytechnic of Wales (now the University of Glamorgan) on 28 January 1990.

p.224 *It's Not By His Beak You Can Judge a Woodcock*: The title is a literal translation of the Welsh idiom, 'nid wrth ei big y mae prynu [barnu] cyffylog', 'do not judge by appearances'. The phrase appears in the *'Idioms' Notebook*.

p.224 *Jim Saer*: see Note to p.167.

p.224 *like something green brought by a far-off pigeon*: the image, appropriately for a minister, draws on the story of the dove returning to Noah with an olive leaf as the Flood subsides (Genesis 8.8–11).

p.225 *put his shoulder under the ark*: see Note to p.151.

p.225 *the unsearchable riches*: St. Paul wrote to the Ephesians, 'Unto me, who am less than the least of all saints, is this grace given, that I should preach among the

Gentiles the unsearchable riches of Christ' (Ephesians 3.8). The phrase is used to refer to the gospel and its benefits.

p.225   *lake-bank of the Means*: The 'Means' are the means of grace, *moddion gras* (i.e. public prayer, preaching and exhortation as well as the Lord's Supper); 'the lake-bank' refers to John 5.1–9, where Jesus heals the lame man beside the lake of Bethesda where the the sick come for healing. The phrase *wrth lyn y moddion* became a metaphor for public worship through which the healing presence of Christ would be mediated in the preaching of the gospel.

p.225   *Good night*: see note to p.151.

p.226   *you are like a gunbarrel*: that is, straight, honest. Listed in the *'Idioms' Notebook*.

p.226   *nant*: Welsh, 'stream'.

p.226   *a hair of my nose*: see Note to p.170.

p.226   *Yr argian fawr*: Welsh exclamation, 'Good Lord!', 'Good gracious!' (presumably an elision of *Yr Arglwydd Mawr!*).

p.227   *blue himself*: listed in the *'Idioms' Notebook*, where GJ glosses it as 'bruise himself'.

p.227   *Ahab's Welsh*: one of the few points in GJ's stories where it is explicit that the characters are in fact speaking Welsh; cf. Note to 'Price-Parry' (p.166) and 'Lias Lewis' (p.325).

p.227   *the belly of your hand*: a play on the Welsh *tor y llaw*, the palm of the hand, *tor* also meaning 'belly'.

p.228   *gambo*: see Note to p.161.

p.228   *Twm Tircoch*: cf. Note to p.69, Tom of Tircoch ('Redland').

p.228   *With considering Gwilym considered this*: This somewhat ungainly sentence appears in all printings of the story and is read thus by GJ in his Polytechnic of Wales reading.

p.229   *Elin Tŷ-fri*: cf. Note to p.69, Elin of Tŷ-fri ('House above') .

p.229   *fall to the dogs and the ravens*: a literal translation of the Welsh idiom, *mynd rhwng y cŵn a'r brain*, 'to go to wrack and ruin, to be dissipated (of wealth, estate)' (*Geiriadur Prifysgol Cymru*).

p.230   *out of the mouths . . . came forth wisdom*: 'Out of the mouths of babes and sucklings hast thou ordained strength because of thine enemies, that thou mightest still the enemy and the avenger' (Psalms 8.2); the psalm is alluded to in St. Matthew's Gospel: 'And Jesus saith unto them, Yea; have ye never read, Out of the mouth of babes and sucklings thou hast perfected praise?' (Matthew 21.16).

Textual note

The text of 'It's Not by His Beak. . .' in *SSS* is a slightly revised version of that which was published in *Stand*, although the details and sequence of the narrative are unaltered.

Four Tales

The TSS entitled *The Golden Pony* at Trinity College, Carmarthen, contains typescripts of each of the 'Four Tales' published in *Welsh Heirs*, with the overall title of 'The Jeffreys Family'. The sequence is not placed at the opening of the collection, however, as it is in the published collection, and is in a different order.

Robert Jeffreys

In *The Golden Pony* TSS, the story is placed first in 'The Jeffreys Family' but is entitled 'Dafydd Morris'. The TS contains numerous minor holograph revisions by GJ. It seems likely that 'Dafydd Morris' was the '12,000 word story' that GJ tells Gwyn Jones he has 'just finished' in a letter dated 8 May 1949 (Professor Gwyn Jones Papers II, 9/2, NLW). The story's only publication was in *Welsh Heirs* .

p.231 *the Ystrad Valley*:   based on the Merthyr Valley (cf. Note to 'I Was Born in the Ystrad Valley' (p.1). In the TS the location is simply 'the valley'.

p.231 *Robert Jeffreys*: 'Bona Jeffreys' in the TS. The TS version does not have the details of Jeffreys's family given in the opening paragraph.

p.231 *miching*: see Note to p.190.

p.235 *cwm*: see Note to p.105.

p.235 *his Saviour stood among myrtles, or strode out of Edom conquering*: Dafydd is remembering two famous hymns of the Welsh Independents (*Yr Annibynwyr*), which GJ himself would have known throughout his life. The first is by the great hymn-writer Ann Griffiths, Dolwar Fach, (1776–1805): 'Wele'n sefyll rhwng y myrtwydd / Wrthych teilwng o'm holl fryd, / Er mai o ran yr wy'n adnabod / Ei fod uwchlaw gwrthrychau'r byd; / Henffych fore / Caf ei weled fel y mae' (trans. by Tony Conran as: 'Look, between the myrtles standing / A true object of my thought – / Though I know only in part now / He surpasses the worldly sort, / Yet come morning, I shall see him as he is', *Welsh Verse* (Bridgend: Seren, 1986), 239.) The other is a hymn by John Williams, Saint Athan, (1728–1806): 'Pwy welaf o Edom yn dod / Mil harddach na thoriad y wawr? / Yn sathru dan wadan ei droed / Elynion yn lluoedd i'r llawr: / Ei wisg wedi ei lliwio gan waed, / Ei saethu a'i gleddyf yn llym: / Ei harddwch yn llanw'r holl wlad, / Yn ymdaith yn amlder ei rym!' ('Who do I see coming from Edom, a thousand times more beautiful than the break of the dawn? Trampling hosts of enemies into the ground beneath the soles of His feet: His robe is stained by blood, His arrows and his sword are sharp: His beauty fills the whole land, marching in the greatness of His power.')

p.236 *as Ehedydd Iâl the poet says*: Ehedydd Iâl was the bardic name of William Jones (1815–99). The verse referred to is from the hymn by which he is best remembered: 'Er nad yw 'nghawd ond gwellt, / A'm hesgyrn ddim ond clai, / Mi ganaf yn y mellt, / Maddeuodd Duw fy mai; / Mae Craig yr Oesoedd dan fy nhraed, / A'r mellt yn diffodd yn y gwaed' ('Although my flesh is but grass, / And my bones only clay, / I sing in the lightning, / God forgave my sin; / The Rock of Ages is beneath my feet, / And the lightning is quenched in the blood').

p.236 *seiat*: chapel meeting, involving discussion of members' spiritual experience.

p.236 *steel curling box*: A curling box was a pan with a long, handle attachment which colliers (or their 'boys') used to scoop up fallen coal, thus clearing/cleaning the coal-face.

p.236 *eisteddfod*: Originally meaning an assembly of poets (from Welsh, *eistedd*, to sit), the word, has come to denote a festival which includes not only literature but also music and the graphic arts, usually in a competitive context. The tradition can be traced back to the fifteenth century, and probably earlier; the National Eisteddfod is held annually during the first week in August, alternately in north and south Wales, but regional and, as here, local *eisteddfodau* are also still held.

p.236   *about that time . . . religious revival*: In his jacket note to *Welsh Heirs*, GJ says: 'The earliest historical event referred to in [these stories] is I believe the religious revival which was in progress in 1905, the year I was born.'

p.238   *people of the certainty*: The revival – usually called the 'Evan Roberts Revival' after its most charismatic leader – began in the autumn of 1904 and spread throughout Wales until mid-1905, when its vitality abated. One effect of the revival was to create a very intense, pietistic, sect-like Christianity (outside the main denominations) whose members set much store on spiritual experience and the assurance of personal salvation. These were the 'people of the certainty' – *pobl y sicrwydd* – who felt that much chapel religion was lukewarm and compromised. Many of them consequently withdrew from the chapels and formed their own independent 'mission halls'. The term *pobl y sicrwydd* is very much that of industrial south Wales, and was quite common until comparatively recently.

p.239   *the Saviour who blasted the fig-tree . . . from the Temple with twisted cords*: In St. Matthew's Gospel, Christ sees a fig-tree with no fruit and says 'Let no fruit grow on thee henceforward for ever' and the tree withers and dies; he says to the disciples that, if they have absolute faith, they will not only blast fig-trees but move mountains (Matthew 21.19-21); in the same Gospel, Christ tells his disciples, 'Think not that I am come to send peace on earth; I came not to send peace, but a sword' (Matthew 10.34); in St. John, Christ drives the money-changers and merchants out of the temple in Jerusalem: 'And when he had made a scourge of small cords, he drove them all out of the temple . . . and poured out the changers' money, and overthrew the tables' (John 2.13–16).

p.242   *backward glancing . . . the damnation of Lot's wife*: As the Lord rains brimstone and fire on Sodom and Gomorrah, Lot and his wife flee. But despite the Lord's previous injunction that they should not look back, Lot's wife does so and is turned into a pillar of salt (Genesis 19.24–6); in view of later events in the story, the allusion to Lot's wife has particular resonance.

p.244   *Maldwyn bach*: see Note to p.58.

p.245   *nystagmus*: 'an involuntary oscillation of the eyeball, usually laterally, . . . especially common among miners' (*OED*).

p.245   *on strap*: see Note to p.213.

p.245   *the wagon would be in the ditch*: a version of a Welsh idiom which seems to have various local variants including, in parts of Carmarthenshire, *wedi mynd i'r clawdd*, 'gone into the hedge'.

p.245   *down on the bones of her behind*: It is unclear whether this idiom (cf. 'on her uppers') was ever idiomatic in south Wales, though GJ records in the *'Idioms' Notebook* a more demotic version: 'Right down on the bones of my arse'.

p.246   *on the floor of your pocket*: Seemingly a south Walian idiom, possibly from *yng ngwaelod dy boced*; 'the floor of my pocket' appears in GJ's *'Idioms' Notebook*.

p.246   *Phoebe fach*: see Note to p.58.

p.246   *Crugybar*: another famous hymn tune, somewhat funereal in tone; the hymn invariably sung to it is that of David Charles, Carmarthen (1762–1834), the well-known final verse of which begins 'O fryniau Caersalem ceir gweled / Holl daith yr anialwch i gyd'. (The tune is also sometimes known as 'Tôn y Botel' because of its attractiveness to lachrymose drinkers.) Maldwyn himself is not, of course, being entirely devout in humming the tune. The narrator observes that 'Maldwyn expected the storm' as he begins to hum; the final verse of the hymn goes on 'Cawn edrych ar stormydd ac ofnau / Ac angau dychrynllyd, a'r bedd' ('We can look at storms and fears / And terrible death and the grave'). Mrs. Morris recognizes the allusion and rebukes his impertinence.

p.247   *the neck of Abel . . . the knife of Cain*: In Genesis, Abel is killed by his brother Cain (Genesis 4.2–15).

p.247   *gymanfa*: see Note to p.187.

p.249   *duck*: a strong, untwilled, cotton fabric, lighter and finer than canvas, used for sails and for men's (including sailors') outer garments.

p.249   *sitting by 'ere*: see Note to p.58.

p.249   *Hallelujah Chorus*: the most famous chorus from *The Messiah*, by George Frideric Handel (1685–1759), an oratorio much performed by chapel choirs and amateur choral societies. 'King of Kings, and Lord of Lords!' is a part of this chorus.

p.249   *cymanfaoedd*: plural of 'cymanfa'. See Note to p.187.

p.250   *laus Deo*: Latin, praise of God; i.e. the Hallelujah Chorus.

p.250   *Harry the Boot*: In the TS he is 'Harry Cuba . . . because he had been brought up in a house that had once been the Cuba Inn'.

p.252   *poor dab*: see Note to p.130.

p.254   *'goats' pen'*: the back row, downstairs, of the chapel, where those whose commitment was less than total (last in and first out) would sit during the service: thus the goat's pen (*gorlan y geifr*) rather than 'the sheep pen' (*corlan y defaid*), see John 10.1–21.

p.254   *Ishmael*: the archetypal outsider, exile; see Genesis 16.1–16; 21.8–21.

Textual note
As well as the numerous minor revisions in the TS, a comparison of the TS with the published version indicates that the story has undergone a further stage of revision before publication, although the events and sequence of the narrative remain unaltered.

Mrs. Jeffreys
In *The Golden Pony* TSS 'Mrs. Jeffreys' is placed as the third story in 'The Jeffreys Family', and listed as such on the Contents page. The TS contains minor holograph emendations by GJ. The story's only publication was in *Welsh Heirs*.

The story would appear to date from the 1950s; the story is first referred to in a diary entry in 1952, and in an entry in May 1954 GJ makes a note to himself: 'cobwebs in roof in Mrs. Jeffreys story'.

p.256   *Two men were circling*: The description of the fight in the TS is briefer and less graphic. (Cf. the passage quoted in the Introduction from an unpublished piece, written in 1965, in which GJ describes a boyhood memory of seeing a bare-knuckle fight on the mountain above Merthyr.)

p.257   *The 'Court'*: Tudor Bevan notes that GJ based the Court on an actual lodging house in Merthyr (Bevan 40).

p.257   *Without the shedding of blood . . . there is no forgiveness*: The words are those of St. Paul: 'And almost all things are purged with blood; and without the shedding of blood is no remission' (Hebrews 9.22).

p.259   *read his Bible aloud*: The figure is based on a blind man 'who used to read or, rather, intone from a braille Bible outside the main door of the market in Merthyr' (Bevan 40).

p.260   *my mother's death*: the reasons for the mother's death are not in the TS.

p.261   *And in the sixth month . . . He shall be great . . . the Lord God*: The words are those of Luke 1.26–7, the account of the angel Gabriel's annunciation to Mary of Christ's coming.

p.262   *Nhad*: Welsh, 'My father' (*fy nhad*).

p.262   *kind to my mother*: The references to Probert's protection of mother and daughter, and thus the motivation for the father's smashing of the statue, are not in the TS.

p.262   *And his mercy . . . is on them . . . that fear him . . . imagination of their hearts*: the words are those of Mary in the Magnificat; see Luke 1.50–1.

p.263   *the old viaduct*: in the TS the viaduct is called 'Pandy Viaduct'. Cf. the viaduct which Karl climbs in *The Island of Apples*.

p.264   *getting very near the river*: that is, to the River Jordan, to death. See Note to p.214.

p.264   *In the darkness*: This paragraph, ending with the father's direct plea for Lowri's forgiveness, is not in the TS.

p.264   *Though your sins . . . as snow*: The words are those of Isaiah, urging the people to 'put away the evil of their doings' and turn to God (Isaiah 1.16–20).

p.264   *lost sheep, and the missing coin, and the younger son*: In St. Luke's Gospel, all three are parables of Christ's love and forgiveness; see Luke 15.4; 15.8–10; 15.11–32.

p.264   *Lord . . . now lettest*: The words are those of the old man, Simeon, on seeing the infant Christ; he had been promised that he would see the Child before his own death (see Luke 2.29). The words are sometimes sung as the canticle *Nunc Dimittis* (Latin, 'now lettest thou go').

pp.264–5   *I raised my head*: The final two paragraphs of the published version are not in the TS; only one sentence – 'In that way, at the death of my father, I was forgiven' – follows the blind man's reading from words of Simeon (Luke 2.25–32).

p.265   *I have overcome the World*: The words are those of Christ: 'In the world ye shall have tribulation: but be of good cheer; I have overcome the world' (John 16.33).

Textual note

A comparison of the TS with the published version indicates that the story has undergone a further stage of revision before publication, in addition to the minor holograph revisions in the TS, though the events and sequence of the narrative remain unaltered.

The TS version of the story does not contain the opening paragraph, related by Mr. Herbert, the curate who narrates 'Robert Jeffreys', but begins 'My husband had come out of the pit early . . .' The various direct references to Mr. Herbert as auditor of the story are also absent from the TS version. Some other variations are noted above.

Myra Powell

In *The Golden Pony* TSS, the fourth story of 'The Jeffreys Family' is listed as 'The Return' on the title page; it is unclear as to whether this was an earlier version of 'Myra Powell' since the TS of this story is missing. (The reference on p.260 of 'Mrs. Jeffreys' to her daughter Myra is not in the TS.)

A reading of 'Myra Powell' was broadcast as the 'Morning Story' on the Light Programme of BBC Radio (the forerunner of Radio 2) on 9 July 1965. The script of this version varies only slightly from the published story. The story's only appearance in print was in *Welsh Heirs*.

p.267 *three half crowns*: In Carmarthenshire, there was a tradition of giving a baby a half-a-crown when he/she was born. The giving of three half-crowns to this particular baby is thus, presumably, an act of especial generosity (with perhaps a reference to the gifts of the Magi?).

p.267 *cariad*: see Note to p.120.

Gari

In *The Golden Pony* TSS at Trinity College, Carmarthen, 'Gari' is entitled 'Nebo' and is placed as the second story in 'The Jeffreys Family' (and listed as such on the Contents page). The story's only publication was in *Welsh Heirs*.

p.270 *Dinas*: Welsh, 'city'. 'Dinas' is the location of the university attended by Trystan Morgan in GJ's novel *The Valley, The City, The Village* (1956). The location of the university is not given in the 'Nebo' TS, nor is there any reference to 'Ystrad' as the home of the narrator and Nebo.

p.272 *materials he had rubbed into it*: Nebo's attempts to get his hair to grow with a series of bizarre 'cures' echo the efforts of Dewi Davies's father to arrest his baldness in Ch. 5 of *The Island of Apples*.

p.272 *Band of Hope*: a society for children and young people, promoting total abstinence from alcohol. Formed in England in 1855, branches were formed in Wales by the Nonconformist chapels.

p.273 *jellygraph*: a machine for duplicating documents (such as examination papers), a forerunner of the Roneo or Gestetner duplicators.

p.273 *in Gloucestershire*: the school is not located in the TS.

p.274 *bread faggot*: made of minced offal and breadcrumbs.

p.274 *Alcwyn*: 'Alcwyn' is also the name of one of Trystan's college friends in *The Valley, The City, The Village*, although in the novel it is Trystan's friend Gwydion, not Alcwyn, who has 'been all over the world'. (In the TS Nebo's actual name is 'Gareth Davies'.) Nebo's capacity to 'mesmerize' those around him, especially Gari (p.276), is reminiscent of Karl Anthony's similar power over Dewi and his friends in *The Island of Apples*.

p.274 *ten bob note*: a banknote for ten shillings. Pre-decimalization (1971), there were twenty shillings in a pound. Thus, mathematically, the equivalent would be 50p, but the actual monetary value at the time of the story would have been substantially more, several pounds in present-day purchasing power.

p.275 *Turandot*: The story about *Turandot* and the black make-up is not in the

TS, where he has merely, 'spilt a few drops of ink over the sheets doing some studying in bed'.

p.276   *jube*: a fruit pastille, a colloquial usage.

p.277   *out of her sock*: out of the state of inattentiveness into which she has been lulled. The south Walian idiom to be 'in a sock' (or 'soc') is to be dreamy, inattentive to, or unconscious of, what is going on around one. Cf. 'lying sog' in 'Cadi Hughes' (p.72).

p.279   *up in the bows*: The phrase appears in the *'Idioms' Notebook*, where GJ glosses it as 'off the deep end'.

p.285   *rather down* danz la boosh: a comic translation into 'Franglais' of 'down in the mouth' (*bouche* = French, 'mouth').

p.285   *a real Shoni*: an unsophisticated or uncouth person, especially one who dresses poorly (a south Walian usage, from *Sioni*, Johnny).

p.286   *Rilke*: Rainer Maria Rilke (1875–1926), German lyric poet.

p.287   *wedi popi*: 'done for', a version of the Welsh idiom, *wedi pobi*, baked, cooked; possibly once current in GJ's form among non-Welsh-speakers in the Merthyr Valley,

p.291   *But Nebo . . . text-book fund*: there is no reference in the TS to Nebo's stealing of the text-book fund.

Textual note

Although the TS contains only a few minor holograph revisions, a comparison of the TS with the published version indicates that the story has undergone a further stage of revision before publication, although the events and sequence of the narrative remain unaltered. Some of the variations are given in the notes.

The Tower of Loss

A TS of 'The Tower of Loss' is included in *The Golden Pony* TSS at Trinity College, Carmarthen. The story's only publication was in *Welsh Heirs* .

The story would appear to date from the 1960s; in an entry in his diary in 1967 GJ writes: 'For story – "The Tower of Loss" – things in lavatory for wiping with – "or a lump of wadding out of the teddy bear"' (cf. p.297)

In February 1981, GJ gave a lecture entitled 'The Tower of Loss' at a conference on the short story; a TS of this lecture, with holograph revisions, is in the Glyn Jones papers at NLW. (It is referred to in the notes that follow as 'Lecture'.) In the lecture, having summarized the narrative, GJ comments on the characters and notes that the story 'is intended. . . as satire, although by no means very fierce satire':

It is important to realize that the story is set in the Thirties, a time of wide-spread unemployment and of dreadful suffering here in South Wales, and in other parts of Great Britain. One of the two dominant intellectual figures of this period was Karl Marx, and to be a Marxist then was very fashionable among the young. Of course, not everyone who claimed to be a Marxist had made much of a study of the subject, or could swear that he had read *Das Kapital* . . . Even so apolitical a figure as Dylan Thomas at one time wanted to be, or wanted to be thought to be, a Communist [. . . It was a time] of wide-spread and idealistic belief among the young, particularly among the artistic and intellectual young, that to be a Marxist, to be on the side of the workers, the proletariat, was the thing for an artist to be. Even people whose background was privileged, or wealthy, people who had personally no, or only the flimsiest, contact with the workers themselves, seemed to be convinced that Marxism was the answer to all the ills of society.

The one representing this attitude in my story is of course Loss Llewellyn . . . Loss becomes a figure of satire not, certainly, because at one point he takes up the cause of the workers, and the workless, and the poor. Many honourable and dedicated men at the time did this and some . . . gave their lives for democracy fighting in Spain. What is contemptible, it seems to me, in Loss, is his shallowness, his inconstancy, his humbug and hypocrisy. He's not so much wicked as ridiculous. He turns from a life supposedly dedicated to art, first to left-wing ideals because he thinks it's the done thing, and then to a life of service – how long will *that* last one wonders – when all the time what he is doing, is merely indulging his own whims and selfishness and his pursuit of sex. Such people were not at all uncommon during the Thirties. What they wished to get into their work was 'social awareness' – that is they wanted to be concerned as writers with the workers and their problems They were the sort of people described by Dylan Thomas in one of his broadcasts – 'How to be a Poet'. [Here GJ read from 'How to be a Poet', *Prospect of the Sea* (London: Dent, 1955) 104–15.] Can one imagine such people really hunger-marching all the way from Merthyr to London as so many did – much less going to fight and die in Spain? Can one imagine Carlos Llewellyn doing anything so positive and disagreeable and dangerous? . . .

The other type whose antics give rise to Gronow's laughter are the bohemians, who gather in Hoverington's flat. These are the hangers-on who exist in vast numbers about the fringes of art, as it were, in great cities. They are the novelists who don't write novels (or only very occasional bad ones), painters who can't paint pictures, poets who pretend to write poems, etc. The life they lead is pleasant, especially if you have – as many of these people seem or seemed to have in the Thirties – an allowance from their families, sufficient to keep them in fairly comfortable idleness, without having to work very seriously at anything. Hoverington, in the story, is obviously a nice and harmless chap but he is a parasite on parasites, and he's going, unless he changes radically, to fritter his life away in feebleness, and pretence, and self-deception, enjoying the flattery and the support of the would-be artists around him. In this he and Carlos are very similar. Their lives don't appear to be in contact with seriousness and reality. In the midst of the perils and the horrors of conditions in the Thirties . . . Hoverington and his friends can believe that 'sex is the over-riding problem of our generation as faith was that of our grandfathers'. Gronow believes differently, and that's why in his laughing exit from Hoverington's flat, he claims he is going to write a chant with a chorus denouncing religion, justice, peace, philosophy – all the values and ideals by which civilized society is sustained – all these are to be deemed secondary to the supremacy of the external genitalia. That is what strikes Gronow as so hilariously absurd that all he can do is laugh uncontrollably . . .

p.294 *the ferry*: see Note to p.111. In *The Dragon Has Two Tongues*, GJ mentions visiting the estuary with Dylan Thomas in the 1930s: 'I cannot remember if this was Dylan's first visit ever to Laugharne. It was almost certainly his first for many years, as his obvious unfamiliarity with his surroundings showed' (*DTT* 193). The name of the ferryman who rowed them on that occasion, Jack Roberts, appears in a scribbled note at the end of GJ's lecture notes. The tower itself is in fact based on Paxton's Tower, a folly and noted landmark further up the Towy valley (Bevan 70). Although in the published version of the story the walking tour takes place in the 'wild country of West Wales', the TS has simply 'this wild country' and neither does the final section locate the ferry in Wales.

p.294   *Gronow*:

> Gronow Lloyd . . . is described as a Welsh poet, but the language of his poetry, English or Welsh, is left unspecified. He appears in all the scenes and is intended as the pivotal point of the story; he represents the attitudes, the values perhaps, from which the attack on the other characters is launched. His solid appearance is intended to suggest his character. Although a poet, he is unpoetic and unromantic; he is too fat, he is plain and he sweats. He wears thick glasses, a workman's shirt and heavy black boots. He is intended to represent the gifted, clear-sighted, confident, Valleys man, humorous, and combative, and sceptical. His weapon of destruction is laughter. In Hoverington's party he is shown as being quickly bored by the theories of amateurs talking about literature; but he recognizes with compassion the true position where Tessa, Hoverington's wife, is concerned. He is very observant and watchful. His friend Dewi, the narrator, is rather a neutral figure, not too bright and an ignoramus – more than once he claims not to be able to understand what's going on. ('Lecture')

p.294   *tussore*: a coarse silk.

p.296   *Hoverington*: 'He's liberal, or tolerant, or supine, to the point of incapacity, or anarchism. That we first encounter him lying down flat on his back is supposed to hint at his character and attitudes' ('Lecture'). In *The Golden Pony* TS the character's name is 'Witherington'.

p.297   *having dead-born babies*: 'I think it was Byron who pointed out that in the Shelley household in spite of the Shelleys' high idealism, all the babies died. Gronow's feelings were something similar' ('Lecture').

p.297   *poor dab*: see Note to p.130.

p.299   *ganzy*: a jersey or sweater, a version of 'guernsey' (see Partridge, 'gansi, gansy').

p.299   *dubliws*: see Note to p.133.

p.300   *I think they called Loss's girl Jersey*: This paragraph is not in the TS, which contains no reference to Loss's girlfriend.

p.301   *some writer . . . pox*: in the TS he is named as 'Sir William Davenant' (1606–68).

p.301   *any talk . . . except about culture*: In 'Eighteen Poems Again', *Poetry Wales*, 9/2 (1973): 22–6, GJ remembers: 'I was once with Dylan Thomas in London in the Thirties in the company of several young poets and literary people and during the talk I whispered to him, "I have never before been in a place where surrealism is discussed". "I have been in a place", he whispered back, "where *only* surrealism is discussed".' The account of the bohemian life in Hoverington's flat should be compared with the account GJ gives of visits in the 1930s to the house in London which Dylan Thomas shared with the artists Mervyn Levy and Alfred Janes; see *DTT* 182–3.

p.301   *to discuss some theory or other*: in the TS: 'a discussion of poetry and phallic worship'.

p.301   *sex . . . the over-riding problem of our generation*: GJ had written in his journal in December 1939: 'How comical sounds I. A. Richards that "the problem of our generation is sex" – when there are Hitler, unemployment, war, etc. etc etc.'

p.304   *Tiger Bay*: Dinas (Welsh, 'city') is evidently based on Cardiff; Butetown, the multiracial dockland area of Cardiff, was popularly known as 'Tiger Bay', given its reputation, especially in the 1930s, for violence. This section of 'The Tower of Loss' might be compared to the protagonist's visit to the same district of Cardiff in 'I Was Born in the Ystrad Valley'. Neither 'Tiger Bay' nor 'Dinas' are referred to by name in the TS, nor is it indicated directly that the city is in Wales.

p.304   *melodeon* : a type of accordion.

p.304   *bats-wing burner*: see Note to p.64.

p.307   *donkeyman* : a man in charge of a donkey-engine, a small steam engine on board ship, used for subsidiary jobs such as feeding the boilers of the main engine.

p.309   *another ex-artist . . . cela*: Arthur Rimbaud (1854–91).

p.310   *inglorious Welsh Christopher*: St. Christopher is the patron saint of travellers; a giant who, after being converted, devoted his life to carrying travellers across a river, usually represented in art as carrying the Christ child on his back. The phrase also echoes 'mute inglorious Milton', in Thomas Gray's 'Elegy Written in a Country Churchyard', referring to the talented countryman who, because he lives in an out-of-the-way place, has no opportunity to develop his gifts and receives no recognition. The TS has 'inglorious Christopher'.

p.312   *gutser*: a belly-flop, a painfully inelegant dive.

p.312   *in a very posh English accent*: not in TS.

p.312   *Christophero Sly*: Christopher Sly, in the 'induction' to Shakespeare's *The Taming of the Shrew*, is a drunken tinker who is picked up in an alehouse by a lord and and his huntsman and, despite his protestations to the contrary, assured he is a lord who has been out of his mind. He is feasted sumptuously at the castle and the action of the play, is performed for his benefit. Loss has suffered from contact with a bottle in a more directly physical way than Sly. (Gronow is also possibly suggesting that the play's theme is relevant to the relationship between Loss and his English lady.)

Textual note
The TS in *The Golden Pony* TSS contains few revisions, but the story has been considerably revised between that version and the published text, although the events and sequence of the narrative remain unaltered. Some of the more interesting or significant revisions are given in the notes.

Rhysie at Auntie Kezia's
A TS of 'Rhysie at Auntie Kezia's', there entitled 'Rhysie', is included in *The Golden Pony* TS at Trinity College, Carmarthen. The story was first published in *Leek Broth* Christmas 1949: 21–5. (This magazine was published in Cardiff, under the auspices of Toc-H.)
   WH.

A portion of the story was included in Dewi Roberts, ed., *Christmas in Wales* (Bridgend: Seren, 1997), 30–2.

p.315   *mich*: see Note to p.190.
p.315   *ash-boxes*: rubbish bins.
p.317   *twtied down*: see Note to p.164..

Textual note
Several minor emendations, in GJ's handwriting, in his own copy of *Leek Broth* have been incorporated into *The Golden Pony* TS, indicating that the TS post-dated the story's first publication. The text of the story in *Welsh Heirs*, although in narrative detail that of *Leek Broth* and *The Golden Pony* TS, has been substantially revised and, in the process, slightly lengthened.

Lias Lewis

A TS of 'Lias Lewis', with minor holograph emendations by GJ, is included in *The Golden Pony* TSS at Trinity College, Carmarthen. A further TS, also with minor holograph emendations by GJ, is in the Gwyn Jones Papers, NLW 39/77. The story was accepted for publication in *Welsh Review* in a letter from Gwyn Jones to GJ, 1 January 1946. The story was published in *Welsh Review*, 5/4 (1946): 233–45.
     WH.

p.318   *the blazing bush . . . bullock-burning Tishbite*: The angel of the Lord appears to Moses 'in a flame of fire out of the midst of a bush' in Exodus 3.2–3; 'Nebo's patriarchal bones': Nebo was the mountain near Canaan where Moses died (see Deuteronomy 32.49); Enoch is 'unburied' because 'By faith Enoch was translated that he should not see death, and was not found because God had translated him' (Hebrews 11.5); in the Epistle of Jude, Enoch is described as 'the seventh from Adam' (Enoch, verse 14). The 'bullock-burning Tishbite' is Elijah (after whom Elias is named), who defeats the priests of Baal (1 Kings 18.21–30); in 2 Kings 2.11–12 there appears a chariot of fire, 'the chariot of Israel', and Elijah is taken up by a whirlwind into heaven.
p.318   *the holy jumpers*: the more enthusiastic converts of the 1904–5 Revival; see Note to p.238.
p.318   *Cadi Bryncoed*: Cf. Note to p.69, Cadi of Bryncoed ('Woodhill').
p.318   *Maddox the Minister*: 'Morris the Minister' throughout in *Welsh Review* version (*WR*).
p.319   *raised the text*: a literal translation of the Welsh idiom *codi testun*, to take a text for the sermon.
p.319   *hwyl*: see Note to p.184. (The phrase 'in his *hwyl*' does not appear in *WR*.)
p.319   *Jonah . . . the whale*: Jonah is swallowed by 'a great fish' in Jonah 1.17–2.10.
p.319   *Kerith*: Elijah is told by the Lord to 'hide thyself by the brook Cherith, that is before Jordan. And the ravens brought him bread and flesh in the morning and bread and flesh in the evening; and he drank of the brook' (1 Kings 17.3–6).
p.319   *bach*: see Note to p.58.
p.320   *potch*: mess, a south Walian idiom, used both as a verb ('He's always potching/messing with something in the garage') and a noun ('She's made a real

potch of it'). The Welsh 'potsh' is a mash of boiled vegetables, especially potatoes mashed with milk or with another vegetable. Thence 'potsh' and 'poitsh' are used figuratively as 'a mess'.

p.322 *Ishmael*: see Note to p.254.

p.322 *rod of Aaron*: When Pharaoh challenges Moses and Aaron to show him a miracle, Aaron casts down his rod and it turns into a serpent (Exodus 7.9-10).

p.322 *groat* : a (silver) fourpenny piece.

p.322 *Lonso lowered the fish. 'Thruppence then,'*: 'Lonso lowered the fish. "You've got a plaster for every sore," he said. Then he lifted it up close to Lias's face again. "Thruppence then",' (*WR*). In *WR* Lonso's sewin weighs 'three pounds'.

p.322 *What is the matter with you, Lias?*: 'What is the matter with you, Lias you are like a bull with a stung rump lately. Lie down, Fan, lie down will you. I must have food like everyone else, Lias, and those hatched from hens must scratch for a living, remember' (*WR*).

p.322 *sweating to reach the 'Black Horse'*: 'all sweat and snobs to reach the Black Horse' (*WR*).

p.322 *bring him over Jordan*: that is, to convert him, bring him to faith, to the Promised Land; cf. 'leave the wilderness . . . possess the land' (p.323).

p.323 *talu pump*: 'bomberino', a (fairly physically robust) children's team-game.

p.323 *like Joshua possess the land*: after Moses' death it was Joshua who led the Israelites out of the wilderness and into the Promised Land.

p.323 *try washing the feet of the ducks*: cf. the line from the *hen bennill* (lit. 'old verse'): 'Ofer golchi traed hwyaden' ('It's useless to wash the feet of ducks'). See *A People's Poetry: Hen Benillion*, trans. Glyn Jones (Bridgend: Seren, 1997), 126–7.

p.323 *preaching to me?*: 'preaching to me? You've got the wrong pig by the ear, Lias' (*WR*).

p.323 *went through the wood . . . branch*: the phrase appears in the *'Idioms' Notebook*, as does 'the more you tread on mud' (p.124).

p.325 *laughing at him*: 'laughing at him behind her teeth' (*WR*).

p.325 *understand Welsh*: Again, clearly, the reader is to assume that the characters are in fact speaking in Welsh. Cf. Notes to 'Price-Parry' (p.166), 'It's Not By His Beak . . .' (p.227).

p.325 *wetting your beak*: a literal translation of the Welsh idiom, *gwlychu dy big* (also *gwlychu dy lwnc*), wet your whistle, take a drink.

p.325 *tipped her head in the tar bucket*: in the early years of the century, a Carmarthenshire idiom for one who had transgressed, especially a woman who had transgressed sexually.

p.325 *thick tongue or what?*: 'thick tongue or what? Who do you think you are, Lias Lewis, the marble of the hill?' (*WR*).

p.325 *a bit more of food*: a literal translation of the Welsh idiom, *ychwaneg o fwyd*.

p.325 *Jezebel . . . dogs*: Jezebel 'painted her face, and tired her hair' to tempt Jehu, who was anointed by the Lord; she is killed 'and they found no more of her than the skull, and the feet, and the palms of her hands'; Jehu relates Elijah's prophecy: 'In the portion of Jezreel shall dogs eat the flesh of Jezebel' (2 Kings 9.30–7).

p.326 *swingle-tree*: a plough or carriage cross-bar, pivoted at the middle.

p.326 *like a new Elias*: see Note to p.318.

p.327 *put my foot to the earth*: see Note to p.156.

p.327   *my piece myself I am*: '"... my piece myself I am." Lonso grinned at her over-ripe body.' (*WR*).

p.328   *poor old dab*: see Note to p.130.

p.328   *like poor Lias?*:

'... like poor Lias?' 'I dropped hard, Mr. Morris,' the old man went on. 'I heard the screeching branches and I felt the claws of the darkness; as I fell the winds went flapping past me from open holes in the earth and the ground rose up and kicked me in the face. I was sick and giddy, and somebody began banging me on the head with a bell. Who is banging me on the head with a bell, Mr. Morris? Who has got a bell for banging me on the head?' He groaned, rolling his white eyes in misery, and the clock went *tack-tick*, *tack-tick* into the silence of the little barn. (*WR*)

p.328   *forehead of my knee*: a play on the Welsh *pen-glin*, the knee (*pen*=Welsh, 'head'.), and also *tal fy nglin* (*ar dal ei lin* = on his knees; *tal* also means 'forehead').

p.328   *draw in my feet and die*: The phrase 'pulled his feet in and died' appears in GJ's *'Idioms' Notebook*.

p.329   *fat arms ... over her bosom*: 'fat arms ... over her bosom, they looked as though they had been broken off short and fingers were sprouting from the elbows' (*WR*).

p.329   *every chance she gets*: 'every chance she gets. I know I've been a scamp, but there's no need for her to chuck grease on the fire the way she is doing. And if it comes to clecks, what about her, the slut, Mr. Morris? Everybody knows you can't go in her house on horseback' (*WR*).

p.329   *muscles of his back?*: 'muscles of his back? That has got her stammering, that has. That has got her with her boots in the bushes, Mr. Morris' (*WR*).

p.331   *put the wool on the pins*: to begin something, to 'cast on' a piece of knitting, onto the needles.

p.331   *The minister ... opened the half-door of the barn to the night*: 'The minister .. opened the half-door of the barn upon the night. "He is born again," he whispered' (*WR*).

Textual note

The text which appears in *Welsh Review* has been considerably revised before being reprinted in *Welsh Heirs*; some of the more interesting or significant revisions have been given in the notes. The events and sequence of the narrative remain altered.

Rhamant Drist

A TS of 'Rhamant Drist', with minor holograph emendations by GJ, is included in *The Golden Pony* TSS at Trinity College, Carmarthen, under the the title 'Hope'. The story's only publication was in *Welsh Heirs*.

p.332   *Rhamant Drist*: Welsh, 'a sad tale'.

p.332   *a heavy load* : In the TS the boy moves 'as though dragging behind him a great weight'. This is followed by a passage which, although unmarked in the TS, has been deleted in later revision:

His eye was upon a star moving before him and he wept. He had not wanted to set out on this journey; he had heard much of its cruelty and suffering, but it had been his destiny to come. The star shaped like a tinsel decoration, would guide him, so it was determined, to the house at which he must knock for entrance.

Seeing the star halt he felt in his cold heart a colder stab.

This is followed by the description of the cottage in the moonlight.

p.332 *The child longed to join them*: In the TS the child is 'the watcher behind the panes, forgetting what he had been told about this journey'.

p.333 *her yellow-haired girl*: 'a little golden headed boy' in the TS.

p.333 *the child could see dimly*: 'When the unborn looked at the door again he could discern' in the TS. Again, in the TS, it is 'the unborn' whose heart is 'filled with protest' at the man's actions.

p.333 *the lover*: In the TS, the figure in this section is not referred to as 'the lover' but as 'he' or, twice, as 'the seeker'. In the following section, the male figure is again referred to as 'the seeker' (four times) but also (twice) as a 'lover'. In the fourth and fifth sections of the story, the protagonist is not referred to as 'the soldier' but as 'the seeker'.

p.336 *ban-dog*: a guard dog, 'tied or chained up, either to guard a house or on account of its ferocity' (*OED*).

p.339 *a strange emotional stirring* : in the TS this penultimate sentence is followed by a passage which, although unmarked in the TS, has been deleted in later revision:

So much evil had he seen, so much cruelty, so much suffering of the innocent that, like a sick child, he could not understand or name the bewildering changes within himself. And yet he dimly recognised this emotion as one he had experienced before and repeatedly rejected. The love, the courage, the remorse, the pity he had also encountered, when he remembered them, threw as it were a powerful upward beam upon him and in this illumination he recognised the stirring as hope.

Textual note

The TS of 'Hope' in *The Golden Pony* contains few revisions but the story has been much revised between that version and that which appears as 'Rhamant Drist' in *Welsh Heirs*, although the events and sequence of the narrative remain the same. The most significant textual variations are given in the notes above.

The Golden Pony

A TS of the story, with minor holograph emendations by GJ, is in *The Golden Pony* TSS at Trinity College, Carmarthen. The story was first published in *Chance*, 4 (1953): 11–22. It was reprinted in *The Penguin Book of Welsh Short Stories*, ed. Alun Richards (Harmondsworth: Penguin, 1976), 29–46, before being collected in *Welsh Heirs*.

WH, GWWY.

p.340 *the wooden holder*: the children's pens, and here the teacher's red-ink pen, comprised a wooden handle (holder) with a metal bracket at its end into which the nib slotted.

p.340   *the golden pony*: GJ's uncle, John Ifans, who lived on the farm called 'Y Lan', between Johnstown and Llangynog, Carmarthenshire, bred horses and it was here that GJ spent several summer holidays (*MPi* 76). GJ told Tudor Bevan that 'there was a magnificent golden pony on the farm, which he was enchanted by and which would come to him when he called' (Bevan 62). Cf. the 'lovely slender mare with a pale golden coat' which the narrator's father buys in 'Wat Pantathro' (p.142).

p.341   *the island*: GJ told Tudor Bevan that the vivid account of the crossing to the island 'is based on the many crossings from Ferryside to Llansteffan that Glyn Jones made from an early age,' although 'the island itself is a composite and generally unlocated place' (Bevan 75).

p.343   *to keep the sun off the fire*: cf. the Note to p.101.

p.343   *dock and feverfew*: herbs.

p.345   *Mamgu*: see Note to p.185.

Textual note

The text of 'The Golden Pony' in *Welsh Heirs* is identical to that in *The Penguin Book of Welsh Short Stories*. The version in *Chance*, however, does not contain the opening section of the *Welsh Heirs/Penguin* version, set in Rhodri's schoolroom; it begins with the second section of the *Welsh Heirs/Penguin* version: 'The child had come to the island . . .' The final sentences of the *Welsh Heirs/Penguin* version also differ slightly, but significantly, from the *Chance* version:

> The child recognized it at once. It was the head of the golden pony. They were swimming her back to the island. [*Welsh Heirs/Penguin*]

> The child recognised it at once. It was the golden pony returning to the island. [*Chance*]

The TS included in *The Golden Pony* TSS contains the *Chance* version of the ending. However, it also includes a version of the schoolroom scene at the beginning. It seems likely that the TS post-dates *Chance*, but variations between the TS and the *Welsh Heirs/Penguin* version, and holograph revisions in GJ's own copy of *Chance*, not included in the TS, indicate that at least one further stage of revision took place before the publication of the story in *The Penguin Book of Welsh Short Stories*.